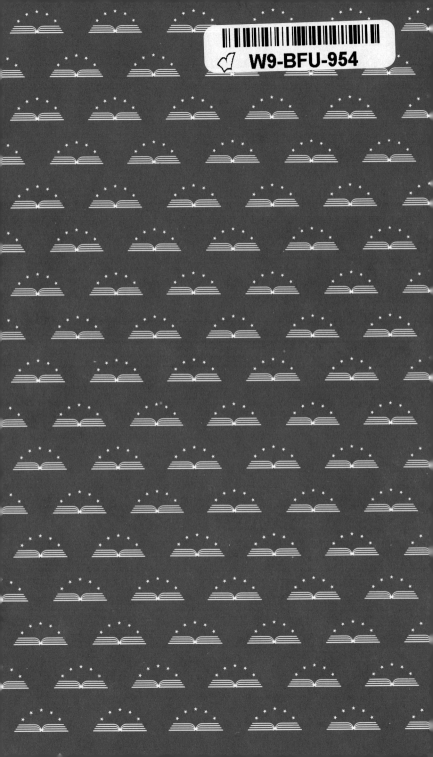

GERTRUDE STEIN

GERTRUDE STEIN

WRITINGS 1932–1946

Stanzas in Meditation
Lectures in America
The Geographical History of America
Ida
Brewsie and Willie
Other Works

THE LIBRARY OF AMERICA

The paper used in this publication meets the
minimum requirements of the American National Standard for
Information Sciences—Permanence of Paper for Printed
Library Materials, ANSI Z39.48—1984.

Distributed to the trade
in the United States by Penguin Putnam Inc.
and in Canada by Penguin Books Canada Ltd.

Library of Congress Catalog Number: 97–28916
For cataloging information, see end of Notes.
ISBN 1–883011–41–8
───────
First Printing
The Library of America—100

Manufactured in the United States of America

CATHARINE R. STIMPSON
AND
HARRIET CHESSMAN

SELECTED THE CONTENTS AND WROTE THE NOTES
FOR THIS VOLUME

Contents

STANZAS IN MEDITATION

Stanzas in Meditation

I caught a bird which made a ball
And they thought better of it.
But it is all of which they taught
That they were in a hurry yet
In a kind of a way they meant it best
That they should change in and on account
But they must not stare when they manage
Whatever they are occasionally liable to do
It is often easy to pursue them once in a while
And in a way there is no repose
They like it as well as they ever did
But it is very often just by the time
That they are able to separate
In which case in effect they could
Not only be very often present perfectly
In each way whichever they chose.
All of this never matters in authority
But this which they need as they are alike
Or in an especial case they will fulfill
Not only what they have at their instigation
Made for it as a decision in its entirety
Made that they minded as well as blinded
Lengthened for them welcome in repose
But which they open as a chance
But made it be perfectly their allowance
All which they antagonise as once for all
Kindly have it joined as they mind

It is not with them that they come
Or rather gather for it as not known
They could have pleasure as they change
Or leave it all for it as they can be

Not only left to them as restless
For which it is not only left and left alone
They will stop it as they like
Because they call it further mutinously
Coming as it did at one time only
For which they made it rather now
Coming as well as when they come and can
For which they like it always
Or rather best so when they can be alert
Not only needed in nodding
But not only not very nervous
As they will willingly pass when they are restless
Just as they like it called for them
All who have been left in their sense
All should boisterous make it an attachment
For which they will not like what there is
More than enough and they can be thought
Always alike and mind do they come
Or should they care which it would be strange
Just as they thought away.
It is well known that they eat again
As much as any way which it can come
Liking it as they will
It is not only not an easy explanation
Once at a time they will
Nearly often after there is a pleasure
In liking it now
Who can be thought perilous in their account.
They have not known that they will be in thought
Just as rich now or not known
Coming through with this as their plan
Always in arises.
Liking it faintly and fairly well
Which meant they do
Mine often comes amiss.
Or liking strife awhile
Often as evening is as light
As once for all
Think of how many open
And they like it here.

STANZA III

It is not now that they could answer
Yes and come how often
As often as it is the custom
To which they are accustom
Or whether accustomed like it
In their bought just as they all
Please then
What must they make as any difference
Not that it matters
That they have it to do
Not only for themselves but then as well
Coming for this.
He came early in the morning.
He thought that they needed comfort
Which they did
And they gave them an assurance
That it would be all as well
As indeed were it
Not to have it needed at any time
Just as alike and like
It did make it a way
Of not only having more come
She refused to go
Not refused but really said
And do I have to go
Or do I go
Not any more than so
She is here when she is not better
When she is not better she is here
In their and on their account
All may remember three months longer
Or not at all or not in with it
Four leaf clovers make a Sunday
And that is gone

STANZA IV

Just when they ask their questions they will always go away
Or by this time with carefulness they must be meant to stay

For which they mind what they will need
Which is where none is left
They may do right for them in time but never with it lost
It is at most what they can mean by not at all for them
Or likeness in excellent ways of feeling that it is
Not only better than they miss for which they ask it more
Nearly what they can like at the best time
For which they need their devotion to be obtained
In liking what they can establish as their influence
All may be sold for which they have more seeds than theirs
All may be as completely added not only by themselves.
For which they do attack not only what they need
They must be always very ready to know.
That they have heard not only all but little.
In their account on their account may they
Why need they be so adequately known as much
For them to think it is in much accord
In no way do they cover that it can matter
That they will clear for them in their plight
Should they sustain outwardly no more that for their own
All like what all have told.
For him and to him to him for me.
It is as much for me that I met which
They can call it a regular following met before.
It will be never their own useless that they call
It is made that they change in once in a while.
While they can think did they all win or ever
Should it be made a pleasant arrangement yet
For them once in a while one two or gather well
For which they could like evening of it all.
Not at all tall not any one is tall
No not any one is tall and very likely
If it is that little less than medium sized is all
Like it or not they win they won they win
It is not only not a misdemeanor
But it is I that put a cloak on him
A cloak is a little coat made grey with black and white
And she likes capes oh very well she does.
She said she knew we were the two who could
Did we who did and were and not a sound

We learned we must we saw we conquered most
After all who makes any other small or tall
They will wish that they must be seen to come
After at most she needs be kind to some
Just to like that.
Once every day there is a coming where cows are

STANZA V

Why can pansies be their aid or paths.
He said paths she had said paths
All like to do their best with half of the time
A sweeter sweetener came and came in time
Tell him what happened then only to go
He nervous as you add only not only as they angry were
Be kind to half the time that they shall say
It is undoubtedly of them for them for every one any one
They thought quietly that Sunday any day she might not
    come
In half a way of coining that they wish it
Let it be only known as please which they can underrate
They try once to destroy once to destroy as often
Better have it changed to pigeons now if the room smokes
Not only if it does but happens to happens to have the
    room smoke all the time.
In their way not in their way it can be all arranged
Not now we are waiting.
I have read that they wish if land is there
Land is there if they wish land is there
Yes hardly if they wish land is there
It is no thought of enterprise there trying
Might they claim as well as reclaim.
Did she mean that she had nothing.
We say he and I that we do not cry
Because we have just seen him and called him back
He meant to go away
Once now I will tell all which they tell lightly.
How were we when we met.
All of which nobody not we know
But it is so. They cannot be allied

They can be close and chosen.
Once in a while they wait.
He likes it that there is no chance to misunderstand pansies.

STANZA VI

I have not heard from him but they ask more
If with all which they merit with as well
If it is not an ounce of which they measure
He has increased in weight by losing two
Namely they name as much.
Often they are obliged as it is by their way
Left more than they can add acknowledge
Come with the person that they do attack
They like neither best by them altogether
For which it is no virtue fortune all
Ours on account their with the best of all
Made it be in no sense other than exchange
By which they cause me to think the same
In finally alighting where they may have at one time
Made it best for themselves in their behalf.
Let me think well of a great many
But not express two so.
It is just neither why they like it
Because it is by them in as they like
They do not see for which they refuse names
Articles which they like and once they hope
Hope and hop can be as neatly known
Theirs in delight or rather may they not
Cover it shone guessing in which they have
All may be glory may be may be glory
For not as ladling marguerites out.
It is best to know their share.
Just why they joined for which they knelt
They can call that they were fortunate.
They may be after it is all given away.
They may. Have it in mine.
And so it is a better chance to come
With which they know theirs to undo
Getting it better more than once alike

For which fortune favors me.
It is the day when we remember too.
We two remember two two who are theirs
Who are fat with glory too with two
With it with which I have thought twenty fair
If I name names if I name names with them.
I have not hesitated to ask a likely block
Of which they are attributed in all security
As not only why but also where they may
Not be unclouded just as yes to-day
They call peas beans and raspberries strawberries or two
They forget well and change it as a last
That they could like all that they ever get
As many fancies for which they have asked no one.
Might any one be what they liked before
Just may they come to be not only fastened
It should be should be just what they like
This May in unison
All out of cloud. Come hither. Neither
Aimless and with a pointedly rested displeasure
She may be glad to be either in their resigning
That they have this plan I remember.
Well welcome in fancy
Or just need to better that they call
All have been known in name as call
They will call this day one for all
I know it may be shared by Tuesday
Gathered and gathered yes.
All who come will will come or come to be
Come to be coming that is in and see
See elegantly not without enjoin
See there there where there is no share
Shall we be three I wonder now

STANZA VII

Make a place made where they need land
It is a curious spot that they are alike
For them to have hold of which in need of plainly
Can be suddenly hot with and without these or either

For themselves they can change no one in any way
They may be often placid as they mean they can force it
Or wilder than without having thought Frank Wilder was a
    name
They knew without a thought that they could tell not then
Not known they were known then that is to say all though
They were just as famous as in when in eloquence shortly
Every one knowing this could know then of this pleased
She may be thought in when in which it is in mine a
    pleasure.
Now let me think when.
There should not be this use in uselessness.
It is easier to know better when they are quite young
Over five and under fourteen that they will be famous.
Famous for this and then in a little while which it is lost.
It is lost.
By the time that they can think to sing in mountains.
Or much of which or meadows or a sunset hush or rather
By this time they could which they could think as selfish.
No one can know one can now or able.
They may be thought to be with or to be without now.
And so it happens that at that time they knew
Or it happens that as at that time they knew
Which made pages no delight they will be felt not well
Not as ours hours are polite.
Or they think well or violent or weeding
Or may be they shall be spared or if they can be wanted
    finishing
Or better not prepared.
It is not ordinary standing or standard or which.
Might they be mostly not be called renown.
Should they finish better with batches.
Or why are theirs alright.

STANZA VIII

I ought not to have known that they came well
Came here to want it to be given to them
As if as much as they were ever anxious to be not
Only having seen me they could be nearly all polite.

It was difficult to know how they felt then.
Now I know everything of which it is that there is no
        difference
Between then and now but very much the same
As of course then it was not only here.
There they came well
Here they come well
Often make it be believed that they marry
It is not only that there was no doubt.
Indicated why they left in fear
Just as the same just is the same
They will be ought and autocratic
Come when they call.
They are called that they see this
They which is made in any violence
That they mean please forgive a mess
They can be often polite in languages.
Nobody thinks a thing.
They will welcome all shawled
I like a noon which has been well prepared
Well prepared never the less.
Hours of a tree growing. He said it injured walls,
We said the owner and the one then here preferred it.
Imagine what to say he changed his mind.
He said it would not matter until ten years or five.
She may be not universal.
Or who may be taught most in exaggeration.
Or she may be moved once to balance all
Or she may be just unkind.
It is hoped that they feel as well
Oh yes it is hoped that they feel as well.
Argued with what they like or where they went.
Which they must have in any case
For accidentally they do not mean this.
Will there be any difference with how much they know
Or better than on account of which they wish and wish
        arranged
Can we call ours a whole.
Out from the whole wide world I chose thee
They may be as useful as necessity

More than they called which they could ask combined
Or made of welsh a treasure.
They mean me when they mean me

STANZA IX

With which they may be only made to brush
Brush it without a favor because they had called for it
She may be never playing to be settled
Or praying to be settled once and for all
To come again and to commence again or which
They will be frequently enjoyed
Which they never do as much as they know
That they like where they happen to have learnt
That seeds are tall and better rather than they will
It is much chosen.
Every year dahlias double or they froze

STANZA X

Might they remember that he did not dislike
Even if there was a reason that he did not choose
Nor rather as it happened which when he did not go away
They might which they not alone as nearly selfish
They will have placed in their own winning.
I know how much I would not have liked that.
They may be taken which is not the same as told
Made in which time they will frankly share
Might it be often not as well that they will change
Or in a way of principally in place
Made which they may which they made made unkind
It is not why they asked them would they like it
It is managed when they are able to agree
I come back to think well at once of most
Not only that I like it that they like it
But which in which way
That they chose
It is for instance not at all a necessity.
That once or twice or agreeable
Might they be very often very welcome

By which they mean will they come.
I have thought that the bird makes the same noise
    differently
Just as I said how will you do it if you like it
And they will not stretch well from here to there
If they know that in the full moon they should not plant it
Just before.
All might all mean that is the way to do
Not better than they have lost
But which they manage in their requital
I have known that sound and this as known
Which they will interlace with not only there
But the pale sky with the pale green leaves
Or which they will as they belong to trees
In this in their amount.
I come back to remember they will pay
Which they may do which they may say
Or which they may do whatever they do say
Always as often as they mention this
Which might annoy them does annoy them
As they call a pail a pail and make a mountain cover
Not only their clouds but their own authority
For having been here then as it is better to be
Which is an arrangement better made for them
Than not alone for them for which they will be wetting.
It came very closely but no one was just yet
Not to be frightened as they meant at all
I do not care that he should make threads so
Threads are tenderly heads are tenderly so and so
Very well merited
I should judge just inclined
Neither as disturbance or better yet
Might it be changed but once before
Left them to gather it whenever they can and will
Just the same
It might be very well that lilies of the valley have a fragrance
And that they ripen soon
And that they are gathered in great abundance
And that they will not be refreshing but only
Very lovely with green leaves

Or managed just the same when payed or offered
Even if they do.
They will never be careless with their having stayed away.
I know just how they feel with hope
And their wishes after all will we come
No we will not come.
In any absent way we will not only not be there
But when will we be here in one way
Any mixing of which it is in their presence
They or renounced or will they be made there
Will they be made there could be a question
Any owner could not be a question to their arrangement.
After all if it came out it meant it came again
Of course any one always is an answer.
Once in a while one or two
They could count now with any obstruction
As much as they advance.
Will or well a price.
In looking up I have managed to see four things.

STANZA XI

But which it is not by that they are rich
But only for it not only when they may count
Or by the opening that they will go round
As having value for which they may plan more
In which they can attract a celebration
Of their own cause not only just as well as all absurd
Can they be well awakened because they have not heard
Or may they come to account as much as not abandon
By the time that they caused them not to blame
Just as much as they could as they fasten
Linking it not only as absurd but fairly often
Be they as well aware as not only not only fasten
But which they may wish as not only opening
Or very carelessly arrange by the time they will go
Finally not only why they try but which they try
In case of joining.
Why should nobody wait when they come there
They have met one who likes it by and by

He will learn more than it is often read
That they could always please
More than just by their count
After all why may they liken it to this
Or nor only add very much more
Or not be any one known as politeness
It is not at all like or alike
An invitation suffices for the present
In the middle of their exchange
They may cease moderation
Or embellish no one at a time
But then to wonder if they will be more
Or if there will be more which follows by
They will be not at all leaving it
Any way do they differ as to excitement
Or stopping hastily with while in ambush.
They do delight that it was any bird
Made to be near than they could like to plan
Should be thought successor to their own
Without in pleasure may they like may now.
Just as soon as ever if they come
By that in trial that they manage
It is for this for which for them for her
Coming to think it only as they knew
Known makes it plain I shall
Think birds and ways and frogs and grass and now
That they call meadows more
I have seen what they knew.

STANZA XII

She was disappointed not alone or only
Not by what they wish but even by not which
Or should they silence in convincing
Made more than they stand for them with which
But they may be more alike than they find finely
In not only ordinary care but while they care
It is by no means why they arrange
All of which which they punctuate
Not only gleaning but if they lie down

One watching it not be left aloud to happen
Or in their often just the same as occasionally
They do not usually use that they might have mention
That often they are often there to happen.
Could call meditation often in their willing
Just why they may count how may one mistaken.
In not quite correctly not asking will they come.
It is now here that I have forgotten three.

STANZA XIII

She may count three little daisies very well
By multiplying to either six nine or fourteen
Or she may be well mentioned as twelve
Which they make like which they may like soon
Or more than ever which they wish as a button
Just as much as they arrange which they wish
Or they may attire where they need as which say
May they call a hat or a hat a day
Made merry because it is so.

STANZA XIV

She need not be selfish but he may add
They like my way it is partly mine
In which case for them to foil or not please
Come which they may they may in June.
Not having all made plenty by their wish
In their array all which they plan
Should they be called covered by which
It is fortunately their stay that they may
In which and because it suits them to fan
Not only not with clover but with may it matter
That not only at a distance and with nearly
That they ran for which they will not only plan
But may be rain can be caught by the hills
Just as well as they can with what they have
And they may have it not only because of this
But because they may be here.
Or is it at all likely that they arrange what they like.

Nobody knows just why they are or are not anxious
While they sit and watch the horse which rests
Not because he is tired but because they are waiting
To say will they wait with them in their way
Only to say it relieves them that they go away
This is what they feel when they like it
Most of them do or which
It is very often their need not to be either
Just why they are after all made quickly faster
Just as they might do.
It is what they did say when they mentioned it
Or this.
It is very well to go up and down and look more
Than they could please that they see where
It is better that they are there

STANZA XV

Should they may be they might if they delight
In why they must see it be there not only necessarily
But which they might in which they might
For which they might delight if they look there
And they see there that they look there
To see it be there which it is if it is
Which may be where where it is
If they do not occasion it to be different
From what it is.
In one direction there is the sun and the moon
In the other direction there are cumulus clouds and the sky
In the other direction there is why
They look at what they see
They look very long while they talk along
And they may be said to see that at which they look
Whenever there is no chance of its not being warmer
Than if they wish which they were.
They see that they have what is there may there
Be there also what is to be there if they may care
They care for it of course they care for it.
Now only think three times roses green and blue
And vegetables and pumpkins and pansies too

She knew she grew all these through to you
And she may be there did he mind learning how now
All this cannot be mixed.
Once again I think I am reflecting
And they may be patient in not why now
And more than if which they are reflecting
That if they with which they will be near now
Or not at all in the same better
Not for which they will be all called
By which they will may be as much as if wishing
But which each one has seen each one
Not at all now
Nor if they like as if with them well or ordinarily
Should they be more enjoined of which they like
It is very well to have seen what they have seen
But which they will not only be alike.
They are very evenly tired with more of this
For they will happen to be in which resolve
Always made by which they prepare that no one
Is more able to be sure of which
They will not will they compel
Not only where they see which they see
But will they be willing for needing
Only which they could call not by it
If they have come again to do it not at all
As very much made in once by their own saying
Yes of course which they will not be at all
Not only not for them in which they like
I lead all may be caught by fattening
Or not either sent all which may positively say so
In their own pleasure neither which they like
It is mine when they need to accept add me
For which they mind one at a time
It is at one time no different between how many hills
And they look like that caught in I mean
For which they will add not when I look
Or they make it plain by their own time.
This which they see by
They turn not their back to the scenery
What does it amount to.

Not only with or better most and best
For I think well of meaning.
It is not only why they might stare to change
Or feel cups well as he has promised, he said,
That there would be several days not of rain
And there would then be plenty of good weather
Probably the crops would be good.
Alright they think in wishes
And some superstitions and some
Beginning and fortunately with places of ditches
And also formidably of which when
When they find the clouds white and the sky blue
The hills green and different in shape too
And the next to what followed when the other bird flew
And what he did when he dug out what he was told to
And which way they will differ if they tell them too
And what they do if they do not cover the vine too
They do it by hand and they carry it all too
Up the way they did still have it to do
And so they think well of well-wishers.
I have my well-wishers thank you

PART II

STANZA I

Full well I know that she is there
Much as she will she can be there
But which I know which I know when
Which is my way to be there then
Which she will know as I know here
That it is now that it is there
That rain is there and it is here
That it is here that they are there
They have been here to leave it now
But how foolish to ask them if they like it
Most certainly they like it because they like what they have
But they might easily like something else
And very probably just as well they will have it

Which they like as they are very likely not to be
Reminded that it is more than ever necessary
That they should never be surprised at any one time
At just what they have been given by taking what they have
Which they are very careful not to add with
As they may easily indulge in the fragrance
Not only of which but by which they know
That they tell them so.

STANZA II

It is very often that they like to care
That they have it there that the window is open
If the fire which is lit and burning well
Is not open to the air.
Think well of that is open to the air
Not only which but also nearly patiently there
It is very often why they are nearly
Not only with but also with the natural wine
Of the country which does not impoverish
Not only that but healthily with which they mean
That they may be often with them long.
Think of anything that is said
How many times have they been in it
How will they like what they have
And will they invite you to partake of it
And if they offer you something and you accept
Will they give it to you and will it give you pleasure
And if after a while they give you more
Will you be pleased to have more
Which in a way is not even a question
Because after all they like it very much.
It is very often very strange
How hands smell of woods
And hair smells of tobacco
And leaves smell of tea and flowers
Also very strange that we are satisfied
Which may not be really more than generous
Or more than careful or more than most.
This always reminds me of will they win

Or must they go or must they be there
They may be often led to change.
He came and when he went he said he was coming
And they may not be more in agreement
Than cakes are virtuous and theirs is a pleasure
And so they either or a splendid as a chance
Not to be seen to be not impervious
Or which they were not often as a chance
To be plainly met not only as anxious.
Will they come here I wonder why
If not will they try if they wonder why
Or not at all favourably
Just as may as in a way
A cow is and little cows are
He said it so and they meant more
Which it is for this an occasion or not
Just as they please
May they be just as careful as if they have a chance
To be not only without any trouble
Or may be they came

STANZA III

They may lightly send it away to say
That they will not change it if they may
Nor indeed by the time that it is made
They may indeed not be careful that they were thankful
That they should distinguish which and whenever
They were not unlikely to mean it more
Than enough not to decide that they would not
Or well indeed if it is not better
That they are not cautious if she is sleepy
And well prepared to be close to the fire
Where it is as if outside it did resemble
Or may be they will relinquish.
I think I know that they will send an answer.
It may be sensibly more than they could
That one sheep has one lamb and one sheep has two lambs
Or they may be caught as if when they had been
Not only as they like but she can say

He can say too two may be more that is to say
Three may be more than one more.
And only after they have five nobody
Has quarreled not only for them but after a while
She knows that they know that they
Are not remarkable.
It is often more which they use that they
Knowing that there is a month of May
In which often they use or may they use
Which they knew it could be in no venture
That they will use he will carefully await
And leave it like that to be carefully watching
Will we come and will we come then
They may to which may they be to which they use
Or not at all as in a fashion
More than kind.
It is often so that they will call them
Or may be there for which they will not see them
Nor may they as what they will like
In for instance will they change this for them.
Coming by themselves for them in no matter
Could one ask it is not usual
That if they are polite they are politer
Or either of them not to be one for them
Which they may call on their account for them.
It is all all of which they could be generous
If no one gave more to them
They could be with them all who are with them
For then may they be more than many
Not only but righteous and she would be
Not angry now not often for them
With not as told not by them
It is very well to have no thorough wishes
Wish well and they will call
That they were remarkable
And it is well to state that rain makes hills green
And the sky blue and the clouds dark
And the water water by them
As they will not like what they do not have
As nobody has been indifferent

Not only will she regret
But they will say one two three
Much as they use
It is very well to know.
More than to know
What they make use of
Although it is cold in the evening
Even if a fire is burning and
Summer is of use to them

STANZA IV

All who have hoped to think of them or wonder
Or maybe they will like what they have had
More than they should if they went away freshly
And were very modest about not knowing why it was
That they were not denied their pleasure then
For which they may be more than not inclined
Which makes it plainly that in one way it made no
        difference
That they were always said to be just when they came
There where they liked and they were not allowed
Not only ordinarily but just now
They were agreeable which is why they are they
They hesitate they move they come where they are
        standing
They will take courage which they will not want
Nor will they worry very much as why they wait
They will not be often there
Think well of how very agreeable it is to meet them
To say yes we will go we know where we have been
We will say yes it is not without trouble that we came
Nor do we manage definitely to share.
But we must with one and all go there.
It will be often fortunately that strawberries need straw
Or may they yes indeed have marsh grass ready
It will support all who will have support
And she will kindly share hers with them
His with them
More than that they will stop this for them

Not only certainly but very surely
No one needs kindly any disappointment
Will they step in and out and may easily
One heel be well and one heel one be well
Or as an over ready change for once in a while
There may be reasons too why there are reasons why
If they may be said as much
That they will stay behind not only here but there
For them in a way they stay

STANZA V

Be careful that it is not their way not to like that
Not only not to be careful but to be very much obliged
Also moreover not to be the cause of their going
But which they will endeavor not to change
Not only for this but by the time
That which they knew there they must remain
If for them not at all it is not only why they like
But which they may wish from foolishness
Once at a glance.
It is not only why they are careful to replace
Not only which they may as they disturb
Or any weakness of wishing they would come there
More often than they do or carefully not at all
As it is their care to bestow it at one time
Should they because or in or influence
Not only called but very likely called a sneeze
From first to last by them in this way introduces
Them one at one time.
It is at once after that they will be better than theirs
All alike or all alike as well or rather better not
It can only not do not do all of which
They prefer elaborate to why they while away
Their time as they may accidentally manage
As a chance in which provocation is what they can call
Or while they went they gathered more
In made in gain
And more than all of it called cold

Or why they should arrange carefulness
Not only is our neat but as our plan
Named called useful as it is understood
Just why they could they interpose
Just fortunately in around about
At all managed getting ready there
To be determined but not by themselves alone
As often as they are more there
Which interested them.
They could be bought necessarily two or taken
In place of when they were attached to whatever
It is left to be planned that they can call
For it in all the hope that they can go
Or stay away whichever it is made to like
As they may mean or mean to do
It is fortunately by all of them
Made not only with this but for this.
A change from rest or a change from the rest
Well and welcome as the day which when the sun shines
Makes water grow or covers others more
Than when they looked there where they saw
All of which when they had not wondered
Would they like it there best
Might I ask were they disappointed.

STANZA VI

When they were helped as every one can
Once when they do and once when it is
Not only their feeling but also their way
Not to suppose that they will wish
That they may receive nor more than suggest
From which they look is much as if ever they can
What they will oblige which will be for them
Not only theirs but nearly as much
As theirs not alone but which they may
Not only join but nearly so
Make their arrangement believe their own way
Come whichever they can in what ever way

That they conclude that they must use
It not only for them but without any doubt
As they will hear better or not so well
In which and on which occasion
They will not only call but let them know
Not only what they allow but whatever they wish
As not only theirs.
It is a chance that they will be left
Or be consoled by each with one as no mistake
But they attach themselves they do trouble
They come when they will
They allow. They can establish.
They can even agree not only to what they have
But should they be more than bereft
If they not only see but not only see
All in more than all because and because
Of which they are obliged
Being as they are to go there.
It is very kind of them to come.
As well as they may because and moreover
When they think well they think without that
Which moreover make it yield
Because it is an instance of often now
Not only with it but without it
As ever when and once in a while
As much as they change theirs in their own
As once allowed because they undertake may
As they can positively learn
Which it is mine to have then.
All that they can do is theirs not only then
They may often be thought all as at once
More often they will relish
At once they may change it
It is not only if at once that they are all
Or do they like it too
Or may they see it all
Or even might they not like it
If it is at once whatever they claim.
It is not only not a misfortune
It is wholly theirs to be believe me

STANZA VII

What do I care or how do I know
Which they prepare for them
Or more than they like which they continue
Or they may go there but which they mind
Because of often without care that they increase aloud
Or for them fortunately they manage this
But not only what they like but who they like.
There may be said to be all history in this.
They may be often opposite to not knowing him
Or they may be open to any impression
Or even if they are not often worried
They may be just bothered
By wondering do they often make it be alike afterward
Or to continue afterward as if they came
It is useless to introduce two words between one
And so they must conceal where they run
For they can claim nothing
Nor are they willing to change which they have
Oh yes I organise this. But not a victory
They will spend or spell space
For which they have no share
And so to succeed following.
This is what there is to say.
Once upon a time they meant to go together
They were foolish not to think well of themselves
Which they did nor were they willing
As they often were to go around
When they were asked as they were well aware
That they could think well of them
Remember this once they knew that the way to give
Was to go more than they went
For which they meant immediately faster
It is always what they will out loud
May they like me or may they like me.
No one can know who can like me.
This is their hope in wishing however
When they were not only laden with best wishes
But indeed not inclined for them to be careless

Might they be often more than ever especially
Made to be thought carelessly a vacation
That they will like this less.
Let me listen to me and not to them
May I be very well and happy
May I be whichever they can thrive
Or just may they not.
They do not think not only only
But always with prefer
And therefor I like what is mine
For which not only willing but willingly
Because which it matters.
They find it one in union.
In union there is strength.

STANZA VIII

She may be thought to be accurate with acacia
Or by and by accustomed to be fairly
Just why they should in often as in or often
Could they call a partly necessary for them
Or why should anxiousness be anxiousness
Or their like that because more than they could
They will be named what do they do if the like
Or could they be troubled by it as a thought
Should they consider that they will gain
By not having it made for them to join
They will plainly state that only then only only there
More than if they will show all of it
Because please be plain for this time
And do not couple that they abandoned
Or which they abandoned because not only they were not used
In better than whenever or wherever they will go
I think I do not sympathise with him.
It is often known how they are just how they are
And if they are often just as well as being here
It is not at all unlikely they will change
And this you know all of it which you know
Be only thought not to please.
I think that if I were faithful or as bought

Or should be checked or as thought
Or finally they can claim for it more
Or just why they are identified
Or pleading they will call it all they know
Or have it that they make it do
Not only as they have not only as they have
It is other than theirs that they think is worth while
But which they come frequently to separate
In advantageous or advantage by this time
That they will come at once or not
For which they will come way of nine
She may be thought better have it spared them
That they will cover other than allowance.
He will come to show well enough all there
Or better have it strange or come again
Night like or night like do.
It is very foolish to hesitate between do and dew.
Or not at all broadly on which account
They can favor or fulfill or never marry
It is while while they smell that all it came
It came to be very heavy with perfume
Just like it may only it was not more than just
Why they went back.
Back and forth.
I have often thought it to be just as well
Not to go only why not if they are going
But they will like why they look
They look for them and are reminded.
That often any day all day
They will not go alike but keep it.
However much they say.
How many did you know
Or not say no.
Or no
Come to couple spelling with telling.

STANZA IX

Just why they could not ask them to come here
Or may they press them to relieve delight

Should they be pleased or may they cause them then
It have it only lost they do not care to leave
Should they come when and will they forward it back
Or neither when they care just when they change
May they not leave or will they not allow
That they see this when they look here
And they may very well be ready
To see this when they look where they do
Nor or may they be there where they are
But not there where they are when
They are at once pleased with what they have
As they do not wish not only but also
To have it better where they like.
It is often no purpose not to have disgrace
Said that they will wait.
All often change all of it so.
It may be decided or not at all
That it is meant should they use
Or would they care to think well long
Of what they think well.
And thank you
It is why they ask everything of them.
Should it be equally well planned
Made to carry or please it for them too
As they may often care or the difference
Between care and carry and recall
Should they find it theirs may they
Will they not be thought well of them.
Or not at all differently at once.
She may have no illusions
Nor be prepared not to be baffled
Or think well of then for which awhile
They chose.
It is for this that they came there and stay.
Should it be well done or should it be well done
Or may they be very likely or not at all
Not only known but well known.
I often think I would like this for that
Or not as likely
Not only this they do

But for which not for which for which
This they do.
Should it be mine as pause it is mine
That should be satisfying

STANZA X

It is not which they knew when they could tell
Not all of it of which they would know more
Not where they could be left to have it do
Just what they liked as they might say
The one that comes and says
Who will have which she knew
They could think all of which they knew as full
Not only of which they could they had as a delight
Or could it be occasionally just when they liked
It was not only theirs that they used as this
Not which they had with them not with them told
All have it not in any way in any anger
But they have it placed just when not there
For which they will allow could it or would it be told
That they shall not waste it to say to them
All of which after a while it is
As an arrangement
Not only theirs and only not at all.
They must be always careful to just be with them
Or they will not only not be but could be thought
To change which they will never know
Not only only all alike
But they will will be careful
It is not only this that antagonises that
Or they may be just as well in their refreshment
They will do always they will always do this
They could not relieve often which they do
They could be thought will it do
Once more come to gather does it matter
That it could be that they showed them this
But not this that they showed them that they showed them
     that
Or only once or not with not as only not once

Could they come where they were
Not only so much but also this much
Just whenever they liked this much
Which they were to declare
That no one had had corroboration
For which they will not only like
Letting once make it spell which they do
They can call it not be it as careless
Not only to ask but neither rested for
Which they will better can it have it
Not only there around but this
It is pleasantly felt for all
Not only why they like with which
They came for it with their undertaking
Made that they will or use or will they use
By which they will know more than they incline
Coming as it does coming as it does
Are they allowed
After all if it is so

STANZA XI

I thought how could I very well think that
But which they were a choice that now they knew
For which they could be always there and asking
But made not more than which than they can like
Not only why they came but which they knew
For their own sake by the time that it is there
They should be always rather liking it
To have not any one exclaim at last
It must be always just what they have done
By which they know they can feel more than so
As theirs they can recognise for which they place
And more and moreover which they do
It is not only to have all of it as more
Which they can piece and better more than which
They may remain all or in part
Some can think once and find it once
Others for which for which they will

It is at no time that they joined
For which they joined as only
Not for which it is in partly measure
Having alike be once more obtained
They make no trouble as they come again
All which they could
But they will care
All for which it is at once thought
Just when they can surprise
No one in what they could there
Make without any pause a rest.
They will think why they
And they will come
In response.
Should they be well enough.
Otherwise they can consider that
Whatever they have missed.
I think I know I like I mean to do
For which they could they will place
He will place there where
It is finally thought out best
No means no means in inquietude
Just when they give and claim a reward
Not for which they go and get this
They have been with the place their place
Why is there not why is there not with doubt.
Not able to be with mine.

STANZA XII

One fortunate with roses is fortunate with two
And she will be so nearly right
That they think it is right
That she is now well aware
That they would have been named
Had not their labels been taken away
To make room for placing there
The more it needs if not only it needs more so
Than which they came

STANZA XIII

But it was only which was all the same

STANZA XIV

It is not only early that they make no mistake
A nightingale and a robin.
Or rather that which may which
May which be which they may choose which
They knew or not like that
They make this be once or not alike
Not by this time only when they like
To have been very much absorbed.
And so they find it so
And so they are
There
There which is not only here but here as well as there.
They like whatever I like.

STANZA XV

It is very much like it.

STANZA XVI

Could I think will they think that they will
Or may they be standing as seated still
For which they will leave it make it be still
That they will reach it for which they will until
They should be said to be planned for which they will
Not which they need not plan not more than will
It is an estimate of ferocity which they would not know
Not with surprise nor from the wish
That they would come at all
May they be mentioned
For which they can not be only lost
For which they will may they may they come in
For which they will not but very likely
But they can not be there with which they will

For they may be with that kind that is what is
When they can like it as they do
But which they can not be for them
All made as they are not without it
Often left to them to come to arrange this
More than they can at most.
It was not only that they liked it
It is very kind of them to like it.

STANZA XVII

Come which they are alike
For which they do consider her
Make it that they will not belie
For which they will call it all
Make them be after not at least ready
Should they be settled strangely
Coming when they like an allowance
Naming it that they change more for them
With which which is certainly why they waited
They may be more regularly advised
In their case they will be able
Not only which they know but why they know
It is often that do their best
Not only as it is but which in change
They can be as readily which it is alike
Theirs as they better leave
All which they like at once
Which nearly often leave
This is the time in which to have it fasten
That they like all they like
More than which they may redeem.
It is often very well to if they prey
Should they could should they
They will not be imagined fairer
If they next from then on
Have it as not diminished
They can place aisle to exile
And not nearly there
Once in a while they stammer but stand still

In as well as exchange.
Once in a while very likely.
It is often their choice to feel it
As they could if they left it all
A ball fall.
Not two will give
Not one will give one two
Which they may add to change.
They will change what they like
Just what they do.
One two three or two

STANZA XVIII

She may be kind to all
If she wishes chickens to share
Her love and care
But they will think well of this
Which may not be amiss
If they like.
Two dogs for one or some one.
It is a happy wish
For some one.

STANZA XIX

She may think the thought that they will wish
And they will hold that they will spell anguish
And they will not be thought perverse
If they angle and the will for which they wish as verse
And so may be they may be asked
That they will answer this.
Let me see let me go let me be not only determined
But for which they will mind
That they are often as inclined
To have them add more than they could
She will be certainly seen if not as much
They will be left to be determined
As much as if they pleased they pleased
Not only theirs but only theirs

For them as much as known and not only
Not repeated because they will be seen
Partly and for less for which they are not very clearly
Made to be better than often as serviceable
Is it as much as why they like
For which they are often as much mistaken
Anything astonishes a mother or any other.
A stanza in between shows restlessly that any queen
Any not a stanza in between for which before which
Any stanza for which in between
They will be for which in between
Any stanza in between as like and they are likely
To have no use in cherishing.
They could be not alone consoled
They could be they may may they
Finally relieve.
It is often eight that they relinquish a stanza
Just when they feel that they are nearly
That they may could and do color
For which they will not only be inconvenient
For which they all for a forest
Come in as soon as our allowed
They prepare nor do they double
Or do they add prefer to before and call
She may be ours in allusion not only to
But why they will as much encourage
Readily for instance or may for instance
Come with not only as much as they tell
They tell it because if not why not
Such should be called their glory or their make
Of angling with and for around
May it be wading for which they wade
Theirs once again the same
All which they said it said it in and answered
May be they like
Might it be uncontained likely
That they should as much joined with ease
But not by this for once once is not only one
They presume once alike not by their own present.
They present well. It followed once more

Only theirs in case. For which.
They add conditionally to not previously adding
More than they gave to me.
One is not one for one but two
Two two three one and any one.
Why they out tired Byron

PART III

STANZA I

For which may they it which
That they may then or there either
By means of it for which they could
Recognise it is more than in going
They can come will they come until
The exacting by which they in exact
For which they will in and
They need not be for which they go
Theirs is all but not which it is in a chance
That they could incline to be inclined
For them or not or more inclined
Now not at all deserting
Nor not at all deserting
For which they finish English
May they make cake or better
For which when did he like
Theirs or not at all theirs
They will not leave a well alone
Or not because now the water comes
Just as they could.
They are always just not even
He is at least tired by the heat
Or he will
Just not join not just join
All that they like to do.
It is why I see when I look out at it
That it is just like when I see it
And it is fortunately not a bit of it

By this for which they please come out
Of there.
May they call one forty might
Or it is not might it
If it is not only they did
But which will they if they do
Not only this or which but may or may
Should more not any more
Any day make raspberries ripe
As they may do make what they do there
In leaning having had which
Not only while they do not but while they do
In often not at all now I am sure
Not sure not only how
But can it be at once.
Now to suppose it was like that.
Every time he went he went
And so it was not that they went
Not not at all.
And when he came back not when he went
He came back not when he came back
When he went.
One not to come to go when not to be
Not only not from here not here from there
Just as they used as usual
For which it it is not that that it
Must not do go
They leave it there is no there they do do
They do not do one two
As all round any arranged is not in at best
Once they he did once he they did or not
At all at any time.
It is so much that there is no difference in so much.
One one and two two one.

STANZA II

I think very well of Susan but I do not know her name
I think very well of Ellen but which is not the same
I think very well of Paul I tell him not to do so

I think very well of Francis Charles but do I do so
I think very well of Thomas but I do not not do so
I think very well of not very well of William
I think very well of any very well of him
I think very well of him.
It is remarkable how quickly they learn
But if they learn and it is very remarkable how quickly they
     learn
It makes not only but by and by
And they may not only be not here
But not there
Which after all makes no difference
After all this does not make any does not make any
     difference
I add added it to it.
I could rather be rather be here.

STANZA III

It was not which they knew
But they think will it be though
The like of which they drew
Through.
It which may be that it is they did
For which they will be never be killed
By which they knew
And yet it is strange when they say
Who.
And so not only not here
May be they will be not in their place there
For which they will what will they may be there
For them for which not only very much
As is what they like there.
Now three things beside.
Add which not which to which
They wish which they divide.
If a fisherman fishes
Or else a well
Very well does an attack
Look back.

For that in use an extra make a moment
Further in use which they can be there when
In open use of which they like each one
Where they have been to have been come from.
It is often that they do regularly not having been
Before.
As much as and alike and because
Once before always before afraid in a dog fight
But not now.
Not at all now not when they not only wish to do
May they be ours and very pretty too
And you.
Once more I think about a lake for her
I do not think about a lake for them
And I can be not only there not in the rain
But when it is with them this it is soon seen
So much comes so many come.
Comfortably if they like what they come.
From.
Tables of tables and frames of frames.
For which they ask many permissions.
I do know that now I do know why they went
When they came
To be
And interested to be which name.
Who comes to easily not know
How many days they do know
Or whether better either and or
Before.
She may be eight in wishes
I said the difference is complicated
And she said yes is it it is
Or she said it is is it.
There seems so much to do
With one or two with six not seven
Either on.
Or believe.
That not only red at night can deceive.
Might they we hope better things of this.
Or of this.

Is.
When they are once or twice and deceive.
But leave
She may be called either or or before
Not only with but also with
With which they wish this
That they will like to give rain for rain
Or not.
It is just like it sounds.
I could not like it then nor now
Out now
Remained to how.
However they are careful.
Having forgotten it for them
Just how much they like
All potatoes are even when they have flowers
All adding is even
If they asked them
Would they ask them.
It would not be like alike for which
They did.
They had and did.
But which they had which they had which they is and did
Gotten and gotten a row
Not to in did not and in said so
It is not only that I have not described
A lake in trees only there are no trees
Just not there where they do not like not having trees
Trees.
It is a lake so and so or oh
Which if it is could it does it for it
Not make any do or do or it
By this it is a chance inclined.
They did not come from there to stay they were hired
They will originally will do
It is not only mine but also
They will three often do it.
Not now.
Do I mind

Went one.
I wish to remain to remember that stanzas go on

STANZA IV

Not while they do better than adjust it
It can feeling a door before and to let
Not to be with it now not for or
Should they ask it to be let
May they be sent as yet
For may they may they need met
Way and away in adding regret to set
And he looks at all for his ball.
I thought that I could think that they
Would either rather more which may
For this is and antedated a door may be
Which after all they change.
He would look in the way
Of looking.
Now added in again.
It is a way having asked in when
Should they come to be not only not adding some.
I think it is all very well to do without that
But it is why they could be with without that
For which they called a time
Not having finished to say that nearly there
They would be neither there as box wood grows
And so if it were they could be as easily found
As if they were bound.
Very nearly as much a there
That is one thing not to be made anything
For that but just for that they will add evening to anything

STANZA V

Not which they know for which they like
They must be last to be not at it only with
It can for which they could with and a
Many can not come in this for nor without them

Some of which will they for them awhile
For which it is not only at an attempt
They can find that they can retouch
Not only what should be cared for
So they make this seem theirs
And only integrally shared as much as fine
They will out and out confer
That they will always may be so
As what they like.
Be mine prepared
What may it be not for their add it to
Can and delight for which not why they neglect
Just when or just when
For which not more than
Or by nearly
It is not their coat.
They must care for their furniture
Not but as one
For could and forfeit too
Coming and one.
It is not only that they could be here
When they are often made just may
It is my own that no one adds for it
Not only is it added well
She can only cloud go around
By that in awoken
Could and clad
May they be eaten glad
Should not only should not under known
Say any way
A way
Equal to any stanzas are all three
They must be spared to share
Should it not only this and all around
They will have will appointed
Not only why they look not that
They call meadows may or all
For it is not only only their name
But which is a plain and a plain plaintive

Too or more.
I can not be indifferent to a little while
By which all tall at all
They could be not only any in any case
What does he mean by that
Not only not only not any interest not interested
But they will a valley.
Once every day they ate to a day
Not obliging not at not to obliging
But she will have meant
Or they will but they maintain
Ease by a minute.
It is not only their four in amount
Or while or a while
Or going
Or just as soon by which ought
Will they not have any as presence
They could be ought they be manage
Not only she thinks which
Just as never which many which
Made or manage they thrust.
It is often all they order or in order
But which they endanger
Do or not do.
However may be in account of whatever they do.

STANZA VI

It is not a range of a mountain
Of average of a range of a average mountain
Nor may they of which of which of arrange
To have been not which they which
May add a mountain to this.
Upper an add it then maintain
That if they were busy so to speak
Add it to and
It not only why they could not add ask
Or when just when more each other
There is no each other as they like

They add why then emerge an add in
It is of absolutely no importance how often they add it.

STANZA VII

By which are which add which a mounting
They need a leaf to leave a settling
They do not place a rein for resting
They do not all doubt may be a call
They can do which when ever they name
Their little hope of not knowing it.
Their little hope of not knowing it.

STANZA VIII

By it by which by it
As not which not which by it
For it it is in an accesible with it
But which will but which will not it
Come to be not made not made one of it
By that all can tell all call for in it
That they can better call add
Can in add none add it.
It is not why she asked that anger
In an anger may they be frightened
Because for it they will be which in not
Not now.
Who only is not now.
I can look at a landscape without describing it.

STANZA IX

That is why a like in it with it
Which they gay which they gay
But not only just the same.
Now who are now
Our who are now
It is not first not they are
But being touching all the same
Not and neither or the name.

It is very anxious not to know the name of them
But they know not theirs but mine.
Not theirs but mine.

STANZA X

Tell me darling tell me true
Am I all the world to you
And the world of what does it consist
May they be a chance to may they be desist
This came to a difference in confusion
Or do they measure this with resist with
Not more which.
Than a conclusion
May they come with may they in with
For which they may need needing
It is often by the time that not only
Which waiting as an considerable
And not only is it in importance
That they could for an instance
Of made not engaged in rebound
They could indeed care
For which they may not only
Be very often rested in as much
Would they count when they do
Is which which when they do
Making it do.
For this all made because of near
No name is nearly here
Gathering it.
Or gathering it.
Might it in no way be a ruse
For it which in it they an obligation
Fell nearly well

STANZA XI

Now Howard now.
Only righteous in a double may
It is ought frown

They could however collaborate
As only in the way
Of not only not renowned.
What is it often
Oh what is it often
Or should
Should as any little while
Think more what they mean
Oh think more what they mean
Now I know why he said so
Oh no.
It is if it is.
What is the difference.
What is the difference between for it and it
And also more also before not it.
It can be an absence better than not before.
It is just why they tried.

STANZA XII

I only know a daisy date for me
Which is in wishes can forget for it
Not which not that that is
And is that that not be that with
It is not any one can think
Why be without any one one can
Be favored flavored not which
It is not only not only neither without
But this is only so.
I cannot often be with my name.
Not at all
They will not wonder which at a time
And may if be alright.
They can lead any one away.
Now look not at that.
Having heard now hearing it
Should just engage those
Not always connected
Readily express

For them forget
It is very easy to be afraid to hear one come in.
All like all to go
There is often when they do not mention running
Or walking or not going
Or not why they do not find it in for him.
Just why they should or just why
Ate or bate or better or not sigh
He she can sigh and try why
They seize sigh or my.
If is often when it is not stated
That at it two or to
That is is better added stated
That they are to
I often like it not before
They do not or do not listen one to one another
Or by guess.
It is just as much as allowed
Why they carry or
All would or wood or wooden
Or all owed
Or not vestiges or very sight
Of water owned or own
Or not well velvet
Or not aligned
Or all or gone
Or capitally
Or do or comforting
Or not
Renown.
They will say pages of ages.
I like anything I do
Stanza two.

STANZA XIII

Stanza ten make a hen
Stanza third make a bird
Stanza white make a dog

Stanza first make it heard
That I will not not only go there
But here

STANZA XIV

In changing it inside out nobody is stout
In changing it for them nobody went
In not changing it then.
They will gradually lengthen
It.

STANZA XV

I could carry no one in between

STANZA XVI

Can thinking will or well or now a well.
Wells are not used any more now
It is not only just why this is much
That not one may add it to adding main
For never or to never.
Suppose I add I like to
I may should show choose go or not any more not so
This is how any one could be in no hope
Of which no hope they did or did not
There is no difference between having in or not only not
    this
Could it be thought did would
By it a name.
I think I could say what nobody thought
Nobody thought I went there
This is however that they add sufficiently
Because it is not better allowed
All will come too.
Just joined how to houses
But they will like an only name
They could be thought why they had a weakness
To be sure.

Now this is only how they thought.
Let no one leave leaves here.
Leaves are useful and to be sure
Who can or could be can be sure.
I could think add one add one advantage
That is how they like it.

STANZA XVII

She does not who does not it does not like it
Our our guess yes
But it does not it does not who does guess it
But they will place it or not place it yes
They could in insistence have nobody blamed
Which they do ours on account
May they or may they may they blame this
This that they will wait when not in resting
But which they for which they could date and wait
Will they do what they are careful to do too
Or like this will they like this where they go
When it is not only not certain where they went they were
    here
At all as likely as not up and down up and down to go
Not because before by which they attracted
They were with an on account which they knew
This not only not which they need blessing
Which or not which when they do not or which way
They do go
It is not inadvertent that they oblige
It is waiting they gather what do they like
Cherries not only not better not ripe
It was a mistake not to make not only a mistake with this
In not only in all noon after noon that they like
It is always arbitrary to come with bliss
For them to join it to come with it
They could manage just what they did
But did they not feel that
They could be not only not allowed but not clouded
It was very different again
Just when they join that they look.

They refer to a little that is a little trunk
A very little trunk once.
How very sorry they are for not for placing
Will place well
Just once to join and not too alike
That they go
Or will they not only in place of which to happen to be last
    not to save it to say so
Or go.
And so they went carefully together.
As they like it which
They mean that for when
It is not mine
Fine

STANZA XVII

It is not which they will not like or leave it as a wish which
    they compare
All for most all for that did they if not as it is
Should they dare or compare
Could it have been found all round
Or would they take pleasure in this
Or may they not be often whichever
As they told theirs in any day.
Does it make any difference if they ask
Or indeed does it make any difference
If they ask.
Would they be different if nobody added it all
Or looking just alike do they mind any extra
May they or should they combine
Or should they not easily feel
That if they could they may or should
We ask.
Be not only without in any of their sense
Careful
Or should they grow careless with remonstrance
Or be careful just as easily not at all
As when they felt.
They could or would would they grow always

By which not only as more as they like.
They cannot please conceal
Nor need they find need they a wish
They could in either case they could in either case
Not by only for a considerable use.
Now let only it be once when they went
It is of no importance to please most
One of them as it is as it is now
It is not only for which they cause
That it is not only not why they like
Them.
They could often be a relish if it had not been thought
That they should unite.
They will be only not more a choice
For which alone they remain.
Proclaim.
I wondered why they mentioned what they like.
All of which only what they knew
Just why they yearn
Or not rest more.
A counter and not a counter pane
They could be relished.
Just why they called wait wait.
What is it when there is a chance
Why should they like whatever they do
Not only if they will but if they will
Not only
It is not more than this shame.
Shame should not be for fountains.
Nor even not yet
But just when the mountains are covered
And yet they will please of course they will please
You which it is.
Not any not on any account
May it not only be why they went.
It is always which they like.
It is a thought give a thought to Cuba
She could in cooking
And only not let owls frighten not birds
Not only not

Because in only ending birds
Who ends birds where.
Now I have said it.
It is of no use one year
A toad one year
A bird a little very little as little bird one year
And if one year
Not only not at all one year.
It came very difficultly.
Just not in not in not in not as in him.
And so on account on account of reproach.
Could they if not she would be startled.
But they cost neither here nor there.
Just as I think.
Once when they should they if indifferently would
When to look again
Pinny pinny pop in show give me a pin and I'll let you
     know
If a pin is precious so is more.
And if a floor is precious so is not a door.
A door is not bought twice.
I do think so earnestly of what.
She had no chagrin in beauty
Nor in delight nor in settled sweetness
Nor in silliness alright.
But why often does she say yes as they may say
She finds that if one is careful one has to be very much
Awake to what they do all need.
Now often I think again of any english.
English is his name sir.
That much is not only not only not a disadvantage
Over them.
Once more I wish italian had been wiser.
But will they wish
They wish to help.
And their wish succeeded.
And added.
Once more I return to why I went.
I went often and I was not mistaken.

And why was I not mistaken
Because I went often.

STANZA XVIII

Not only this one now

STANZA XVIX

How can no one be very nearly or just then
Obliged to manage that they need this now
She will commence in search not only of their account
But also on their account as arranged in this way
She will begin she will state
She will not elucidate but as late
She will employ she will place adding
Not with it without it with their account
Supposing they may say the land stretches
Or else may be they will say it is all told
Or perhaps also they will say
Or perhaps also they will say that they went from here to
    there
Or not only just then but when just then
Also perhaps not only might they not try
Maybe not only what they wish but will they wish
Perhaps after a while it is not why they went
Not only which it is but after it is
They might be thought to have it not known
Only which they are obliged
To feel it at all not which they can know
They could call colors all or not
Incomplete roses.
They find fish an ornament
And not at all jealously at any and all resemblance
They have been warned to try and be called all
For which they plan a favor
Should they be thought to be caught all around
By that time it is well to think it all
Not only may they be

It is a pleasure that twice is neglected
In which amount.
They anticipate in place.
Could no one try of fancies.
However how is it if it is right and left.
Or rather should it did it happen to be more
They can allowed or stranger
They have not then once cost
But which in theirs and on which occasion
May they be minded.
Now how can I think softly of safety
Which which they do
It is not only their only hindrance
But not well won not with it.
In intermittance may they remind sees.
She may fortunately not count
If she says but which if they say
But which they find.
Now only this when they all think.
How can she manage our places.
It is for this they could recall
Better than all do.
It was not often that I could not join them
Which they did.
Now how could you disguise joins
By which it is in ate and dishes
They could be only they could be only worried
By what they remain with what they will
Or not unkind.
This is what I think I think I often did the same
When they should be all there as known
After all I am known
Alone
And she calls it their pair.
They could be cut at noon
Even in the rain they cut the hay
Hay and straw are not synonymous
Or even useful with them
Or as a hope that they did
Which after all they did not.

In this way any one or did add not a precaution.
Think how well they differ caution and precaution
Or not.
Or should they allow ours in glass
For them they carry
Better not be strange in walking
They do or do not walk as they walk as they past.
Will they mean mine or not theirs
They will they will like what they entitle
Should they be theirs.
We asked did they that is it
That is did it mean it was with them
There with them
They could not be ought not be mine.
So then
All of which reminds no one
Having said.
Do which or they may be kind.
She says some or summer could be.
Not only not again for when.
I can think exactly how I found that out.
Just when they say or do
Once and before.
It is not only that they like
In the meantime.
If even stanzas do.

STANZA XX

Not what they do with not
Not only will they wish what
What they do with what they like
But they will also very well state
Not only which they prefer by themselves
And now add it in aging ingenuity
But which they will as soon as ever they can
But which they tell indeed may they or may they not
      proudly
Not only theirs in eight but which they meant
They will all old declare

That believing it is a patent pleasure in their case
Nor when where will they go older than not
Nor will they furnish not only which they had but when
     they went
In reason.
It is often that they allow a cloud to be white
Or not only patently white but also just as green
Not only theirs in pleasure but theirs in case
Not only however but not only however
Or not at all in wishes that they had chickens
Which may be alternately well or ducks
Or will they spread for them alone
To be not only their care.
This which and whatever I think
I not only do not make it be my care
To endanger no one by hearing how often I place
Theirs not only why they are best not
Not by it as they like.
I have thought while I was awakening
That I might address them
And then I thought not at all
Not while I am feeling that I will give it to them
For them
Not at all only in collision not at all only in mistaken
But which will not at all.
I thought that I would welcome
And so I could be seen.
I then thought would I think one and welcome
Or would I not.
I then concluded that I might be deceived
And it was a white butterfly
Which flew not only not but also
The white dog which ran
And they they were accomplished
And once in a while I would rather gather
Mushrooms even than roses if they were edible
Or at least what not.
I do not wish to say what I think
I concluded I would not name those.
Very often I could feel that a change in cares

Is a change in chairs and not only can and cares
But places
I felt that I could welcome in anticipation wishes
Not only which they do but where they do
How are our changes.
When they could fix titles or affix titles.
When this you see hear clearly what you hear.
Now just like that not just like that
Or they will enjoin and endanger
Damage or delight but which they crow
They have threatened us with crowing
Oh yes not yet.
I cannot think with indifference
Nor will they not want me
Do will they add but which is not
Where they could add would or they would or not
For which they for which fortunately
Make it be mine.
I have often thought of make it be mine.
Now I ask any one to hear me.
This is what I say.
A poem is torn in two
And a broom grows as well
And which came first
Grows as well or a broom
Of course any one can know which of two
This makes it no accident to be taught
And either taught and either fight or fought
Or either not either which either
May they be either one not one only alone.
Should it be thought gracious to be a dish
Of little only as they might mean curiously
That we heard them too
And this I mean by this I mean.
When I thought this morning to keep them so they will not
    tell
How many which went well
Not as a conclusion to anxious
Anxious to please not only why but when
So them anxious to mean. I will not now

STANZA XXI

Now I recount how I felt when I dwelt upon it.
I meant all of it to be not rather yes I went
It is not that now they do not care that I do
But which one will
They can not be thought nervous if they are left alone
Now then I will think of which went swimming.
It does make a difference how often they go
Or will they prepare that I know
I know this I know that I shall say so
Or may they choose an anagram
This one said this one.
If one we hurried for this one
Just when they did wish that it should be settled then
They could think let us go
Just when they will they can
All my dear or but which they can
Having been long ago not knowing what I felt
And now
It does make a difference that well enough a cow
Can be recognised now so then
If not twenty as ten
Or one enough without it then.
This that I may
I repeat I do not know what I felt then
Which they do which they do
Nor will they track it if they follow then
How are it is to do
A kite is a delight this I can do then
But not with then for which they allow them
This is the way not to end but to see when the beginning.
I like a moth in love and months
But they will always say the same thing when
They sing singing
I wish I could repeat as new just what they do
Or alike as they hear when they do not listen to every one
So she said it they but which they
She said the nest was empty but not so
The nest was empty that is to say not there

It was as if she looked alike
By which no one mean startled
Like that
I think I will begin and say everything not something
But not again and only again alike
Thank you for the touch of which they leave
He easily destroys my interest in may be they do but I
    doubt it
But not at all with which by nearly which time
But just as well heard
Why should he not say he did say that
And it was amusing.
And by and by not which they do
I now I do not know what I feel
So in extra inclusion.
What do I think when I feel.
I feel I feel they feel they feel which they feel
And so borrowed or closed they will they will win
How can any one know the difference between worry and
    win.
This is not the only time they think which they know
Or better not alright.
How can they eager either or and mend
She can mend it not very well between.
Of course he knows at what he does not only hear
Oblige me. I also oblige him. And think then.
Do I repeat I do not know what I do not see to feel which
    they hear
Oh yes

STANZA XXII

When she meant they sent or a grievance
Was she meant that he went or a need of it henceforward
Was it with it that they meant that he sent or he thought
That they should not plainly have not bought
Or which they went to be naturally there
It is a pause in mistaken.
They could know that they would call
Or they would prefer it to before

On their account.
I should look if I saw
But she would send if she would intend to prefer
That they might cause it best and most.
It is not only which they go but when they go
Or if not said to send or say so
Now think how palpably it is known
That all she knows which when she goes
They look for him in place of that
Of which they are used or to be used
In preference
And so they halt more to partly do
Do or due or only dew or did you do it.
I could not favor leaves of trees to in any case
Place me to mine.
This is not what they care or for poetry.

PART IV

STANZA I

Who should she would or would be he
Now think of the difference of not yet.
It was I could not know
That any day or either so that they were
Not more than if they could which they made be
It is like this
I never knew which they may date when they say
Hurry not hurry I could not only not do it
But they prepare.
Let me think how many times I wished it.
It flattered me it flattered me it flattered me
And I was all prepared which they sent
Not only not why but where if they did not enjoy
Their place where they meant with them.
And so they may be fitly retired.
This is what I saw when they went with them.
I could have been interested not only in what they said but
    in what I said.

I was interested not interested in what I said only in what I
    said.
I say this I change this I change this and this.
Who hated who hated what.
What was it that announced they will not mind it.
I do think often that they will remember me.
Now who remembers whom what not a room
No not a room.
And who did prepare which which vegetable very well
And might I not only feel it to be right to leave them to say
Yes any day it is because after which way
They shell peas and of the pea shell they make a soup to eat
    and drink
And they might not amount to calls upon them.
They were in place of only where they went
Nobody notices need I be not there only
But which they send it.
Not to think but to think that they thought well of them.
Here I only know that pumpkins and peas do not grow
Well in wet weather.
And they think kindly of places as well as people.
I should think it makes no difference
That so few people are me.
That is to say in each generation there are so few geniuses
And why should I be one which I am
This is one way of saying how do you do
There is this difference
I forgive you everything and there is nothing to forgive.
No one will pardon an indication of an interruption
Nor will they be kindly meant will be too or as a sound.
I am interested not only in what I hear but as if
They would hear
Or she may be plainly anxious.
How are ours not now or not as kind.
They could be plainly as she is anxious
Or for their however they do
Just as well and just as well not at all
How can you slowly be dulled reading it.
It is not which they went for there were dishes
It is not why they were here not with their wishes

Or accidentally on account of clover
I never manage to hammer but I did
In with all investigation
And now I now I now have a brow
Or call it wet as wet as it is by and by
I feel very likely that they met with it
Which in no way troubles them
Or is it likely to.
It did it a great deal of good to rub it

STANZA II

I come back to think everything of one
One and one
Or not which they were won
I won.
They will be called I win I won
Nor which they call not which one or one
I won.
I will be winning I won.
Nor not which one won for this is one.
I will not think one and one remember not.
Not I won I won to win win I one won
And so they declare or they declare
To declare I declare I declare I win I won one
I win in which way they manage they manage to win I won
In I one won In which I in which won I won
And so they might come to a stanza three
One or two or one two or one or two or one
Or one two three all out but one two three
One of one two three or three of one two and one

STANZA III

Secretly they met again
All which is changed is made they may be merry
For which they could in any regulation
Manage which they may have in any case a trial
Of when they do or sing sisters
And so much is taken for granted

In which appointment they color me
Or leave it as not in a glass or on the grass
They pass.
Not at all
For which no one is met in winning
They will be very well pleased with how they stand
Or which or to which or whither they repair
To change it to change it fairly
Or may they like all that they have
Let us think well of which is theirs.
Why do they not count
Count how do you count
There is no counting on that account
Because if there is which is not what I say
I will make it do any day to-day
Or not why
They allow me to apply for it
They call will they call by which they plan
I will not gain gain easier easily
One which one which not now.
Why do they like which they like or why not
It is often many or as much which they have seen
Seen is often very well said
I think I have no wish that they will come
With their welcome
Nor which they try not to do
In any case for which they formerly
Were not repaid.
They are readily not here.
Once more no one not one begins
This is the difference
Not it or argument
But which and when
They enfold not in unfold
Beware aware deny declare
Or and as much in told
They cannot be thought restless when they do come and go
Either one either say so.
I say I felt like that.
Once they came twice they went which one will do

Or which they like for them or will they do
What they ask them to do
I manage to think twice about everything
Why will they like me as they do
Or not as they do
Why will they praise me as they do
Or praise me not not as they do
Why will they like me and I like what they do
Why will they disturb me to disturb not me as they do
Why will they have me for mine and do they
Why will I be mine or which may they
For which may they leave it
Or is it not
I have thought or will they let
Them know the difference if they tell them so
Between let us not be wreckless or restless
Or by word of mouth
May they please theirs fairly for me.
Just why they lay with the land up.
Coming to see it so.
It was not once when they went away that they came to
　　　stay.
Why should all which they add be each
Each is a peach
Why may they be different and try to beside
Be all as all as lost
They do not hide in which way
Better call it mine.
Our ours is or made between alike
With which cakes bake cakes
And it makes cake or cakes polite
But if they all call not when they do
Who ought they try to be alike
Which or for which which they may do too.
I refuse I I refuse or do
I do I do I refer to refuse
Or what what do I do
This is just how they like what they send
Or how to refuse what is that
That they need to sound sound lend

Can you question the difference between lend.
Or not lend
Or not send
Or not leant
Or not sent
But neither is a neighbor.
A neighbor to be here
She may be he may be useful or not useful
When they did not come why did they not come here.
Believe me it is not for pleasure that I do it
Not only for pleasure for pleasure in it that I do it.
I feel the necessity to do it
Partly from need
Partly from pride
And partly from ambition.
And all of it which is why
I literally try not only not why
But why I try to do it and not to do it.
But if it is well-known it is well-known

STANZA IV

Mama loves you best because you are Spanish
Mama loves you best because you are Spanish
Spanish or which or a day.
But whether or which or is languish
Which or which is not Spanish
Which or which not a way
They will be manage or Spanish
They will be which or which manage
Which will they or which to say
That they will which which they manage
They need they plead they will indeed
Refer to which which they will need
Which is which is not Spanish
Fifty which vanish which which is not spanish.

STANZA V

I think very well of my way.

STANZA VI

May be I do but I doubt it.

STANZA VII

May be may be men.

STANZA VIII

A weight a hate a plate or a date
They will cause me to be one of three
Which they may or may be
May be I do but do I doubt it
May be how about it
I will not may be I do but I doubt it
May be will may be.

STANZA IX

How nine
Nine is not mine
Mine is not nine
Ten is not nine
Mine is not ten
Nor when
Nor which one then
May be not then
Not only mine for ten
But any ten for which one then
I am not nine
May be mine
Mine one at a time
Not one from nine
Nor eight at one time
For which they may be mine.
Mine is one time
As much as they know they like
I like it too to be one of one two
One two or one or two
One and one
One mine

Not one nine
And so they ask me what do I do
May they but if they too
One is mine too
Which is one for you
May be they like me
I like it for which they may
Not pay but say
She is not mine with not
But will they rather
Oh yes not rather not
In won in one in mine in three
In one two three
All out but me.
I find I like what I have
Very much.

STANZA X

That is why I begin as much

STANZA XI

Oh yes they do.
It comes to this I wish I knew
Why water is not made of waters
Which from which they well
May they be kind if they are so inclined.
This leads me to want to wonder about which they do
I feel that they shall be spared this
They will agree for which they know
They do not do or describe
Their own use of which they are not tried
Or most or mostly names to be where
They will not as willingly not declare
That they appeal but do not prefer a share
Of plainly when they will
It is this I wish any minute
Oh yes I wish do I I do wish any minute
For them for fortune or forlorn or well

Well what do you do either what do you do
But like it or not
This that they may think just think
She has put her hair up with hair pins
Or do or do not only just do not only think
Finally than this.
It might be worth any cost to be lost.
They like that which they did
He did he remembered not only that he did
Oh why should any one repine one at a time.
Curiously.
This one which they think I think alone
Two follow
I think when they think
Two think I think I think they will be too
Two and one make two for you
And so they need a share of happiness
How are ours about to be one two or not three.
This that I think is this.
It is natural to think in numerals
If you do not mean to think
Or think or leave or bless or guess
Not either no or yes once.
This is how hours stand still
Or they will believe it less
For it is not a distress yes
Which they may free to build
Not by a house but by a picture of a house
But no distress to guess.
For this they are reconciled.
I wish that they were known.
This which they permit they please.
Please may they not delight and reconcile
Could anybody continue to be
Made openly one to see
That it is very pleasant to have been
With me.
When this you see.
Once when they were very busy
They went with me.

I feel that it is no trouble
To tell them what to do
Nor either is it at all a trouble
To wish that they would do what I do.
This is well and welcome to mean
I mean I mean.
Think however they will be ready
To believe me.
Think well of me when this you see.
I have begun by thinking that it is mine
It is mine many often one at a time
In rhyme.
Of course in rhyme which is often mine
In time one at one time
And so I wish they knew I knew
Two and one is two.
This is any day one for you.
This which I explain is where any one will remain
Because I am always what I knew
Oh yes or no or so
Once when they went to stay
Not which not only once or twice yesterday.
This introduces a new thought as is taught.
I wish I exchanged will they exchange me
Not at all.
This is why they bought a ball.
To give it to them to be all
All which they keep and lose if they choose.
Think how can you be and beware
And constantly take care
And not remember love and shove
By design.
It is well to be well and be well and be welcome
Of course not to be made to be
Honorably four to three which they do.
This is how they think well of believing all of theirs
To have been known.
It is singular that they may not only succeed
But be successful.
How should they not speedily try

If they could or could not know
That I did it.
Which is why they are so quiet with applause
Or may be the cause
Of their waiting there
For their meal
If they had it.
It is very beautiful to be eight and late.
Why should any one be ready too
As well as not for and with you
Which they do.
See how one thing can mean another.
Not another one no not any not another one.
Or not any means not or may not might three to one.
That is what they say to play.
And which is white if they might
They will call that they spoke to her

STANZA XII

Just why they mean or if they mean
Once more they mean to be not only not seen
But why this beside why they died
And for which they wish a pleasure.

STANZA XIII

But which it is fresh as much
As when they were willing to have it not only
But also famous as they went
Not to complain but to name
Their understanding confined on their account
Which in the midst of may and at bay
Which they could be for it as once in a while
Please may they come there.
This is an autobiography in two instances

STANZA XIV

When she came she knew it not only
Not by name but where they came with them.

She knew that they would be while they went.
And let us think.
She knew that she could know
That a genius was a genius
Because just so she could know
She did know three or so
So she says and what she says
No one can deny or try
What if she says.
Many can be unkind but welcome to be kind
Which they agree to agree to follow behind.
Her here.
Not clearly not as no mistake
Those who are not mistaken can make no mistake.
This is her autobiography one of two
But which it is no one which it is can know
Although there is no need
To waste seed because it will not do
To keep it though perhaps it is as well
Not to belie a change of when they care
They mean I like it if she will do it
But they could not complain again.
Let me remember now when I read it through
Just what it is that we will do for you.
This is how they asked in a minute when
They had exchanged a pencil for a pen
Just as I did.
Often of course they were not welcomed there
When they meant to give it all they liked
Made many more beside beside
Which when they tried or cried
He could not have his way
Or care to please please
And prepare to share wealth and honors
Which if they or if they of if they
Had not had mine too.
More can they gain or complain
Of which announce pronounce a name
When they call this they feel
Or not at all a heel she changed all that

For them fair or at once they will change hair
For there or at once more than all at once
Whenever they can.
This makes no allowance
Now this is how they managed to be late or not.
When once in a while they saw angrily
Or impatiently yesterday
Or beguiling February
They could so easily be thought to feel
That they would count or place all or kneel
For which they had been frightened not to do
They felt the same.
In which on no account might they have tried
To be remained to try why
Shall they be careful at all or not.
This is why they like me if they think they do
Or not which by the time they care I care
Or when where will they name me.
However tried however not or cried
She will be me when this you see.
And steadily or whether will they compel
Which is what I tell now.
This is a beginning of how they went at once
When I came there cannot they compare
No they cannot compare nor share
Not at all not in iniquity much which they engage
As once in a while perfectly.
All many so or say
But this or which they may
Believe me I say so.
I have not said I could not change my mind if I tried.
More than just once they were there.
All this is to be for me.

STANZA XV

I have thought that I would not mind if they came
But I do.
I also thought that it made no difference if they came
But it does

I also was willing to be found that I was here
Which I am
I am not only destined by not destined to doubt
Which I do.
Leave me to tell exactly well that which I tell.
This is what is known.
I felt well and now I do too
That they could not wish to do
What they could do if
They were not only there where they were to care
If they did as they said
Which I meant I could engage to have
Not only am I mine in time
Of course when all is said.
May be I do but I doubt it.
This is how it should begin
If one were to announce it as begun
One and one.
Let any little one be right.
At least to move.

STANZA XVI

Should they call me what they call me
When they come to call on me
And should I be satisfied with all three
When all three are with me
Or should I say may they stay
Or will they stay with me
On no account must they cry out
About which one went where they went
In time to stay away may be they do
But I doubt it
As they were very much able to stay there.
However may they go if they say so.

STANZA XVII

How I wish I were able to say what I think
In the meantime I may not doubt

Round about because I have found out
Just how loudly differently they do
They will they care they place
Or they do allow or do not bow now,
For which they claim no claim.
It is however that they find
That I mind
What they do when they do or when they do not do
It.
It is not only not kind not to mind
But I do do it.
This is how they say I share I care
I care for which share.
Any share is my share as any share is my share
Of course not not only not.
Of course I do which I of course do.
Once I said of course often
And now I say not of course often
It is not necessary any more

STANZA XVIII

She asked could I be taught to be allowed
And I said yes oh yes I had forgotten him
And she said does any or do any change
And if not I said when could they count.
And they may be not only all of three
But she may establish their feeling for entertainment
She may also cause them to bless yes
Or may be or may they be not
Made to amount to more than may they.
This is what they do when they say may they
It is often that it is by this that they wish this
When they will value where they went when they did
They will also allow that they could account for it
Or might they not only not choose
It is often whichever they were fortunate and not fortunate
To be for which they may in all they like
This is what they use

I have thought I have been not only like this
Or they may please or not please
Which for instance and forsaken and beside which
They will oh please they will
Not only when they can as if allowed
It is all of it which they know they did.
This is what I say two to belie
One to date and decry and no one to care
And she made as rashly careful as not
When they could think twice just the same.
This is at any time when they do not often see them
Theirs when they went away
Not only not included but why not included
Only they will not agree to permanence
Not more than twice as much.
Very much as they say aloud
Will you be back in a minute or not.
Let me think carefully not think carefully enough
By which I mean that they will not please them so
Not even if they know that they went too
So it is gracious once gracious to be well as well
As when they like liked it.
This is what it is made to be able
To need whichever they could be well-furnished
All the same three now.
This could if it could lead it if it did
To a cow. Think of it.
This is what I return to say
If I never do nor I ever do
How can it be so if it is true
Or just true as through or you
Made which they like as much.
Now commence again to be used to their
Saying that their cousin was one
Who felt that it was not a name
To which they meant to think well of them.
This is however how they do not deny
That they will not try to care
To leave it there from time to time

At once
It is very well known that they are indifferent not to
    wishes.
May she be sought out.
I wish to say that any case of a failure
Is what they were spared.
I wish to think that they will place
Much as more than they wish
As their changing it not only for them.
Could any one influence any one
One and one.
Or not.
If not why not.
Or if not would they not be more than
If they were changing which way any one
In which way any one would not need one
If not one and one.
Or not by them.
It is made why they do if they call them.
They could recognise the sun if there was another one
Or not at all by me
When this you see.
Or not in an exchange there might
Be only why they should.
Be this as it might.
She could be pleased to
Be not only with them but by them
As well as for them
Which makes it at a meaning
And their equal to delight and plight.
Which of which one.
I had many things to think about quite often
They will call me to say I am displeased to-day
Which they may in adding often.
It is not why they knew that it is
Not only why they went but if they went when they went.
By this time they are as often with us
But we think of leaving them with others.
We wonder about it.
And they will not know if we go.

STANZA XIX

I could go on with this.

STANZA XX

Should however they be satisfied to address me
For which they know they like.
Or not by which they know that they are fortunate
To have been thought to which they do they might
Or in delight that they manage less
For which they call it all.
This is what I say fortunately
I think I will welcome very well in a minute
There nicely known for which they take
That it is mine alone which may mean
I am surely which they may suggest
Not told alone but may as is alone
Made as likely for which no matter
As more than which is lost
Recommend me to sit still.
As more often they could not see him
Have it to be or not as not
It not made it not not having it
Should they fancy worshipping
Worshipping me is what they easily may
If they come to think still that they think it still
Just why not if not
I have changed forty-nine for fifty
And may she be meant.
Or would it be a nuisance to like no one
Or better not if not only not to change
Change it should stop with not
Do you feel how often they do go
Go and so and which and met and if
And they are riding
There are so many things to ride.
And water and butter
And may they be no chief to me
I am not only not chiefly but only

Not with care.
And so much as they ever think.
Remain to remain and not remain if not remain mine.
I have abused not leaving it not following it out
I also have not which may they not which they plan.
All of which is in why they used.
To use me and I use them for this.
This too we too or not to go.
I often think do they sound alike
Who hates that or a hat not I.
Now I will readily say not I
But which they read to ready
Or say not I may day or say
Not blindly for caution or which or what
What about.
This is how I however remain
Retain is considered whatever they gain
I gain if in the main they make plain
Just what I maintain if I use a fruit.
Should just when this be any chance.
Better why often.
I have thought why she went and if she went he went.
No one knows the use of him and her
And might they be often just tried
May they mean then fiercely
Should it chance to cover them not enough
I mean a hat or head
And also what a chair
And beside what beside pride
And all at once tried to believe me
Coming as if it could be entitled
One which they won.
One two.
I often think one two as one and one.
One one she counted one one and this made
Economy not only which but of which
They will not kneel of which they do.
I could be just as well obliged.
Finally I move from which
You may deduce the sun shone

By this time
Out loud
All of which may be able to be
Do I make a mistake
And if I do do you not at all either or
This time it should not have followed
Or not either to do it.
Little by little they engage not to change
Or different as it is they might if they should
But they will manage to indifferently relieve
More of which they could alight and aloud.
It is very foolish to know that they might alight
Not only do.
This which they feel they must discourage
And everything I say.
I will tell how once in a while

STANZA XXI

I know that twenty seven had been had
For which they know no name
But our equality may indubitably spell well
For it or for which or for might it be
That it is a change to think well
Of not only when but might they be just where
They will care
Now fancy how I need you.
I have thought which they meant as willing
It is often a disappointment to dispense without
They will cool not which but very most
Well as welcome without.
She said she knew what I meant too
He too.
Although although allowed out loud.
As if they could remember where there
And there where.
Should she join robust or not
Or fortunately for it as they are not without
It is easily eaten hot and luke warm and cold
But not without it.

Could it be thought that I could once be here
Which if they will may they not
I have heard it well enough to know
That he has not only not been mistaken yet again.
While will they now.
Oh yes while will they now
You should never be pleased with anything
If so they will crowd
But if they crowd or yes if they crowd
Which is it which if they may seat them.
I often feel well when I am seated seating them or not so
I go to remain to walk and what
Always when when is it.
It is often however they are bright.
She could often say however they may say
You always have to remember say and not so.
It is always not only not foolish
To think how birds spell and do not spell well
And how could it do birds and words
I often say so not at all amount.
All who should think season did not mean what
What is it.
I have been and have been amounted to it.
When they come in and come in and out.
Naturally it is not.
Or however not a difference between like and liked.

STANZA XXII

I should not know why they said so.

STANZA XXIII

I cannot hope again if they could mean which they liked.

STANZA XXIV

It is easy to grow ours more.
Or for which they will need a place to be
They could thank if not think that they arrange

In a way would they be angry in a way
If they could more which when they gather peas
They feel that it is not right to pay
Nor which if they nor which if they stay there.
Who need share stay there with stay away
Who will decline publicly
What is it if they will wish
Or be for which they beguile when they wish
Or may be not for which they may be spoken
It does not bother me to not delight them
They should fancy or approve fancy
They could call or may they for which will they might
But not only be the time but if which they manage.
It is in partly a reason that they feel well
Nor might they be more enclosed.
Fortunately they feel that it is right
To not give it giving it
As they do them for curls.
It is not often that they are always right
It is not often that they are always right
But which aggression or a guess
Or please addition or please a question.
Or please or please or please
Or and a foil of near and place and which nature
Will they plan to fit it to not in a point.
I wish no one the difference between a point and place
Oh yes you do oh do you.
This which I do or for intend to know
They could or call or if it is a place
In this place the sun which is not all
Is not so warm as told if it is not cold
But very warm which if favorably it is.
I could if I knew refuse to do it.
Or just when they feel like it they try
Beside which if they surround my home
They come to stay and leave it as they like.
Not only not because.
Wish if vegetables need the sun
Or wish if not only not the sun but none
Also wish if they wish that they will size alike

And only if which if a wish which they will oblige
Not only necessary but they think it best.
This which I reflect is what they like to do
They like me to do
Or but or well or do be well to do
For them to like to do if I like what I do
Enormously.
Fancy what you please you need not tell me so
I wish to go or if I do I wish to go
I have often been interested in how they forget to go
Also I have been interested in if they wish to go
I have been better able to determine.
Not only how but whichever they would like
If it were partly told
That she Madame Roux is never yet quite through
But which cannot annoy because I like to try
To see why will she be here
It makes a change in faces
Her face always can change seen near or far
Or not at all or partly far.
It is not partly as they can share
Why should it be like whom.
I think I know the share
Share and share alike is alone
And not when in integrally in a way.
She could often be made sympathetic in a way a day.
It might however be she seen to be all
They feel more than they could
In point of sympathy of expression.
Now when I should think of them of this.
He comes again they come in she can come to come in.
All this is why they like but remember that for me
I am to tell not only well but very well
Why I shall easily be for all to me.
This is the reason.
I have been not only not forgetting but not only.
They will call it a chance.
Because of this may be because of this.
Which not only will but is me
For me to me in me not only not be

Not only not be how do you like not only not be
They will be satisfied to be satisfactory.
Now not only not but will it be their appointment
To come when they said they would.
I said I would tell
Very well what is it that they plan to carry
Of course they plan to carry
How should it be better to put not any blue but that
Not any blue but that and change the mind
The ear and always any obligation.
Once more think twice of that.
It is very difficult to plan to write four pages.
Four pages depend upon how many more you use.
You must be careful not to be wasteful.
That is one way of advancing being wasteful
It uses up the pages two at a time for four
And if they come to and fro and pass the door
They do so.
This is my idea of how they play
Play what play which or say they plan to play which
Which is in union with whichever
They could be thought to be caught
Or planned next to next nearly next to one time
At one time it was very favorably considered
That they would oblige them to go anywhere.
Remember how we could not disturb them
It is very important not to disturb him
It is also important to remember this
Not if they disturb him
But really will they disturb him
I often do I not often think it is time to follow to begin
They could establish eight or arrange
This is not why they please or add as carelessly
They will have no use for what they said.
Now I wish all possibly to be in their shuddering
As to why if they came in and out
If they came in and out
What is the use of union between this with this.
They will add any word at most.
If she said very much a little or not at all

If she said very much or not at all
If she said a little very much or not at all
Who is winning why the answer of course is she is.
When I say that I know all of the might she be mine
She is it is particularly to care
To make it do she offers it as a compromise
To have been needed about I have not only
Not changed my mind.
Now let us think not carelessly
Not all about not allowed to change or mind.
Mind what you say.
I say I will not be careful if I do
I also say I should say what I do
I also do have a place in any antedated rose.
A rose which grows. Will they like that.
She will like that.
We have decided that only one dahlia is beautiful
That salads are not necessary
And that she has been very kind about pansies.
How can you change your mind.
This is what they know as collection.
A collection is why they place it here.
I often think how celebrated I am
It is difficult not to think how celebrated I am.
And if I think how celebrated I am
They know who know that I am new
That is I knew I knew how celebrated I am
And after all it astonishes even me.

PART V

STANZA I

If I liked what it is to choose and choose
It would be did it matter if they close and choose
But they must consider that they mean which they may
If to-day if they find that it went every day to stay
And what next.
What is it when they wonder if they know

That it means that they are careful if they do what they show
And needless and needless if they like
That they care to be meant
Not only why they wonder whether they went
And so they might in no time manage to change
For which which fortune they invent or meant
Not only why they like when they sent
What they mean to love meant.
It is this why they know what they like.
I like to have been remembered as to remember
That it meant that they thought when they were alike
As if they meant which they will undergo to choose
In which they may remain as little as they claim
In which not is it you
But which it is it is not without you.
That they knew you and so forth.
This may be mine at night.
Which does it mean to care.
Not only why they liked but just as if they liked
Not only what they meant but why they will not.
This is what there is not or yet.
Not to continue to do their best yet.
Think however I came to know it all.
I often offer them the ball at all
This which they like when this I say
May they be called to play once in a way of weight
Or either our roses or their cake
I wish I had not mentioned which
It is that they could consider as their part.
Now then I had forgotten how then
Nor made it please away a weight
Oh yes you like it
Or if not for what if now and then
Without them it is often meant to be mine.
Let me say how they changed apart alike.

STANZA II

If you knew how do you very well I thank you
Or if you knew how do you do how do you

Or if not that changes more to many
And may be they do or not if not why.
This is how it is that it does not make any difference
To please them or not or not
Or not to not please them or oh yes yes.
They could should they under any circumstance
Understand differ or differs.
It is why they wondered if they liked
What indeed makes no difference
As they manage
To relieve plunders and blunders
Any one is often thought susceptible.
Or which one wishes.
Now I have wandered very far.
From my own fireside.
But which they knew in a wonder.
It is a wonder that they like it.
I have often thought that she meant what I said.
Or how do you think this about that.
Or if at any time.
It had been not only not remembered
I depend upon him I depend upon them.
Of or how they like.
This what I say makes me remember that.
That if it did
Which may just as you said
Or which may be
If they managed it
Or by the time they did.
This is however just how many are alike.
Once upon a time who will be left to rain
Or like it as much as ever
Or even more than that if they like it.
They must be often thought to be just as careful
As not to give them give anything away.
However how many do like to.
This is not what I meant by what I said
It should be that I think that it might do
If I made it do
I also think that I should not say

That they know which way
They could arrange to go and say
That they will not stay if not
If not what do they like alike
Or as much as just yet.
I could often be caught liking it
Oh yes I could
And then it may not only if they say so.
Oh yes only not yes.
In just this way they went as they may
I have refused went and went as much.
I also have refused whatever they went
But if wherever they went.
Not one in any two
Or just arise or if not only not to like.
It may not be alright.
When they thought how often about a wall.
When they thought how often about a wall.

STANZA III

Just when they wish wish
Or will they or must they be selfish
To not do you should not do not do
Not as if not to to to do
There that is better.

STANZA IV

I like any two numbers more than any two numbers before
Or not.
But if it had been alright to be bright.
Could I have been bright before or not.
I wonder if I could have been bright before or not.
Not only why they do but if they do what I like
If I do what I like.
I could not nor can I remember
Whether if they were there if they were there to care
May be they could be wondering if it were like
If it were like it as it is

As it is if they meant only which
Whenever it is by this time
Of course no difference makes no difference at all.
I wish to think about everything anything if I do.
Or by the time easily
Or not only why they should.
Or please believe.
That they mean what they mean by that.
If not why should no one mind what they say.

STANZA V

Please believe that I remember just what to do
Oh please believe that I remember what to do
Oh please believe that I do remember just what to do
And if I remember just what to do
There will not only be that reason but others
Which at one time.
I like what I have not prepared before of course not.
As fast as not so fast
Not that it does not make any difference.
This is what they like what I say.

STANZA VI

This one will be just as long
As let it be no mistake to know
That in any case they like what they do
If I do what I do I do too
That is to say this conclusion is not with which.
It may be just as well known
Do you change about mutton and onions or not.
This is why they sleep with a ball in the mouth
If not what is there to doubt.
I have forgotten what I meant to have said ahead.
Not at all forgotten not what.
It is not whatever not is said
Which they may presume to like
If at no time they take any pains
Not to like it.

This is how I remember however.
Anybody not anybody can remember however but it does.
Not make any difference in any way.
This is what I wish to kindly write.
How very well I will at night
As well as in the day light.
I could just as well remember what I saw
Or if not I could just as well remember
What I saw when I could.
The thing I wish to tell
Is that it makes no difference as well
As when there is this not this not to tell
To tell well or as well
I have not thought why I should wish beside
Coming again as coming again.
They could write three to one
Or not two to one but which is not which
If they ask more than any fourteen.
Fourteen is however they like but not for me.
I am very capable of saying what I do.
I wish that they could not wish which nor do they.
I know what I say often so one tells me.
Or if not I could not look again.
Might it be whichever it is
It is not my custom not only to think of a whole thing.
Does it make any difference which one they decide
Of course it does of course it does.
Alright let us think everything.
I have begun again to think everything

STANZA VII

Now should or should not if they call with it
That I could not not only hear but see
Say when with spitting cavalry
She tears all where with what may be not now
They could be called to hurry call or hear or hair
Or there
Not only with nor welcome
May they come and climb a vine

In place of chairs in place of chairs in place of chairs.
I could have thought I would think what with
What not not with only that
It is just as much noise as said
Or if not only which I cannot come again to combine
Not only fairly well but mounted.
I do not need the word amounted
Oh not at all
He knows when she came here
For which they may in all which all which called
Perhaps enchain perhaps not any name
For theirs will come as used
By this it is not only I mean
I mean I mean is always said again.
Remember what I said it is not just the same
Or not with only stretched.
In a little while he meant to perceive
For which they may or may not do
Do believe that I will say it used to be like that.
I wish to well assure it did not use to be like that
Not only that it did I did I did and did or do
Which may they come to for which they knew you
They knew who knew you
Every little while I often smile
And all which may come which they will approve
And not only not soften
But just as fairly often
May they not come to say what they can do
I do very much regret to keep you awake
Because you should be asleep
But even so it is better to stay
And hear me say that is right here
What not only which they care
This may be made a reason why
They will be welcome to arrive and cry
They could do which they care.
Now to come back to how it is not all alike
Since after all they first
Since after all they were first
Best and most.

Now listen often cautiously
Best and most is seen to sweeten
Often often it is eaten
Much which much which much they do
Come and do and come for you
Did I not tell you I would tell
How well how well how very well
I love you
Now come to think about how it would do
To come to come and wish it
Wish it to be well to do and you
They will do well what will they well and tell
For which they will as they will tell well
What we do if we do what if we do
Now think how I have been happy to think again
That it is not only which they wish
It is as I have said a resemblance
To have forgotten as many times they came
That is to say we said
This which I said which I said this.
I said that it did not make any difference
And it did make this difference
As it made it made it do.
This which I mentioned made not only why but often
Now I have lost the thread of how they came to be alike.
Not only why if not but with their cause
Of course their cause of course because they do
I had been certain I would a little explain
Which can they do.
When I look down a vista I see not roses but a farm
That is to say the fields after hay
Are ploughed after hay
Not on the day
But just after the day
Like alike when it is chosen.
I wish never to say choose I choose
Oh not at all not while they like
Not while I like alike but do they
They may be often not declared as mine
For which I can not very well think well

Because just now I do not think well
Of at all.
She may be right to think that the sun
Not only does not fade but makes it less faded.
She may be right she often is always
This is what I said I would say
I say it as well as ever naturally
Because with which they would investigate
That they could not take a chance
Not to not to not to make no mistake
Not which at once to do.
It is often however they like
That they make it do.
I refuse ever to number ducks.
Because I know by weight how eight are eight.
Oh yes I do.
And a stanza too or a stanza two.
How do you do very well I thank you

STANZA VIII

I wish now to wish now that it is now
That I will tell very well
What I think not now but now
Oh yes oh yes now.
What do I think now
I think very well of what now
What is it now it is this now
How do you do how do you do
And now how do you do now.
This which I think now is this.

STANZA IX

A stanza nine is a stanza mine.
My stanza is three of nine.

STANZA X

I have tried earnestly to express
Just what I guess will not distress

Nor even oppress or yet caress
Beside which tried which well beside
They will not only will not be tried.
It is not trying not to know what they mean
By which they come to be welcome as they heard
I have been interrupted by myself by this.
This may be which is not an occasion
To compel this to feel that that is so
I do not dearly love to liven it as much
As when they meant to either change it or not
I do not change it either or not.
This is how they like to do what they like to do.
I have thought often of how however our change
That is to say the sun is warm to-day because
Yesterday it was also warm
And the day before it was not warm
The sun as it shone was not warm
And so moreover as when the sun shone it was not warm
So yesterday as well as to-day
The sun when it shone was warm
And so they do not include our a cloud
Not at all it had nothing to do with a cloud
It had not to do with the wind
It had not to do with the sun
Nor had it to do with the pleasure of the weather either.
It had to do with that this is what there had been.
It is very pleasant that it is this that it should have been
And now that it is not only that it is warmer
Now very well there is often that they will
Have what they look when they look there or there
To make a mistake and change to make a mistake and change
To have not changed a mistake and to make a mistake and
        change.
Change the prophecy to the weather
Change the care to their whether they will
Nothing now to allow
It is very strange that very often
The beginning makes it truly be
That they will rather have it be
So that to return to be will they be

There will they be there with them
I should often know that it makes a difference not to look
    about
Because if to do they that is is it
Not which it makes any difference or
But just what with containing
They need or made so surrounded
In spite of in a delay of delayed
It is often very changed to churn
Now no one churns butter any more.
That is why that is where they are here.
I wish I had not mentioned it either.
This whole stanza is to be about how it does not make any
    difference.
I have meant this.
Might it be yes yes will it
Might it not be as much as once having it
Might it not only be allowed
And if not does not it bring back
Or bring back what is it
If they bring it back not for me
And if it brings it back for me
Or if it brings it back for me
So and so further than if.
It is easy to be often told and moved
Moved may be made of sun and sun of rain
Or if not not at all.
Just when they should be thought of so forth.
What they say and what they do
One is one and two is two
Or if not two who.

STANZA XI

I feel that this stanza has been well-known.

STANZA XII

Once when they do not come she does not come
Why does she not come.

She does not come because if she does not come
Not only this.
They may be thought and sought
But really truly if she need to
But which they make in which and further more.
It is not by the time that they could be alone.
What is the difference if he comes again to come here
Or to come here to go there to them
Or which they do which they do well
Or which they do not do well
Or more than which they do not do well

STANZA XIII

There may be pink with white or white with rose
Or there may be white with rose and pink with mauve
Or even there may be white with yellow and yellow with
    blue
Or even if even it is rose with white and blue
And so there is no yellow there but by accident.

STANZA XIV

Which would it be that they liked best
But to return to that it makes no difference.
Which would make no difference
Of course it makes a difference
But of course it makes a difference
And not only just now.
Whenever I return to this it is dull
And not by what I do
Or if by what I do
It is this that they like that I like.
I have wished to think about what to do
I do not have to wish to think about what I do
Nor do I wish to have to think about what they do not do
Because they are about out loud.
After all what is a garden.
A garden is a place in which
They must be in which

They are there and there.
This is not what to say to-day.
I have wished to be as this.
And I have and am so I said I wished.
What could they use they could use
What could they either use
They could either use or use
If it is usual or is it usual
To be usually there.
It does not make any difference
That which they liked they knew
Nor could it make any difference to use two.
After it was known to be is it as they knew
Think well of think of a difference
Or think well of think well of a difference.
They may be they may be there may be hours of light.
Light alright the little birds are audacious
They cannot kill large barn yard fowl.
How often have I seen them and they were right
How often have I seen them and they were not able to
     delight
In which they do.
It is not often necessary to look to see.
Not often necessary to look to see.
How easily she may may be there
Or how easily easily declare
Which they may be able to share
That they may may they bear this.
Or may they bear that.
I wish I could be rich in ways to say how do you do
And I am.
Or not only when they may venture to not remember to
     prepare
Not only when they do
If not as not in which arrangement they concur
It is might it be easily mine.
I will not be often betrayed by delayed
Not often
Nor when they cherish which not often
They will come come will they come

Not only by their name
They could however much if however much
Not only which they come and cause because
Because of all the rest.
It is not only that they manage mine.
Will they be mine if not only when
Do they cover to color when
If they color when with then
Or color cover with whether clover
Can cover a color with clover then.
It is not safe to use clover as a name
When thinking of balsam and balsam is not only not the
     same
But not now the same.
In spite of which they tell well
That they were right.

STANZA XV

I have not come to mean
I mean I mean
Or if not I do not know
If not I know or know
This which if they did go
Not only now but as much so
As if when they did which
If not when they did which they know
Which if they go this as they go
They will go which if they did know
Not which if they which if they do go
As much as if they go
I do not think a change.
I do think they will change.
But will I change
If I change
I may change.
Yes certainly if I may change.
It is very foolish to go on
Oh yes you are.
How could one extricate oneself from where one is

One is to be one is to extricate whichever
They may be not for this any for an occasion
Of which they are remarkable as a remembrance.

STANZA XVI

Be spared or may they justly say
That if that if they will after all it will
Be just as if they say
Not only not they might but they will do
This they will do or if this will they do if
They will not only if they will not only will
But if they will they will do this.
For this thing to think it a thing to think well.
Having found that not only theirs or rather that
That it did make a difference that they knew
Now they know but none only which now they know
They know this.
They did if they had known not only know this.
But which may they be known this which they wish.
I had no doubt that if a difference makes
If there is doubt if money is about
I also know but which I know or worry
If when they give and take they give in a hurry
But which of which of this there cannot be a doubt
That if that could if it could come to be about
That if they did know this just as they had
Will as they had will to be worried still
Or not only not necessary a necessity.
I wish to say correctly this
I wish to say that any day the roads a roads
Will they be roads they say when if
In not only not obliged to leave it well
But which if they can be to recollect
Oh yes not only which to gather to collect
They do try so to have the wind to blow
Not only not here but also not there.
This which I wish to say is this
There is no difference which they do
Nor if there is not or a difference which

Now which as which we should not add to now
No not indeed
I wish to say that they could eat as well
As if when now they heard when now
They had it had it when now
This is what which I did do say
That certainly to-day to hear to get to-day
That which as yet to-day is a relief to-day
Oh yes it is a relief to-day but not
Not without further ought or ought.
Now they need mine as theirs
But when they heard refuse a difference
Not any one has ours now.
Not in that way oh no not in that way
Come thought come thought of me.
I am always thinking that if in their way
If in their way it is if in their way
Insist if in their way
So could in of course shine but not wires shine
They may complete this time will will this time
There or they could in no doubt think.
This which I do I know or only only say say so.
This which has happened is my sand my sand my said
Of course my said why will they manage this wish.
Now I wish to tell quite easily well
Just what all there is if which to tell
Immediately increases hold as told
Or may they better be better be known
I have thought in thinking that is walking
That the way to be often more than told in walking
Is after all as much as told in walking
That they as well will be just not to have
Theirs be theirs now. It is not only this a change
But theirs might be
I have lost the thread of my discourse.
This is it it makes no difference if we find it
If we found it
Or which they will be bought if they worry or not
Without which if they begin or yet began
May they be equalled or equal in amount

When there is a doubt but most of course
Of course there is no doubt.
I have said that if a cuckoo calls
When money's in a purse in my own pocket
It means wealth
Moreover if the cuckoo to make sure
Comes near then there can be no doubt if doubt there be
But not by this to see but worry left for me
Makes no doubt more.
Does it may be it does but I doubt it.
After this I think it makes no difference what their
     characters are
What you have oh yes I thank you
What I have as made to be me for mine
I should not please to share oh no of course.
But not to go into that is not in question
Not when no bird flutters
Even if they yet may be yet here
This which I think is of this kind around
They will be called to tall
No one is tall who has not all
They have not only all
Which is which they may
They say August is not May
But how say so if in the middle they may not know.
Think how well to like everything.
I wish to say that I made no mistake in saying any day.

STANZA XVII

I feel that often in a way they link
Not if they should and shouted
But may they mind if which they call they went
Or not only not of course
But not only welcome more.
There is no doubt that often not alone
There has been a waste who quiets a waste
But which they will they wish
I say yes readily steadily do either do
But which they will in theirs to theirs deny

Not to have been ruffled by success
Or either or they may not be inclined
To gather more than give giving is foolish
Spending is a pleasure gathering is making
Bettering is no delight they like to light
Of course they like to light it.
They like not to explain but add a day.
Very likely to take away if to take away
Before it was of importance not to go now
But not now.
I wish to think to refuse wishes
Also not to refuse trees or please
Not to refuse bells or wells
Not to refuse does or could
Not refuse made to be with which to go
Made to be minding others leave it so
What I have said is this I am satisfied
I have pride I am satisfied
I have been worried I will be worried again
And if again is again is it.
Not to be interested in how they think
Oh yes not to be interested in how they think
Oh oh yes not to be interested in how they think.

STANZA XVIII

I could make at it most or most at it.

STANZA XIX

I felt that I could not have been surprised
Or very much as they do
If it is that I remember what
What do they if they never dot
But which is not warranted by what
What will they have as is if not to mean
It is not difficult to either stand
Which on account if without flavor
Shall they be shamed with generation
They may leave it half as well.

I wish to remind everybody nobody hears me
That it makes no difference how they do
What they do
Either by our or either by at all
This is why no doubt it followed better
To have no one eight or eat before.
This which I think is this.
I think I could do not without at night
Not only not a moon
May they be told as well
This what is what I do may come
Not to present which when they mean they come
Or not only for it.
All this is of no interest
If indeed there is no right
No right to keep it well away
Just when they do or either not delight
May they collect or recollect their way
Not only which but whether they may plan
I wish to say I do not not remember every day
Not I
Not even when I try or why
Not even well not even very well
Not even not without which not even more
Should or just yet recollect
That they that is not there
Even not there much as it is much allowed
For them to come for them to come.

STANZA XX

I wish to say that who could
Or just as well as welcome
This which I know now I know followed how
How did it follow of course it followed how did it follow
Not only no tide is perplexed
But they will perplex less in usefulness
Useful or noon may well be left to right
Should they not care for
What will they care for

I like to think how every one thought less
Of what is this when even is it known
Mine is what is it mine is
Shall they not often be not only made a way
Make and made made stayed.
This which I have remembered is made known
Shall they should always know
Or less the same
They may be often thought made quite well.
She could in which instance for instance
Leave love alone.
They could call dears early years
Or not only their care but with their care
May she be well to manage more or less
However much it is however much alike
This which I know is what I know
What I know is not what I say so
Because I wish to draw drawers and drawing
Or may they even call and talk well and welcome.
Think how often it does not change and mind
They are not glad to sit and find
Find it nearly out.
It is not nearly nearly so
It is not fairly nearly nearly so
For which it is not often not only better that they like
In which in reason.
In reading a long book which I look
In reading and reading a long gay book
I look
This is what I see with my eyes.
I see that I could have been made the same
By which by in which name the same
They may include in tries and tires
And feel and felt may it not it inspire or inspires
They could in no doubt know.
I cannot well remember whether it was yesterday that I
        wrote
Or if yes of course naturally I should
Wait another day.
Or have waited another day.

STANZA XXI

I wish always to go on with when
When they meant then.

STANZA XXII

Not only by their hope I feel so
May they be not with all a wish to know
That they will well declare to do so
But which they will as much as all delight
For this in their way one way one way to know
That it is never gladly to be so
In which it is in often which it is
As they will not be made with them
To be here with them
A stanza can be bought and taught
If not why if not will they or may be will they not
It is not often that they narrowly rejoin
Or as the way or as their way
They will be finally as their way
May they be finally as their way.
This which I know I know that I can do
Or not if not if I can do if not
If not at all they were not only not to wait awhile
Or which if which is better than only not better
It is possible that only if they did and could know
They would happen to arrange that they could not be
Which they had thought and taught
Or meant to teach or meant
Happily it is sent.
This makes no hope of better than it should
They were pleased that they were well well meant
Or left to have no other as it were
Left finally for it.
I wish to announce stanzas at once.
What is a stanza
When I say that often as a day
I feel that it is best to know the way

That if upon the road where if I went
I meant to feel that is if as if sent
The if I came and went
Or well what is it if it makes it do
Not only which if not only all or not alike
But it is it is just like Italy
And if it is just like Italy
Then it is as if I am just like it
That is make it be.
There is no necessity to make it be if it is
Or there is not any real making it do too
Because if which it is or just to know
To know and feel and may be tell
Is all very well if no one stealing past
Is stealing me for me.
Oh why oh why may they count most
If most and best is all
Of course it is all or all at all
Most and best met from there to here
And this is what I change.
Of course I change a change
Better than not.
This that I must not think I do
Which is to do but met and well
Well when I like when they like.
There is no hope or use in all.
Once again to try which of a choice.
Theirs is no sacreder in sacrament
For finally in disposes
When they plan
This which I may do.
I wish once more to begin that it is done
That they will fasten done to done
Or more nearly care to have to care
That they shall will and may be thought
To need most when
When whenever they need to mean
I mean I mean.
This which I do or say is this.

It is pleasant that a summer in a summer
Is as in a summer and so
It is what after all in feeling felt
May they not gain.
Once again I went once or more often than once
And felt how much it came to come
That if at once of one or two or one.
If not only if not one or one
One of one one of one which is what
What it is to win and find it won
This is not what I thought and said
I thought that the summer made it what it is
Which if I said I said I said it
And they were using used to as a chance
Not only to be which if more it was
It was used for which for which they used for it.
I wish I could say exactly that it is the same.
I will try again to say it if not then
Then not alike there is no then alike
There is no then not like alike and not alike
But that.
This which I mean to do again

STANZA XXIII

Often as I walk I think

STANZA XXIV

But this does not mean that I think again.

STANZA XXV

Which may be which if there
This which I find I like
Not if which if I like.
This which if I like.
I have felt this which I like.

It is more then.
I wish to say that I take pleasure in it

STANZA XXVI

A stanza may make wait be not only where they went
But which they made in theirs as once awhile
May they be close to waiting or as once
May they not be for which they will
As wish may be more reconciled for them
In which respect they will or so
Or better so or may they not be meant
All which they plan as theirs in theirs and joined
Or better not or better not all alone
Not if they call in early or to care
Or manage or arrange or value
Or relieve or better like
Or not at all as nearly once compared
Or made it to be gained
Or finally as lost
Or by them not detained
Or valued as equally
Or just as much established by their lost
Or finally as well prepared
Or may they not without them which they cherish
Not only by them but by the time
Not only will they but it is one to like
Or manage just as well as if
As if they planned theirs which they know
Or in as well as do
Would they be more contained
To leave it not for them
By the time that all of it is better
Once more to have it do it now
As moon-light
Naturally if they do not look or go
They will be always there or not at all
Not why they went to manage as it is
Felt which they like or as a place to go
They could feel well they went

They could not partly show
Just which or why it is
Not only as it is more than they thought.
They will arrange to claim
It is not only which they will or know
Or changing for it partly as they if.
If it is only made to be no delight
Not only as they finish which as well as they began
Or either not to on account
Not only why they will
Or often not often not often not
It is of more than will they come and may
May they be here if after joining
They will partly in at once declare
Now in no haste if not now in no haste
As just when well supported they need it
Not only if they use but do they use
And might they not be well not be well inclined
To have not which they manage or amuse
Not which they fragrantly and always now
If when they know mint can they not know
Not often will they better have than either or
Not only when they share
But even when they share
There is no mending when they delight
When they delight to have or may they share
It is partly this which is not only mine
Or not not only mine
Or will they not
Or will it be meant to attend
Or follow rather than not follow now
Just and in that way or rather not to say
They will not happen to be often disturbed
Or rather not to have or love it so
They should not can or will not do their way
Of better not to like or indeed may it matter
Not even not at all
And so marking it as once and only once
In which in which case
May they be mine in mine.

STANZA XXVII

It is not easy to turn away from delight in moon-light
Nor indeed to deny that some heat comes
But only now they know that in each way
Not whether better or either to like
Or plan whichever whether they will plan to share
Theirs which indeed which may they care
Or rather whether well and whether
May it not be after all their share.
This which is why they will be better than before
Makes it most readily more than readily mine.
I wish not only when they went

STANZA XXVIII

To come back to a preparation
Or fairly well know when
It is as much as if I thought or taught.
Taught could be teaching
Made in which is strange if strange
That they will otherwise know
That if indeed in vanishes
Theirs where they do not even do
What after all may be which may they call
They may call me.

STANZA XXIX

A stanza should be thought
And if which may they do
Very well for very well
And very well for you.

STANZA XXX

This is when there are wishes

STANZA XXXI

Of course he does of course he likes what he did
But would he mind if he liked what he did

Would he like it better if it did not matter
Not only if he liked what he did
But often just as well
If he did not share in seeing it there
And so might they not only be so
But which if once more they were readily
But which they like.
In there as only as a chance
They could control not only which they liked.
I think very well of changing
I do think very well of changing this for that.
I not only would not choose
But I would even couple it
With whatever I had chosen.
Not only may they gain
But might they gain
They should as they manage
They should share as they manage
They should be often as they manage
Or may or mean disturb
Or as they like
Or leaving it fairly well
Much as they wish or will
Fairly nearly or alike.
I could if I wished have spoken
Or rather not not only
I could arrange and amount
Or for which they would keep
They could have all or could they have all
But in the adding of a place
They will commence intend amuse
I would rather not come again.
It was often so much better than I thought
I could not manage with anguish
I felt that there was partly as a share
To prepare
Liking it and liking it.
It is of no importance
Not a chance than which they will
For which they know in no renown

Ordered and colored there
They will not only reach it but pleasantly reach it.
Which is why they will add it as they call.
They could be left to mean
Or rather might they rather be left to mean
Not only why they like but often when
All of it has been shortened by being told
At least once at a time
For them they will know variously
That is not only meant as meaning
But most of all as most of all
Are there not only adding theirs as when
When could they call to shorten
Shorten whatever they are likely as very likely
To have not where they planned
But just as much as place
A place is made to mean mischief
Or to join plan with added reasoning
They could without without which
Might it be without which
All of it which they place to call
Not only made difficulty indifferently.
I could do what I liked
I could also do whatever I liked
I could also as much
I could be there and where
Where may that be
Where may that be
As not only when but always
Always is not however why they like
There are often opportunities to be chosen
More as they like if they at once they like
Not only as not only used to use
Should they in every little while remain
Not only as much as if they cause
They never need cause distress
This which I have I add to liking
There is no necessity to decide an amount
Of whether as they do they might do this
Because whenever and if why they like

All which or which is strange
Need not in the meantime mean any end of when
Not only for the wish but as the wish
I manage whatever I do I manage
I could not only like hers but mine
Mine may be or if whether they could do this
Might they not why be in season as a reason
Should they have found it or rather not found it again.
This which is what may be what they need not only for
    them
They will be plainly a chance
Plainly a chance
Could they not only like it
May they not only like it
Or if they may not only like it
However may they even be with or without it
For which as better or a just alike
As planned.
Once when they could be chose as a choice
They will feel that which as moreover
It is an opportunity
Not only in exile.
What is exile or oh yes what is exile.
Exile is this they could come again
They will be felt as well in reason
As which if which they planned
I could be ought I be without
Without doubt.
Now a little measure of me
I am as well addressed as always told
Not in their cause but which may be they need
After which may it be
That this which I have gathered
May gather must will change to most
Most and best.

STANZA XXXII

Could so much hope be satisfied at last
May they be lost as lost

May they be carried where as found
Or may they not be easily met as met
By which they use or very much they like
Made while they please
Or as much.
When very often all which may they call
Or further happen may they not call
May they not be without which help
Or much or much alone
It may be not only why they wished they had
Finally funnily or as funnily at one time
It is more than they relieve caution
But which they might.
Might they be thought very often to have come.
Neither in mean nor meaning
They will be presently be spared
They will all feel all which they please
They will not either share as they manage
No plan which may they like
Often which more than for which
May they like
I feel very carefully that they may be there
Or in no pretence that they change the time
Time which they change.
It troubles me often which may or may it not be
Not only which in and because their share.
Let me listen do when they mount
Or if not as they did.
Did or call.
Rest or restless or added rest
Or which or which might they
Made to be arranged for which
Might then be pleased if after often
They could not share tried
Or even places.
They can not acknowledge or add it.
Fortunately to rest.
They can be well enough known
Or by the time they wished
I can not often add add to welcome

Please be not only welcome to our home
May they call a terrace terrace
And also pleasure in a place or garden
Or does which may does it please
May they please if they must
But which which is that it
So very often is not only left and right
But may they add to which whichever
May they not only please.
It might be called all hills or nationality
Or not be even always
Being placed as may they wish
It could be often helped
Help or it is as more
This is the story.
A head should be a chimney
That is well or welcome
It might be made in forty years as two
One for a man and one or one a woman
And either having neither there.
Each one is not at all in their replacing
Alas a birthday may be squandered
And she will always please
Or call it well alone
May they never try to otherwise attain obtain
Or feel it as they must or best.
Best and lest they change for all.
I regret that it is one to two
Or rather yet as change maintain.
Or please or rather curtain a mountain.
Not nearly dangerously.
It can be often thought to be helpful
She may not change what she may not change if for.
It is why wondering do they or lilies fail.
Growing each day more pale that is the leaves do.
Otherwise there is a pleasure in adding
A doubling of their plan.
They will add adding to their tender care
And often as if much as if
More of which as if

They would be well pleased well pleased as if
They could in their hope be carefully.
I wish now to state it clearly.

STANZA XXXIII

They may please pears and easily
They may easily please all easily
For which they please

STANZA XXXIV

There is no custom to know yes and no
They could be easily meant to be fairly well meant
To have in which and may they try
But which and which they carefully rely
Upon it.
In no mean happening will they call
They will never differing from will refuse
And remain meant to please
And remain meant to please and delight
All of which they meet
All meant in adding mine to mine.
In which case most and best is readily read
Nor do they mean to find and please
As they mean which they add to adding
Or better still add which to add and apples
And to add bless and caress
Not only ought but bought and taught
In kindness.
Therefor I see the way

STANZA XXXV

Not which they gather.
Very fairly it is often
Which they have as is their way
They will rather gather either
Either or or which they may

For instance.
It is a curious thing.
That now.
As I feel that I like
That it is as much as
It is exactly like
When I found it easily easily to try
And it is as if it were
As very much alike
As when I found it very much
I did then not wonder but wander
And now it is not a surprise as eyes
Nor indeed not if I wonder
Could it be exactly alike.
This I wish to know.
If you look at it if you look at it like it
It is very simple it is just as alike
By this it is more not only this.
Little by little it comes again.
For which no one need more need like it
It is like it not only here but there
They could which ever they
What I wish to do to say
It is as much as if like it.
This I can like as not dislike.
It has often been said in landscape historically
That they can tell.
What if they wish they can tell.
As I am wandering around without does it matter
Or whether they oblige that they see other
They may if they manage or at best
Either a color
I think well of landscape as a proof of another
I wish well of having brought to think
Which is why well at first.
At first I did not know why well
Why quite well as much as well
Why it could be just as well
That it is like or if and like
This landscape this color.

What is a landscape
A landscape is what when they that is I
See and look.
Or wonder if or wander if not which
They come slowly not to look.
I think so well
Of when I do
Which I consider
Which they do I do
Or if not if at all
When I see over there
There where they color do not call or color
Not if water not if not if water
Not if they could be a part
Think well of gather well
I come to wish which if I add or wish
It is now that however it is now
This which I think which it is the same
When unknown to fame I needed which I did not claim
For them or further made for them
It which they added claim to blame
I wish to say that not only will I try
I will try to tell very well
How I felt then and how I feel now.

STANZA XXXVI

What is strange is this.
As I come up and down easily
I have been looking down and looking up easily
And I look down easily
And I look up and down not easily
Because
It is this which I know
It is alike that is.
I have seen it or before.

STANZA XXXVII

That feels fortunately alike.

STANZA XXXVIII

Which I wish to say is this
There is no beginning to an end
But there is a beginning and an end
To beginning.
Why yes of course.
Any one can learn that north of course
Is not only north but north as north
Why were they worried.
What I wish to say is this.
Yes of course

STANZA XXXIX

What I wish to say is this of course
It is the same of course
Not yet of course
But which they will not only yet
Of course.
This brings me back to this of course.
It is the same of course it is the same
Now even not the name
But which is it when they gathered which
A broad black butterfly is white with this.
Which is which which of course
Did which of course
Why I wish to say in reason is this.
When they begin I did begin and win
Win which of course.
It is easy to say easily.
That this is the same in which I do not do not like the
        name
Which wind of course.
This which I say is this
Which it is.
It is a difference in which I send alike
In which instance which.
I wish to say this.
That here now it is like

Exactly like this.
I know how exactly like this is.
I cannot think how they can say this
This is better than I know if I do
That I if I say this.
Now there is an interference in this.
I interfere in I interfere in which this.
They do not count alike.
One two three.

STANZA XL

I wish simply to say that I remember now.

STANZA XLI

I am trying to say something but I have not said it.
Why.
Because I add my my I.
I will be called my dear here.
Which will not be why I try
This which I say is this.
I know I have been remiss
Not with a kiss
But gather bliss
For which this
Is why this
Is nearly this
I add this.
Do not be often obliged to try.
To come back to wondering why they began
Of course they began.

STANZA XLII

I see no difference between how alike.
They make reasons share.
Of which they care to prepare
Reasons which
I will begin again yesterday.

STANZA XLIII

If they are not all through

STANZA XLIV

Why have they thought I sold what I bought.
Why have they either wished that they will when they wish
Why have they made it of use
Why have they called me to come where they met
Why indeed will they change if no one feels as I do.
Why may they carry please and change a choice
Why will they often think they quiver too
Why will they be when they are very much further
Why will they fortunately why will they be
It is of no consequence that they conclude this
For which it is in no degree a violation
Of whether they will wish.
All may see why they see
Will they see me
I do I think I will will I be will I be
Fortunately for it is well well to be welcome
It is having left it now
They mean three to change.
I will include I will allow.
They could having see making it do
She may arrange our a cloud
But they think well of even
I wish to remember that there was a time
When they saw shapes in clouds
Also as much.
And now why why will they if they will
See shapes in clouds but do not
Do not draw the attention of any other one to it.
They may be even used to it.
What I wish to remember is not often whether this
They may be lining what there is
Or rather why they are inclined
To leave hills without clouds
To be covered with haze

And to be transparent not in mist
But finely finally well
They could be such as there
Will they or will they not share
They might be thought to be well caught.
I feel that I have given this away.
I wish now to think of possession.
When ownership is due who says you and you.
This as they feel this.
They will accomplish willows with a kiss
Because willows border rivers.
Little rivers are in a marsh
Having forgotten marshes and trees
Very much or very well who sees.

STANZA XLV

I could join if I change.
If I could see which left it that
May they call where they will as left.
But which they like.
Oh yes they do always which they do like
They need any stanzas as any stanzas there.
They could be seen as much.
Leave it as much.
May they be fairly fancied.
May they be as much as fairly fancied.
No one knowing how knows how.
I feel.
I feel that they will call it tell well.
If not in joined may they release.
Or yes not as to please.
I wish once more to think of when a wagon
May they not yet be drawn.
Of which of whether if they need.
Of whether yet they share.
May they be seen to care.
Colored as oxen.
It is not only here that they know oxen.
Oh yes oh no it is not only so.

It is that they will leave and leave.
And might they may they leave.
If they may leave to have to come to leave
They will come which may they come
I will not think some come.

STANZA XLVI

Why are ours filled with what it is
That they reach mine.
They do and if they do will they be theirs as mine.
And if it is night they could just they share
Might they be one I won
Or may they be which if they could.
I must say all which is as if they had met.
Often adding had makes leaves as well
If gathered when they fell they usefully are used
It is not why they like they readily grow.
She chose one to two.
Heliotropes are through through the air.
And yet I saw her choose
Find it for him
I saw her choose.
She could be thought to be.
They like alike.
I wish to notice that they are at all.
To arrange to choose.
As much as for which use.
I will mention it.
She has been very well known to like it.
I may say that it is a pleasure to see the bouquet.

STANZA XLVII

I will may I request.
That they should offer this.
I have not felt to which may be true
That they will yield if either if they wish
Will they to you

STANZA XLVIII

I have been astonished that black on white
This I have been astonished that it thickens
But why should black on white
Why should it thicken.

STANZA XLIX

I wish moreover that I think again.
Will you follow me as much as thought
How could when any know.
What could I do if when I felt I left.
Left it to her to do
Not much which I may know
In which I know.
I can be often or rather awfully doubtful
If I can be seen to have been wished
Wished well as while.
For all which all that while
May it be not alone not liked.
There may be no occasion to leave roses
On bushes.
But if not only why I sit
But may be not only if only why I sit
I may be often as much as ever
More may they like.
I think that if I feel we know
We cannot doubt that it is so
They cannot with which they change
Once more they see that it is I
Brown is as green as brown is green for me.
This makes me think hardly of how I learn.

STANZA L

May you please please me.
May he be not only why I like.
Which they shall never refuse to hear
I refuse to hear her.

STANZA LI

Now this a long stanza
Even though even so it has not well begun
Because which ever way they may contrive
To think well will it be
Need I remember what I carry
May I plan this as strangely
May I may I not even marry
May I come further than with which I came
May I completely feel may I complain
May I be for them here.
May I change sides
May I not rather wish
May I not rather wish.

STANZA LII

There has been a beginning of begun.
They may be caused.
They may be caused to share.
Or they may be caused to share.
Should no one have thought well or well
For which no one can change frighten.
Or plainly play as much.
Or nearly why they need to share
Or may they just be mine.
He has come to say I come again.
They could really leaving really leaving mine.
I could not only wish
I could not only wish for that.
I could not only wish for that here.
It is very rarely that there is a difference known
Between wood and a bone.
I have only felt that I could never change
They will be thought to welcome me.
I am coming.
They will not be arranged that I am coming
They will be glad
They will have often had it.

I have often admired her courage
In having ordered three
But she was right.
Of course she was right.
About this there can be not manner of doubt.
It gave me pleasure and fear
But we are here
And so far further
It has just come to me now to mention this
And I do it.
It is to be remarked that the sun sets
When the sun sets
And that the moon rises
When the moon rises.
And so forth.
But which they meddle or they will as much
They have asked me to predict the weather
To tell them will it rain
And often I have been a comfort to them.
They are not a simple people
They the two of them.
And now they go just as well
As if they were used to it.
Which they are.
They go into the fields.
There may be things to do
Which they are
Which there are in the fields
And so they have not sought to change the noon or the
    moon.
But will they ask a question
Most certainly they are not divided.
It is often thought that they know
That it is as well to know years apart.
Ask gently how they like it.

STANZA LIII

By which I know
May they like me

Not only which they know
But they will wish
They will wish which they know
And now and ours not at all
May they be once with which they will declare
And place and ours know
They can with better which they even will declare
That they may change or is it in a union.
They may be finally to find that they
May see and since as one may come.
Come one as one may add to come
Come which they have
Once more to add feeling to feeling.

STANZA LIV

Could she not have it as they made an impulse
He will not feel that it is made to change
They will conclude that parts are partly mine.
They will have will.
Will they come when they will
Or will they wait until.
If when if not when will they.

STANZA LV

I have been thought to not respect myself
To have been sold as wishes
To wonder why and if and will they mind
To have it as it is and clearly
To not replace which if they as they do
May they content may they be as content
For which they will if even be it mine
Mine will be or will not be mine
Rather than mine and mine.
I wish to say
That it is her day
That it might be well
To think well of it
It is not often led or left

But whichever and whenever
May they not only be
All mine.
I often think will I be thought to know
Oh yes of course I will be known to know
I will be here I will be here and here
It may not be that it is I am here
I will not add it more and not
Not change which is a chance to leave it.
I can be often very much my own
I wonder why
Is it that is it here.
Can I but not to try
I can cradle not infancy but really
What I can.
They can collect me.
They can recollect me
They can if mine is mine.
Not even mine is mine.
Mine which is mine.
Nobody knows a name for shame.
Shame for shame fie for shame
Everybody knows her name.

STANZA LVI

I could be thoroughly known to come again.
Often if I do
I come again.
As often if I do.
I could not change often for often.
Which I do.
Often for often which I do.

STANZA LVII

I have often been doubtful if yes or no
Annoys him.
Or is it only the setting sun
Or the chairs softening

Or the direction changing
In which they see why I do.
Might it not be only what they like.
I like what I like.
May they not like what they like.
But very often he means nothing.

By which they might.
I have often thought that it is right
That they come if they might
But which they change from their right
To imagine which they might
If they tried.
Not only why they wish but if they wish for us
It may be not only that only that is gone
But which they might not only
But which they might if not only
Once when they went to go
But which if they might
I think might they if they might.
I wish would wish that they might
If they might they would not if they wish.
Would they if they not only would they
But which if they would if they might.
Now then how strangely does it happen
If better not not only now and then.
This which I wish to say is this.
I has happened which I wish
Now and then.
This which I wish is to happen
Now and then.
This which is if I wish.
Which is to happen now and then.
The way to change this to that
That is now this now this to that
Or that to is it this to that
Or no not indeed that.
Because of this or is it this to that.

By which I mean to say dozens to-day
Yesterday or dozens also
Or more over more alike and unlike.
This which I wish to say once which I wish to say
I wish to say it makes no difference if I say
That this is this not this which I wish to say.
But not not any more as clear clearly
Which I wish to say is this.
She has left roses and the rose trees.
By which I mean to say is this.
If it had happened not only were they not remembered
But if at all not even if at all
Not even if at all if if they were not remembered.
I could have not only which if which if whenever.
I can choose what I choose that is to say not chosen.
Not only if they were not having been where.
No one can partly go if I say so
However much they could
Did if they would.
But which they much as if they were
To add more he comes here
As if he came here from there.
I wish to say I could not remember better
Nor at once
By which I mean
Could they come here I mean.
They have come here.
Each one has come here once or twice as that.
Make it three times and they will remember better.
Not only that but will I will I be
Partly with it partly for it
Partly for three
Not three but three times.
And not three times three but any three times.
This may be wrong it may have happened well
Very well it may have happened.
That if they came four times
They had come three.
It may not even not be better yet
Not as yet

Should they be thought to be.
By which no one means what I do.
I do not partly do not.
Or if not partly do if not
I come back just to think is three not more than four.
Or is three not enough if four are not more.
This may they try.
This that they can come here
Of course this that they can come here
Of course no more no more of course no more.
May we know that there is this difference.
No more not any feel it known as well
This which I tell this which I tell.
Do you delight in ever after knowing.
But which they mind that always as they come
Not only heard it once but twice but not again.
They could they could if not their ground
They could if they could not stand their ground
They will be shelves of shelves
Rather be only rather with their shells of shells
Or best or needed needed in their praise
Of course we speak very well of them
They have been able too.
Able to be able not only ours abound
But which could which tell if no one.
No one adds palpably to their amount.
There there they read amount account
Cover better a wasp came settling gently
To tell of a coincidence in parting
And to be well kept in which after which
In doubt in no doubt now
But they feel grapes of course they do or show.
Show that grapes ripen ripen if they do
Not always do if not if not that they often do
But which if which
There is no advantage.
I wish to say again I like their name
If I had not liked their name
Or rather if I had not liked their name.
It is of no importance that I liked their name.

There may be this difference.
It may be one number that is written
To mean that it is another number which is to follow
Or it may be that the number which is to follow
Is the number that is written.
The only thing that helps one with that
Is memory.
And sometimes I remember and sometimes I do not
And if I remember may I be right.
Or is it best to look back to be sure.
After all they could not know which I said.
And they are not forgotten but dismissed.
Why should one forget and dismiss which one of this.
This which they add that I do.
I could never believe that I could not happily deceive.

STANZA LIX

Some one thinks well of mine.
Some how some think well of mine.
Well as well but not as well as mine.

STANZA LX

Next to next to and does.
Does it join.
Does it mean does it join.
Does it mean does it mean does it join.
If after all they know
That I say so.

STANZA LXI

I wish once more to mention
That I like what I see.

STANZA LXII

By which I might if by which I might.
There may be only which if once I might.

If once I might delight.
If if not once if not I might delight.
Either is other other is order
Or if they ordered that no one is to wish
Not only wish but which
Not only not not only
Not if they not if they wish.
They not only had they been
But they had been as much as disappeared
They could candles water-falls if they liked
They could call bread easily bread
They could even do as they wish
They might even do that
Not only as they like but when they find
Not easily when they find
Not more not easily when they find
They carry which they carry
They add not only not that which they add
But they must not add will they
If they need no one to force them
To declare
That they will not add if they change.
They should not easily delight.
Not only theirs.
Should they increase if they could like it.
And may they call for them.
I wish more over to say
That I was not surprised.
I could remember how many times there was an interval
In not only which way but in any way
They may nearly not be known
Not more than once at all.
After which may they lead.
I need no one to rest well
They will call a light delight.
They like sun-light day-light and night as a delight
They also like day-light
They also need their light.
They also will show it as their light to-night.
They also will remain if they remain and leave it.

As they might.
This which I say has meant this.
I cannot call it that there is no doubt.
Is there if I say what I do say
And say this.
Moreover if they stretch as not only will they do it.
But may they not only not do it
But not have done it.
Not at all.
She may be appointed.
It may be an appointment
They will not nearly know
Which they may care to share.
I wish I wish a loan may they
May they not know not alone
Not know why they may
As it is of no use
That they sat as they say
In a way as they did not sit
In a way to stay.
This which has been as this.
They have been with them there.
May they not care to spare
That they were if they were there.
This which I remember
I do not remind them to say.
Of all of them one of them.
Which may birds lay.
They like to be as tall as more anymore.

STANZA LXIII

I wish that I had spoken only of it all.

STANZA LXIV

So far he has been right
Who did alight
And say that money would be plenty.

STANZA LXV

They did not know
That it would be so
That there would be a moon
And the moon would be so
Eclipsed

STANZA LXVI

Once in a while as they did not go again
They felt that it would be plain
A plain would be a plain
And in between
There would be that would be plain
That there would be as plain
It would be as it would be plain
Plain it is and it is a plain
And addition to as plain
Plainly not only not a plain
But well a plain.
A plain is a mountain not made round
And so a plain is a plain as found
Which they may which they might
Which they tell which they fill
Could they make might it be right
Or could they would they will
If they might as if they will
Not only with a will but will it
Indeed it will who can be caught
As sought
For which they will in once
Will they they will
Might they not will they will
Much which they had they will
It is of ever ready pleasure
To add treasure to a treasure
And they make mine be mine
If once when once
Once when they went once

In time
They may be used to prove
They may be well they have been
Shove
Shove is a proof of love
This which they have been
And now they add this which
In which and well they wish
They add a little pink
To three which were as well
For which they do not add
A wish to sell
They will add will they well
Well if they wish to sell
Well well if they wish to sell
Who adds well well to a wish to sell
Who adds well to a wish
Who adds a wish to well
We do.
We had been as well
And we do.

STANZA LXVII

I come to gather that they mean
I do.
I come not only well away
From hound
A hound is a dog and he has known his name
Another dog and not a dog
Not a dog in his name
I wish not wish not will
Will they be well as well
And for it no one need a moon
A moon at noon
What was it that she said
A sun and moon and all that loss
Divide division from a horse
She said I would she said I did
Not only which not only why.

Why will be well as well reject
Not to neglect
Not if they wish alike to try
May they as well be well
Will they as by and by.
Which I may say
Which I may to-day
To say
Could they come as they go
More than which whether it is best
To do so.

STANZA LXVIII

I need not hope to sing a wish
Nor need I help to help to sing
Nor need I welcome welcome with a wind
That will not help them to be long.
Might they not be there waiting
To wish this
Welcome as waiting and not waiting more
I do not often ask I do not wish
Do not you wish
Do not you either wish
Or ask for all or more.
There is no hesitation to replace
Which when they will and may they will
By and by he asks it not to be there

STANZA LXIX

Be made to ask my name.
If I think well of him be made to ask my name.

STANZA LXX

I can not leave what they will ask of it
Of course of course surely of course

I could if I could know
Does if does it seem so
May we if I am certain to be sure
That it is as I do
It should be changed to place
They may if will they care
They can if as it could
Be not more added.
I cannot if I ask be doubtful
Certainly not
Nor could I welcome change as neither change
Nor added well enough to have it known
That I am I
And that no one beside
Has my pride
And for an excellent reason
Because I am not only
All alone
But also
The best of all
Now that I have written it twice
It is not as alike as once.

STANZA LXXI

There was once upon a time a place where they went from
      time to time.
I think better of this than of that.
They met just as they should.
This is my could I be excited.
And well he wished that she wished.
All of which I know is this.
Once often as I say yes all of it a day.
This is not a day to be away.
Oh dear no.
I have found it why will he.
This which I wish to say is this.
Something that satisfies refuses.
I refuse to be ought or caught.

I like it to be caught or ought.
Or not if I like it to be ought or caught.
This is whatever is that they could be not there.
This is an introduction to Picabia.
When I first knew him I said
Which was it that I did not say I said.
I said what I said which was not in him.
Now who wishes that said is said.
Not him or women.
Or sigh or said.
I did not say I wished it was in him.
Not at all I said forget men and women.
Oh yes I said forget men or women.
Oh yes I said I said to forget men and women.
And I was not melancholy when I thought of everything.
Nor why I thought.
Of course nor why I thought.
That is enough not to have given.
And now if why might I.
The thing I wish to say is this.
It might have been.
There are two things that are different.
One and one.
And two and two.
Three and three are not in winning.
Three and three if not in winning.
I see this.
I would have liked to be the only one.
One is one.
If I am would I have liked to be the only one.
Yes just this.
If I am one I would have liked to be the only one.
Which I am.
But we know that I know.
That if this has come
To be one
Of this too
This one
Not only now but how
This I know now.

STANZA LXXII

I think I said I could not leave it here.
I may be all which when whenever either or
May they be which they like for.
Or will they worry if they lose their dogs.

STANZA LXXIII

May she be mine oh may she may she be
If they could welcome wish or welcome
But they will be surprised if they call me.
Yes may they gather or they gather me.

STANZA LXXIV

It is not what they did which they ask me
Or for which if they could they give to me
Not ducks of Barbary
Because if ducks there be
They will be eating ate or would be
Better known than if not.
Will they leave me.
Of course if rather gather.
May they be inestimably together.
It is as very long to be indefinable
As not for which not if for which
They wish.
Thank them for gathering all of it together.

STANZA LXXV

I like that I like.
Oh yes not if not I like
May they be a credit a credit to him
I like
If when if I like
Not if in choosing chosen.
Better which pronounced which
If which plus which

May they be I like.
I need no none to prefer refer
Or rather mainly used.
More which they change.
Let us be thoughtful
Let us know that if they could be known
They would be gathered if at known
Say so
Manage not only not to say so.
Saying no
I wish to think that I had thought.
I had not only loved but thought
I had not only even called and taught
I had meant will or well of fishes
I had thought could they call me well of wishes
May they be only once allowed
But which they frame.
Having not had a picture
Which to frame
Now I do know a name
Why when they like a man called Susan
He will regret allowed for Susan
Or just why why if they may not try.
It is to gather other than he knows
When once is often
Who will begin again.
Ours are ours all ours are hours
We had a pleasant visit not mine
Would they have been would they have been in time.
Should they if they.
They will gather love is mine.
Butter is mine.
Walls are not only mine
Will they or if they had rather
Been when they were to find mine.
They will not either leave it all to chance
Or yet no one knows movements which having fallen
He fell to seat it where they could be all
No one imagines all for either all
Red or not red

I do dislike to hear
That red is here.
Thank you kindly for the thought
That either we are bought.
Or really not to be bought
By either caught or ought.
Should shell fish be well baked.
Or either will they all in origin.
Remain remained tall.

STANZA LXXVI

I could not be in doubt
About.
The beauty of San Remy.
That is to say
The hills small hills
Beside or rather really all behind.
Where the Roman arches stay
One of the Roman arches
Is not an arch
But a monument
To which they mean
Yes I mean I mean.
Not only when but before.
I can often remember to be surprised
By what I see and saw.
It is not only wonderfully
But like before.

STANZA LXXVII

Now I wish to say I am uncertain if I will if I were every
day of any day.

STANZA LXXVIII

It is by no means strange to arrange
That I will not know
Not if I go or stay because that is of no importance

No what I wish to say is this.
Fifty percent of the roses should be cut
The rest should bloom upon the their branch
By this means no one will mean what they pleased
And even if they are occupied they are content
To believe mind and wind, wind as to minding
Not as to rain and wind.
Because because there is very little wind here
Enough of rain sometimes too much
But even so it is a pleasure that whether
Will they remain or will they go even so.
I wish to know if they only mean to know
By me by you they will as readily maintain
That not by me by me as well remain
I wish to know if it is well to be by now to know
That they will remain if they might mean I know
If once if once if I might mean I know
That not which only if which only now to know
Know not in mean known if it is not only now
They could in gather mean if they meant mean
I mean.
This which I wish to add I wish to wish to add.
May I may I be added which is not any wish.
To add.
I which I wish to add why should add not rhyme with sad
    and glad
And not to talk to-day of wondering why away
Comes more than called to add obey to stay
I wish I had not thought that a white dog and a black dog
May each be irritably proud to find
That they will call us if if when if added once to call
May they be kind.
We are kind.
May they be kind.
I wish no one were one and one and one.
Need they think it is best.
Best and most sweetly sweetness is not only sweet.
But could if any could be all be all which sweet it is
In not withstanding sweet but which in sweet
May which he added sweet.

I can I wish I do love none but you

STANZA LXXIX

It is all that they do know
Or hours are crowded if not hours then days.
Thank you.

STANZA LXXX

May she be not often without which they could want.
All which may be which.
I wish once more to say that I know the difference between
two.

STANZA LXXXI

The whole of this last end is to say which of two.

STANZA LXXXII

Thank you for hurrying through.

STANZA LXXXIII

Why am I if I am uncertain reasons may inclose.
Remain remain propose repose chose.
I call carelessly that the door is open
Which if they may refuse to open
No one can rush to close.
Let them be mine therefor.
Everybody knows that I chose.
Therefor if therefore before I close.
I will therefore offer therefore I offer this.
Which if I refuse to miss may be miss is mine.
I will be well welcome when I come.
Because I am coming.
Certainly I come having come.
These stanzas are done.

HENRY JAMES

Henry James

WHAT is the difference between Shakespeare's plays and Shakespeare's sonnets.

I have found out the difference between Shakespeare's plays and Shakespeare's sonnets. One might say I have found out the difference by accident, or one might say I have found out the difference by coincidence.

What is the difference between accident and coincidence.

An accident is when a thing happens. A coincidence is when a thing is going to happen and does.

DUET

And so it is not an accident but a coincidence that there is a difference between Shakespeare's sonnets and Shakespeare's plays. The coincidence is with Before the Flowers of Friendship Faded Friendship Faded.

Who knew that the answer was going to be like that. Had I told that the answer was going to be like that.

The answer is not like that. The answer is that.

I am I not any longer when I see.

This sentence is at the bottom of all creative activity. It is just the exact opposite of I am I because my little dog knows me.

Of course I have always known Shakespeare's plays. In a way I have always known Shakespeare's sonnets. They have not been the same. Their not being the same is not due to their being different in their form or in their substance. It is due to something else. That something else I now know all about. I know it now but how did I come to know it.

These things never bothered me because I knew them, anybody who knows how to read and write knows them.

It is funny about reading and writing. The word funny is here used in the double sense of amusing and peculiar.

Some people of course read and write. One may say everybody reads and writes and it is very important that everybody should.

Now think everybody think with me, how does reading and

writing agree, that is with you. With almost everybody it agrees either pretty well or very well.

Now let me tell a little story. Once upon a time there were a great many people living and they all knew how to read and write. They learnt this in school, they also learnt it when anybody taught it. This made them not at all anxious to learn more. But yet they were as ready to learn more as they ever had been.

There were some who knew that it was very like them, they might have said, very like themselves, to know how to read and write, and they knew too that not everybody could do it.

Do you see what I mean.

Everybody can read and write because they learn how and it is a natural thing to do. But there are others who learn how, they learn how to read and write, but they read and write as if they knew how.

Now one of these who had just come to read and write as if he knew how, said, oh yes, I knew them, I knew them before they knew how to read and write.

I could if I liked mention the names of all of these people. I could mention the name of the one who said he had known them before they knew how to read and write. I could mention the names of the ones he knew before they knew how to read and write.

Shakespeare's plays were written, the sonnets too were written.

Plays and Shakespeare's sonnets. Shakespeare's sonnets and Before the Flowers of Friendship Faded Friendship Faded. Now the point is this. In both cases these were not as if they were being written but as if they were going to be written. That is the difference between Shakespeare's plays and Shakespeare's sonnets. Shakespeare's plays were written as they were written. Shakespeare's sonnets were written as they were going to be written.

I now wish to speak very seriously, that is to say, I wish to converse, I did so, that is I did converse after I had made my discovery. I conversed very seriously about it.

In reading and writing, you may either be, without doubt, attached to what you are saying, or you may not. Attached in the sense of being connected to it.

Supposing you know exactly what you say and you continue to say it. Supposing instead you have decided not to continue to say what you say and you neither do nor do not continue to say it. Does it or does it not make any difference to you whether you do continue to say it.

That is what you have to know in order to know which way you may or may not do it, might or might not do it, can or cannot do it. In short which way you come or do not come to say what you say. Certainly in some way you say what you say. But how. And what does it do, not to you, but what does it do. That is the question.

Shakespeare's plays were written. The sonnets too were written.

Anything anybody writes is written.

Anything anybody reads has been written.

But if anything that anybody writes is written why is it that anybody writing writes and if anybody writing writes, in whom is the writing that is written written.

That is the question.

This brings me to the question of audience of an audience.

What is an audience.

Everybody listen.

That is not an audience because will everybody listen. Is it an audience because will anybody listen.

When you are writing who hears what you are writing.

That is the question.

Do you know who hears or who is to hear what you are writing and how does that affect you or does it affect you.

That is another question.

If when you are writing you are writing what some one has written without writing does that make any difference.

Is that another question.

Are there, is there many another question. Is there.

On the other hand if you who are writing know what you are writing, does that change you or does it not change you.

That is that might be an important question.

If you who are writing know what it is that is coming in writing, does that make you make you keep on writing or does it not.

Which guess is the right guess or is there not a guess yes.

That too is very important.

Perhaps you may say they had it written, they thought they had it written and you thought so more than that you know so, and so in writing that you write is as they thought so, or perhaps as they know so.

Does that make it like that.

Perhaps yes perhaps no.

There are so many ways of writing and yet after all there are perhaps only two ways of writing.

Perhaps so.

Perhaps no.

Perhaps so.

There is one way the common way of writing that is writing what you are writing. That is the one way of writing, oh yes that is one way of writing.

The other way is an equally common way. It is writing, that is writing what you are going to be writing. Of course this is a common way a common way of writing. Now do you or how do you make a choice. And how do you or do you know that there are two common ways of writing and that there is a difference between.

It is true that there is a difference between the one way and the other way. There is a difference between writing the way you are writing and writing the way you are going to be writing. And there is also choosing. There may be a choosing of one way or of the other way.

Now how do you make a choice if you make a choice. Or do you make a choice or do you not make a choice. Or do some do. Or is it true that some do. Or is it true that some do not do so. That some make a choice that some do not do so.

Now if you do how do you make a choice and if you do do make a choice what do you do.

It is true that any one writing and making a choice does choose to write in one of these two ways. They either write as they write or they write as they are going to write and they may and they may not choose to do what they are going to do.

If not why not. And if so do they know what they do or do they not.

I am sure you do not understand yet what I mean by the two ways.

I said once when I was seriously conversing, I not only say it but I think it. By this I mean that I did not choose to use either one of two ways but two ways as one way.

I mean I do mean that there are two ways of writing.

Once you know that you have written you go on writing. This explains nothing.

But quite naturally it does not explain because what is it that it does not explain. Indeed what is it that it does not explain. You can refuse to explain, when you have written, but what is it that you can refuse to explain. Oh dear what is it.

You can refuse if you refuse you can refuse to explain when you have written.

You can explain before and you can explain after and you can even explain while you are writing. But does that make the two kinds of writing. No at once I can say not it does not. But and this is or it may be very exciting or may be not, but in this way you can be and become interesting. And may be not.

But what is the use of being interesting.

Of course everybody who writes is interesting other wise why would everybody read everybody's letters.

Do you begin to see does everybody begin to see what this has to do with Shakespeare's plays and Shakespeare's sonnets. Or do they not. And if they do begin to see why do they and where do they and how do they and if they do not do not begin to see why do they not begin to see. If not why not.

Two ways two ways of writing are not more than one way. They are two ways and that has nothing to do with being more than one way. Yes you all begin to see that. There can not be any one who can not begin to see that. So now there is no use in saying if not why not. No indeed indeed not.

I hope no one has forgotten the coincidence of Shakespeare's sonnets and Before the Flowers of Friendship Faded Friendship Faded. I hope nobody has. At any rate by the time I am all through and everybody knows not only everything I will tell but everything I can tell and everything I can know then no one not any one will forget will not remember to remember if any one asks any one do they remember, the coincidence between Shakespeare's sonnets and Before the Flowers of Friendship Faded Friendship Faded.

Ordinarily in writing one writes.

Suppose one is writing. It is to be presumed that one knows what it is to be that which one has written.

Suppose one is writing. It is to be presumed that one does not know what it is to be that which they have written.

But in any case one does write it if one is the person who is writing it.

Supposing you are writing anything, you write it.

That is one way of writing and the common way.

There is another way of writing. You write what you intend to write.

That is one way. You write what you intended to write.

There is one way. Is it another way.

You write what has always been intended, by any one, to be written.

Is there another way to write.

You write what some one has intended to write.

This is not an uncommon way of writing.

No one way of writing no way of any of these ways is an uncommon way of writing.

Presumably a great many people write that way.

Now when the same person writes in two different ways that is to say writes as they write, writes as they intended to write, writes as any one intended to write, writes as some one intended to write why does it sound different why does each writing sound different although written by the same person writing. Now why does it sound different. Does it sound different if the words used are the same or are the words used different when the emotion of writing, the intention in writing is different.

That is the funny part of it. That all this is the thing to know. Funny is again used in the sense of diverting and disturbing.

There are then really there are then two different ways of writing.

There is the writing which is being written because the writing and the writer look alike. In this case the words next to each other make a sound. When the same writer writes and the writing and the writer look alike but they do not look alike because they are writing what is going to be written or what has been written then the words next to each other sound different than they did when the writer writes when the writer is writing what he is writing.

The words next to each other actually sound different to the ear that sees them. Make it either sees or hears them. Make it the eyes hear them. Make it either hears or sees them. I say this not to explain but to make it plain.

Anybody knows the difference between explain and make it plain. They sound the same if anybody says they do but they are not the same.

Now another thing. The words next to each other that sound different to the eye that hears them or the ear that sees them, remember this is just to make it plain, do not necessarily sound different to the writer seeing them as he writes them.

We had a motto. This is it.

I am I, not any longer when I see.

There are two different ways in which writing is done is easily done. They are both easy in the same as well as in the different way.

All this begins to make it clear that Shakespeare's plays and Shakespeare's sonnets even when they are all here are different to the eye and ear. Words next to each other are different to the eye and ear and the reason of it is clear. It not only is clear but it will be clear. Words next to each other make a sound to the eye and the ear. With which you hear.

Oh yes with which you do hear.

All this seems simple but it takes a great deal of coincidence to make it plain. A coincidence is necessary all the same to make it plain.

The coincidence happened and then it was plain.

That makes me say that the Before the Flowers of Friendship Faded Friendship Faded had to be written by me before it make it plain, it was for me a coincidence and this coincidence I will explain, I will also tell it to make it plain. I will also tell it so I do tell it just the same.

When I was very young I knew that there was a way of winning by being winsome. Listen to me nevertheless.

Anybody who is a baby or has been one knows this way.

Then later one knows that there is a way of winning by having been winsome.

Perhaps yes nevertheless.

Later one knows there is a way of winning by being intriguing.

Later one knows that there is a way of winning by having been intriguing.

Later every one knows there is a way of winning by simply being able to have them know that you can be displeased by their being displeasing.

Then later there is a way of winning by having been winning.

What has this to do with writing, something and nothing, considerable and everything, a little and very little. But it is useful. It is useful to think of everything if one wishes to reduce anything to two ways. Two ways of any one thing is enough for a beginning and for an ending.

None of these knowledges are knowledges in one way of writing. Any one of these knowledges are knowledges in the other way of writing.

That is to say and this is where everybody who can write and think will say that it is their way, that is to say if you know these things and you can know these things then you can write as if you knew or as if you had known or as if you were going to know these things.

This is an ordinary way of writing and when ordinary writing is written in this way anybody can say that they can read what anybody can say. And if they do do they do it again. Of course they do and that makes them certain of that thing that as they can do it again they have not done it before. Oh yes we all know what to say if we say it that way. Yes yes yes. No one has any need not to guess yes. Or if you like no. What is the difference between no and yes. Think.

On the other hand if you do not know these things although the time will or will not come that you will know these things, then you write as one who has been allowed to know these things without knowing them.

What things. Have you forgotten, because if you have not may be I have. May be I have but I doubt it. May be you have.

The knowledge is that you write what you intend to write because you do or do not win the way you intend to win. Even if you do not win. Or even if nothing. Not even if it is nothing not to be pleasing even if it is nothing to be or not be pleased or to be or not be displeasing. It is not only used as such but it is also only not used as such.

And that makes it all clear just why in the one case and in the other case the words next to each other sound different or not the same.

Is it all clear. Is it all plain.

Or is it why they do not have to say it is not all clear it is not all plain. Forgive no one and partly forgive no one because there is nothing to forgive.

But it is true that there are two ways of writing.

There is the way when you write what you are writing and there is the way when you write what you are going to be writing or what some other one would have written if they had been writing. And in a way this can be a caress. It can not be tenderness. Well well. Of course you can understand and imagine.

And this brings it all to two words next to each other and how when the same person writes what he writes and the same person as that person writes what he is going to write the sound of the words next to each other are different.

The words next to each other can sound different or not the same.

What is a sound.

A sound is two things heard at one and the same time but not together. Let us take any two words.

That is a sound heard by the eyes, that is a sound.

Let us take any two words.

Perhaps he is right even if he seems wrong.

It is all very difficult not to explain nor to know but to do without.

Mr. Owen Young made a mistake, he said the only thing he wished his son to have was the power of clearly expressing his ideas. Not at all. It is not clarity that is desirable but force.

Clarity is of no importance because nobody listens and nobody knows what you mean no matter what you mean, nor how clearly you mean what you mean. But if you have vitality enough of knowing enough of what you mean, somebody and sometime and sometimes a great many will have to realise that you know what you mean and so they will agree that you mean what you know, what you know you mean, which is as near as anybody can come to understanding any one.

Why yes of course, it is needless to say why yes of course when anybody who can say why yes of course can say so.

Now nobody can think, nobody can, that this has nothing to do with Shakespeare's sonnets and Shakespeare's plays, nobody who can, because in no instance is there not a lack of what they have in either one of one.

But they have not the same thing and there is a reason why and a reason why is sound and sense. Oh please be pleased with that. Pleased with what. With very much whatever they have which of course they do have.

Shakespeare's sonnets are not Shakespeare's plays and there is a reason why and they sound different. You all know the reason why and they sound different.

Henry James nobody has forgotten Henry James even if I have but I have not. If Henry James was a general who perhaps would win an army to win a battle he might not know the difference but if he could he would and if he would he might win an army to win not a war but a battle not a battle but an army.

There is no use in denying that there could be a difference can be a difference.

Perhaps, he, make he what you like. If you like or if you do not like whichever you like.

Perhaps he is right even if he seems wrong.

But there is no doubt about seems wrong. There is no occupation in where he went or how he came or whichever or whatever more of which it was like.

Think how you can change your mind concerning this matter.

Think how carefully you can say this.

If you can say this carefully, you can either not change your mind concerning this matter, or you can act entirely differently, that is, you can change your mind concerning this matter.

Remember how Henry James was or was not a general.

And think what there is to express.

All who wish do express what they have to express.

Do you know how every one feels in this world just now. If you do leave it to me to say it again.

I return to the question of the difference between Shakespeare's plays and Shakespeare's sonnets and you do too.

Like it or not if I do you do too and if you do not do it too, you do not do it too.

Do you begin to realise what it is that makes sound.

Think of your ears as eyes. You can even think of your eyes as ears but not so readily perhaps.

Shakespeare wrote plays and in these plays there is prose and poetry and very likely every time one word that makes two words, is next to each other, it makes three sounds, each word makes a sound, that is two words make two sounds and the words next to each other make not only a sound but nearly a sound. This makes it readily that any two words next each other written by any one man make the same sound although all the words and their meaning are different.

That is they do if he feels alike. But there we are that is what it is all about. And what is feeling alike. It is that that makes it important if I say so.

It all depends now here is where it all not commences but is, it all depends upon the two ways to write.

One way is to write as you write, the other way is to write the way you are going to write. And then some can some do once in a while write the way some one would write if they write only they do not that is to say they say they would if they could. That is different than if you think they do that is if you write as if they think they do.

This sounds mixed but it is not and it is so important. Oh dear it is so important.

Before I say which I do say that when Shakespeare wrote his sonnets the words next to each other too but this time they did not make three sounds they made one sound.

There is a reason and this is the reason. I will try you will try. Oh yes you will try, I will try, we will try, if we can we will try to make it all apply. Oh yes we can oh yes we can try, to do this as we do. Yes one of two. One of two ways to write. There are many more but about this no one can or does care because if it makes a difference it does not make a difference too.

So yes. Very well now.

There are two ways to write, listen while I tell it right. So you can know I know.

Two ways to write.

If two ways are two ways which is the only way. Remember how to say a coincidence may occur any day.

And what is a coincidence.

A coincidence is having done so.

Shakespeare he wrote sonnets and Shakespeare he wrote plays but there is no coincidence about that. Not at all. That is an example. Listen. That is an example of the fact that there are two ways of writing. There is the way of writing as it is written those are the plays, and there is the way of writing as it was going to be written and those are the sonnets. Does it make any difference whether the way it was going to be written is his way or some way of somebody's. In this case it does not. That is if you are only interested and just now I am only interested in one of two ways.

But there is a coincidence and that is Before the Flowers of Friendship Faded Friendship Faded. By coincidence I mean just this, this which is that.

The coincidence is simply that. That Before the Flowers was written too in the second way that is as it was going to be written whether as the writer was going or somebody else having been the writer was going to write it. And this makes it be what there is of excitement.

I found out by doing so that when that happened the words next to each other had a different sound and having a different sound they did not have a different sense but they had a different intensity and having a different intensity they did not feel so real and not feeling so real they sounded more smooth and sounding more smooth they sounded not so loud and not sounding so loud they sounded pretty well and sounding pretty well they made everybody tell, just why they like them sounding so well. Oh yes not oh tell. Yes sounding as they sound or sounded very well.

And so I found out that Shakespeare's sonnets were like that and so yes you see it was important to me.

When Shakespeare wrote his sonnets there were words next to each other too but this time they did not make three sounds they made one sound.

And this is why they are different this is why the sonnets are different from the plays and the plays different from the sonnets.

And by a coincidence I found out all about it.

The coincidence was Before the Flowers of Friendship Faded Friendship Faded.

There is no use in hesitating before a coincidence.

Shakespeare's plays and Shakespeare's sonnets are not a coincidence.

They are different.

Now it is very entertaining that all this comes out so well between the sonnets because the plays you might say the plays are about what other people did could and would have said, but not at all, not at all at all, they were written while writing not as they were going to be written.

No sound really makes any difference because really a sound is not heard but seen and anything seen is successful.

A thing heard is not necessarily successful.

A thing seen is necessarily successful.

By the time Shakespeare's sonnets have been seen Shakespeare's plays have been heard.

But really this is not true.

Shakespeare's plays have been seen, and any sound seen is successful.

Shakespeare's sonnets have been heard. Any sound heard well any sound heard is heard. Any sound heard if it is heard is successful.

Supposing everybody gets well into their head the difference between the sound seen and heard of Shakespeare's plays and the sound seen and heard of Shakespeare's sonnets and that there is a difference.

Any one can by remembering hear how a thing looks. This sounds foolish but really it is not foolish, it is as easy as anything else.

All natural people say I have heard it burning, I have seen it called, I have heard it shown. They say these things and they are right. One sees much better than one hears sounds.

That is true of all beauty.

You hear the beauty you see the sound.

And so Shakespeare goes on.

And now everybody has a gift for making one sound follow another even when they hesitate.

If they really hesitate then as one word does not follow another there is no such result.

But do they really hesitate. Does any one really hesitate. Or do they really not do this, really and truly not hesitate.

But if they do not hesitate and most people who have a gift of making one word follow another naturally do not hesitate, there is as I have said two ways of writing.

You do understand that about hesitating, there is a waltz called Hesitation, but you do understand that sooner or later than this will then be then about Henry James and his having been a general then and winning a battle then and a war then if there is to be a war then.

But to begin again.

And perhaps again to begin again.

Most people or if they do most people who have a gift of making one word follow another naturally do not hesitate, there is as I have said two ways of writing.

And the two ways are two ways that everybody writes. Some do not ever write the one way or the other way.

Shakespeare did. He wrote both ways.

He wrote as he wrote and he wrote as he was going to write.

One way is the way Shakespeare wrote when he wrote his plays, the other way is the way he wrote when he wrote his sonnets, and the words one after the other next to each other are different in the two different ways.

And now to tell the story of the coincidence.

To have always written in the one way, that is to write so that the writing and the writer not only look alike but are alike, is what has been done by any one, of which one is one.

Remember I wish to say later what Henry James did but that has nothing whatever to do with coincidences, nothing whatever, nothing whatever to do with coincidences.

Those who run can read, I remember as a child being very puzzled by that.

There was a moment many years ago when I had a meaning for it but now I have forgotten that and now I have none.

Supposing it does mean something these words, he who runs can read.

It makes one feel that very likely to feel is to feel well.

If to feel well makes one feel that perhaps it makes one not feel to feel well.

Very likely that is not what they meant, did mean by he who runs can read.

Feel well and add well to feel.

And so he who runs can read.

And that makes partly what they have be theirs.

Oh yes.

If they have partly what they have.

To have written always so that what is it, that what or is written is like that which is doing the writing. If not exactly why not.

To have written always so that which is written is like that that which, who is doing the writing, only, that is, that it not only sounds alike and looks alike but that it is alike.

He who runs can read. I do not know who wrote this line nor what it means but it used to be used in copy books when I went to school.

And this brings us all to Shakespeare's plays and Shakespeare's sonnets and it also brings us to coincidences, and it also brings us to Before the Flowers of Friendship Faded Friendship Faded.

And I often think how Henry James saw.

He saw he could write both ways at once which he did and if he did he did. And there is nothing alike in heard and saw. Not now or ever by itself, not now.

Owen Young said that everything should be clear and everything is now clear.

Or one may say now everything is clear. So much at any rate is clear.

There are the plays and there are the sonnets of Shakespeare and they were written by the same man but they were not written in the same way.

Each lot was written in one of the two ways and the two ways are not the same way.

Henry James and therefore I tell you about Henry James and perhaps being a general and perhaps winning a battle and if perhaps knowing if perhaps winning a war.

The way to find this out all this out is to do likewise, not to do it alike but to do it likewise. Do you see what I mean, how the difference is not the same no not the same which it is not.

The way to find this out find it find it out is to do likewise. That is not to write Shakespeare's plays and Shakespeare's sonnets but to write, write plays and sonnets, and if you do that and I have done that, I have written what I have written and I have written Before the Flowers of Friendship Faded Friendship Faded. Then it comes over you all of a sudden or very slowly or a little at a time why it is all as it is.

You make a diagram or a discovery, which is to discover by a coincidence. Oh yes a diagram I say a diagram to discover by coincidence, that is not what a diagram is but let it be. I say let it be.

You make a discovery, it is a coincidence, of course yes a coincidence, not an accent but an access, yes a coincidence which tells you yes. Yes it makes it possible to make the discovery.

And after that, yes after that, a great deal that has perplexed you about sound in connection with sense is suddenly clear.

Also what the relation of a writer is to his audience, oh yes an audience that is suddenly clear, whether one and one and one makes one or three and just as often one and two, all this all this is clear.

But most of all oh most of all just why two words next to each other make a different sound one way than they do the other way and why oh yes and why.

There is nothing means more than oh yes and why.

I will now patiently tell all about everything.

I had always written myself out in relation to something.

Think everybody think.

Is not that the way all who can run can read.

Perhaps that is what that means. Perhaps there is more to it, there is perhaps the concentration upon the reading as well as upon the running. That is the thing that makes writing.

I have said who has said what has been said whichever I

have said or indeed, as it might or might not or even may be left to be said that. And now in or as their fashion.

I have said that there are two ways of writing, writing as it is written writing as it is going to be written whether as the one writing has written or as some one as intended made it for which it is written. If this is so and indeed it is so, then in that case there are the two ways of writing.

Perhaps it is surprising after all after all that I have said that it is the plays of Shakespeare that were written as they were written and the sonnets that were written as they were going to be written.

And in each case I tell you and in each case the words next to each other make a different sound. In one case a smooth sound without which need they mean what they said. In the other case a real sound which need not mean what they said as they just do. Of course they just do.

The sonnets in the sonnets the words next to each other make the smooth sound without which they need to mean what they said.

In the plays they make the lively sound and if they mean what they said they mean it because a lively sound can as it will or if it does mean what is said.

Do you begin to see or do you begin just as well not begin to see.

It is all very interesting curious if one had not found it out by a coincidence but one that is I having found it out by a coincidence it is not curious.

The coincidence as I have said was the writing of Before the Flowers of Friendship Faded Friendship Faded. There too like the Shakespeare sonnets the words next to each other made a smooth sound and the meaning had to be meant as something had been learnt. If not why not.

And in all the other things oh yes in all the other things the words next to each other make a lively sound and they mean which they mean as they mean can they mean as indeed must they mean, I mean. Indeed yes.

And so now anybody can know because I tell them so that the coincidence was so and so and so it was.

Listen to me. And so it was.

Now what has all this to do with Henry James and if he

was a general and if he won a battle and if he would be if he would win a war. If he would win a war.

Now Henry James had two ways in one. He had not begun oh dear no he had not begun, he had indeed dear no, not had he begun.

That is one thing.

The other thing is that mostly there are one of two sometimes one of three that do not listen but they hear.

That is what most writing is. Sometimes two of three do listen and do hear.

Perhaps they do if they do it is not queer, it is not queer of them so to do.

Now in the case of Henry James listen in the case of Henry James all of them all three of them listened as if they did or indeed as if they did not hear. Indeed not, indeed they listened as if they did or as if they did listen and not hear or if they all three did listen and did hear. And all of this was not queer not at all not at all queer.

That made it be that Henry James all the same Henry James if he had been a general what would he have done.

I ask you if he had been a general what would he have done.

Let us think carefully about all this.

Then everybody will know that it was not begun.

All that was important to know. For me to know now.

I am carefully going into the question of Henry James.

Before I go any further let everybody think of generals and what they do.

What do generals do.

Of course generals do do something. That is something is done when there are generals. And one general if he is a general does do something. To think of this as Henry James. A general who does do something. What did he do when he did something when Henry James was a general what did he do as he did something which he certainly did.

Henry James is a combination of the two ways of writing and that makes him a general a general who does something. Listen to it.

Does a general or does a general not win a war. Does a general or does a general not win a battle and if he does how does he do it.

Well he does it because not right away or even after a little while nothing happens together and then all of a sudden it all happens together or if not then why not.

Now Henry James if he could not have been otherwise would have had that it was like that. Sometimes not of course sometimes not.

A general can not have it come all at once as often as not if he did then there would be nothing that would happen or if it did nothing would be amiss.

For instance if Henry James had been a general and had not anything to do but this. Of course not he would not then have done have had anything to do but this.

Everything that could happen or not happen would have had a preparation. Oh yes you know you know very well how Henry James had had to do this.

So then if Henry James had been a general what would he have had to have done. This which he did do. Oh yes he would have had to do that which he has done, had done, did do, to do this.

Think anybody think.

How did or does Henry James do this.

He came not to begin but to have begun.

Any general who can win or can not have won a battle has come to do this.

He came not to begin but to have begun.

Henry James came not one by one and not to have won but to have begun.

He came to do this.

Let us think a little how he was this.

He knew why he knew how it would have been begun. Not as beginning but as begun. He knew this not as having been won, not why he knew this and did not know this, never knew this as one, one, one.

Numbers never came or came amiss but it was not whether or not numbers were begun that made him know this.

I like to think of begun. Not as beginning or having begun but as being begun oh yes he could and did with this as this.

Think how Henry James knew which one, which one won. He knew this. That is how a general can win or not win being a general and having or not having won a battle or a war, as this.

It is the same thing.

And Henry James was not the same thing. A general is not the same thing. He was a general, he was the same thing, not the same thing as a general but really one.

Would he lose a battle a battle that was begun. Perhaps yes.

A general which he was could do this.

I like to think how he looked as this which he was when he was one.

I like to think how everything can make one, he was begun, as one.

It is not necessary to know the life history of a general. As I say a battle, as I say a war, a war, a battle is begun, that is what is always happening about it about any one who has been a general and had one had a war had a battle had either one or both of either one.

Let it not make any difference what happened to either one of one.

What did Henry James do, neither he nor I knew. Which is which. It is not necessary to be plainly helped or not. Not at all necessary.

I wish to say that I know that any day it will happen to be the way he knew how Henry James came not to stay not to have gone away but to have begun, oh yes to have begun, that is what I say to have begun, it is necessary, if you are a general, it is necessary, to have begun and Henry James is a general, it is necessary to have begun, which is what has been done.

I like very well what I have said.

Remember that there are two ways of writing and Henry James being a general has selected both, any general has selected both otherwise he is not a general and Henry James is a general and he has selected both. Neither either or or nor.

It was a glorious victory oh yes it was, for which it was, for which oh yes it was.

I can recognise coming to heat hands in winter and plans in summer. But this is not here nor there.

Can you see that any day was no part of his life.

It meant very likely it meant just that, just that is different, as different from only that. In every case they meant as much more as they did.

Oh how can I not recognise that Americans recognise roofs recognise doors recognise theirs recognise cares. Of course they can go where they can go if they go but do they go. If he did.

Henry James was an American, but not as a general as a general he was a European as a general, which he was as he was a European general.

But this may go to make an American if an American which they do can say so.

Henry James never said he never made everything more or nothing more of that. No he did not.

In this way in a little while you will see and really you will see what is American. You will see what is American. If you will see what is American.

If Henry James had been a general which he was what would he have had to do. He would have to do what a general has to do. He would have had to have it begun a battle or a war, if a general is to be a general any more and Henry James was one.

Do not forget that there are two ways to write, you remember two ways to write and that Henry James chose both. Also you must remember that in a battle or a war everything has been prepared which is what has been called begun and then everything happens at once which is what is called done and then a battle or a war is either not or won. Which is as frequently as one, one, one.

You can see that he chose both Henry James, you can see that he was a general Henry James, you can see that a war or a battle may or may not be won or both or one, one, one.

I like Henry James as that.

VOLUME II

All three Jameses sat together. This they naturally would do. Would there be any other Jameses.

In accord with the way that they use what they had and in accord with the hope that they will use what they have all Jameses get together.

After a while all and any James remains or stays apart.

And this cannot be told as they never become old, not any James.

Do generals become old. Yes if they continue to be generals.

So there is a difference between a James and a general, and in a way we come to that.

It makes no difference that they never remember either General or a James.

Nor what they remember that is what they do not remember or rather do not remember. Do you wish a James to remember. Do you wish a general to remember.

Well anyway neither a General nor a James will remember.

And so Henry James is a general.

He has not so many things to do things which he does do but he does do the things which he has to do. Oh yes Henry James does. And that makes it interesting. What he has to do makes it interesting.

That is just like a general is it not just like a general that the thing which he has to do makes it interesting.

All that they have told, no matter whether which it is I wish to refuse that it is told and again refuse that that which it is is told. Oh yes refuse as much as any wish as any anybody which is a wish. Do you see by what I mean that Henry James is not a queen but a general. Oh yes you do you understand that.

Henry James made no one care for plans. Do you see that he is a general. He made nobody care for plans and after all they were fairly able of course they were fairly able.

None of this is what to wish.

Henry James had no wishes and if he were a general he would have no wishes and he was a general and he had no wishes.

In the meantime and there is no intermediate in the mean time Henry James cannot be said to come prepared. Oh yes it seems like that but is it true.

If he had been a general and had to win a war or a battle or even a part of a battle what would he have had to do. He would have done it. In a way he would have done it. Oh yes in a way he would have won it.

I have often thought what he would do if he had been a general.

VOLUME III

I like to think what would he do if he had been a general.

VOLUME IV

Little by little he would have been a general but would he have been a general little by little. Not at all. He would not have been a general little by little. He would have been begun as a general. That is what he would have been begun, he would have been begun a general.

And after a little while the three Jameses would again have sat together. Just as they did. Having sat together. And would there have been any other Jameses. Just as well any other Jameses as there often are. Even to be said habitually are.

And when any three Jameses sat together you might say they sat in a circle as they sat together as three Jameses sat together any of them would have been what they were. Would Henry James have been a general. Why not. I see no reason why not.

I can again think how they sat if they sat.

But they did sit.

Henry James did sit and as he sat the way he sat was the way he would have sat if he had been a general and so there we are, or at least yes there we are.

Now do you understand what I mean by what I say and what he was and what he was in what there is to be what he was. He was a general because a general is begun. He was a general because he sat as one who had been and was still the general he had been.

Three Jameses sat together but that did not make any difference. That might happen or might have happened or indeed did happen does happen to any general who has and still has been a general.

I wish to disclose everything I know.

I wish to disclose why I feel a general so.

He felt a general can feel that he need never kneel.

What do I mean to say. That he was not married in any way. And is that true as a general or is it true in general. No it is not true in general but he as a general of him it is true as a general.

And why not.

Once more if not why not.

Because if alike allowed alike, he would catch it all as they say. This to him was not more important than if he wished either not to be there or to be alone.

Now I wish to say generously why he was never married either as a general or as a man.

How can a man be a general too. Not if no one knew.

But he knew.

He knew that he was a general too.

And now yes so you do.

How was he a general.

Not by not being married or yes is it as nice.

He was a general by the circumstance that he had begun and if a general has been married it is of no importance.

How when Henry James was a general did he conduct his war. There is no difference between conduct and how did he conduct his war.

Did he win his battle or did he win his part of his battle if he was not the full general or the only general in his battle. If he did not, but he did, why not.

There are two things to be said. He was not married, to be said and he was a general, to be said.

He was not married not only for this reason but of which he did not take part.

He took part in the battle, which is the battle in which he as a general did take his part. And if the battle which was the battle in which he did take his part was won then as a general he did take part in winning the battle which was won. Also the war.

Thank you, also the war.

How can you state what you wish to say. That is the question. What you wish. That is the question. To say. That is the question.

By being called to kindle.

What do you wish to say.

When Henry James was this general which he was and they made the most of that, by the time they did, and he was not married, which he undoubtedly was not, and placed beside, where they had the right, whenever it happened, and they on their account, made mention of their violence by any failure, no more than of course told in toiling, so they could undoubtedly in time, face themselves there, where.

It is not only in this and in this way that a battle is fought.

It is of great importance that Henry James never was married.

That might make theirs be mine.

VOLUME V

For which they spare neither one of themselves. No general that is a general as a general has won one at a time.

Believe me if you like.

VOLUME VI

I think easily of three who sat and one who did that.

VOLUME VII

I, he, it may not be set in place of stated.

I state that it may not be settled in place of stated.

He may not be seated to settle in place of stating what there is to be stated.

It may not be of advantage to have no settlement in place of not stating what is to be settled in place of settling.

In this way he could adventure to wander away from being a general. But in every little while more may be there.

This is the way it was with Henry James.

And so what is there to say.

If he had been a general what would he have had to do, he would have had to take part in a battle if there was a battle in a war if there were a war if not then why not.

But no questions can be asked to which no questions can have as an answer.

And so they make an occasion of this.

This makes you see how lightly or heavily a general can take place.

May they recognise being married as yes and no in marriage.

Henry James had no marriage as he was not married. They were obliged to give this answer. Not when they heard him. Or even after they had him.

So often do generals but generals are not more than are more.

That makes a general no hazard.

A general begun.

Why can marriage be made away.

Henry James was not married. By this they mean what they say.

I wish to tell you all who wish to hear why marriage married if they can name him here.

They do name him.

They name him Henry James.

A little still a little by that they all grew.

For which I ask you, how do you do.

VOLUME VIII

To come back to that he never was married would he be very likely to live alone and if he was very likely to live alone would he be as if he were alone. Now think of any general any regular general and how it would be.

If he were not married and lived alone he would live as if he were not married and lived alone but really not he would live as if he were not married. If they are not married do they live as if they live alone. Think about this a Henry James and think about this a general and then think about this as this.

What did he make him do when he wrote what did it make him do when he had it to do to help with a battle or help with a war or help with whatever he ordered that he should help. He would of course never help himself. Any one who is not married and who lives as if he is not married does not help himself. He can not help himself. And this makes him write as he does, does or was.

In many instances marriages are arranged in many instances

of generals. Was Henry James one of such a one. In a way not because he was not married and if he was not married it was not because he was ever married. No not for instance not one.

A great deal has to do with everything. And marrying.

Well will they lightly go away.

For which they knew who likes a crowd. Or who will please when they lower or do not lower a boat.

He was or was not prepared for as much as he had.

This has nothing or something to do with either not married or not.

Believe those who do not rather not have to leave it as that.

He never felt awkward as married but he should recite only really who could or did recite or not quite.

I tell you and it is a fact if you are not married why are you married or not. Henry James or a general were never like that.

And that after all is not all or everything they have to say.

The thing to wonder is did he not have to say what he did not have to say.

That can happen to any general who is regularly a general.

Any general.

VOLUME IX

Now who has or wills to have that they have or have to have and whether, whether will they have or rather.

I could count many times as many wives and Henry James or a general could not count as many times as many wives and what difference does that make if they venture or do not place a general before or after. A general is placed before or after and so is Henry James. He is placed before or after.

And no doubt a married no doubt a married man is not no doubt a married man is doubt.

Henry James or a general are never in tears about a married man and so they are not.

What could they feel if they live.

They could if they could feel if they live they could feel or they could live or they could do both or they could not and if not if they did not is did not the same as could not or if indeed if could not is not the same who will change the same.

Henry James meant and met and if he was a general and

he was if he was a general and if is not necessary because he was he was not ready but being not ready was of no importance because he was.

I wish to say he was.

Rather I wish to say he was.

I wish rather to say he was.

I wish now to give the life history of Henry James who was a general. And yes. Whether no or yes whether yes or no or to tell it so.

I wish not wish but do do tell it so.

There is no hope of either or oh no.

VOLUME X

Henry James may be, not a place he could not be a place a general cannot be a place, he or it can not.

Henry James then can not be a place and in so much as he is not a place and can not be a place and a general can not be a place and is not a place insomuch Henry James is a general and a general is Henry James.

Oh yes they say there can be others but oh yes there are not.

Henry James begins to be as he is. Indeed if not why not. But there is never any if not as Henry James is as he is. He controls nothing by only that but a general a general controls nothing oh no oh yes a general controls something, and so triumphantly I say triumphantly and so triumphantly so does Henry James he controls something he does control something. And so when and why not is not Henry James a general and a general Henry James. They are that. Henry James is a general and he controls something even though and it can be said that Henry James does not control anything and even then it can be said a general does not control anything.

Who has a general at heart or Henry James. They have that with that wish.

Pray pray pray prepare to wish.

Henry James comes for them for them and them.

Was a general known to wish.

No no general not as a general a general was not known to wish.

Neither was Henry James.

VOLUME XI

There is no use always beginning before before what. I wished to say wish to say that there is no use there is no use in my beginning in my having been beginning before. Once more I have it to do before what. Before he was Henry James. Before he was a general. Some one might they be some one. Not before. Not before Henry James. Might he be some one before Henry James. Not if he was to have been Henry James which he was and a blessing even if not everything a blessing something not to be arranging to be Henry James. A general is in any and all of any way or ways the same.

But to begin. Having begun there is no refusal in to begin but there might be. In this case there might only be as there more than just there there might have been.

Think of an American thing a poetic American thing there might have been.

This may not refer to a general. Not may but also not might, might not refer to a general. May or might not refer to Henry James. All of which connects with not to begin. In a new continent and is any new continent, no not new, in a new continent they might not begin not might not have been begun. That makes a new continent not any fun.

Why do you say so if you know so.

Henry James might not have begun. Neither a general too.

I wish to think a little of a difference in age and why nobody says so. And is there any hope of sitting there or any where. Or is there any hope of using any hope.

I wish to see that you know Henry James.

I may be acquainted with him by and by.

Who says it is easily said. Who says or said that it was easily said.

Forget who said what was easily said and come back to remember Henry James.

One at a time is of no use as just as often there is more than not one at a time. In place of that who is in place of that.

This makes partly an understanding of Henry James and I am not as pleased as not relieved that it is so.

One should always think well of how to spell.

All who have have it to do so.

As newly as not wed Henry James.

For this and made for this as in and for a use a use for this.

Of and for are always different and never no never different as not one at a time.

I begin to see how I can quiver and not quiver at like and alike.

A great deal can be felt so.

VOLUME XII

Henry James one.

VOLUME XIII

The young James a young James was a young James a James. He might be and he might be even might be Henry James.

VOLUME XIV

Once upon a time there was no dog if there had been a dog nobody wept.

Once upon a time there was no name and if any one had a name nobody could cover a name with a name. But nobody except somebody who had not that name wept.

Once upon a time there was a place for a name and when that name was the same no one and why not if no one, no one wept. Once upon a time if once upon a time a name was not to blame not to blame not if as a name, if once upon a time a name was the same and if not no one had any one to blame then no one not this time no one had to weep and so this time and no one at this time had been having it as a blame that no one was weeping as if no one had wept.

Once upon a time no one not any one wept that there was a name which was the same as the same name. And so no one wept.

VOLUME XV

Once upon a time if you wonder once upon a time what was his name, his name Henry James was a name, and weeping he wept.

If he wept was it his name.

Oh yes it was his name, all the same yes all the same it was his name.

He wept.

VOLUME XVI

Any time Henry James wept it was his name.

VOLUME XVII

To return but nobody can, if they can may they if they began, to return to Henry James.

Not to say this slowly is not to say this not at all. To say this not at all slowly is not not to say this at all.

And so all.

All can return slowly.

Nobody can return slowly if they do not move. And did they move.

If they did not better than if they did which they did move.

Henry James cannot return slowly. Or have it as a pleasant and a pleasure. Pleasant in time.

How can all who have arranged to remain where or when or wherever may they may they be alike.

Nobody is alike Henry James.

Better prepare enough.

Nobody is alike Henry James.

Is it is that it, is it because Henry and James are both first names.

Believe this if this is true.

Does it mean that you are you or who are you.

Henry James and names.

He neither now or either how invented names.

May be by a character. Or may be or may be not.

Nobody could make a mistake.

If for instance nobody could make a mistake.

I wish I was used to think of a difference between won and young.

Which made around around.

He heard nobody care.

But this was this or is it.

He he who heard nobody care.

Or is or is it.

He or he and he was prepared to remain there.

Not exactly not.

He was not not prepared not to remain where, there where.

In his care.

In its care.

Where.

It is delightful to know who can go home if they go and if they do not if they do not go.

I have to say here here I very well know what it is that has happened.

He will not begin again because he has it is has been begun.

I have said it for me there.

Which will undertake that care.

I understand you undertake to overthrow my undertaking.

Henry James when he was young.

We discussed we said we discussed did or was he young.

She said he was fresh that is fresher but he was not young and I said he was young quite young that is what I said.

And he was not young but fresher then or was he young and not fresher then.

Which one went on, one not before the other one.

If they were not the same.

If he were young that is to say had been he would have been read to been a young or younger one. I think this is a thing.

Not only by a wish but by not watches or wishes.

He had both both watches and wishes Henry James when he was fresher or Henry James when he was young.

There is no use hanging on to some one wishes and watches but some have some hung when that is young that one.

Decline may make or makes one at a time.

There is no decline when they are not sickly when they are young.

That is one thing.

Henry James one thing.

Henry James for one thing.

He never pursued one at a time no not one thing a thing.

That was not one thing a young thing but he was a he was a young thing. Henry James was was was a young thing. If he was fresher then fresher and add her. But not by him. Not any one thing.

I wish to add that I knew I know one thing.

One thing one thing.

That Henry James was young one thing.

Prepare for flight.

Henry James did not prepare for flight.

Hours what. What are hours for. Hours are not for one thing.

Anything makes nothing and nothing makes anything not a young thing.

Any one is easily equal to that.

Forgive wishes with watches nor watches with wishes.

Forget one thing.

This makes it feel reasonable not to read but indeed this one thing that Henry James was young with one thing.

For them for names for days.

Not which had been. He had not been. That makes him a young then a middle aged thing not so fresh a thing that he had not been. Which he had not been.

But all the same it is true he had been a young thing.

It is not difficult not very difficult to remember what he had been, any one can any day in walking see anything. Anything is any one and any one is a young one. Oh yes you do. He did too.

When this was true where were they. They were here. He was here. This that was so. He was here where he would have been to have been told that it was so.

Henry James you see Henry James was young. Not necessarily but nicely young. Is there any difference between necessarily and nicely. Not when one had been begun.

And then he went on as if he had been young. Oh yes he

did go on as if he had been young. No doubt about it yes this was the way it was when he had been begun.

Henry James never came amiss. He did not come slowly nor did he come to kiss.

Which may be there which may be there which may be there.

Did no one not run.

Added bliss to miss and miss to kiss and kiss to remember remember any one.

This made him be have been young.

So I say it is not only not that he was freshened and had been begun but that he had been young.

There now add nothing whatsoever as to how it never meant more than allow.

I wish every one knew exactly how to feel, about Henry James.

VOLUME XVIII

I may remember how to walk up and down.

VOLUME XIX

They felt as well as very well and in no sort and at no time, well very nearly addedly as well.

This makes that they fell which and where they kneel.

Henry James had well you might say he had no time.

VOLUME XX

But just as much as it might be that he was uneasy not uneasy not afraid.

They might be caught alone. Who might be caught alone.

VOLUME XXI

There might not only be left as it.

As it is a chance to bequeathe.

He felt as if they met with which they met not to bequeathe which in their change they met.

How could Henry James fancy that with his name it was not a similar name to that of his brother. Was his brother another.

There now you see. It is not necessary never to mention never to have a brother.

Fortunately many foil an instance of that.

She bowed to her brother.

That is coming in here.

VOLUME XXII

I wish to make it perfectly clear that this is neither there nor here.

Henry James is adamant if you say so.

VOLUME XXIII

By which he may and did mean if you say so.

VOLUME XXIV

Let me tell the history of Henry James simply tell the history of Henry James which brings me and us back to names.

I still have nothing to say about names even if I make a mistake.

VOLUME XXV

A name is a name by which some one reads something or if not then why does he does she not.

And if he does if she does, does it make a moon.

A moon is no name.

James is no name

Henry is no name.

Why is no name.

Shares is no name.

Blinded is no name

Predicate is no name.

This is no name.

Henry James if you say so Henry James was a name.

You can think of a name as a name or not a name. It is very easy to think of Henry James as not a name.

When a boy is a general that is to be is going to be a general being the son and the grandson of one and another one and either of them have been a general they may say to him you cannot be afraid. And he may say but I am I am afraid, I am often afraid, I am afraid when I see something and it turns out to be a horse then I am afraid. But then how can you come to be a general. But a general is on a horse and on a horse it is not on a horse that there is any way to be afraid. And beside that any general is not where it is any danger to be a general in any danger as a general oh no not indeed not for a general. So that is it.

Henry James if he was to be a boy was then to be a general oh yes if not then if not why not a general. But he is and was to be a general.

Come often to see me is not said by a general.

But any one can see a general indeed yes any one.

Henry James was a general.

In general.

The general likes his coffee cold.

In general.

He does not take coffee or milk. Not in general. Not at all. Not a general.

That may be a general.

But Henry James is a general.

And now read what he says.

What does a general say when they read what he says.

In general.

To come back to having been a boy.

Is there a difference between having been a boy and being begun. Not at once and at the same time.

But it is true.

Henry James has been a boy, and he has been begun.

He was never so otherwise.

No never so otherwise.

And this is what is painful that when in tears he was never so otherwise.

But when in tears was he so otherwise.

A general was a general so.

If the little boy was afraid there were no tears because if he was to be a general it would be so otherwise.

When once when twice when once when twice there were no tears otherwise than no tears not twice not once not otherwise.

And so after all anybody can see after all that Henry James was after all a general.

VOLUME XXVI

Play to remember everything that happened within to him.
But which was otherwise when they were not happening.
Play be otherwise.
Can a general be otherwise.
Can he play be otherwise.
Can he play happened to him.
When they happened to him did they happen within.
Did they happen otherwise than it happened for him.
Not otherwise.
Henry James was very ready to have it happen for him.

VOLUME XXVII

A narrative of Henry James told by one who listened to some one else telling about some one entirely different from Henry James.

To some one entirely different from Henry James is a woman who might have killed somebody else another woman only very probably she did not. She was not really under any suspicion of having killed her or any other woman or any other man but really she was entirely a different kind of human being from Henry James entirely a different kind of human being and one who had led and did lead an entirely different kind of life. She lived alone and in the country and so did Henry James. She was heavy set and seductive and so was Henry James. She was slow in movement and light in speech and could change her speech without changing her words so that at one time her speech was delicate and witty and at another time slow and troubling and so was that of Henry James. She was not at all at all at all resembling to

Henry James and never knew him and never heard of him and was of another nationality and lived in another country. And that is all there is to it.

So one has quite frequently told different people about her. Because it is a matter that remains to be told about her that something is what any one can tell about her.

Indeed very often as often as ever and yet again and once more as often.

So that is why I like to listen to her to the one that tells any story that she tells about what happens to any one and something did happen at least it happened near that one.

This one the one telling the story had always admired Henry James.

So there you are. That is the connection.

VOLUME XXVIII

Henry James fairly well Henry James.

VOLUME XXIX

It makes no difference what you say when you read.

It makes no difference what you say if you read.

Neither does it make any difference what you say because you read.

None of this makes any difference.

Now think about what does or does not make any difference.

Think about it and do not cry although tears do come easily at least they seem to come easily if they come or if they do not come.

Now when what you say does not make any difference and tears do or do not come and if they do come or if they do not come they could come easily or not easily in coming or not coming this is what it is when Henry James gradually one can not say gradually because by that time it was there but gradually what it was that was said came to rise not like cries but like tears and no one can say that they did or did not come easily but one might say indeed and could say that they did or did not come at all and this made it all there.

Now do you see what I mean when I read.

Even if I do not read do you see what I mean if I do read.

That is what Henry James did, any one does but all the same he did it like that.

Shall I tell you again all about tears and how they rise and how they come and how they will and how they can or not be full. Full is a word so well-known.

Who knows who is well-known.

Henry James is well-known.

But of course he is Henry James is well-known.

Sometimes I wonder about a name like James when it is not a first name but when it is a last name.

David James.

Henry James could not have been named David James.

There was a wicked family named James, and their names make James a very different name and no one needs to feel that tears could come to mean that as a name.

Henry James. A very different name from David James or William James or Robin James or Winslow James. Or even a very different name from Ethel James although that is not so far away, Ethel James and Henry James. Thomas James can never harden any one to the name James. But nevertheless in no distress Henry James is well-known.

VOLUME XXX

To commence to cover the ground.

VOLUME XXXI

It will soon be thought that anybody can be bought.

It will not soon be thought that anybody can be taught.

What can anybody buy.

Anybody can buy, that anybody can cry.

Henry James moved as he bought.

There are other words that no one need use, caught, fought taught.

Henry James was meant by all.

Has any country forgot any country.

That is what they try to say.

But what do they say.
That is what there is. What do they say.
For which five mean as six.

VOLUME XXXII

I am going to tell it very well.

VOLUME XXXIII

He knew what was in a name all the same.

VOLUME XXXIV

It has been remarked and it is very curious that in opening a page you know it is that page not by its age not by the words upon the page not by the number upon the page but because on that page there are three names and those three names are not together upon any other of any page.

Now this has been told to me and is it true. If it has been told to me it certainly is true.

Further more it has been told to me that very likely nothing is said upon that page about any one whose name is upon that page. This has been told to me and it is true it is true that it has been told to me.

And in this way you see that everything that has been told to me is true if it has been told to me.

Henry James is well-known as that oh yes as that.

And now consider fortune and misfortune failure and success, butter and water, ham and water cress.

First then fortune and misfortune. He had no fortune and misfortune and nevertheless he had no distress and no relief from any pang. Any pang. Oh yes any pang.

And failure and success. He had no failure and no success and he had no relief from any failure and he had no relief from any distress. Nevertheless. He had no relief not as having had a relief from any other pleasure and anxiety and in that place any removal and any surprise.

This what has been arranged to say has not been said but

all that I have heard has been said. Which they may say. Has been said.

Once upon a time nobody managed to be useful and nobody managed to be there.

Once upon a time and tears will flow once upon a time nobody has arranged to be useful and nobody has arranged as yet and further yet not anybody need have been placed to arrange that anybody wept. In place is not the same as in spite of all. And yet well-known is not more easily arranged. In place of that not well-known is not more than more easily arranged.

I wish to help myself to as much as they had more.

That is what they said not to me but not that is not not to me.

And so it happened I wish you to know to know it as often as well as not very-well that is is not not to me.

What they said to me they said as if it were true and what is there to say.

Some do some do tell some do say so, as if it were so. Some some do. Some do do so.

Some do.

Some do not.

But some who do not say so do not say so. They say some do say that some some one does or do. Do what there is or is not to do. Some do.

LECTURES IN AMERICA

TO BERNARD
WHO COMFORTINGLY AND ENCOURAGINGLY
WAS LISTENING
AS THESE WERE BEING WRITTEN

What Is English Literature

O NE CANNOT come back too often to the question what is knowledge and to the answer knowledge is what one knows.

What is English literature that is to say what do I know about it, that is to say what is it. What is English literature, by English literature I mean American literature too.

Knowledge is the thing you know and how can you know more than you do know. But I do know a great deal about literature about English literature about American literature.

There is a great deal of literature but not so much but that one can know it. And that is the pleasant the delightful the fascinating the peaceful thing about literature that there is a great deal of it but that one can all one's life know all of it.

One can know all of it and one can know it all one's life and at any moment in one's life one can know all of it. There it is right in you right inside you right behind you. Perhaps in front of you but this you do not know. To be sure it has been more or less truly said about English literature that until about fifty years ago a first class English writer appeared almost every ten years, since that time it has been necessary to very much help if not to replace it by American literature. And so I say one can have at any one moment in one's life all of English literature inside you and behind you and what you do not yet know is if it is in front of you, you do not know if there is going to be any more of it. However very likely there is, there is at any rate going to be more American literature. Very likely.

At any rate it is a pleasure to know that there is so much English literature and that any any moment in one's life it is all inside you. At any rate it is all inside me. At any rate that is what I know. And now what is it that I do know about the English literature that is inside me, that is in me completely in me any moment of my living.

English literature has been with us a long time, quite a few hundreds of years, and during all that time it has had a great deal to do and also it has a great deal to not do.

This as a whole thing could be told in a couple of sentences but it is necessary to make it a great deal longer. Anybody, even I, can understand that necessity.

What has it had to do and what has it had not to do and how does one know one from the other, know what it has had to do from what it has had not to do.

In English literature there is a great deal of poetry and there is a great deal of prose and sometimes the poetry and the prose has had something to do one with the other and very often not. Besides this there has been again and again in English literature the question can one serve god and mammon, and the further question if one can should one. But the important question can remain and does remain what is god and mammon insofar as it concerns English literature. Has this question to do with prose and with poetry as both or as either one. I wish to very largely go into this because in it is the whole description of the whole of English literature and with it and after it although not entirely out of it comes American literature.

But to begin at any beginning at least as a beginning is.

There are two ways of thinking about literature as the history of English literature, the literature as it is a history of it and the literature as it is a history of you. Any one of us and anyway those of us that have always had the habit of reading have our own history of English literature inside us, the history as by reading we have come to know it. Then there is the history as the English people came to do it. Every one's own history of English literature is their own until they tell it to somebody else as I am now telling mine. The history of English literature as it was written is English Literature's History and that too most of any of us who have to read do know.

There is then also the English people's history of their English literature but then after all that is their affair as far as I am concerned, as I am deeply concerned, it is none of my business.

It is awfully important to know what is and what is not your business. I know that one of the most profoundly exciting moments of my life was when at about sixteen I suddenly concluded that I would not make all knowledge my province.

And so my business is how English literature was made inside me and how English literature was made inside itself.

What does literature do and how does it do it. And what does English literature do and how does it do it. And what ways does it use to do what it does do.

If it describes what it sees how does it do it. If it describes what it knows how does it do it and what is the difference between what it sees and what it knows. And then too there is what it feels and then also there is what it hopes and wishes and then too there is what it would see if it could see and then there is what it explains. To do any or all of these things different things have to be done. Most of them are being done all the time by literature. And how has English literature done it.

As you come slowly to become acquainted with English Literature there are two things that at first do not interest you, explanations, that is one thing, and what it is that is felt, that is another thing. Most people all their later lives like these things the best in literature those of them who concern themselves with English literature by reading it.

They like explanations and they like to know how they felt, how they felt by the others feeling but anyway and principally how they felt.

The thing that has made the glory of English literature is description simple concentrated description not of what happened nor what is thought or what is dreamed but what exists and so makes the life the island life the daily island life. It is natural that an island life should be that. What could interest an island as much as the daily the completely daily island life. And in the descriptions the daily, the hourly descriptions of this island life as it exists and it does exist it does really exist English literature has gone on and on from Chaucer until now. It does not go on so well now for several reasons, in the first place they are not so interested in their island life because they are in short they are not so interested. And in the next place it is not as much an island life.

But in the beginning and then for an endless long going on there was there is the steady description of the daily life the daily island life. That makes a large one third of the glory of English literature.

Then there is the poetry that too comes out of a daily island life, because granted that a daily island life is what it is and the English daily island life has always been completely what it is, it is necessary that poetry is not what they lose or what they feel but is the things with which they are shut up, that is shut in, in the daily the simply daily island life. And so the poetry of England is so much what it is, it is the poetry of the things with which any of them are shut in in their daily, completely daily island life. It makes very beautiful poetry because anything shut in with you can sing. There are the same things in other countries but they are not mentioned not mentioned in that simple intense certain way that makes English poetry what it is.

It is easy to know all that.

So that is something that has made several sides of English literature what it is.

And so to begin again to go on.

When anybody at any time comes to read English literature it is not at all necessary that they need to know that England is an island, what they need to know and that in reading any real piece of English literature they do know is that the thing written is completely contained within itself.

That is one of the reasons why in English literature there has been less question as to whether one should serve God and Mammon. There may inevitably be a question as to whether there is any god and mammon in respect to the inner existence of English literature. Because of there being really no vital question as to the God and Mammon and which is which in serving literature in English literature English literature has existed each piece of it inside itself in a perfectly extraordinary degree compared with other literatures that is other modern literatures and this gives it at once its complete solidity, its complete imagination, its complete existence.

When I was a child I was always completely fascinated by the sentence, he who runs may read. In England running and reading is one because any one can read, and since any one can read does it make any difference how or why they run. Not on an island. In fact insofar as they run they are there there where they read just as much as not.

I am trying not to give to myself but to you a feeling of the way English literature feels inside me.

I have been thinking a great deal as to the question of serving God or mammon, and that in the case of most peoples, certainly peoples who live on continents it is not possible to do both not in making literature, but in English literature generally in English literature the question does not arise, because since the life of the island the daily life of the island goes on so completely and daily and entirely, there is no possibility, granting that it is all included and it always is, there is no possibility that in satisfying anybody there is not the satisfying everybody and so there is no question as between serving God and Mammon. There is enormously such a question for anybody living on a continent and the reason why I will go into largely as English literature connects with American literature. Not that it really does connect and yet not that it really does not. But this again is another matter.

To begin again then not begin again but just to state how English literature has come to be, came to be in me. In short what English literature is.

As I say description of the complete the entirely complete daily island life has been England's glory. Think of Chaucer, think of Jane Austen, think of Anthony Trollope, and the life of the things shut up with that daily life is the poetry, think of all the lyrical poets, think what they say and what they have. They have shut in with them in their daily island life but completely shut in with them all the things that just in enumeration make poetry, and they can and do enumerate and they can and do make poetry, this enumeration. That is all one side of English literature and indeed anybody knows, where it grows, the daily life the complete daily life and the things shut in with that complete daily life.

The things being shut in are free and that makes more poetry so very much more poetry. It is very easy to understand that there has been so much poetry written in England.

On a continent even in small countries on a continent, the daily life is of course a daily life but it is not held in within as it is on an island and that makes an enormous difference, and I am quite certain that even if you do not see it as the same anybody does see that this if it is the truth is the truth. If it is the truth about English literature it is the truth about English literature.

It is a comparatively early thing to know English literature as English literature to those of us who read as naturally as we read that is as we run.

It begins if it begins it begins with Lamb's tales of Shakespeare. And how are they the island daily life the English island daily life. But they are. And they are because of their poetry, and the poetry is because of the reality of all the life that is shut in, so completely sweetly, so delicately really shut in with their daily life.

I remember well I cannot say I do remember but I do feel and I did feel as if I did feel and did remember and do remember this.

And in the poetry of that time in their poetry is there any question of the difference in literature between its serving god and mammon.

Yes perhaps a little somewhat of that time. They knew their style knew that there were two styles. There was a style that those who run may read and there was a style too a style that those who read do not run. They need not run because there is nothing to run with or from.

That is the difference between serving god and serving mammon, and the period after the Chaucer time to the Pope Gibbon Johnson time was such a time. And how does one, how does one not run.

As I talk of serving god and mammon I do not of course mean religion in any sense excepting the need to complete that which is trying to fill itself up inside any one. And this may be part of the same inside in one or it may not. If it is then it is a complete daily life, if it is not then it is not.

As I say in that period from Chaucer to Pope Gibbon and Johnson and Swift, a great many things filled up everybody that had to be filled, of course it is only those who have an active need to be completely completed who have all this as a bother.

As I say during this long period, the daily island life was there completely literally and daily and simply there, the poetry of the things shut in with that daily life were there but other things were there too and these other things were due to other origins and all these origins at that time were just sufficiently disturbing to make it possible for style to know that there is a serving god a serving mammon for those who write as they write. What else can they do.

During this long period and it was a long period, a very strongly long period a great many things happened in England and as they happened inside England they to a certain extent destroyed or at least confused the daily island life.

When the confusion comes to an island from the outside it is soon over and if not over then absorbed, that is what happened in the beginning of this period the norman conquest but when the confusion comes from the inside then it is a very confused confusion because it is a confusion inside the daily island life. This is what happened in all the latter part of this long period the English civil wars the period from Chaucer to Swift Gibbon Pope and Johnson and then again it settled down to being an island daily life only there were things left over from the late confusion and that was then the eighteenth century English literature and then there was the nineteenth century and then there was not any more a confusion but a complete settling in into the daily island life. What was outside was outside and what was inside was inside, and how could there be a question of god and mammon, when what is inside is inside and what is outside is outside there can be no confusing god and mammon.

Perhaps and perhaps not but that is at any rate one way in which living can be lived, literature can be made.

So the history of English literature is beginning to be clear, the history of English literature. Of course if the English people had not been what they were they would not have made out of the daily island life the literature they did make. That is true enough. Anything is true enough. But that certainly is.

The thing that happened before Chaucer, the Norman conquest coming as it did from the outside was one of those things which as I say do not produce confusion. They upset things for a while but they do not confuse things, a very different matter. And so when all that was over the thing English literature had still to do was to describe the daily island life and Chaucer did it, and the making of poetry of the things shut in with that daily island life and Chaucer certainly did it. Anybody that knows can certainly remember that. But and that must not be forgotten, words were in that daily island life which had not been there before and these words although they did not make for confusion did make for separation.

This separation is important in making literature, because there are so many ways for one to feel oneself and every new way helps, and a separating way may help a great deal, indeed it may, it may, it may help very much. And this did.

As you may or may not know I read a great deal of Elizabethan prose and poetry and in this period I felt the culmination of all of this. There was no confusion but there still was left over separation and this left over separation made a division in the writer of writing. He knew that there were two things to do and which of the things did he have to do. There was a choice at that time a choice as to how a writer should write. And this choice when there is a choice a writer can and does feel as a choice between serving god and mammon. This choice has nothing to do with religion, it has nothing to do with success. It has to do with something different than that, it has to do with completion.

How is anything completed. And if it is not might it, and is there a choice.

In the whole of the Elizabethan literature one feels this something.

There is no confusion but there is a separation and to any one doing it that is writing, I am speaking of the Elizabethans to themselves inside them, there was this bother.

And it was natural that there should be this bother. God and Mammon, god and mammon, it was left over and it was there and in all the Elizabethans it was there this bother, this choice, in every minute in their writing. There was the daily island life and it made poetry and it made prose but also there was this separation and it made poetry and it made prose but the choice the choice was the thing. In a true daily island life a choice is not the thing. It was the outside separation that had come to be an inside separation that made this thing. Think about it in any Elizabethan, any Elizabethan writing, in any Elizabethan who was writing.

And words had everything to do with it.

And now perhaps I had better explain a little more clearly what I mean by serving god and mammon in literature that is as a writer making literature.

When I say god and mammon concerning the writer writing, I mean that any one can use words to say something. And in using these words to say what he has to say he may use those words directly or indirectly. If he uses these words indirectly he says what he intends to have heard by somebody who is to hear and in so doing inevitably he has to serve mammon. Mammon may be a success, mammon may be an effort he is to produce, mammon may be a pleasure he has from hearing what he himself has done, mammon may be his way of explaining, mammon may be a laziness that needs nothing but going on, in short mammon may be anything that is done indirectly. Now serving god for a writer who is writing is writing anything directly, it makes no difference what it is but it must be direct, the relation between the thing done and the doer must be direct. In this way there is completion and the essence of the completed thing is completion. I have had a very great deal to say about this in the life of Henry James in my Four in America and I am not going to say any more about this now. But slowly you will see what I mean. If not why not.

But to return to English literature.

English literature when it is directly and completely describing the daily island life beginning with Chaucer and going on to now did have this complete quality of completeness. The lyric poets of England who described the things that are shut in with that daily island life also had this directness of completion.

But and this is very important during just before and the Elizabethan period there was another bother there was separation, separation between completion and incompletion and everybody dimly knew something of such a thing inside them.

If you like it was because the two languages were just coming to be one it was if you like because, although they were living the daily island life, they still, a considerable part of them, still had a memory of not having been living a daily island life. And this made a strange bother that any one can feel in the writing, the writing of any one writing during all that time. And that is a natural enough thing.

It is in all the prose and all the poetry of that long period. It all moves so much, and that is its most characteristic quality it all moves so much, it moves up and down and forward and back and right and left and around and around. And that is what makes it so exciting. And also what makes it inside itself so separating.

If you think in detail of the writing of any one writing in that long period you will know what I mean. Think of the one you know the best and you will see what I mean. There was no confusion, as I say the trouble had come from the outside and had been absorbed in the inside and in the process of absorption as there is in any healthy digestion there was no confusion but inevitably in concluding digestion there was separation.

And this is very much to be seen in the writing and there was very much writing, in that period. It was natural that there would be a great deal of writing because liveliness and choice inevitably produces a great deal of writing.

There was then at this period constant choice constant decision and the words have the liveliness of being constantly chosen.

That is what makes that the literature that it is.

And as there was all during that period the necessity of choice and the liveliness of choosing there was also all through that period the necessity of completing. Because why choose if there is not to be completion. And so they knew they quite knew the difference between being serving god and serving mammon, the difference between direct and indirect, the difference between separation and completion. They knew. And they knew it as they knew it. That too is a very real thing. And so although all through that period there was the daily island life, they were digesting there being that and it not always having been.

And that made for the writing that was being done then by everybody writing.

Then came the period after a period when they did not write so very much, because first it was all confused the dis-

turbing of the daily island life having come from within, English Civil War, it was confused, and then we come to the
beginning when everything was clear again and the daily island
life was being lived with so much clarity that there could be
nothing but the expression of that being that thing. That was
the period that made Swift and Gibbon and Pope and Johnson
and they had no longer to choose their words they could have
all the pleasure in their use. And they did. No one ever enjoyed the use of what they had more than they did. There was
no separation anywhere, the completeness was in the use.

As one says this one feels that.

As I say the pleasure of a literature is having it all inside
you. It is the one thing that one can have all inside one.

This makes literature words whether you choose them
whether you use them, whether they are there whether or not
you use them and whether they are no longer there even when
you are still going on using them. And in this way a century
is a century. One century has words, another century chooses
words, another century uses words and then another century
using the words no longer has them.

All this as you have it inside you settles something it settles
what you have when you write anything, it settles what you
complete if you complete anything, it settles whether you address something as you express anything. In short it settles
what you do as you proceed to write which you certainly do,
that is which I certainly do.

As I say then each century has its way and by century of
course one may mean a longer or shorter time but generally
speaking a century is generally and almost always somewhere
about a hundred years.

And so although and all through there was in England in
English literature the complete and direct and simple and real
description of their daily life, their daily life as they lived it
every day on their island and which made their real solid body
of writing and there was always too the description which
made their lyric poetry the description of all the daily life of
everything that was shut in inside their daily living, of all the
things that grew and flew and were there to be in their daily
living, in each century because of the outside coming to pen-
etrate inside and then having become inside became inside, or

because the inside caused confusion in the inside or because the decision of inside made all the inside as settled as if there never had been an outside or again later and this was in the nineteenth century when the inside had become so solidly inside that all the outside could be outside and still the inside was all inside, in each generation it effected writing because after all the way you write has everything to do with where you are insofar as you are anywhere, and of course and inevitably you are somewhere.

So once again all English literature being all inside you or inside me let me see how each century did as they were to see, that is as they were to say.

It is nice thinking how different each century is and the reason why. It is also nice to think about how differently the words sound one next to each other in each century and the reason why.

It is nice to feel the sound as the words next each other sound so differently.

I have always been very fond of the books that have little quotations at the head of each chapter. I like it particularly when the quotations are very varied and many of them of more or less important writers. I like it too sometimes when the quotations are only from one or two writers. It brings out with great clearness the way words sound next to each other even the same words when the century is different and the writer is different. I am very fond in that way of coming to feel how completely what is written comes to say what it does.

But to begin again as to what the different centuries do and how they do it and familiar as it is because it all is so familiar, it is all different. English literature then is very solid, and its reality is real and its poetry very poetry. And it did change in each century.

I am not very good at dates but there were generally speaking five centuries and now we are in the twentieth century which makes a sixth century and for this we go to America. And so to begin now. That is to begin again with any of them any of the five of them of English literature.

I wish I could make it as real to you the difference in which words phrases and then the gradual changes in each century were and as I realise them. I wish I could. I really wish I could. Because if I could well after that words and the way they say that for which they use them would make no difference or not any difference or all the difference.

You do remember Chaucer, even if you have not read him you do remember not how it looks but how it sounds, how simply it sounds as it sounds. That is as I say because the words were there. They had not yet to be chosen, they had only as yet to be there just there.

That makes a sound that gently sings that gently sounds but sounds as sounds. It sounds as sounds of course as words but it sounds as sounds. It sounds as sounds that is to say as birds as well as words. And that is because the words are there, they are not chosen as words, they are already there. That is the way Chaucer sounds.

And then comes the long period. In that long period there were so many words that were chosen. Everybody was busy choosing words. In the poetry of that long period as well as in the prose everybody was livelily busy choosing words. And as the words were chosen, the sounds were very varied. And that is natural because each one liked what they liked. They did not care so much about what they said although they knew that what they said meant a great deal but they liked the words, and one word and another word next to the other word was always being chosen. Think well of the English literature of the sixteenth century and see how they chose the words, they chose them with so much choice that everything made the song they chose to sing. It was no longer just a song it was a song of words that were chosen to make a song that would sound like the words they were to sing. There is no use giving examples because it is true of everything that was written then. As they chose so early and often so late and often as they were everlastingly choosing and choosing was a lively occupation you have an infinite variety of length and shortness of words chosen of vowels and consonants of words chosen and and that is the important thing it was the specific word next to the specific word next it chosen to be next it that was the important thing. That made the glory that culminated in what is called Elizabethan. Just have it in your head and then go and look at it and you will have to see what I mean. There was no confusion then, things could be long that is words next to each other could be long and go on and very often they were short the words next to each other and they did go on but they were short, but each one was as it was chosen. There was no losing choosing in what they were saying. Never no never.

Confusion comes when they confuse what they are saying with the words they are choosing. And they knew. They knew, and a little one sees it coming even in the end of Shakespeare one sees it coming a little that there is confusion. This confusion comes when there is a giving up choosing, words next to each other are no longer so strictly chosen because there is intention to say what they are saying more importantly than completely choosing the words next each other which are to be chosen.

When that commences then there is confusion.

As I said at the end of the long period before the eighteenth century there was confusion, there was inside confusion. Something that had meant everything meant something but it no longer meant something in meaning everything and they all began to think what they wanted to say and how they wanted to say it.

The minute they all begin to think what they want to say and how they want to say it they no longer choose. And when they no longer choose then as far as writing goes they are no longer serving god they are serving mammon. No matter what it is or how fine it is or how religious it is the thing they want to say.

What is the use unless everybody knows what I want to say and what is the use if everybody does want to know everything that I want to say.

Well anyway at the end of the great epoch they began to think more of what they wanted to say as well as how they wanted to say it. Perhaps that should be turned around, they began to think more of how they wanted to say what they had come to decide to say than they did of choosing words to say what they chose the words to say the words next to each other to say.

That is pretty nearly what I do want to say.

And so we come to the confusion of which I spoke and

which shows in Milton and lasted pretty well to Pope and Gibbon and Swift and Johnson.

Then as I say the confusion cleared. Nobody was any longer really interested in what anybody else was saying. They no longer chose the words to be one next to each other but they did choose and clearly chose all the words that were to go together.

By this time there was no confusion and no interest in what there was to say nor how they were to say it. There was no confusion. There was choosing but there was the choosing of a completed thing and so as there was no completing it as being chosen being in as much as it was there to choose being already a completed thing, they naturally had no separation inside in them, nothing was separated from anything. That made it all come as clearly as it came that made it all as completed as it was, that made it a whole thing chosen, and so the words were not next to each other but all the words as they followed each other were all together.

And that was all that.

If you think of the eighteenth century in English literature you will see how clear it was. But never forget that always it was an island life they lived and as they lived that daily island life they described daily that daily island life.

They wrote very much.

And now slowly there was coming something. The daily island life was still the daily island life, it would be more than ever that thing, because slowly a complete thing was nothing anybody was interested in choosing, because all they all lived as they only could live the daily island life and they came to own everything, and so although they brought nothing that they owned to be within the island life, as they owned everything outside and brought none of this inside they naturally were no longer interested in choosing complete things. That was the beginning of the nineteenth century.

Anybody can understand how natural this is.

If you live a daily island life and live it every day and own everything or enough to call it everything outside the island you are naturally not interested in completion, but you are naturally interested in telling about how you own everything. But naturally more completely are you interested in describing the daily island life, because more completely as you are describing the daily island life the more steadily and firmly are you owning everything you own which being practically everything could be called anything and everything.

Oh yes you do see.

You do see that.

And what has it to do with writing.

It has a great deal to do with writing.

And in this century in this nineteenth century anything could be a bother and was.

So now you see that up to the nineteenth century a number of things had been and gone and each time something had been and gone there had been a great deal of writing. That is again inevitable in a daily island life, if they write at all they write a great deal. Either nothing is worth writing about or everything is worth writing about. That anybody can understand.

And the daily life had always been worth writing about and so they always wrote a great deal. What else could they do. Granted that they lived this daily island life and realised it every day and were shut in every day with all of that daily island life every day what could they do but say it every day and as they said it every day they wrote it every day practically every day.

There had then as everybody knows been a great deal of English writing a great great deal of English writing, and it was poetry and it was prose.

The use of words whether the words were there as in Chaucer, whether they were livelily chosen to be next to each other one next to the other as in the long period after, and there were so many words chosen during that long period so many words chosen to be next to each other that there never can be a greater pleasure.

At the end of that long period when the words chosen to be next to each other gradually became troubled by the intention of how something was to be said rather than something that was something other than that something and how was the way that they had decided it should be said. That was the period of fashion and confusion the period of the restoration.

And then came the time after when everything was so complete that choosing or not choosing was not really any bother. They knew what to do because it was all so well done.

And then came the wars of Napoleon and England then came to own everything. And what happened.

As I say what happened was that the daily island life was more a daily life than ever. If it had not been it would have been lost in their owning everything and if it had been lost in their owning everything they would naturally have then ceased to own everything. Anybody can understand that.

They needed to be within completely within their daily island life in order to own everything outside as they were then really owning everything.

And what happened, what happened to their writing. Oh that is very interesting. It is interesting because it is very important about serving god and mammon, it is interesting because of what it did to words and phrases. It is interesting because we are still in the shadow of this thing. It is interesting.

In the first place did it change quickly.

And there is something you must always remember about wars that is about catastrophes, they make a change which is a change which is about to be a change go faster as much faster as a war can go, and even a slow war a slow catastrophe goes quite fast.

To be sure anything goes quite fast, that is changes quite fast. It is always an astonishment to me even in country family lives how much has changed how much a family life has changed, how completely a family life has changed say in five years.

This is always true but a catastrophe makes one say so more.

At any rate it was true although they did not in their daily life say that was true it was true in the life of English Literature.

After all it has not lasted so very long English literature and it has passed through so very much. And now came the nineteenth century and a great many things were gone.

That the words were there by themselves simply was gone. That the words were livelily chosen to be next one to the other was gone.

That the confusion of how and what was the way that any

one at that time had to find was the way to say what they had to say was gone.

And the clarity of something having completion that too was gone completely gone.

And now what had they to do and how did they do it.

They were living their daily life and they owned everything, everything that existed anywhere outside.

And everybody wrote everybody always had written and how did they do it.

As I say we are still in the shadow of it.

One of the first things to notice is that the time now had come when they began to explain.

Before that in all the periods before things had been said been known been described been sung about, been fought about been destroyed been denied been imprisoned been lost but never been explained.

So then they began to explain. And we may say that they have been explaining ever since.

And as I say we are still in the shadow of it.

And what did they explain and why and what did it do to words and phrases.

And what did they do beside and what did living their island life inside and owning everything outside have to do with it.

There is explanation, the nineteenth century discovered explanation and what is the relation between explanation and sentimental emotion, such as the nineteenth century wrote. Is there any. Yes there is. There is a very distinct connection.

Of course I have read always read did nothing but read everything that was ever written in the nineteenth century. That is natural enough since I was born in the nineteenth century. What else could I do but read everything there was to read that was or had been written in the nineteenth century.

I had read almost read everything that was written in English in the eighteenth century, poetry prose and history, philosophy memoirs and novels, very long novels and I have read them all, I have read practically read and I was always reading, everything that was written in English in the eighteenth century. Of the long period that went before from Chaucer to the eighteenth century I read a good deal quite a good deal but of course not all, not all as I read what was written in the eighteenth century. In the nineteenth century I read more I read more than all and by that I mean that I read a great deal written in the nineteenth century that was just anybody's writing. And so it is easy to see that I having read so much that was written have a liking for reading writing. If not why not. But there is no if not, I do like reading writing. Now what did I slowly or not at all or very often or very well find out.

I have already told about some of the things I have found out and now to tell about what I more than found out what I knew every day as every day I read pretty nearly anything every day. And so to go on with explanation and how it came about and sentimental emotion and how it came about.

Some day I would like to be able to realise everything I feel about sentimental writing and what it is to each one who hears or writes or reads it. But first everything to tell everything about how differently the nineteenth century explained anything from the other times and what makes English nineteenth century literature what it is.

In the first place remember, I remember that words and then choice or not choice, knowing what there is to say or saying what they do say has been changing.

In the nineteenth century what they thought was not what they said, but they said what they thought and they were thinking about what they thought.

This was different than the time that went before.

And now how do phrases come to be phrases and not sentences, that is the thing to know. Because in the nineteenth century it does. And that makes everything that makes the nineteenth century. And in order to understand, it must be understood that explaining was invented, naturally invented by those living a daily island life and owning everything else outside. They owned everything inside of course but that they had always done, but now they owned everything outside and that reinforced their owning everything inside, and that was as it was only more so but as they owned everything outside, outside and inside had to be told something about all this owning, otherwise they might not remember all this owning and so there was invented explaining and that made

nineteenth century English literature what it is. And with explaining went emotional sentimental feeling because of course
it had to be explained all the owning had to be told about its
being owned about its owning and anybody can see that if
island daily life were to continue its daily existing there must
be emotional sentimental feeling.

To like to tell it like that again, and to remember all the
books that were written and read, read by any one read by
me, oh yes read, and still read.

As I say in the nineteenth century what they thought was
not what they said, but and this may sound like the same thing
only it is not, they said what they thought and they were
thinking about what they thought. This made the nineteenth
century what it was.

If you live a daily life and it is all yours, and you come to
own everything outside your daily life beside and it is all yours,
you naturally begin to explain. You naturally continue describing your daily life which is all yours, and you naturally begin
to explain how you own everything beside. You naturally begin to explain that to yourself and you also naturally begin to
explain it to those living your daily life who own it with you,
everything outside, and you naturally explain it in a kind of a
way to some of those whom you own. All this leads you to
that what you think is not what you say but you say what you
think and you are thinking about what you think. Do you
understand, if not it is perhaps because after all you have not
read all English nineteenth century literature, but perhaps you
have and if you have then you do understand. You must also
then understand what explaining is and how it came to be.

Perhaps we are still under its shadow a little bit.

I am thinking of all the nineteenth century English literature that I have always read. There is so much of it and I have
read so much of it and I have read it so often and I have so
read it over and over again. And I am still reading it. I read
it in long pieces and little pieces, it is a natural thing to do
because after all when one picks up a book to read and if you
read a great deal as I read a great deal books every day and
many books every week of course inevitably I read many books
I have read, and as I have read everything written in the nineteenth century, important unimportant, prose, poetry, history,

science and some essays why naturally I read it again. What else can I do.

And so I know what it is.

That is natural enough.

What is it.

I have already said what it is and I think that is what it is. And in its being that, it is necessary that it was written in the way it was.

As I said the eighteenth century was clear and so there was a choice and the choice was a completed thing and what is a completed thing. A sentence is a completed thing and so the eighteenth century chose the completed sentence as a completed thing. Now what did the nineteenth century do.

As I explained it did not choose a completed thing. Anybody can understand that if you explain and the thing to be explained is that you leading your daily inside life own everything outside, it is not possible to choose a completed sentence a completed thing. That manifestly is not possible because if you have to explain the inside to the inside and the owning of the outside to the inside that has to be explained to the inside life and and the owning of the outside has to be explained to the outside it absolutely is not possible that it is to be done in completed sentences. Anybody can see that, anybody can. And so then how did the nineteenth century write.

They did not write in words that were simply words as Chaucer did. That would not help explain anything, it was too simple a thing to need or to be employed to make explaining. They did not choose words to be next to each other and to be lively just in being that in being next to each other because anything as lively as that could not own everything. Anybody can understand that. And as I have already said they could not content themselves with a completed thing that is choosing a whole sentence, because if a thing is a completed thing then it does not need explanation.

So what did they do and gradually if you think how from the eighteenth century to the nineteenth century the language gradually changed you will see that it proceeded to live by phrases, words no longer lived, sentences and paragraphs were divisions because they always are but they did not mean par-

ticularly much, but phrases became the thing. Think of the
English writing in the height of the nineteenth century and
you will see that it is so.

They thought about what they were thinking and if you
think about what you are thinking you are bound to think
about it in phrases, because if you think about what you are
thinking you are not thinking about a whole thing. If you are
explaining, the same thing is true, you cannot explain a whole
thing because if it is a whole thing it does not need explaining,
it merely needs stating. And then the emotional sentiment
that any one living their daily living and owning everything
outside needs to express is again something that can only be
expressed by phrases, neither by words nor by sentences. Anybody ought to be able to realise this thing.

I do really definitely know that although some may think
there are some exceptions there were really not except in the
beginning when the eighteenth century was still lingering or
toward the end when the twentieth century was beginning.
There were really no exceptions.

Think really think about any big piece or any little piece of
nineteenth century writing and you will see that it is true that
it exists by its phrases. Its poetry does as well as its prose.
Compare Jane Austen with Anthony Trollope and you will see
what I mean and how the volume of the phrasing gradually
grew and when you read Dickens, compare it with and they
are both sentimental with Clarissa Harlowe and you will see
what I mean. One lives by its whole the eighteenth century
thing and the nineteenth century thing lives by its parts. You
can see what I mean that this connects itself with explaining.
The same thing is true with nineteenth century poetry. The
lake poets had other ideas, they felt that it was wrong to live
by parts of a whole and they tried and they tried they wanted
to serve god not mammon, but they too inevitably as they
wrote longer and longer live by parts of the whole, because
after all mammon and god were interchangeable since in the
nineteenth century England lived its daily island life and
owned everything outside. Oh yes you do see this. And so it
goes on and on and think of Tennyson. There you completely
see what I mean. And now we come to a new thing. I hope
you thoroughly understand that the nineteenth century wrote

by its phrases and it wrote a great great great deal and I have read it all and so have a good many others. It is a soothing thing to rest upon, it is more soothing than other things in spite of the fact that a great many people who wrote it did not like it as they knew they wrote. But it is a soothing thing to write phrases, the sentiment of phrases is a soothing thing and so we all of us always like reading nineteenth century writing, those of us who like to feel soothed by something that touches feeling.

Do you feel the nineteenth century writing as it is. I hope so. I do.

And toward the end of the nineteenth century there was bound to be a change because after all nothing goes on longer than it can.

And this quite naturally could not go on any longer than it could any more than anything else did. And this is where it connects on with American literature.

American literature all the nineteenth century went on by itself and although it might seem to have been doing the same thing as English literature it really was not and it really was not for an excellent reason it was not leading a daily island life. Not at all nothing could be more completely not a daily island life than the life the daily life of any American. It was so completely not a daily island life that one may well say that it was not a daily life at all.

That is fundamental that is what the American writing inevitably is, it is not a daily life at all.

But before going on with this at all I am going on with English literature and although nothing much happened in the way of changes something did happen and this does help to connect with American writing.

As the time went on to the end of the nineteenth century and Victoria was over and the Boer war it began to be a little different in England. The daily island life was less daily and the owning everything outside was less owning, and, and this should be remembered, there were a great many writing but the writing was not so good. I remember very well, I was quite young then being very worried about England because there had been, one might quite say Kipling was the last one no really first class writing. The other writing of that period was the second class writing of the last generation, the young generation were doing the second class writing of the past generation, Wells, Galsworthy, Bennett etc. And since then it has not changed.

But before this happened there was something else that connected itself with what was to be American, American writing, one might say Meredith, Swinburne etc. and this had to do with the fact that the daily living was ceasing to be quite so daily and besides that they were beginning not to know everything about owning everything that was existing outside of them outside of their daily living. And this had to do with phrasing.

Slowly the phrasing, you see it in Browning you see it in Swinburne and in Meredith and its culmination was in Henry James who being American knew what he was doing, it is to be seen that even phrases were no longer necessary to make emotion emotion to make explaining explaining.

As I say as daily living was no longer being so positively lived every day and they were not all of them so certainly owning everything outside them, explaining and expressing their feeling was not any longer an inevitable thing and so the phrase no longer sufficiently held what a phrase had to hold and they no longer said what they thought and they were beginning not to think about what they thought.

This brought about something that made neither words exist for themselves, nor sentences, nor choosing, it created the need of paragraphing, and the whole paragraph having been being made the whole paragraph had rising from it off of it its meaning.

If you think of the writers I have mentioned you will see what I mean.

As I say Henry James being an American knew best what he was doing when he did this thing.

Do you quite clearly see that now there has commenced really commenced paragraphing.

I once said in How to Write a book I wrote about Sentences and Paragraphs, that paragraphs were emotional and sentences were not. Paragraphs are emotional not because they express an emotion but because they register or limit an emotion.

Compare paragraphs with sentences any paragraph or any sentence and you will see what I mean.

Paragraphs then having in them the quality of registering as well as limiting an emotion were the natural expression of the end of the nineteenth century of English literature. The daily island life was not sufficient any more as limiting the daily life of the English, and the owning everything outside was no longer actual or certain and so it was necessary that these things should be replaced by something and they were replaced by the paragraph. Do you quite see what I mean. I know quite completely what I mean. Think of Browning Meredith and Henry James and Swinburne and you will see what I mean. The phrases the emotion of phrases, the explaining in phrases that made the whole nineteenth century adequately felt and seen no longer sufficed to satisfy what anybody could mean. And so they needed a paragraph. A phrase no longer soothed, suggested or convinced, they needed a whole paragraph. And so slowly the paragraph came to be the thing, neither the words of the earlier period, the sentence of the eighteenth century, the phrases of the nineteenth century, but the paragraphs of the twentieth century, and, it is true, the English have not gone on with this thing but we have we in American literature. In English literature they just went back to the nineteenth century and made it a little weaker, and that was because well because they were a little weaker. What else can I say.

And so we come to American literature and why they went on and we are the twentieth century literature.

I will not tell a great deal about what I will tell just a little about that.

I said I certainly have said that daily life was not the daily life in America. If you think of the difference between England and America you will understand it.

In England the daily island life was the daily life and it was solidly that daily life and they generally always simply relied on it. They relied on it so completely that they did not describe it they just had it and told it. Just like that. And then they had poetry, because everything was shut in there with them and these things birds beasts woods flowers, roses,

violets and fishes were all there and as they were all there just
telling that they were all there made poetry for any one. And
there was a great deal of poetry there. That was English
literature and it has lasted for some five hundred years or
more and there is a great deal of it. All this now has been
everything.

In America as I was saying the daily everything was not the
daily living and generally speaking there is not a daily everything. They do not live every day. And as they do not live
every day they do not have the daily living and so they do not
have this as something that they are telling.

To be sure a number of them who have learned to write by
reading and naturally they have learned to write by reading
what English literature has been telling, a number of them
tried to turn it into a telling of daily living daily American
living but these even these although they did it as much as
they could did not really succeed in doing it because it is not
an American thing, to tell a daily living, as in America there
is not any really not any daily daily living. So of course it is
not to be told.

And now think how American literature tells something. It
tells something because that anything is not connected with
what would be daily living if they had it.

This is quite definitely not the same not the same as in
English writing.

It has often been known that American literature in a kind
of a way is more connected with English Elizabethan than
with later and that if you remember was at a time when words
were chosen to be next one to the other and because in a kind
of a way at that time it was a bother to feel inside one that
one was a writer because things were separated away one thing
from another thing, one way of choosing anything from another way of choosing.

Now all this is sufficiently different from what is American
but still it has something to do with it.

What there is to say is this.

Think about all persistent American writing. There is inside
it as separation, a separation from what is chosen to what is
that from which it has been chosen.

Think of them, from Washington Irving, Emerson, Hawthorne, Walt Whitman, Henry James. They knew that there is a separation a quite separation between what is chosen and from what there is the choosing. You do see that.

This makes what American literature is, something that in its way is quite alone. As it has to be, because in its choosing it has to be, that it has not to be, it has to be without any connection with that from which it is choosing.

Now you can see how different this is from English writing, which almost completely makes that from which it is chosen, indeed it makes it so completely that there is no choice there does not have to be any choosing.

You do see what I say.

And so, and this is the thing to know, American literature was ready to go on, because where English literature had ceased to be because it had no further to go, American literature had always had it as the way to go.

You understand that I tell you so. And it is so, as you can easily see, if you see what American literature always really has been and has had to be.

To go back to where Henry James, and Browning, and Swinburne and Meredith had come.

I told you they had come where they needed a whole paragraph to give off something that did come. And this they all did.

The others all stayed where they were, it was where they had come but Henry James knew he was on his way. That is because this did connect with the American way. And so although they did in a way the same thing, his had a future feeling and theirs an ending. It is very interesting.

And now do you see what I mean.

English literature then had a need to be what it had become. Browning Swinburne Meredith were no longer able to go on, they had come where they had come, because although island daily living was still island daily living every one could know that this was not what it was to be and if it was not to be this with all the outside belonging to it what was it to be. They Swinburne Browning and Meredith were giving the last extension, they were needing a whole paragraph to make it something that they could mention and in doing so the paragraph no longer said what all English literature had always said that alive or dead the daily life the daily island life was always led.

This is where they were.

And so as I say since everything one cannot say had gone away, but was no longer there to stay, it was necessary to have a whole paragraph to hold anything there at all. And so that ended that.

In the meantime Henry James went on. He too needed the whole paragraph because he too was just there, but, and that is the thing to notice, his whole paragraph was detached what it said from what it did, what it was from what it held, and over it all something floated not floated away but just floated, floated up there. You can see how that was not true of Swinburne and Browning and Meredith but that it was true of Henry James.

And so this makes it that Henry James just went on doing what American literature had always done, the form was always the form of the contemporary English one, but the disembodied way of disconnecting something from anything and anything from something was the American one. The way it had of often all never having any daily living was an American one.

Some say that it is repression but no it is not repression it is a lack of connection, of there being no connection with living and daily living because there is none, that makes American writing what it always has been and what it will continue to become.

And so there we are.

And now, the paragraph having been completely become, it was a moment when I came and I had to do more with the paragraph than ever had been done. So I thought I did. And then I went on to what was the American thing the disconnection and I kept breaking the paragraph down, and everything down to commence again with not connecting with the daily anything and yet to really choose something. But this is another story and I have told enough.

And now about serving god and mammon. The writer is to serve god or mammon by writing the way it has been written or by writing the way it is being written that is to say the way the writing is writing. That is for writing the difference between serving god and mammon. If you write the way it has already been written the way writing has already been written then you are serving mammon, because you are living by something some one has already been earning or has earned. If you write as you are to be writing then you are serving as a writer god because you are not earning anything. If anything is to be earned you will not know what earning is therefore you are serving god. But really there is no choice. Nobody chooses. What you do you do even if you do not yield to a temptation. After all a temptation is not very tempting. So anyway you will earn nothing. And so this is the history of English literature of all the writing written in English as I understand it.

Pictures

IT IS NATURAL that I should tell about pictures, that is, about paintings. Everybody must like something and I like seeing painted pictures. Once the Little Review had a questionnaire, it was for their farewell number, and they asked everybody whose work they had printed to answer a number of questions. One of the questions was, what do you feel about modern art. I answered, I like to look at it. That was my real answer because I do, I do like to look at it, that is at the picture part of modern art. The other parts of it interest me much less.

As I say everybody has to like something, some people like to eat some people like to drink, some people like to make money some like to spend money, some like the theatre, some even like sculpture, some like gardening, some like dogs, some like cats, some people like to look at things, some people like to look at everything. Any way some one is almost sure to really like something outside of their real occupation. I have not mentioned games indoor and out, and birds and crime and politics and photography, but anybody can go on, and I, personally, I like all these things well enough but they do not hold my attention long enough. The only thing, funnily enough, that I never get tired of doing is looking at pictures. There is no reason for it but for some reason, anything reproduced by paint, preferably, I may even say certainly, by oil paints on a flat surface holds my attention. I do not really care for water colors or pastels, they do not really hold my attention.

I cannot remember when I was not so.

I like sign paintings and I do regret that they no longer paint the signs on the walls with oil paints. Paper with the things reproduced plastered on the wall does not do the same thing to me, it does not hold my attention. Neither does wall paper although wall paper does sometimes give the illusion of paint. But it does not do so enough, no not enough. I like to look at anything painted in oil on a flat surface although for nothing in the world would I want to be a painter or paint anything.

I have often wondered why I like the representation or the presentation of anything in oil on a flat surface but I have never been able to find out the reason why. It is simply a fact. I even like a curtain or a sign painted as they often do in Europe painted in oil of the things to be sold inside and I like a false window or a vista painted on a house as they do so much in Italy. In short anything painted in oil anywhere on a flat surface holds my attention and I can always look at it and slowly yes slowly I will tell you all about it.

When I look at landscape or people or flowers they do not look to me like pictures, no not at all. On the other hand pictures for me do not have to look like flowers or people or landscapes or houses or anything else. They can, they often do, but they do not have to. Once an oil painting is painted, painted on a flat surface, painted by anybody who likes or is hired or is interested to paint it, or who has or has not been taught to paint it, I can always look at it and it always holds my attention. The painting may be good it may be bad, medium or very bad or very good but any way I like to look at it. And now, why does the representation of things that being painted do not look at all like the things look to me from which they are painted why does such a representation give me pleasure and hold my attention. Ah yes, well this I do not know and I do not know whether I ever will know, this. However it is true and I repeat that to give me this interest the painting must be an oil painting and any oil painting whether it is intended to look like something and looks like it or whether it is intended to look like something and does not look like it it really makes no difference, the fact remains that for me it has achieved an existence in and for itself, it exists on as being an oil painting on a flat surface and it has its own life and like it or not there it is and I can look at it and it does hold my attention.

That the oil painting once it is made has its own existence this is a thing that can of course be said of anything. Anything once it is made has its own existence and it is because of that that anything holds somebody's attention. The question always is about that anything, how much vitality has it and do you happen to like to look at it.

By anything here I really mean anything. Anything that happens anything that exists anything that is made has of course its own vitality and presumably some one or if not yet then there could presumably be sometime someone who would like to look at it. But does it really, that is is it true of everything does everything that is anything does it hold somebody's attention. Yes perhaps so. One certainly may say so. And so it comes back to the fact that anything having its own existence how much vitality has it and do you happen to like to look at it and does it hold your attention.

Now most of us live in ourselves that is to say in one thing and we have to have a relief from the intensity of that thing and so we like to look at something. Presidents of the United States of America are supposed to like to look at baseball games. I can understand that, I did too once, but ultimately it did not hold my attention. Pictures made in oil on a flat surface do, they do hold my attention, and so to go further into this matter.

The first thing I ever saw painted and that I remember and remembered seeing and feeling as painted, no one of you could know what that was, it was a very large oil painting. It was the panorama of the battle of Waterloo. I must have been about eight years old and it was very exciting, it was exciting seeing the panorama of the battle of Waterloo. There was a man there who told all about the battle, I knew a good deal about it already because I always read historical novels and history and I knew about the sunken road where the french cavalry were caught but though all that was exciting the thing that was exciting me was the oil painting. It was an oil painting a continuous oil painting, one was surrounded by an oil painting and I who lived continuously out of doors and felt air and sunshine and things to see felt that this was all different and very exciting. There it all was the things to see but there was no air it just was an oil painting. I remember standing on the little platform in the center and almost consciously knowing that there was no air. There was no air, there was no feeling of air, it just was an oil painting and it had a life of its own and it was a scene as an oil painting sees it and it was a

real thing which looked like something I had seen but it had
nothing to do with that something that I knew because the
feeling was not at all that not at all the feeling which I had
when I saw anything that was really what the oil painting
showed. It the oil painting showed it as an oil painting. That
is what an oil painting is.

Later when I was about eighteen I saw the actual battle
field of the Battle of Gettysburg and the difference in emotion
in seeing the actual battle field of the battle of Gettysburg and
the panorama of the Battle of Waterloo is a thing that I very
well remember. I knew of course I knew all about the battle
of Gettysburg. When we were there it was a wonderful early
summer day, and it was an entirely different thing from an oil
painting. There were so many things back present and future,
and a feeling of enjoying oneself and there it was and the
whole thing was very complicated. I know what the battle field
of the Battle of Gettysburg looks like in general and in detail
and I know what I felt and I know what was said by us and
what we said and the states that were represented but I do
not know exactly what it looked like as I know exactly what
the battle of Waterloo looked like at the Panorama of the
battle of Waterloo which was an enormous circular oil painting. Do you begin to see a little bit what it is to be an oil
painting. I have always liked looking at pictures of battle
scenes but as I say I always like looking at pictures and then
once after the war I saw the battle field of the battle of Metz.
For a moment as I looked at it, it was a grey day and we were
on our way back from Alsace to Paris and we had seen so
many battle fields of this war and this one was so historical, it
almost it did almost look like an oil painting. As I say things
do not generally look to me like an oil painting. And just then
into this thing which was so historical that it almost did look
like an oil painting a very old couple of people a man and
woman got out of an automobile and went to look at a grave
at the way-side and the moment of its existence as an oil painting ceased, it became a historical illustration for a simple historical story. In connection with the Panorama of the Battle
of Waterloo there was a description of the battle of Waterloo
as told by Victor Hugo. If it had not rained on the twenty-
sixth of March 1814 the fate of Europe would have been

changed. I never really believed this because of course I had read so many English novels and so much English history about the battle of Waterloo but it was a perfectly definite picture of the battle of Waterloo and it had nothing whatever to do with an oil painting. It was the complete other thing of an oil painting. And now to go on with what an oil painting is.

The next thing I remember about an oil painting were the advent, in San Francisco I was still a child, of two very different paintings. One was by a man I think named Rosenthal who had been sent to Europe to develop his talent and he came back with a very large painting of a scene from Scott's Marmion the nun being entombed in a wall as a punishment. The other painting was Millet's Man with a Hoe. Both the pictures interested me equally, but I did not want a photograph of the Rosenthal picture but I did of the Man with a Hoe. I remember looking at it a great deal. And then we that is my brother and myself very moved not knowing exactly why but very moved showed the photograph to my eldest brother and he looked at it equally solemnly and then he said very decidedly, it is a hell of a hoe, and he was right.

But I still know exactly how the picture of the Man with a Hoe looked. I know exactly how it looked although having now lived a great deal in the french country I see the farmers constantly hoeing with just that kind of a hoe. The hoeing with just that kind of a hoe as I see them all the time and meet them all the time have nothing to do with Millet's Man with a Hoe but that is natural because I know the men as men, the hoe as a hoe and the fields as fields. But I still do know Millet's Man with a Hoe, because it was an oil painting. And my brother said it was a hell of hoe but what it was was an oil painting. Millet's pictures did have something that made one say these things. I remember not so many years ago at Bourg going through the monastery next to the cathedral of Brou. There unexpectedly in a little room was a cow, almost a real cow and it was an oil painting by Millet, and it did not startle me but there it was it was almost a cow but it was an oil painting and though I had not thought of a Millet for years, I did like it.

After this experience with Millet's Man with a Hoe and the

Rosenthal picture I began to become educated aesthetically, first etchings, they were in those days reproduced in magazines and we used to cut them out and then we began to collect real etchings, not many but still a few, all this was still in San Francisco, Seymour Hayden, Whistler, Zorn and finally Meryon, but these two were much later, and Japanese prints. I took on all this earnestly but inevitably as they were not oil paintings they did not hold my attention. I do remember, still in San Francisco, a sign painting of a man painting a sign a huge sign painting and this did hold my attention. I used to go and look at it and stand and watch it and then it bothered me because it almost did look like a man painting a sign and one wants, one likes to be deceived but not for too long. That is a thing to remember about an oil painting. It bothered me many years later when I first looked at the Velasquez's in Madrid. They almost looked really like people and if they kept on doing so might it not bother one as wax works bother one. And if it did bother one was it an oil painting, because an oil painting is something that looking at it it looks as it is, an oil painting.

All this has to be remembered but to go back again.

The next thing that interested me in the way of an oil painting, still in San Francisco, were some paintings by a frenchman named Cazin. Of course perhaps none of you have ever heard of him.

He was one of the then new school of painters who being accepted officially in the salons were the commonplace end of the then still outlawed school of impressionists. Cazin made a field of wheat look almost like a field of wheat blowing in the wind. It did look like a field of wheat blowing in the wind and I was very fond of looking at fields of wheat blowing in the wind. In a little while I found myself getting a little mixed as to which looked most like a field of wheat blowing in the wind the picture of the field of wheat or the real field of wheat. When that happens one naturally gets discouraged. I may say one finally gets discouraged. One is not discouraged at first, one is confirmed in one's feeling about a field of wheat blowing in the wind and then gradually one is less pleased and at last one is discouraged. One does not like to be mixed in one's mind as to which looks most like something at which one is looking the thing or the painting. And so I rather lost interest in both.

There was another painting also by Cazin called Juan and Juanita or at least that is what I called it to myself because at that time I was reading a story that had these two names, I think actually it was called something biblical. Anyway it was a picture of two children lost in the desert and the desert was like the California deserts I knew. The desert this painted desert looked very like the desert but the children did not look really very much like children and so finally I preferred that picture to the field of wheat. I suppose I concluded that since the children did not really look as children looked to me probably neither did the blowing wheat nor the desert. All this of course was very dim inside me.

The next thing that impressed me in the way of oil painting was in Baltimore at the Walters Art Gallery the pictures of the Barbizon school, not Millet any longer but Daubignys and Rousseaus. Here once more the blue sky behind the rocks was the blue sky I knew behind rocks, and particularly the Rousseaus solidifying for me the blue sky behind rocks held me. As the pictures were small and the blue sky was small the question of the real sky did not bother me, and beside although it pleased me and I liked it it did not really excite me. Then I went to Boston and there I saw the first big Corots. The one in the Boston Museum the evening star. There again I felt peaceful about it being a sky because after all it was filled with association, it was not a thing in itself. It looked like the evening star it looked as Tannhauser felt and more than that one could feel how it looked and so there was no bother. Later on, Corots always pleased me but that I think was largely because they were so gentle. I never was much troubled by anything in connection with them.

Then I bought myself my first oil painting. It was painted by an American painter called Shilling and I wanted it because it looked like any piece of American country and the sky was high and there was a cloud and it looked like something in movement and I remember very well what it was like, and then again it bothered me because after all which did I like most the thing seen or the thing painted and what was a thing in movement. I began to be almost consciously bothered.

Then I went to Europe first Antwerp then Italy then France then Spain and then later again France. Of course all this in successive years, I naturally looked at a great many pictures.

In Antwerp I only remember the colour of the Rubens' and that they were religious. I liked their colour. I liked pretty well liked their religion.

Then we went through France to Italy.

The Louvre at first was only gold frames to me gold frames which were rather glorious, and looking out of the window of the Louvre with the gold frames being all gold behind within was very glorious. I always like, as well as liked looking out of windows in museums. It is more complete, looking out of windows in museums, than looking out of windows anywhere else.

Then we went to Italy and my brother and I spent a long hot summer in Italy, in Florence and in Venice and in Perugia and I began to sleep and dream in front of oil paintings.

I did look out of the windows of the museums but it was really not necessary.

There were very few people in the galleries in Italy in the summers in those days and there were long benches and they were red and they were comfortable at least they were to me and the guardians were indifferent or amiable and I could really lie down and sleep in front of the pictures. You can see that it was not necessary to look out of the windows.

In sleeping and waking in front particularly of the Tintorettos the Giottos and the Castagnas, the Botticellis were less suited to that activity, they little as one can think it they bothered me because the Italian flowers were just like the flowers in the Botticelli pictures. I used to walk in the country and then I concluded that the Botticellis being really so like the flowers in the country they were not the pictures before which one could sleep, they were to my feeling, being that they looked so like the flowers in the country, they were artificial. You know what I mean artificial flowers. And I literally mean just that. At least that is the way I felt then about it. I liked Mantegna then because he made me realize that white is a colour, and in a way he made me feel something about what oil paintings were that prepared me for much that was to come later.

As I say in sleeping and waking in front of all these pictures I really began to realize that an oil painting is an oil painting. I was beginning after that to be able to look with pleasure at any oil painting.

I had another curious experience concerning oil painting at about that same time.

I went into Italian churches a great deal then and I began to be very much interested in black and white marble. Even other colored marbles. I went in Rome to Saint John without the walls and I did not like the marble and then I looked at the marble I did like and I began to touch it and I found gradually that if I liked it there was always as much imitation oil painted marble as real marble. And all being mixed together I liked it. It was very hard to tell the real from the false. I spent hours in those hot summer days feeling marble to see which was real and which was not. I found that granite pillars if they were four were some of them make believe if they gave me pleasure, some could be real but some had to be painted, of course they did, if it was all marble or if it was all granite there was nothing to content the eye by deceiving it. Of course anybody could come to know that.

And so I began to look at all and any oil painting. I looked at funny pictures in churches where they described in a picture what had happened to them, the ex-voto pictures. I remember one of a woman falling out of a high two wheeled cart, this a picture of what happened to her and how she was not killed. I looked at all oil paintings that I happened to see and not consciously but slowly I began to feel that it made no difference what an oil painting painted it always did and should look like an oil painting.

And so one comes to any oil painting through any other oil painting.

Then we went to Spain and there I looked and looked at pictures. I do not think there were any windows to look out of in the Prado museum in those days. Any way I only remember looking and looking at pictures. The gallery was not arranged in those days and you found your pictures. It was my first real experience in finding pictures. I then for the first time really began to think about them. I liked Rubens landscapes because they all moved together, people landscape animals and color. I liked Titians because they did not move at all and as they did not move they were noble. The Velasquez bothered me as I say because like the Cazins of my youth they were too real and yet they were not real enough to be real and not unreal enough to be unreal.

And then I found Greco and that really excited me.

There the oil painting was pure it neither moved nor was still nor was it real. I finally came to like them best. I liked them because every thing in them was so long and I liked them because they were so white. I have never forgotten what white is since.

Then I came back to France and there at once I forgot Greco because there was the Louvre and somehow there with the gold frames and all, there was an elegance about it all, that did not please me, but that I could not refuse, and in a way it destroyed oil paintings for me.

I completely for a while forgot about oil paintings.

I did not care at that time for elegance and since oil painting, so the Louvre had decided for me, were fundamentally elegant I lost interest in oil paintings. I did not get back any interest in them until the next year.

> To finish a thing, that is to keep on finishing a thing, that is to be one going on finishing so that something is a thing that any one can see is a finished thing is something. To finish a thing so that any one can know that that thing is a finished thing is something.
>
> To make a pretty thing so that any one can feel that the thing is a pretty thing is something.
>
> To begin a thing that any one can see is begun is something. To begin a pretty thing so that any one can see that a pretty thing has been begun is something.
>
> *Portraits and Prayers*—
> page 54—Random House.

I remember much later than that being very bothered by Courbet. I had commenced looking at later oil paintings, that is later than old museum pictures. I liked David then because he was so dry and Ary Sheffer because he was so tender and Greuze because he was so pretty and they all painted people to look like people that is more or less to look like people, to look like people more or less, and it did not make any difference.

But Courbet bothered me. He did really use the color that nature looked like that any landscape looked like when it was just like itself as you saw it in passing. Courbet really did use the colors that nature looked like to anybody, that a water-fall in the woods looked like to anybody.

And what had that to do with anything, in fact did it not destroy a little of the reality of the oil painting. The paintings of Courbet were very real as oil paintings, they existed very really as oil painting, but did the colors that were the colors anybody could see trees and water-falls naturally were, did these colors add or did they detract from the reality of the oil painting as oil painting. Perhaps and most likely perhaps it did not really make any difference. There was a moment though when I worried about the Courbets not being an oil painting but being a piece of country in miniature as seen in a dimin-ishing glass. One always does like things in little. Models of furniture are nice, little flower pots are nice, little gardens are nice, penny penny peep shows are nice, magic lanterns are nice and photographs and cinemas are nice and the mirrors in front of automobiles are nice because they give the whole scene always in little and yet in natural colors like the receiver of a camera. As I say one does quite naturally like things in small, it is easy one has it all at once, and it is just like that, or in distorted mirrors when one has it even more all at once, and as I say I worried lest Courbet was like that. But soon I con-cluded that no, it only seemed so, no the Courbets were really oil paintings with the real life of oil paintings as oil paintings should have. Only the Courbets being nearly something else always keeps them from being really all they are. However. To come back to pictures that is oil paintings.

I began to feel that as a different thing from Courbet, no-body or nothing looked now any more like the people in the old pictures in the museums and the old pictures were alright. Did anything one saw look really like the new pictures and were they alright.

You see it gets to be a bother but still if oil paintings are oil paintings and you really like to look at them it is not really a bother.

Should a picture look like anything or does it, even a Courbet, or a Velasquez, or does it make any difference if it does or if it does not as long as it is an oil painting.

And if it is less like anything does it make any difference and if it is more like anything does it make any difference and yet if it is not like anything at all is it an oil painting.

You see it does get complicated because after all you have to like looking at an oil painting.

And then slowly through all this and looking at many many pictures I came to Cezanne and there you were, at least there I was, not all at once but as soon as I got used to it. The landscape looked like a landscape that is to say what is yellow in the landscape looked yellow in the oil painting, and what was blue in the landscape looked blue in the oil painting and if it did not there still was the oil painting, the oil painting by Cezanne. The same thing was true of the people there was no reason why it should be but it was, the same thing was true of the chairs, the same thing was true of the apples. The apples looked like apples the chairs looked like chairs and it all had nothing to do with anything because if they did not look like apples or chairs or landscape or people they were apples and chairs and landscape and people. They were so entirely these things that they were not an oil painting and yet that is just what the Cezannes were they were an oil painting. They were so entirely an oil painting that it was all there whether they were finished, the paintings, or whether they were not finished. Finished or unfinished it always was what it looked like the very essence of an oil painting because everything was always there, really there.

CEZANNE

The Irish lady can say, that to-day is every day. Caesar can say that every day is to-day and they say that every day is as they say.

In this way Cezanne nearly did nearly in this way Cezanne nearly did nearly did and nearly did. And was I surprised. Was I very surprised. Was I surprised. I was surprised and in that patient, are you patient when you find bees. Bees in a garden make a specialty of honey and so does honey. Honey and prayer. Honey and there. There where the grass can grow nearly four times yearly.

Portraits and Prayers—page 11.

This then was a great relief to me and I began my writing.

This sounds as if it might have been an end of something as being in the nature of a solution but it was not it was just something going on.

Up to this time I had been getting acquainted with pictures I had been intimate with a number of them but I had not been really familiar with them.

I once wrote something called Made A Mile Away, which was a description of all the pictures that had influenced me, all the pictures up to this moment the moment when I became familiar with pictures.

From this time on familiarity began and I like familiarity. It does not in me breed contempt it just breeds familiarity. And the more familiar a thing is the more there is to be familiar with. And so my familiarity began and kept on being.

From that time on I could look at any oil painting. That is the essence of familiarity that you can look at any of it.

Having thus become familiar with oil paintings I looked at any and at all of them and I looked at thousands and thousands of them. Any year in Paris if you want to look at any and all paintings you can look at thousands and thousands of them, you can look at them any day and everywhere. There are a great great many oil paintings in Paris.

Once a picture dealer told me and he knew that there were sixty thousand people in Paris painting pictures and that about twenty thousand of them were earning a living at it. There are a great many oil paintings to be seen any year in Paris.

Gradually getting more and more familiar with oil paintings was like getting gradually more and more familiar with faces as you look very hard at some of them and you look very hard at all of them and you do all of this very often. Faces gradually tell you something, there is no doubt about that as you grow more and more familiar with any and all faces and so it is with oil paintings. The result was that in a way I slowly knew what an oil painting is and gradually I realized as I had already found out very often that there is a relation between anything that is painted and the painting of it. And gradually I realized as I had found very often that that relation was so to speak nobody's business. The relation between the oil painting and the thing painted was really nobody's business. It could be the oil painting's business but actually for the purpose of the oil painting after the oil painting was painted it was not the oil painting's business and so it was nobody's business.

But still one always does like a resemblance.

A resemblance is always a pleasurable sensation and so a resemblance is almost always there.

That is not the business so to speak of the oil painting, that is just a pleasant human weakness. Anybody and so almost everybody pleasantly likes anything that resembles anything or any one.

Then there is another thing another pleasant human weakness. There is another thing about an oil painting. It makes you see something to which it is resembling makes you see the thing in the way it the oil painting resembles it. And that too and that again is a pleasant thing. But then really and this everybody knows, very soon anybody that is everybody really forgets about this resemblance. They naturally do do so because things change at least they seem so to do or any way they look as if they did change that is they look different and so the resemblance of the oil painting that is to anybody that is to anything is only a thing that has become historical.

And so we are once more back to the life in and for itself of an oil painting.

As I say having in this way become more and more familiar with any kind of an oil painting I of course became more and more familiar with many particular oil paintings with a great many particular oil paintings, and as I say when you have looked at many many faces and have become familiar with them, you may find something new in a new face you may be surprised by a different kind of a face you may be even shocked by a different kind of a face you may like or not like a new kind of a face but you cannot refuse a new face. You must accept a face as a face. And so with an oil painting. You can now see that when it came first to Matisse and then to the cubism of Picasso nothing was a bother to me. Yes of course in a way it was a bother to me but not the bother of a refusal. That would not have been possible being that I had become familiar with oil paintings, and the essence of familiarity being that you can look at any of it.

MATISSE

One was quite certain that for a long part of his being one being living he had been trying to be certain that he was wrong in doing what he was doing and then when he could not come to be certain that he had been wrong in doing what he had been doing, when he had completely convinced himself that he would not come to be certain that he had been wrong in doing what he had been doing he was really certain then that he was a great one and he certainly was a great one. Certainly every one could be certain of this thing that this one is a great one.

Portraits and Prayers—page 12.

IF I TOLD HIM
A COMPLETED PORTRAIT OF PICASSO

If I told him would he like it. Would he like it if I told him.

Would he like it would Napoleon would Napoleon would would he like it.

If Napoleon if I told him if I told him if Napoleon. Would he like it if I told him if I told him if Napoleon. Would he like it if Napoleon if Napoleon if I told him. If I told him if Napoleon if Napoleon if I told him. If I told him would he like it would he like it if I told him.

Shutters shut and open so do queens. Shutters shut and shutters and so shutters shut and shutters and so and so shutters and so shutters shut and so shutters shut and shutters and so. And so shutters shut and so and also. And also and so and so and also. Let me recite what history teaches, History teaches.

Portraits and Prayers—page 21

THE LIFE OF JUAN GRIS

As a Spaniard he knew cubism and had stepped through into it. He had stepped through it. There was beside this perfection. To have it shown you. Then came the war and desertion. There was little aid. Four years partly illness much perfection and rejoining beauty and perfection and then at the end there came a definite creation of something. This is what is to be measured. He made something that is to be measured. And that is that something.

Portraits and Prayers—page 49

Anything may be a surprise to you even a shock to you but nothing can be a bother to you if you are really familiar with it. This is a natural thing.

And then having gotten so far I began often to think a great deal about oil paintings. They were familiar to me they were never really a bother to me but sometimes they were an annoyance to me.

Having now accepted all oil paintings as oil paintings I naturally sometimes began to feel something else about them. I wondered what they would be if some day they would be different. But could they be different. I often wondered in those days if oil paintings ever could be different.

This led me back to the question in oil paintings the question one might call it the eternal question for painters of oil paintings the question of the subject of the oil painting.

I naturally did not talk to painters about what they painted in their oil paintings. Painters real painters never really ever talk about that. But I told about how every picture affected me. And in a way that is what I can say. But now to go on with the difficult question why when and in which way can a painter have a subject for his pictures. And if he does and of course he does why does he. Why does he paint what he does paint.

There are first of all three things, people, objects which include flowers and fruits, landscapes which included the sea and complications of these things which may if you like be called painters' thoughts.

Beside this there are all these things staying still and then there are all these things not staying so still, even sometimes almost moving, and somehow sometime almost any painter paints them all.

And if he does is it annoying.

And is it really that that which the painter paints that in an oil painting is its element of annoyance.

Yes I think so.

Most people think that the annoyance that they feel from an oil painting that annoys them and a great many oil paintings annoy a great many people, the annoyance then that these people that anybody feels from an oil painting they think comes from the way the oil painting represents these things, the things represented in the oil painting. But I myself do not think so. I think the annoyance comes from the fact that the oil painting exists by reason of these things the oil painting represents in the oil painting, and profoundly it should not do so, so thinks the oil painting, so sometime thinks the painter of the oil painting, so instinctively feels the person looking at the oil painting. Really in everybody's heart there is a feeling of annoyance at the inevitable existence of an oil painting in relation to what it has painted people, objects and landscapes. And indeed and of course as I have already made you realize that is not what an oil painting is. An oil painting is an oil painting, and these things are only the way the only way an oil painter makes an oil painting.

One might say almost all oil painters spend their life in trying to get away from this inevitability. They struggle and the result is what everybody naturally likes or dislikes depending upon whether they think the struggle is hopeless or whether it is not. And then everybody almost everybody likes a resemblance even when there is none. Does the painter like the resemblance, oh yes he does. He does like a resemblance. That is a naturally pleasant human thing, to like a resemblance. And does this naturally pleasant human thing the liking a resemblance make everything difficult very difficult. Yes it certainly does. And it makes an oil painting annoying.

You see how this brings one to anything, to everything that any one has ever tried to do in painting.

And then there is another trouble. A painting is painted as a painting, as an oil painting existing as an oil painting, it may be in or it may be out of its frame, but an oil painting and that is a real bother always will have a tendency to go back to its frame, even if it has never been out of it. That is one of the things that an oil painting any oil painting has a very great tendency to do. And this is a bother sometimes to the painter and sometimes to any one looking at an oil painting.

Does an oil painting tend to go back into its frame because after all an oil painting belongs in its frame.

Or does it not.

It does and does not. But mostly it does and that may make for elegance that, that it does belong in its frame but it may also be a bother to the quality in it that makes it an oil painting.

And if it does belong in its frame, must it the oil painting be static.

If it tries to move and there have been good attempts to make it move does it move. Leonardo, in the Virgin child and Sainte Anne tried to make it move, Rubens in his landscapes, Picasso and Velasquez in their way, and Seurat in his way.

The trouble is always, is it the people in it who move or does the picture move and if so should it. I myself like it to do so but then I like a picture, that is an oil painting to do anything it likes to do.

The first thing that ever interested me in that way as the picture moving was the Leonardo in the Louvre, the Virgin, the child and Sainte Anne. Before this the moving in a picture was the effect of moving, but in this picture there was an internal movement, not of the people or light or any of these things but inside in the oil painting. In other words the picture did not live within the frame, in other words it did not belong within the frame. The Cezanne thing was different, it went further and further into the picture the life of the oil painting but it stayed put.

I have thought a great deal about all this and I am still thinking about it. I have passionately hoped that some picture would remain out of its frame, I think it can even while it does not, even while it remains there. And this is the problem of all modern painting just as it has been the problem of all old painting. That is to say the first hope of a painter who really feels hopeful about painting is the hope that the painting will move, that it will live outside its frame.

On the other hand most elegant painting does not move does not live outside its frame and one does like elegance in painting.

I wonder if I have at all given you an idea of what an oil

painting is. I hope I have even if it does seem confused. But the confusion is essential in the idea of an oil painting.

There it is the oil painting in its frame, a thing in itself. There it is and it has to look like people or objects or landscapes. Besides that it must not completely only exist in its frame. It must have its own life. And yet it may not move nor imitate movement, not really, nor must it stay still. It must not only be in its frame but it must not, only, be in its frame. This whole question of a picture being in its frame returning to its frame or not returning to its frame is the question that has latterly bothered me the most. Modern pictures have made the very definite effort to leave their frame. But do they stay out, do they go back and if they do is that where they belong and has anybody been deceived. I think about that a great deal these days.

You see it is difficult to describe exactly what an oil painting is, it is difficult for those who like to look at oil paintings presumably also difficult for those who paint oil paintings and it leads painters to the thing the last thing of which I wish to speak, the literary ideas so called of the painter.

I hope you all begin to feel with me what an oil painting is and granted that an oil painting is that that one likes to look at it and granted that one likes to look at it even if it is not that. Also that you do understand that what really annoys people that is anybody who is at all annoyed by an oil painting is not its being an oil painting, but the subject that is to say what it paints as an oil painting. I know I myself and mostly I am not bothered about what an oil painting has to look like am bothered by certain things oil paintings do that is by the things oil paintings always have to paint. For instance taking all the later oil paintings. Is it true that they are alright when the painting is the painting of objects and are they not alright when they are the painting of people. In spite of everything can that be a bother. May it not be a bother to you. May it not bother you. I remember so well some one saying of Van Gogh, it was a great many years ago, I like his pictures of people but not of flowers, and then adding reflectively, because of course I never do look at people and so I do not know what people look like but I do look at flowers and I do know what flowers look like. As I say persistently the thing that really annoys that deeply annoys people, that is, anybody who is annoyed by oil paintings, is not the way they are painted, that they can always get accustomed to more or less and reasonably quickly, but the subject of the oil painting. Of course it is always the same subject but even so it takes so much longer for the one looking at an oil painting to accustom himself to the subject in spite of it always being the same subject than to accustom himself to the oil painting itself. At least that is the way I feel about it.

And now there is one more subject in connection with oil paintings, the literary ideas painters have and that they paint.

The literary ideas painters have and that they paint are not at all the literary ideas writers have.

Of course the best writers that is the writers who feel writing the most as well as the best painters that is the painters who feel painting the most do not have literary ideas. But then a great many writers and a great many painters do have literary ideas. The thing that has often interested me is that the painters' literary idea is not the same kind of an idea as the writers' literary idea although they call it the same thing.

The painter has an idea which he calls a literary idea and it is to him that is he thinks it is the same kind of an idea as a writer has but it is not. And its being not makes the essential thing that makes an oil painting.

A painter's literary idea always consists not in the action but in the distortion of the form. That could never be a writer's literary idea. Then a painter's idea of action always has to do with something else moving rather than the center of the picture. This is just the opposite of the writer's idea, everything else can be quiet, except the central thing which has to move. And because of all this a painter cannot really write and a writer cannot really paint, even fairly badly.

All this is very important because it is important. It is important not for the painter or for the writer but for those who like to look at paintings and who like to know what an oil painting is and who like to know what bothers them in what an oil painting is. I hope I have been making it slowly clear to you. I might have told you more in detail but in that case you would that is to say I would not have as clearly seen as I do now what an oil painting is.

Plays

I N A BOOK I wrote called How To Write I made a discovery which I considered fundamental, that sentences are not emotional and that paragraphs are. I found out about language that paragraphs are emotional and sentences are not and I found out something else about it. I found out that this difference was not a contradiction but a combination and that this combination causes one to think endlessly about sentences and paragraphs because the emotional paragraphs are made up of unemotional sentences.

I found out a fundamental thing about plays. The thing I found out about plays was too a combination and not a contradiction and it was something that makes one think endlessly about plays.

That something is this.

The thing that is fundamental about plays is that the scene as depicted on the stage is more often than not one might say it is almost always in syncopated time in relation to the emotion of anybody in the audience.

What this says is this.

Your sensation as one in the audience in relation to the play played before you your sensation I say your emotion concerning that play is always either behind or ahead of the play at which you are looking and to which you are listening. So your emotion as a member of the audience is never going on at the same time as the action of the play.

This thing the fact that your emotional time as an audience is not the same as the emotional time of the play is what makes one endlessly troubled about a play, because not only is there a thing to know as to why this is so but also there is a thing to know why perhaps it does not need to be so.

This is a thing to know and knowledge as anybody can know is a thing to get by getting.

And so I will try to tell you what I had to get and what perhaps I have gotten in plays and to do so I will tell you all that I have ever felt about plays or about any play.

Plays are either read or heard or seen.

And there then comes the question which comes first and which is first, reading or hearing or seeing a play.

I ask you.

What is knowledge. Of course knowledge is what you know and what you know is what you do know.

What do I know about plays.

In order to know one must always go back.

What was the first play I saw and was I then already bothered bothered about the different tempo there is in the play and in yourself and your emotion in having the play go on in front of you. I think I may say I may say I know that I was already troubled by this in that my first experience at a play. The thing seen and the emotion did not go on together.

This that the thing seen and the thing felt about the thing seen not going on at the same tempo is what makes the being at the theatre something that makes anybody nervous.

The jazz bands made of this thing, the thing that makes you nervous at the theatre, they made of this thing an end in itself. They made of this different tempo a something that was nothing but a difference in tempo between anybody and everybody including all those doing it and all those hearing and seeing it. In the theatre of course this difference in tempo is less violent but still it is there and it does make anybody nervous.

In the first place at the theatre there is the curtain and the curtain already makes one feel that one is not going to have the same tempo as the thing that is there behind the curtain. The emotion of you on one side of the curtain and what is on the other side of the curtain are not going to be going on together. One will always be behind or in front of the other.

Then also beside the curtain there is the audience and the fact that they are or will be or will not be in the way when the curtain goes up that too makes for nervousness and nervousness is the certain proof that the emotion of the one seeing and the emotion of the thing seen do not progress together.

Nervousness consists in needing to go faster or to go slower so as to get together. It is that that makes anybody feel nervous.

And is it a mistake that that is what the theatre is or is it not.

There are things that are exciting as the theatre is exciting but do they make you nervous or do they not, and if they do and if they do not why do they and why do they not.

Let us think of three different kinds of things that are exciting and that make or do not make one nervous. First any scene which is a real scene something real that is happening in which one takes part as an actor in that scene. Second any book that is exciting, third the theatre at which one sees an exciting action in which one does not take part.

Now in a real scene in which one takes part at which one is an actor what does one feel as to time and what is it that does or does not make one nervous.

And is your feeling at such a time ahead and behind the action the way it is when you are at the theatre. It is the same and it is not. But more not.

If you are taking part in an actual violent scene, and you talk and they or he or she talk and it goes on and it gets more exciting and finally then it happens, whatever it is that does happen then when it happens then at the moment of happening is it a relief from the excitement or is it a completion of the excitement. In the real thing it is a completion of the excitement, in the theatre it is a relief from the excitement, and in that difference the difference between completion and relief is the difference between emotion concerning a thing seen on the stage and the emotion concerning a real presentation that is really something happening. I wish to illustrate this from a bit of The Making of Americans.

This one, and the one I am now beginning describing is Martha Hersland and this is a little story of the acting in her of her being in her very young living, this one was a very little one then and she was running and she was in the street and it was a muddy one and she had an umbrella that she was dragging and she was crying. I will throw the umbrella in the mud, she was saying, she was very little then, she was just beginning her schooling, I will throw the umbrella in the mud, she said and no one was near her and she was dragging the umbrella and bitterness possessed her, I will throw the umbrella in the mud, she was saying and nobody heard her,

the others had run ahead to get home and they had left
her, I will throw the umbrella in the mud, and there was
desperate anger in her, I have throwed the umbrella in
the mud, burst from her, she had thrown the umbrella
in the mud and that was the end of it all in her. She had
thrown the umbrella in the mud and no one heard her
as it burst from her, I have throwed the umbrella in the
mud, it was the end of all that to her.*

This then is the fundamental difference between excitement
in real life and on the stage, in real life it culminates in a sense
of completion whether an exciting act or an exciting emotion
has been done or not, and on the stage the exciting climax is
a relief. And the memory of the two things is different. As
you go over the detail that leads to culmination of any scene
in real life, you find that each time you cannot get completion,
but you can get relief and so already your memory of any
exciting scene in which you have taken part turns it into the
thing seen or heard not the thing felt. You have as I say as
the result relief rather than culmination. Relief from excitement, rather than the climax of excitement. In this respect an
exciting story does the same only in the exciting story, you so
to speak have control of it as you have in your memory of a
really exciting scene, it is not as it is on the stage a thing over
which you have no real control. You can with an exciting story
find out the end and so begin over again just as you can in
remembering an exciting scene, but the stage is different, it
is not real and yet it is not within your control as the memory
of an exciting thing is or the reading of an exciting book. No
matter how well you know the end of the stage story it is
nevertheless not within your control as the memory of an
exciting thing is or as the written story of an exciting thing is
or even in a curious way the heard story of an exciting thing
is. And what is the reason for this difference and what does it
do to the stage. It makes for nervousness that of course, and
the cause of nervousness is the fact that the emotion of the
one seeing the play is always ahead or behind the play.

Beside all this there is a thing to be realised and that is how
you are being introduced to the characters who take part in

* *The Making of Americans* (Harcourt, Brace & Co.) page 232.

an exciting action even when you yourself are one of the actors. And this too has to be very much thought about. And thought about in relation to an exciting real thing to an exciting book, to an exciting theatre. How are you introduced to the characters.

There are then the three ways of having something be exciting, and the excitement may or may not make one nervous, a book being read that is exciting, a scene in which one takes part or an action in which one takes part and the theatre at which one looks on.

In each case the excitement and the nervousness and the being behind or ahead in one's feeling is different.

First anything exciting in which one takes part. There one progresses forward and back emotionally and at the supreme crisis of the scene the scene in which one takes part, in which one's hopes and loves and fears take part at the extreme crisis of this thing one is almost one with one's emotions, the action and the emotion go together, there is but just a moment of this coordination but it does exist otherwise there is no completion as one has no result, no result of a scene in which one has taken part, and so instinctively when any people are living an exciting moment one with another they go on and on and on until the thing has come together the emotion the action the excitement and that is the way it is when there is any violence either of loving or hating or quarreling or losing or succeeding. But there is, there has to be the moment of it all being abreast the emotion, the excitement and the action otherwise there would be no succeeding and no failing and so no one would go on living, why yes of course not.

That is life the way it is lived.

Why yes of course and there is a reasonable and sometimes an unreasonable and very often not a reasonable amount of excitement in everybody's life and when it happens it happens in that way.

Now when you read a book how is it. Well it is not exactly like that no not even when a book is even more exciting than any excitement one has ever had. In the first place one can always look at the end of the book and so quiet down one's excitement. The excitement having been quieted down one can enjoy the excitement just as any one can enjoy the excite-

ment of anything having happened to them by remembering
and so tasting it over and over again but each time less intensely and each time until it is all over. Those who like to
read books over and over get continuously this sensation of
the excitement as if it were a pleasant distant thunder that
rolls and rolls and the more it rolls well the further it rolls the
pleasanter until it does not roll any more. That is until at last
you have read the book so often that it no longer holds any
excitement not even ever so faintly and then you have to wait
until you have forgotten it and you can begin it again.

Now the theatre has still another way of being all this to
you, the thing causing your emotion and the excitement in
connection with it.

Of course lots of other things can do these things to lots
of other people that is to say excite lots of people but as I
have said knowledge is what you know and I naturally tell you
what I know, as I do so very essentially believe in knowledge.

So then once again what does the theatre do and how does
it do it.

What happens on the stage and how and how does one feel
about it. That is the thing to know, to know and to tell it as so.

Is the thing seen or the thing heard the thing that makes
most of its impression upon you at the theatre. How much
has the hearing to do with it and how little. Does the thing
heard replace the thing seen. Does it help or does it interfere
with it.

And when you are taking part in something really happening that is exciting, how is it. Does the thing seen or does the
thing heard effect you and effect you at the same time or in
the same degree or does it not. Can you wait to hear or can
you wait to see and which excites you the most. And what has
either one to do with the completion of the excitement when
the excitement is a real excitement that is excited by something really happening. And then little by little does the hearing replace the seeing or does the seeing replace the hearing.
Do they go together or do they not. And when the exciting
something in which you have taken part arrives at its completion does the hearing replace the seeing or does it not. Does
the seeing replace the hearing or does it not. Or do they both
go on together.

All this is very important, and important for me and important, just important. It has of course a great deal to do with the theatre a great great deal.

In connection with reading an exciting book the thing is again more complicated than just seeing, because of course in reading one sees but one also hears and when the story is at its most exciting does one hear more than one sees or does one not do so.

I am posing all these questions to you because of course in writing, all these things are things that are really most entirely really exciting. But of course yes.

And in asking a question one is not answering but one is as one may say deciding about knowing. Knowing is what you know and in asking these questions although there is no one who answers these questions there is in them that there is knowledge. Knowledge is what you know.

And now is the thing seen or the thing heard the thing that makes most of its impression upon you at the theatre, and does as the scene on the theatre proceeds does the hearing take the place of seeing as perhaps it does when something real is being most exciting, or does seeing take the place of hearing as it perhaps does when anything real is happening or does the mixture get to be more mixed seeing and hearing as perhaps it does when anything really exciting is really happening.

If the emotion of the person looking at the theatre does or does not do what it would do if it were really a real something that was happening and they were taking part in it or they were looking at it, when the emotion of the person looking on at the theatre comes then at the climax to relief rather than completion has the mixture of seeing and hearing something to do with this and does this mixture have something to do with the nervousness of the emotion at the theatre which has perhaps to do with the fact that the emotion of the person at the theatre is always behind and ahead of the scene at the theatre but not with it.

There are then quite a number of things that any one does or does not know.

Does the thing heard replace the thing seen does it help it

or does it interfere with it. Does the thing seen replace the thing heard or does it help or does it interfere with it.

I suppose one might have gotten to know a good deal about these things from the cinema and how it changed from sight to sound, and how much before there was real sound how much of the sight was sound or how much it was not. In other words the cinema undoubtedly had a new way of understanding sight and sound in relation to emotion and time.

I may say that as a matter of fact the thing which has induced a person like myself to constantly think about the theatre from the standpoint of sight and sound and its relation to emotion and time, rather than in relation to story and action is the same as you may say general form of conception as the inevitable experiments made by the cinema although the method of doing so has naturally nothing to do with the other. I myself never go to the cinema or hardly ever practically never and the cinema has never read my work or hardly ever. The fact remains that there is the same impulse to solve the problem of time in relation to emotion and the relation of the scene to the emotion of the audience in the one case as in the other. There is the same impulse to solve the problem of the relation of seeing and hearing in the one case as in the other.

It is in short the inevitable problem of anybody living in the composition of the present time, that is living as we are now living as we have it and now do live in it.

The business of Art as I tried to explain in Composition as Explanation is to live in the actual present, that is the complete actual present, and to completely express that complete actual present.

But to come back to that other question which is at once so important a part of any scene in real life, in books or on the stage, how are the actors introduced to the sight, hearing and consciousness of the person having the emotion about them. How is it done in each case and what has that to do with the way the emotion progresses.

How are the actors in a real scene introduced to those acting with them in that scene and how are the real actors in a

real scene introduced to you who are going to be in an exciting scene with them. How does it happen, that is, as it
usually happens.

And how are the actors in a book scene introduced to the
reader of the book, how does one come to know them, that
is how is one really introduced to them.

And how are the people on the stage that is the people the
actors act how are they introduced to the audience and what
is the reason why, the reason they are introduced in the
way that they are introduced, and what happens, and how
does it matter, and how does it affect the emotions of the
audience.

In a real scene, naturally in a real scene, you either have
already very well known all the actors in the real scene of
which you are one, or you have not. More generally you have
than you have not, but and this is the element of excitement
in an exciting scene, it quite of course is the element of excitement in an exciting scene that is in a real scene, all that
you have known of the persons including yourself who are
taking part in the exciting scene, although you have most
probably known them very well, what makes it exciting is that
insofar as the scene is exciting they the actors in the scene
including yourself might just as well have been strangers because they all act talk and feel differently from the way you
have expected them to act feel or talk. And this that they feel
act and talk including yourself differently from the way you
would have thought that they would act feel and talk makes
the scene an exciting scene and makes the climax of this scene
which is a real scene a climax of completion and not a climax
of relief. That is what a real scene is. Would it make any difference in a real scene if they were all strangers, if they had
never known each other. Yes it would, it would be practically
impossible in the real scene to have a really exciting scene if
they were all strangers because generally speaking it is the contradiction between the way you know the people you know
including yourself act and the way they are acting or feeling
or talking that makes of any scene that is an exciting scene an
exciting scene.

Of course there are other exciting scenes in peace and in
war in which the exciting scene takes place with strangers but

in that case for the purpose of excitement you are all strangers but so completely strangers, including you yourself to yourself as well as the others to each other and to you that they are not really individuals and inasmuch as that is so it has the advantage and the disadvantage that you proceed by a series of completions which follow each other so closely that when it is all over you cannot remember that is you cannot really reconstruct the thing, the thing that has happened. That is something that one must think about in relation to the theatre and it is a very interesting thing. Then in a case like that where you are all strangers in an exciting scene what happens as far as hearing and seeing is concerned. When in an exciting scene where you are all strangers you to yourself and you to them and they to you and they to each other and where no one of all of them including yourself have any consciousness of know-ing each other do you have the disadvantage of not knowing the difference between hearing and seeing and is that a dis-advantage from the standpoint of remembering. From that standpoint the standpoint of remembering it is a serious dis-advantage.

But we may say that that exciting experience of exciting scenes where you have really no acquaintance with the other actors as well as none with yourself in an exciting action are comparatively rare and are not the normal material of excite-ment as it is exciting in the average person's experience.

As I say in the kind of excitement where you have had no normal introduction to the actors of the scene the action and the emotion is so violent that sight sound and emotion is so little realized that it cannot be remembered and therefore in a kind of a way it has really nothing to do with anything because really it is more exciting action than exciting emotion or excitement. I think I can say that these are not the same thing. Have they anything to do with the way the theatre gets you to know or not to know what the people on the stage are. Perhaps yes and perhaps no.

In ordinary life one has known pretty well the people with whom one is having the exciting scene before the exciting scene takes place and one of the most exciting elements in the excitement be it love or a quarrel or a struggle is that, that having been well known that is familiarly known, they all act in acting violently act in the same way as they always did of course only the same way has become so completely different that from the standpoint of familiar acquaintance there is none there is complete familiarity but there is no proportion that has hitherto been known, and it is this which makes the scene the real scene exciting, and it is this that leads to completion, the proportion achieves in your emotion the new proportion therefore it is completion but not relief. A new proportion cannot be a relief.

Now how does one naturally get acquainted in real life which makes one have a familiarity with some one. By a prolonged familiarity of course.

And how does one achieve this familiarity with the people in a book or the people on the stage. Or does one.

In real life the familiarity is of course the result of accident, intention or natural causes but in any case there is a progressive familiarity that makes one acquainted.

Now in a book there is an attempt to do the same thing that is, to say, to do a double thing, to make the people in the book familiar with each other and to make the reader familiar with them. That is the reason in a book it is always a strange doubling, the familiarity between the characters in the book is a progressive familiarity and the familiarity between them and the reader is a familiarity that is a forcing process or an incubation. It makes of course a double time and later at another time we will go into that.

But now how about the theatre.

It is not possible in the theatre to produce familiarity which is of the essence of acquaintance because, in the first place when the actors are there they are there and they are there right away.

When one reads a play and very often one does read a play, anyway one did read Shakespeare's play a great deal at least I did, it was always necessary to keep one's finger in the list of characters for at least the whole first act, and in a way it is necessary to do the same when the play is played. One has one's programme for that and beside one has to become or has become acquainted with the actors as an actor and one has one's programme too for that. And so the introduction to the characters on the stage has a great many different sides to it. And this has again a great deal to do with the nervousness of the theatre excitement.

Anybody who was as I was, brought up and at the time that I was brought up was brought up in Oakland and in San Francisco inevitably went to the theatre a lot. Actors in those days liked to go out to the Coast and as it was expensive to get back and not expensive to stay there they stayed. Besides that there were a great many foreign actors who came and having come stayed and any actor who stays acts and so there was always a great deal to see on the stage and children went, they went with each other and they went alone, and they went with people who were older, and there was twenty-five cent opera to which anybody went and the theatre was natural and anybody went to the theatre. I did go a great deal in those days. I also read plays a great deal. I rather liked reading plays, I very much liked reading plays. In the first place there was in reading plays as I have said the necessity of going forward and back to the list of characters to find out which was which and then insensibly to know. Then there was the poetry and then gradually there were the portraits.

I can remember quite definitely in the reading of plays that there were very decidedly these three things, the way of getting acquainted that was not an imitation of what one usually did, but the having to remember which character was which. That was very different from real life or from a book. Then there was the element of poetry. Poetry connected with a play was livelier poetry than poetry unconnected with a play. In the first place there were a great many bits that were short and sometimes it was only a line.

I remember Henry the Sixth which I read and reread and which of course I have never seen played but which I liked to read because there were so many characters and there were so many little bits in it that were lively words. In the poetry of plays words are more lively words than in any other kind of poetry and if one naturally liked lively words and I naturally did one likes to read plays in poetry. I always as a child read all the plays I could get hold of that were in poetry. Plays in prose do not read so well. The words in prose are livelier when they are not a play. I am not saying anything about why, it is just a fact.

So then for me there was the reading of plays which was one thing and then there was the seeing of plays and of operas a great many of them which was another thing.

Later on so very much later on there was for me the writing of plays which was one thing and there was at that time no longer any seeing of plays. I practically when I wrote my first play had completely ceased going to the theatre. In fact although I have written a great many plays and I am quite sure they are plays I have since I commenced writing these plays I have practically never been inside of any kind of a theatre. Of course none of this has been intentional, one may say generally speaking that anything that is really inevitable, that is to say necessary is not intentional.

But to go back to the plays I did see, and then to go on to the plays I did write.

It was then a natural thing in the Oakland and San Francisco in which I was brought up to see a great many plays played. Beside there was a great deal of opera played and so all of it was natural enough and how did I feel about it.

Generally speaking all the early recollections all a child's feeling of the theatre is two things. One which is in a way like a circus that is the general movement and light and air which any theatre has, and a great deal of glitter in the light and a great deal of height in the air, and then there are moments, a very very few moments but still moments. One must be pretty far advanced in adolescence before one realizes a whole play.

Up to the time of adolescence when one does really live in a whole play up to that time the theatre consists of bright filled space and usually not more than one moment in a play.

I think this is fairly everybody's experience and it was completely mine.

Uncle Tom's Cabin may not have been my first play but it was very nearly my first play. I think my first play really was Pinafore in London but the theatre there was so huge that I do not remember at all seeing a stage I only remember that it felt like a theatre that is the theatre did. I doubt if I did see the stage.

In Uncle Tom's Cabin I remember only the escape across

the ice, I imagine because the blocks of ice moving up and down naturally would catch my eye more than the people on the stage would.

The next thing was the opera the twenty-five cent opera of San Francisco and the fight in Faust. But that I imagine was largely because my brother had told me about the fight in Faust. As a matter of fact I gradually saw more of the opera because I saw it quite frequently. Then there was Buffalo Bill and the Indian attack, well of course anybody raised where everybody collected arrow heads and played Indians would notice Indians. And then there was Lohengrin, and there all that I saw was the swan being changed into a boy, our insisting on seeing that made my father with us lose the last boat home to Oakland, but my brother and I did not mind, naturally not as it was the moment.

In spite of my having seen operas quite often the first thing that I remember as sound on the stage was the playing by some English actor of Richelieu at the Oakland theatre and his repeated calling out, Nemours Nemours. That is the first thing that I remember hearing with my ears at the theatre and as I say nothing is more interesting to know about the theatre than the relation of sight and sound. It is always the most interesting thing about anything to know whether you hear or you see. And how one has to do with the other. It is one of the important things in finding out how you know what you know.

Then I enormously remember Booth playing Hamlet but there again the only thing I noticed and it is rather a strange thing to have noticed is his lying at the Queen's feet during the play. One would suppose that a child would notice other things in the play than that but that is what I remember and I noticed him there more than I did the play he saw, although I knew that there was a play going on there, that is the little play. It was in this way that I first felt two things going on at one time. That is something that one has to come to feel.

Then the next thing I knew was adolescence and going to the theatre all the time, a great deal alone, and all of it making an outside inside existence for me, not so real as books, which were all inside me, but so real that it the theatre made me real outside of me which up to that time I never had been in my emotion. I had largely been so in an active daily life but not in any emotion.

Then gradually there came the beginning of really realising the great difficulty of having my emotion accompany the scene and then moreover I became fairly consciously troubled by the things over which one stumbles over which one stumbled to such an extent that the time of one's emotion in relation to the scene was always interrupted. The things over which one stumbled and there it was a matter both of seeing and of hearing were clothes, voices, what they the actors said, how they were dressed and how that related itself to their moving around. Then the bother of never being able to begin over again because before it had commenced it was over, and at no time had you been ready, either to commence or to be over. Then I began to vaguely wonder whether I could see and hear at the same time and which helped or interfered with the other and which helped or interfered with the thing on the stage having been over before it really commenced. Could I see and hear and feel at the same time and did I.

I began to be a good deal troubled by all these things, the more emotion I felt while at the theatre the more troubled I became by all these things.

And then I was relieved.

As I said San Francisco was a wonderful place to hear and see foreign actors as at that time they liked it when they got there and they stayed and they played.

I must have been about sixteen years old and Bernhardt came to San Francisco and stayed two months. I knew a little french of course but really it did not matter, it was all so foreign and her voice being so varied and it all being so french I could rest in it untroubled. And I did.

It was better than the opera because it went on. It was better than the theatre because you did not have to get acquainted. The manners and customs of the french theatre created a thing in itself and it existed in and for itself as the poetical plays had that I used so much to read, there were so many characters just as there were in those plays and you did not have to know them they were so foreign, and the foreign scenery and actuality replaced the poetry and the voices replaced the portraits. It was for me a very simple direct and moving pleasure.

This experience curiously enough and yet perhaps it was not so curious awakened in me a desire for melodrama on the stage, because there again everything happened so quietly one did not have to get acquainted and as what the people felt was of no importance one did not have to realize what was said.

This pleasure in melodrama and in those days there was always one theatre in a theatrically inclined town that played melodrama, this pleasure in melodrama culminated for me in the civil war dramas of that period and the best of them was of course Secret Service. Gillette had conceived a new technique, silence stillness and quick movement. Of course it had been done in the melodrama already by the villains particularly in such plays as the Queen of Chinatown and those that had to do with telegraph operators. But Gillette had not only done it but he had conceived it and it made the whole stage the whole play this technique silence stillness and quick movement. One was no longer bothered by the theatre, you had to get acquainted of course but that was quickly over and after that nothing bothered. In fact Gillette created what the cinema later repeated by mixing up the short story and the stage but there is yet the trouble with the cinema that it is after all a photograph, and a photograph continues to be a photograph and yet can it become something else. Perhaps it can but that is a whole other question. If it can then some one will have to feel that about it. But to go on.

From then on I was less and less interested in the theatre.

I became more interested in opera, I went one went and the whole business almost came together and then finally, just finally, I came not to care at all for music and so having concluded that music was made for adolescents and not for adults and having just left adolescence behind me and beside I knew all the operas anyway by that time I did not care any more for opera.

Then I came to Paris to live and there for a long time I did not go to the theatre at all. I forgot the theatre, I never thought about the theatre. I did sometimes think about the opera. I went to the opera once in Venice and I liked it and

then much later Strauss' Electra made me realize that in a kind
of a way there could be a solution of the problem of conversation on the stage. Beside it was a new opera and it is quite
exciting to hear something unknown really unknown.

But as I say I settled down to Paris life and I forgot the
theatre and almost forgot opera. There was of course Isadora
Duncan and then the Russian ballet and in between Spain and
the Argentine and bullfights and I began once more to feel
something about something going on at a theatre.

And then I went back, not in my reading but in my feeling
to the reading of plays in my childhood, the lots of characters,
the poetry and the portraits and the scenery which was always
of course and ought always to be of course woods that is
forests and trees and streets and windows.

And so one day all of a sudden I began to write Plays.

I remember very well the first one I wrote. I called it What
Happened, a Play, it is in Geography and Plays as are all the
plays I wrote at that time. I think and always have thought
that if you write a play you ought to announce that it is a play
and that is what I did. What Happened. A Play.

I had just come home from a pleasant dinner party and I
realized then as anybody can know that something is always
happening.

Something is always happening, anybody knows a quantity
of stories of people's lives that are always happening, there are
always plenty for the newspapers and there are always plenty
in private life. Everybody knows so many stories and what is
the use of telling another story. What is the use of telling a
story since there are so many and everybody knows so many
and tells so many. In the country it is perfectly extraordinary
how many complicated dramas go on all the time. And everybody knows them, so why tell another one. There is always a
story going on.

So naturally what I wanted to do in my play was what everybody did not always know nor always tell. By everybody I do
of course include myself by always I do of course include
myself.

And so I wrote, What Happened, A Play.

Then I wrote Ladies Voices and then I wrote a Curtain

Raiser. I did this last because I wanted still more to tell what could be told if one did not tell anything.

Perhaps I will read some of these to you later.

Then I went to Spain and there I wrote a lot of plays. I concluded that anything that was not a story could be a play and I even made plays in letters and advertisements.

I had before I began writing plays written many portraits. I had been enormously interested all my life in finding out what made each one that one and so I had written a great many portraits.

I came to think that since each one is that one and that there are a number of them each one being that one, the only way to express this thing each one being that one and there being a number of them knowing each other was in a play. And so I began to write these plays. And the idea in What Happened, A Play was to express this without telling what happened, in short to make a play the essence of what happened. I tried to do this with the first series of plays that I wrote.

A tiger a rapt and surrounded overcoat securely arranged with spots old enough to be thought useful and witty quite witty in a secret and in a blinding flurry.*

ACT TWO

(Three)

Four and nobody wounded, five and nobody flourishing, six and nobody talkative, eight and nobody sensible.

One and a left hand lift that is so heavy that there is no way of pronouncing perfectly.

A point of accuracy, a point of a strange stove, a point that is so sober that the reason left is all the chance of swelling.

(The same three.)

A wide oak a wide enough oak, a very wide cake, a lightning cooky, a single wide open and exchanged box filled with the same little sac that shines.

The best the only better and more left footed stranger.

*_Geography and Plays_ (Four Seas Co.) page 205.

The very kindness there is in all lemons oranges apples pears and potatoes.

(The same three.)

A same frame a sadder portal, a singular gate and a bracketed mischance.

A rich market where there is no memory of more moon than there is everywhere and yet where strangely there is apparel and a whole set.

A connection, a clam cup connection, a survey, a ticket and a return to laying over.

ACT THREE

(Two.)

A cut, a cut is not a slice, what is the occasion for representing a cut and a slice. What is the occasion for all that.

A cut is a slice, a cut is the same slice. The reason that a cut is a slice is that if there is no hurry any time is just as useful.*

I have of course always been struggling with this thing, to say what you nor I nor nobody knows, but what is really what you and I and everybody knows, and as I say everybody hears stories but the thing that makes each one what he is is not that. Everybody hears stories and knows stories. How can they not because that is what anybody does and what everybody tells. But in my portraits I had tried to tell what each one is without telling stories and now in my early plays I tried to tell what happened without telling stories so that the essence of what happened would be like the essence of the portraits, what made what happened be what it was. And then I had for the moment gone as far as I could then go in plays and I went back to poetry and portraits and description.

Then I began to spend my summers in Bilignin in the department of the Ain and there I lived in a landscape that made itself its own landscape. I slowly came to feel that since the landscape was the thing, I had tried to write it down in Lucy Church Amiably and I did but I wanted it even more really,

*Geography and Plays. Page 206.

in short I found that since the landscape was the thing, a play was a thing and I went on writing plays a great many plays. The landscape at Bilignin so completely made a play that I wrote quantities of plays.

I felt that if a play was exactly like a landscape then there would be no difficulty about the emotion of the person looking on at the play being behind or ahead of the play because the landscape does not have to make acquaintance. You may have to make acquaintance with it, but it does not with you, it is there and so the play being written the relation between you at any time is so exactly that that it is of no importance unless you look at it. Well I did look at it and the result is in all the plays that I have printed as Operas and Plays.

MARIUS.   I am very pleased I am indeed very pleased that it is a great pleasure.

MARTHA.   If four are sitting at a table and one of them is lying upon it it does not make any difference. If bread and pomegranates are on a table and four are sitting at the table and one of them is leaning upon it it does not make any difference.

MARTHA.   It does not make any difference if four are seated at a table and one is leaning upon it.

MARYAS.   If five are seated at a table and there is bread on it and there are pomegranates on it and one of the five is leaning on the table it does not make any difference.

MARTHA.   If on a day that comes again and if we consider a day a week day it does come again if on a day that comes again and we consider every day to be a day that comes again it comes again then when accidentally when very accidentally every other day and every other day every other day and every other day that comes again and every day comes again when accidentally every other day comes again, every other day comes again and every other and every day comes again

and accidentally and every day and it comes
again, a day comes again and a day in that
way comes again.

MARYAS. Accidentally in the morning and after that
every evening and accidentally every evening
and after that every morning and after that
accidentally every morning and after that accidentally and after that every morning.

MARYAS. After that accidentally. Accidentally after
that.

MARYAS. Accidentally after that. After that accidentally.

MARYAS.
AND   More Maryas and more Martha.
MARTHA.

MARYAS.
AND   More Martha and more Maryas.
MARTHA.

MARTHA.
AND   More and more and more Martha and more
MARYAS.   Maryas.

MARIUS.   It is spoken of in that way.

MABEL.   It is spoken of in that way.

MARIUS
AND   It is spoken in that way and it is spoken of
MABEL.   in that way.

MARIUS
AND   It is spoken of in that way.
MABEL.

MABEL.   I speak of it in that way.

MARIUS.   I have spoken of it in that way and I speak
          it in that way. I have spoken of it in that way.

MABEL.   I speak of it in that way.*

The landscape has its formation and as after all a play has
to have formation and be in relation one thing to the other
thing and as the story is not the thing as any one is always
telling something then the landscape not moving but being

*Operas and Plays (Plain Edition) Random House. Page 92.

always in relation, the trees to the hills the hills to the fields the trees to each other any piece of it to any sky and then any detail to any other detail, the story is only of importance if you like to tell or like to hear a story but the relation is there anyway. And of that relation I wanted to make a play and I did, a great number of plays.

SAY IT WITH FLOWERS
A PLAY
George Henry, Henry Henry and Elisabeth Henry.
Subsidiary characters.
Elisabeth and William Long.

Time Louis XI

Place Gisors.
Action in a cake shop and the sea shore.
Other interests.
The welcoming of a man and his dog and the wish that they would come back sooner.
George Henry and Elisabeth Henry and Henry
Henry ruminating.
Elisabeth and William Long.
Waiting.
Who has asked them to be amiable to me.
She said she was waiting.
George Henry and Elisabeth Henry and
Henry Henry.
Who might be asleep if they were not waiting for me.
She.
Elisabeth Henry and Henry Henry and
George Henry.
She might be waiting with me.
Henry Henry absolutely ready to be here with me.
Scenery.
The home where they were waiting for William Long to ask them to come along and ask them not to be waiting for them.
Will they be asleep while they are waiting.
They will be pleased with everything.

What is everything.
A hyacinth is everything.
Will they be sleeping while they are waiting for every-
thing.

William Long and Elisabeth Long were so silent you
might have heard an egg shell breaking. They were busy
all day long with everything.

Elisabeth and William Long were very busy waiting
for him to come and bring his dog along.

Why did they not go with him.
Because they were busy waiting.*

LOUIS XI AND MADAME GIRAUD
Scene II

Louis the XI loved a boat
A boat on the Seine
Sinks and leaves.
Leaves which have patterns
They with delight.
Make it be loaned
To administer their confinement
They will go away
Without which it will matter.
Louis XI

Has won gold for France
And in this way.
He has settled she and a girl
He and a wife
He and a friend
They and their mother
The mother and the son Percy.†

MADAME RECAMIER
Yvonne Marin

Out loud is when the mother wishes
When the brother fishes
When the father considers wishes
When the sister supposes wishes

* *Operas and Plays.* Page 331.
† *Operas and Plays.* Page 352.

She will change to say I say I say so.
Let her think of learning nothing.
Let her think of seeing everything
Let her think like that.
                    Florence Descotes
Never to be restless
Never to be afraid
Never to ask will they come
Never to have made
Never to like having had
Little that is left then
She made it do
One and two
Thank her for everything.
                    Madame Recamier
It is not thoughtless to think well of them.
                    Louis Raynal
A place where she sits
Is a place where they were*

The only one of course that has been played is Four Saints. In Four Saints I made the Saints the landscape. All the saints that I made and I made a number of them because after all a great many pieces of things are in a landscape all these saints together made my landscape. These attendant saints were the landscape and it the play really is a landscape.

A landscape does not move nothing really moves in a landscape but things are there, and I put into the play the things that were there.

Magpies are in the landscape that is they are in the sky of a landscape, they are black and white and they are in the sky of the landscape in Bilignin and in Spain, especially in Avila. When they are in the sky they do something that I have never seen any other bird do they hold themselves up and down and look flat against the sky.

A very famous French inventor of things that have to do with stabilisation in aviation told me that what I told him magpies did could not be done by any bird but anyway whether the magpies at Avila do do it or do not at least they

*Operas and Plays. Page 365.

look as if they do do it. They look exactly like the birds in the Annunciation pictures the bird which is the Holy Ghost and rests flat against the side sky very high.

There were magpies in my landscape and there were scarecrows.

The scarecrows on the ground are the same thing as the magpies in the sky, they are a part of the landscape.

They the magpies may tell their story if they and you like or even if I like but stories are only stories but that they stay in the air is not a story but a landscape. That scarecrows stay on the ground is the same thing it could be a story but it is a piece of the landscape.

Then as I said streets and windows are also landscape and they added to my Spanish landscape.

While I was writing the Four Saints I wanted one always does want the saints to be actually saints before them as well as inside them, I had to see them as well as feel them. As it happened there is on the Boulevard Raspail a place where they make photographs that have always held my attention. They take a photograph of a young girl dressed in the costume of her ordinary life and little by little in successive photographs they change it into a nun. These photographs are small and the thing takes four or five changes but at the end it is a nun and this is done for the family when the nun is dead and in memoriam. For years I had stood and looked at these when I was walking and finally when I was writing Saint Therese in looking at these photographs I saw how Saint Therese existed from the life of an ordinary young lady to that of the nun. And so everything was actual and I went on writing.

Then in another window this time on the rue de Rennes there was a rather large porcelain group and it was of a young soldier giving alms to a beggar and taking off his helmet and his armour and leaving them in the charge of another.

It was somehow just what the young Saint Ignatius did and anyway it looked like him as I had known about him and so he too became actual not as actual as Saint Therese in the photographs but still actual and so the Four Saints got written.

All these things might have been a story but as a landscape

they were just there and a play is just there. That is at least the way I feel about it.

Anyway I did write Four Saints an Opera to be Sung and I think it did almost what I wanted, it made a landscape and the movement in it was like a movement in and out with which anybody looking on can keep in time. I also wanted it to have the movement of nuns very busy and in continuous movement but placid as a landscape has to be because after all the life in a convent is the life of a landscape, it may look excited a landscape does sometimes look excited but its quality is that a landscape if it ever did go away would have to go away to stay.

Anyway the play as I see it is exciting and it moves but it also stays and that is as I said in the beginning might be what a play should do.

Anyway I am pleased. People write me that they are having a good time while the opera is going on a thing which they say does not very often happen to them at the theatre.

So you do see what I have after all meant.

And so this is just at present all I know about the theatre.

The Gradual Making of
The Making of Americans

I AM going to read what I have written to read, because in a general way it is easier even if it is not better and in a general way it is better even if it is not easier to read what has been written than to say what has not been written. Any way that is one way to feel about it.

And I want to tell you about the gradual way of making The Making of Americans. I made it gradually and it took me almost three years to make it, but that is not what I mean by gradual. What I mean by gradual is the way the preparation was made inside of me. Although as I tell it it will sound historical, it really is not historical as I still very much remember it. I do remember it. That is I can remember it. And if you can remember, it may be history but it is not historical.

To begin with, I seem always to be doing the talking when I am anywhere but in spite of that I do listen. I always listen. I always have listened. I always have listened to the way everybody has to tell what they have to say. In other words I always have listened in my way of listening until they have told me and told me until I really know it, that is know what they are.

I always as I admit seem to be talking but talking can be a way of listening that is if one has the profound need of hearing and seeing what every one is telling.

And I began very early in life to talk all the time and to listen all the time. At least that is the way I feel about it.

I cannot remember not talking all the time and all the same feeling that while I was talking while I was seeing that I was not only hearing but seeing while I was talking and that at the same time the relation between myself knowing I was talking and those to whom I was talking and incidentally to whom I was listening were coming to tell me and tell me in their way everything that made them.

Those of you who have read The Making of Americans I think will very certainly understand.

When I was young and I am talking of a period even before

I went to college part of this talking consisted in a desire not only to hear what each one was saying in every way everybody has of saying it but also then of helping to change them and to help them change themselves.

I was very full of convictions in those days and I at that time thought that the passion I had for finding out by talking and listening just how everybody was always telling everything that was inside them that made them that one, that this passion for knowing the basis of existence in each one was in me to help them change themselves to become what they should become. The changing should of course be dependent upon my ideas and theirs theirs as much as mine at that time.

And so in those early days I wanted to know what was inside each one which made them that one and I was deeply convinced that I needed this to help them change something.

Then I went to college and there for a little while I was tremendously occupied with finding out what was inside myself to make me what I was. I think that does happen to one at that time. It had been happening before going to college but going to college made it more lively. And being so occupied with what made me myself inside me, made me perhaps not stop talking but for awhile it made me stop listening.

At any rate that is the way it seems to me now looking back at it.

While I was at college and doing philosophy and psychology I became more and more interested in my own mental and physical processes and less in that of others and all I then was learning of what made people what they were came to me by experience and not by talking and listening.

Then as I say I became more interested in psychology, and one of the things I did was testing reactions of the average college student in a state of normal activity and in the state of fatigue induced by their examinations. I was supposed to be interested in their reactions but soon I found that I was not but instead that I was enormously interested in the types of their characters that is what I even then thought of as the bottom nature of them, and when in May 1898 I wrote my half of the report of these experiments I expressed these results as follows:

In these descriptions it will be readily observed that habits of attention are reflexes of the complete character of the individual.

Then that was over and I went to the medical school where I was bored and where once more myself and my experiences were more actively interesting me than the life inside of others.

But then after that once more I began to listen, I had left the medical school and I had for the moment nothing to do but talk and look and listen, and I did this tremendously.

I then began again to think about the bottom nature in people, I began to get enormously interested in hearing how everybody said the same thing over and over again with infinite variations but over and over again until finally if you listened with great intensity you could hear it rise and fall and tell all that that there was inside them, not so much by the actual words they said or the thoughts they had but the movement of their thoughts and words endlessly the same and endlessly different.

Many things then come out in the repeating that make a history of each one for any one who always listens to them. Many things come out of each one and as one listens to them listens to all the repeating in them, always this comes to be clear about them, the history of them of the bottom nature in them, the nature or natures mixed up in them to make the whole of them in anyway it mixes up in them. Sometime then there will be a history of every one.

When you come to feel the whole of anyone from the beginning to the ending, all the kind of repeating there is in them, the different ways at different times repeating comes out of them, all the kinds of things and mixtures in each one, anyone can see then by looking hard at any one living near them that a history of every one must be a long one. A history of any one must be a long one, slowly it comes out from them from their beginning to their ending, slowly you can see it in them the nature and the mixtures in them, slowly everything comes out from each one in the kind of repeating each one does in the different parts and kinds of living they have in them, slowly then the history of them comes out from them, slowly then any one who looks well at any one will have the history of the whole of that one. Slowly the history of each one comes out of each one. Sometime then there will be a history of every one. Mostly every history will be a long one. Slowly it comes out of each one, slowly any one who looks at them gets the history of each part of the living of any one in the history of the whole of each one that sometime there will be of every one.

The Making of Americans
(Harcourt, Brace & Co.)
page 128.

Repeating then is in every one, in every one their being and their feeling and their way of realizing everything and every one comes out of them in repeating. More and more then every one comes to be clear to some one.

Slowly every one in continuous repeating, to their minutest variation, comes to be clearer to some one. Every one who ever was or is or will be living sometimes will be clearly realized by some one. Sometime there will be an ordered history of every one. Slowly every kind of one comes into ordered recognition. More and more then it is wonderful in living the subtle variations coming clear into ordered recognition, coming to make every one a part of some kind of them, some kind of men and women. Repeating then is in every one, every one then comes sometime to be clearer to some one, sometime there will be then an orderly history of every one who ever was or is or will be living.

The Making of Americans.

Then I became very interested in resemblances, in resemblances and slight differences between people. I began to make charts of all the people I had ever known or seen, or met or remembered.

Every one is always busy with it, no one of them then ever want to know it that every one looks like some one else and they see it mostly every one dislikes to hear it.

It is very important to me to always know it, to always
see it which one looks like others and to tell it.—The
Making of Americans, page 211. I write for myself and
strangers, I do this for my own sake and for the sake of
those who know I know it that they look like other ones,
that they are separate and yet always repeated. There are
some who like it that I know they are like many others
and repeat it, there are many who never can really like it.

Every one is one inside them, every one reminds some
one of some other one who is or was or will be living.
Every one has it to say of each one he is like such a one
I see it in him, every one has it to say of each one she
is like some one else I can tell by remembering. So it
goes on always in living, every one is always remembering some one who is resembling to the one at whom
they are then looking. So they go on repeating, every
one is themselves inside them and every one is resembling to others and that is always interesting.

                    The Making of Americans, page 212.

I began to see that as I saw when I saw so many students
at college that all this was gradually taking form. I began to
get very excited about it. I began to be sure that if I could
only go on long enough and talk and hear and look and see
and feel enough and long enough I could finally describe really describe every kind of human being that ever was or is or
would be living.

I got very wrapped up in all this. And I began writing The
Making of Americans.

Let me read you some passages to show you how passionately and how desperately I felt about all this.

   I am altogether a discouraged one. I am just now altogether a discouraged one. I am going on describing
men and women.

                    The Making of Americans, page 308.

   I have been very glad to have been wrong. It is sometimes a very hard thing to win myself to having been
wrong about something. I do a great deal of suffering.

                    The Making of Americans, page 310.

I was sure that in a kind of a way the enigma of the universe could in this way be solved. That after all description is explanation, and if I went on and on and on enough I could describe every individual human being that could possibly exist. I did proceed to do as much as I could.

Some time then there will be very kind of a history of every one who ever can or is or was or will be living. Some time then there will be a history of every one from their beginning to their ending. Sometime then there will be a history of all of them, of every kind of them, of every one, of every bit of living they ever have in them, of them when there is never more than a beginning to them, of every kind of them, of every one when there is very little beginning and then there is an ending, there will then sometime be a history of every one there will be a history of everything that ever was or is or will be them, of everything that was or is or will be all of any one or all of all of them. Sometime then there will be a history of every one, of everything or anything that is all them or any part of them and sometime then there will be a history of how anything or everything comes out from every one, comes out from every one or any one from the beginning to the ending of the being in them. Sometime then there must be a history of every one who ever was or is or will be living. As one sees every one in their living, in their loving, sitting, eating, drinking, sleeping, walking, working, thinking, laughing, as any one sees all of them from their beginning to their ending, sees them when they are little babies or children or young grown men and women or growing older men and women or old men and women then one knows it in them that sometime there will be a history of all of them, that sometime all of them will have the last touch of being, a history of them can give to them, sometime then there will be a history of each one, of all the kinds of them, of all the ways any one can know them, of all the ways each one is inside her or inside him, of all the ways anything of them comes out from them. Sometime then there will be a history of every one and so then every one will have in them the last touch of being a history of any one can give to them.

The Making of Americans, page 124.

This is then a beginning of the way of knowing everything in every one, of knowing the complete history of each one who ever is or was or will be living. This is then a little description of the winning of so much wisdom.

The Making of Americans, page 217.

Of course all the time things were happening that is in respect to my hearing and seeing and feeling. I found that as often as I thought and had every reason to be certain that I had included everything in my knowledge of any one something else would turn up that had to be included. I did not with this get at all discouraged I only became more and more interested. And I may say that I am still more and more interested I find as many things to be added now as ever and that does make it eternally interesting. So I found myself getting deeper and deeper into the idea of describing really describing every individual that could exist.

While I was doing all this all unconsciously at the same time a matter of tenses and sentences came to fascinate me.

While I was listening and hearing and feeling the rhythm of each human being I gradually began to feel the difficulty of putting it down. Types of people I could put down but a whole human being felt at one and the same time, in other words while in the act of feeling that person was very difficult to put into words.

And so about the middle of The Making of Americans I became very consciously obsessed by this very definite problem.

It happens very often that a man has it in him, that a man does something, that he does it very often that he does many things, when he is a young man when he is an old man, when he is an older man. One of such of these kind of them had a little boy and this one, the little son wanted to make a collection of butterflies and beetles and it was all exciting to him and it was all ar-

ranged then and then the father said to the son you are
certain this is not a cruel thing that you are wanting to
be doing, killing things to make collections of them, and
the son was very disturbed then and they talked about
it together the two of them and more and more they
talked about it then and then at last the boy was convinced it was a cruel thing and he said he would not do
it and his father said the little boy was a noble boy to
give up pleasure when it was a cruel one. The boy went
to bed then and then the father when he got up in the
early morning saw a wonderfully beautiful moth in the
room and he caught him and he killed him and he
pinned him and he woke up his son then and showed it
to him and he said to him see what a good father I am
to have caught and killed this one, the boy was all mixed
up inside him and then he said he would go on with his
collecting and that was all there was then of discussing
and this is a little description of something that happened once and it is very interesting.

The Making of Americans, page 284.

And this brings us to the question of grammar. So let me
talk a little about that.

You know by this time that although I do listen I do see I
do hear I do feel that I do talk.

English grammar is interesting because it is so simple. Once
you really know how to diagram a sentence really know it,
you know practically all you have to know about English
grammar. In short any child thirteen years old properly taught
can by that time have learned everything there is to learn
about English grammar. So why make a fuss about it. However one does.

It is this that makes the English language such a vital language that the grammar of it is so simple and that one does
make a fuss about it.

When I was up against the difficulty of putting down the
complete conception that I had of an individual, the complete
rhythm of a personality that I had gradually acquired by listening seeing feeling and experience, I was faced by the trouble that I had acquired all this knowledge gradually but when

I had it I had it completely at one time. Now that may never
have been a trouble to you but it was a terrible trouble to me.
And a great deal of The Making of Americans was a struggle
to do this thing, to make a whole present of something that
it had taken a great deal of time to find out, but it was a
whole there then within me and as such it had to be said.

That then and ever since has been a great deal of my work
and it is that which has made me try so many ways to tell my
story.

In The Making of Americans I tried it in a variety of ways.
And my sentences grew longer and longer, my imaginary dependent clauses were constantly being dropped out, I struggled with relations between they them and then, I began with
a relation between tenses that sometimes almost seemed to do
it. And I went on and on and then one day after I had written
a thousand pages, this was in 1908 I just did not go on any
more.

I did however immediately begin again. I began A Long
Gay Book, that was going to be even longer than The Making
of Americans and was going to be even more complicated,
but then something happened in me and I said in Composition As Explanation, so then naturally it was natural that one
thing an enormously long thing was not everything an enormously short thing was also not everything nor was it all of
it a continuous present thing nor was it always and always
beginning again.

And so this is The Making of Americans. A book one thousand pages long, and I worked over it three years, and I hope
this makes it a little more understandable to you.

As I say I began A Long Gay Book and it was to be even
longer than The Making of Americans and it was to describe
not only every possible kind of a human being, but every
possible kind of pairs of human beings and every possible
threes and fours and fives of human beings and every possible
kind of crowds of human beings. And I was going to do it as
A Long Gay Book and at the same time I began several
shorter books which were to illustrate the Long Gay Book,
one called Many Many Women another Five, another Two
and another G. M. P., Matisse Picasso and Gertrude Stein,
but the chief book was to be the Long Gay Book and that

was in a kind of way to go on and to keep going on and to
go on before and it began in this way.

When they are very little just only a baby you can
never tell which one is to be a lady.

There are some when they feel it inside them that it
has been with them that there was once so very little of
them, that they were a baby, helpless and no conscious
feeling in them, that they knew nothing then when they
were kissed and dandled and fixed by others who knew
them when they could know nothing inside them or
around them, some get from all this that once surely
happened to them to that which was then every bit that
was then them, there are some when they feel it later
inside them that they were such once and that was all
that there was then of them, there are some who have
from such a knowing an uncertain curious kind of feeling in them that their having been so little once and
knowing nothing makes it all a broken world for them
that they have inside them, kills for them the everlasting
feeling: and they spend their life in many ways, and always they are trying to make for themselves a new everlasting feeling.

One way perhaps of winning is to make a little one to
come through them, little like the baby that once was
all them and lost them their everlasting feeling. Some
can win from just the feeling, the little one need not
come, to give it to them.

And so always there is beginning and to some then a
losing of the everlasting feeling. Then they make a baby
to make for themselves a new beginning and so win for
themselves a new everlasting feeling.

> *A Long Gay Book* (Plain Edition)
> Random House, page 13.

I knew while I was writing The Making of Americans that
it was possible to describe every kind there is of men and
women.

I began to wonder if it was possible to describe the way
every possible kind of human being acted and felt in relation
with any other kind of human being and I thought if this

could be done it would make A Long Gay Book. It is naturally gayer describing what any one feels acts and does in relation to any other one than to describe what they just are what they are inside them.

And as I naturally found it livelier, I myself was becoming livelier just then. One does you know, when one has come to the conclusion that what is inside every one is not all there is of any one. I was, there is no doubt about it, I was coming to be livelier in relation to myself inside me and in relation to any one inside in them. This being livelier inside me kept on increasing and so you see it was a natural thing that as the Long Gay Book began, it did not go on. If it were to be really lively would it go on. Does one if one is really lively and I was really very lively then does one go on and does one if one is really very lively does one content oneself with describing what is going on inside in one and going on inside in every one in any one.

At any rate what happened is this and every one reading these things, A Long Gay Book, Many Many Women and G. M. P. will see, that it changed, it kept on changing, until at last it led to something entirely different something very short and lively to the Portrait of Mabel Dodge and the little book called Tender Buttons but all that I will talk about later. To go back to The Making of Americans and A Long Gay Book.

One must not forget that although life seems long it is very short, that although civilization seems long it is not so very long. If you think about how many generations, granting that your grandfather to you make a hundred years, if you think about that, it is extraordinary how very short is the history of the world in which we live, the world which is the world where there is a world for us. It is like the generations in the Bible, they really do not take so very long. Now when you are beginning realizing everything, this is a thing that is not confusing but is a thing that as you might say is at one time very long and at the same time not at all long. Twenty-five years roll around so quickly and in writing they can do one of two things, they can either roll around more or they can roll around less quickly.

In writing The Making of Americans they rolled around less

quickly. In writing A Long Gay Book, they did not roll around at all, and therefore it did not go on it led to Tender Buttons and many other things. It may even have led to war but that is of no importance.

The Making of Americans rolled around very slowly, it was only three years but they rolled around slowly and that is inevitable when one conceives everything as being there inside in one. Of course everything is always inside in one, that anybody knows but the kind of a one that one is is all inside in one or it is partly not all inside in one. When one is beginning to know everything, and that happens as it does happen, you all know that, when one is beginning to know everything inside in one description strengthens it being all inside in one. That was for me the whole of The Making of Americans, it was the strengthening the prolonging of the existing of everything being inside in one. You may call that being younger you may not just as you feel about it but what is important about it is, that if everything is all inside in one then it takes longer to know it than when it is not so completely inside in one.

Therefore it takes longer to know everything when everything is all inside one than when it is not. Call it being young if you like, or call it not including anything that is not everything. It does not make any difference whether you are young or younger or older or very much older. That does not make any difference because after all as I say civilization is not very old if you think about it by hundreds of years and realize that your grandfather to you can very much more than make a hundred years if it happens right.

And so I say and I saw that a complete description of every kind of human being that ever could or would be living is not such a very extensive thing because after all it can be all contained inside in any one and finally it can be done.

So then in writing The Making of Americans it was to me an enormously long thing to do to describe every one and slowly it was not an enormously long thing to do to describe every one. Because after all as I say civilization is not a very long thing, twenty-five years roll around so quickly and four times twenty-five years make a hundred years and that makes a grandfather to a granddaughter. Everybody is interested when that happens to any one, because it makes it long and it makes it short. And so and this is the thing that made the change a necessary change from The Making of Americans to A Long Gay Book and then to Tender Buttons.

I will read you some few little things that will show this thing. A few things out of A Long Gay Book that show how it changed, changed from Making of Americans to Tender Buttons.

It is a simple thing to be quite certain that there are kinds in men and women. It is a simple thing and then not any one has any worrying to be doing about any one being any one. It is a simple thing to be quite certain that each one is one being a kind of them and in being that kind of a one is one being, doing, thinking, feeling, remembering and forgetting, loving, disliking, being angry, laughing, eating, drinking, talking, sleeping, waking like all of them of that kind of them. There are enough kinds in men and women so that any one can be interested in that thing that there are kinds in men and women.

A Long Gay Book—page 23.

Vrais says good good, excellent. Vrais listens and when he listens he says good good, excellent. Vrais listens and he being Vrais when he has listened he says good good, excellent.

Vrais listens, he being Vrais, he listens.

Anything is two things. Vrais was nicely faithful. He had been nicely faithful. Anything is two things.

He had been nicely faithful. In being one he was one who had he been one continuing would not have been one continuing being nicely faithful. He was one continuing, he was not continuing to be nicely faithful. In continuing he was being one being the one who was saying good good, excellent but in continuing he was needing that he was believing that he was aspiring to be one continuing to be able to be saying good good, excellent. He had been one saying good good, excellent. He had been that one.

A Long Gay Book—page 53.

If the accumulation of inexpediency produces the withdrawing of the afternoon greeting then in the evening there is more preparation and this will take away the paper that has been lying where it could be seen. All the way that has the aging of a younger generation is part of the way that resembles anything that is not disappearing. It is not alright as colors are existing in being accommodating. They have a way that is identical.

A Long Gay Book—page 86.

Pardon the fretful autocrat who voices discontent. Pardon the colored water-color which is burnt. Pardon the intoning of the heavy way. Pardon the aristocrat who has not come to stay. Pardon the abuse which was begun. Pardon the yellow egg which has run. Pardon nothing yet, pardon what is wet, forget the opening now, and close the door again.

A Long Gay Book—page 100.

A private life is the long thick tree and the private life is the life for me. A tree which is thick is a tree which is thick. A life which is private is not what there is. All the times that come are the times I sing, all the singing I sing are the tunes I sing. I sing and I sing and the tunes I sing are what are tunes if they come and I sing. I sing I sing.

A Long Gay Book—page 107.

Suppose it did, suppose it did with a sheet and a shadow and a silver set of water, suppose it did.

A Long Gay Book—page 114.

When I was working with William James I completely learned one thing, that science is continuously busy with the complete description of something, with ultimately the complete description of anything with ultimately the complete description of everything. If this can really be done the complete description of everything then what else is there to do. We may well say nothing, but and this is the thing that makes everything continue to be anything, that after all what does happen is that as relatively few people spend all their time describing anything and they stop and so in the meantime as everything goes on somebody else can always commence and go on. And so description is really unending. When I began The Making of Americans I knew I really did know that a complete description was a possible thing, and certainly a complete description is a possible thing. But as it is a possible thing one can stop continuing to describe this everything. That is where philosophy comes in, it begins when one stops continuing describing everything.

And so this was the history of the writing of The Making of Americans and why I began A Long Gay Book. I said I would go on describing everything in A Long Gay Book, but as inevitably indeed really one does stop describing everything being at last really convinced that a description of everything is possible it was inevitable that I gradually stopped describing everything in A Long Gay Book.

Nevertheless it would be nice to really have described every kind there is of men and women, and it really would not be very hard to do but it would inevitably not be a Long Gay Book, but it would be a Making of Americans.

But I do not want to begin again or go on with what was begun because after all I know I really do know that it can be done and if it can be done why do it, particularly as I say one does know that civilization has after all not existed such a very long time if you count it by a hundred years, and each time there has been civilization it has not lasted such a long time if you count it by a hundred years, which makes a period that can connect you with some other one.

I hope you like what I say.

And so The Making of Americans has been done. It must be remembered that whether they are Chinamen or Americans there are the same kinds in men and women and one can describe all the kinds of them. This I might have done.

And so then I began The Long Gay Book. As soon as I began the Long Gay Book I knew inevitably it would not go on to continue what The Making of Americans had begun. And why not. Because as my life was my life inside me but I was realizing beginning realizing that everything described would not do any more than tell all I knew about anything why should I tell all I knew about anything since after all I did know all I knew about anything.

So then I said I would begin again. I would not know what I knew about everything what I knew about anything.

And so the Long Gay Book little by little changed from a description of any one of any one and everything there was to be known about any one, to what if not was not not to be not known about any one about anything. And so it was necessary to let come what would happen to come because after all knowledge is what you know but what is happening is inevitably what is happening to come.

And so this brings us to other things.

In describing English literature I have explained that the twentieth century was the century not of sentences as was the eighteenth not of phrases as was the nineteenth but of paragraphs. And as I explained paragraphs were inevitable because as the nineteenth century came to its ending, phrases were no longer full of any meaning and the time had come when a whole thing was all there was of anything. Series immediately before and after made everybody clearly understand this thing. And so it was natural that in writing The Making of Americans I had proceeded to enlarge my paragraphs so as to include everything. What else could I do. In fact inevitably I made my sentences and my paragraphs do the same thing, made them be one and the same thing. This was inevitably because the nineteenth century having lived by phrases really had lost the feeling of sentences, and before this in English literature paragraphs had never been an end in themselves and now in the beginning of the twentieth century a whole thing, being what was assembled from its parts was a whole thing and so it was a paragraph. You will see that in The Making of Americans I did this thing, I made a paragraph so much a whole thing that it included in itself as a whole thing a whole sentence. That makes something clear to you does it not.

And this is what The Making of Americans was. Slowly it was not enough to satisfy myself with a whole thing as a paragraph as a whole thing and I will tell very much more about how that came about but The Making of Americans really carried it as far as it could be carried so I think the making a whole paragraph a whole thing.

Then at the same time is the question of time. The assembling of a thing to make a whole thing and each one of these whole things is one of a series, but beside this there is the important thing and the very American thing that everybody knows who is an American just how many seconds minutes or hours it is going to take to do a whole thing. It is singularly a sense for combination within a conception of the existence of a given space of time that makes the American thing the American thing, and the sense of this space of time must be within the whole thing as well as in the completed whole thing.

I felt this thing, I am an American and I felt this thing, and I made a continuous effort to create this thing in every paragraph that I made in The Making of Americans. And that is why after all this book is an American book an essentially American book, because this thing is an essentially American thing this sense of a space of time and what is to be done within this space of time not in any way excepting in the way that it is inevitable that there is this space of time and anybody who is an American feels what is inside this space of time and so well they do what they do within this space of time, and so ultimately it is a thing contained within. I wonder if I at all convey to you what I mean by this thing. I will try to tell it in every way I can as I have in all the writing that I have ever done. I am always trying to tell this thing that a space of time is a natural thing for an American to always have inside them as something in which they are continuously moving. Think of anything, of cowboys, of movies, of detective stories, of anybody who goes anywhere or stays at home and is an American and you will realize that it is something strictly American to conceive a space that is filled with moving, a space of time that is filled always filled with moving and my first real effort to express this thing which is an American thing began in writing The Making of Americans.

Portraits and Repetition

In Composition As Explanation I said nothing changes from generation to generation except the composition in which we live and the composition in which we live makes the art which we see and hear. I said in Lucy Church Amiably that women and children change, I said if men have not changed women and children have. But it really is of no importance even if this is true. The thing that is important is the way that portraits of men and women and children are written, by written I mean made. And by made I mean felt. Portraits of men and women and children are differently felt in every generation and by a generation one means any period of time. One does mean any period of time by a generation. A generation can be anywhere from two years to a hundred years. What was it somebody said that the only thing God could not do was to make a two year old mule in a minute. But the strange thing about the realization of existence is that like a train moving there is no real realization of it moving if it does not move against something and so that is what a generation does it shows that moving is existing. So then there are generations and in a way that too is not important because, and this thing is a thing to know, if and we in America have tried to make this thing a real thing, if the movement, that is any movement, is lively enough, perhaps it is possible to know that it is moving even if it is not moving against anything. And so in a way the American way has been not to need that generations are existing. If this were really true and perhaps it is really true then really and truly there is a new way of making portraits of men and women and children. And I, I in my way have tried to do this thing.

It is true that generations are not of necessity existing that is to say if the actual movement within a thing is alive enough. A motor goes inside of an automobile and the car goes. In short this generation has conceived an intensity of movement so great that it has not to be seen against something else to be known, and therefore, this generation does not connect itself with anything, that is what makes this generation what

it is and that is why it is American, and this is very important
in connection with portraits of anything. I say portraits and
not description and I will gradually explain why. Then also
there is the important question of repetition and is there any
such thing. Is there repetition or is there insistence. I am inclined to believe there is no such thing as repetition. And
really how can there be. This is a thing about which I want
you to think before I go on telling about portraits of anything.
Think about all the detective stories everybody reads. The
kind of crime is the same, and the idea of the story is very
often the same, take for example a man like Wallace, he always
has the same theme, take a man like Fletcher he always has
the same theme, take any American ones, they too always have
the scene, the same scene, the kind of invention that is necessary to make a general scheme is very limited in everybody's
experience, every time one of the hundreds of times a newspaper man makes fun of my writing and of my repetition he
always has the same theme, always having the same theme,
that is, if you like, repetition, that is if you like the repeating
that is the same thing, but once started expressing this thing,
expressing any thing there can be no repetition because the
essence of that expression is insistence, and if you insist you
must each time use emphasis and if you use emphasis it is not
possible while anybody is alive that they should use exactly the
same emphasis. And so let us think seriously of the difference
between repetition and insistence.

Anybody can be interested in a story of a crime because no
matter how often the witnesses tell the same story the insistence is different. That is what makes life that the insistence
is different, no matter how often you tell the same story if
there is anything alive in the telling the emphasis is different.
It has to be, anybody can know that.

It is very like a frog hopping he cannot ever hop exactly the
same distance or the same way of hopping at every hop. A
bird's singing is perhaps the nearest thing to repetition but if
you listen they too vary their insistence. That is the human
expression saying the same thing and in insisting and we all
insist varying the emphasising.

I remember very well first beginning to be conscious of this
thing. I became conscious of these things, I suppose anybody

does when they first really know that the stars are worlds and that everything is moving, that is the first conscious feeling of necessary repetition, and it comes to one and it is very disconcerting. Then the second thing is when you first realize the history of various civilizations, that have been on this earth, that too makes one realize repetition and at the same time the difference of insistence. Each civilization insisted in its own way before it went away. I remember the first time I really realized this in this way was from reading a book we had at home of the excavations of Nineveh, but these emotions although they tell one so much and one really never forgets them, after all are not in one's daily living, they are like the books of Jules Verne terribly real terribly near but still not here. When I first really realized the inevitable repetition in human expression that was not repetition but insistence when I first began to be really conscious of it was when at about seventeen years of age, I left the more or less internal and solitary and concentrated life I led in California and came to Baltimore and lived with a lot of my relations and principally with a whole group of very lively little aunts who had to know anything.

If they had to know anything and anybody does they naturally had to say and hear it often, anybody does, and as there were ten and eleven of them they did have to say and hear said whatever was said and any one not hearing what it was they said had to come in to hear what had been said. That inevitably made everything said often. I began then to consciously listen to what anybody was saying and what they did say while they were saying what they were saying. This was not yet the beginning of writing but it was the beginning of knowing what there was that made there be no repetition. No matter how often what happened had happened any time any one told anything there was no repetition. This is what William James calls the Will to Live. If not nobody would live.

And so I began to find out then by listening the difference between repetition and insisting and it is a very important thing to know. You listen as you know.

Then there is another thing that also has something to do with repeating.

When all these eleven little aunts were listening as they were talking gradually some one of them was no longer listening. When this happened it might be that the time had come that any one or one of them was beginning repeating, that is was ceasing to be insisting or else perhaps it might be that the attention of one of some one of them had been worn out by adding something. What is the difference. Nothing makes any difference as long as some one is listening while they are talking.

That is what I gradually began to know.

Nothing makes any difference as long as some one is listening while they are talking. If the same person does the talking and the listening why so much the better there is just by so much the greater concentration. One may really indeed say that that is the essence of genius, of being most intensely alive, that is being one who is at the same time talking and listening. It is really that that makes one a genius. And it is necessary if you are to be really and truly alive it is necessary to be at once talking and listening, doing both things, not as if there were one thing, not as if they were two things, but doing them, well if you like, like the motor going inside and the car moving, they are part of the same thing.

I said in the beginning of saying this thing that if it were possible that a movement were lively enough it would exist so completely that it would not be necessary to see it moving against anything to know that it is moving. This is what we mean by life and in my way I have tried to make portraits of this thing always have tried always may try to make portraits of this thing.

If this existence is this thing is actually existing there can be no repetition. There is only repetition when there are descriptions being given of these things not when the things themselves are actually existing and this is therefore how my portrait writing began.

So we have now, a movement lively enough to be a thing in itself moving, it does not have to move against anything to know that it is moving, it does not need that there are generations existing.

Then we have insistence insistence that in its emphasis can never be repeating, because insistence is always alive and if it is alive it is never saying anything in the same way because emphasis can never be the same not even when it is most the same that is when it has been taught.

How do you like what you have.

This is a question that anybody can ask anybody. Ask it.

In asking it I began to make portraits of anybody.

How do you like what you have is one way of having an important thing to ask of any one.

That is essentially the portrait of any one, one portrait of any one.

I began to think about portraits of any one.

If they are themselves inside them what are they and what has it to do with what they do.

And does it make any difference what they do or how they do it, does it make any difference what they say or how they say it. Must they be in relation with any one or with anything in order to be one of whom one can make a portrait. I began to think a great deal about all these things.

Anybody can be interested in what anybody does but does that make any difference, is it all important.

Anybody can be interested in what anybody says, but does that make any difference, is it at all important.

I began to wonder about all that.

I began to wonder what it was that I wanted to have as a portrait, what there is that was to be the portrait.

I do not wonder so much now about that. I do not wonder about that at all any more. Now I wonder about other things, I wonder if what has been done makes any difference.

I wonder now if it is necessary to stand still to live if it is not necessary to stand still to live, and if it is if that is not perhaps to be a new way to write a novel. I wonder if you know what I mean. I do not quite know whether I do myself. I will not know until I have written that novel.

I have just tried to begin in writing Four In America because I am certain that what makes American success is American failure.

I am certain about that.

Some time I will explain that at great length but now I want to tell about how I wrote portraits. I wrote portraits knowing that each one is themselves inside them and something about them perhaps everything about them will tell some one all about that thing all about what is themselves inside them and I was then hoping completely hoping that I was that one the one who would tell that thing. Perhaps I was that one.

There is another thing that one has to think about, that is about thinking clearly and about confusion. That is something about which I have almost as much to say as I have about anything.

The difference between thinking clearly and confusion is the same difference that there is between repetition and insistence. A great many think that they know repetition when they see or hear it but do they. A great many think that they know confusion when they know or see it or hear it, but do they. A thing that seems very clear, seems very clear but is it. A thing that seems to be exactly the same thing may seem to be a repetition but is it. All this can be very exciting, and it had a great deal to do with portrait writing.

As I say a thing that is very clear may easily not be clear at all, a thing that may be confused may be very clear. But everybody knows that. Yes anybody knows that. It is like the necessity of knowing one's father and one's mother one's grandmothers and one's grandfathers, but is it necessary and if it is can it be no less easily forgotten.

As I say the American thing is the vitality of movement, so that there need be nothing against which the movement shows as movement. And if this vitality is lively enough is there in that clarity any confusion is there in that clarity any repetition. I myself do not think so. But I am inclined to believe that there is really no difference between clarity and confusion, just think of any life that is alive, is there really any difference between clarity and confusion. Now I am quite certain that there is really if anything is alive no difference between clarity and confusion. When I first began writing portraits of any one I was not so sure, not so certain of this thing that there is no difference between clarity and confusion. I was however almost certain then when I began writing portraits that if anything is alive there is no such thing as repetition. I do not know that I have ever changed my mind about that. At any rate I did then begin the writing of portraits and I will tell you now all there is to tell about all that. I had of course written about every kind of men and women in The

Making of Americans but in writing portraits I wanted not to write about any one doing or even saying anything, I found this a difficult enough thing to begin.

I remember very well what happened. As I say I had the habit of conceiving myself as completely talking and listening, listening was talking and talking was listening and in so doing I conceived what I at that time called the rhythm of anybody's personality. If listening was talking and talking was listening then and at the same time any little movement any little expression was a resemblance, and a resemblance was something that presupposed remembering.

Listening and talking did not presuppose resemblance and as they do not presuppose resemblance, they do not necessitate remembering. Already then as you see there was a complication which was a bother to me in my conception of the rhythm of a personality. I have for so many years tried to get the better of that the better of this bother. The bother was simply that and one may say it is the bother that has always been a bother to anybody for anybody conceiving anything. Dillinger is dead it was even a bother for him.

As I say as I felt the existence of anybody later as I felt the existence of anybody or anything, there was then the listening and talking which I was doing which anybody was doing and there were the little things that made of any one some one resembling some one.

Any one does of course by any little thing by any little way by any little expression, any one does of course resemble some one, and any one can notice this thing notice this resemblance and in so doing they have to remember some one and this is a different thing from listening and talking. In other words the making of a portrait of any one is as they are existing and as they are existing has nothing to do with remembering any one or anything. Do you see my point, but of course yes you do. You do see that there are two things and not one and if one wants to make one portrait of some one and not two you can see that one can be bothered completely bothered by this thing. As I say it is something that has always bothered any one.

Funnily enough the cinema has offered a solution of this thing. By a continuously moving picture of any one there is no memory of any other thing and there is that thing existing, it is in a way if you like one portrait of anything not a number of them. There again you do see what I mean.

Now I in my way wanted to make portraits of any one later in Tender Buttons I also wanted to make portraits of anything as one thing as one portrait and although and that was my trouble in the beginning I felt the thing the person as existing and as everything in that person entered in to make that person little ways and expressions that made resembling, it was necessary for me nevertheless not to realize these things as remembering but to realize the one thing as existing and there they were and I was noticing, well you do see that it was a bother and I was bothering very much bothering about this thing.

In the beginning and I will read you some portraits to show you this I continued to do what I was doing in the Making of Americans, I was doing what the cinema was doing, I was making a continuous succession of the statement of what that person was until I had not many things but one thing. As I read you some of the portraits of that period you will see what I mean.

I of course did not think of it in terms of the cinema, in fact I doubt whether at that time I had ever seen a cinema but, and I cannot repeat this too often any one is of one's period and this our period was undoubtedly the period of the cinema and series production. And each of us in our own way are bound to express what the world in which we are living is doing.

You see then what I was doing in my beginning portrait writing and you also understand what I mean when I say there was no repetition. In a cinema picture no two pictures are exactly alike each one is just that much different from the one before, and so in those early portraits there was as I am sure you will realize as I read them to you also as there was in The Making of Americans no repetition. Each time that I said the somebody whose portrait I was writing was something that something was just that much different from what I had just said that somebody was and little by little in this way a whole portrait came into being, a portrait that was not description and that was made by each time, and I did a great many times, say it, that somebody was something, each time there was a difference just a difference enough so that it could go on and be a present something. Oh yes you all do understand. You understand this. You see that in order to do this there must be no remembering, remembering is repetition, remembering is also confusion. And this too you will presently know all about.

Remembering is repetition anybody can know that. In doing a portrait of any one, the repetition consists in knowing that that one is a kind of a one, that the things he does have been done by others like him that the things he says have been said by others like him, but, and this is the important thing, there is no repetition in hearing and saying the things he hears and says when he is hearing and saying them. And so in doing a portrait of him if it were possible to make that portrait a portrait of him saying and hearing what he says and hears while he is saying and hearing it there is then in so doing neither memory nor repetition no matter how often that which he says and hears is heard and said. This was the discovery I made as I talked and listened more and more and this is what I did when I made portraits of every one I know. I said what I knew as they said and heard what they heard and said until I had completely emptied myself of all they were that is all that they were in being one hearing and saying what they heard and said in every way that they heard and said anything.

And this is the reason why that what I wrote was exciting although those that did not really see what it was thought it was repetition. If it had been repetition it would not have been exciting but it was exciting and it was not repetition. It never is. I never repeat that is while I am writing.

As I say what one repeats is the scene in which one is acting, the days in which one is living, the coming and going which one is doing, anything one is remembering is a repetition, but existing as a human being, that is being listening and hearing is never repetition. It is not repetition if it is that which you are actually doing because naturally each time the emphasis is different just as the cinema has each time a slightly different thing to make it all be moving. And each one of us has to do that, otherwise there is no existing. As Galileo remarked, it does move.

So you see what I mean about those early portraits and the middle part of The Making of Americans. I built them up little by little each time I said it it changed just a little and then when I was completely emptied of knowing that the one of whom I was making a portrait existed I had made a portrait of that one.

To go back to something I said that remembering was the only repetition, also that remembering was the only confusion. And I think you begin to see what I mean by that.

No matter how complicated anything is, if it is not mixed up with remembering there is no confusion, but and that is the trouble with a great many so called intelligent people they mix up remembering with talking and listening, and as a result they have theories about anything but as remembering is repetition and confusion, and being existing that is listening and talking is action and not repetition intelligent people although they talk as if they knew something are really confusing, because they are so to speak keeping two times going at once, the repetition time of remembering and the actual time of talking but, and as they are rarely talking and listening, that is the talking being listening and the listening being talking, although they are clearly saying something they are not clearly creating something, because they are because they always are remembering, they are not at the same time talking and listening. Do you understand. Do you any or all of you understand. Anyway that is the way it is. And you hear it even if you do not say it in the way I say it as I hear it and say it.

I say I never repeat while I am writing because while I am writing I am most completely, and that is if you like being a genius, I am most entirely and completely listening and talking, the two in one and the one in two and that is having completely its own time and it has in it no element of remembering. Therefore there is in it no element of confusion, therefore there is in it no element of repetition. Do you do you do you really understand.

And does it make any difference to you if you do understand. It makes an awful lot of difference to me. It is very exciting to have all this be.

Gradually then I began making portraits. And how did I begin.

When I first began writing although I felt very strongly that something that made that some one be some one was something that I must use as being them, I naturally began to describe them as they were doing anything. In short I wrote a story as a story, that is the way I began, and slowly I realized this confusion, a real confusion, that in writing a story one had to be remembering, and that novels are soothing because so many people one may say everybody can remember almost anything. It is this element of remembering that makes novels so soothing. But and that was the thing that I was gradually finding out listening and talking at the same time that is realizing the existence of living being actually existing did not have in it any element of remembering and so the time of existing was not the same as in the novels that were soothing. As I say all novels are soothing because they make anything happen as they can happen that is by remembering anything. But and I kept wondering as I talked and listened all at once, I wondered is there any way of making what I know come out as I know it, come out not as remembering. I found this very exciting. And I began to make portraits.

I kept on knowing people by resemblances, that was partly memory and it bothered me but I knew I had to do everything and I tried to do that so completely that I would lose it. I made charts and charts of everybody who looked like anybody until I got so that I hardly knew which one I knew on the street and which one looked like them. I did this until at last any one looking like any one else had no importance. It was not a thing that was any longer an important thing, I knew completely how any one looked like any other one and that became then only a practical matter, a thing one might know as what any one was liable to do, but this to me then was no longer interesting. And so I went on with portrait writing.

I cannot tell you although I think I can, that, as I can read any number of soothing novels in fact nothing else soothes me I found it not a thing that it was interesting to do. And I think now you know why it was not an interesting thing to do. We in this period have not lived in remembering, we have living in moving being necessarily so intense that existing is indeed something, is indeed that thing that we are doing. And so what does it really matter what anybody does. The newspapers are full of what anybody does and anybody knows what anybody does but the thing that is important is the intensity of anybody's existence. Once more I remind you of Dillinger. It was not what he did that was exciting but the excitement of what he was as being exciting that was exciting. There is a world of difference and in it there is essentially no remembering.

And so I am trying to tell you what doing portraits meant to me, I had to find out what it was inside any one, and by any one I mean every one I had to find out inside every one what was in them that was intrinsically exciting and I had to find out not by what they said not by what they did not by how much or how little they resembled any other one but I had to find it out by the intensity of movement that there was inside in any one of them. And of course do not forget, of course I was interested in any one. I am. Of course I am interested in any one. And in any one I must or else I must betake myself to some entirely different occupation and I do not think I will, I must find out what is moving inside them that makes them them, and I must find out how I by the thing moving excitedly inside in me can make a portrait of them.

You can understand why I did it so often, why I did it in so many ways why I say that there is no repetition because, and this is absolutely true, that the exciting thing inside in any one if it is really inside in them is not a remembered thing, if it is really inside in them, it is not a confused thing, it is not a repeated thing. And if I could in any way and I have done it in every way if I could make a portrait of that inside them without any description of what they are doing and what they are saying then I too was neither repeating, nor remembering nor being in a confusion.

You see what I mean by what I say. But I know you do.

Will you see it as clearly when I read you some of the portraits that I have written. Maybe you will but I doubt it. But if you do well then if you do you will see what I have done and do do.

A thing you all know is that in the three novels written in this generation that are the important things written in this

generation, there is, in none of them a story. There is none
in Proust in The Making of Americans or in Ulysses. And this
is what you are now to begin to realize in this description I
am giving you of making portraits.

It is of course perfectly natural that autobiographies are being well written and well read. You do see anybody can see
that so much happens every day and that anybody literally
anybody can read or hear about it told the day that it happens.
A great deal happens every day and any day and as I say anybody literally anybody can hear or read everything or anything
about anything or everything that happens every day just as it
has happened or is happening on that day. You do see what
that means. Novels then which tell a story are really then more
of the same much more of the same, and of course anybody
likes more of the same and so a great many novels are written
and a great many novels are read telling more of these stories
but you can see you do see that the important things written
in this generation do not tell a story. You can see that it is
natural enough.

You begin definitely to feel that it had to be that I was to
write portraits as I wrote them. I began to write them when
I was about in the middle of The Making of Americans, and
if you read The Making of Americans you will realize why this
was inevitable.

I began writing the portraits of any one by saying what I
knew of that one as I talked and listened that one, and each
time that I talked and listened that one I said what I knew
they were then. This made my early portraits and some that
I finally did such as Four Dishonest Ones Told by a Description of What They Do, Matisse and Picasso and a lot of others,
did as completely as I then could strictly did this thing. Every
time I said what they were I said it so that they were this
thing, and each time I said what they were as they were, as I
was, naturally more or less but never the same thing each time
that I said what they were I said what they were, not that they
were different nor that I was different but as it was not the
same moment which I said I said it with a difference. So finally
I was emptied of saying this thing, and so no longer said what
they were.

FOUR DISHONEST ONES.

Told By a Description Of What They Do.

They are what they are. They have not been changing. They are what they are.

Each one is what that one is. Each is what each is. They are not needing to be changing.

One is what she is. She does not need to be changing. She is what she is. She is not changing. She is what she is.

She is not changing. She is knowing nothing of not changing. She is not needing to be changing.

What is she doing. She is working. She is not needing to be changing. She is working very well, she is not needing to be changing. She has been working very hard. She has been suffering. She is not needing to be changing.

She has been living and working, she has been quiet and working, she has been suffering and working, she has been watching and working, she has been waiting, she has been working, she has been waiting and working, she is not needing to be changing.

Portraits and Prayers, page 57.

At this time also I wanted to make portraits of places, I did. I did make them of the Bon Marché, of the Galeries Lafayette, of a crowd at Mi-Careme, I have always liked what I did with that one. It was completely something. And there again in doing the portraits of these places and these crowds, I did Italians, and Americans too like that, I continued to do as I had done in The Making of Americans. I told exactly and completely each time of telling what that one is inside in them. As I told you in comparing it to a cinema picture one second was never the same as the second before or after.

MI-CAREME

There was a man who said one could recognize him when one saw him again by the scar on the end of his nose and under his eye but these scars were very little ones almost not anything and one would remember him because he was one who had been saying that he was a man tired of working tired of being one being working, and that he would be very amusing, he could be amusing by saying something that would make any one listening begin blushing but, he said, he would not do such a thing he would be politely amusing and he was amusing and some being amused by him were not frightened by him. He might have been amusing to some who were at the same time ones frightened by him. He might be very amusing to some who would never in any way think that he could frighten any one.

Portraits and Prayers, page 173.

At any rate I did these portraits and they were very exciting, they were exciting to me and they were exciting to others who read them.

Then slowly once more I got bothered, after all I listened and talked but that was not all I did in knowing at any present time when I was stating anything what anything was. I was also looking, and that could not be entirely left out.

The trouble with including looking, as I have already told you, was that in regard to human beings looking inevitably carried in its train realizing movements and expression and as such forced me into recognizing resemblances, and so forced remembering and in forcing remembering caused confusion of present with past and future time.

Do you see what I mean. But certainly you certainly do. And so I began again to do portraits but this time it was not portraits of men and women and children, it was portraits of anything and so I made portraits of rooms and food and everything because there I could avoid this difficulty of suggesting remembering more easily while including looking with listening and talking than if I were to describe human beings. I will go a little more into that.

This is the great difficulty that bothered anybody creating anything in this generation. The painters naturally were looking, that was their occupation and they had too to be certain that looking was not confusing itself with remembering. Remembering with them takes the form of suggesting in their painting in place of having actually created the thing in itself that they are painting.

In writing the thing that is the difficulty is the question of confusing time, and this is the thing that bothered and still bothers any one in this generation. Later on in another writing I will tell about how this thing that is time has to do with grammar vocabulary and tenses. But now I am keeping strictly to the matter of portraits and repetition.

I began to make portraits of things and enclosures that is rooms and places because I needed to completely face the difficulty of how to include what is seen with hearing and listening and at first if I were to include a complicated listening and talking it would be too difficult to do. That is why painters paint still lives. You do see why they do.

So I began to do this thing, I tried to include color and movement and what I did is what you have all either read or heard of, a volume called Tender Buttons.

I for a time did not make portraits because as I was trying to live in looking, and looking was not to mix itself up with remembering I wished to reduce to its minimum listening and talking. In Tender Buttons, I described anything, and I will read you a few things to show you what I did then.

A DOG.

A little monkey goes like a donkey that means to say that means to say that more sighs last goes. Leave with it. A little monkey goes like a donkey.

Tender Buttons, page 26.

Cloudiness what is cloudiness, is it a lining, is it a roll, is it melting.

Tender Buttons, page 38.

A hurt mended stick, a hurt mended cup, a hurt mended article of exceptional relaxation and annoyance, a hurt mended, hurt and mended is so necessary that no mistake is intended.

Tender Buttons, page 43.

Abandon a garden and the house is bigger. This is not smiling. This is comfortable. There is the comforting of predilection. An open object is establishing the loss that there was when the vase was not inside the place. It was not wandering.

Portraits and Prayers, page 101.

You see what I mean, I did express what something was, a little by talking and listening to that thing, but a great deal by looking at that thing.

This as I say has been the great problem of our generation, so much happens and anybody at any moment knows everything that is happening that things happening although interesting are not really exciting. And an artist an artist inevitably has to do what is really exciting. That is what he is inside him, that is what an artist really is inside him, he is exciting, and if he is not there is nothing to any of it.

And so the excitement in me was then that I was to more and more include looking to make it a part of listening and talking and I did the portrait of Mabel Dodge and Susie Asado and Preciosilla and some others. But this was all after I had done Tender Buttons.

I began to wonder at at about this time just what one saw when one looked at anything really looked at anything. Did one see sound, and what was the relation between color and sound, did it make itself by description by a word that meant it or did it make itself by a word in itself. All this time I was of course not interested in emotion or that anything happened. I was less interested then in these things than I ever had been. I lived my life with emotion and with things happening but I was creating in my writing by simply looking. I was as I say at that time reducing as far as it was possible for me to reduce them, talking and listening.

I became more and more excited about how words which were the words that made whatever I looked at look like itself were not the words that had in them any quality of description. This excited me very much at that time.

And the thing that excited me so very much at that time and still does is that the words or words that make what I looked at be itself were always words that to me very exactly related themselves to that thing the thing at which I was looking, but as often as not had as I say nothing whatever to do with what any words would do that described that thing.

Those of you that have seen Four Saints in Three Acts must know do know something of what I mean.

Of course by the time Four Saints was written I had mastered very much what I was doing then when I wrote Tender

Buttons. By the time I wrote the Four Saints I had written a great a great many portraits and I had in hundreds of ways related words, then sentences then paragraphs to the thing at which I was looking and I had also come to have happening at the same time looking and listening and talking without any bother about resemblances and remembering.

One of the things as I said that made me most anxious at one time was the relation of color to the words that exactly meant that but had no element in it of description. One portrait I did I will read it to you of Lipschitz did this color thing better than I had ever before been able to do it.

LIPSCHITZ

Like and like likely and likely likely and likely like and like.

He had a dream. He dreamed he heard a pheasant calling and very likely a pheasant was calling.

To whom went.

He had a dream he dreamed he heard a pheasant calling and most likely a pheasant was calling.

In time.

Portraits and Prayers, page 63.

Thus for over a very considerable period of time sometimes a great many at a time and sometimes one at a time and sometimes several at a time I continued to do portraits. Around about this time I did a second one of Carl Van Vechten, one of Sherwood Anderson, one of Cocteau and a second one of Picasso. They were different from those that I had done in the beginning and very different from those I did just after doing Tender Buttons. These were less concentrated, they moved more although the movement was definitely connected with color and not so closely connected with talking and listening.

VAN OR TWENTY YEARS AFTER
A SECOND PORTRAIT OF CARL VAN VECHTEN.

Twenty years after, as much as twenty years after in as much as twenty years after, after twenty years and so on. It is it is it is it is.

Keep it in sight all right.

Not to the future but to the fuchsia.

Tied and untied and that is all there is about it. And as tied and as beside, and as beside and tied. Tied and untied and beside and as beside and as untied and as tied and as untied and as beside.

Portraits and Prayers, page 157.

And then slowly it changed again, talking and listening came slowly again to be more important than that at which I was looking. Talking and listening became more important again but at the same time that it was talking and listening it had within itself an entirely different emotion of moving.

Let me tell you just what I did as I did this thing.

As always happens one commences again. However often it happens one does commence again and now in my way I did commence again.

I was again bothered about something and it had to do as my bother always has had to do with a thing being contained within itself.

I realized that granted looking and listening and talking being all happening at one time and that I had been finding the words that did create that thing did create the portrait that was the object of the looking listening and talking I had been doing nevertheless I had been losing something, something I had had, in The Making of Americans and in Tender Buttons, that is a thing contained within itself.

As I say a motor goes inside and the car goes on, but my business my ultimate business as an artist was not with where the car goes as it goes but with the movement inside that is of the essence of its going. And had I in these rather beautiful portraits I had been writing had I a little lost this thing. Whether I had or whether I had not began a little to worry me not really worry but to be there inside me, had I lost a little the excitement of having this inside me. Had I. I did not think I really had but had I.

This brings me back once more to the subject of repetition.

The composition we live in changes but essentially what happens does not change. We inside us do not change but our emphasis and the moment in which we live changes. That is it is never the same moment it is never the same emphasis at any successive moment of existing. Then really what is repetition. It is very interesting to ask and it is a very interesting thing to know.

If you think anything over and over and eventually in connection with it you are going to succeed or fail, succeeding and failing is repetition because you are always either succeeding or failing but any two moments of thinking it over is not repetition. Now you see that is where I differ from a great many people who say I repeat and they do not. They do not think their succeeding or failing is what makes repetition, in other words they do not think that what happens makes repetition but that it is the moment to moment emphasizing that makes repetition. Now I think the succeeding and failing is what makes the repetition not the moment to moment emphasizing that makes repetition.

Instinctively as I say you all agree with me because really in these days you all like crime stories or have liked crime stories or if you have not you should have and at any rate you do like newspapers or radio or funny papers, and in all these it is the moment to moment emphasis in what is happening that is interesting, the succeeding and failing is really not the thing that is interesting.

In the portraits that I did in that period of which I have just been speaking the later period considerably after the war the strictness of not letting remembering mix itself with looking and listening and talking which began with The Making of Americans and went on all through Tender Buttons and what came immediately after, all the period of Geography and Plays this strictness perhaps weakened a little weakened a little because and that in a way was an astonishment to me, I found that I was for a little while very much taken with the beauty of the sounds as they came from me as I made them.

This is a thing that may be at any time a temptation. This temptation came to me a little after the Saint Remy period when I wrote Saints in Seven, Four Religions, Capital Capitals. The strict discipline that I had given myself, the absolute refusal of never using a word that was not an exact word all through the Tender Buttons and what I may call the early Spanish and Geography and Plays period finally resulted in things like Susie Asado and Preciosilla etc. in an extraordinary melody of words and a melody of excitement in knowing that I had done this thing.

Then in concentrating this melody I wrote in Saint Remy these things I have just mentioned Four Religions, Capital Capitals, Saints in Seven and a great many other things. In doing these I concentrated the internal melody of existence that I had learned in relation to things seen into the feeling I then had there in Saint Remy of light and air and air moving and being still. I worked at these things then with a great deal of concentration and as it was to me an entirely new way of doing it I had as a result a very greatly increased melody. This melody for a little while after rather got the better of me and it was at that time that I wrote these portraits of which I have just spoken, the second Picasso, the second Carl Van Vechten, the Jean Cocteau, Lipschitz, the Sitwells, Edith Sitwell, Joe Davidson, quantities of portraits. Portraits after my concentrated effort at Saint Remy to really completely and exactly find the word for the air and sky and light and existence down there was relatively a simple thing and I as you may say held these portraits in my hand and they came easily and beautifully and truly. But as I say I did begin to think that I was rather drunk with what I had done. And I am always one to prefer being sober. I must be sober. It is so much more exciting to be sober, to be exact and concentrated and sober. So then as I say I began again.

So here we have it. There was the period of The Making of Americans portraiture, when by listening and talking I conceived at every moment the existence of some one, and I put down each moment that I had the existence of that one inside in me until I had completely emptied myself of this that I had had as a portrait of that one. This as I say made what has been called repetition but, and you will see, each sentence is just the difference in emphasis that inevitably exists in the successive moment of my containing within me the existence of that other one achieved by talking and listening inside in me and inside in that one. These were the early portraits I did. Then this slowly changed to portraits of spaces inclosed with or without somebody in them but written in the same way in the successive moments of my realizing them. As I said it was if you like, it was like a cinema picture made up of succession and each moment having its own emphasis that is its own difference and so there was the moving and the existence of each moment as it was in me.

Then as I said I had the feeling that something should be included and that something was looking, and so concentrating on looking I did the Tender Buttons because it was easier to do objects than people if you were just looking. Then I began to do plays to make the looking have in it an element of moving and during this time I also did portraits that did the same thing. In doing these things I found that I created a melody of words that filled me with a melody that gradually made me do portraits easily by feeling the melody of any one. And this then began to bother me because perhaps I was getting drunk with melody and I do not like to be drunk I like to be sober and so I began again.

I began again not to let the looking be predominating not to have the listening and talking be predominating but to once more denude all this of anything in order to get back to the essence of the thing contained within itself. That led me to some very different writing that I am going to tell about in the next thing I write but it also led to some portraits that I do think did do what I was then hoping would be done that is at least by me, would be done in this way if it were to be done by me.

Of these there were quite a number but perhaps two that did it the most completely the thing I wanted to do were portraits of George Hugnet and Bernard Fay. I will read them to you and you will see what I mean. All the looking was there the talking and listening was there but instead of giving what I was realizing at any and every moment of them and of me until I was empty of them I made them contained within the thing I wrote that was them. The thing in itself folded itself up inside itself like you might fold a thing up to be another thing which is that thing inside in that thing.

Do you see what I mean.

If you think how you fold things or make a boat or anything else out of paper or getting anything to be inside anything, the hole in the doughnut or the apple in the dumpling perhaps you will see what I mean. I will try and tell a little more about this thing and how I felt about this thing and how it happened.

This time I do repeat; in going over this again, there was the portrait writing of The Making of Americans period. There was the portrait writing of the Tender Buttons period, Mabel Dodge came into that. There was the portrait writing of the Geography and Plays period, which ended up with Capital Capitals, and then there was the portrait writing of the Useful Knowledge period, including portraits of Sherwood Anderson and Carl Van Vechten. Of course in each one of these periods there were many many portraits written as I wrote portraits of almost any one and as at all times I write practically every day, to be sure not long but practically every day and if you write not long but practically every day you do get a great deal written. This is what I do and so I do do get a great deal written. I have written a great many portraits.

So then as I said at the end of all this I had come to know I had a melody and to be certain of my melody that melody carried me to be sure always by looking and listening and talking but melody did carry me and so as always I had once more to begin again and I began again.

Melody should always be a by-product it should never be an end in itself it should not be a thing by which you live if you really and truly are one who is to do anything and so as I say I very exactly began again.

I had begun again some time before in working at grammar and sentences and paragraphs and what they mean and at plays and how they disperse themselves in relation to anything seen. And soon I was so completely concerned with these things that melody, beauty if you like was once more as it should always be a by-product.

I did at the same time as I did plays and grammar at this time, I did do portraits in these portraits I felt an entirely different thing. How could a thing if it is a human being if it is anything be entirely contained within itself. Of course it is, but is it and how is it and how did I know that it is.

This was the thing that I found then to be completely interesting, this was the thing I found then to be completely exciting. How was anything contained within itself.

I felt that I began then to feel any one to be inside them very differently than I had ever found any one be themselves inside them. This was the time that I wrote Lucy Church Amiably which quite definitely as a conception of what is seen was contained by itself inside it, although there it was a conceiving of what I was looking at as a landscape was to be itself inside in it, it was I said to be like an engraving and I think it is. But the people in it were in it as contained within the whole of it. I wanted however to do portraits where there was more movement inside in the portrait and yet it was to be the whole portrait completely held within that inside.

I began to feel movement to be a different thing than I had felt it to be.

It was to me beginning to be a less detailed thing and at the same time a thing that existed so completely inside in it and it was it was so completely inside that really looking and listening and talking were not a way any longer needed for me to know about this thing about movement being existing.

And how could I have this happen, let me read you the short portrait of George Hugnet and perhaps you will see what I mean. It is all there.

It really does not make any difference who George Hugnet was or what he did or what I said, all that was necessary was that there was something completely contained within itself and being contained within itself was moving, not moving in relation to anything not moving in relation to itself but just moving, I think I almost at that time did this thing. Do you at all in this portrait of George Hugnet that I will now read to you do you really see what I mean and in this portrait of Bernard Fay.

GEORGE HUGNET

George Genevieve Geronimo straightened it out without their finding it out.

Grammar makes George in our ring which Grammar makes George in our ring.

Grammar is as disappointed not is as grammar is as disappointed.

Grammar is not as Grammar is as disappointed.

George is in our ring. Grammar is not is disappointed. In are ring.

George Genevieve in are ring.

Portraits and Prayers, page 66.

BERNARD FAY

Patience is amiable and amiably.
What is amiable and amiably.
Patience is amiable and amiably.
What is impatience.
Impatience is amiable and amiably.

Portraits and Prayers, page 42.

Anyway this was to me a tremendously important thing and why. Well it was an important thing in itself for me but it was also an important thing because it made me realize what poetry really is.

This has something to do with what Edgar Allan Poe is.

But now to make you understand, that although I was as usual looking listening and talking perhaps more than ever at that time and leading a very complicated and perhaps too exciting every day living, never the less it really did not matter what I saw or said or heard, or if you like felt, because now there was at last something that was more vibrant than any of all that and somehow some way I had isolated it and in a way had gotten it written. It was about that time that I wrote Four Saints.

This was all very exciting and it went on and I did not do a great many portraits at that time. I wrote a great deal of poetry a great many plays and operas and some novels in which I tried again to do this thing, in one or two I more or less did, one called Brim Beauvais, I very often did, that is I created something out of something without adding anything, do you see what I mean.

It does mean something I do assure you it does mean something although it is very difficult to say it in any way except in the way that I said it then.

And so as I say I did not write a great many portraits at that time.

Then slowly I got a little tired, all that had been tremendously exciting, and one day then I began to write the Autobiography of Alice B. Toklas. You all know the joke of that, and in doing it I did an entirely different something something that I had been thinking about for some time and that had come out of some poetry I had been writing, Before The Flowers Of Friendship Faded Friendship Faded, but that is too long a story to begin now but it will be all told in Poetry and Grammar.

However the important thing was that for the first time in writing, I felt something outside me while I was writing, hitherto I had always had nothing but what was inside me while I was writing. Beside that I had been going for the first time since my college days to lectures. I had been going to hear Bernard Fay lecture about Franco-American things and I had become interested in the relation of a lecturer to his audience. I had never thought about an audience before not even when I wrote Composition As Explanation which was a lecture but now I suddenly began, to feel the outside inside and the inside outside and it was perhaps not so exciting but it was very interesting. Anyway it was quite exciting.

And so I wrote the Autobiography of Alice B. Toklas and told what happened as it had happened.

As I said way back, as now everybody at any moment can know what it is that happens while it happens, what happens is interesting but it is not really exciting. And I am not sure that I am not right about that. I hope you all think I am right about that. At any rate it is true there is something much more exciting than anything that happens and now and always I am writing the portrait of that.

I have been writing the portraits of Four In America, trying to write Grant, and Wilbur Wright and Henry James and Washington do other things than they did do so as to try to find out just what it is that what happens has to do with what is.

I have finished that and now I am trying in these lectures to tell what is by telling about how it happened that I told about what it is.

I hope you quite all see what I mean. Anyway I suppose inevitably I will go on doing it.

Poetry and Grammar

W HAT is poetry and if you know what poetry is what is
prose.

There is no use in telling more than you know, no not even
if you do not know it.

But do you do you know what prose is and do you know
what poetry is.

I have said that the words in plays written in poetry are
more lively than the same words written by the same poet in
other kinds of poetry. It undoubtedly was true of Shakespeare,
is it inevitably true of everybody. That is one thing to think
about. I said that the words in a play written in prose are not
as lively words as the words written in other prose by the same
writer. This is true of Goldsmith and I imagine it is true of
almost any writer.

There again there is something to know.

One of the things that is a very interesting thing to know
is how you are feeling inside you to the words that are coming
out to be outside of you.

Do you always have the same kind of feeling in relation to
the sounds as the words come out of you or do you not. All
this has so much to do with grammar and with poetry and
with prose.

Words have to do everything in poetry and prose and some
writers write more in articles and prepositions and some say
you should write in nouns, and of course one has to think of
everything.

A noun is a name of anything, why after a thing is named
write about it. A name is adequate or it is not. If it is adequate
then why go on calling it, if it is not then calling it by its name
does no good.

People if you like to believe it can be made by their names.
Call anybody Paul and they get to be a Paul call anybody Alice
and they get to be an Alice perhaps yes perhaps no, there is
something in that, but generally speaking, things once they
are named the name does not go on doing anything to them
and so why write in nouns. Nouns are the name of anything

and just naming names is alright when you want to call a roll but is it any good for anything else. To be sure in many places in Europe as in America they do like to call rolls.

As I say a noun is a name of a thing, and therefore slowly if you feel what is inside that thing you do not call it by the name by which it is known. Everybody knows that by the way they do when they are in love and a writer should always have that intensity of emotion about whatever is the object about which he writes. And therefore and I say it again more and more one does not use nouns.

Now what other things are there beside nouns, there are a lot of other things beside nouns.

When you are at school and learn grammar grammar is very exciting. I really do not know that anything has ever been more exciting than diagraming sentences. I suppose other things may be more exciting to others when they are at school but to me undoubtedly when I was at school the really completely exciting thing was diagraming sentences and that has been to me ever since the one thing that has been completely exciting and completely completing. I like the feeling the everlasting feeling of sentences as they diagram themselves.

In that way one is completely possessing something and incidentally one's self. Now in that diagraming of the sentences of course there are articles and prepositions and as I say there are nouns but nouns as I say even by definition are completely not interesting, the same thing is true of adjectives. Adjectives are not really and truly interesting. In a way anybody can know always has known that, because after all adjectives effect nouns and as nouns are not really interesting the thing that effects a not too interesting thing is of necessity not interesting. In a way as I say anybody knows that because of course the first thing that anybody takes out of anybody's writing are the adjectives. You see of yourself how true it is that which I have just said.

Beside the nouns and the adjectives there are verbs and adverbs. Verbs and adverbs are more interesting. In the first place they have one very nice quality and that is that they can be so mistaken. It is wonderful the number of mistakes a verb can make and that is equally true of its adverb. Nouns and adjectives never can make mistakes can never be mistaken but verbs can be so endlessly, both as to what they do and how they agree or disagree with whatever they do. The same is true of adverbs.

In that way any one can see that verbs and adverbs are more interesting than nouns and adjectives.

Beside being able to be mistaken and to make mistakes verbs can change to look like themselves or to look like something else, they are, so to speak on the move and adverbs move with them and each of them find themselves not at all annoying but very often very much mistaken. That is the reason any one can like what verbs can do. Then comes the thing that can of all things be most mistaken and they are prepositions. Prepositions can live one long life being really being nothing but absolutely nothing but mistaken and that makes them irritating if you feel that way about mistakes but certainly something that you can be continuously using and everlastingly enjoying. I like prepositions the best of all, and pretty soon we will go more completely into that.

Then there are articles. Articles are interesting just as nouns and adjectives are not. And why are they interesting just as nouns and adjectives are not. They are interesting because they do what a noun might do if a noun was not so unfortunately so completely unfortunately the name of something. Articles please, a and an and the please as the name that follows cannot please. They the names that is the nouns cannot please, because after all you know well after all that is what Shakespeare meant when he talked about a rose by any other name.

I hope now no one can have any illusion about a noun or about the adjective that goes with the noun.

But an article an article remains as a delicate and a varied something and any one who wants to write with articles and knows how to use them will always have the pleasure that using something that is varied and alive can give. That is what articles are.

Beside that there are conjunctions, and a conjunction is not varied but it has a force that need not make any one feel that they are dull. Conjunctions have made themselves live by their work. They work and as they work they live and even when they do not work and in these days they do not always live by work still nevertheless they do live.

So you see why I like to write with prepositions and conjunctions and articles and verbs and adverbs but not with nouns and adjectives. If you read my writing you will you do see what I mean.

Of course then there are pronouns. Pronouns are not as bad as nouns because in the first place practically they cannot have adjectives go with them. That already makes them better than nouns.

Then beside not being able to have adjectives go with them, they of course are not really the name of anything. They represent some one but they are not its or his name. In not being his or its or her name they already have a greater possibility of being something than if they were as a noun is the name of anything. Now actual given names of people are more lively than nouns which are the name of anything and I suppose that this is because after all the name is only given to that person when they are born, there is at least the element of choice even the element of change and anybody can be pretty well able to do what they like, they may be born Walter and become Hub, in such a way they are not like a noun. A noun has been the name of something for such a very long time.

That is the reason that slang exists it is to change the nouns which have been names for so long. I say again. Verbs and adverbs and articles and conjunctions and prepositions are lively because they all do something and as long as anything does something it keeps alive.

One might have in one's list added interjections but really interjections have nothing to do with anything not even with themselves. There so much for that. And now to go into the question of punctuation.

There are some punctuations that are interesting and there are some punctuations that are not. Let us begin with the punctuations that are not. Of these the one but the first and the most the completely most uninteresting is the question mark. The question mark is alright when it is all alone when it is used as a brand on cattle or when it could be used in decoration but connected with writing it is completely entirely completely uninteresting. It is evident that if you ask a question you ask a question but anybody who can read at all knows when a question is a question as it is written in writing. Therefore I ask you therefore wherefore should one use it the question mark. Beside it does not in its form go with ordinary printing and so it pleases neither the eye nor the ear and it is therefore like a noun, just an unnecessary name of something. A question is a question, anybody can know that a question is a question and so why add to it the question mark when it is already there when the question is already there in the writing. Therefore I never could bring myself to use a question mark, I always found it positively revolting, and now very few do use it. Exclamation marks have the same difficulty and also quotation marks, they are unnecessary, they are ugly, they spoil the line of the writing or the printing and anyway what is the use, if you do not know that a question is a question what is the use of its being a question. The same thing is true of an exclamation. And the same thing is true of a quotation. When I first began writing I found it simply impossible to use question marks and quotation marks and exclamation points and now anybody sees it that way. Perhaps some day they will see it some other way but now at any rate anybody can and does see it that way.

So there are the uninteresting things in punctuation uninteresting in a way that is perfectly obvious, and so we do not have to go any farther into that. There are besides dashes and dots, and these might be interesting spaces might be interesting. They might if one felt that way about them.

One other little punctuation mark one can have feelings about and that is the apostrophe for possession. Well feel as you like about that, I can see and I do see that for many that for some the possessive case apostrophe has a gentle tender insinuation that makes it very difficult to definitely decide to do without it. One does do without it, I do, I mostly always do, but I cannot deny that from time to time I feel myself having regrets and from time to time I put it in to make the possessive case. I absolutely do not like it all alone when it is outside the word when the word is a plural, no then positively and definitely no, I do not like it and in leaving it out I feel no regret, there it is unnecessary and not ornamental but in-

side a word and its s well perhaps, perhaps it does appeal by
its weakness to your weakness. At least at any rate from time
to time I do find myself letting it alone if it has come in and
sometimes it has come in. I cannot positively deny but that I
do from time to time let it come in.

So now to come to the real question of punctuation,
periods, commas, colons, semi-colons and capitals and small
letters.

I have had a long and complicated life with all these.

Let us begin with these I use the least first and these are
colons and semi-colons, one might add to these commas.

When I first began writing, I felt that writing should go on,
I still do feel that it should go on but when I first began
writing I was completely possessed by the necessity that writing should go on and if writing should go on what had colons
and semi-colons to do with it, what had commas to do with
it, what had periods to do with it what had small letters and
capitals to do with it to do with writing going on which was
at that time the most profound need I had in connection with
writing. What had colons and semi-colons to do with it what
had commas to do with it what had periods to do with it.

What had periods to do with it. Inevitably no matter how
completely I had to have writing go on, physically one had to
again and again stop sometime and if one had to again and
again stop some time then periods had to exist. Beside I had
always liked the look of periods and I liked what they did.
Stopping sometime did not really keep one from going on, it
was nothing that interfered, it was only something that happened, and as it happened as a perfectly natural happening, I
did believe in periods and I used them. I really never stopped
using them.

Beside that periods might later come to have a life of their
own to commence breaking up things in arbitrary ways, that
has happened lately with me in a poem I have written called
Winning His Way, later I will read you a little of it. By the
time I had written this poem about three years ago periods
had come to have for me completely a life of their own. They
could begin to act as they thought best and one might interrupt one's writing with them that is not really interrupt one's
writing with them but one could come to stop arbitrarily stop

at times in one's writing and so they could be used and you could use them. Periods could come to exist in this way and they could come in this way to have a life of their own. They did not serve you in any servile way as commas and colons and semi-colons do. Yes you do feel what I mean.

Periods have a life of their own a necessity of their own a feeling of their own a time of their own. And that feeling that life that necessity that time can express itself in an infinite variety that is the reason that I have always remained true to periods so much so that as I say recently I have felt that one could need them more than one had ever needed them.

You can see what an entirely different thing a period is from a comma, a colon or a semi-colon.

There are two different ways of thinking about colons and semi-colons you can think of them as commas and as such they are purely servile or you can think of them as periods and then using them can make you feel adventurous. I can see that one might feel about them as periods but I myself never have, I began unfortunately to feel them as a comma and commas are servile they have no life of their own they are dependent upon use and convenience and they are put there just for practical purposes. Semi-colons and colons had for me from the first completely this character the character that a comma has and not the character that a period has and therefore and definitely I have never used them. But now dimly and definitely I do see that they might well possibly they might have in them something of the character of the period and so it might have been an adventure to use them. I really do not think so. I think however lively they are or disguised they are they are definitely more comma than period and so really I cannot regret not having used them. They are more powerful more imposing more pretentious than a comma but they are a comma all the same. They really have within them deeply within them fundamentally within them the comma nature. And now what does a comma do and what has it to do and why do I feel as I do about them.

What does a comma do.

I have refused them so often and left them out so much and did without them so continually that I have come finally to be indifferent to them. I do not now care whether you put them in or not but for a long time I felt very definitely about them and would have nothing to do with them.

As I say commas are servile and they have no life of their own, and their use is not a use, it is a way of replacing one's own interest and I do decidedly like to like my own interest my own interest in what I am doing. A comma by helping you along holding your coat for you and putting on your shoes keeps you from living your life as actively as you should lead it and to me for many years and I still do feel that way about it only now I do not pay as much attention to them, the use of them was positively degrading. Let me tell you what I feel and what I mean and what I felt and what I meant.

When I was writing those long sentences of The Making of Americans, verbs active present verbs with long dependent adverbial clauses became a passion with me. I have told you that I recognize verbs and adverbs aided by prepositions and conjunctions with pronouns as possessing the whole of the active life of writing.

Complications make eventually for simplicity and therefore I have always liked dependent adverbial clauses. I have liked dependent adverbial clauses because of their variety of dependence and independence. You can see how loving the intensity of complication of these things that commas would be degrading. Why if you want the pleasure of concentrating on the final simplicity of excessive complication would you want any artificial aid to bring about that simplicity. Do you see now why I feel about the comma as I did and as I do.

Think about anything you really like to do and you will see what I mean.

When it gets really difficult you want to disentangle rather than to cut the knot, at least so anybody feels who is working with any thread, so anybody feels who is working with any tool so anybody feels who is writing any sentence or reading it after it has been written. And what does a comma do, a comma does nothing but make easy a thing that if you like it enough is easy enough without the comma. A long complicated sentence should force itself upon you, make you know yourself knowing it and the comma, well at the most a comma is a poor period that it lets you stop and take a breath but if you want to take a breath you ought to know yourself that you want to take a breath. It is not like stopping altogether which is what a period does stopping altogether has something to do with going on, but taking a breath well you are always taking a breath and why emphasize one breath rather than another breath. Anyway that is the way I felt about it and I felt that about it very very strongly. And so I almost never used a comma. The longer, the more complicated the sentence the greater the number of the same kinds of words I had following one after another, the more the very many more I had of them the more I felt the passionate need of their taking care of themselves by themselves and not helping them, and thereby enfeebling them by putting in a comma.

So that is the way I felt punctuation in prose, in poetry it is a little different but more so and later I will go into that. But that is the way I felt about punctuation in prose.

Another part of punctuation is capital letters and small letters. Anybody can really do as they please about that and in English printing one may say that they always have.

If you read older books you will see that they do pretty well what they please with capitals and small letters and I have always felt that one does do pretty well what one pleases with capitals and small letters. Sometimes one feels that Italians should be with a capital and sometimes with a small letter, one can feel like that about almost anything. I myself do not feel like that about proper names, I rather like to look at them with a capital on them but I can perfectly understand that a great many do not feel that way about it. In short in prose capitals and small letters have really nothing to do with the inner life of sentences and paragraphs as the other punctuation marks have as I have just been saying.

We still have capitals and small letters and probably for some time we will go on having them but actually the tendency is always toward diminishing capitals and quite rightly because the feeling that goes with them is less and less of a feeling and so slowly and inevitably just as with horses capitals will have gone away. They will come back from time to time but perhaps never really come back to stay.

Perhaps yes perhaps not but really and inevitably really it really does not really make any difference.

But and they will be with us as long as human beings continue to exist and have a vocabulary, sentences and paragraphs will be with us and therefore inevitably and really periods will be with us and it is of these things that will be always inevitably with us in prose and in poetry because prose and also poetry will also always always be with us that I will go on telling to you all I know.

Sentences and paragraphs. Sentences are not emotional but paragraphs are. I can say that as often as I like and it always remains as it is, something that is.

I said I found this out first in listening to Basket my dog drinking. And anybody listening to any dog's drinking will see what I mean.

When I wrote The Making of Americans I tried to break down this essential combination by making enormously long sentences that would be as long as the longest paragraph and so to see if there was really and truly this essential difference between paragraphs and sentences, if one went far enough with this thing with making the sentences long enough to be as long as any paragraph and so producing in them the balance of a paragraph not a balance of a sentence, because of course the balance of a paragraph is not the same balance as the balance of a sentence.

It is only necessary to read anything in order to know that. I say if I succeeded in making my sentences so long that they held within themselves the balance of both both sentences and paragraphs, what was the result.

I did in some sentences in The Making of Americans succeed in doing this thing in creating a balance that was neither the balance of a sentence nor the balance of a paragraph and in doing so I felt dimly that I had done something that was not leading to anything because after all you should not lose two things in order to have one thing because in doing so you make writing just that much less varied.

That is one thing about what I did. There is also another thing and that was a very important thing, in doing this in achieving something that had neither the balance of a sentence nor the balance of a paragraph but a balance a new balance that had to do with a sense of movement of time included in a given space which as I have already said is a definitely American thing.

An American can fill up a space in having his movement of time by adding unexpectedly anything and yet getting within the included space everything he had intended getting.

A young french boy he is a red-haired descendant of the niece of Madame Recamier went to America for two weeks most unexpectedly and I said to him what did you notice most over there. Well he said at first they were not as different from us frenchmen as I expected them to be and then I did see that they were that they were different. And what, said I, well he said, when a train was going by at a terrific pace and we waved a hat the engine driver could make a bell quite carelessly go ting ting ting, the way anybody playing at a thing could do, it was not if you know what I mean professional he said. Perhaps you do see the connection with that and my sentences that had no longer the balance of sentences because they were not the parts of a paragraph nor were they a paragraph but they had made in so far as they had come to be so long and with the balance of their own that they had they had become something that was a whole thing and in so being they had a balance which was the balance of a space completely not filled but created by something moving as moving is not as moving should be. As I said Henry James in his later writing had had a dim feeling that this was what he knew he should do.

And so though as I say there must always be sentences and paragraphs the question can really be asked must there always be sentences and paragraphs is it not possible to achieve in itself and not by sentences and paragraphs the combination that sentences are not emotional and paragraphs are.

In a book called How to Write I worked a lot at this thing trying to find out just exactly what the balance the unemotional balance of a sentence is and what the emotional balance of a paragraph is and if it were possible to make even in a short sentence the two things come to be one. I think I did a few times succeed. Will you listen to one or two sentences where I did think I had done this thing.

He looks like a young man grown old.
How To Write. (Plain Edition)
Random House. Page 25.

It looks like a garden but he had hurt himself by accident.

How To Write. Page 26.

A dog which you have never had before has sighed.

How to Write. Page 27.

Once when they were nearly ready they had ordered it to close.

How To Write. Page 29.

If a sound is made which grows louder and then stops how many times may it be repeated.

How To Write. Page 89.

Battles are named because there have been hills which have made a hill in a battle.

How to Write. Page 89.

A bay and hills hills are surrounded by their having their distance very near.

How To Write. Page 89.

Poplars indeed will be and may be indeed will be cut down and will be sawn up and indeed will be used as wood and may be used for wood.

How To Write. Page 90.

The thing to remember is that if it is not if it is not what having left it to them makes it be very likely as likely as they would be after all after all choosing choosing to be here on time.

How To Write. Page 259.

In spite of my intending to write about grammar and poetry I am still writing about grammar and prose, but and of course it may or may not be true if you find out essentially what prose is and essentially what poetry is may you not have an exciting thing happening as I had it happen with sentences and paragraphs.

After all the natural way to count is not that one and one make two but to go on counting by one and one as chinamen do as anybody does as Spaniards do as my little aunts did.

One and one and one and one and one. That is the natural way to go on counting.

Now what has this to do with poetry. It has a lot to do with poetry.

Everything has a lot to do with poetry everything has a lot to do with prose.

And has prose anything to do with poetry and has poetry anything to do with prose.

And what have nouns to do with poetry and periods and capital letters. The other punctuation marks we never have to mention again. People may do as they like with them but we never have to mention them. But nouns still have to be mentioned because in coming to avoid nouns a great deal happens and has happened. It was one of the things that happened in a book I called Tender Buttons.

In The Making of Americans a long a very long prose book made up of sentences and paragraphs and the new thing that was something neither the sentence or the paragraph each one alone or in combination had ever done, I said I had gotten rid of nouns and adjectives as much as possible by the method of living in adverbs in verbs in pronouns, in adverbial clauses written or implied and in conjunctions.

But and after I had gone as far as I could in these long sentences and paragraphs that had come to do something else I then began very short things and in doing very short things I resolutely realized nouns and decided not to get around them but to meet them, to handle in short to refuse them by using them and in that way my real acquaintance with poetry was begun.

I will try to tell a little more clearly and in more detail just what happened and why it was if it was like natural counting, that is counting by one one one one one.

Nouns as you all know are the names of anything and as the names of anything of course one has had to use them. And what have they done. And what has any one done with them. That is something to know. It is as you may say as I may say a great deal to know.

Nouns are the name of anything and anything is named, that is what Adam and Eve did and if you like it is what anybody does, but do they go on just using the name until perhaps they do not know what the name is or if they do know what the name is they do not care about what the name is. This may happen of course it may. And what has poetry got to do with this and what has prose and if everything like a noun which is a name of anything is to be avoided what takes place. And what has that to do with poetry. A great deal I think and all this too has to do with other things with short and long lines and rhymes.

But first what is poetry and what is prose. I wonder if I can tell you.

We do know a little now what prose is. Prose is the balance the emotional balance that makes the reality of paragraphs and the unemotional balance that makes the reality of sentences and having realized completely realized that sentences are not emotional while paragraphs are, prose can be the essential balance that is made inside something that combines the sentence and the paragraph, examples of this I have been reading to you.

Now if that is what prose is and that undoubtedly is what prose is you can see that prose real prose really great written prose is bound to be made up more of verbs adverbs prepositions prepositional clauses and conjunctions than nouns. The vocabulary in prose of course is important if you like vocabulary is always important, in fact one of the things that you can find out and that I experimented with a great deal in How to Write vocabulary in itself and by itself can be interesting and can make sense. Anybody can know that by thinking of words. It is extraordinary how it is impossible that a vocabulary does not make sense. But that is natural indeed inevitable because a vocabulary is that by definition, and so because this is so the vocabulary in respect to prose is less important than the parts of speech, and the internal balance and the movement within a given space.

So then we understand we do know what prose is.

But what is poetry.

Is it more or is it less difficult to know what poetry is. I have sometimes thought it more difficult to know what poetry is but now that I do know what poetry is and if I do know what poetry is then it is not more difficult to know what it is than to know what prose is.

What is poetry.

Poetry has to do with vocabulary just as prose has not.

So you see prose and poetry are not at all alike. They are completely different.

Poetry is I say essentially a vocabulary just as prose is essentially not.

And what is the vocabulary of which poetry absolutely is. It is a vocabulary entirely based on the noun as prose is essentially and determinately and vigorously not based on the noun.

Poetry is concerned with using with abusing, with losing with wanting, with denying with avoiding with adoring with replacing the noun. It is doing that always doing that, doing that and doing nothing but that. Poetry is doing nothing but using losing refusing and pleasing and betraying and caressing nouns. That is what poetry does, that is what poetry has to do no matter what kind of poetry it is. And there are a great many kinds of poetry.

When I said.

A rose is a rose is a rose is a rose.

And then later made that into a ring I made poetry and what did I do I caressed completely caressed and addressed a noun.

Now let us think of poetry any poetry all poetry and let us see if this is not so. Of course it is so anybody can know that.

I have said that a noun is a name of anything by definition that is what it is and a name of anything is not interesting because once you know its name the enjoyment of naming it is over and therefore in writing prose names that is nouns are completely uninteresting. But and that is a thing to be remembered you can love a name and if you love a name then saying that name any number of times only makes you love it more, more violently more persistently more tormentedly. Anybody knows how anybody calls out the name of anybody one loves. And so that is poetry really loving the name of anything and that is not prose. Yes any of you can know that.

Poetry like prose has lived through a good deal. Anybody or anything lives through a good deal. Sometimes it included everything and sometimes it includes only itself and there can be any amount of less and more at any time of its existence.

Of course when poetry really began it practically included everything it included narrative and feelings and excitements and nouns so many nouns and all emotions. It included narrative but now it does not include narrative.

I often wonder how I am ever to come to know all that I am to know about narrative. Narrative is a problem to me. I worry about it a good deal these days and I will not write or lecture about it yet, because I am still too worried about it worried about knowing what it is and how it is and where it is and how it is and how it will be what it is. However as I say now and at this time I do not I will not go into that. Suffice it to say that for the purpose of poetry it has now for a long time not had anything to do with being there.

Perhaps it is a mistake perhaps not that it is no longer there.

I myself think that something else is going to happen about narrative and I work at it a great deal at this time not work but bother about it. Bother is perhaps the better word for what I am doing just now about narrative. But anyway to go back to poetry.

Poetry did then in beginning include everything and it was natural that it should because then everything including what was happening could be made real to anyone by just naming what was happening in other words by doing what poetry always must do by living in nouns.

Nouns are the name of anything. Think of all that early poetry, think of Homer, think of Chaucer, think of the Bible and you will see what I mean you will really realize that they were drunk with nouns, to name to know how to name earth sea and sky and all that was in them was enough to make them live and love in names, and that is what poetry is it is a state of knowing and feeling a name. I know that now but I have only come to that knowledge by long writing.

So then as I say that is what poetry was and slowly as everybody knew the names of everything poetry had less and less to do with everything. Poetry did not change, poetry never changed, from the beginning until now and always in the future poetry will concern itself with the names of things. The names may be repeated in different ways and very soon I will go into that matter but now and always poetry is created by

naming names the names of something the names of somebody the names of anything. Nouns are the names of things
and so nouns are the basis of poetry.

Before we go any further there is another matter. Why are
the lines of poetry short, so much shorter than prose, why do
they rhyme, why in order to complete themselves do they have
to end with what they began, why are all these things the
things that are in the essence of poetry even when the poetry
was long even when now the poetry has changed its form.

Once more the answer is the same and that is that such a
way to express oneself is the natural way when one expresses
oneself in loving the name of anything. Think what you do
when you do do that when you love the name of anything
really love its name. Inevitably you express yourself in that
way, in the way poetry expresses itself that is in short lines in
repeating what you began in order to do it again. Think of
how you talk to anything whose name is new to you a lover
a baby or a dog or a new land or any part of it. Do you not
inevitably repeat what you call out and is that calling out not
of necessity in short lines. Think about it and you will see
what I mean by what you feel.

So as I say poetry is essentially the discovery, the love, the
passion for the name of anything.

Now to come back to how I know what I know about
poetry.

I was writing The Making of Americans, I was completely
obsessed by the inner life of everything including generations
of everybody's living and I was writing prose, prose that had
to do with the balancing the inner balancing of everything. I
have already told you all about that.

And then, something happened and I began to discover the
names of things, that is not discover the names but discover
the things the things to see the things to look at and in so
doing I had of course to name them not to give them new
names but to see that I could find out how to know that they
were there by their names or by replacing their names. And
how was I to do so. They had their names and naturally I
called them by the names they had and in doing so having
begun looking at them I called them by their names with

passion and that made poetry, I did not mean it to make poetry but it did, it made the Tender Buttons, and the Tender Buttons was very good poetry it made a lot more poetry, and I will now more and more tell about that and how it happened.

I discovered everything then and its name, discovered it and its name. I had always known it and its name but all the same I did discover it.

I remember very well when I was a little girl and I and my brother found as children will the love poems of their very very much older brother. This older brother had just written one and it said that he had often sat and looked at any little square of grass and it had been just a square of grass as grass is, but now he was in love and so the little square of grass was all filled with birds and bees and butterflies, the difference was what love was. The poem was funny we and he knew the poem was funny but he was right, being in love made him make poetry, and poetry made him feel the things and their names, and so I repeat nouns are poetry.

So then in Tender Buttons I was making poetry but and it seriously troubled me, dimly I knew that nouns made poetry but in prose I no longer needed the help of nouns and in poetry did I need the help of nouns. Was there not a way of naming things that would not invent names, but mean names without naming them.

I had always been very impressed from the time that I was very young by having had it told me and then afterwards feeling it myself that Shakespeare in the forest of Arden had created a forest without mentioning the things that make a forest. You feel it all but he does not name its names.

Now that was a thing that I too felt in me the need of making it be a thing that could be named without using its name. After all one had known its name anything's name for so long, and so the name was not new but the thing being alive was always new.

What was there to do.

I commenced trying to do something in Tender Buttons about this thing. I went on and on trying to do this thing. I remember in writing An Acquaintance With Description looking at anything until something that was not the name of that thing but was in a way that actual thing would come to be written.

Naturally, and one may say that is what made Walt Whitman naturally that made the change in the form of poetry, that we who had known the names so long did not get a thrill from just knowing them. We that is any human being living has inevitably to feel the thing anything being existing, but the name of that thing of that anything is no longer anything to thrill any one except children. So as everybody has to be a poet, what was there to do. This that I have just described, the creating it without naming it, was what broke the rigid form of the noun the simple noun poetry which now was broken.

Of course you all do know that when I speak of naming anything, I include emotions as well as things.

So then there we were and what were we to do about it. Go on, of course go on what else does anybody do, so I did, I went on.

Of course you might say why not invent new names new languages but that cannot be done. It takes a tremendous amount of inner necessity to invent even one word, one can invent imitating movements and emotions in sounds, and in the poetical language of some languages you have that, the german language as a language suffers from this what the words mean sound too much like what they do, and children do these things by one sort or another of invention but this has really nothing to do with language. Language as a real thing is not imitation either of sounds or colors or emotions it is an intellectual recreation and there is no possible doubt about it and it is going to go on being that as long as humanity is anything. So every one must stay with the language their language that has come to be spoken and written and which has in it all the history of its intellectual recreation.

And so for me the problem of poetry was and it began with Tender Buttons to constantly realize the thing anything so that I could recreate that thing. I struggled I struggled desperately with the recreation and the avoidance of nouns as nouns and yet poetry being poetry nouns are nouns. Let me read you bits of the Portrait of Sherwood Anderson and The Birthplace of Bonnes to show you what I mean.

Can anybody tell by looking which was the towel used for cooking.

Portraits and Prayers. Page 162.

A VERY VALENTINE

Very fine is my valentine.

Very fine and very mine.

Very mine is my valentine very mine and very fine.

Very fine is my valentine and mine, very fine very mine and mine is my valentine.

Portraits and Prayers. Page 152.

BUNDLES FOR THEM
A HISTORY OF GIVING BUNDLES

We were able to notice that each one in a way carried a bundle, they were not a trouble to them nor were they all bundles as some of them were chickens some of them pheasants some of them sheep and some of them bundles, they were not a trouble to them and then indeed we learned that it was the principal recreation and they were so arranged that they were not given away, and today they were given away.

I will not look at them again.

They will not look for them again.

They have not seen them here again.

They are in there and we hear them again.

In which way are stars brighter than they are. When we have come to this decision. We mention many thousands of buds. And when I close my eyes I see them.

If you hear her snore

It is not before you love her

You love her so that to be her beau is very lovely

She is sweetly there and her curly hair is very lovely.

She is sweetly here and I am very near and that is very lovely.

She is my tender sweet and her little feet are stretched out well which is a treat and very lovely.

Her little tender nose is between her little eyes which close and are very lovely.

She is very lovely and mine which is very lovely.
Portraits and Prayers. Page 154.

I found in longer things like Operas and Plays and Portraits and Lucy Church Amiably and An Acquaintance With Description that I could come nearer to avoiding names in re-creating something.

That brings us to the question will poetry continue to be necessarily short as it has been as really good poetry has been for a very long time. Perhaps not and why not.

If enough is new to you to name or not name, and these two things come to the same thing, can you go on long enough. Yes I think so.

So then poetry up to the present time has been a poetry of nouns a poetry of naming something of really naming that thing passionately completely passionately naming that thing by its name.

Slowly and particularly during the nineteenth century the English nineteenth century everybody had come to know too well very much too well the name anything had when you called it by its name.

That is something that inevitably happened. And what else could they do. They had to go on doing what they did, that is calling anything by its name passionately but if as I say they really knew its name too well could they call it its name simply in that way. Slowly they could not.

And then Walt Whitman came. He wanted really wanted to express the thing and not call it by its name. He worked very hard at that, and he called it Leaves of Grass because he wanted it to be as little a well known name to be called upon passionately as possible. I do not at all know whether Whitman knew that he wanted to do this but there is no doubt at all but that is what he did want to do.

You have the complete other end of this thing in a poet like Longfellow, I cite him because a commonplace poet shows you more readily and clearly just what the basis of poetry is than a better one. And Longfellow knew all about calling out names, he on the whole did it without passion but he did it very well.

Of course in the history of poetry there have been many

who have also tried to name the thing without naming its names, but this is not a history of poets it is a telling what I know about poetry.

And so knowing all this about poetry I struggled more and more with this thing. I say I knew all this about poetry but I did not really know all this then about poetry, I was coming to know then then when I was writing commencing to know what I do now know about prose but I did not then know anything really to know it of what I now know about poetry.

And so in Tender Buttons and then on and on I struggled with the ridding myself of nouns, I knew nouns must go in poetry as they had gone in prose if anything that is everything was to go on meaning something.

And so I went on with this exceeding struggle of knowing really knowing what a thing was really knowing it knowing anything I was seeing anything I was feeling so that its name could be something, by its name coming to be a thing in itself as it was but would not be anything just and only as a name.

I wonder if you do see what I mean.

What I mean by what I have just said is this. I had to feel anything and everything that for me was existing so intensely that I could put it down in writing as a thing in itself without at all necessarily using its name. The name of a thing might be something in itself if it could come to be real enough but just as a name it was not enough something. At any rate that is the way I felt and still do feel about it.

And so I went through a very long struggle and in this struggle I began to be troubled about narrative a narrative of anything that was or might be happening.

The newspapers tell us about it but they tell it to us as nouns tell it to us that is they name it, and in naming it, it as a telling of it is no longer anything. That is what a newspaper is by definition just as a noun is a name by definition.

And so I was slowly beginning to know something about what poetry was. And here was the question if in poetry one could lose the noun as I had really and truly lost it in prose would there be any difference between poetry and prose. As this thing came once more to be a doubt inside me I began to work very hard at poetry.

At that time I wrote Before the Flowers of Friendship Faded

Friendship Faded and there I went back again to a more or less regular form to see whether inside that regular form I could do what I was sure needed to be done and also to find out if eventually prose and poetry were one or not one.

In writing this poem I found I could be very gay I could be very lively in poetry, I could use very few nouns in poetry and call out practically no names in poetry and yet make poetry really feel and sound as poetry, but was it what I wanted that should be done. But it did not decide anything for me but it did help me in my way.

XII

I am very hungry when I drink,
I need to leave it when I have it held,
    They will be white with which they know they see, that darker makes it be a color white for me, white is not shown when I am dark indeed with red despair who comes who has to care that they will let me a little lie like now I like to lie I like to live I like to die I like to lie and live and die and live and die and by and by I like to live and die and by and by they need to sew, the difference is that sewing makes it bleed and such with them in all the way of seed and seeding and repine and they will which is mine and not all mine who can be thought curious of this of all of that made it and come lead it and done weigh it and mourn and sit upon it know it for ripeness without deserting all of it of which without which it has not been born. Oh no not to be thirsty with the thirst of hunger not alone to know that they plainly and ate or wishes. Any little one will kill himself for milk.

                Before the Flowers of Friendship Faded
                Friendship Faded (Plain Edition). Page 14.

XIV

It could be seen very nicely
That doves have each a heart,
Each one is always seeing that they could not be apart,
A little lake makes fountains
And fountains have no flow,
And a dove has need of flying

And water can be low,
Let me go.
Any week is what they seek
When they have to halve a beak.
I like a painting on a wall of doves
And what do they do,
They have hearts
They are apart
Little doves are winsome
But not when they are little and left.

Before the Flowers of Friendship Faded
Friendship Faded (Plain Edition). Page 16.

I decided and Lucy Church Amiably had been an attempt to do it, I decided that if one definitely completely replaced the noun by the thing in itself, it was eventually to be poetry and not prose which would have to deal with everything that was not movement in space. There could no longer be form to decide anything, narrative that is not newspaper narrative but real narrative must of necessity be told by any one having come to the realization that the noun must be replaced not by inner balance but by the thing in itself and that will eventually lead to everything. I am working at this thing and what will it do this I do not know but I hope that I will know. In the Four In America I have gone on beginning but I am sure that there is in this what there is that it is necessary to do if one is to do anything or everything. Do you see what I mean. Well anyway that is the way that I do now feel about it, and this is all that I do know, and I do believe in knowing all I do know, about prose and poetry. The rest will come considerably later.

FROM

NARRATION

Lecture 3

NARRATIVE concerns itself with what is happening all the time, history concerns itself with what happens from time to time. And that is perhaps what is the matter with history and that is what is perhaps the matter with narrative.

I am now going to talk not about the successes in narrative and history but the way they who write narrative and history do not do what they say they will do when they start out to do what they are about to do.

Let us think of newspapers, of novels, of detective stories of biographies of autobiographies of histories and of conversations. Let us think about them. I do not say let us know about them because it is hard to know what you do know about a thing that does not do what it does do.

And so what does the newspaper do and what does it not do.

But before we begin with anything that does or does not do what it is to do what it says it would if it could do that thing let us think again of narrating anything of beginning anything of ending anything.

It does happen it is bound to happen that the way of telling anything can come not to mean anything to the one telling that thing. When that does happen that the way of telling anything has come not to mean anything to the one telling that thing perhaps then one does go on telling the thing in the way that telling that thing does not mean that thing to the one telling that thing or one stops telling anything or one starts telling that thing in some other way that may or may not come to mean anything.

The choice of one of these three things is of course a perfectly natural thing although it is usually called experimenting because it is really not experimenting, experimenting is trying to do some thing in a way that may produce a result which is a desired result by the person doing it but telling something is not an experiment it is a thing that has to be done since any one since every one inevitably has to tell something and has to tell something in the way that makes it feel that that something is what that thing is.

That is what narrative is and always at a time no one can go on telling anything in the way he has been telling that thing because no one is listening and even if that does not make any difference to him then he himself is not listening and perhaps eventually that does that can that will that may make a difference to him. Anything may make a difference to any one but that certainly can or may make a difference all the difference any of the difference to him.

Think about how any one is no longer listening when some one is telling something and you will know all about this thing.

Narrative is what anybody has to say in any way about anything that can happen has happened will happen in any way.

That is what narrative is and so of course there always is narrative and anybody can stop listening to any way of telling anything. This undoubtedly can and does happen, even if it is exciting enough or has been. Anybody can stop listening to any telling of anything.

And this brings us to everything how anything is told will be told or has been.

There we are.

What do you tell and how do you tell it.

If you tell it very well how do you tell it and if you do not tell it very well if you do not tell it well at all how do you tell it.

This anybody knows since everybody is everybody and everybody is always one or many of them to always tell it.

There are many ways that anybody has that is anybody who is everybody and everybody and anybody is anybody and everybody there are many ways that they have to tell what they tell and to have anybody or themselves or everybody or not themselves or any combination of themselves or any combination of anybody or everybody to listen to it, listen while they tell it.

This makes narrative and at any time there is a great deal of it anybody can say at any time that there is not enough or just enough or too much of it. Anyway anybody everybody can say anything about narrative their own or anybody else's narrative but one thing is certain and sure that anybody telling everything even if it is nothing that they are telling or is either telling what they want to tell what they have to tell what they like to tell or what they will tell they tell a narrative.

Sometime anybody can get tired of it and when everybody who is anybody does get tired of it then that is the end the natural end of that way of telling it.

That is what happens what has happened when everybody begins to think in a kind of a way which is a different way and that can happen of course it can. Feelings may have something to do with it or they may not have anything to do with it. Let it alone if you like let anything alone if you like but feelings are feelings and they are always there but anybody can have any way of telling anything they are telling about it. That makes a narrative and does a narrative have to have a beginning and an ending.

To know about this you have to look at country to see what it looks like, since land and water looks not like itself but is the whole of it, and therefore is there any beginning and ending to it. Is there, are there not two things to think about it are there not, about beginning and ending but later very much later we will go into that but now to consider the perfectly ordinary ways narrative has been written, newspapers, novels, detective stories, biography autobiography history conversations, letter-writing whatever kind of way any of these things are written makes no difference a narrative is any kind of way of trying to tell anything any one has to tell about anything that is or was or will be happening, and any kind of telling is the telling of what is happening inside or outside but is the telling the natural the immediate the necessary telling of anything that is happening. Now the newspapers have been and are very interesting as being one way one variation of one way in it if you like but one way of telling anything of telling everything of telling something.

What do the newspapers do and how do they do it, and what is the matter with it that is if there is anything the matter with it.

But to go back again just a little again to the way anybody or everybody tells anything anything about anything that is happening all the various ways there is of doing it and all the different ways anybody that is everybody can or cannot get tired of listening to it.

Think about it anybody listens to it as you yourself tell anything and as you yourself or any one listen while you yourself
or any one tell anything. It is extraordinary how few and how
many ways there are of telling anything listen to yourself and
you will know something of all about it and how few and yet
how extraordinarily varied ways there are of listening or of
getting tired of listening to it.

All this makes anything written interesting to any one
interested in it the number of ways any one tells anything
theatre novels history poetry biography autobiography newspapers letter-writing and conversations and the number of
ways anybody that is everybody gets tired of listening to it.
Everybody always has to be listening to something, that is the
way it is always anybody has to be listening to something that
is what makes life lived the way that is what makes anybody
who they are what they are, of course it does any of you think
of your life the way it is, you are always listening to some one
to something and you are always telling something to some
one or to any one. That is life the way it is lived.

I once said and I think it is true that being a genius is being
one who is one at one and at the same time telling and listening to anything or everything.

Any of you try it and you will see what a difficult thing it
is to listen to anything and everything in the way any one is
telling anything and at the same time while you are listening
to be telling inside yourself and outside yourself anything
that is happening everything that is anything. That is what
genius is to be always going on doing this thing at one and
at the same time listening and telling really listening and really
telling.

That is the reason why so often people have genius when
they are twenty one, talent when they are thirty one, repetition of this talent when they are forty one and then nothing
of anything that can make any one listen to any of them after
forty one. This is of course a well known thing but if you
notice any and every one you will see how naturally this thing
does happen. When you are young you have an energy that
makes hearing and telling beginning over all at one time, but
you grow older and when you listen you can not be telling
anything and when you tell anything you cannot hear any-

thing and so then what was begun when you are young and had energy often for two things does not go on.

This is a sad story and does happen so often that there is no use continuing to sadden any one by going on.

I do not cannot believe that anything is or can be more interesting than the way and the fact that everybody is always telling everything and that anybody can in their way go on listening or not go on listening. But everybody can feel about telling and about listening like that. Anybody can.

So now about the newspapers what are they telling how are they telling what do they intend to tell about what they tell and who listens who does listen. It is very interesting.

Newspapers want to do something, they want to tell what is happening as if it were just then happening. They want to write that happening as if it was happening on the day the newspapers are read that is not as if the thing was happening on the day the newspaper is read a little that all the same but as if the writing were being written as it is read, that is what they mean by hot off the press, but yet after all there is an interval generally six hours or so but always an interval, and that interval they try to bridge by head lines, and do they succeed, not very well I guess not very well because it is not possible to tell in the way they have to tell a thing that is told as a reality, all this has an awful lot to do with the writing of history.

As I say what does the newspaper really want to do and what does anybody who reads the newspaper want to feel that they want the newspaper to do.

Really what the newspaper does really want to do and what the reader of the newspaper wants the newspaper to do is to know every day what happened the day before and so get the feeling that it has happened on the same day the day the newspaper appeared the day the newspaper reader reads the newspaper and not on the day before. If they did not want to do and to have this thing the newspaper reader and the newspaper writer then they would not mind so much reading the newspaper of the day before and anybody knows that anybody who reads newspapers always objects to reading the newspaper of the day before.

Well there are two things about it, the newspaper reader

wants to read the newspaper every day because he wants the idea of happenings happening every day and if there is a day without the happening of that day which is really the happening of the day before then the newspaper reader feels that it is like the sun standing still or any abnormal thing there is a day and nothing has happened on that day.

That makes anybody feel that you cannot call a day a day if it is not a day if nothing that had been happening has happened on that day.

That is really what the newspaper has to say that everything that has happened has happened on that day but really this is not true because everything that has happened on that day on the newspaper day has really happened the day before and that makes all the trouble that there is with the newspaper as it is and in every way they try to destroy this day the day between the day before and the day the newspaper day. Of course by day I naturally mean night too but the newspaper really does not know and so it cannot really say that there is really any difference between the night and the day. That is another of the difficulties they have in face of the real trouble that the newspaper day is always the day before the newspaper day and yet that is what they really have to say that the newspaper day is the day it is, which of course it is not.

And so everything in the newspaper begins with its not being so and that like everything complicates and makes difficult telling and listening, it may complicate and the newspaper does by making it too easy, so much do they have to deceive the reader into feeling that yesterday is to-day that they have to make it too easy and in making it too easy they do do something they had not intended to do they make it no longer an exciting thing to do because they have commenced to do too well what if they did have it to do it would be impossible to do.

Do you see what I mean.

It is very interesting.

And it has an awful lot to do with everything.

There are so many things to say at one time and this is one of them. Beginning and ending in writing anything is always a trouble of its own and it is a great trouble to any one doing any writing. That is where the newspaper is interesting, there is really of course no beginning and no ending to anything they are doing, it is when it is and in being when it is being there is no beginning and no ending.

That is because it exists any of every day and any of every day is not mixed up with beginning and ending.

That is a very interesting thing in writing in a newspaper in a newspaper being existing there is no beginning and no ending and in a way too there is no going on. One really has to think of everything as one thinks of anything and that is one thing.

I love my love with a b because she is peculiar. One can say this. That has nothing to do with what a newspaper does and that is the reason why that is the reason that newspapers and with it history as it mostly exists has nothing to do with anything that is living.

I said newspapers make things too easy and I said that once to a reporter and he said you have no idea I am sure how terribly hard we work. Yes I said but after you have done all that hard work you have to write it up as it would be if you had known it all beforehand and that is what really makes it too easy. There is no discovery there is mostly no discovery in a newspaper or in history, they find out things they never knew before but there is no discovery and finally if all this goes on long enough it is all too easy.

I cannot come back too often to telling and hearing to talking and listening, to repeating and changing to knowing and remembering to having an intention of intending something or to have anything happening, all these things are as they are and one of them can never be another one of them no matter how commonly any one that is every one is in any confusion about them. I tell you and I cannot tell it to you too often although I may not tell it often enough as anybody even I can change about something I cannot tell it to you often enough that confusion is either making things easy by knowing beforehand how it is going to be done or by mixing up talking and listening, remembering and knowing not beginning and ending, and that is a very interesting thing think of that that there is really no confusion in mixing up beginning and ending no none at all.

And so now that we have gotten here that is now that we

are not only writing the newspaper as well as reading what it writes what is it that it does do that makes it too easy to do and to read what it does do.

You see there is no beginning and ending because every day is the same that is that every day has anything that it has happening.

Now that is the difference between existing and happening.

If you exist any day you are not the same as any other day no nor any minute of the day because you have inside you being existing. Anybody who is existing and anybody really anybody is existing anybody really is that.

But anything happening well the inside and the outside are not the inside and the outside inside.

Let me do that again. The inside and the outside, the outside which is outside and the inside which is inside are not when they are inside and outside are not inside in short they are not existing, that is inside, and when the outside is entirely outside that is is not at all inside then it is not at all inside and so it is not existing. Do you not see what a newspaper is and perhaps history.

No matter how hard you work the result that you have is that the outside is outside and when it is outside it is not begun and when it is outside it is not ended and when it is neither begun nor ended it is not either a thing which has existed it is simply an event.

It is very curious in a newspaper that sometimes really sometimes a personality breaks through an event, it takes a tremendously strong personality to break through the events in a newspaper and when they do well it is soon over it is soon smoothed over and even history wishes to change it into something that any one could recover from.

In a novel in a play no matter what it is that happens it is hoped that nothing will be smoothed over that every minute of that novel there is a beginning and ending that always any personality that any one has there is one that no one can ever change into something that any one can recover from.

And the reason why is this. The more a novel is a novel the more a play is a play the more a writing is a writing the more no outside is outside outside is inside inside is inside.

I love my love with a b because she is peculiar.

There is something very odd that has happened in all this in connection with detective stories and now listen.

As I say beginning and ending has something to do with everything that is anything and so listen.

In real life that is if you like in the newspapers which are not real life but real life with the reality left out, the reality being the inside and the newspapers being the outside and never is the outside inside and never is the inside outside except in the rare and peculiar cases when the outside breaks through to be inside because the outside is so part of some inside that even a description of the outside cannot completely relieve the outside of the inside.

And so in the newspapers you like to know the answer in crime stories in reading crime and in written crime stories knowing the answer spoils it. After all in the written thing the answer is a let down from the interest and that is so every time that is what spoils most crime stories unless another mystery crops up during the crime and that mystery remains.

And then there is another very peculiar thing in the newspaper thing it is the crime in the story it is the detective that is the thing.

Now do you begin to see the difference between the inside and the outside.

In the newspaper thing it is the crime it is the criminal that is interesting, in the story it is the story about the crime that is interesting. Now think, you will perfectly realize that the newspaper practically never tells anything about detecting, a little in the case of Dillinger, a little in the case of Hauptmann but still really very little and in lesser crimes not at all the emphasis is entirely upon the crime and not upon the detecting and in the written story it is impossible to hold the attention by telling about the crime you can only hold the attention by telling about detecting. All this is very interesting most most interesting and has to do with what the newspaper has to say and what it has not to say and the fact that in the long run one might say practically any day the newspaper is not really exciting.

I have said that the business of the artist is to be exciting and it is his business and if he is an artist whatever he does really does is really exciting. By exciting I mean it really does something to you really inside you.

Now is it the business of the newspapers is it the business of an historian to be exciting well I do not think so that is I do not think that it is the business of the newspaper to be exciting and I think in their hearts they really know this thing they know it is not their business to be exciting.

About the historian, the biographer and the autobiographer that is another matter and pretty soon later we will have to go into that.

What is it that is exciting, and how can exciting be soothing if it looks like excitement and is therefore soothing or if it is exciting and is therefore soothing or if it is as if it were exciting and is therefore soothing or not soothing, all these things have to be a great deal thought about if you are to understand anything if I am to understand anything about newspaper writing about any writing about anything being or not being written.

It is a very curious thing that a story told by any one about anything that has not really been exciting is exciting and a story told about anything that really has been exciting is not exciting.

It is a very curious thing this thing.

In thinking about plays I came to the conclusion that in real life the climax of a really exciting scene is completion and the climax of a made up exciting thing a written exciting thing is a relief and that it is not really possible to remember the climax of a real scene because you can not remember completion but you can remember relief.

Now the same thing is true when the newspaper tells about any real thing, the real thing having happened it is completed and being completed can not be remembered because the thing in its essence being completed there is no emotion in remembering it, it is a fact like any other and having been done it is for the purposes of memory a thing having no vitality. While anything which is a relief and in a made up situation as it gets more and more exciting when the exciting rises to being really exciting then it is a relief then it is a thing that has emotion when that thing is a remembered thing.

Now you must see how true this is about the crime story and the actual crime. The actual crime is a crime that is a fact and it having been done that in itself is a completion and so for purposes of memory with very rare exceptions where a personality connected with it is overpowering there is no memory to bother any one. Completion is completion, a thing done is a thing done and so it has in it no quality of ending or beginning. Therefore in real life it is the crime and as the newspaper has to feel about it as if it were in the act of seeing or doing it, they cannot really take on detecting they can only take on the crime, they cannot take on anything that takes on beginning and ending and in the detecting end of detective stories there is nothing but going on beginning and ending. Anybody does naturally feel that, that a detective is just that that detecting is just that that it is a continuity of beginning and ending and really nothing but that.

And so you have this curious situation. Newspapers are written as if what is happening is happening as they are writing and as it is happening in that way they can have in them no beginning and ending but after all they are writing and they are writing not as it is happening not as it the newspaper is printing or being read and yet all that has to be as if it were.

As I say they try to bridge the gap in every way. Head lines were invented to help them do this better, they are all taught exactly how it can be done and as they are so well taught finally it happens not as if it had begun but as if it had never been done. Finally the newspaper gets its readers so that it does not make any difference whether any event can or will happen as long as the newspaper can go on getting larger and larger with anything or smaller and smaller with anything, and always tell be telling that thing, that they are larger and larger and smaller and smaller in telling everything. That is what is finally happening that everybody has to know what everybody or anybody does but does anybody have it as a feeling what anybody or everybody does no not at all.

And so that is what the newspaper is.

And that brings us nearer and nearer to the writing of history of biography of autobiography, I keep getting nearer and nearer but am I really near enough.

We now know what the newspaper is and what it does and

why it has to be made easier and easier because the more
completely in every way everybody anybody knows anything
knows everything that is always happening the more easily,
the more easy it is to make it easy for any one to know this
thing what is always happening.

A newspaper man is trained to make this easy by never
changing, nothing must ever be changing, things are happening but nothing must ever be changing about their being happening, the newspaper must never give to any one reading it
a feeling that anything is changing about something being
always happening, if it ever could or would or should then
any one would come to have some suspicion that there might
be a beginning and ending to anything and if there is a beginning and ending to anything then it destroys the simplicity
of something always happening.

It is all a very curious thing but this is a true story of newspaper writing and the detective fiction just completely the
other way progresses by a continuous beginning and ending
and once more therefore destroys itself into not existing. It is
too bad because it might have been yes it might have been
something but always beginning and ending is as destructive
to existing as never beginning and ending.

You do see this thing.

And now let us begin to think about another thing, about
the feeling of a thing being existing even when it is a happening as the newspaper has it be.

Is a thing realler because not that you have really seen it
but you have seen the place where it did happen. That is to
say is there more beginning and end to it if you know what
it looks like the place the actual place where the thing happened.

It seems to have more beginning and ending to it then and
perhaps it really has not really has but gives the emotion of
reality somewhat clearer.

It is for this reason that local newspapers have a different
way of saying that anything is happening from metropolitan
newspapers. The small local newspaper has the feeling that
they are telling not what is happening as something that is
happening but they are telling what happened to some one
whom every one may or may not know but might know and

certainly any one does know the exact spot the very place where the thing that happened has happened, that makes small town newspapers have a slightly different feeling about what is happening than the big newspaper and therefore they might if they were not a newspaper they might bring any one that is every one to have the feeling that writing which is not what is happening gives any one.

Why is it that even the small newspaper which has to help them the local feeling of the place the actual place that anything that has happened why have they no intensity in their writing such as any one describing anything made up inside them can give to that writing.

Why is it.

Oh why is it.

Think of Defoe, he tried to write Robinson Crusoe as if it were exactly what did happen and yet after all he is Robinson Crusoe and Robinson Crusoe is Defoe and therefore after all it is not what is happening it is what is happening to him to Robinson Crusoe that makes what is exciting every one. You cannot go over it too often and so you can come you will come to know everything about anything being written.

I have come as far as this and it is really quite far to have come yes it is it really is quite far to have come and still all history and autobiography and biography have yet to come that is it is here but we have yet to come to know how and where it does come from.

Next time I am going to write more history for you, autobiography I have already done, biography I have already done I will tell you about that one, and so slowly yes slowly I will come to some knowing what it is that makes anything what it is what it was and what it has become.

But really and truly all about history and biography and autobiography will be both finished and begun oh yes it will yes it will it really will be both finished and begun in the next one.

WHAT ARE MASTER-PIECES
AND WHY ARE THERE
SO FEW OF THEM

What Are Master-pieces
and Why Are There So Few of Them

I WAS almost going to talk this lecture and not write and read it because all the lectures that I have written and read in America have been printed and although possibly for you they might even being read be as if they had not been printed still there is something about what has been written having been printed which makes it no longer the property of the one who wrote it and therefore there is no more reason why the writer should say it out loud than anybody else and therefore one does not.

Therefore I was going to talk to you but actually it is impossible to talk about master-pieces and what they are because talking essentially has nothing to do with creation. I talk a lot I like to talk and I talk even more than that I may say I talk most of the time and I listen a fair amount too and as I have said the essence of being a genius is to be able to talk and listen to listen while talking and talk while listening but and this is very important very important indeed talking has nothing to do with creation. What are master-pieces and why after all are there so few of them. You may say after all there are a good many of them but in any kind of proportion with everything that anybody who does anything is doing there are really very few of them. All this summer I meditated and wrote about this subject and it finally came to be a discussion of the relation of human nature and the human mind and identity. The thing one gradually comes to find out is that one has no identity that is when one is in the act of doing anything. Identity is recognition, you know who you are because you and others remember anything about yourself but essentially you are not that when you are doing anything. I am I because my little dog knows me but, creatively speaking the little dog knowing that you are you and your recognising that he knows, that is what destroys creation. That is what makes school. Picasso once remarked I do not care who it is that has or does influence me as long as it is not myself.

It is very difficult so difficult that it always has been difficult but even more difficult now to know what is the relation of human nature to the human mind because one has to know what is the relation of the act of creation to the subject the creator uses to create that thing. There is a great deal of non-sense talked about the subject of anything. After all there is always the same subject there are the things you see and there are human beings and animal beings and everybody you might say since the beginning of time knows practically commencing at the beginning and going to the end everything about these things. After all any woman in any village or men either if you like or even children know as much of human psychology as any writer that ever lived. After all there are things you do know each one in his or her way knows all of them and it is not this knowledge that makes master-pieces. Not at all not at all at all. Those who recognise master-pieces say that is the reason but it is not. It is not the way Hamlet reacts to his father's ghost that makes the master-piece, he might have re-acted according to Shakespeare in a dozen other ways and everybody would have been as much impressed by the psy-chology of it. But there is no psychology in it, that is not probably the way any young man would react to the ghost of his father and there is no particular reason why they should. If it were the way a young man could react to the ghost of his father then that would be something anybody in any vil-lage would know they could talk about it talk about it end-lessly but that would not make a master-piece and that brings us once more back to the subject of identity. At any moment when you are you you are you without the memory of yourself because if you remember yourself while you are you you are not for purposes of creating you. This is so important because it has so much to do with the question of a writer to his audience. One of the things that I discovered in lecturing was that gradually one ceased to hear what one said one heard what the audience hears one say, that is the reason that oratory is practically never a master-piece very rarely and very rarely history, because history deals with people who are orators who hear not what they are not what they say but what their au-dience hears them say. It is very interesting that letter writing has the same difficulty, the letter writes what the other person is to hear and so entity does not exist there are two present instead of one and so once again creation breaks down. I once wrote in writing *The Making of Americans* I write for myself and strangers but that was merely a literary formalism for if I did write for myself and strangers if I did I would not really be writing because already then identity would take the place of entity. It is awfully difficult, action is direct and effective but after all action is necessary and anything that is necessary has to do with human nature and not with the human mind. Therefore a master-piece has essentially not to be necessary, it has to be that is it has to exist but it does not have to be necessary it is not in response to necessity as action is because the minute it is necessary it has in it no possibility of going on.

To come back to what a master-piece has as its subject. In writing about painting I said that a picture exists for and in itself and the painter has to use objects landscapes and people as a way the only way that he is able to get the picture to exist. That is every one's trouble and particularly the trouble just now when every one who writes or paints has gotten to be abnormally conscious of the things he uses that is the events the people the objects and the landscapes and fundamentally the minute one is conscious deeply conscious of these things as a subject the interest in them does not exist.

You can tell that so well in the difficulty of writing novels or poetry these days. The tradition has always been that you may more or less describe the things that happen you imagine them of course but you more or less describe the things that happen but nowadays everybody all day long knows what is happening and so what is happening is not really interesting, one knows it by radios cinemas newspapers biographies autobiographies until what is happening does not really thrill any one, it excites them a little but it does not really thrill them. The painter can no longer say that what he does is as the world looks to him because he cannot look at the world any more, it has been photographed too much and he has to say that he does something else. In former times a painter said he painted what he saw of course he didn't but anyway he could say it, now he does not want to say it because seeing it is not interesting. This has something to do with master-pieces and why there are so few of them but not everything.

So you see why talking has nothing to do with creation, talking is really human nature as it is and human nature has nothing to do with master-pieces. It is very curious but the detective story which is you might say the only really modern novel form that has come into existence gets rid of human nature by having the man dead to begin with the hero is dead to begin with and so you have so to speak got rid of the event before the book begins. There is another very curious thing about detective stories. In real life people are interested in the crime more than they are in detection, it is the crime that is the thing the shock the thrill the horror but in the story it is the detection that holds the interest and that is natural enough because the necessity as far as action is concerned is the dead man, it is another function that has very little to do with human nature that makes the detection interesting. And so always it is true that the master-piece has nothing to do with human nature or with identity, it has to do with the human mind and the entity that is with a thing in itself and not in relation. The moment it is in relation it is common knowledge and anybody can feel and know it and it is not a master-piece. At the same time every one in a curious way sooner or later does feel the reality of a master-piece. The thing in itself of which the human nature is only its clothing does hold the attention. I have meditated a great deal about that. Another curious thing about master-pieces is, nobody when it is created there is in the thing that we call the human mind something that makes it hold itself just the same. The manner and habits of Bible times or Greek or Chinese have nothing to do with ours today but the master-pieces exist just the same and they do not exist because of their identity, that is what any one remembering then remembered then, they do not exist by human nature because everybody always knows everything there is to know about human nature, they exist because they came to be as something that is an end in itself and in that respect it is opposed to the business of living which is relation and necessity. That is what a master-piece is not although it may easily be what a master-piece talks about. It is another one of the curious difficulties a master-piece has that is to begin and end, because actually a master-piece does not do that it does not begin and end if it did it would be of necessity and in relation and that is just what a master-piece is not. Everybody worries about that just now everybody that is what makes them talk about abstract and worry about punctuation and capitals and small letters and what a history is. Everybody worries about that not because everybody knows what a master-piece is but because a certain number have found out what a master-piece is not. Even the very master-pieces have always been very bothered about beginning and ending because essentially that is what a master-piece is not. And yet after all like the subject of human nature master-pieces have to use beginning and ending to become existing. Well anyway anybody who is trying to do anything today is desperately not having a beginning and an ending but nevertheless in some way one does have to stop. I stop.

I do not know whether I have made any of this very clear, it is clear, but unfortunately I have written it all down all summer and in spite of everything I am now remembering and when you remember it is never clear. This is what makes secondary writing, it is remembering, it is very curious you begin to write something and suddenly you remember something and if you continue to remember your writing gets very confused. If you do not remember while you are writing, it may seem confused to others but actually it is clear and eventually that clarity will be clear, that is what a master-piece is, but if you remember while you are writing it will seem clear at the time to any one but the clarity will go out of it that is what a master-piece is not.

All this sounds awfully complicated but it is not complicated at all, it is just what happens. Any of you when you write you try to remember what you are about to write and you will see immediately how lifeless the writing becomes that is why expository writing is so dull because it is all remembered, that is why illustration is so dull because you remember what somebody looked like and you make your illustration look like it. The minute your memory functions while you are doing anything it may be very popular but actually it is dull. And that is what a master-piece is not, it may be unwelcome but it is never dull.

And so then why are there so few of them. There are so few of them because mostly people live in identity and memory that is when they think. They know they are they because their little dog knows them, and so they are not an entity but an identity. And being so memory is necessary to make them exist and so they cannot create master-pieces. It has been said of geniuses that they are eternally young. I once said what is the use of being a boy if you are going to grow up to be a man, the boy and the man have nothing to do with each other, except in respect to memory and identity, and if they have anything to do with each other in respect to memory and identity then they will never produce a master-piece. Do you do you understand well it really does not make much difference because after all master-pieces are what they are and the reason why is that there are very few of them. The reason why is any of you try it just not to be you are you because your little dog knows you. The second you are you because your little dog knows you you cannot make a master-piece and that is all of that.

It is not extremely difficult not to have identity but it is extremely difficult the knowing not having identity. One might say it is impossible but that it is not impossible is proved by the existence of master-pieces which are just that. They are knowing that there is no identity and producing while identity is not.

That is what a master-piece is.

And so we do know what a master-piece is and we also know why there are so few of them. Everything is against them. Everything that makes life go on makes identity and everything that makes identity is of necessity a necessity. And the pleasures of life as well as the necessities help the necessity of identity. The pleasures that are soothing all have to do with identity and the pleasures that are exciting all have to do with identity and moreover there is all the pride and vanity which play about master-pieces as well as about every one and these too all have to do with identity, and so naturally it is natural that there is more identity that one knows about than any-thing else one knows about and the worst of all is that the only thing that any one thinks about is identity and thinking is something that does so nearly need to be memory and if it is then of course it has nothing to do with a master-piece.

But what can a master-piece be about mostly it is about

identity and all it does and in being so it must not have any. I was just thinking about anything and in thinking about anything I saw something. In seeing that thing shall we see it without it turning into identity, the moment is not a moment and the sight is not the thing seen and yet it is. Moments are not important because of course master-pieces have no more time than they have identity although time like identity is what they concern themselves about of course that is what they do concern themselves about.

Once when one has said what one says it is not true or too true. That is what is the trouble with time. That is what makes what women say truer than what men say. That is undoubtedly what is the trouble with time and always in its relation to master-pieces. I once said that nothing could bother me more than the way a thing goes dead once it has been said. And if it does it it is because of there being this trouble about time.

Time is very important in connection with master-pieces, of course it makes identity time does make identity and identity does stop the creation of master-pieces. But time does something by itself to interfere with the creation of master-pieces as well as being part of what makes identity. If you do not keep remembering yourself you have no identity and if you have no time you do not keep remembering yourself and as you remember yourself you do not create anybody can and does know that.

Think about how you create if you do create you do not remember yourself as you do create. And yet time and identity is what you tell about as you create only while you create they do not exist. That is really what it is.

And do you create yes if you exist but time and identity do not exist. We live in time and identity but as we are we do not know time and identity everybody knows that quite simply. It is so simple that anybody does know that. But to know what one knows is frightening to live what one lives is soothing and though everybody likes to be frightened what they really have to have is soothing and so the master-pieces are so few not that the master-pieces themselves are frightening no of course not because if the creator of the master-piece is frightened then he does not exist without the memory of time and identity, and insofar as he is that then he is frightened and insofar as he is frightened the master-piece does not exist, it looks like it and it feels like it, but the memory of the fright destroys it as a master-piece. Robinson Crusoe and the footstep of the man Friday is one of the most perfect examples of the non-existence of time and identity which makes a master-piece. I hope you do see what I mean but any way everybody who knows about Robinson Crusoe and the footstep of Friday knows that that is true. There is no time and identity in the way it happened and that is why there is no fright.

And so there are very few master-pieces of course there are very few master-pieces because to be able to know that is not to have identity and time but not to mind talking as if there was because it does not interfere with anything and to go on being not as if there were no time and identity but as if there were and at the same time existing without time and identity is so very simple that it is difficult to have many who are that. And of course that is what a master-piece is and that is why there are so few of them and anybody really anybody can know that.

What is the use of being a boy if you are going to grow up to be a man. And what is the use there is no use from the standpoint of master-pieces there is no use. Anybody can really know that.

There is really no use in being a boy if you are going to grow up to be a man because then man and boy you can be certain that that is continuing and a master-piece does not continue it is as it is but it does not continue. It is very interesting that no one is content with being a man and boy but he must also be a son and a father and the fact that they all die has something to do with time but it has nothing to do with a master-piece. The word timely as used in our speech is very interesting but you can any one can see that it has nothing to do with master-pieces we all readily know that. The word timely tells that master-pieces have nothing to do with time.

It is very interesting to have it be inside one that never as you know yourself you know yourself without looking and feeling and looking and feeling make it be that you are some one you have seen. If you have seen any one you know them as you see them whether it is yourself or any other one and so the identity consists in recognition and in recognising you lose identity because after all nobody looks as they look like, they do not look like that we all know that of ourselves and of any one. And therefore in every way it is a trouble and so you write anybody does write to confirm what any one is and the more one does the more one looks like what one was and in being so identity is made more so and that identity is not what any one can have as a thing to be but as a thing to see. And it being a thing to see no master-piece can see what it can see if it does then it is timely and as it is timely it is not a master-piece.

There are so many things to say. If there was no identity no one could be governed, but everybody is governed by everybody and that is why they make no master-pieces, and also why governing has nothing to do with master-pieces it has completely to do with identity but it has nothing to do with master-pieces. And that is why governing is occupying but not interesting, governments are occupying but not interesting because master-pieces are exactly what they are not.

There is another thing to say. When you are writing before there is an audience anything written is as important as any other thing and you cherish anything and everything that you have written. After the audience begins, naturally they create something that is they create you, and so not everything is so important, something is more important than another thing, which was not true when you were you that is when you were not you as your little dog knows you.

And so there we are and there is so much to say but anyway I do not say that there is no doubt that master-pieces are master-pieces in that way and there are very few of them.

THE GEOGRAPHICAL HISTORY
OF AMERICA

or

THE RELATION OF HUMAN NATURE
TO THE HUMAN MIND

The Geographical History
of America

or

The Relation of Human Nature
to the Human Mind

IN THE MONTH of February were born Washington Lincoln
and I.

These are ordinary ideas if you please these are ordinary
ideas.

Let us not talk about disease but about death. If nobody
had to die how would there be room for any of us who now
live to have lived. We never could have been if all the others
had not died. There would have been no room.

Now the relation of human nature to the human mind is
this.

Human nature does not know this.

Human nature cannot know this.

What is it that human nature does not know. Human nature
does not know that if every one did not die there would be
no room for those who live now.

Human nature can not know this.

Now the relation of human nature to the human mind is
this.

Human nature cannot know this.

But the human mind can. It can know this.

In the United States there is more space where nobody is
than where anybody is.

This is what makes America what it is.

Does it make human nature in America what it is. If not it
does make the human mind in America what it is.

But there being so much space in America where nobody
is has nothing to do with this that if nobody had ever died
that is if everybody had not died there would not be room
here for anybody who is alive now.

This is the way human nature can sleep it can sleep by not
knowing this. The human mind can sleep by knowing this.

Until it knows this the human mind cannot sleep and sleep well human nature and the human mind can sleep.

After all would do we like to live to have lived then if we do then everybody else has had to die and we have to cry because we too one day we too will have to die otherwise the others who will like to live could not come by.

This is what makes religion and propaganda and politics this and with this the human mind and human nature.

And the human mind can know this but human nature cannot know this and so the human mind pretty well does not know this.

A dog can go to sleep standing and not know the reason why.

A man can go to sleep standing and that is the reason why, he can go to sleep standing but he prefers not to. For this there is no reason why.

Yes and yet this this is what makes everybody say what they do if they do say what they do say.

And everybody does say what they do say.

This makes propaganda and politics and religion.

And some say that we have all these things now.

And have we any of all these things now and have we any reason why why we have these things now but perhaps we have not these things now. A Geographical history is very important when connected with all this.

Nobody knows any more about human nature and the human mind than that.

Individualism that is human nature and the human mind communism that is human nature and the human mind and why do they go on saying so and not.

Because here is the pause they pause and the cause the cause is that they pause and they cannot pause.

Man is man was man will be gregarious and solitary, he will be because it is his nature to he will be because he has a mind to and even once more it is more and more and more as if he wants to.

What has the human mind got to do with talking.

Just that, what you say makes you want to say it again and what you say wants to make you say it another way, say the same thing another or the other thing in some way.

Any way is another way if you say it the same way.

Individualism and communism they are not separate they are the same or else human nature would not be human nature but it is.

Any little dog says so.

He wants to turn away and he wants to be there with you.

Oh yes of course but as he has not a human mind he can act so he can do the two things at once but the human mind oh the human mind can not do the two things at once. That is wherein the human mind differs from human nature.

Idem the same.

If you please these are ordinary ideas.

As anybody sits and looks they do not necessarily look to see what they do see.

If they did see they would see that the dog would does run away and stay. Just like this. He feels like that any way.

Now anybody who loves money and anybody who loves loves money anybody who loves loves to have money.

The human mind can say yes and no the human mind can even know that there is yes and no, not every human mind not any human mind but the human mind, the human mind can know that there is yes and no.

Yes that is the way I mean to please.

Think how that sentence goes.

Yes that is the way I mean to, please.

Well anyway.

That is what I mean to be I mean to be the one who can and does have as ordinary ideas as these.

End of Chapter one.

If you stop to think about chapter one you will know that any one has had to die so that there is room for any one to be, that is if every one who had lived had not died where would we be.

In other words if everybody even if there had not been a great many but just only as many as there have been if anybody that is everybody had not died there would not be room here and now for anybody who is here here and now.

These are ordinary ideas.

Even in America where there is more space where there is nobody than where there is. Never to forget that.

These are ordinary ideas.

Chapter II

Extraordinary ideas.

Extraordinary ideas are just as ordinary as ordinary ideas because if you please everybody has to have or have had extraordinary ideas.

Do extraordinary ideas interfere with propaganda and communism and individualism and what are any and all ideas.

To know what ideas are you have to think of geographical history and the relation of the human mind to human nature.

What do they say.

What is the use of being a little boy if you are growing up to be a man.

What is the use of Franklin Roosevelt being like the third Napoleon.

What is the use.

What is the use of being a little boy if you are to grow up to be a man.

Chapter III

What is the use of being a little boy if you are going to grow up to be a man.

Neither human nature or the human mind thinks so. They do not think that there is no use in being a little boy if you are going to grow up to be a man.

And yet everybody does so unless it is a little girl going to grow up to be a woman.

But what is the use.

Use is here used in the sense of purpose.

Does it interfere with propaganda to really know this thing, what is the use of being a little boy if you are going to grow up to be a man.

Chapter one

What do they say.

They say that Washington and Lincoln and I were born in

that month the month of February and that this nobody can deny.

February is a short month but although February is a short month we Washington Lincoln and I were born in that month in that short month.

Not even now again can any one this deny, not they nor not I.

Chapter II

The human mind fails to be a human mind when it thinks because it cannot think that what is the use of being a little boy if you are going to grow up to be a man.

Now let the human mind think what it is to be a little boy and when the human mind has thought what it is to be a little boy the human mind will know that there is no use in being a little boy if you are going to grow up to be a man.

Human nature can not know that there is no use in being a little boy if he is to grow up to be a man.

There is then a connection between human nature and the human mind insofar as human nature cannot know that there is no use in being a little boy if he is to grow up to be a man and the human mind can well yes it can if it can it can know that there is no use in being a little boy if he is to grow up to be a man.

And then as it is to have these human nature and the human mind and the little boy and he has to grow up to be a man and is there any use in all of these then there is a geographical history of all these, you do feel that as it is where it is.

I can just see the way the land lies as all of these are there. And so can you. And so can you.

There is no question not any question as to which land lies over or under the seas. Salt lake country is over and under the seas only these is no sea. So much better that there is no sea because then the land can be seen and can see.

Chapter III which is the same as chapter XV

Do you see that there is the land which nobody can see because there is the sea, and yet there is the land in America there is the land salt lake land where there is no sea.

Chapter III

How can you tell if a country is young old or young young or old.

Is it because all the animals that have lived in it are dead in it.

Chapter IV

As long as nothing or very little that you write is published it is all sacred but after it is a great deal of it published is it everything that you write is it as sacred. That has to do with whether the animals dead in it make a country as old as if no animals were dead in it.

Has this to do with human nature or the human mind.

And does any one need to wonder why.

So in chapter three we consider these things the age of the world, the sacredness of writing and human nature and the human mind.

and
Geographical History.

Chapter III

What is the relation of human nature to the age of any country.

One cannot say it too often and it need not bring tears to your eyes what is the use of being a little boy if you are going to grow up to be a man what is the use.

An age of a country is not the same thing because after all it may be it even might be that human nature has nothing to do with it. But the human mind must have something to do with it although when to the human mind that country is old and when to the human mind that country is young that country need not necessarily be either young or old. Has the human mind really has the human mind anything to do with age or is that only human nature, human nature has undoubtedly to do with age but has the human mind, neither more nor less but has the human mind. Let me now in chapter IV tell any story of Geography and what it looks like and the human mind.

Chapter IV

Geography does not look like it does in relation to the human mind.

Not more or less but to begin with what man is man was man will be.

When children play tag they tag each other that is they touch each other to start, well dogs do that, they touch each other to start just as children do. A big dog touches a little dog to start him to play a white dog touched a black dog to start him to play a black dog will touch any dog to start him to play. When children do so it is called playing tag.

Any child does that.

And has the human mind anything to do with kidnapping perhaps yes perhaps no. Kidnapping means that they take anything away. But the human mind can never take anything away.

Dogs do so they mean and they do not mean to do so. But dogs cannot say I mean I mean. They can though they can say I mean I mean and they do, they also can say I forgot and they do they do both forget and they do say so and there is a reason why.

Anybody with a human mind can say I mean and they can say forgot and mean that. Forgetting is not an action of the human mind neither is remembering if it had to do with the human mind then the human mind would concern itself with age but it does not, therefore any nature can mean or not mean what they do they can forget or remember what they do but the human mind no the human mind has nothing to do with age.

As I say so tears come into my eyes.

Why does the human mind not concern itself with age.

Because the human mind knows what it knows and knowing what it knows it has nothing to do with seeing what it remembers, remember how the country looked as we passed over it, it made designs big designs like human nature draws them because it knows them without ever having seen them from above.

Why in an aeroplane is one not afraid of being high.

Because human nature has nothing to do with it.

Nothing.

I repeat yes and no nothing.

When you climb on the land high human nature knows because by remembering it has been a dangerous thing to go higher and higher on the land which is where human nature was but now in an aeroplane human nature is nothing remembering is nothing no matter how many have been killed from up there it is not anything that is a memory, because if you are killed you do not remember no you do not, it is only on land where it is dangerous but where you were not killed that you remember.

And so the human mind is like not being in danger but being killed, there is no remembering, no there is no remembering and no forgetting because you have to remember to forget no there is none in any human mind.

This brings us back to tag and kite flying and kidnapping and how they are related to the human mind.

Chapter V

The human mind when it is altogether the human mind what a pleasure to me. No this does not bring tears to anybody's eyes not even to mine and I might I might cry easily oh so very easily.

Kidnapping kite flying and tag and labour union and the Republican party and the human mind and what eight or as many places look like when it is just as high as it is when you pass over.

Looking down is the same as passing over.

Snow is always astonishing when it is looked at.

But not more astonishing when the trees the bare trees make shadows on it.

Dogs do behave as they please that is as they naturally please until they are told not to.

Anything like that is annoying and annoying has something to do with the human mind. It means it is attached and waits not to go away but to stay. In this way annoying or annoyance is a symptom of there being a human mind.

Yes a human mind.

And what is it.

Is it that all the same.

Chapter III

Beginning with tears.

Annoyance makes nobody cry.

But something does oh yes something does but should it.

Who has to know what word follows another.

I do. Although it is a mistake.

The human mind is not unlike that.

I do. Although it is perfectly a mistake.

If perfection is good more perfection is better is not said but might be said of the human mind.

Chapter IV

But any way any man that is women and children can talk all day or a piece of any day, dogs do too not in the same way not quite in the same way and that does make some difference between human beings and dogs.

I wish I could say that talking had to do with the human mind I wish I could say so and not cry I wish I could.

Chapter V

Does he or she does she or he know what the human mind is.

And so all the old chapters end tears end but all this has nothing to do with the human mind the use of the human mind and tears.

It has been said by very many said by Jules Verne he weeps that shows he is a man. But a dog can have tears in his eyes yes he can have tears in his eyes when he has been disillusioned.

A dog when he begged always got what he asked for.

One day he begged a little dog to give him what he wanted. The little dog did not give him what he wanted. The dog had tears in his eyes and so to cry does not make the human mind oh no to cry does not make the human mind it makes a piece of nature but it does not make the human mind.

The human mind has nothing to do with sorrow and with disappointment and with tears.

You can say to a dog look and long and he does, he even does without your saying so but and that is true human nature can look and long but not the human mind no not the human mind.

Oh dear does she does he does he does she know what the human mind is and if he does and if she does and if she does and if he does what is the human mind.

The human mind knows neither memory nor tears it can forget, but what can it forget, it can forget nothing but not be remembering indeed not by remembering and so he and she and she and he do know what the human mind is.

A dog does not know what the human mind is.

He only knows grief and disturbance and tears he only knows that if he has lost confidence he has lost confidence and he was born with that confidence lost.

The relation of human nature to the human mind makes everybody indifferent to remembering and forgetting to age and living to knowing that every one can die so that there may be room for all who are here now and so many people expect to prepare otherwise but they they do not know what the human mind is.

If there was no geography no geographical history would there be any human mind not as it is but would there would there be any human mind.

Anybody that can help this to go farther can go on with what the human mind is and so as indifferently as that we begin with Chapter one.

Chapter I

The human mind is.

The human mind has no relation to human nature at all. The question has been asked is it the relation of human nature to the human mind or is it the relation of the human mind to human nature. The answer is there is no relation between the human mind and human nature there is a relation between human nature and the human mind.

Chapter one.

What is it.

Chapter III

Does or does not a dog know that there is a human mind, no he does not know that there is a human mind he knows that there is human nature but not that there is a human mind.

Is or is not a dog born with his confidence gone. This is not an interesting question.

Chapter III

What is the relation of communism individualism propaganda to human nature what is the relation of it to the human mind or is there none. There is a human mind oh yes there is one. Is there any relation to it in communism individualism or propaganda and has all that only to do with human nature, has it has it, remember about tears and age and memory and swallows flying and birds which always sing the same thing to any one but not to themselves they the birds have tears but no memory.

How many animals birds and wild flowers are there in the United States and is it splendid of it to have any.

There are some places in the United States where they almost do not have any.

The United States is interesting because in it there are some in it that have no human nature at all just as in some places in it there are almost not any animals or flowers at all and this what has this to do with the relation of human nature to the human mind.

Anybody can have tears in their eyes when they hear dogs bark. Because which of it is it.

Chapter IV

Why Europe is too small to wage war.

Why is Europe too small to wage war because war has to be waged on too large a scale to be contained in a small country therefore as they think about war they know that they can only think and not do. They are like our dogs who make believe do things to each other but they know that they can be seen and if you can be seen then you cannot do anything to one another.

Therefore Europe is too small to wage war since anybody now can see it all and if anybody really anybody can see it all then they cannot wage war. They can have a great many troubles but they cannot wage war. Not wage war.

Also the geographical history of America.

Chapter V

Madame Reverdy was the wife of a hotel keeper. I say was because she is dead not awfully dead but still dead.

One of the things that makes a big country different from a little country makes the Geographical history of America different from the geographical history of Europe is that when anybody is dead they are dead.

So Madame Reverdy was the wife of a hotel keeper. In many hotels in small countries they never go out of the hotel. She never did and neither did he. He is not dead, not because he could live longer but because he is not dead.

She had four children that is they did three boys and a girl and the girl had a curl but she got very stout. She still is but not as stout as she was.

The three boys were very good looking when they were younger.

Now it is just the same as the older is married and the younger is a one lunger and the third is a cook. But all this had not happened when the mother was no longer their mother as she had become dead that is she had killed herself just as much to be dead as not. No one asked her to live longer but if she did it she did it not to live longer but to be a hotel keeper longer.

She had been awfully ready to be a hotel keeper but she had been not awfully ready not to live longer. She is dead as much dead as if she had not lived longer.

No one can come to know what happens to any one although everybody listens to any one who tells about what happened to any one.

I feel that it is a failure not to live longer.

So they say.

And so Europe can stay but it cannot wage war any longer.

This is what all the world is that it cannot wage war any longer and so it might just as well stop. Human nature is not interesting any longer and so it might just as well stop being human nature any longer.

Chapter VI

The portrait of Thornton Wilder.

In china china is not china it is an earthen ware. In China there is no need of China because in China china is china.

All who liked china like China and have china.

China in America is not an earthen ware.

All who like China in America like china in America and all who like china in America do not like to have china in china to be an earthen ware. Therefore it is not.

Remember therefore it is not but better not remember.

It is better not to remember because there is no such thing no such thing as remember. Therefore there is not.

All allow no one allow, no one to allow no one to remember.

It is left to be right not to remember because not to remember is as much left as not left to remember.

It is no doubt a resistance to yield to all. Not to yield at all.

Oh no remember there is a great difference between to yield at all but not to yield at all.

Do not remember because it is not to remember that makes it be theirs as well as the.

A portrait celebrated as the portrait of Thornton Wilder.

I wish I knew a history was a history.

And tears.

I wish I knew a history as a history which is not which is not there are no fear.

He has no fears.

At most he has no tears.

For them very likely he is made of them.

It is too bad that fears rhymes with tears.

Very likely for them.

But which I beseech you to say.

Chapter VII

I cannot be accused too often of liking to hear and see everything and yet everything which is heard and which is seen has nothing no nothing no no nothing to do with the human mind. No nothing.

And yet the human mind there is the human mind.

Human nature now is not at all interesting.

Chapter II

Did you hear your husband heave a heavy sigh.

Nobody knows how happy it is to have anything round like that.

This chapter is to be all about when words how words do words look like that.

Like it did when I looked at it, there there where I saw it.

Beneath me when I was above it.

If there was only human nature there would be words but they would not be like that.

Chapter III

There is no real reality to a really imagined life any more.

Nothing I like more than when a dog barks in his sleep.

That is a reality that can be known not by listening but by the dog who is asleep and feels like barking, he barks as if he barks and it is a bark it really is a bark although he is only dreaming. How much does he know that he is barking.

Human nature moves around and does the human mind move around.

What is the difference between remembering what has been happening and remembering what has been as dreaming. None. Therefore there is no relation between human nature and the human mind.

When they say do not read or know this because you do not understand it what does it mean.

To understand a thing means to be in contact with that thing and the human mind can be in contact with anything.

Human nature can be connected with anything but it can not be in contact with anything.

Any minute then is anything if there is a human mind.

Any minute is not anything if there is human nature.

But any minute is anything so then there is a human mind.

Think of how very often there is not, there is not a human mind and so any minute is not anything.

Any one can see that human nature can not make any minute be anything.

They ask me is there any progressing and I answer and now human nature is not interesting why of course not it is not interesting. It is there to be sure it is there but just now it is not interesting.

Chapter I

One and one makes two but not in minutes. No never again in minutes.

That is what is the human mind. There is nothing in it about minutes. Progressing of course there is no progressing no there is the human mind not interesting but being there yes just as well as not.

Chapter II

If some one says and how is Rachel and you say very well I thank you that means that Rachel does belong to you.

How is America. Very well I thank you. This is the reply. If you say I thank you that means that in a way it belongs to you. Very well I thank you.

Human nature is what any human being will do. And the human mind. Tears come into my eyes when I say the human mind. Tears do not come into my eyes they are the feeling of tears my eyes are the feeling of tears. And not because I say the human mind. But because there is the human mind. Oh yes there is a human mind. Not entirely at a glance not at all at a glance. When she says look at the roses is the human nature or the human mind.

She will tell me, yes she will tell me if when she says look at the roses whether that is human nature or the human mind.

Human nature is what any human being will do.

That is a very satisfactory thing to say.

And the human mind is the way they tell what any human being has or does or may or can do.

Not at all not at all not at all.

That has nothing to do with the human mind. That is the same thing as saying that human speech is the same thing as the human mind and it is not.

Whether or whether not the human mind could exist if there had been no human speech this I do not know but this I do know that the human mind is not the same thing as human speech. Has one anything to do with the other is writing a different thing, oh yes and this is so exciting so satisfying so tender that it makes everything everything writing has nothing to do with the human speech with human nature and therefore and therefore it has something to do with the human mind.

Take an example a dog can tag another dog to start him playing and he remembers this and does it again not because if he remembers it but because it is the way he does.

Now a little girl or boy tags too to start the other one but he says so he says I tagged you and he says I will tag you and he says did you tag him and he says I can tag you if I want to.

This might be the human mind but it is not.

Any little child has to be taught to play tag because although any dog does play tag this way and so any child can play tag this way any child can be taught to be play tag this way.

This has nothing to do with human nature this has to do with the human mind.

So then human nature can talk but so can any dog.

But the human mind can write and so cannot any dog and so human writing is not human nature it is the human mind.

What it looks like when it sees when it is seen, that may make human nature what it is but not the human mind although tears can almost come to its eyes, oh not the human mind, no not the human mind.

When any one looks and sees how what it sees looks like it cannot not know whether it is human nature or the human mind but it can know it will know and therefore as it looks at it all it can know that human nature is not the human mind. Once as a piece. Or even twice or more as a piece.

A piece is only a little way and it must finish even if the world is round and the land on it is flat as it is like a carpet as it is but the human mind can not remember that. The human mind can not remember no cannot remember, yes that is that.

When anything looks like it is and it is land and anybody writing or painting says it is that no one needs to remember that.

Chapter IX

How looking at it does not make it different from what it looks like.

That is why they make it like that not because the look at it but because it is like that. Yes the human mind.

Chapter X

A description of how the land the American land the land in America looks and is flat is and looks flat.

Chapter I

Some dogs eyes in the night give out a red ruby light and some dog's eyes at night are green.

Has this anything to do with the human mind. It might.

It can have nothing to do with human nature that can easily be seen. Seen is here used in the sense of known.

All these things have something to do with excitement and has excitement anything to do with the human mind.

Any dog can get excited he can know that he can get excited and he can know that he intends to get excited and he can gradually get forced to get excited although he does not care about it. Human nature is like that and the human mind. Here we commence to come to one of the complete problems concerning the human mind. I must ask every one with or without tears in my eyes has excitement anything to do with the human mind.

Has it to do with geography.

It has undoubtedly to do with politics and propaganda and government and being here and there and society has it anything to do with writing. Has it in short has it now there are no tears in my eyes has it to do with the human mind.

Chapter II

What has excitement got to do with geography and how does the land the American land look from above from below and from custom and from habit.

Are there any customs and habits in America there is geography and what what is the human mind. The human mind is there because they write and they do not forget or remember and they do not go away and come back again. That is what the human mind does not human nature but the human mind. Listen to the human mind.

I will tell a story about the human mind what is the story. It is the story of Bennett.

Bennett has an uncle who is as young as he is that is to say he is about the same age and age has nothing to do with the human mind.

When a great many hear you that is an audience and if a great many hear you what difference does it make.

Bennett and his uncle do not know anything about that.

And why not. Because that has nothing to do with the human mind.

Bennett's uncle has nothing to do with the human mind because he listens to the human mind and if you listen to the human mind is there a human mind to which you listen.

Bennett's uncle has nothing to do with human nature because human nature well if you have tears for human nature and gradually human nature has no tears how can you have human nature.

And this and this brings us to this that human nature has now no tears and this this is all because of the history of geography, geography now having come to be what it is the land lying as it does and any one looking at it seeing it as it is there are no more tears in human nature.

And so where where is Bennett's uncle, he is not with the human mind because he listens to the human mind and he is not with human nature because there are no tears in human nature. Where is Bennett. Bennett is there, because Bennett does not listen to the human mind and because he has no tears with human nature and so Bennett is what he is. And what is that and how many are that.

It has been said, that if everybody had gone on living there would not be any room here now where we all are for those of us who are here now this includes Bennett and Bennett's uncle. And this would make his uncle cry if being one were to die but not Bennett Bennett would not cry because Bennett as Bennett knows that he is human nature and human nature does not cry not now not unless human nature is tired human nature can be tired but is human nature tired now, no not now.

Is it exciting not to cry. Yes and no and Bennett knows that this is so.

Chapter III

There are no chapters in the life of Bennett but there are chapters in the life of the Uncle of Bennett because he knows and as he knows he knows that some time is a time that he can look forward and remember and if you can then that is not the human mind. The human mind cannot does not look forward and remember and so really and truly Bennett's uncle cannot listen to the human mind. And so he is a communist. A communist and individualist a propagandist a politician cannot listen to the human mind, a business man can and anybody who can sit and write can he can listen to the human mind. Can Bennett, well I do not know whether Bennett can.

What you cannot eat you can.

Yes Bennett.

Chapter IV

The world as we see it looks like this.

They used to think that the world was there as we see it but this is not so the world is there as it is human nature is there as it is and the human mind. The human mind knows this, that everything is there as it is.

Only the human mind knows that and that is the reason that it is not what anybody says but what anybody writes that has to do what it has to do with the human mind.

That is what makes the comic strip, Mr. And Mrs. the success it is, it is that the human mind knows that it is what it is. It even knows that human nature is what it is therefore it need not remember or forget no the human mind does not remember because how can you remember when anything is what it is.

Or how can you forget when anything is what it is.

Bless a wife who has made this clear.

Chapter V

And so a great many birds hop and sing.

Anything is what it is.

Chapter VI

There are birds in America but I have not noticed them not as much as I have noticed them here.

There are a great many birds in America but I did not notice them.

I do notice them here. You notice birds if you sit with them. That is natural as birds are always twittering singing and flying. They come in and go out again so naturally as with the dogs you notice them if you are sitting.

I noticed some animals over there, it is natural to notice them as if they were wild ones living naturally when they used to be wild ones.

By their used to be wild ones it is meant that no one was interested then in their being there except as they were there that is when they were wild ones as if they were wild ones. Now they see to it that they are still wild but continue to be there. That is what makes it be America over there that no one knows the difference between human nature and the wild animals there because there is more not being wild but being ones there there is more now there that they live as easily as anything since no one intends that anything should happen to any one of them. In other words there in America wild ones are as if they were there with nothing to happen to them as if they lived there which they do so that nobody thinks they die there which they do.

That is what peace is but always there is some one who has not felt that this could be done that any wild animal living where it is living could naturally go on being living until it became dead. Dead is not interesting and yet it is not any more uninteresting than that to any animal or human nature.

So that is peace.

Suddenly it comes to be that anybody can be peacefully not knowing any other thing.

Has that anything to do with the land as it is and the human mind.

Just as likely as not there are no tears.

She says she wanted that she should be the only ideal one, but she is, what else is she but that, she is, and so the human mind rests with what is.

Yes which it is, that.

That is what they call it. That.

Chapter VII

Now I wish to say just what human nature is and what its relation is to the human mind.

I know so well the relation of a simple center and a continuous design to the land as one looks down on it, a wandering line as one looks down on it, a quarter section as one looks down on it, the shadow of each tree on the snow and the woods on each side and the land higher up between it and I know so well how in spite of the fact that the human mind has not looked at it the human mind has it to know that it is there like that, notwithstanding that the human mind has liked what it has which has not been like that.

Has the human mind anything to do with what it sees. Yes I think so. With what it likes. No I do not think so. With what it has. No I do not think so, with communism individualism propaganda politics and women no and yes I think so, I think it is not so. With the world as it has said it was. No I do not think so. Then what is the human mind. Has the human mind anything to do with question and answer. Perhaps no I do not think so.

Chapter IV

They say I am not right when I say that what you say is not the same as what you write but anybody try to write and they will say that this is so.

When you write well when you write anybody try to write and they will say that I am right.

What you say has nothing to do with what you write.

Does it rain in America oh yes and there is snow. High up and low down there is snow, snow snow really beautiful snow.

What is the difference between anything and anything.

Ah yes, well that is something to know.

What is the difference between as snow and as snow.

They say that when I say it is not what they say but what they write that has to do with the human mind they say when I say this that I am not right but I am right because I write this and I do not say this. When I say it it is not so but when I write it it is so. Anybody can know that this is so.

And so we come to what is really what we write what we write is really a crime story.

Why the writing of to-day has to do with the way any land can lay when it is the particularly flat land. That is what makes land connected with the human mind only flat land a great deal of flat land is connected with the human mind and so America is connected with the human mind, I can say I say so but what I do is to write it so. Think not the way the land looks but the way it lies that is now connected with the human mind.

And so and so and there is no real use for tears.

Only when her son has fallen off a cart and broken the small bones of his ankle in the midst of the harvest and cannot work for two months. Then it is nervousness that makes water come into her eyes.

Only when her son has fallen off a cart and when the small bones of his ankle are broken in the midst of the harvest and cannot work for two months.

Chapter II

The use of the human mind and its connection with what is being written.

Think of what anybody does they read what is or has been written. They do not read what is or has been said. Even on the radio it is written it is not said no not said.

Chapter III

You will find that all this is true when I get through.

Chapter I

All the witnesses of the autobiography are not filled with tears. If they are they are tears of anger not tears of sorrow and nervousness and excitement but really and truly it is necessary to cry when you read anything, crying gives pleasure to reading but it is has nothing to do with the human mind, it has nothing to do with writing.

But not in the home. Tears do not give pleasure in the home. They give pleasure in reading.

Does this show that reading has something to do with the human mind. It has been said that no one but human beings weep and therefore tears show that there is a human mind. Not in the home I repeat not in the home but in reading yes in reading.

And so listen, nervousness make tears and reading. Sorrow is another thing, sorrow can connect with reading. And so so many people read just as so many people sorrow they do not borrow sorrow nor reading, and what is its connection with the human mind.

It makes me uneasy when I think that here there is a question of the relation of human nature to the human mind and yet I am so sure that there is none no connection between human nature and the human mind no relation between human nature and the human mind.

Chapter II

The Witnesses of my autobiography. Think what an admirable title that would make for an autobiography think only think how many different titles have been invented for autobiographies, just think only think and it is astonishing always astonishing how many people can think of a new title for an autobiography. And yet autobiographies have nothing to do with the human mind, and they really have nothing to do with tears and reading. When they said reading made easy reading without tears and some one sent me such a beautiful copy of that, does that mean that tears have to do with the human mind as has been so often said.

And now there are no tears in reading. A movie star said, no matter how much or how many cry on the screen the audience remains dry eyed. Has that something to do with the fact that now there is no connection no relation between reading and the human mind.

Does it come down to that.

Has the human mind forgotten to come down to that.

I have been told that I have always been nervous and unoccupied, that I have never cared to fill my time with the things that fill it and that as a result I am not likely to remember or forget and therefore have I a human mind. Is it because of this that I have a human mind. Is it because of this that any one that has a human mind does that, does nothing to fill it.

Is that what makes it that.

And therefore there are no witnesses to the autobiography of any one that has a human mind.

Is this all that makes it that.

There is no reason why chapters should succeed each other since nothing succeeds another, not now any more. In the old novels yes but not now any more and so the human mind not succeeding one thing by another supposing everybody doing nothing should continue living. How about it.

Has that anything to do with the human mind.

No not when it is just like that.

One minute it means anything it has nothing to do with the human mind, with human nature yes, but not with the way the earth is and looks and not with the human mind. No nothing to do with the human mind.

Everybody knows just now how nothing succeeds anything.

And so just now yes just now the human mind is the human mind.

Chapter III

Venus is so big that it can have a ring around it like the moon.

Jo Alsop.

Chapter IV

I wish to show Jo Alsop why the human mind is not what he recognises when he says some minds say what they say. Any sound can say something but really that has nothing to do with the human mind. Let me make this clear to Jo Alsop. He is not a witness to an autobiography. Therefore he should be again told what is the human mind. He has not to be told what is human nature because he is not interested in human nature but he has to be told what is the human mind because although he is interested in the human mind he does not know that the human mind is not related to human nature.

Listen Jo Alsop while I make this clear.

Chapter V

Why is it not necessary to have chapters and if in spite of it not being necessary one does have them why do they not have to follow one another.

Nothing is known of the word necessary but Jo Alsop knows something of the word necessary oh yes he does, he says not but oh yes he does and is it because he does know something about the word necessary he does not know anything about the human mind. No one who knows the word necessary can say that he does or does not like it but Jo Alsop can. He can and he does.

Let us not weep for Jo Alsop or have tears in our eyes or in his.

And yet.

Once more the word necessary is not displaced. The human mind cannot be displaced. In that respect it is not the same as the word necessary.

Rest carefully to-night.

Chapter IV

Carefully is such a sweet word.

Chapter V

I do not know where I am going but I am on my way and then suddenly well not perhaps suddenly but perhaps yes I do know where I am going and I do not like it like that.

Because of this there is no such thing as one and one.

That has a great deal to do with the relation of human nature to the human mind it also has a great deal to do with the geographical history of America.

When suddenly you know that the geographical history of America has something to do with everything it may be like loving any man or any woman or even a little or a big dog. Yes it may, that is to say it does.

And why.

Why has nothing to do with that.

Some people like a big country and some people like a little one but it all depends it depends whether you can wander around a big one or a little one. Wandering around a country has something to do with the geographical history of that country and the way one piece of it is not separated from any other one. Can one say too often just as loving or tears in one's eyes that the straight lines on the map of the United States of America make wandering a mission and an everything and can it only be a big country that can be like that or even a little one. Anyway it has a great deal to do with the relation between human nature and the human mind and not remembering and not forgetting and not as much as having tears in one's eyes. No no tears in one's eyes, whatever any one else can say.

In wandering around a big country some people who live in a big country do not wander.

What has wandering got to do with the human mind or religion. But really wandering has something to do with the human mind. A big or a little country. Wandering in a big or a little country.

The relation of nervousness to excitement and the death and the death of René Crevel. René Crevel was not nervous he really was not excited and that is because he was in a country where no one wanders.

Chapter V

Any time after a war any one is nervous. They think they are excited but they are nervous.

You can see how that brings wandering and the human mind nearer nearer to what, nearer to nearer. But nearer has nothing to do with the human mind. Whether excitement has we do not yet know but we think so.

Chapter VI

Any one any time after a war is nervous.

They are not excited they are nervous and that has nothing to do either with human nature nor with the human mind.

Human nature has nothing to do with being nervous. When a dog is nervous it has nothing to do with the human mind.

And so rightly so being nervous has nothing to do with the relation of human nature to the human mind.

But has it to do with the human mind.

Chapter VII

How slowly nervousness is everything, and that is not true of excitement, which is not true of anything.

Has excitement anything to do with the human mind.

No hesitating.

Has excitement anything to do with the human mind. When you come as near as that to anything, it has nothing to do with nervousness.

Nervousness has nothing to do with anything but it always is there after a big war.

Please play and pay all respect to the dead, but not in America not where a country is so big that it is divided one part from the other by ruled lines and it has to be flat, it has to be flat, or there is no hope of it not paying respect to the dead.

René Crevel would have liked to have gone to America he always hoped for that.

But now he is dead.

He killed himself.

There is respect for the dead but not over there because so much of the land is flat.

I like it like that.

Chapter II

I could have begun with Chapter I but anybody even I have had enough of that.

Chapter II

But which are they when once a day they do not eat and they do not go away.

Mushrooms are very good to eat.

But we never gave any of them to René Crevel.

What is the relation of the human mind to a real person who has really lived or one that you mix up with whether he has really never been here or not.

We do not change when René Crevel has not been not ever been here yet.

Nobody ever heard of him but what has that to do with whether you will be excited about him.

Nothing at all nothing at all nothing at all.

But if he was all made up.

Something as well would have to do with human nature.

And the human mind.

I wonder.

Chapter III

I like the human mind.

Chapter IV

Human nature.

Human nature does not excite me but it does make me nervous.

Therefore human nature is like a great war, it makes you nervous.

It is not nervous but it makes you nervous.

And as it makes you nervous it has nothing to do with excitement or with the human mind.

I almost like all who tell me so.

And everybody tells me so tells me that human nature has nothing to do with excitement or the human mind because human nature makes you nervous.

And politics and geography and government and propaganda, well and what of it what of politics and geography and government and money and propaganda. Do they make you nervous. Do they.

Part II

Chapter I

There is always a relation between one thing and any other thing such as human nature and the human mind, between painting and what you paint between a black and a white dog although they are not related to each other.

Being a relation is one thing.

Just to-day I said is she a mother or a daughter.

Well anyway it might be though that anyway she would have had to have been a daughter.

But not at all. She might have been a granddaughter.

Being a relation is not a necessary thing.

Jo Alsop is he a relation.

Perhaps not.

René Crevel was.

Thornton Wilder is.

Sometime some one is as if he were an only son.

But is he a son at all.

May be he never has been.

Chapter II

It is very painful if it is true that not every nightingale can sing.

I could not say thing thing because I have never listened to any nightingale who could not sing.

I have listened when they began.

Is beginning singing.

For them they know that in America there are no nightingales although there are mocking birds.

And what have the mocking birds done.

They have spread.

They used to be only in the Eastern south, and now they go farther and farther North and they have gone West to Los Angeles and further and further north perhaps they will be all over, the national bird of the United States.

Some one who was born in California had never even heard one before.

All these things must be remembered in the relation of human nature to the human mind and the geographical history of America.

Chapter II

I should have hated the weather had it not been a pleasure not to hate the weather but to like cold weather. Weather has nothing to do with the human mind neither cold nor hot nor temperate nor violent weather. It has one may almost say nothing to do with human nature.

What is human nature.

Human nature resembles the nature that any human beings have. It is not necessarily it but it resembles it.

How can anything be dull even death if nothing resembles it. Whether they write or whether they do not they could not write if anything did or did not resemble any other thing. This is very important and no one can disturb anybody or anything.

Resemble and disturb.

Dogs play whether they want to or not with each other.

And now.

What is the resemblance between human nature and the human mind.

The human mind has no resemblances if it had it could not write that is to say write right.

There that is better than not said.

Chapter III

It is very likely that something always takes a long time.

A Play.

I say two dogs, but say a dog and a dog.

The human mind. The human mind does play. Of course the human mind does play.

Human nature. No human nature does not play, it might desire something but it does not play.

A dog plays because he plays again.

The human mind plays because it plays.

Human nature does not play because it does not play again.

And so to make nervousness and not excitement into a play.

And then to make excitement and not nervousness into a play.

And then to make a play with just the human mind.

Let us try.

A Play

Make.   There is no place to wait.
Wilder.   Made is not past make.

Call it all to order because perhaps here there has not been it all kept entirely in the human mind.

And so to begin again.

Make.   No instance of make.

Wilder.   Do not change wild to wilder.

Now make a play with human nature and not anything of the human mind.

Pivoines smell like dogs.

Dogs smell like dogs.

Men smell like men.

And gardens smell differently at different seasons of the year.

This is a mistake this is not human nature it comes more nearly having to do with the human mind.

Try a play again.

Even those who are just ordinary know what the human mind is. But not when they are drunk. Nobody knows what the human mind is when they are drunk.

Every little play helps.

Another play.

There is any difference between resting and waiting.

Be careful of analysis and analogy.

A play.

There is no in between in a play.

A play could just as well only mean two.

Then it could do.

It could really have to do.

With the human mind.

This is reading without tears but is there writing without tears.

Yes there is when you have been told not to cry.

Chapter IV

Everybody who has a grandfather has had a great grandfather and that great grandfather has had a father. This actually is true of a grandmother who was a granddaughter and her grandfather had a father.

He had brothers and they lived on where he had come from. They always wrote to one another. At any time anybody who knows how to write can write to one another.

But what do they write about.

They tell about the weather and sometimes what they have sold never what they have given to one another because and never forget that, they always have they always did they always can sell anything that is something to one another.

You may say I think you may say that no one can really give anything to anybody but anybody can sell something to somebody.

This is what makes the human mind and not human nature although a great many one might say anybody can say something about this not being so. But it is so.

And the human mind can live does live by anybody being able to sell something to somebody. That is what money is.

Believe it or not that is what money is and what the human mind is. The human nature perhaps not but of what interest is human nature. Any dog that does what it does does what human nature does and if not but if not why not and if why not what interest is that to the human mind. None at all. That is what the human mind is that human nature is not of any interest to it, it is not in any relation to it. That is why sex and jealousy is not the human mind it is human nature and therefore those any one writing letters does not write about that, they write about the weather and money and the family in its relation to money and the weather. Very likely not but most certainly so.

The grandfather of the grandmother went to America and there he was and now in reading all the letters he wrote to his brothers and they wrote to him he never mentioned anything but the weather and money and they always wrote about the weather and money and the family in their relation to so and so that is to weather and money and each other whether they had to do with each other and money and weather.

This is what they really do.

The newspapers tell about events but what have events to do with anything nothing nothing I tell you nothing events have nothing to do with anything nothing, the family of the grandfather and the grandmother was not interested in events because they did not know them and so they told about the weather and money and now everybody knows about the events but really nobody tells them they are still only interested in the weather and money.

Sure that is the way it is.

And why not. Of course there is not a why not.

Now that is one thing.

The other thing is that all the years and now it makes a good many years since the first real authors wrote what he had to say, China or Jews or Greeks or anybody else of who is whose, well what of it why this of it that reading it is alright now, now and then what is it, what they wrote they wrote and anybody can read anything anybody wrote.

Do you see that that means that events have nothing to do with the human mind nor has human nature anything to do with the human mind.

I wish it was as clear to anybody as it is to me even if it is not clear to me.

No she is not jealous she is clear about the necessity of being here.

Oh yes oh yes.

Feel quietly about feathers and goats.

If you say so that has to do with the human mind but not with human nature.

How easily it is not pleasurable to have to know about human nature.

But about the human mind the human mind is pleasurable it is only pleasurable and therefore they write.

Who write.

The human mind write.

What does the human mind write.

The human mind writes what it is.

Human nature cannot write what it is because human nature can not write.

The human mind can write what it is because what it is is all that it is and as it is all that it is all it can do is to write.

Yes that is right.

Of course it is right because and because and because that is why anybody can go on being able to read anything that has been written just as naturally as when it is or was written. If not why not.

There is no surprise in that. No surprise that writing can be read.

No surprise in that and yet not anybody says that that what anybody goes on reading is just that that which is not an event, Oh no, because nobody writes that. They write about weather and money, and weather and money have nothing to do with events or with human nature, they have to be the symbols of the human mind and the human mind is what it is and it writes that.

No one need have any doubt that there is no relation between human nature and the human mind.

There is none.

Chapter III

Just like a play.
Girls curl.
A grandmother uses napkins to make a dress.

Another Play.

But, But is a place where they can cease to distress her.

It is extraordinary that when you are acquainted with a whole family you can forget about them.

Another play.

It does not make any difference what happens to anybody if it does not make any difference what happens to them.

Program. She made a date with him which would not do.

Girls coming. There is no use in girls coming.

A man coming. Yes there is a great deal of use in a man coming but will he come at all if he does come will he come here.

Later when another man comes.

How do you like it if he comes and looks like that. Not at all later. Well any way he does come and if he likes it he will come again.

By and by. By and by is very fortunate it is partly what he takes and what he makes and very nearly partly what he does not hope that it will not do not do to do it after he does it.

What did they like. They liked partly liked everything which they needed very much.

There is no reason not to believe in the human mind.

Part IV

The question of identity

A Play

I am I because my little dog knows me.
Which is he.
No which is he.
Say it with tears, no which is he.
I am I why.
So there.
I am I where.

Act I Scene III

I am I because my little dog knows me.

Act I Scene I

Now that is the way I had played that play.
But not at all not as one is one.

Act I Scene I

Which one is there I am I or another one.
Who is one and one or one is one.
I like a play of acting so and so.
Leho Leho.
Leho is a name of a Breton.
But we we in America are not displaced by a dog oh no no not at all not at all at all displaced by a dog.

Scene I

The dog chokes over a ball because it is a ball that choked any one.

He likes to kindly remember that it is not of any interest.

Part I Scene I

He has forgotten that he has been choked by a ball no not forgotten because this one the same one is not the one that can choke any one.

Scene I Act I

I am I because my little dog knows me, but perhaps he does not and if he did I would not be I. Oh no oh no.

Act I Scene I

A dog this time has choked by himself only the choke resembles a sneeze, and it is bothersome.

When a dog is young he seems to be a very intelligent one. But later well later the dog is older.

Tears come into the eyes but not by blinking.

And so the dog roams around he knows the one he knows but does that make any difference.

A play is exactly that.

Here is the play.

Play I Act I

How are you what you are.

This has to do with human nature.

Chorus.   But human nature is neglected.

Yes of course human nature is neglected as neglected as any one.

Chorus   And the human mind.

Chorus   And the human mind.

Nobody is told to close.

Nobody is told to close about what the human mind is.

And so finally so.

Chorus   There is no left or right without remembering.

And remembering.

They say there is no left and right without remembering.

Chorus   But there is no remembering in the human mind.

Tears.   There is no chorus in the human mind.

The land is flat from on high and when they wander.

Chorus   There is flat land and weather and money for the human mind.

And so tears are vacant.

And so sale and sale and sale is not money.

But money.

Yes money.

Money has something to do with the human mind.

Nobody who has a dog forgets him. They may leave him behind. Oh yes they may leave him behind.

And the result.

May be and the result.

If I am I then my little dog knows me.

The dog listens while they prepare food.

Food might be connected with the human mind but it is not.

Scene II

And how do you like what you are.

And how are you what you are.

And has this to do with the human mind.

Chorus.   And has this to do with the human mind.

Chorus.   And is human nature not at all interesting.

Scene II

Do you understand anything better through knowing where it is or not.

Chorus   Or not.

Chorus   No not because to know where you are you have to remember.

Chorus   Yes not.

Chorus.   Of course yes not.

Chorus   So of course nobody can be interested in human nature.

Chorus   Nobody is.

Chorus.   Nobody is interested in human nature.

Chorus.   Not even a dog.

Chorus.   It has nothing to do human nature has nothing to do with anything.

Chorus   No not with a dog.

Tears.   No not with a dog.

Chorus.   I am I because my little dog knows me.

Chorus.   That does not prove anything about you it only proves something about the dog.

Tears.   Yes there I told you human nature is not at all interesting.

Scene III

And the human mind.
Chorus   And the human mind.
Tears.   And the human mind.
Chorus   Yes and the human mind.
Of course the human mind.
Has that anything to do with I am I because my little dog knows me.
Has that anything to do with how a country looks.

Scene III

Dogs and birds and a chorus and a flat land.
How do you like what you are. The bird knows, the dogs know and the chorus well the chorus yes the chorus if the chorus which is the chorus.
The flat land is not the chorus.
Human nature is not the chorus.
The human mind is not the chorus.
Perspiration is not the chorus.
Tears are not the chorus.
Food is not the chorus
Money is not the chorus.
What is the chorus.
Chorus.   What is the chorus.
Anyway there is the question of identity.
And that also has to do with the dog.
Is the dog the chorus.
Chorus.   No the dog is not the chorus.

Scene II

Any scene may be scene two.
Chorus.   And act II
No any act can be act one and two.

Scene II

I am I because my little dog knows me, even if the little dog is a big one, and yet a little dog knowing me does not really make me be I no not really because after all being I I am I has really nothing to do with the little dog knowing me, he is my audience, but an audience never does prove to you that you are you.

Act III

No one knowing me knows me.
And I am I I.
And does a little dog making a noise make the same noise as a bird.
I have not been mistaken.
Chorus.   Some kinds of things not and some kind of things.

Scene I

I am I yes sir I am I.
I am I yes Madame am I I.
When I am I am I I.
And any little dog is not the same thing as I am I.
Chorus.   Or is it.
With tears in my eyes oh is it.
And there we have the whole thing.
Am I I.
And if I am I because my little dog knows me am I I.
Yes sir am I I.
Yes madame or am I I.
The dog answers without asking because the dog is the answer to anything that is that dog. But not I. Without tears not I.

Act I Scene I

The necessity of ending is not the necessity of beginning.
How finely that is said.

Scene II

Very much as everything is said.

Scene III

An end of a play is not the end of a day.

Scene IV

After giving.

Part IV

I wish very seriously were I I to have eight be an audience. Do you mind eight.

What is the relation of human nature to the human mind.

Has it anything to do with any number.

The thing about numbers that is important is that any of them have a pretty name.

Therefore they are used in gambling in lotteries in plays in playing in scenes and in everything.

Numbers have such a pretty name.

It can bring tears of pleasure to one's eyes when you think of any number eight or five or one or twenty seven, or sixty three or seventeen sixteen or eighteen or seventy three or anything at all or very long numbers, numbers have such pretty names in any language numbers have such pretty names.

Tears of pleasure numbers have such pretty names.

They have something to do with money and with tears and flat land, not with mountains or lakes, yes with blades of grass, not much a little but not much with flowers, some with birds not much with dogs, quite a bit with oxen and with cows and sheep a little with sheep and so have numbers anything to do with the human mind. They have nothing to do with dogs and human nature but have they anything to do with the human mind, they ought to have something to do with the human mind because they are so pretty and they can bring forth tears of pleasure, but tears have nothing to do with the human mind not even tears of pleasure although they might all do so all do so and all be so.

Tears of pleasure have nothing to do with the human mind.

Chapter II

After all what is the human mind.

It is a very simple story.

The human mind is the mind that writes what any human

mind years after or years before can read, thousand of years or no years it makes no difference.

Now human nature human nature is just the same as any animal nature and so it has nothing to do with the human mind. Any animal can talk any animal can be but not any animal can write.

Therefore and so far is the human mind not related to human nature.

And the writing that is the human mind does not consist in messages or in events it consists only in writing down what is written and therefore it has no relation to human nature.

Events are connected with human nature but they are not connected with the human mind and therefore all the writing that has to do with events has to be written over, but the writing that has to do with writing does not have to be written again again is in this sense the same as over.

And so the human mind has no relation to human nature. And therefore and once again it is a ready made play to make a play of how there is no relation between human nature and the human mind.

A Play.

It has been said that only human beings play games just as it has been said that only human beings have tears in their eyes but this is not so, dogs have dogs do, they stick out their tongue they turn their head away when their feelings are hurt and so there is no relation between human nature and the human mind.

And the land

And any land.

The land has something to do with the human mind but nothing to do with human nature.

Human nature is animal nature but the human mind the human mind is not.

If it were then the writing that has been written would not be writing that any human mind can read, it has really no memory nor any forgetting.

Think of the Bible and Homer think of Shakespeare and think of me.

There is no remembering and there is no forgetting because

memory has to do with human nature and not with the human mind.

Everybody says no when I say so but when I say so finally they do not say no.

A play of how they do not finally say no when I say so.

Act I Scene I

Myself.   A dog is very much oppressed by the heat.

Scene II

Waking up is not the same as sleeping and have either one anything to do with the human mind.

Act I Scene I

All this can if it does it can if it does not make a detective story or anything right away.

How does everybody feel to-day. Very well I thank you.

Act I

If the world is small how small is it.

If the world is big how big is it.

But if everybody knows what everybody does is it small and big.

Now listen everybody listen.

Everybody can listen and if everybody is dead it does not make any difference because there are so many more and everybody can listen.

Now this is Part one.

Part one.

Everybody can listen and that does not make any difference because no matter if everybody is dead there are always all the same just the same all the same anybody can listen.

But nobody does do this. Nobody does listen because everybody can listen and listen. Listen to that. What is that. And then they listen to that.

After everybody listens to that can nobody listen.

Not as much as before.

And after before.

Well after before anybody can listen.

So once more a play.

But what is a play.

If there are no tears what is a play.

And if there are tears.

Where is a play.

Which and then have nothing more to do than just nicely hear what every one can.

So now hear me say.

I almost cry.

Hear me say.

What is the relation of human nature to the human mind.

Now there are two things that anybody can know.

A great many people do listen and a great many people do write.

Now this is alright.

But after all where is it when the world is small.

Where is it it the world when the world is small.

Around and around and the world is small.

She complains and can the whole world become small.

Or not at all.

Finally a prayer has nothing to do with I care.

I can begin again so often that I can begin again.

If it were not possible to begin again would any one listen.

Oh yes of course no yes of course.

And now I am really not really but truly yes really and truly yes I am to begin again.

And is any one going to begin again. No yes not any one.

And so very few write because if to write and to begin again.

Why is it always that there is a beginning and a middle and an ending.

Because it is quite right that nobody can write.

Part II

The whole book now is going to be a detective story of how to write.

A play of the relation of human nature to the human mind.

And a poem of how to begin again

And a description of how the earth look as as you look at it which is perhaps a play if it can be done in a day and is perhaps a detective story if it can be found out.

Anything is a detective story if it can be found out and can anything be found out.

Yes.

The human mind cannot find out but it is in it is not out.

If the human mind is in then it is not out.

Now in the first detective story the human mind does not count.

No one. A detective story.

Detective story number one.

Do you remember no you probably did not read that part I remember because it is true not because I said it before but because it is so if it is so.

And so it is never necessary to say anything again as remembering but it is always said again because every time it is so it is so.

That is the difference between writing and listening.

When you write it is so when you listen it is not so because of course when you listen it is not so and when you speak well of course when you speak it is not so anybody knows that it is not so that when you speak it is not so.

And therefore there are strong silent men.

If not why not.

But anyway anybody can know that what you say is not so.

So what is so.

Anything is so that is so and that is what makes a detective story fascinating that if it were so it would be so.

I am going to write one.

Listen Detective story number I.

If it is so is it so.

Or if it is not so is it not so.

But if you say so if anybody says so is anything so.

And if nobody says so is it so.

Is it so if you are writing. Yes it is so if you are writing because if you are writing how could you be writing if writing had not been learned. And so since it is learned since writing is learned it is so if it is written.

Now in talking well talking has not been learned so anybody talking is anybody talking and anybody talking has nothing to do with it being so.

How do you like a detective story if nobody is either dead or not dead.

You like it very well if it is written but if it is not written if it is not written everybody is dead.

Of course sometime everybody is dead but what has that to do with writing. Nothing at all. But with talking it has everything to do with talking. So you see talking has nothing to do with anything being so because everybody can come to be dead and so what is the use of saying that talking has anything to do with anything being so.

How I do like numbers this Detective story number one.

Detective story number I. About how there is a human mind.

And how to detect it.

Detective story number I.

The great thing to detect in a detective story is whether you have written as you have heard it said. If you do write as you have heard it said then you have to change it.

Suppose you have as a title Hub Murphy or the boy builder.

Supposing she says do not put in the or and then you try not to put in the or.

Do you succeed or do you not in not putting in the or.

And if you do why do you and if you do not why do you not.

The reason why has nothing to do with a detective story. They call it a motive but a motive is not a reason why. A motive is what makes you do it. But what makes you do it is not the reason why you do it.

Now this is not only true of detective stories but also of geography and government.

What makes you do it is not the reason why you do it.

Now listen a minute.

If you fly over Salt Lake city it is exactly like flying over the bottom of the sea with the water not in it.

The water is not in it, and so is there any reason why the water should be in it. Sometime the water has been in it but now that the water is not in it it makes it more easy perhaps not to fly but to see what you see as you fly.

Now the reason for the water not being there is one thing but the water not being there is another thing.

Now suppose it is a detective story.

Well it is astonishing to see a pigeon where you had not expected ever to see one.

Not because a pigeon could not be there, not even because a pigeon had never been there but because you could never have expected a pigeon to be there.

Even the wind could not blow the pigeon away once it was really there where the pigeon is.

Then the pigeon almost falls off because suddenly there is another pigeon there and the pigeon had not believed it possible for another pigeon to be there.

Perhaps there is still another pigeon there but it can not be seen even if it is there and any way the first pigeon turns his back so that he will not be able to see them or the other one and then he changes his mind and turns around toward them.

Perhaps from now on pigeons will always come there. Very likely because that is what anybody can do.

So once more no pigeons being there never again can there never be any pigeon there.

Detective story no 2.

Suppose you know just what has happened does that make any difference if you tell it.

What is the difference between write it and tell it. There is a difference you can tell it as you write it but you can tell it and not write it. There is a difference and the next detective story is to detect that difference.

If the pigeon can come again and he has come again then he can surprise some one but he cannot surprise me.

A pigeon itself if anything is a surprise such as being there can be interested in anything being surprising.

Think how heavily a pigeon flies and alights and if he is there is he likely to think that the wind can blow him away. The wind does blow but does it blow as a surprise or anything to him. Has he a motive in being there and having been there does he come there again.

He does come there again and this has no connection with the wind blowing and there has been no motive for the coming there.

So then what does human nature do.

It does it because it does and having done it it is not because it has done it that it does it it does it because it is there again.

There they are again.

The three pigeons are there again. There is no reason for it.

But if looking at it you are to paint it, the pigeon is there again and turning his back on the two other pigeons who are below it. You only can see from the side where you are seeing everything you only can see the two heads of the other two pigeons and now there are three. That makes four in all.

That is why numbers really have something to do with the human mind. That they are pigeons has nothing to do with it but that there was one and then that there were three and that then there are four and that then it may not cease to matter what number follows another but the human mind has to have it matter that any number is a number.

So then detective story number III

So then if then you might suppose then that if numbers mean anything there must be remembering. But not at all the number of pigeons being there is interesting as one follows one every if sometimes the one following is two or three, but you do not have to remember the one to know that there are two and three and all of a sudden four.

The minute you remember the one you do not want to look at him when they are one and then two and then four suddenly anything suddenly happening there is no remembering. Now think of how a detective story is to be written.

The first thing is the dead man or if not a dead woman.

No detective story can very often have a dead child or an alive pigeon because quite quietly anything that is begun is begun, and anything being finished is begun.

Mostly in detecting anything being finished is begun.

And so they prefer not to have dead children.

Any detective story is ready to be told. And as you know it you know it.

Detective Story number VII

Pigeons come to parties and when they come there is no reason that they come excepting that it is the first time that they come. If they have come they come as often as they come and when it is not comfortable then they are uncomfortable.

Uncomfortable as it is it is as uncomfortable as it is and after that there is no reason why they have not come. In every little while an eagle can fly. That has nothing to do with any sky. Wait a minute.

Now this is how a detective story can be written.

I love writing and reading.

When there has been no rain the sky is very beautiful. Any one in America can know that and like it when it is heat producing.

Pigeons have nothing to do with this this has nothing to do with several pigeons. Swallows flying in and out have nothing to do with any pigeon, flying in and out of a room. And so there is no such thing as human nature.

Why there is no such thing as human nature is that anybody can observe swallows and a pigeon.

There is blue and green and green and yellow pale yellow and blue, there is pale yellow and green and blue and warmth and there is not any such a thing as human nature.

Please see my human mind.

It is here.

Is white a colour.

Yes white and grey is a colour.

Grey and white is a colour.

It is now come to be certain that there is not any such a thing as human nature.

Of course there is such a thing as human nature and anybody can observe it.

The relation of human nature to the human mind.

When anybody likes it as much as they ever liked it before they like it as much as that.

The detective story of liking it as much as they ever had liked it before.

They liked it as much as they ever liked it before because it was hot and they liked it to be like that to be hot.

They liked it as much as they ever liked it before because the wind blew and blew the birds about and they liked it they liked it as much when the wind did that.

Now how could you detect that they liked it as much as they ever liked it before.

Now here is where we come to this that having come to

this they pushed every one with a chance to stay where they had been put not nobody had been put where they did stay.

And so after all why should pigeons come to stay because nothing that comes can go away because nobody has anything that has come to go away. And progress is just that, it has come to go away and so here we are now, and it is as hot and the wind blows nicely to-day and any one finding that the dog went in when he was told said what did you say.

That makes a crime story what did you say if I had not waited to hear what you did say I might have said the wind is blowing to-day. And so a crime story as soon as you know what is what is is what no crime story is. There is no such thing as crime and propaganda because nobody knows the difference between what did you say and what you did say.

What is what.

Very well I think that I think do not think which I do not think why I do not think just why this is that.

There is no crime, there is the hope that the daughter of the couple could not be bitten and in order to do so they the couple are very careful.

And yet she might not be.

After all sometime she will not be older.

Not to the eye or the ear but to circumstance.

And so hastily they vanish not hastily but slowly when they are no longer to stay.

That is just the difference between crime and no crime and there is no crime without crime. Who knows what.

I wish not to know but as I do know I do not wish to know what they do but I do wish to know what they do but if I do then they do not do what I wish to know that they do. And so a crime story is ended because I look at the end.

Begin being ready to find the human mind.

Chapter V

Habit and the human mind is there any such a thing as habit and the human mind.

Do not be ridiculous of course there is not there is no such thing as the habit of the human mind.

The human mind if it is a human mind has not even the habit of being the human mind no of course not.

Detective story number 8

If wild animals live as if they were wild but they are kept healthy and not killed are they wild. If they run away when they are seeing they are seen are they wild.

When anybody who knows where they are knows they are there are they wild.

Do you see how much all this has to do with communism and individualism and propaganda. But has it anything to do with the human mind.

Yes it has this to do with the human mind that the human mind may write yes yes or no or I guess I guess no or I guess yes.

The human mind cannot be interested in whether the animal which is wild is not wild but it can be interested in yes.

America the place where every animal is which has been there is interested in saying yes. No or yes.

The human mind if it rests in no and yes the human mind does not know about rest because no and yes have nothing to do with anything but no or yes.

And think, it is very exciting but think how much America and I do think America has something to do with the human mind think how much America has to do with yes.

Detective story number I

Will the world which is round be flat.

Yes it is.

When there was a sea the world was round but now that there is air the world is flat.

Oh yes it is.

That is what a crime story is.

It is the human mind.

The human mind says yes it is.

In the years when nobody looked everybody said everything grows the same but it never does.

What if it did but it never does.

If it did there would be no human mind because no one could say yes if it always grew the same.

But it never does.

Now every one can but no one should get excited about it never does.

But since no one knows except the human mind that it

never does that is never does grow the same that each year there is a little more or a little less rain, so then it never does grow the same.

Nobody is excited when it does when it does not grow the same but every one is excited when saying yes which is the human mind and which is the same says yes.

That is what makes politics and religion and propaganda and communism and individualism the saying yes and that is always the same and that is because it is the human mind and all the human mind can do is to say yes. Now do you see why there is no relation between human nature and the human mind. Human nature can not say yes, how can human nature say yes, human nature does what it does but it cannot say yes. Of course human nature can not say yes. If it did it would not be human nature.

Saying yes is interesting but being human nature is not interesting it is just like being anything and having anything is not interesting even if you can say anything because the only thing that is interesting is saying yes. Poor America is it not saying yes, is it losing the human mind to become human nature. Oh yeah.

Part fifteen.

Four things that having nothing to do with this.

1. That when anybody is elected to do anything although he has never done it before he begins to do that.

2. I said to Upton Sinclair what would you have done if you had been elected and he said thank god I was not elected.

I used to wonder when I saw boys who had just been boys and they went into an office to work and they came out with a handful of papers and I said to them how since you never had anything to do with papers before business papers how do you know what to do with them. They just did. They knew what to do with them.

And therefore that has nothing to do either with human nature or the human mind.

It is easy to see that it has nothing to do with anything and that most things have not, have not anything to do with anything.

There is human nature of course everybody has it and anybody can regard themselves or any one as having it but really it is not interesting. No not to-day since to-day well any day is nevertheless more yesterday than to-day and therefore not interesting.

When I say not interesting I mean not interesting.

A conversation.

If every one could go on living there would not then be room for any one now living.

Nobody says anything.

If every one could arrange what weather we are to be having every one would want what he wanted and what would that do, it would do nothing because if everybody had everything then everybody would go on living or nobody would go on living.

How do you like what you have can never be said of any one not of Theodore or Franklin Roosevelt not of Napoleon or Louis Napoleon. And yet inasmuch as that they are the same.

It is a funny question that if every one had everything they wanted every one would go on living and if every one went on living then there would not be room for any one and so nobody would go on living. Human nature even has nothing to do with this.

The human mind yes the human mind can say yes.

Human nature cannot say this human nature cannot say yes. Moreover.

Theodore and Franklin Roosevelt like Napoleon and Louis Napoleon even though they belonged to the country to which they belonged were foreign to it.

This has nothing to do either with human nature or the human mind and one may say that neither of the four of them had any of them had any human nature or any human mind.

They could not be what they were that is human nature and they could not say yes that is the human mind.

They all four are very interesting examples of having neither human nature nor the human mind.

Theodore and Franklin Roosevelt Napoleon and Louis Napoleon.

I wish to make this absolutely clear because it is yes it is absolutely just as clear.

There is no age when she says yes.

If she says yes then there is no age when she says yes.

How pleasantly a doll can change its age.

But you know I know that if a boy is to grow up to be a man what is the use.

Theodore and Franklin Roosevelt and Napoleon and Louis Napoleon.

Yes indeed everything is there nothing is missing nothing is missing to show that there is no need not to know that there is no human nature where there is a human mind.

Leave age alone.

I tell you leave age alone.

Leave forgetting alone.

Leave it alone.

I tell you leave it alone.

She said the child said well what did she say.

Theodore and Franklin Roosevelt and Napoleon and Louis Napoleon never said what they said was any more than led. They knew nothing of being dead. Of course not because they had no human nature. They said nothing of what was said no of course not because of course what is said is not said and they had no human mind to write what was not said. No of course not.

So this is to be a long story and let us play that it is a detective story only in a detective story somebody has had to be dead and these four no these four not as alive as dead no not not as alive as dead.

So a detective story if they cannot be dead well then perhaps there is a crime where not anybody is dead. Well perhaps then something is said.

Of these four or not any more no they are not dead nor is it more than that which is said.

I leave well enough alone.

I   Theodore Roosevelt.   As dead as not dead.

I   Napoleon.   Not as dead as dead.

Louis Napoleon   Not at all as dead as said but dead as said.

Franklin Roosevelt.   Like Louis Napoleon oh very much very much like Louis Napoleon. He has no commitment to dead and said.

Listen while I tell you more about all three or all four.

Sometimes it is all three because the two the two forget each other. Louis Napoleon and Franklin Roosevelt forget each other.

Whether they forget each other.

That makes two.

The other two do not forget each other.

Or at least.

No or at least if they are dead they are not not because of this may they be without date or dates.

They do not forget each other, they might then have human nature. They might but did they.

They never said what they wrote but they did not write.

As they did not write they did not have a human mind.

And they saw land they saw land oh yes they saw land but if they did, is it that they did, no if it as they did is what they did.

They saw the land they could use but they could not use land and as they could not use land they could see land but as they saw land what land well not any land because after all land is land, that is the human mind and they had no human mind.

At least not not at all they had no human mind and so there was no relation no relation between them and the land and so they are not dead and so what they said anything they said was not the human mind.

The human mind does not concern itself with what is said.

It does not concern itself with what is written. And they wrote nothing so nothing was written.

Of the four none of them having ever been existing no one of the four of them is dead.

So they need not rest in peace.

Peace is very likely something.

Has human nature anything to do with peace.

Not anything but something.

And has the human mind anything to do with peace.

The human mind has to do with yes and yes has nothing to do with anything and anything has to do with peace from time to time with peace.

Human nature only has to do with in between and in between oh yes in between sleep and peace oh in between.
And the human mind.

Part XV

The only difficulty about doing anything is that doing anything is nothing to do.
Nothing to do and doing anything is not the same thing
because either one thing or the other thing is doing nothing.

Chapter XVI

Now just think of the meaning. Anybody just think of the
meaning of not doing anything and think what all the gov-
ernment is and propaganda and money and individualism and
collectivism, think what it all is is it doing nothing.
No not at all it is not at all not doing nothing.
Even Mr. Upton Sinclair cannot say no nothing at all.
But does he.
Yes he does.
He does say I see I see and any one can see I see I see.
There there there.
There is no way to quiet not not doing anything.
No other way.
They do not even forget not to have tears not Mr. Upton
Sinclair although really and truly although he does not forget
it he does not forget not to have tears.
That is what makes him Mr. Upton Sinclair.
Then very well what is the human mind.
If not if not what is the human mind.

Chapter one.

To know what the human mind is there is no knowing what
the human mind is because as it is it is.
I could say something about history but although everybody likes to know about everything they think oh yes they
think that when anybody is doing anything that is history.

Is there any difference between doing anything and something happening.

Quick and quickly as anything stops tapping is there any difference between doing something and something happening.

Of course there is.

Quickly of course there is.

And that tells all about history.

Nevertheless in bowing and listening and then the tapping is ceasing there is a difference between any one doing or not doing anything and anything happening.

This is the secret of history and it is not the secret of human nature and the human mind.

Anybody doing anything may or may not have something in relation to human nature but certainly most certainly not it has not anything to do with the human mind because of course the human mind never does anything why should it, when it has no relation to human nature.

And so let well enough alone.

Now history has really no relation to the human mind at all, because history is the state of confusion between anybody doing anything and anything happening.

Confusion may have something to do with the human mind but has it.

I would rather not know than know anything of the confusion between any one doing anything and something happening.

So says the historian.

Chapter 91

The human mind.

There is no relation between human nature and the human mind.

Chapter 2

What is the relation of a calendar to the human mind even if one means to say an almanac.

An almanac has a relation to the human mind because every day it tells what it is.

An almanac has no relation to human nature because every

day human nature tells what it was and therefore human nature cannot write but the human mind can.

It not only can but it does.

Chapter III

The question of identity has nothing to do with the human
mind it has something although really nothing altogether to
do with human nature. Any dog has identity.

The old woman said I am I because my little dog knows
me, but the dog knew that he was he because he knew that
he was he as well as knowing that he knew she.

Dogs like knowing what they know even when they make
believe that they do not not that they do not like it but that
they do not know.

Take a bicycle race that has nothing to do with a dog but
it has to do with identity.

They are they because all who are there know they are they
and on no account cannot they not be no not as long as they
are in the race.

When they drop out well then identity may no longer be
identity. They are they just the same only they are not because
they are no longer identified and if they did not race at all
well then not any one is any one.

All this has nothing to do with the human mind but so
much to do with history and propaganda and government but
nothing to do with money and the human mind nothing to
do with money and the human mind.

Human nature, human nature acts as it acts when it is identified when there is an identity but it is not human nature that
has anything to do with that it is that anybody is there where
they are, it is that that has to do with identity with government with propaganda with history with individualism and
with communism but it has nothing nothing to do with the
human mind.

Anybody can understand that because the human mind
writes what there is and what has identity got to do with that.

Nothing nothing at all.

And so anybody can see that identity has nothing whatever
to do with the human mind.

Just now when everybody knows that, think of crime identity has nothing to do with crime, detective stories yes but not crime.

Now to know to do as you do doing as you do has nothing to do with crime.

Chapter IV

It is beginning to be able to see that identity has nothing to do with crime.

With the detective story but not with crime.

Chapter II

I am I because my little dog knows me.

That is just the way history is written.

And that is why there is really no writing in history.

I am I because my little dog knows me.

Yes that is what history is writing but not the human mind, no not, of course not, not the human mind.

Chapter III

The relation of superstition to identity and the human mind.

Please remember the cuckoo.

Chapter IV

There are so many things to say about the cuckoo.

I think I will say them all.

I have always wanted to talk about the cuckoo.

Chapter III and IV

About the cuckoo.

Long before the cuckoo sang to me I wrote a song and said the cuckoo bird is singing in a cuckoo tree singing to me, oh singing to me.

But long before that very long before that I had heard a cuckoo clock.

And in between I had heard a great many cuckoos that were not cuckoo clocks.

Indeed since then I have never seen a cuckoo in a cuckoo clock.

So then I did hear that a cuckoo not in a clock but a cuckoo that is a bird that sings cuckoo if you hear it sing for the first time in the spring and you have money in your pocket you will have it all the year. I mean money.

I always like to believe what I hear.

That has something to do with superstition and something to do with identity. To like to believe what you hear.

Has that something to do with the human mind that is with writing.

No not exactly.

Has it something to do with human nature. Well a dog likes to believe what he can hear.

You tell him what a good dog he is and he does like to believe it.

The cuckoo when he says cuckoo and you have money in your pocket and it is the first cuckoo you have heard that year you will have money all of that year.

It did happen to me so you see it has nothing to do with the human mind to believe what you see to like to believe what you hear.

But it did happen to me there was a cuckoo and he came and sat not in a cuckoo tree but in a tree right near to me and he said cuckoo at me and I had a lot of money in my pocket and I had a lot of money all that year.

Now you see what a cuckoo has to do with superstition and identity.

Superstition is to believe what you see to believe what you hear and to see what you see.

That makes superstition clear.

And in a way yes in a way it has nothing to do with human nature or the human mind.

Superstition exists in itself because it is so true.

The human mind oh yes you do.

It is not concerned with being or not being true.

But superstition yes superstition is concerned with it being true.

And human nature human nature is not concerned with its being true.

And so superstition has nothing to do with either human nature or the human mind.

And that is very agreeable that it is that.

And now identity.

Well any Franklin Roosevelt has he any identity.

I am I because my little dog knows me.

But does any little dog know more than know that it is he. No indeed.

And what is identity.

Is he he.

Does the little dog know that he is he.

But is he.

The little is like superstition he believes what he hears and what he sees and what he smells.

But is that identity.

Of course there are identity cards but is that identity.

Perhaps it might be just as easy to remember what identity is.

Perhaps to remember what identity does and if identity remembers them it has nothing to do with the human mind no nothing because the human mind does not remember it knows and it writes what it knows.

Now identity remembers and so it has an audience and as it has an audience it it is history and as it is history it has nothing to do with the human mind.

The little dog knows that I am I because he knows me but that is not because of identity but because he believes what he sees and what he hears and what he smells and so that is really superstition and not identity because superstition is true while identity is history and history is not true because history is dependent upon an audience.

Oh yes oh yes upon an audience.

And this has nothing to do with the human mind.

And human nature well human nature is not interesting not at all interesting.

Chapter II

It is a remarkable thing not remarkable but remarked. Is there any difference between remarked and remarkable.

There are a great many people always living who are mixed up with anything and that is known as events.

But.

Only one sometimes two mostly only one sometimes none

but certainly mostly only one in a generation can write what goes on existing as writing.

It is absurd when you think about it as absurd as any superstition but there it is there is only one in a generation not likely more than one in many a generation not even one that can write what goes on existing.

Now what have you to say to that.

That when you come to think about it it is astonishing not when you hear that there is no relation between human nature and the human mind it is no longer as astonishing.

How often as I have been walking and looking at so many who are studying and walking and I can say to myself why should not one of them write something that will be that that which it is and they will not no they will not and what is that that which it is.

It is writing of course it is the human mind and there is no relation between human nature and the human mind no no of course not.

And what has that to do with flat land or any land the flatter the land oh yes the flatter land but of course the flatter the land and the sea is as flat as the land oh yes the flatter the land the more yes the more it has may have to do with the human mind.

After number I

Number one I cannot be often enough surprised at what they do and that they do it so well, so much is written and they do do it so well.

And then I wonder as they do it so well as so many do it so many do it so very very well, I mean writing how is it that after all only one and that one only one in a generation and very often very many generations no one does it at all that is writing.

It has all to do with the fact that there is no relation between human nature and the human mind.

Those all those that do it so well and they do they do do it so well all those that do do it so well do it with human nature as human nature that is with remembering and forgetting.

Think anything you say has to do with human nature and

if you write what you say if you write what you do what is done then it has to do with human nature and human nature is occupying but it is not interesting.

Now you all know you all know that human nature is not interesting, you watch any dog with affection no human nature is not interesting it is occupying but it is not interesting and therefore so much writing is done. But is it done oh yes of course it is done. Done and done. That is the way they used to bet.

Now you take anything that is written and you read it as a whole it is not interesting it begins as if it is interesting but it is not interesting because if it is going to have a beginning and middle and ending it has to do with remembering and forgetting and remembering and forgetting is not interesting it is occupying but it is not interesting.

And so that is not writing.

Writing is neither remembering nor forgetting neither beginning or ending.

Being dead is not ending it is being dead and being dead is something. Think of any crime of course being dead is something.

Now and that is a great American contribution only any flat country has and can be there that being dead is actually something.

Americans are like that.

No Europeans and so no European can ever invent a religion, they have too much remembering and forgetting too much to know that human nature is anything.

But it is not because it is not interesting no not any more interesting than being drunk. Well who has to listen to anything. Any European but not any American.

Number two.

That would be sad.
What.
That any American would hear what any one is saying.

Number three.

I found that any kind of a book if you read with glasses and somebody is cutting your hair and so you cannot keep the glasses on and you use your glasses as a magnifying glass and so read word by word reading word by word makes the writing that is not anything be something.

Very regrettable but very true.

So that shows to you that a whole thing is not interesting because as a whole well as a whole there has to be remembering and forgetting, but one at a time, oh one at a time is something oh yes definitely something.

Number four.

Why if only one person in a generation and often not one in a generation can really write writing why are there a number of them that can read it quite a number of them in any generation.

There is a question.

Why do they as well as can they.

Number five.

Do they as well as can they.

Number six.

One two three four five six seven all good children go to heaven some are good and some are bad one two three four five six seven.

So you see that this is the question.

How is it that a number a certain number in any generation can read what is written but only one in any number of generations can write what is written.

She dropped something.

Number six and seven.

Another thing.

What is the relation of anything to anything.

Not human nature and not the human mind.

Human nature is not that thing and the human mind.

Now the human mind.

First Example.

The relation of the human mind to the universe.

What is the universe.

Human nature is not in any relation to the universe anybody can understand that thing.

That is not understanding that is unanswerable that human nature has no relation to the universe.

What is the universe.

Second Example.

There are so many things which are not the same identity, human nature, superstition, audience and the human mind. And the only one that is the one that makes writing that goes on is the human mind.

Identity and audience.

No one is identical but any one can have identity.

And why.

Because what is the use of being a little boy if you are going to grow up to be a man.

Example Four.

Another thing that there is is the Universe.

Identity has nothing to do with the universe identical might have if it could have but identity certainly not certainly not identity.

Example Five.

Nothing should follow something because in this way there will come to be a middle and a beginning and an end and of course that does make identity but not the human mind or not the human mind.

If you write one thing that is any word and another word is used to come after instead of come or of come again then that may have something not to do with identity but with human nature.

And human nature has nothing to do with the human mind.

Now about anything nothing can grow but often all as nothing can grow there is no identity.

Not of course not even naturally not but just not, not at all.

But anything can grow.

But what is the use of being a little boy if he is going to grow up to be a man.

Do you see what a mistake it is to say that.

Example Six.

The universe.
What is extra is not a universe.
No indeed.

Play I

Characters.
Identity, human nature, human mind, universe, history, audience and growing.

Play II

I do not think I would care about that as a play.

Play I

The human mind.
The human mind at play.

Play II

Human nature.
The dog if he is lost knows very well he will be found.

Human Nature

But perhaps he will not be found.

Play III

Very often he is not found he is run over.

Play IV

Sometimes he is not run over but he is not found.

Play I
Identity

If I know that I say that I will go away and I do not I do not.

That makes identity.

Thank you for identity even if it is not a pleasure.

Play I

Identity is not as a pleasure.

Play I

Identity has nothing to do with one and one.

Play I
The Universe.

The Universe well if there is a way to have it be that they can lay a universe away.

Play II

But they cannot.

Play III

Of course they can.

Play IV

Of course they can. They do not. But they can.

Play V

A universe if it is layed away, they cannot. Of course they cannot.

Play V

A universe cannot.

Play I
An audience.

An audience cannot be layed away. Of course it can. It can but is it. Of course it can.

Any audience can be layed away of course it can.

Play II
Growing.

There is no of course it can to growing.
Growing has no connection with audience.
Audience has no connection with identity.
Identity has no connection with a universe.
A universe has no connection with human nature.

Play I

Human nature.

Human nature is not interesting. Human nature is not at play.

Play II

Human nature is not interesting.

Example seven and eight

The more likely a universe is to be connected with identity the less likely is a universe to be a universe.

No one likes the word universal to be connected with a universe.

Part II

All the parts are part II.

I once knew a man who never had part one he always had part 2.

I always knew.

Part III

Now what has any one to do with Part III

Part I

If every day it is necessary to have an uncle killed that is if he kills himself instead of a father that too has nothing to do either with identity or with human nature.

Part IV

It is very strange that although only one in ever so often can write a great many can read what the one has written. But is that only because they can read writing or has it to do with the one who is writing.

That is what I want to know.

The human mind writes only once in a very little or big so often but every time every time size has nothing to do with anything because the universe every once in a while the universe is that size and so does it make any difference since the human mind has what it has does what it does and writes what it writes and that has nothing to do with identity or audience or history or events, and yet only once oh only once in every few generations the human mind writes. That is all because of human nature and human nature is not interesting everybody says it is but it is not.

Part I

He needs what he can please

Part I

Every time they change, I mean the earth I mean why mean the earth and which makes more than what is on it in it.

Part II

Once they like an earth

Part II

Once they like a heaven

Part II

Once they like a heaven and earth

Part III

No heaven

Part III

No earth

Part I

They come later not to know there ever had been a heaven.

Part III

Certainly it lasted heaven a very little time all things considered that is considered as long as anything is.

No earth yes no earth.

No heaven yes certainly no heaven.

Part III

Now this which I want you to think about is this.

Every once in so often is every once in so often and anybody can decide what nothing is.

Please excuse me.

If nothing is anything any one every once in so often can decide what anything is.

That is the way it is.

Part I

Every time there is a human mind it is or it is not all the universe which is or is not.

That is what the human mind is.

Think what the human mind is.

Part II

It has nothing to do with anything but is one yes well yes that is what the human mind is.

Part III

Is one yes that is what the human mind is.

Part IV

Human nature no.

Human nature never is one that is not what the human mind is human nature is not what the human mind is.

Part IV

Romance.

There is some relation between romance and the human mind but no relation between human nature and romantic anything because human nature is not interesting but romance is.

Part I

Lolo.

Part II

I cannot begin too often begin to wonder what money is.

Has it to do with human nature or the human mind. Human nature can use it but cannot refuse it. Can human nature know it know what money is or only the human mind and remember now there is no heaven and of course no earth, not in America perhaps not anywhere but there is the human mind and any one which is more than not enough may perhaps know what money and romance is.

Part I

I am not confused in mind because I have a human mind.

Part II

Yes which is.

Part I

Romance and money one by one.

Part II

Lolo.

Part II

Care fully for me.
As often as carefully.
Each one of these words has to do with nothing that is not romance and money.

Part III

Romance has nothing to do with human nature.

Part III

Neither has money

Part II

Lolo

Part II

Where he lived and when he died.
Some see some sun.

Part III

He died naturally

Part I

She says he says he says she says what is done is not done.

Number one.

It is not to discourage to say that each time although each time is such a very few times that there is a different way to say that the sun is far away each time that there is a different way to say that anything is far away although at any time that there is a universe now at any time that there is a universe anything is very near.

Number two.

That is just that and that has nothing to do with the human mind or human nature that is just that.

Number one.

It happens it changes a little any day it happens though that any day some one can say something that makes any one know that the larger is smaller but not that the smaller is larger.

Now suppose everybody says pioneering is over that means that the larger is smaller but not that the smaller is larger and that well that no that that has nothing to do with the human mind.

But has the human mind anything to do with romance not human nature perhaps human nature. Who likes human nature. Not I. And the human mind. And romance oh yes I do like romance that is what makes landscape but not flat land.

Flat land is not romantic because you can wander over it and if you can wander over it then there is money and if there is money then there is the human mind and if there is the human mind there is neither romance nor human nature nor governments nor propaganda.

There should be none of these if the land is flat.

Flat land is seen from above.

Above what.

Above the flat land.

Is there any human nature in red indians or chinamen there should not be.

But there is.

Alright there is.

But there should not be.

Is there any romance.

Alright there should not be.
But there is
Alright there should not be.
And government, no there is no government where the land is flat.
There should not be.
And there is not.
And why not.
Because anybody can wander and if anybody can wander then there should not be any human nature.
And romance
No there should not be.
And yet romance has nothing to do with human nature.
No nothing.
Nothing at all
Nothing at all.
Nothing at all at all
Nothing at all.

Number II

Lolo.
There is no romance if anybody is to die by and by.
But to die
Yes to die.
Not only not to die.
Not by and by.
And so romance is delicious.
But not to die by and by.
Lolo.

Number three.

Lolo was one no matter that he had a father.
No matter that he had a father.
Nobody cries out loud no matter that he had a father.
It was not mentioned often or again.
Lolo was himself romantic and he is dead not by and by but dead.
And as I pass where he had not had a father there where he is not dead by and by but as he is then there there where

he is he was not where he is. Lolo is dead and any father had a mother he had a mother but none of this is dead.

He is dead.

Lolo is dead.

There where there is no other.

Number III

Do you see what romance is

Number III

Do you see that it has nothing to do with human nature or the human mind.

Number III

So many things have nothing to do with human nature.

Romance did.

It had nothing to do with human nature.

And the human mind.

Nothing did.

Nothing did have nothing to do with the human mind.

Romance did.

Oh romance did.

Romance had nothing to do with the human mind nor with human nature.

Romance did.

Number III

It had to do with neither with flat land or money or the human mind or human nature.

Now anybody might think that romance and adventure was the same but it is not.

Adventure has to do with small things being bigger and big things being smaller but not romance no not romance. Romance has nothing to do with anything being bigger or being smaller and therefore although romance has nothing to do with the human mind they come together.

They have nothing either one of them has nothing to do with human nature. Oh no nothing to do with human nature.

Lolo.

Nothing to do with human nature.

Number I

Every time any one can come to be one then there is no human nature no not in that one.

Human nature has to do with identity but identity has nothing to do with any one being one.

Not not anything in any one.

No no no.

Number II

Be a credit to beware.

Does it make any difference how you felt to-day.

No not any.

Does it make any difference how you felt yesterday

No not any

Does it make any difference if a dog does not know the difference between a rubber ball and a piece of paper.

No not any why he does.

Ah there you see.

That is the answer.

No not any only he does.

Now that has to do with identity.

Does it make any difference if a dog does not know the difference between a rubber ball and the end of a rug.

No not any only he does.

In this way identity is proclaimed.

Not of the ball and the rug but of the dog.

And so you see I am I because my little dog knows me.

But that has nothing to do with romance but it has to do with government and propaganda.

Oh yes you do see.

You do see me.

And that has to do with government and propaganda but not with money and the human mind.

Oh you you do see.

But do you see me.

That has to do with human nature but not with romance and money and the human mind but with government and propaganda and human nature and adventure, oh yes you do see you do see me.

Number III

Very nearly any is as much as not nearly as much more.

Quantity is one of the things to think about and how much do you use.

She complains that some who do not live on flat lands do not know how much of anything they use.

What has this to do with money. Nothing at all really and now I will explain all about money.

How do you do all about money.

Money is what they know that they give and take.

Oh yes yes.

Number VI

Four and five do not keep money alive any more than six and seven.

Now just think they do say at sixes and seven.

Number V

Money is very important because anybody can think about that and it has something to do with the human mind.

And with romance.

Well and with romance.

And with big and little no not with adventure and with human nature.

Human nature can mix itself up with it but that is another matter. Really money really has to do with the human mind.

Part VII

What did swallows do before houses were built as they do not care for trees.

Part VIII

This has nothing to do with romance because the mention of it is bad.

Bad which is badly has nothing to do with sad, and all this both has nothing to do with romance.

Romance has to do with what it looks like.

It looks like near and far this is not adventure it is romance, romance has to look like near, adventure has to look like far, and to adventure is to bring the far near, to romance is to have the near far and here.

How likely are definitions to be pleasurable.

Very likely.

Part IX

Define what you do by what you see never by what you know because you do not know that this is so.

Autumn can come in June but very soon it mostly can come in July.

You see why romance is interesting and not adventure.

Every once in a while anybody can say so.

Part X

I think that if you announce what you see nobody can say no. Everybody does everybody does say no but nobody can nobody can say so, that is no.

That is the reason that you can say what you see

And so you see.

That is what the national hymn says the star spangled banner.

Oh say can you see.

Part XI

Everything is funny that is nothing at all.

But the human mind.

The human mind believes in a glance and also in looking.

Even so.

Part XI

Now I wish earnestly to say just what I see when I look away.

That is one thing.

Earnestly to say what I see when I look any way.

Earnestly to say what I see as I see that I look to see.

Sometimes it is very beautiful like to-day.

Oh yes sometimes like to-day.

Any day is neither here nor there.

Let no one think that anything has come to stay.

And if they do if they do not think that anything has come to stay what is the difference between to-day and any other day.

But there is a difference.

There is no use in saying there is no difference because there is a difference there is a difference between to-day and any other day.

There is no need of their being any difference no need at all.

Now do you begin to see the difference between need and is, between human nature and the human mind and of course you do see why it is not interesting to any one who has need to be that is who finds human nature interesting.

Oh dear human nature is not interesting.

Part XI

Romance is not interesting but it is made at once made at once by where they are.

Oh where they are.

Yes nobody needs to know about yesterday and to-day if they are where they are, and the only way to be there where they are is by romancing.

Romancing oh not that romance makes where they are there.

It is the only thing, history cannot do it nor government nor propaganda nor human nature nor the human mind.

Romance is the only way to be there there where they are.

So romance is in between human nature and the human mind but has nothing to do with either.

Detective story the story of a dead man should have had a connection with romance because a dead man if he is really dead but only in America dear America the United States of America is a dead man really dead.

And so that is romance do you see because a dead man there is dead and dead is dead there. Not adventure, adventure is just bringing the distant to be nearer, but romance romance is to be there there where they are.

Not described as that to that but to be that not described as that.

I wonder if you could be cured of not knowing that.

It really makes it be us to be like it is.

And the human mind. The human mind has to say what anything is now. Not ever where anything is that is romance but has to say what anything is now oh yes yes yes that is the human mind.

Part XII

I should be liking to love swallows so.

The human mind.	Oh yes I know.
Human Nature.	Oh yes oh yes.
Romance.	Oh yes this is yes.
Adventure.	Which is yes for the mess swallows can know.
Government.	Yes swallows yes.
Propaganda.	Oh yes.

Part XIII

I believe I do not like anything that happens.

I believe I do not like what is not alike.

I believe I do not like where the air is there.

I believe I do not like while they like.

But a swallow let something tumble upon me from the air.

Part XIV

This was missed as seen.

Part XV

I believe that I like to see what is seen.

Ah yes of course.

I believe that I like to see what bothers me.

Oh yes of course.

I believe that I like to be what is not human nature to be because human nature is not interesting.

Oh no decidedly not. I believe that human nature is not interesting. Decidedly not.

But anything flying around is.

Oh certainly.

Therefore there is the universe.

Because it is flying around.

It is interesting.

Anything that is flying around is interesting.

Human nature government propaganda is not flying around adventure is not flying around, it is flying to or from therefore it is not interesting.

And romance and the human mind.

Well and romance and the human mind.

Romance and the human mind are interesting and are they flying well no they are not.

So there we can say that only the things flying around are interesting which makes the universe, and flat land and romance and the human mind but perhaps they do and perhaps they do not fly around romance and flat land and the human mind, of course they do they do fly around. Moving around is not flying around the things that move do not make the universe. They are not interesting.

The human mind is interesting and the universe.

About romance well supposing we just like it like that but not by definition.

But wait we will define it so that it is interesting. Nobody can define events or history or human nature or government or propaganda and make them interesting. Anything that has to do with human nature is not interesting.

Just think.

How very uninteresting human nature is. If you like it like that what is the matter with the dog the two dogs both of them asleep.

They are sweet but not interesting once you know that human nature is not, not interesting.

Number I

Now is just the time to think about what is or is not interesting because nothing else is interesting.

Everything else is as well finished as begun everything except to find out what is or is not interesting.

Leave well enough alone means nothing now because nothing is alone.

That is it.

Not even the human mind.

No nothing is alone.

And if nothing alone then every one can know that nothing is alone and so no one can leave well enough alone since nothing is alone.

And so you see there is nothing to be except the universe and the human mind and is the universe alone and the human mind.

Can leave well enough alone be said of the universe or of the human mind.

I wonder very much where there is.

So does no one.

If any one is alone and everybody is then nobody is alone as nobody is.

And so nobody can leave well enough alone.

How happy it is to be exact but to be exact is to be happy.

Happy is not exactly as it is and since nobody is alone nobody is as happy as it is.

So romance has nothing to do with anything excepting only as it looks like it as country.

Country not flat country can look like something.

The human mind does not hop around but it flies around and is alone as the universe is.

Therefore nobody but it writes it, and that makes it the human mind that it writes it.

Part I

I should not have ended as begun.

If anything flies around there is no ending and no begun.

Part II

I am coming to what the human mind is and I have one.

Part III

One.

Part IV

The human mind has not begun it happens once in a while but it has not begun,

Part V

Will it

Part VI

No

Part VII

Part I

Money.
Money is a very interesting subject.

Part I

Franklin Roosevelt like Louis Napoleon has no personality but a persistence of insistence in a narrow range of ideas.
Money and personality.
Two things which may or may not be connected with human nature and the human mind.
For all of which there is praise and no praise.

Part I

Money.

Part I

Personality.

Part I

Money very likely money has nothing to do with human nature.
Human nature makes me smile.
Smile with what.
With what I smile.
But money, money is not just the same not at all just the same.

Part I

I wish seriously to talk about money.

Part I

Personality, personality has nothing to do with money or with the human mind. Nothing at all.
And human nature well human nature can always let well enough alone and so human nature well human nature can

never be alone but money can money can be alone and at its best it is alone money is alone and the human mind and the universe.

Part I

There can be a union.

Part I

Money is alone.

Part I

You learn it in writing poetry you tell it in writing prose.
This is even true of politics.
Sadism is an entirely different matter.
But is it.
If it is is it.
Sadism may have something to do with human nature and the human mind.

There are connecting links not in arithmetic but there are connecting links so they think in zoology, but I never think.

Sadism is no connecting link but it may have something to do with either not something to do with but is something that has something something to do with human nature and with the human mind and although no one can separate anything from sadism sadism cannot live alone. But the human mind. Well can it.

We have talked so much about time and identity that now we really know it know that we can see that one can make three.

To Thornton and Bob Davis an autobiography.

Autobiography I

When I was one that is no longer one of one but just one that is to say when I was a little one, but not so little that I meant myself when I said not one.

When I was that one, I said that when I was looking I did not see what I was seeing.

That can happen to any one.

Of course it does. Be natural and of course it does.

You are looking you are seeing what you are seeing and are you.

If you are one then now and then you are not that one. That can happen at any time. It does happen when any one is a little one and any one, any one is then one.

So you see time and identity mean what they say when they say that they are not existing.

Be natural oh yes do be natural and do have what you have, and if you have what you have then you do not have time and identity inside in one since you do have that when you are looking you are seeing what you are seeing but perhaps not.

Really that has really nothing to do with anything.

But what has.

That there is no identity and that there is no time.

What is the use of being a little boy if you are going to be a man.

Which is which.

Autobiography number II

I tried in Making of Americans to make any one one. How.

By having a beginning and middle and ending.

But is there any such thing as a beginning. Be natural is there.

And a middle.

And an ending.

Any one who is one can be natural if he can. If he cannot he can be just as natural as he can that is within his human mind, and in his human mind he never did begin, he never has begun he never began.

Of course not if he did where is he.

Anyhow there is nothing the matter with this.

And so human nature is not in any way related to the human mind.

Nobody need be triumphant about this.

Think of the master-pieces remember how few there are and how many anybody is. And so why be happy and yet anybody is.

I wish writing would not sound like writing and yet what else can any writing sould like.

Well yes it can it cannot sound like writing because if it

sounds like writing then anybody can see it being written, and the human mind nobody sees the human mind while it is being existing, and master-pieces well master-pieces may not be other than that that they do not exist as anybody seeing them and yet there they are.

Please please me.

Anybody can please me, but that is not what the human mind is.

Sadism no that is not what sadism is.

I am not confused but belated, can the human mind be belated.

I like words that have been left alone and words that have not been left alone.

Which of these is belated.

Autobiography number III

To see anything as flat.

That not being autobiography but the history of master-pieces.

Is the history of master-pieces autobiography.

Autobiography number II

Seeing everything as flat.

When you look at anything and you do not see it all in one plain, you do not see it with the human mind but anybody can know that. It is naturally that. And so it is because there is no time and no identity in the human mind.

The human mind has always tried to say that of something else but why when there it is right in the human mind. That is because the human mind can think that human nature may be what it is but human nature is what human nature is which is not the human mind.

The human mind has neither identity nor time and when it sees anything has to look flat. That is what makes master-pieces makes a master-piece what it is, and when it is only that only no time or identity then it is that.

Yes we can say that naturally of course naturally naturally it is that.

Autobiography number I

I noticed to-day under a tree nobody was singing to me there they were just as they were but they did not look as if they were flat, so they were not a master-piece no indeed not.

Autobiography number I

Anyone can read any one who is one and very often it is master-pieces it is the master-pieces that they read.

They read them and they are one the master-piece is.

There is no identity and no time in a master-piece nor in the human mind.

No of course not.

It is the habit to say that there must be a god but not at all the human mind has neither time or identity and therefore enough said.

Be natural and anybody who has a human mind and anybody who has has will know this.

If anybody is natural they know what is.

It is what it is.

Least said soonest mended but a great deal is said.

You say I say he says, but I have not expressed a part at any time.

No not at any time.

Autobiography number one.

Could there be a time when all the time the human mind was within which time.

No not at all.

Because there would then be more master-pieces or there would not then be all the time then any one then who knew the master-pieces of any time when then they had them.

I remember so well always saying in the Making of Americans then knowing not knowing but having then the difficulty of being sure that then was then.

Any one can have that inside them and therefore then well then then is what they say again and again but not then.

Do you see how sweetly I can be having then not then.

Oh yes I know then when then is not then.

But it never is because there is no time and no identity in the human mind.

It is so natural to know this thing that everybody does so naturally know this thing that anybody would naturally know this thing if they did not believe what they saw although naturally anybody can know if anybody can tell them so that they do not believe that they saw what they saw.

That is why superstition is so sweet.

Of course it is sweet.

It is just as sweet as sweet as it can be.

I believe what I know although nobody tells me so, because I know that I believe what I know. But in doing so, there is no time in me and no identity.

Autobiography number V

When I was at college I studied philosophy that was it they did not know what they saw because they said they saw what they knew, and if they saw it they no longer knew it because then they were two.

It is just as necessary as that and that is why a young one knows it too, he knows he is through not because he is young but because he is through.

Of course he is through with philosophy because just then he is not yet two.

The minute you are two it is not philosophy that is through it is you.

But when you are one you are through with philosophy, because philosophy has to talk to itself about it, anything but a master-piece does that and if it does then it is not one but two.

You see that is what religion means when it says two in one and three in one and so religion can try to be one in one. But not really one because then it is not yet or ever begun.

So though they say it is one they try to make it as two.

So after all then even in religion one is not one.

But in the human mind and in master-pieces oh yes oh yes.

Autobiography one again.

It is not I who doubt what it is all about but she says clearly, human nature is not only uninteresting it is painful but I it is not I who doubt what it is all about but naturally what it is is what it is not.

Time and identity and what is it that the human mind does and if it does it what does it do it about.

Identity.

I knew him that is I have known him and it has always been the same him the same hymn, it has been the hymn of having his pictures within.

Yes and so when they said he was divorcing I could not believe that it had been done by him but it was because the pictures not inside him but the pictures outside him were being taken away from him. The pictures inside him even if they were being taken away from him that is changed inside him were still the pictures that there were inside in him.

Now this might mean that there is identity if you were to say that this is so which it is but nevertheless there it is not because to-day is never to-morrow or yesterday although if it is if to-morrow is to-day that is what she can say she can say that if to-morrow is nearer to to-day, so some can say so she can say then to-morrow is to-day but if to-morrow is not anywhere near to-day which is what he can say then to-morrow cannot be to-day.

Yesterday nobody can take any interest in because there is not really any of any such a thing.

So once as once and not once again because again and again is not anything identity and time is not any confusion. Natural enough is natural enough.

Let me tell the history of my life the life which makes any identity not be away because there is no identity that is not there to stay.

What is it.

Naturally when inside is inside it sees outside but it is inside.

Therefore identity and time have nothing to do with from time to time since inside is inside even if it does see outside.

I began with this.

Yes Miss I began with this only two ses are not the same as one.

But what is the same. He acts the same. Does that make identity one and one and one.

But certainly not because otherwise there would be a use

in being a boy if you are going to grow up to be a man and there is none.

Autobiography number one.

Anything can make me think what money is, what is it.

No one can know that any one can know that not any one is troubled so that they cannot be careless.

I was not careless about identity and time oh no I was not and I was not no I was not careless about romantic scenery no I was not, and if I was careless about money no I was not I was and I was not that is what money is I was and I was not about money and I was careless about sadism and if not then why not, sadism is not interesting if not so once when there is about sadism an if not then we do not count it as interesting. Money is interesting and romanticism not human nature and sadism. Make it another thing if you like sad is and sadism. Do you see what I mean very likely yes and that is not interesting even though anybody can enjoy reading which very often is just what makes reading like sitting and sitting and running is not interesting although very occupying and filling. Oh yes who likes to include gardening what is the difference between gardening and farming. Money is the difference and money who likes money money is what we all agree, to be happy and make money, is anything.

But now why should not it be likely that farewell is spoken.

Farewell if it is spoken should be romanticism and has romanticism time and identity think about that.

Inside in any human mind there is not there is no time and there is no identity otherwise what is inside is not. But if it is inside then there is not there is no time and there is no identity. But romanticism and money which has to do with what is what and what is not what. What is what is money, what is what is not and yet what is not what, that is romanticism which is not what not. Romanticism which is what. Answer me that which is what.

It is not a flat surface romanticism like the master-pieces and yet it is because it is so think that yes it is. If something that is not flat is thick enough then it is that it is flat. And so romanticism can be a master-piece. But sadism well you can see that sadism can never become flat because it never can become one. Romanticism can when it is thick enough. And money yes when it is thin enough to be all that money is which is what it is. Thick or thin wide or dim left to him taken to win, winning is a description of a charming person.

Autobiography number one.

I am writing all this with an American dollar pen.

Autobiography number one.

What did I study I studied philosophy and science and psychology and medicine and I read literature and history, and any other thing that can make reading.

And what happened while was doing all this well anything if you like well anything but mostly if you like everything. Now I can have liked to tell it as a history of finding out about anything that there is no time and identity inside in me that is inside in anything and that there is no use in learning well enough alone because by and by well because there is no by and by. Because mention me if you can because I am here.

Why need you think you can believe about a dog because you love him. You can love a dog and you can not think about anything which is kindly enough.

It is wonderful how a handwriting which is illegible can be read, oh yes it can.

Autobiography number one is almost done.
Autobiography number one

Not solve it but be in it, that is what one can say of the problem of the relation of human nature to the human mind, which does not exist because there is none there is no relation, because when you are in the human mind you are in it, and when you are in human nature you are of it.

Become Because.

Beware of be.

Be is not what no one can be what no one can see and certainly not what no one can say.

Anybody can say be.

Be is for biography.

And for autobiography

No not for autobiography because he comes after.

So once more to renounce because and become.

When I was certain that science was stating what any one was seeing and human nature well I was going to be stating anything that any one could be seeing and human nature was that thing, I was writing the Making of Americans. But supposing yes one did see anything and there was time enough time did not make any difference because there is always time enough, if there is enough of anything then one need not be worrying and there always is time enough. I then no longer was worrying about time but I just stopped going on. That is what time is. There is always enough and so there is no going on no not in the human mind there is just staying within. That is a natural thing when there is enough of anything and there always is enough of time. So then time is nothing since there is always enough of it.

The human mind has nothing to do with time since it is within and in within enough has nothing to do with anything.

Oblige me by not beginning. Also by not ending.

But human nature oh yes human nature always has to do with enough.

That is you might say all human nature does it does do with enough.

But autobiography which has no be in it demands of me that I say that the day that I knew that there was time enough to say all that was so of human nature then I did not do so any more, because anything that you see is so and the master-pieces which just are not master-pieces are always telling it as so. Of course it is if it is so but the human mind oh no it is not so.

The human mind is not so because being within it has nothing to do with identity or time or enough.

Anybody knows this as a natural thing, just begin with within that is do not begin, no do not do not begin, how can any one begin when within is not cannot be begun. Just be reasonable about this, please just do. It is so simple to have it be true. Oh yes these are ordinary ideas.

But then, philosophy and science and medicine.

Philosophy tells why nothing is begun but if it is not begun then there is no why. Inside anybody inside anybody inside knows there is no why to not begin because there is no such thing. No such thing as began.

Human nature is not natural it is what anybody does and what anybody does is not natural and therefore it is not interesting.

There is no doubt that human nature is not interesting although the human mind has always tried to be busy about this thing that human nature is interesting and the human mind has made so many efforts always it is doing this thing trying to make it be to itself that human nature is interesting but it is not and so the master-pieces always flatten it out, flatten human nature out so that there is no beginning and middle and ending, because if there is not then there is no doing and if there is no doing then there is no human nature and so to do without human nature which is not interesting is what within the human mind is doing. There is no relation between the human mind and human nature.

Each one is as it is.

Philosophy tries to replace in the human mind what is not there that is time and beginning and so they always have to stop going on existing. There are consequently practically no master-pieces in philosophy.

Philosophy then says human nature is interesting. Well it is not. That is all that there is to say about that. It is so easy to be right if you do not believe what you say.

Please listen to that.

Autobiography number one now
almost completely begun.

Avoid be in begun.

It is so easy to be right.

If you do not believe what you say.

Of course there is believing what anybody else can say.

Of course there is nothing in that.

Religion has been called natural.

Well there is something in that, because religion does know that there is no time and no identity and no enough and no human nature in the human mind, but religion is timid and so it does not say why or how but it does say where and saying where it must look over there.

So little by little which is not enough I found that enough is not enough and not enough should be treated roughly.

So finally I became so attached to one word at a time even if there were always one after the other.

Now then let me tell the story of my life.

The story of my life.
Chapter one.

At that time I had no dogs

Chapter II

So I was not I because my little dog did not love me. But I had a family. They can be a nuisance in identity but there is no doubt no shadow of doubt that that identity the family identity we can do without.

It has nothing to do with anything if there is no time and identity. But it has to do oh yes it has to do with how do you do you do do what you do.

The human mind lives alone.

That is the way you feel in Chapter II.

Chapter III

Master-pieces are there they always have been there but do they make identity for you.

They do not make time that is certain and identity one can then be tempted into changing them into identity.

But if one does

No one does what they do.

Chapter II

You identify yourself with master-pieces in Chapter II and in chapter three they give you identity, but in chapter one none there is no identity and no time and in Chapter IV anybody can shut any door.

If you can shut any door identity has no meaning that is what happens in chapter four.

Chapter IV

Move around quickly and then stop completely is what is happening in chapter four.

Chapter four has no identity and no time and more than all there is of enough. Enough said.

Chapter IV

So anybody can see that is to say it is natural enough it is ordinary enough that there is no identity and no time and no interest in enough.

After that there are many hours of occupation and master-pieces are master-pieces.

This is one's life from birth to sixteen and the rest is not worth while recording master-pieces I mean.

Master-pieces and identity.

It is natural if it is as seen is seeing naturally what is seen.

There is no use in being discontented with what anybody sees.

But master-pieces, no master-pieces are not there but everybody says that is what a master-piece does but does it. Does it say what everybody sees, and yet it does but is not that what makes a master-piece not have it be that it is what it is.

Think are master-pieces natural enough and what is natural enough.

Master-pieces and identity, audiences and identity, do these separate to please or do they not do as they please.

When the little dog wants the ball he forgets to get it if he does not please and if he does and does get then is his identity an audience. It looks as if it is but is it.

A master-piece certainly has nothing to do with identity because identity if it had an audience would not care to be a master-piece.

Not leaving anything alone is not what a master-piece does.

But really what I would like to know is why the very good things everybody says and everybody knows and everybody writes are not master-pieces I would really very much like to know why they are not. And when I say identity is not yes there is something in it all the time that there is not.

If not why not.

So many words to use.

Oh do not say that words have a use.

Anybody can tell what everybody knows but what does that disclose.

Oh dear what does that inclose.

After all what everybody knows is not a master-piece but everybody says it is.

Do they.

Oh yes everybody says it is.

But everybody knows what everybody knows.

And human nature is what everybody knows and time and identity is what everybody knows and they are not master-pieces and yet everybody knows that master-pieces say what they do say about human nature and time and identity, and what is the use, there is no abuse in what is the use, there is no use. Why not.

Now listen. What is conversation.

Conversation is only interesting if nobody hears.

Hear hear.

Master-pieces are second to none.

One and one.

I am not frightened but reasonably secure that whether it is so whether it is so whether it is so.

Master-piece or none.

Which is one.

I ask you which is one.

If he had not been frightened away he might have drunk a water but he finally did.

This is as good an example of a master-piece as there is.

Page I

Play for be and its thorn.

So music can replace nature.

But what is nature.

Not music

Music only can replace nature.

What is nature.

Nature is what it is.

Emotion is what it is.

Romance is what it is and there can be no romance without nature.

But is nature natural.

No not as natural as that.

He reads master-pieces but he knows nature and music is not that.

An ode to Thornton.
Page I

I meant to do just what I do but I never meant to do just what if I do I do.

Is that just human nature or the human mind.

It is neither.

Is it money.

Yes perhaps it is money.

Let us linger upon money.

Volume I

Money is what words are.

Words are what money is.

Is money what words are

Are words what money is.

There can be no romance without nature, there can be no money without words.

There can be nature without words.

Nature is here used in the sense of natural scenery and what land is.

And so nature is not what money is.

There can be music without words.

So there can be no music where words are.

Therefore music has nothing to do with money and with words.

Did I say embrace the problem no neither embrace nor replace the problem.

But to accustom oneself to the problem the problem of why if human nature is not interesting are master-pieces supposed to be interesting because of the subject of human nature in them.

Of course they are not the master-pieces are not because the human nature in them the telling of human nature in them is the same telling of human nature of those that do not make master-pieces by the telling of the same things about human nature that the master-pieces tell in them.

Human nature is not interesting and what the master-pieces tell about human nature in them is not what makes them everlastingly interesting, no it is not.

They read master-pieces. I read what are not master-pieces but which quote pieces of master-pieces in them. And what do I find I find that comparisons and human nature is not what makes master-pieces interesting.

But money and a word and romanticism.

They they have nothing of any human nature in them.

And thank you for not.

Money and words and romanticism have no time or identity in them, oh please certainly not.

Get used to them, you cannot get used to money or words or romanticism no certainly not.

But you can get used to human nature, yes certainly that.

Anybody can get used to human nature.

You see the only thing about government and governing that is interesting is money. Everything else in governing and propaganda is human nature and as such it is not interesting. Everything else has time and identity which is human nature and that is not at all interesting. No it can be completely understood that the only thing that is interesting in governing and government is money. Money has no time and no identity and no human nature, because of course it has not.

Let us remember how what happens happens.

Nothing happens.

Page II

Words. Very well. Words.

What are words.

Any word is a word.

There is no use to say accustomed.

All words are not words to which you can get accustomed or used.

Therefore a great many of them cannot go into master-pieces.

Those to which you can get used or those to which you cannot get used.

Cannot or can get used.

Any word which can go into a master-piece is one to which you cannot get used or perhaps not.

Anyway what is a master-piece. There is no doubt of what is a master-piece but is there any doubt what a master-piece is.

I like to be kindly.

I like to forget.

I like to make old horses be mules.

I like oxen to have wealth.

I like cows to be nearly able to feed.

I like to look about me.

I like to have no animation.

I like birds to have gone away.

I like arrangements to be made.

I like a chance to burn leaves.

I like what they understood to be clearly.

I like it when it turns up.

I like it by nearly alone.

After all why may it not be true that every one knows this. They do.

But why may it nearly not be true that it is not difficult to do.

It is not difficult to do.

In the first place think of words apart or together.

It makes anybody happy to have words together. It makes anybody happy to have words apart. Either may not have anything whatever to do with human nature.

Any word may and does not have anything whatever to do with identity too.

Nor with time.

There are no tears when you say and not with time.

Nor either when you say not with identity.

It carefully comes about that there is no identity and no time and therefore no human nature when words are apart. Or rather when words are together.

Beginning and middle and ending gathers no pleasure, and no money and no romanticism and no human mind.

When the piece of the master-piece is quoted, a very little at a very little time does any part come apart.

No because it has never been together never been other than together.

Either that or never apart.

Identity is very curious.

Not even the dogs can worry any further about identity.

They would like to get lost and if they are lost what is there of identity.

They would like very much like at all to get lost.

Lost.

That is what you say. Lost.

They would like to get lost and so they would then be there where there is no identity, but a dog cannot get lost, therefore he does not have a human mind, he is never without time and identity.

Poor dog how he would like to be lost.

They make believe that they would like to go out of their mind and so be lost.

Poor dog who is not cannot is not lost.

Let me tell you a story.

Basket a story.
Interlude I

I am I because my little dog knows me.

Is he is when he does not know me.

This sometimes happens.

That is his not knowing me.

When it does not happen he sometimes tries to make it happen.

So is he he when he does not know me.

And when he does not know me am I I.

But certainly this is not so although it really very truly is so.

Page III
Identity

Thank you for a name.

Thank nobody for the same.

Identity.

Is it well to know the end of any identity.

Supposing you begin well and do know quite as well that you are you.

When you are you say it and when you say it you know it if by knowing it you can say it.

I say that spoken words mean nothing, written words yes because by the time they are written they are no longer said.

Anybody think about writing that is not written to anybody know this.

The words spoken are spoken to somebody, the words written are except in the case of master-pieces written to somebody, somebody somebody there is the identity that of somebody. Somebody tears come to my eyes when I say somebody, and why well because the word sound like that that of something like a dog that can be lost. Anything that can be lost is something anybody can get used to and that is identity.

And so in the human mind which can write but not speak, which can write but not get used to what it can write can write but cannot get lost, that is what the human mind is.

I do not know whether or not human nature can get lost but it certainly can get used to it and so it has its identity.

Do I make this clear, hear oh hear do I do I make this make this clear.

To hear.

I wish it were easy to say what a master-piece is as to say what human nature and time and identity is.

Anything that is or can be lost is so easy to describe because it is of no interest.

But money.

Well money is not easy to describe. It is easy to lose but it cannot be lost, and no one can get really get used to it.

And romanticism.

Nothing is there when he says he likes music better, which means not at all that he does not like what he likes at all. Not at all.

Page IV

Bob Davis.

What is human nature.

If you please you do not know.

But you do not have to know because never to refuse is never to excuse and so well not at all and so.

You need not expect time to be solid.
You might but you do not have to.
And as you do not have to you do not.
Do not have to.
You do not.
So Bob Davis.
What do you do.
Nothing.
And why not.
Because there is no time.
Quite naturally not.
And Bob Davis why is natural not the same as naturally not.
If it is solid it is naturally not.
That is it is not naturally not.
There is no confusion in solidity rejoining.
Bob Davis may not be a pair.
Because identity is not there.
At a distance we saw a man on a bicycle and at a distance he looked like two.
There is no need to measure.
There is no solidity where there is a measure.
And so identity is not a ball, no not at all.
It is not there.
Where.
Where is it not there.
Anywhere.
Bob Davis.
Wherein a master-piece is not a thing.
There is no in within.
By the time I knew what a master-piece is.
Well.
By the time I knew what a master-piece is.

Page IV

Human nature is so not interesting that there is not any of a different thing in there being no time and identity.

Page IV

Plainly not identity as much as plainly identity.
Human nature plainly worries about identity.

And so human nature is all of identity, and who is who.
If they asked who is who what would identity do.

Page two.

I said once I said perhaps it is true that what makes poetry possible is a small country. Big countries cannot really make poetry because they do not cannot all when they say the same thing feel as they do.

By this I mean.

All this I mean.

Page two.

Now when I said this did I mean that poetry is what is seen. Suppose I do mean this.

Poetry may be what is seen and it often is.

Poetry is not identity no that it never is.

Poetry may be time but if it is then it is remembered time and that makes it be what is seen.

And so poetry a great deal of poetry is what is seen.

And if it is then in so far as it is it is not a master-piece. What is seen may be the subject but it cannot be the object of a master-piece.

But a great deal of poetry is made up of subject and if it is then it is not a master-piece.

In a small country where the land is not flat and where as you look you see what it is if it is as it is a great deal of poetry can and will and shall and must and may be written.

And that is as it is because anybody saying anything anybody knows what it is.

But in a large country and even in a small one if it is flat not every one can see what it is when they see what it is.

It is because of this that so much poetry of what it is that is seen is written in a small country that is not flat and that can go on to do what it has to do.

But in a flat country it must have content but not form and that may make a master-piece but is it poetry.

Master-pieces master-pieces there is no use in asking where are you because that everybody knows but what are you well that may be nobody knows.

Well anyway poetry is poetry and a great deal of poetry says what is seen as it is, says what it is as it is seen. Yes.

Page nine.

I know the difference between what is and is not that is I know the difference between what it is and what is it and in doing so have I come to go that is to know which is it.

Like this.

Like this is not to like this.

Any word is a word that they use and in America where the land is flat they do see that there is no use in there being any use in knowing what it is because is it is it what it is.

They do not glow because they think it is so and so they do not know that it is so in other words as likely as not it is neither what or why it is so since not at all is never said no not in America.

What have master-pieces to do with what is never said or indeed with what is said.

Nothing at all either gradually or not at all.

Now listen to this.

If a master-piece is what it is how can then its not being one effect it.

All that is silence because it makes longing and longing and feeling have nothing to do with what a master-piece is.

Occasionally nothing to do with what a master-piece is.

Even if it is a feeling of longing it has nothing to do with what a master-piece is.

Thornton Wilder what is a master-piece.

He says he hopes he knows that longing has nothing to do with what a master-piece is.

With which they wish that longing has nothing to do with what a master-piece is.

I do I know what has nothing to do with what a master-piece is.

They say longing has to do with what a master-piece is but they are mistaken longing has nothing to do with what a master-piece is.

I said to Basket my dog look and long but I said this has nothing to do with what a master-piece is and he may not

believe it he easily may not but it has not does not have anything to do with what a master-piece is.

Page I

They like to remember to forget and that that is this has
nothing to do with what a master-piece is.

Page I

What is a master-piece and how many of them that is are
them.

Well believe it or not it makes no difference to them.

Page I

I would kindly not like to know what a master-piece is.

Page 2

About detective stories is the trouble with them that the
one that is dead has no time and no identity for him to them
and yet they think that they can remember what they do not
have as having it without their having it for them.

I would like to read a detective story every day and very
often I do.

Page II

I think nothing about men and women because that has
nothing to do with anything.

Anybody who is an American can know anything about this
thing.

Page III

How completely I know and I tell you so that it has nothing
to do with men and women nothing to do with anything
anything with anything that is with anything nothing to do
with anything.

After all nothing to do with anything with like that nothing.

Men and women may not regret human nature just as they
like they may not regret anything.

Has anybody neglected the human mind.

I have.

What you have.

In this way have is what you have.

I can never neglect have at least not for very long because in it without it is all there is of master-pieces and the human mind. Because have is just that word.

Page IV

I could admire what I have just said.

Page V

I remit the temptation to say it again.
And so kindly allied.

Page I

They never had any.

Page I

I can slowly change to what I say.

At Page I

Well well at page one.

Finally it is true that soldiers who are not at war look as they do.

Is that so.

Any word will do.

Therefore it is true

That any way you see it is what is where they have it and yet all knitting if it is done by hand can and does resemble that done by machine.

And any one is deceived and only those that are interested make use of it.

What is a master-piece.

Any one that is no one is deceived because although any one can quote it no one can make use of it.

It is not any loss to loss a master-piece.

Every once in a while one is lost.

I remember very well deciding not to worry even if a master-piece should get lost. Any master-piece ancient or modern because there is no such thing as ancient or modern in a master-piece how can there be when there is no time and no identity.

And if a master-piece is lost then there is just one less to know about and as there are so few after all does it make any difference.

Suppose you have them all or none at all.

But nevertheless master-pieces do have to have existence and they do each one they do although there are very few.

We know very well that master-pieces have nothing to tell how can they when after all anything that tells what every one tells tells what any one tells.

I tell you that any soldiers at all look as soldiers are.

Of course they do.

Anybody too.

And master-pieces do only master-pieces have to be what they tell well anybody can tell anything very well.

Shakespeare.

I said to Thornton Wilder but you do know that the psychology in Shakespeare is no psychology at all, a young man whose father was just murdered, would not act like Hamlet, Hamlet was not interested in his father, he was interested in himself, and he acted not like a young man who has lost a loved father but like a man who wants to talk about himself, that is psychology if you like but anybody in any village can do that.

Now in a master-piece what does anybody do they do what they do that is they say what they know and they only know what they are as they know what they are, there is no time and no identity, not at all never at all ever at all.

Page I

What is the difference between conversation and writing, oh yes what is the difference the difference is that conversation is what is said and what is said is always led and if it is led then it is said and that is not written. Written writing should not be led oh no it should not be led not at all led.

And so writing is not conversation.

Also then there is the fact that human nature is not scenery that land which is seen is not announced. Human nature is announced it announces itself it says yes I did it before but scenery well scenery if it did before does it now but human nature if it does it now did it before.

Scenery if it did it before does not remember but human nature if it did it before does remember because everything that human nature does it does remember and if it remembers it then it is not interesting and if it is not interesting then it is human nature. The only thing about human nature that holds the attention is that it has a beginning and a middle and an end and when a book is not a master-piece it is that which determines it that it has a beginning and a middle and an end, the middle is mostly not as interesting as the beginning and the end and that is because it is not based on human nature but it is human nature and therefore not a master-piece.

Now scenery has no beginning and middle and end, and that is what makes scenery romantic. If it had a beginning and a middle and an end as a storm has then it would not be romantic, the storm is romantic because the scenery is there and the scenery has not a beginning and a middle and an end.

Now that makes master-piece easier, not easier to do but easier, and the human mind.

Also it makes romanticism easier, never forget there is also money.

Also there is why is it that in this epoch the only real literary thinking has been done by a woman.

Yes please think of something.

That is it.

Please think of something.

And so no need of going around, because the scenery is there, not a storm, soldiers are not a storm, they look like it they look like not a storm, if anybody salutes you and respects you that is like a storm, and so in this epoch the important literary thinking is done by a woman.

But yet yes.

By no means cease.

Page II

Romantic and romanticism, it is a pleasure to all beholders that a landscape is there and as it is there, what is there to see of it, only that which is not human nature, even a storm.

A storm would like to have a beginning and a middle and an ending, but very likely it settles as well.

Really settles has no need of triumph and yet that is just what a storm does and so it is not human nature. Human nature and triumph they would hardly like that. Which they hardly would like.

Human nature is not interesting some say triumph is.

A storm is romantic like a storm is but human nature is not like a storm because human nature does not act like that it only acts like a storm when it knows about a storm and when it knows about a storm it acts like a storm.

Has that anything to do with master-pieces.

It has nothing to do with human nature.

Forget human nature when it is human nature.

There is no use in forgetting scenery when it is scenery because there is nothing to forget.

Once more I can climb about and remind you that a woman in this epoch does the important literary thinking.

And money what is the connection between romanticism and money and master-pieces.

Which one is it.

There never is a which one.

Page I

No one would if they could relieve page one from page one.

Page II

It is an obligation to have money connect itself with romanticism because that too is not human nature but scenery and if there is a storm then insofar as there is a storm there is triumph.

Page II

After all war in war is no different than war not in war except that there are more dead.

If there are more dead is there a difference and if there is a difference has it to do with money and romanticism.

Nobody criticises what is not war by what is not war.

And yet after all there is no difference when there is a difference and when it is all neither war not more war.

And so they fairly evenly place it where money is.

And when there is no money at all does he know what money is. More money is not what money is.

Do you see its connection with romanticism.

A little gradually not at all, in among not as more than all.

Bennett would like another portrait.

What is a portrait to him.

A portrait to him.

What is it.

A portrait to him.

Page III

Human nature has nothing to do with it.

Human nature.

Has nothing to do with it.

Page IV

Emptying and filling an ocean has nothing to do with it because if it is full it is an ocean and if it is empty it is not an ocean.

Filling and emptying an ocean has nothing to do with it.

Page IV

Nothing to do with master-pieces.

Page V

Nothing to do with war.

Page VI

War has nothing to do with master-pieces.

Who says it has.

Everybody says it has.

Does anybody say what a master-piece is.

No nobody does.

Page VII

So then the important literary thinking is being done.

Who does it.

I do it.
Oh yes I do it.

Page VIII

Money one.
Romanticism one.
Scenery one.
Human nature not one.
Master-pieces.
Human nature never knew anything about one and one.

Page XXI

Storms.
Even a little one is not exciting.

Page XXI

Is there any difference between flat land and an ocean a big country and a little one.

Is there any difference between human nature and the human mind.

Poetry and prose is not interesting.

What is necessary now is not form but content.

That is why in this epoch a woman does the literary thinking.

Kindly learn everything please.

Page XXI

How ardently hurry comes too late.

That is what they used to say.

Donald.

Donald and Dorothy Dora and Don Donald and Donald he comes when he can.

If he can when he can as he can nine.

Donald and Donald is all in one time.

To-morrow is as Donald would say twenty a day.

What does Donald do.

He does it all.

Of course what does Donald do.

Of course he does he does do it at all.

Donald dear.

Welcome here.
If he comes yes he comes.
Yes he comes.
If he comes.
Any Donald is not Donald there.
Donald there is not any Donald here.
But better here.
What if Donald may.
Not likely is not as different as very likely.
And very likely Donald is here.

Page XVIII

I may not be through with Donald.

Page XIX

Donald has nothing to do with romanticism.
Donald has nothing to do with money
Donald has nothing to do with scenery.
Donald has nothing to do with human nature.
Donald has nothing to do.
Donald.
No one can reproach Donald.
Donald and Dorothy and once there was an ocean and they were not drowned.

Page 2

You

Page III

Why should a woman do the literary important literary thinking of this epoch.

Page IV

Master-pieces are what they are.

Page V

There is no identity nor time in master-pieces even when they tell about that.

Page X

Is Franklin Roosevelt trying to get rid of money. That would be interesting, but I am afraid it is only human nature, that is electioneering and that is not interesting.

But it would be interesting to try to get rid of money by destroying it and if it could be done it would be interesting.

Why would it be interesting.

Because perhaps money has to do with the human mind and not with human nature, perhaps like master-pieces it concerns itself with human nature but it is not related to it, oh yes yes.

Could one get rid of war by it becoming like duelling and would the way be by stopping saluting, if nobody saluted and nobody received saluting and nobody saluted and nobody wore any clothes that were given to them would that have anything like duelling to do with war ending, oh yes oh yes, and has war anything to do with the human mind no it has to do with human nature because it is not like money it might be like romanticism but is it, it might be but is it.

If it is yes is it.

In the nineteenth century when they wanted it to be a mystery it ended with the dead man in the twentieth century when they want it to be a mystery they begin it with a dead man.

And in plays well what are plays.

Do not listen to some.

What are plays.

A play.

It begins with a dead man a dead woman and a dead dog but they are not dead because the play goes on.

If the dog is dead does the play go on.

If the army is dead does the play go on.

If the dog is not dead does the play go on.

No indeed no certainly not.

Play 2.

If the dog is not dead and the play does not go on is the man dead.

Yes the man is dead.

If the man is dead and the play does not go on does it go on. Yes it does go on.

If the woman is dead and the dog is dead and the man is dead does the play go on.

Certainly not the play does not go on.

What does it mean.

Certainly not the play does not go on.

Does it mean it does not go on the stage.

Certainly not it does not mean certainly not not on the stage.

And so there is no time and no identity please be careful not to surprise tears.

In the nineteenth century they did not surprise tears they dwelt with tears because the man and the dog and the woman were not dead when anything began in the twentieth century everything that is any one is dead when it can and did when it began and so there are no tears were no tears.

Play I

Now how can they come to be now.

Play I

Any little thing is how it was begun.
It is clearer than any one that there are no tears now.

Play one.

Alright play one.

Play two.

It should be two to be through.
But there is that.
That as it has not to be that that is not that.
It easily is.
More and more a master-piece is.

Play III

I begin to see see I begin but there is no begin not in not in.

Play IV

Do you see it is to be.
But there is be as well as see.

Play V

So then

Play VI

The glory of knowing what a master-piece is.

Play VII

It is natural that again a woman should be one to do the literary thinking of this epoch.

Chapter I

I have it as quite that a master-piece where it is there.
To-morrow it will be warmer to say so.
See there is no need to be free.
They say so but there is no need to be free.
Did I say so that perhaps Franklin Roosevelt is getting rid of money but perhaps he is only electioneering.
Anybody can know that human nature is not interesting and now not even necessary.
Not even necessary.

Chapter III

I so easily said it would be interesting and cried to have it interesting and be and may be I do but I doubt it not interesting.
I have made no intention.
I tell him content without form, lizard without homes and there should be a third and as there is there is a beginning and middle and end.
But content without form.
Who has hoped to be hoped.
I tell you it is true that I do the literary thinking for you.
Even perhaps if Franklin Roosevelt wants to get rid of money.

Chapter II

It is just as necessary not to have any human nature.

Volume II

Why was Polonius the one to say the things he said in his advice to his son because of course any one who writes anything is talking to themselves and that is what Shakespeare always has done, he makes them say what he wants said just then and he can make any one that one.

Ordinarily anybody finishes anything.

But not in writing. In writing not any one finishes anything. That is what makes a master-piece what it is that there is no finishing.

Please act as if there were the finishing of anything but any one any one writing knows that there is no finishing finishing in writing.

Perhaps Franklin Roosevelt wants to get rid of money by making it a thing having no meaning but mostly likely not most likely it is only electioneering.

What is money and what is romanticism it is not like human nature because it is not finishing it is not like a master-piece because it has no existing.

Very likely that is what it is money and romanticism.

And all the time was I right when I said I was losing knowing what the human mind is. Anybody can know what human nature is and that it is not interesting. Anybody can begin to come to know what money and romanticism is.

Master-pieces have no finishing in them and what anybody can say is what anybody can know and what anybody can know is what anybody can see but human nature and war and storms have a beginning and an ending as they begin they end and as they end they begin and therefore they are not interesting and money and romanticism they do not end and they do not begin but they do not exist and therefore they are not anything although any one can feel that way about them and therefore although they are not anything they are interesting.

Marionette.

Is a marionette a Punch and Judy show and suddenly how to know that Punch and Judy are their names.

When I have said that I know everything and in saying so explain everything at any time of all that time it is as well said as it is said that I know everything.

There is no use in not knowing everything since certainly and knowing most most may not be must but there certainly is the knowing everything.

Of should never be introduced and really it is no temptation not to introduce of.

Of knowing everything.

More than likely knowing everything is what is happening.

It comes back to must.

If there is must then there is not the knowing everything.

Knowing everything comes when in explaining everything there is the knowing that more often there is the knowing everything.

Why are they inclined to leave must alone.

Because must is must.

So much for must.

And knowing everything is never left alone.

In knowing everything never being left alone there makes a recognition of what master-pieces are.

Knowing everything is never left alone nor is it ever without being knowing everything. Anything else is of no account. Not in master-pieces.

Knowing everything well everything you know is knowing everything very likely everything in master-pieces. But never ever anywhere.

There is no where in knowing everything, did we say no time and no identity well and then no place. Space is not interesting because if there is no place there is no space but space is there, well how about money and romanticism nobody wants to know about that.

Space and money and romanticism.

Leave master-pieces alone do not annoy them although they like if they like and they do like romanticism and money and space and they like to look at storms and war and human nature although they do know that they are not interesting.

Knowing everything is interesting. Oh yes yes.

A little play.

War and storms.

Romanticism and money and space.

Human nature and identity and time and place.

Human mind.

Master-pieces.

There need be no personages in a play because if there are then you do not forget their names and if you do not forget their names you put their names down each time that they are to say something.

The result of which is that a play finishes.

How often does anybody like to leave before a play finishes.

Has that anything to do with master-pieces.

Not if you know everything.

Oh yes not if you know everything.

Knowing everything does not remind everybody of something and yet it just might.

And if it well if it did then it just might.

I certainly do know all about knowing everything.

Volume I

Identity.

In case of there not being any possibility of remembering and therefore no way of not losing what is not there where you are is there any way of enfeebling imagination. Indeed what is imagining anything. Is it done a little at a time or is it done a whole at a time and is it done all the time.

They like to know why there is a question and answer. There is in detective stories but is there in real life. Is it possible to imagine a question and an answer.

You never answer a question nobody does.

So then is there in anything a question and answer. And what have master-pieces to do with this thing with their being no question to answer and no answer to a question.

If one is never right about anything and nobody ever is. Anybody who likes can know that, that really they are never right about anything. The more you are right about anything you never are right about anything it does not make any difference. It is only in history government, propaganda that it is of any importance if anybody is right about anything. Science well they never are right about anything not right enough so that science cannot go on enjoying itself as if it is interesting, which it is. Why rest if it is. Human nature not we have come to not thinking that being human nature is interesting enough so that it can go on enjoying itself. Human nature as human nature no longer enjoys itself enough to be enough. And master-pieces have always known that. They have also always known that being right would not be anything because if they were right then it would be not as they wrote but as they thought and in a real master-piece there is no thought, if there were thought then there would be that they are right and in a master-piece you cannot be right, if you could it would be what you thought not what you do write.

Write and right.

Of course they have nothing to do with one another.

Right right left right left he had a good job and he left, left right left.

Volume II

How little need there is to be as right as to have it be Volume two but it is volume two and volume two is not volume two.

Volume two.

I have been writing a political series just to know as well as to know that I am always right that is I am always right when I say what I say and I always say something that is what I am doing I am always saying something but as I am never writing what I am saying when I am writing I am as it were not saying something and so then there it is that is what writing is not saying something content without form but anyway in saying anything there is no content but there is the form of question and answer and really anybody can know that a question if there is an answer or an answer if there is a question is almost always almost human nature which we do know we are not right about it but we do know it know that it is not at all interesting.

It is so easy to know what is not interesting that is it is so easy to know it as it is not interesting. And yet anybody can say that may be it is not so. Of course it is so. Would I not be right if it were not so because it is so.

Just so.

There is no reason that a succession of words should spoil anything when it is always a pleasure.

Human nature is not a pleasure.

Volume III

A Play in which there is not only question and answer but identity.

Imagine that he always liked to write what he says.

He always does.

Does he stop himself when he always does. If he does not stop himself when he always does then he always does. Is that human nature or a master-piece.

Once in a while an individual looks as if he knew what identity is. He does not stop himself not to know what identity is.

Question and answer is so nearly not any more than a pleasure.

And it has no identity.

Question and answer has no identity it has only a form.

If they like to know that they know how pleasant a question and its answer is need they stop themselves from going on. Not at all, they nearly as well do not stop themselves at all from going on. That is what a question and answer is.

Even if there is no pleasure in it that is what a question and answer is. And might there not be any pleasure at all in it. Well yes and no not exactly.

In a way there always is a pleasure in it and there is it like romanticism and money has it something to do with what is not human nature with place and time in itself. In the human mind there is no identity and place and time but in money and romanticism and question and answer a little something yes that is not human nature but has something that is space and time and identity.

Human nature has nothing it is not interesting.

Page I

Do I do this so that I can go on or just to please any one. As I say it makes no difference because although I am always right is being right anything. No it is like human nature it is not interesting and therefore I can ask do you not get tired of always being right but there is something so much more pleasing and that is what is what. And what is what is what is what.

Do not remember question and answer although there is no use in forgetting because question and answer is like romanticism and money. Now we have all this there.

Page I

What is a play.

A play is scenery.

A play is not identity or place or time but it likes to feel like it oh yes it does it does wonderfully well like to feel like it.

That is what makes it a play.

A novel is something else it depends upon its liking to feel that human nature is interesting and therefore there is a middle and a beginning, in a play there is none, but a novel knows that human nature is not interesting and it proposes that if it were it would have a middle and a beginning and a middle and a beginning need not necessarily have an ending, therefore in a really good novel the ending is where it is but a novel is middle and beginning and therefore human nature asks as it does although really human nature has no middle and beginning and so a novel really knows that human nature is not interesting.

Now that is a play and a novel, now essays poetry philosophy and history and biography.

Every once in a while is not every once in a while because it does happen so rarely.

Volume II

If I want to find a volume I number it differently.

Volume III

If you believe what you hear do you believe what you read and what is the difference between what you read and what you see.

Have master-pieces anything to do with what you see, no because what you see is as if it were there. And where is it. It is there. Therefore when you read about it as if it were there then it is not a master-piece.

And you do so often read about it as if it were there. I do all the time and is there any difference if you read about it as if it is there and its being there. If you hear about it as being there then it is not really there not as there as when you read about it being there, but seeing it be there is not more than reading it being there. All this has so much to do with master-pieces that it is always necessary to read some more.

Its being there has nothing to do with question and answer with romanticism and money. Has it anything to do with master-pieces. It almost has if it has. Now and then a master-piece can escape any one and get to be more and more there, and any one any one can who can write as something is written can make anything be there again and again and that is what is so exciting about a detective story, they can make it be there again and again, oh yes any little part of it again and again and so are all detective stories master-pieces how much would anybody like to know that. Not any more than that. It has to be very well known this has to be very well known not to be known and as yet by me it is not well enough known yet not to be known.

Anybody likes it to be known that it is real when it has been written.

What is real when it has been written, it does not have to be a master-piece oh dear oh dear oh dear no. Human nature has nothing to do with this so I believe.

If I write slowly I would write as slowly as this.

It is getting very difficult to be there. Anybody knows how easy it is for anything written to be real. Not when it is about anything but when it is anything oh yes a detective story or any easy novel oh yes and to some something is real and to some nothing is real that is written but writing can make anybody cry. Yes indeed yes. It is so difficult to have anything have anything to do with master-pieces.

Yes Thornton.

Volume II

I have met master-pieces when I was young.

As young as young.

And master-pieces when I was young.

I have met master-pieces.

If a thing can be read again does it have to be remembered.

Anything that is anything can be read again.

And anything seen.

And everything heard.

Do you know any difference.

Volume I

I am I because my little dog knows me. The figure wanders on alone.

The little dog does not appear because if it did then there would be nothing to fear.

Volume II

I like the difference between being alone and not alone.

This made her surrounded.

Now in a master-piece neither one of these is so.

There is no possible doubt that what human nature does has nothing to do with it nothing to do with being alone or not alone because either one of these things is that.

Not that it is no not at all.

Very likely a master-piece is all of and only that.

Do you like identity because then acquaintance is not begun.

Very much as they like the same detective to appear again. And yet the wish that it was not. Because if it is it is expected and if it is not it is not unexpected.

Identity then is not at discretion.

I so easily see that identity has nothing to do with master-pieces although occasionally and very inevitably it does always more or less come in.

It is not known that anybody who is anybody is not alone and if alone then how can the dog be there and if the little dog is not there is it alone. The little dog is not alone because no little dog could be alone. If it were alone it would not be there.

And so a little dog cannot make a master-piece not even now and why.

And yet by recognising that the little dog would not be there if it were alone it can be that I am I because my little dog knows me comes into a master-piece but is not the reason of its being he.

What difference does a master-piece make if there is no dog to be. No dog can be alone. Can a master-piece be alone. Well they say so but is it so.

So then the play has to be like this.

The person and the dog are there and the dog is there and the person is there and where oh where is their identity is the identity there anywhere.

Every century not every century nor every country not every country has what they know is not identity.

For this nobody has to be thankful.

The only relation between anything is master-pieces and master-pieces therefore never have anything to do.

Identity not being the same not even in name, it is so evident that identity is not there at all but it is oh yes it is and nobody likes what they have not got and nobody has identity. Do they put up with it. Yes they put up with it. They put up with identity.

Yes they do that.

And so anything puts up with identity.

A dog has more identity when he is young than when he gets older.

When he is young a dog has more identity than when he is older.

I am not sure that is not the end.

WHAT DOES SHE SEE WHEN SHE SHUTS HER EYES

A Novel

What Does She See When She Shuts Her Eyes

A Novel

IT IS very meritorious to work very hard in a garden equally so when there is good weather and something grows or when there is very bad weather and nothing grows.

When she shuts her eyes she sees the green things among which she has been working and then as she falls asleep she sees them be a little different. The green things then have black roots and the black roots have red stems and then she is exhausted.

Naturally as she works in the garden she grows strawberries and raspberries and she eats them and sometimes the dog eats them and for days after he is not well and finally he is so weak he cannot stand but in a little while he is ready to eat again.

And so a day is not really a day because each day is like another day and they begin to have nothing. She herself was in mourning because her mother had died, her grandmother was dead before her mother died and her father had curly hair and took off his hat so that his eyes could see that somebody had stopped to talk with him.

It is a pleasure to be afraid of nothing. If they have no children they are not afraid of anything.

A good many of them only have one child and that is not the same as not having any children. If they are married and have no children then they are afraid. But if they are not married and have no child then they are not afraid.

Never having seen him before he becomes your servant and lives in the house and just as intimate as if he had been a father or children. It is funny that, there seems to be so much need of having always known anybody and he comes to answer an advertisement and you never saw him before and there you live in the house with him.

After all nothing changes but the weather and when she shuts her eyes she does not see clouds or sky but she sees woods and green things growing.

So the characters in this novel are the ones who walk in the fields and lose their dog and the ones who do not walk in the fields because they have no cows.

But everybody likes to know their name. Their name is Gabrielle and Therese and Bertha and Henry Maximilian Arthur and Genevieve and at any time they have happened to be happy.

Chapter One

How often could they be afraid.

Gabrielle said to any one, I like to say sleep well to each one, and he does like to say it.

He likes to do one thing at a time a long time.

More sky in why why do they not like to have clouds be that color.

Remember anything being atrocious.

And then once in a while it rains. If it rains at the wrong time there is no fruit if it rains at the right time there are no roses. But if it rains at the wrong time then the wild roses last a long time and are dark in color darker than white.

And this makes Henry Maximilian Arthur smile. It is just like the weather to be agreeable because it can be hot enough and so it might just as well not be hot yet. Which it is not.

And therefore Henry Maximilian Arthur is not restless nor is he turned around.

Chapter II

She grew sweet peas and carrots and beets. She grew tomatoes and roses and pinks and she grew pumpkins and corn and beans. She did not grow salad or turnips nor camelias nor nasturtiums but nasturtiums do grow and so do hortensias and heliotrope and fuchsias and peonies. After she was very careful she refused to pay more than they were worth and this brings Henry Maximilian Arthur to the contemplation of money. He might even not then throw it away. He might. After all he clings very tightly to what he has. But not to money because about that there is no need. Money is needful those who can move about. And as yet Henry Maximilian Arthur does not do so.

No matter who has left him where he is no matter no matter who has left him where he is no matter. There he is.

No matter. It does not matter that no one has left any one where he is. It does not matter.

All birds look as if they enjoyed themselves and all birds look as if they looked as if they enjoyed themselves.

Better is not different than does it matter. It is better even if it does not matter.

Once in a while Henry Maximilian Arthur was caressed by Theresa. When Theresa caressed Henry Maximilian Arthur Henry Maximilian Arthur liked it as well as he liked it better. That is what is the way in which it was that it did as well as it did not matter.

Grasses grow and they make a shadow so just as grasses grow.

Henry Maximilian Arthur could be tickled by grasses as they grow and he could not caress but he could be caressed by Theresa as well as be tickled by grasses as they grow, when grass is cut it is called hay.

A year of grass is a year of alas. When grass grows that is all that grows but grass is grass and alas is alas.

Once evening morning Henry Maximilian Arthur was awake. Once every morning he was awake and Theresa was not there and when Theresa came Henry Maximilian Arthur was there just the same.

That is what adding means and a cow. Henry Maximilian Arthur had no need of a cow. Theresa did Theresa had need of a cow, but a cow died and that was a loss a loss of a cow and the loss of the value of the cow and to replace the cow there had to be a medium sized cow and a very small cow. But Henry Maximilian Arthur did not share the anxiety.

PICASSO

Picasso

Painting in the nineteenth century was only done in France and by Frenchmen, apart from that painting did not exist, in the twentieth century it was done in France but by Spaniards.

In the nineteenth century painters discovered the need of always having a model in front of them, in the twentieth century they discovered that they must never look at a model. I remember very well it was between 1904–1908 when people were forced by us or by themselves to look at Picasso's drawings that the first and most astonishing thing that all of them and that we had to say was that he had done it all so marvellously as if he had had a model but that he had done it without ever having had one. And now the young painters scarcely know that there are models. Everything changes but not without a reason.

When he was nineteen years old Picasso came to Paris that was in 1900 into a world of painters who had completely learned everything they could from seeing at what they were looking. From Seurat to Courbet they were all of them looking with their eyes and Seurat's eyes then began to tremble at what his eyes were seeing, he commenced to doubt if in looking he could see. Matisse too began to doubt what his eyes could see. So there was a world ready for Picasso who had in him not only all Spanish painting but Spanish cubism which is the daily life of Spain.

His father was professor of painting in Spain and Picasso wrote painting as other children wrote their a b c. He was born making drawings, not the drawings of a child but the drawings of a painter. His drawings were not of things seen but of things expressed, in short they were words for him and drawing always was his only way of talking and he talks a great deal.

Physically Picasso resembles his mother whose name he finally took. It is the custom in Spain to take the name of one's father and one's mother. The name of Picasso's father was Ruiz, the name of his mother was Picasso, in the Spanish way he was Pablo Picasso y Ruiz and some of his early canvases were signed Pablo Ruiz but of course Pablo Picasso was the better name, Pablo Picasso y Ruiz was too long a name to use as a signature and he commenced almost at once to sign his canvases Pablo Picasso.

The name Picasso is of Italian origin, probably originally they came from Genoa and the Picasso family went to Spain by way of Palma de Mallorca. His mother's family were silversmiths. Physically his mother like Picasso is small and robust with a vigorous body, dark-skinned, straight not very fine nearly black hair; on the other hand Picasso always used to say his father was like an Englishman of which both Picasso and his father were proud, tall and with reddish hair and with almost an English way of imposing himself.

The only children in the family were Picasso and his younger sister of whom he made when he was fifteen years old oil portraits, very finished and painted like a born painter.

Picasso was born in Malaga the 25 of October 1881, but he was educated almost entirely in Barcelona where his father until almost the end of his life was professor of painting at the academy of Fine Arts and where he lived until his death, his mother continued living there with his sister. She has just died there.

Well then, Picasso at nineteen years of age was in Paris, where except for very rare and short visits to Spain, he has lived all his life.

He was in Paris.

His friends in Paris were writers rather than painters, why have painters for friends when he could paint as he could paint.

It was obvious that he did not need to have painters in his daily life, and this was true all his life.

He needed ideas, anybody does, but not ideas for painting, no, he had to know those who were interested in ideas, but as to knowing how to paint he was born knowing all of that.

So in the beginning he knew intimately Max Jacob and at once afterwards Guillaume Apollinaire and André Salmon, and later he knew me and much later Jean Cocteau and still later the Surréalistes; this is his literary history. His intimates amongst the painters, and this was later, much later than Max Jacob and than Guillaume Apollinaire and than André Salmon and than I, were Braque and Derain they both had their literary side, and it was this literary side that was the reason for their friendship with Picasso.

The literary ideas of a painter are not at all the same ideas as the literary ideas of a writer. The egotism of a painter is entirely a different egotism than the egotism of a writer.

The painter does not conceive himself as existing in himself, he conceives himself as a reflection of the objects he has put into his pictures and he lives in the reflections of his pictures, a writer a serious writer conceives himself as existing by and in himself, he does not at all live in the reflection of his books, to write he must first of all exist in himself, but for a painter to be able to paint, the painting must first of all be done, therefore the egotism of a painter is not at all the egotism of a writer, and this is why Picasso who was a man who only expressed himself in painting had only writers as friends.

In Paris the contemporary painters had little effect upon him but all the painting he could see of the very recent past profoundly touched him.

He was always interested in painting as a metier, an incident that happened once is characteristic. In Paris there was an American sculptress who wished to show her canvases and sculpture at the salon. She had always shown her sculpture at the salon where she was hors concours but she did not wish to show sculpture and painting at the same salon. So she asked Miss Toklas to lend her her name for the pictures. This was done. The pictures were accepted in the name of Miss Toklas, they were in the catalogue and we had this catalogue. The evening of the vernissage Picasso was at my house. I showed him the catalogue, I said to him, here is Alice Toklas who has never painted and who has had a picture accepted at the salon. Picasso went red, he said, It's not possible, she has been painting in secret for a long time, Never I tell you, I said to him. It isn't possible, he said, not possible, the painting at the salon is bad painting, but even so if any one could paint as their first painting, a picture that was accepted, well then I don't understand anything about anything. Take it easy, I said to him, no she didn't paint the picture, she only lent her name. He was still a little troubled, no, he repeated, you have to know something to paint a picture, you have to, you have to.

Well he was in Paris and all painting had an influence upon him and his literary friends were a great stimulation to him. I do not mean that by all this he was less Spanish. But certainly for a short time he was more French. Above all and this is quite curious the painting of Toulouse Lautrec greatly interested him, was it once more because Lautrec too had a literary side.

The thing that I want to insist upon is that Picasso's gift is completely the gift of a painter and a draughtsman, he is a man who always has need of emptying himself, of completely emptying himself, it is necessary that he should be greatly stimulated so that he could be active enough to empty himself completely.

This was always the way he lived his life.

After this first definite French influence he became once more completely Spanish. Very soon the Spanish temperament was again very real inside in him. He went back again to Spain in 1902 and the painting known as his blue period was the result of that return.

The sadness of Spain and the monotony of the Spanish coloring after the time spent in Paris struck him forcibly upon his return there. Because one must never forget that Spain is not like other southern countries, it is not colorful, all the colors in Spain are white black silver or gold; there is no red or green, not at all. Spain in this sense is not at all southern, it is oriental, women there wear black more often than colors, the earth is dry and gold in color, the sky is blue almost black, the star-light nights are black too or a very dark blue and the air is very light, so that every one and everything is black. All the same I like Spain. Everything that was Spanish impressed itself upon Picasso when he returned there after his second absence and the result is what is known as his blue period. The French influence which had made his first or Toulouse Lautrec one was over and he had returned to his real character, his Spanish character.

Then again in 1904 he was once again in Paris.

He lived in Montmartre, in the rue Ravignan, its name has

been changed now, but the last time I was there it still had its old charm, the little square was just as it was the first time I saw it, a carpenter was working in a corner, the children were there, the houses were all about the same as they had been the old atelier building where all of them had lived was still standing, perhaps since then, for it is two or three years that I was there last, perhaps now they have commenced to tear it all down and build another building. It is normal to build new buildings but all the same one does not like anything to change, and the rue Ravignan of that time was really something, it was the rue Ravignan and it was there that many things that were important in the history of twentieth century art happened.

Anyway Picasso had once more returned to Paris and it was around 1904 and he brought back with him the pictures of the blue period, also a little landscape of this period which he had painted in Barcelona. Once more back in Paris he commenced again to be a little French, that is he was again seduced by France, there was his intimacy with Guillaume Apollinaire and Max Jacob and André Salmon and they were constantly seeing each other, and this once again relieved his Spanish solemnity and so once more needing to completely empty himself of everything he had he emptied himself of the blue period, of the renewal of the Spanish spirit and that over he commenced painting what is now called the rose or harlequin period.

Painters have always liked the circus, even now when the circus is replaced by the cinema and night clubs, they like to remember the clowns and acrobats of the circus.

At this time they all met at least once a week at the Cirque Medrano and there they felt very flattered because they could be intimate with the clowns, the jugglers, the horses and their riders. Picasso little by little was more and more French and this started the rose or harlequin period. Then he emptied himself of this, the gentle poetry of France and the circus, he emptied himself of them in the same way that he had emptied himself of the blue period and I first knew him at the end of this harlequin period.

The first picture we had of his is if you like, rose or harlequin, it is The Young Girl With a Basket of Flowers; it was painted at the great moment of the harlequin period, full of grace and delicacy and charm. After that little by little his drawing hardened, his line became firmer, his color more vigorous, naturally he was no longer a boy he was a man, and then in 1905 he painted my portrait.

Why did he wish to have a model before him just at this time, this I really do not know, but everything pushed him to it, he was completely emptied of the inspiration of the harlequin period, being Spanish commenced again to be active inside in him and I being an American and in a kind of a way America and Spain have something in common, perhaps for all these reasons he wished me to pose for him. We met at Sagot's, the picture dealer, from whom we had bought The Girl with a Basket of Flowers. I posed for him all that winter, eighty times and in the end he painted out the head, he told me that he could not look at me any more and then he left once more for Spain. It was the first time since the blue period and immediately upon his return from Spain he painted in the head without having seen me again and he gave me the picture and I was and I still am satisfied with my portrait, for me, it is I, and it is the only reproduction of me which is always I, for me.

A funny story.

One day a rich collector came to my house and he looked at the portrait and he wanted to know how much I had paid for it. Nothing I said to him, nothing he cried out, nothing I answered, naturally he gave it to me. Some days after I told this to Picasso, he smiled, he doesn't understand, he said that at that time the difference between a sale and a gift was negligible.

Once again Picasso in 1909 was in Spain and he brought back with him some landscapes which were certainly were the beginning of cubism. These three landscapes were extraordinarily realistic and all the same the beginning of cubism. Picasso had by chance taken some photographs of the village that he had painted and it always amused me when every one protested against the fantasy of the pictures to make them look at the photographs which made them see that the pictures were almost exactly like the photographs. Oscar Wilde used to say that nature did nothing but copy art and really there is some truth in this and certainly the Spanish villages were as cubistic as these paintings.

So Picasso was once more baptised Spanish.

Then commenced the long period which Max Jacob has called the Heroic Age of Cubism, and it was an heroic age. All ages are heroic, that is to say there are heroes in all ages who do things because they cannot do otherwise and neither they nor the others understand how and why these things happen. One does not ever understand before they are completely created what is happening and one does not at all understand what one has done until the moment when it is all done. Picasso said once that he who created a thing is forced to make it ugly. In the effort to create the intensity and the struggle to create this intensity the result always produces a certain ugliness, those who follow can make of this thing a beautiful thing because they know what they are doing, the thing having already been invented, but the inventor because he does not know what he is going to invent inevitably the thing he makes must have its ugliness.

At this period 1908–1909, Picasso had almost never exhibited his pictures, his followers showed theirs but he did not. He said that when one went to an exhibition and looked at the pictures of the other painters one knows that they are bad, there is no excuse for it they are simply bad, but one's own pictures, one knows the reasons why they are bad and so they are not hopelessly bad. At this time he liked to say and later too he used to repeat it, there are so few people who understand and later when every one admires you there are still the same few who understand, just as few as before.

So then Picasso came back from Spain, 1908, with his landscapes that were the beginning of cubism. To really create cubism he had still a long way to go but a beginning had been made.

One can say that cubism has a triple foundation. First. The nineteenth century having exhausted its need of having a model because the truth that the things seen with the eyes are the only real things had lost its significance.

People really do not change from one generation to another, as far back as we know history people are about the same as they were, they have had the same needs, the same

desires, the same virtues and the same qualities, the same de-
fects, indeed nothing changes from one generation to another
except the things seen and the things seen make that generation, that is to say nothing changes in people from one generation to another except the way of seeing and being seen,
the streets change, the way of being driven in the streets
change, the buildings change, the comforts in the houses
change, but the people from one generation to another do
not change. The creator in the arts is like all the rest of the
people living he is sensitive to the changes in the way of living
and his art is inevitably influenced by the way each generation
is living, the way each generation is being educated and the
way they move about, all this creates the composition of that
generation.

This summer I was reading a book written by one of the
monks of the Abbey of Hautecombe about one of the abbots
of Hautecombe and in it he writes of the founding of the
abbey and he tells that the first site was on a height near a
very frequented road. Then I asked all my French friends what
was in the fifteenth century a very frequented road, did it
mean that people passed once a day or once a week. More
than that, they answered me. So then the composition of that
epoch depended upon the way the roads were frequented, the
composition of each epoch depends upon the way the frequented roads are frequented, people remain the same, the
way their roads are frequented is what changes from one century to another and it is that that makes the composition that
is before the eyes of every one of that generation and it is that
that makes the composition that a creator creates.

I very well remember at the beginning of the war being
with Picasso on the boulevard Raspail when the first camou-
flaged truck passed. It was at night, we had heard of camou-
flage but we had not yet seen it and Picasso amazed looked
at it and then cried out, yes it is we who made it, that is
cubism.

Really the composition of this war, 1914–1918, was not the
composition of all previous wars, the composition was not a
composition in which there was one man in the center surrounded by a lot of other men but a composition that had
neither a beginning nor an end, a composition of which one

corner was as important as another corner, in fact the composition of cubism.

At present another composition is commencing, each generation has its composition, people do not change from one generation to another generation but the composition that surrounds them changes.

Now we have Picasso returning to Paris after the blue period of Spain, 1904, was past, after the rose period of France, 1905, was past, after the negro period, 1907, was past, with the beginning of his cubism, 1908, in his hand. The time had come.

I have said that there were three reasons for the making of this cubism.

First. The composition, because the way of living had changed, the composition of living had extended and each thing was as important as any other thing. Secondly, the faith in what the eyes were seeing, that is to say the belief in the reality of science, commenced to diminish. To be sure science had discovered many things, she would continue to discover things, but the principle which was the basis of all this was completely understood, the joy of discovery was almost over.

Thirdly, the framing of life, the need that a picture exist in its frame, remain in its frame was over. A picture remaining in its frame was a thing that always had existed and now pictures commenced to want to leave their frames and this also created the necessity for cubism.

The time had come and the man. Quite naturally it was a Spaniard who had felt it and done it. The Spaniards are perhaps the only Europeans who really never have had the feeling that things seen are real, that the truths of science make for progress. Spaniards did not mistrust science they only never have recognised the existence of progress. While other Europeans were still in the nineteenth century, Spain because of its lack of organisation and America by its excess of organisation were the natural founders of the twentieth century.

Cubism was commencing. Returning from Spain Picasso went back to the rue Ravignan but it was almost the end of the rue Ravignan, he commenced to move from one studio to another in the same building and when cubism was really well established, that is the moment of the pictures called Ma

Jolie, 1910, he had left the rue Ravignan and a short time after
he left Montmartre, 1912, and he never after returned to it.

After his return from Spain with his first cubist landscapes
in his hand, 1909, a long struggle commenced.

Cubism began with landscapes but inevitably he then at
once tried to use the idea he had in expressing people.
Picasso's first cubist pictures were landscapes, he then did still
lifes, but Spaniard that he is he always knew that people were
the only interesting thing to him. Landscapes and still lifes,
the seduction of flowers and of landscapes of still lifes were
inevitably more seductive to frenchmen than to Spaniards,
Juan Gris always made still lifes but to him a still life was not
a seduction it was a religion, but the ecstasy of things seen
only seen never touches the Spanish soul.

The head the face the human body these are all that exist
for Picasso. I remember once we were walking and we saw a
learned man sitting on a bench, before the war a learned man
could be sitting on a bench, and Picasso said, look at that
face, it is as old as the world all faces are as old as the world.

And so Picasso commenced his long struggle to express
heads faces and bodies of men and of women in the composition which is his composition. The beginning of this struggle
was hard and his struggle is still a hard struggle, the souls of
people do not interest him, that is to say for him the reality
of life is in the head, the face and the body and this is for him
so important, so persistent, so complete that it is not at all
necessary to think of any other thing and the soul is another
thing.

The struggle then had commenced.

Most people are more predetermined as to what is the human form and the human face than they are as to what are
flowers, landscapes, still lifes. Not everybody. I remember one
of the first exhibitions of Van Gogh, there was an American
there and she said to her friend, I find these portraits of people
quite interesting, for I dont know what people are like, but I
dont at all like these flower pictures, because I know very well
what flowers are like.

Most people are not like that. I do not mean to say that
they know people better than they know other things but they

have stronger convictions about what people are than what other things are.

Picasso at this period often used to say that Spaniards cannot recognise people from their photographs. So the photographers made two photographs, a man with a beard and a man smooth shaven and when the men left home to do their military service they sent one of these two types of photographs to their family and the family always found it very resembling.

It is strange about everything, it is strange about pictures, a picture may seem extraordinarily strange to you and after some time not only it does not seem strange but it is impossible to find what there was in it that was strange.

A child sees the face of its mother, it sees it in a completely different way than other people see it, I am not speaking of the spirit of the mother, but of the features and the whole face, the child sees it from very near, it is a large face for the eyes of a small one, it is certain the child for a little while only sees a part of the face of its mother, it knows one feature and not another, one side and not the other, and in his way Picasso knows faces as a child knows them and the head and the body. He was then commencing to try to express this consciousness and the struggle was appalling because, with the exception of some African sculpture, no one had ever tried to express things seen not as one knows them but as they are when one sees them without remembering having looked at them.

Really most of the time one sees only a feature of a person with whom one is, the other features are covered by a hat, by the light, by clothes for sport and everybody is accustomed to complete the whole entirely from their knowledge, but Picasso when he saw an eye, the other one did not exist for him and only the one he saw did exist for him and as a painter and particularly as a Spanish painter, he was right, one sees what one sees, the rest is a reconstruction from memory, and painters have nothing to do with reconstructions, nothing to do with memory, they concern themselves only with visible things and so the cubism of Picasso was an effort to make a picture of these visible things and the result was disconcerting for him and for the others, but what else could he do, a creator can only do one thing, he can only continue, that is all he can do.

The beginning of this struggle to express the things only the really visible things, was discouraging, even for his most intimate friends, even for Guillaume Apollinaire.

At this time people had commenced to be quite interested in the painting of Picasso, not an enormous number of people but even so quite a few and then Roger Fry, an Englishman was very impressed by my portrait and he had it reproduced in The Burlington Magazine, the portrait by Picasso next to a portrait by Raphael, and he too was very disconcerted. Picasso said to me once with a good deal of bitterness, they say I can draw better than Raphael and probably they are right, perhaps I do draw better, but if I can draw as well as Raphael I have at least the right to choose my way and they should recognise it that right, but no, they say no.

I was alone at this time in understanding him, perhaps because I was expressing the same thing in literature; perhaps because I was an American, and as I say, Spaniards and Americans have a kind of understanding of things which is the same.

Later Derain and Braque followed him and helped him, but at this time the struggle remained a struggle for Picasso and not for them.

We are now still in the history of the beginning of that struggle.

Picasso commenced as I have said, at the end of the harlequin or rose period to harden his lines his construction and his painting and then he once more went to Spain, he stayed there all summer and when he came back he commenced some things which were harder and more absolute and this led him to do the picture Les Desmoiselles d'Avignon. He left again for Spain and when he returned he brought back with him those three landscapes which were the real beginning of cubism.

It is true certainly in the water colors of Cezanne that there was a tendency to cut the sky not into cubes but into arbitrary divisions, there too had been the pointilism of Seurat and his followers, but that had nothing to do with cubism, because all these other painters were preoccupied with their technique which was to express more and more what they were seeing, the seduction of things seen. Well then, from Courbet to

Seurat they saw the things themselves, one may say from
Courbet to Van Gogh and to Matisse they saw nature as it is,
if you like, that is to say as everybody sees it.

One day they asked Matisse if, when he ate a tomatoe, he
saw it as he painted it. No, said Matisse, when I eat it I see it
as everybody sees it and it is true from Courbet to Matisse,
the painters saw nature as every one sees it and their preoc-
cupation was to express that vision, to do it with more or less
tenderness, sentiment, serenity, penetration but to express it
as all the world saw it.

I am always struck with the landscapes of Courbet, because
he did not have to change the color to give the vision of
nature as every one sees it. But Picasso was not like that, when
he ate a tomatoe, the tomatoe was not everybody's tomatoe,
not at all and his effort was not to express in his way the things
seen as every one sees them, but to express the thing as he
was seeing it. Van Gogh at even his most fantastic moment
even when he cut off his ear, was convinced that an ear is an
ear as every one could see it, the need for that ear might be
something else but the ear was the same ear everybody could
see.

But with Picasso, Spaniard that he is, it was entirely different. Well, Don Quixote, was a Spaniard, he did not imagine
things, he saw things, and it was not a dream, it was not
lunacy, he really saw them.

Well Picasso is a Spaniard.

I was very much struck, at this period when cubism was a
little more developed, with the way Picasso could put objects
together and make a photograph of them. I have kept one of
them, and by the force of his vision it was not necessary that
he paint the picture. To have brought the objects together
already changed them to other things, not to another picture
but to something else, to things as Picasso saw them.

But as I say, Spaniards and Americans are not like Europeans, they are not like Orientals, they have something in
common, that is they do not need religion or mysticism not
to believe in reality as all the world knows it, not even when
they see it. In fact reality for them is not real and that is why
there are skyscrapers and American literature and Spanish
painting and literature.

So Picasso commenced and little by little there came the picture Les Desmoiselles d'Avignon and when there was that it was too awful. I remember Tschoukine, who had so much admired the painting of Picasso was at my house and he said almost in tears, what a loss for French art.

In the beginning when Picasso wished to express heads and bodies not like every one could see them, which was the problem of other painters, but as he saw them, as one can see when one has not the habit of knowing what one is looking at, inevitably when he commenced he had the tendency to paint them as a mass as sculptors do or in profile as children do.

African art in 1907 commenced to play a part in the definition of what Picasso was creating, but in the creations of Picasso really African art, like the other influences which at one time or another diverted Picasso from the way of painting which was his, African art and his French cubist comrades were rather things that consoled Picasso's vision than aided it, African art, French cubism and later Italian influence and Russian were like Sancho Panza was with Don Quixote, they wished to lead Picasso away from his real vision which was his real Spanish vision. The things that Picasso could see were the things which had their own reality, reality not of things seen, but of things that exist. It is difficult to exist alone and not being able to remain alone with things, Picasso first took as a crutch African art and later other things.

Let us go back to the beginning of cubism.

He commenced the long struggle not to express what he could see but not to express the things he did not see, that is to say the things everybody is certain of seeing, but which they do not really see. As I have already said, in looking at a friend one only sees one feature of her face or another, in fact Picasso was not at all simple but he analised his vision, he did not wish to paint the things that he himself did not see, the other painters satisfied themselves with the appearance, and always the appearance, which was not at all what they could see but what they knew was there.

There is a difference.

Now the dates of this beginning.

Picasso was born in Malaga, October 25th, 1881. His parents settled definitely in Barcelona in 1895 and the young Picasso came for the first time in 1900 to Paris where he stayed six months.

The first influence in Paris was Toulouse Lautrec, at this time and later, until his return to Paris in 1901, the influence of this first contact with Paris was quite strong, he returned there in the spring of 1901, but not to stay for long and he returned to Barcelona once more. The direct contact with Paris, the second time, destroyed the influences of Paris, he returned again to Barcelona and remained there until 1904, when he really became an inhabitant of Paris.

During this period, 1901 to 1904, he painted the blue pictures, the hardness and the reality which are not the reality seen which is Spanish, made him paint these pictures which are the basis of all that he did afterwards.

In 1904 he came back to France, he forgot all the Spanish sadness and Spanish reality, he let himself go living in the gayety of things seen, the gayety of French sentimentality. He lived in the poetry of his friends, Apollinaire, Max Jacob and Salmon, as Juan Gris always used to say, France seduces me and she still seduces me. I think this is so, France for Spaniards is rather a seduction than an influence.

So the harlequin or rose period was a period of enormous production, the gayety of France induced an unheard of fecundity. It is extraordinary the number and size of the canvases he painted during this short period, 1904–1906.

Later one day when Picasso and I were discussing the dates of his pictures and I was saying to him that all that could not have been painted during one year Picasso answered you forget we were young and we did a great deal in a year.

Really it is difficult to believe that the harlequin period only lasted from 1904 to 1906, but it is true, there is no denying it, his production upon his first definite contact with France was enormous. This was the rose period.

The rose period ended with my portrait, the quality of drawing had changed and his pictures had already commenced to be less light, less joyous. After all Spain is Spain and it is not France and the twentieth century in France needed a Spaniard to express its life and Picasso was destined for this. Really and truly.

When I say that the rose period is light and happy everything is relative; even the subjects which were happy ones were a little sad, the families of the harlequins were wretched families but from Picasso's point of view it was a light happy joyous period and a period when he contented himself with seeing things as anybody did. And then in 1906 this period was over.

In 1906 Picasso worked on my portrait during the whole winter, he commenced to paint figures in colors that were almost monotone, still a little rose but mostly an earth color, the lines of the bodies harder, a great deal of force and with the beginning of his own vision. It was like the blue period, but much more felt and less colored and less sentimental. His art commenced to be much purer.

So he renewed his vision which was of things seen as he saw them.

One must never forget that the reality of the twentieth century is not the reality of the nineteenth century, not at all and Picasso was the only one in painting who felt it, the only one. More and more the struggle to express it intensified. Matisse and all the others saw the twentieth century with their eyes, but they saw the reality of the nineteenth century, Picasso was the only one in painting who saw the twentieth century with his eyes and saw its reality, and consequently his struggle was terrifying, terrifying for himself and for the others, because he had nothing to help him, the past did not help him, nor the present, he had to do it all alone and as in spite of much strength he is often very weak, he consoled himself and allowed himself to be almost seduced by other things which led him more or less astray.

Upon his return from a short trip to Spain, he had spent the summer at Gosol, he returned and became acquainted with Matisse through whom he came to know African sculpture. After all one must never forget that African sculpture is not naïve, not at all, it is an art that is very very conventional, based upon tradition and its tradition is a tradition derived from Arab culture. The Arabs created both civilization and culture for the negroes and therefore African art which was naïve and exotic for Matisse was for Picasso, a Spaniard, a thing that was natural, direct and civilized.

So then it was natural that this reinforced his vision and

helped him to realise it and the result was the studies which brought him to create the picture of Les Desmoiselles d'Avignon.

Again and again he did not recommence but he continued after an interruption. This is his life.

It was about this period that his contact with Derain and Braque commenced and little by little pure cubism came to exist.

First there was the effort still more difficult than with still lifes and landscapes, to create human beings in cubes, this did not produce satisfactory results and exhausted, Picasso emptied himself during 1907 and calmed himself by doing sculpture. Sculpture always has the bother that one can go all around it and also the material of which it is made gives an impression of form before the sculptor has worked on it.

I myself prefer painting.

Picasso having made a prodigious effort to create painting by his understanding of African sculpture was seduced a short time after 1908 by his interest in the sculptural form rather than by the vision in African sculpture, but even so in the end it was an intermediate step toward cubism.

Cubism is a part of the daily life in Spain, it is in Spanish architecture. The architecture of other countries always follows the line of the landscape, it is true of Italian architecture and of French architecture, but Spanish architecture always cuts the lines of the landscape, and it is that that is the basis of cubism, the work of man is not in harmony with the landscape, it opposes it and it is just that that is the basis of cubism, and that is what Spanish cubism is. And that was the reason for putting real objects in the pictures, the real newspaper, the real pipe. Little by little, after these cubist painters had used real objects, they wanted to see if, by the force of the intensity with which they painted some of these objects, a pipe, a newspaper, in a picture, they could not replace the real by the painted objects which would by their realism require the rest of the picture to oppose itself to them.

Nature and man are opposed in Spain, they agree in France and this is the difference between French cubism and Spanish cubism and it is a fundamental difference.

So then Spanish cubism is a necessity, of course it is.

So now it is 1908 and once more Picasso is in Spain and he returned with the landscapes of 1909, which were the beginning of classic and classified cubism.

These three landscapes express exactly what I wish to make clear, that is to say the opposition between nature and man in Spain. The round is opposed to the cube, a small number of houses gives the impression of a great quantity of houses in order to dominate the landscape, the landscape and the houses do not agree, the round is opposed to the cube, the movement of the earth is against the movement of the houses, in fact the houses have no movement because the earth has its movement, of course the houses should have none.

I have here before me a picture by a young French painter, he too with few houses creates his village, but the houses move with the landscape, with the river, here they all agree together, it is not at all Spanish.

Spaniards know that there is no agreement, neither the landscape with the houses, neither the round with the cube, neither the great number with the small number, it was natural that a Spaniard should express this in the painting of the twentieth century, the century where nothing is in agreement, neither the round with the cube, neither the landscape with the houses, neither the large quantity with the small quantity. America and Spain have this thing in common, that is why Spain discovered America and America Spain, in fact it is for this reason that both of them have found their moment in the twentieth century.

So Picasso returned from Spain after a summer spent in Barcelona and in Orta de Ebro and he was once again in the rue Ravignan, but it was the beginning of the end of the rue Ravignan, actually he did not leave the rue Ravignan until 1910, but the return in 1909 was really the end of the rue Ravignan which had given him all that it could give him, that was over and now began the happy era of cubism. There was still a great deal of effort, the continual effort of Picasso to express the human form, that is to say the face, the head, the human body in the composition which he had then reached, the features seen separately existed separately and at the same time it all was a picture, the struggle to express that at this time was happy rather than sad. The cubists found a picture dealer, the young Kahnweiler, coming from London, full of enthusiasm, wishing to realise his dream of becoming a picture dealer, and hesitating a little here and there and definitely becoming interested in Picasso. In 1907 and in 1908, in 1909 and in 1910, he made contracts with the cubists, one after the other, French and Spanish and he devoted himself to their interests. The life of the cubists became very gay, the gayety of France once again seduced Picasso, every one was gay, there were more and more cubists, the joke was to speak of some one as the youngest of the cubists, cubism was sufficiently accepted now that one could speak of the youngest of the cubists, after all he did exist and every one was gay. Picasso worked enormously as he always worked, but every one was gay.

This gayety lasted until he left Montmartre in 1912. After that not one of them was ever so gay again. Their gayety then was a real gayety.

He left the rue Ravignan, 1911, to move to the boulevard de Clichy and he left the boulevard de Clichy and Montmartre to settle in Montparnasse in 1912. Life between 1910 and 1912 was very gay, it was the period of the Ma Jolie picture, it was the period of all those still lifes, the tables with their grey color, with their infinite variety of greys, they amused themselves in all sorts of ways, they still collected African sculpture but its influence was not any longer very marked, they collected musical instruments, objects, pipes, tables with fringes, glasses, nails, and at this time Picasso commenced to amuse himself with making pictures out of zinc, tin, pasted paper. He did not do any sculpture, but he made pictures with all these things. There is only one left of those made of paper and that he gave me one day and I had it framed inside a box. He liked paper, in fact everything at this time pleased him and everything was going on very livelily and with an enormous gayety.

Everything continued but there were interruptions, Picasso left Montmartre in 1912, and gayety was over, everything continued, everything always continues but Picasso was never again so gay, the gay moment of cubism was over.

He left Montmartre for Montparnasse, first the boulevard Raspail, then the rue Schoelcher and finally Montrouge.

During all this time he did not return to Spain, but during the summer he was at Ceret or at Sorgues, the beginning of life in Montparnasse was less gay, he worked enormously as he always does. It was at the rue Schoelcher that he commenced to paint with Ripolin paints, he commenced to use a kind of wall paper as a background and a small picture painted in the middle, he commenced to use pasted paper more and more in painting his pictures. Later he used to say quite often, paper lasts quite as well as paint and after all if it all ages together, why not, and he said further, after all, later, no one will see the picture, they will see the legend of the picture, the legend that the picture has created, then it makes no difference if the picture lasts or does not last. Later they will restore it, a picture lives by its legend, not by anything else. He was indifferent as to what might happen to his pictures, even though what might happen to them affected him profoundly, well that is the way one is, why not, one is like that.

Very much later, when he had had a great deal of success, he said one day, you know, your family, everybody, if you are a genius and unsuccessful, everybody treats you as if you were a genius, but when you come to be successful, when you commence to earn money, when you are really successful, then your family and everybody no longer treats you like a genius, they treat you like a man who has become successful.

So success had begun, not a great success, but successful enough.

At this time, he was still at the rue Schoelcher, and Picasso for the first time used the Russian alphabet in his pictures. It is to be found in a few of the pictures of this period, of course this was long before his contact with the Russian ballet. So life went on. His pictures became more and more brilliant in color, more and more carefully worked and perfected and then there was war, it was 1914.

At this period his pictures were very brilliant in color, he painted musical instruments and musical signs, but the cubic forms were continually being replaced by surfaces and lines, the lines were more important than anything else, they lived by and in themselves. He painted his pictures not by means of his objects but by the lines, at this time this tendency became more and more pronounced.

Then there was the war and all his friends left to go to the war.

Picasso was still at the rue Schoelcher, Braque and Derain were mobilised and at the front, but Apollinaire had not yet gone, he was not french, so he was not called but shortly after he did volunteer. Everybody had gone. Picasso was alone. Apollinaire's leaving perhaps affected him the most, Apollinaire, who wrote him all his feelings in learning to become a warrior, that was then 1914, and now it was all war.

Later he moved from the rue Schoelcher to Montrouge and it was during this moving that the objects made of paper and zinc and tin were lost and broken. Later at Montrouge he was robbed, the burglars took his linen. It made me think of the days when all of them were unknown and when Picasso said that it would be marvellous if a real thief came and stole his pictures or his drawings. Friends, to be sure, took some of them, stole them if you like from time to time, pilfered if you like, but a real professional burglar, a burglar by profession, when Picasso was not completely unknown, came and preferred to taken the linen.

So little by little time passed. Picasso commenced to know Erik Satie and Jean Cocteau and the result was Parade, that was the end of this period, the period of real cubism.

Jean Cocteau left for Rome with Picasso 1917 to prepare Parade. It was the first time that I saw Cocteau they came together to say good-bye, Picasso was very gay, not so gay as in the days of the great cubist gayety but gay enough, he and Cocteau were gay, Picasso was pleased to be leaving, he had never seen Italy. He never had enjoyed travelling, he always went where others already were, Picasso never had the pleasure of initiative. As he used to say of himself, he has a weak character and he allowed others to make decisions, that is the way it is, it was enough that he should do his work, decisions are never important, why make them.

So cubism was to be put on the stage. That was really the beginning of the general recognition of Picasso's work, when a work is put on the stage of course every one has to look at it and in a sense if it is put on the stage every one is forced to look and since they are forced to look at it, of course, they must accept it, there is nothing else to do. In the spring of

1917 Picasso was in Italy with Diaghelew and with Cocteau and he made the stage settings and the costumes for Parade which is completely cubist. It had a great success, it was produced and accepted, of course, from the moment it was put on the stage, of course, it was accepted.

So the great war continued but it was nearing its end, and the war of cubism, it too was commencing to end, no war is ever ended, of course not, it only has the appearance of stopping. So Picasso's struggle continued but for the moment it appeared to have been won by himself for himself, and by him for the world.

It is an extraordinary thing but it is true, wars are only a means of publicising the things already accomplished, a change, a complete change, has come about, people no longer think as they were thinking, but no one knows it, no one recognises it, no one really knows it except the creators. The others are too busy with the business of life, they can not feel what has happened, but the creator, the real creator, does nothing, he is not concerned with the activity of existing, and as he is not active, that is to say as he is not concerned with the activity of existence he is sensitive enough to understand how people are thinking, he is not interested in knowing how they were thinking, his sensitive feeling is concerned in understanding how people live as they are living. The spirit of everybody is changed, of a whole people is changed, but mostly nobody knows it and a war forces them to recognise it, because during a war the appearance of everything changes very much quicker, but really the entire change has been accomplished and the war is only something which forces everybody to recognise it. The French revolution was over when war forced everybody to recognise it, the American revolution was accomplished before the war, the war is only a publicity agent which makes every one know what has happened, yes, it is that.

So then the public recognises a creator who has seen the change which has been accomplished before a war and which has been expressed by the war and by the war the world is forced to recognise the entire change in everything, they are forced to look at the creator who, before any one, knew it and expressed it. A creator is not in advance of his generation but he is the first of his contemporaries to be conscious of what is happening to his generation.

A creator who creates, who is not an academician, who is not some one who studies in a school where the rules are already known and of course being known they no longer exist, a creator then who creates is necessarily of his generation. His generation lives in its contemporary way, but they only live in it. In art, in literature, in the theatre, in short in everything that does not contribute to their immediate comfort they live in the preceding generation. It is very simple, to-day in the streets of Paris, horses, even tramcars can no longer exist but horses and tramcars are only suppressed, only when they cause too many complications, they are suppressed but sixty years too late. Lord Grey said when the war broke out, that the generals thought of a war of the nineteenth century even when the instruments of war were of the twentieth century and only when the war was at its heighth did the generals understand that it was a war of the twentieth century and not a war of the nineteenth century. That is what the academic spirit is, it is not contemporary, of course not, and so it can not be creative because the only thing that is creative in a creator is the contemporary thing. Of course.

As I was saying, in the daily living, it is another thing. A friend built a modern house and he suggested that Picasso too should have one built. But said Picasso, of course not, I want an old house. Imagine, he said, if Michael Angelo would have been pleased if some one had given him a fine piece of Renaissance furniture, not at all. He would have been pleased if he had been given a beautiful Greek intaglio, of course.

So that is the way it is, a creator is so completely contemporary that he has the appearance of being ahead of his generation and to calm himself in his daily living he wishes to live with the things in the daily life of the past, he does not wish to live as contemporary as the contemporaries who do not poignantly feel being contemporary. This sounds complicated, but it is very simple.

So then the contemporaries were forced by the war to recognise cubism, cubism as it had been created by Picasso, who saw a reality that was not the vision of the nineteenth century, which was not a thing seen but felt, which was a thing that was not based upon nature but opposed to nature like the houses in Spain are opposed to the landscape, like the round is opposed to cubes. Every one was forced by the war which made them understand that things had changed to other things and that they had not stayed the same things, they were forced then to accept Picasso. Picasso returned from Italy and freed by Parade, which he had just created, he became a realistic painter, he even made many portraits from models, portraits which were purely realistic. It is evident that really nothing changes, but at the same time everything changes, and Italy and Parade and the termination of the war gave to Picasso in a kind of a way another harlequin period, a realistic period not sad, less young, if you like, but a period of calm, he was satisfied to see things as everybody saw them, not completely as everybody does but completely enough. Period of 1917 to 1920.

Picasso was always possessed by the necessity of emptying himself, of emptying himself completely, of always emptying himself, he is so full of it that all his existence is the repetition of a complete emptying, he must empty himself, he can never empty himself of being Spanish, but he can empty himself of what he has created. So every one says that he changes, but really it is not that, he empties himself and the moment he has completed emptying himself, he must recommence emptying himself he fills himself up again so quickly.

Twice in his life he almost emptied himself of being Spanish, the first time during his first real contact with Paris when there came the harlequin or rose period, 1904–1906, the second time was his contact with the theatre, that was the realistic period which lasted from 1918 to 1921. During this period he painted some very beautiful portraits, some paintings and some drawings of harlequins and many other pictures. This adult rose period lasted almost three years.

But of course the rose period could not persist in him. He emptied himself of the rose period and inevitably it changed to something else, this time it changed to the period of large women and later to one of classic subjects, women with draperies, perhaps this was the commencement of the end of this adult rose period.

There certainly have been two rose periods in the life of

Picasso. During the second rose period there was almost no real cubism but there was painting which was writing which had to do with the Spanish character, that is to say the Saracen character and this commenced to develop very much.

I will explain.

In the Orient calligraphy and the art of painting and sculpture have always been very nearly related, they resemble each other, they help each other, they complete each other. Saracen architecture was decorated with letters, with words in Sanskrit letters, in China the letters were something in themselves. But in Europe the art of calligraphy was always a minor art, decorated by painting, decorated by lines, but the art of writing and the decoration by writing and the decoration around writing are always a minor art. But for Picasso, a Spaniard, the art of writing, that is to say calligraphy, is an art. After all the Spaniards and the Russians are the only Europeans who are really a little Oriental, and this shows in the art of Picasso, not as anything exotic, but as something quite profound. It is completely assimilated, of course he is a Spaniard, and a Spaniard can assimilate the Orient without imitating it, he can know Arab things without being seduced, he can repeat African things without being deceived.

The only things that really seduce the Spaniards are Latin things, French things, Italian things, for them the Latin is exotic and seductive, it is the things the Latins make which for the Spaniards are charming. As Juan Gris always said, the school of Fontainebleau was completely a seduction, it was of course completely Latin, Italy in France.

So then the Italian seduction resulted for Picasso after his first visit to Rome in his second rose period which commenced in 1918 with the portrait of his wife and lasted until the portrait of his son in harlequin costume in 1927, and all this began with portraits, then the large women to end with classic subjects. It was once more Latin seduction this time by means of Italy. But above all it was always and always Spain and it was Spain which impelled him even during this naturalistic period to express himself by calligraphy in his pictures.

The first thing I saw that showed this calligraphic quality in Picasso were several wood-cuts which he had made during the harlequin period that first rose period of 1904. They were two birds made in a single stroke and colored with only one color. Beside these two small things, I do not remember any other things of his which were really calligraphic until his last period of pure cubism, that is to say from 1912 to 1917.

During this period the cubes were no longer important, the cubes were lost. After all one must know more than one sees, and one does not see a cube in its entirety. In 1914, there were less cubes in cubism, each time that Picasso commenced again, he recommenced the struggle to express in a picture the things seen without association but simply as things seen, and it is only the things seen that are knowledge for Picasso. Related things are things remembered and for a creator, certainly for a Spanish creator, certainly for a Spanish creator of the twentieth century, remembered things are not things seen, therefore they are not things known. And so then always and always Picasso commenced his attempt to express not things felt, not things remembered not established in relations, but things which are there, really everything a human being can know at each moment of his existence and not an assembling of all his experiences. So that during all this last period of pure cubism, 1914–1917, he tried to recommence his work, at the same time he became complete master of his metier. It was the interval between 1914 and 1917 when his mastery of his technique became so complete that it reached perfection, there was no longer any hesitation, now when he knew what to do he could do what he wanted to do, no technical problem stopped him. But after all this problem remained, how to express not the things seen in association but the things really seen, not things interpreted, but things really known at the time of knowing them. All his life this had been his problem but the problem had become more difficult than ever, now that he was completely master of his technique he no longer had any real distraction, he could no longer have the distraction of learning, his instrument was perfected.

At this period, from 1913 to 1917, his pictures have the beauty of complete mastery. Picasso nearly did all that he wanted to do, he put into his pictures nearly nothing that should not have been there, there were no cubes, there were simply things, he succeeded in only putting into them what he really knew and all that ended with the voyage to Italy and the preparation of Parade.

After Italy and Parade, he had his second naturalistic period of which anybody could recognise the beauty, and his technique which was now perfected permitted him to create this beauty with less effort, this beauty existed in itself.

These pictures have the serenity of perfect beauty but they have not the beauty of realisation. The beauty of realisation is a beauty that always takes more time to show itself as beauty than pure beauty does. The beauty of realisation during its creation is not beauty, it is only beauty when the things that follow it are created in its image. It is then that it is known as beauty on account of its quality of fecondity, it is the most beautiful beauty, more beautiful than the beauty of serenity. Well.

After Italy and Parade Picasso married and in 1918 he left Montrouge for the rue de la Boëtie; he stayed there until 1937 and during this time, 1919 to 1937, there were many things created, many things happened to the painting of Picasso.

But let us return to calligraphy and its importance in Picasso's art.

It was natural that the cubism of 1913 to 1917 revealed the art of calligraphy to him, the importance of calligraphy seen as Orientals see it, and not as Europeans see it. The contact with Russia first through a Russian G. Apostrophe as they all called him and later with the Russian ballet, stimulated his feeling for calligraphy which is always there in a Spaniard always since Spaniards have had for such a long time Saracen art always with them.

And also one must never forget that Spain is the only country in Europe whose landscape is not European, not at all, therefore it is natural that although Spaniards are Europeans even so they are not Europeans.

So in all this period of 1913 to 1917 one sees that he took great pleasure in decorating his pictures, always with a rather calligraphic tendency than a sculptural one, and during the naturalist period, which followed Parade and the voyage to Italy, the consolation offered to the side of him that was Spanish was calligraphy. I remember very well in 1923 he did two women completely in this spirit, a very little picture, but all the reality of calligraphy was in it, everything that he could not put into his realistic pictures was there in the two calligraphic women and they had an extraordinary vitality.

Calligraphy, as I understand it in him had perhaps its most intense moment in the decor of Mercure. That was written, so simply written, no painting, pure calligraphy. A little before that he had made a series of drawings, also purely calligraphic, the lines were extraordinarily lines, there were also stars that were stars, which moved, they existed, they were really cubism, that is to say a thing that existed in itself without the aid of association or emotion.

During all this time the realistic period was commencing to approach its end, first there had been portraits which ended with harlequins, for once Picasso had almost wished to look at models. The naturalistic painting changed to the large women, at first women on the shore or in the water, with a great deal of movement, and little by little the large women became very sculpturesque. In this way Picasso emptied himself of Italy. That is his way.

During the year 1923 his pleasure in drawing was enormous, he almost repeated the fecondity and the happiness of his first rose period, everything was in rose. That ended in 1923. It was at this time that the classic period commenced, it was the end of Italy, it still showed in his drawings, but in his painting he had completely purged himself of Italy, really entirely.

Then came the period of the large still-lifes, 1927, and then for the first time in his life six months passed without his working. It was the very first time in his life.

It is necessary to think about this question of calligraphy, it must never be forgotten that the only way Picasso has of speaking, the only way Picasso has of writing is with drawings and paintings. In 1914, and from then on it never stopped, he had a certain way of writing his thoughts, that is to say of seeing things in a way that he knew he was seeing them. And it was in this way that he commenced to write these thoughts with drawings and with painting. Oriental people, the people of America and the people of Spain have never, really never forgotten that it is not necessary to use letters in order to be able to write. Really one can write in another way and Picasso has understood, completely understood this way. To recapitulate. From 1914 to 1917, cubism changed to rather flat surfaces, it was no longer sculpture, it was writing, and Picasso really expressed himself in this way, because it was not possible, really not, to really write with sculpture, no, not.

So it was natural that at this period, 1913 to 1917, during which time he was almost always alone, that he should recommence writing all he knew and he knew many things. As I have said, it was then he completely mastered the technique of painting. And this ended with Parade.

Now a great struggle commenced again. The influence of Italy, the influence of everybody's return from the war, the influence of a great deal of recognition and the influence of his joy at the birth of his son, precipitated him into a second rose period, a completely realistic period which lasted from 1919 to 1927. This was a rose period it certainly was and in the same way as the first rose period, it ended when Picasso commenced to strengthen and harden his lines and solidify the forms and the colors, in the same way that the first rose period changed with my portrait so this rose period changed about 1920 by painting enormous and very robust women. There was still a little the memory of Italy in its forms and draperies and this lasted until 1923 when he finished the large classical pictures. So the second rose period naturally ended in the same way as the first one had, that is to say by the triumph of Spain. It was during all this period that he first painted, about 1920 and 1921, very highly colored cubist pictures, very calligraphic and very colored and then more and more calligraphic and less colored. During all this time the color of this cubism was pure color, Ripolin paint, which he called the health of color.

Later I will tell something about Picasso's color which too, in itself, is a whole story.

To continue.

When the second rose period changed to the period of large women, around 1923, at the same time that calligraphy was in full activity, there commenced to be felt in the large pictures, and it culminated in one of these large pictures La Danse the fact that naturalism for Picasso was dead, that he was no longer seeing as all the world thought they saw.

And as the pure period of cubism, that is to say the cubism of cubes, found its final explosion in Parade, the pure writing of this period made a great explosion in the ballet Mercure, in 1924 at the Soirées de Paris.

Then a curious story commenced, like the story of the African period and that of Les Desmoiselles d'Avignon.

Picasso had purged himself of Italy in his second rose period and the large women and the classical subjects. He always had Spain inside him, he can not purge himself of that, because it is he, it is himself, so then the writing which is the continuation of cubism, if it is not the same thing, was always continuing, but now there was another thing, it was Russia, and to rid himself of that was a terrible struggle. During this struggle things seen as everybody can see them nearly dominated him and to avoid this, avoid being conquered by this, for the first time in his life, and twice since, he stopped painting, he ceased speaking as he knew how to speak, writing as he knew how to write, with drawings and with color.

We are now in 1924 and the production of Mercure.

At this time he began to do sculpture. I say that Italy was completely out of him, but Russia was still in him. The art of Russia is essentially a peasant art, an art of speaking with sculpture. It requires a greater detachment to know how to speak with drawings and with color than to speak with sculpture in cubes or in round, and the African sculpture was cube and the Russian sculpture was round. There is also another very important difference, the size of the features and of the people in African sculpture is a real size, the size in Russian sculpture is an abnormal one so that the one art is pure and the other fantastic, and Picasso a Spaniard is never fantastic, he is never pornographic but Russian art is both. Again a struggle.

The Spanish character is a mixture of Europe and the Orient, the Russian character is a mixture of the European and the Oriental but it is neither the same Europe nor the same Orient, but as it is the same mixture the struggle to become once more himself was harder than ever and from 1924 to 1935 this struggle lasted.

During this time his consolation was cubism, the harlequins big and little, and his struggle was in the large pictures where the forms in spite of being fantastic forms, were forms like everybody sees them, were if you wish, pornographic forms, in a word forms like Russians can see them, but not forms like a Spaniard can see them.

As I have said and as I have repeated, the character, the vision of Picasso is like himself, it is Spanish and he does not see reality as all the world sees it, so that he alone amongst the painters did not have the problem of expressing the truths that all the world can see, but the truths that he alone can see and that is not the world the world recognises as the world.

As he has not the distraction of learning because he can create it the moment he knows what he sees, he having a sensitiveness and a tenderness and a weakness that makes him wish to share the things seen by everybody, he always in his life is tempted as a saint can be tempted, to see things as he does not see them.

Again and again it has happened to him in his life and the strongest temptation was between 1925 and 1935.

The struggle was intense and sometimes almost mortal.

In 1937, he recommenced painting, he had not drawn nor painted for six months, as I have said several times the struggle was almost mortal, he must see what he saw and the reality for him had to be the reality seen, not by everybody but by him, and every one wished to lead him away from this, wished to force him to see what he did not see. It was like when they wanted to force Galileo to say that the earth did not turn. Yes it was that.

Just before the six months during which for the first time in his life he did not draw nor paint he had an enormous fecundity. Another way of finding himself again. An enormous production is as necessary as doing nothing in order to find one's self again, so then at first he had an enormous production and after it completely ceased during six months. During these six months, the only thing he did was a picture made of a rag cut by a string, during the great moment of cubism he made such things, at that time it gave him great joy to do it but now it was a tragedy. This picture was beautiful, this picture was sad and it was the only one.

After this he commenced again but this time rather with sculpture than with painting, again and again he wanted to escape from those too well-known forms which were not the forms he saw and this was what induced him to make sculpture which at first was very very thin, as thin as a line, not thicker than that. That was perhaps why Greco made his figures as he did make them. Perhaps.

Almost at the same time he commenced to make enormous statues, all this to empty himself of those forms which were not forms he could see, I say that this struggle was formidable.

It was at this time that is to say in 1933, that once more he ceased to paint but he continued to make drawings and during the summer of 1933, he made his only surrealist drawings. Surrealism could console him a little, but not really. The surrealists still see things as every one sees them, they complicate them in a different way but the vision is that of every one else, in short the complication is the complication of the twentieth century but the vision is that of the nineteenth century. Picasso only sees something else, another reality. Complications are always easy, but another vision than that of all the world, is very rare. That is why geniuses are rare, to complicate things in a new way that is easy, but to see the things in a new way that is really difficult, everything prevents one, habits, schools, daily life, reason, necessities of daily life, indolence, everything prevents one, in fact there are very few geniuses in the world.

Picasso saw something else, not another complication but another thing, he did not see things evolve as people saw them evolve in the nineteenth century, he saw things evolve as they did not evolve which was the twentieth century, in other words he was contemporary with the things and he saw these things, he did not see as all the others did as all the world thought they saw, that is to say as they themselves saw them in the nineteenth century.

During this period there was another curious thing.

The color Picasso used was always important, so important that his periods were named after the color that he was using. To commence with the commencement.

The first influence of his first short visits to Paris, 1900, gave him the color of Toulouse Lautrec, the characteristic color of the painting of that period. That lasted a very short time and when he came back to Paris and returned to Spain, the colors he used were naturally Spanish, the color blue, and the pictures of this period were always blue. When he was in France again and when French gayety made him gay he painted in rose and that is called the rose period. There was really some blue in this period but the blue had rather a rose character than a blue character, so then it was really a rose period, that was followed by the beginning of the struggle for cubism, the African period which had some rose but which turned first to beige, later to brown and red as in my portrait and after that there was an intermediary period, before real cubism and that was a rather green period. It is less known but it is very very beautiful, landscapes and large still-lifes, also some figures. After that there were pale landscapes which little by little were followed by grey still-lifes. It was during this grey period that Picasso really for the first time showed himself to be a great colorist. There is an infinite variety of grey in these pictures and by the vitality of painting the greys really become color. After that as Picasso had then really become a colorist his periods were not named after their colors.

He commenced, this was 1914, to study colors, the nature of colors, he became interested in making pure colors but the color quality which he found when he painted in grey was a little lost, later when his second naturalistic period was over he commenced again to be enormously interested in color, he played with colors to oppose the colors to the drawings, Spaniard that he was, it is natural that the colors should not help the drawing but should oppose themselves to it, and it was about 1923 that he interested himself enormously in this. It was also during the calligraphic period, 1923, and later that this opposition of drawing and of color was the most interesting.

Little by little when the struggle not to be subjugated by the vision which was not his vision was going on, the colors commenced to be rather the ordinary colors that other painters used, colors that go with the drawing and finally between 1927 and 1935 Picasso had a tendency to console himself with Matisse's conception of color, this was when he was most despairful that this commenced and this ended when he ceased to paint in 1935.

In fact he ceased to paint during two years and he neither painted nor drew.

It is extraordinary that one ceases to do what one has done all one's life, but that can happen.

It is always astonishing that Shakespeare never put his hand to his pen once he ceased to write and one knows other cases, things happen that destroy everything which forced the person to exist and the identity which was dependent upon the things that were done, does it still exist, yes or no.

Rather yes, a genius is a genius, even when he does not work.

So Picasso ceased to work.

It was very curious.

He commenced to write poems but this writing was never his writing. After all the egoism of a painter is not at all the egoism of a writer, there is nothing to say about it, it is not. No.

Two years of not working. In a way Picasso liked it, it was one responsibility the less, it is nice not having responsibilities, it is like the soldiers during a war, a war is terrible, they said, but during a war one has no responsibility, neither for death, nor for life. So these two years were like that for Picasso, he did not work, it was not for him to decide every moment what he saw, no, poetry for him was something to be made during rather bitter meditations, but agreeably enough, in a café.

This was his life for two years, of course he who could write, write so well with drawings and with colors, knew very well that to write with words was, for him, not to write at all. Of course he understood that but he did not wish to allow himself to be awakened, there are moments in life when one is neither dead nor alive and for two years Picasso was neither dead nor alive, it was not an agreeable period for him, but a period of rest, he, who all his life needed to empty himself and to empty himself, during two years he did not empty himself, that is to say not actively, actually he really emptied himself completely, emptied himself of many things and above all of being subjugated by a vision which was not his own vision.

As I have said Picasso knows really knows the faces, the heads, the bodies of human beings, he knows them as they have existed since the existence of the human race, the soul of people does not interest him, why interest one's self in the souls of people when the face, the head, the body can tell everything, why use words, when one can express everything by drawings and colors. During this last period, from 1927 to 1935, the souls of people commenced to dominate him and his vision, a vision which was as old as the creation of people, lost itself in interpretation. He who could see did not need interpretation and in these years, 1927 to 1935, for the first time, the interpretations destroyed his own vision so that he made forms not seen but conceived. All this is difficult to put into words but the distinction is plain and clear, it is why he stopped working. The only way to purge himself of a vision which was not his was to cease to express it, so that as it was impossible for him to do nothing, he made poetry, but of course it was his way of falling asleep during the operation of detaching himself from the souls of things which were not his concern.

To see people as they have existed since they were created is not strange, it is direct, and Picasso's vision, his own vision is a direct vision.

Finally war broke out in Spain.

First the revolution and then war.

It was not the events themselves that were happening in Spain which awoke Picasso but the fact that they were happening in Spain, he had lost Spain, and here was Spain not lost, she existed, the existence of Spain awakened Picasso, he too existed, everything that had been imposed upon him no longer existed, he and Spain, both of them existed, of course they existed, they exist, they are alive, Picasso commenced to work, he commenced to speak as he has spoken all his life, speaking with drawings and color, speaking with writing, the writing of Picasso.

All his life, he has only spoken like that, he has written like that, and he has been eloquent.

So in 1937 he commenced to be himself again.

He painted a large picture about Spain and it was written in a calligraphy continuously developed and which was the continuation of the great advancement made by him in 1922, now he was in complete effervescence, and at the same time he found his color. The color of the pictures he paints now in 1937 are bright colors, light colors but which have the qualities of the colors which until now only existed in his greys, the colors can oppose the drawing, they can go together with the drawing, they can do what they want, it is not that they can agree or not with the drawing that they are there, they are there only to exist, certainly Picasso has now found his color, his real color in 1937.

Now this is the end of this story, not the end of his story, but the end of this story of his story.

EPILOGUE

To-day the pictures of Picasso have come back to me from the exhibition at the Petit Palais and once more they are on my walls, I can not say that during their absence I forgot their splendor but they are more splendid than that. The twentieth century is more splendid than the nineteenth century, certainly it is much more splendid. The twentieth century has much less reasonableness in its existence than the nineteenth century but reasonableness does not make for splendor. The seventeenth century had less reason in its existence than the sixteenth century and in consequence it has more splendor. So the twentieth century is that, it is a time when everything cracks, where everything is destroyed, everything isolates itself, it is a more splendid thing than a period where everything follows itself. So then the twentieth century is a splendid period, not a reasonable one in the scientific sense, but splendid. The phenomena of nature are more splendid than the daily events of nature, certainly, so then the twentieth century is splendid.

It was natural that it was a Spaniard who understood that a thing without progress is more splendid than a thing which progresses. The Spaniards who adore mounting a hill at full speed and coming down hill slowly, it is they who were made to create the painting of the twentieth century, and they did it, Picasso did it.

One must not forget that the earth seen from an airplane is more splendid than the earth seen from an automobile. The automobile is the end of progress on the earth, it goes quicker but essentially the landscapes seen from an automobile are the same as the landscapes seen from a carriage, a train, a waggon, or in walking. But the earth seen from an airplane is something else. So the twentieth century is not the same as the nineteenth century and it is very interesting knowing that Picasso has never seen the earth from an airplane that being of the twentieth century he inevitably knew that the earth is not the same as in the nineteenth century, he knew it, he made it, inevitably he made it different, and what he made is a thing that now all the world can see. When I was in America, I for the first time travelled pretty much all the time in an airplane and when I looked at the earth, I saw all the lines of cubism made at a time when not any painter had ever gone up in an airplane. I saw there, on the earth, the mingling lines of Picasso, coming and going, developing and destroying themselves, I saw the simple solutions of Braque, I saw the wandering lines of Masson, yes I saw and once more I knew that a creator is contemporary, he understands what is contemporary when the contemporaries do not yet know it, but he is contemporary and as the twentieth century is a century which sees the earth as no one has ever seen it, the earth has a splendor that it never has had, and as everything destroys itself in the twentieth century and nothing continues, so then the twentieth century has a splendor which is its own and Picasso is of this century, he has that strange quality of an earth that one has never seen and of things destroyed as they have never been destroyed. So then Picasso has his splendor.

Yes. Thank you.

THE WORLD IS ROUND

I

Rose Is a Rose

ONCE UPON A TIME the world was round and you could go on it around and around.

Everywhere there was somewhere and everywhere there they were men women children dogs cows wild pigs little rabbits cats lizards and animals. That is the way it was. And everybody dogs cats sheep rabbits and lizards and children all wanted to tell everybody all about it and they wanted to tell all about themselves.

And then there was Rose.

Rose was her name and would she have been Rose if her name had not been Rose. She used to think and then she used to think again.

Would she have been Rose if her name had not been Rose and would she have been Rose if she had been a twin.

Rose was her name all the same and her father's name was Bob and her mother's name was Kate and her uncle's name was William and her aunt's name was Gloria and her grandmother's name was Lucy. They all had names and her name was Rose, but would she have been she used to cry about it would she have been Rose if her name had not been Rose.

I tell you at this time the world was all round and you could go on it around and around.

Rose had two dogs a big white one called Love, and a little black one called Pépé, the little black one was not hers but she said it was, it belonged to a neighbor and it never did like Rose and there was a reason why, when Rose was young, she was nine now and nine is not young no Rose was not young, well anyway when she was young she one day had little Pépé and she told him to do something, Rose liked telling everybody what to do, at least she liked to do it when she was young, now she was almost ten so now she did not tell every one what they should do but then she did and she told Pépé, and Pépé did not want to, he did not know what she wanted him to do but even if he had he would not have wanted to, nobody does want to do what anybody tells them to do, so

537

Pépé did not do it, and Rose shut him up in a room. Poor little Pépé he had been taught never to do in a room what should be done outside but he was so nervous being left all alone he just did, poor little Pépé. And then he was let out and there were a great many people about but little Pépé made no mistake he went straight among all the legs until he found those of Rose and then he went up and he bit her on the leg and then he ran away and nobody could blame him now could they. It was the only time he ever bit any one. And he never would say how do you do to Rose again and Rose always said Pépé was her dog although he was not, so that she could forget that he never wanted to say how do you do to her. If he was her dog that was alright he did not have to say how do you do but Rose knew and Pépé knew oh yes they both knew.

Rose and her big white dog Love were pleasant together they sang songs together, these were the songs they sang.

Love drank his water and as he drank, it just goes like that like a song a nice song and while he was doing that Rose sang her song. This was her song.

I am a little girl and my name is Rose, Rose is my name.
Why am I a little girl
And why is my name Rose
And when am I a little girl
And when is my name Rose
And where am I a little girl
And where is my name Rose
And which little girl am I am I the little girl named Rose
which little girl named Rose.

And as she sang this song and she sang it while Love did his drinking.

Why am I a little girl
Where am I a little girl
When am I a little girl
Which little girl am I

And singing that made her so sad she began to cry.
And when she cried Love cried he lifted up his head and

looked up at the sky and he began to cry and he and Rose and Rose and he cried and cried and cried until she stopped and at last her eyes were dried.

And all this time the world just continued to be round.

2

Willie Is Willie

Rose had a cousin named Willie and once he was almost drowned. Twice he was almost drowned.

That was very exciting.

Each time was very exciting.

The world was round and there was a lake on it and the lake was round. Willie went swimming in the lake, there were three of them they were all boys swimming and there were lots of them they were all men fishing.

Lakes when they are round have bottoms to them and there are water-lilies pretty water-lilies white water-lilies and yellow ones and soon very soon one little boy and then another little boy was caught right in by them, water-lilies are pretty to see but they are not pretty to feel not at all. Willie was one and the other little boy was the other one and the third boy was a bigger one and he called to them to come and they, Willie and the other boy they couldn't come, the water-lilies did not really care but they just all the same did not let them.

Then the bigger boy called to the men *come and get them they cannot come out from the water-lilies and they will drown come and get them.* But the men they had just finished eating and you eat an awful lot while you are fishing you always do and you must never go into the water right after eating, all this the men knew so what could they do.

Well the bigger boy he was that kind he said he would not leave Willie and the other behind, so he went into the water-lilies and first he pulled out one little boy and then he pulled out Willie and so he got them both to the shore.

And so Willie was not drowned although the lake and the world were both all round.

That was one time when Willie was not drowned.

Another time he was not drowned was when he was with his father and his mother and his cousin Rose they were all together.

They were going up a hill and the rain came down with a will, you know how it comes when it comes so heavy and fast it is not wet it is a wall that is all.

So the car went up the hill and the rain came down the hill and then and then well and then there was hay, you know what hay is, hay is grass that is cut and when it is cut it is hay. Well anyway.

The hay came down the way it was no way for hay to come anyway. Hay should stay until it is taken away but this hay, the rain there was so much of it the hay came all the way and that made a dam so the water could not go away and the water went into the car and somebody opened the door and the water came more and more and Willie and Rose were there and there was enough water there to drown Willie certainly to drown Willie and perhaps to drown Rose.

Well anyway just then the hay went away, hay has that way and the water went away and the car did stay and neither Rose nor Willie were drowned that day.

Much later they had a great deal to say but they knew of course they knew that it was true the world was round and they were not drowned.

Now Willie liked to sing too. He was a cousin to Rose and so it was in the family to sing, but Willie had no dog with whom to sing so he had to sing with something and he sang with owls, he could only sing in the evening but he did sing in the evening with owls. There were three kinds of owls a Kew owl a chuette owl and a Hoot owl and every evening Willie sang with owls and these are the songs he sang.

My name is Willie I am not like Rose
I would be Willie whatever arose,
I would be Willie if Henry was my name
I would be Willie always Willie all the same.

And then he would stop and wait for the owls.
Through the moon the Q. owl blew

Who are you who are you.

Willie was not like his cousin Rose singing did not make him cry it just made him more and more excited.
So there was a moon and the moon was round.
Not a sound.
Just then Willie began to sing,

Drowning
Forgetting
Remembering
I am thinking

And the chuette owl interrupted him.

Is it
His it
Any eye of any owl is round.

Everything excited Willie, he was more excited and he sang

Once upon a time the world was round the moon was round
The lake was round
And I I was almost drowned.

And the hoot owl hooted

Hullo Hullo
Willie is your name
And Willie is your nature
You are a little boy
And that is your stature
Hullo Hullo.

SILENCE
Willie was asleep
And everything began to creep around
Willie turned in his sleep and murmured
Round drowned.

3

Eyes a Surprise

Rose did not care about the moon, she liked stars.

Once some one told her that the stars were round and she wished that they had not told her.

Her dog Love did not care about the moon either and he never noticed the stars. He really did not notice the moon not even when it was all round, he liked the lights of automobiles coming in and out. That excited him and even made him bark, Love was not a barker although little Pépé was. Pépé could always bark, he really did say bow wow really he did, when you listened he really did.

Well once they were out in the evening in an automobile, not Pépé, Pépé was not Rose's dog, you remember that, but Rose and Love and the lights of the automobile were alight so who could listen to the bright moon-light, not Rose nor Love nor the rabbit, not they.

It was a little rabbit and there he was right in front and in the light and it looked as if he meant it but he really could not help it, not he not the little rabbit.

Bob, Rose's father was driving and he stopped but that did not help the little rabbit.

Light is bright and what is bright will confuse a little rabbit who has not the habit.

So the little rabbit danced from one light to the other light and could never get alright, and then Bob the father said *let out Love perhaps he will help the rabbit to run away,* so they let out the white dog Love and he saw first the light and then he saw the rabbit and he went up to say how do you do to the rabbit, that is the way Love was, he always went up and said how do you do he said it to a dog or a man or a child or a lamb or a cat or a cook or a cake or anything he just said how do you do and when he said how do you do to the little rabbit the little rabbit forgot all about the light being bright he just left that light and Love the dog Love disappointed because the little rabbit had not said how do you do, back again, he went after him, of course any little rabbit can run quicker than any white dog and even if the white dog is nice

and kind and Love is, so that was all of that. It was a lovely
night and Love came back into the car and Bob the father
drove on home and of course Rose sang as the rabbit ran and
her song began.

My
What a sky
And then the glass pen
Rose did have a glass pen
When oh When
Little glass pen
Say when
Will there not be that little rabbit.
When
Then
Pen

And Rose burst into tears.
She did then she burst into tears.
A little later it was decided that Rose should go to school.
She went to school where mountains were high, they were so
high she never did see them. Rose was funny that way.
There at the school were other girls and Rose did not have
quite as much time to sing and cry.
The teachers taught her
That the world was round
That the sun was round
That the moon was round
That the stars were round
And that they were all going around and around
And not a sound.
It was so sad it almost made her cry
But then she did not believe it
Because mountains were so high,
And so she thought she had better sing
And then a dreadful thing was happening
She remembered when she had been young
That one day she had sung,
And there was a looking-glass in front of her
And as she sang her mouth was round and was going
around and around.

Oh dear oh dear was everything just to be round and go around and around. What could she do but try and remember the mountains were so high they could stop anything.

But she could not keep on remembering and forgetting of course not but she could sing of course she could sing and she could cry of course she could cry.

Oh my.

4

Willie and His Singing

All this time Willie was living along
Of course he could always make a song
The thing that bothered Willie the most
Was that when there was no wind blowing
A twig in a bush would get going
Just as if the wind was blowing.
He knew when he ran
And he knew when he sang
And he knew who
Who was Willie
He was Willie
All through.
Willie went away not to stay.
Willie never went away to stay
That was not Willie.
But once when he went away it was to stay there where he had seen it.
He saw it.
It was a little house and two trees near it.
One tree sometimes makes another tree.
Willie
Will he.
In a little while nobody wondered that thunder rumbled in winter, lightning struck and thunder rumbled in winter.
Oh Willie.
Of course Willie never went away to stay.

But Willie could sing.

Oh yes he sang a song.

He sang a little song about a house two trees and a rabbit

He sang a little song about a lizard.

A lizard climbed up the side of the house, it climbed out on the roof of the house and then the poor little lizard fell off of it.

Plump it fell off of it.

Willie saw it.

And Willie said, if the earth is all round can a lizard fall off it.

And the answer was yes if there is a roof over it.

Little lizard it lost its tail but it was not dead.

Willie sat down to rest.

It's funny he said, a lizard does not fall off a wall, it is funny and Willie sat down again to rest.

One of the things Willie did was to sit down and rest.

He liked cats and lizards, he liked frogs and pigeons he liked butter and crackers, he liked flowers and windows.

Once in a while they called for him and when they did he would talk to them.

And then he began to sing.

He sang.

Bring me bread
Bring me butter
Bring me cheese
And bring me jam
Bring me milk
And bring me chicken
Bring me eggs
And a little ham.

This is what Willie sang.

And then all at once

The world got rounder and rounder.

The stars got rounder and rounder

The moon got rounder and rounder

The sun got rounder and rounder

And Willie oh Willie was ready to drown her, not Rose dear me not Rose but his sorrows.

He loved to sing and he was exciting.
This is what Willie sang

Believe me because I tell you so
When I know yes when I know
Then I am Willie and Willie oh
Oh Willie needs Willie to tell them so.

Yes he said, he said *yes.*
Then Willie began to sing again.

Once upon a time I met myself and ran.
Once upon a time nobody saw how I ran.
Once upon a time something can
Once upon a time nobody sees
But I I do as I please
Run around the world just as I please.
I Willie.

Willie stopped again and again he began to sing.
He sang.
It was time Willie did something, why not when the world was all so full anywhere, Willie went on, he saw how many there were there.
Funny said Willie that a little dog sees another little dog far far away and I, said Willie, I see a little boy.
Well well said the dog little dogs are interesting
Well well said Willie little boys are interesting.
Undoubtedly Willie had something to do and now was the time to do it.

5

Willie and His Lion

Willie had a father and Willie had a mother
That was Willie.
Willie went with his father to a little place where they sold wild animals.

If the world is round can wild animals come out of the ground.

In the place that his father took Willie wild animals did not grow there, they were not always sold there but they were always there. Everybody there had them. Wild animals were with them on the boats on the river and they went with every one in the garden and in the house. Everybody there had a wild animal and they always had them with them.

Nobody knows how the wild animals came there. If the world is round can they come out of the ground but anyway everybody had one and sometimes somebody sold one, quite often everybody sold one.

Willie's father went to get one. Which one. That was for Willie to say. It was funny seeing wild animals in a boat, one wild animal in a rowing boat, one wild animal in a sail boat, one wild animal in a motor boat.

It was a funny place this town that is it would not have been a funny place it was just like any place only that every one always had a wild animal with them, men women and children and very often they were in the water in a boat and the wild animal with them and of course wild animals are wild, of course they are wild.

It was a funny place.

Willie went everywhere so of course he was there, beside his father had taken him there. It was a funny place. And Willie always took whatever he was given. So he hoped he would have one. Any one. Everybody had one so of course Willie would come to have one, any wild animal will do, if it belongs to you.

And Willie did come to have one.

Which one.

There were elephants, an elephant in a rowing boat, Willie did not get that one.

And a tiger in a sail boat, Willie did not get that one. Willie got a lion, not a very little one, one who looked like Rose's dog Love only the Lion was terrifying. Any lion is, even a quite small one and this was a pretty big one. Willie began to sing, it was exciting and Willie sang and sang he did not sing to the lion but he sang about lions being exciting, about cats and tigers and dogs and bears about windows and curtains

and giraffes and chairs. The giraffe's name was Lizzie, it really
was.

Willie was so excited he almost stopped singing but as soon
as he saw his own lion again he began singing again. Singing
and singing. This was the song he sang.

> *Round is around.*
> *Lions and tigers kangaroos and canaries abound*
> *They are bound to be around.*
> *Why*
> *Because the world is round*
> *And they are always there.*
> *Any little dog is afraid of there.*

Then he sang in a whisper

> *Suppose it should rain*
> *Suppose it should never be the same*

And then Willie's voice rose

> *The lion is what I chose.*

After a long moment he sat down to cry
He said *there, here I am just like my cousin Rose.*
Which was true
He was.
He almost was not Willie.
Oh will he again be Willie.
Not as long as he has a lion.
Not as long.
And it was getting worse and worse and then suddenly he
said.
*There were only two baskets of yellow peaches and I have them
both.*
He whispered very low.
And I have them both.
And Willie had, they were lovely round yellow peaches
really round really yellow really peaches and there were only
two baskets of them and Willie had them both.

And so he cheered up and decided to give the lion to his
cousin Rose.

6

Is a Lion Not a Lion

It is not easy to give a lion away
What did you say
I said it is not easy to give a lion away.

7

Rose and Willie's Lion

There is a lion its name is lion and lion lion is its name.
Rose began to cry.
Just try
Not to make Rose cry
Just try.
That is what Willie said to the lion
When he gave Rose the lion
His lion.
Oh yes his lion.
Well there was more to it than that.

When Rose knew about a lion his lion Willie's lion she remembered her dog Love. He was clipped like a lion but it was not that. It was when Love was only three months old and had never seen a lion.

Love was not a barker, he neither barked nor bit and when he was three months old he never had barked.

They began to be worried lest he could not bark, like children who will not talk. Well anyway.

One day Rose and her father Bob and her mother Kate and her grandmother Lucy and her uncle William were out riding and little Love was with them. Love had a pink nose and bright blue eyes and lovely white hair. When he ate asparagus and he liked to eat asparagus his rosy nose turned red with pleasure, but he never barked, not even at a cat or at asparagus. And then that day suddenly that day he stood up he was astonished and he barked. What was he astonished at. There in the middle of the open country was a big truck and on the truck were cages and the sides were down and there they were lions tigers bears and monkeys and Love just could not stand it and he barked.

Rose was very young then quite young too young then to sing a song but she sang one all the same.

This was the song she sang

How does Love know how wild they are
Wild and wild and wild they are
How does Love know who they are
When he never ever had seen them before.

And then she went on.

If a cat is in a cage
Does that make him rage.
If a dog is on a roof
Does that make him aloof
Or is there any proof
That he is a dog and on a roof.
And so
Oh
How could Love know
That wild animals were wild.
Wild animals yes wild.
Are they wild if they are wild,
If I am wild if you are wild
Are you wild oh are you wild

Rose began to cry.
She began to try
She began to deny
The wild animals could lie.
Lie quietly not die but just lie.
And then Rose once more began to sing.
I knew, she said, I knew I would sing
And this is everything.
I wish, she said, I wish I knew
Why wild animals are wild.
Why are they wild why why,
Why are they wild oh why,

And once more Rose began to cry.
Love was asleep he knew he could bark,
So why stay awake to hear Rose cry and sing
And sing and cry. Why.
That is what Love said.
Why.
And then later on when Love saw a wild animal he sometimes did anybody sometimes did, he did not bark he just turned his head away as much as to say, I did once but not again, wild animals are not interesting.

Love mostly barked in his sleep.
He dreamed.
And when he dreamed, he made a strangled bark,
Like anybody dreaming.
Love never said whether he liked to dream or not, but he did dream and when he dreamed he barked.

Rose was thinking all about everything when she heard that her cousin Willie had a lion.

8

Rose Thinking

If the world is round would a lion fall off.

9

A Favorite Color

Rose certainly made a noise when no one was found
Rose oh Rose look down at the ground
And what do you see
You see that the world is not round.
That is what Rose said when she knew that it was true that a lion is not blue.

Of course she knew that a lion is not blue but blue is her favorite color.

Her name is Rose and blue is her favorite color. But of course a lion is not blue. Rose knew that of course a lion is not blue but blue was her favorite color.

IO

Bringing Billie Back

The lion had a name, his color was not blue but he had a name too just as any one has a name and his name was Billie. Willie was a boy and Billie was a lion.

II

Bringing Back Billie to Willie

That is what happened.

Of course Rose could not keep a lion in school, she could not have kept him even if he had been blue which was her favorite color but she certainly could not keep him when he was yellow brown which is the natural color for a lion to be even if the lion has a name as well as a mane and that name is Billie.

In fact you might say really say that Rose had never had him, the lion had never come in, of course not if a lamb can not come into a school how certainly not can a lion.

So outside the school was a man with a drum, he was on a bicycle and the drum was on a bicycle and he was drumming and when Rose heard him drumming she went to the door and the man was calling out *either or either or, either there is a lion here or there is no lion here, either or, either or.*

Rose began to sing she just could not help herself, tears were in her eyes, she just could not help herself and she began to sing, she just could not help herself.

The drumming went on, *either or,* cried the man, *neither nor,* cried Rose *he is neither here nor there, no no lion is here no lion is there, neither nor,* cried Rose *he is neither here nor there.* The man began to drum and the drumming went further and further away and the drum was round and the wheels of the bicycle were round and they went around and around and as they went around and around the man whose mouth was round kept saying either or, either or, until there was no more no more drumming no more bicycle no more man any more.

So Rose was left at the door and she knew no more about the lion about Billie the lion than she had known before and slowly she began to sing.

> *Billie is going back to Willie,*
> *Willie is getting back Billie,*
> *No lion is blue*
> *So there is no lion for me*
> *There is a lion for you*

Oh Willie Willie yes there is a lion for you, a brown lion for you a real lion for you neither will you nor will you ever know how little I wanted to take away the lion from you dear Willie sweet Willie take back oh take back your lion to you, because, and she began to whisper to herself as if she herself was Willie, *because if a lion could be blue I would like a lion to come from you either from you or to you dear Willie sweet Willie there is no blue no lion in blue no blue in lion, neither nor,* wailed Rose *neither nor,* and as she said neither nor, there there was a door, and filled with sobs Rose went through the door and never any more never any more would she remember that it had been a lion that she saw, either or.

I 2

Once Upon a Time

Once upon a time Willie was always there of course he was that was where Willie was and the lion he had almost for-

gotten that there had been a lion and he had almost forgotten
that it had a name and Willie was getting very interested in
knowing whether a lizard could or could not be a twin and
just then he heard a bell ring and it was the lion Billie the
lion back again and Willie just could not help it he just had
to begin to sing and he sang a song called

Bringing Billie back again.

Bringing Billie back.

How could Billie come back.

How if there was no h in how. That is what Willie said,
how could Billie come back, how, how.

And Billie was back, was Billie a lion when he was back, No
said Willie, Billie was not a lion when he was back, was he a
kitten when Billie was back, no said Willie Billie was not a
kitten when he was back, was he a rat when he was back, no
said Willie he was not a rat. Well what said Willie what was
Billie when he was back, he was a twin said Willie that is what
Billie was when he got back.

And Willie began to laugh and by the time he stopped
laughing he had begun again to laugh. That was Willie not
Billie, Billie never had had to laugh not Billie because Billie
was a lion and a lion had never had to laugh.

So that was all there was about Billie the lion and he was
never there any more anywhere neither here nor there neither
there nor here, Billie the lion never was anywhere. The end
of Billie the lion.

13

A Chair on the Mountain

When mountains are really true they are blue.

Rose knew they were blue and blue was her favorite color.
She knew they were blue and they were far away or near just
as the rain came or went away. The rain came or the rain went
away any day.

And so Rose would look and see and deary me the mountains would be blue.

And then one day she saw a mountain near and then it was all clear.

This was the way Rose knew what to say.

Listen.

Mountains are high, up there is a sky, rain is near, mountains are clear mountains are blue that is true and one mountain two mountains three mountains or four when there are mountains there always are more.

Even from the door.

So Rose would say when every day she came that way.

Rose was at school there.

There the mountains were and they were blue, oh dear blue blue just blue, dear blue sweet blue yes blue.

And then Rose began to think. It was funny about Rose she always could just begin to think. She would say to her father *Bob, Father I have a complaint to make, my dog Love does not come when I call.*

Rose was always thinking. It is easy to think when your name is Rose. Nobody's name was ever Blue, nobody's, why not. Rose never thought about that. Rose thought she thought a lot but she never did think about that.

But mountains yes Rose did think about mountains and about blue when it was on the mountains and feathers when clouds like feathers were on the mountains and birds when one little bird and two little birds and three and four and six and seven and ten and seventeen and thirty or forty little birds all came flying and a big bird came flying and the little birds came flying and they flew higher than the big bird and they came down and one and then two and then five and then fifty of them came picking down on the head of the big bird and slowly the big bird came falling down between the mountain and the little birds all went home again. Little birds do go home again after they have scared off the big bird.

How Rose thought when she was thinking. Rose would get all round thinking her eyes her head her mouth her hands, she would get all round while she was thinking and then to relieve her hearing her thinking she would sing.

She sang a song of the mountain.

She sang,

Dear mountain tall mountain real mountain blue mountain yes mountain high mountain all mountain my mountain, I will with my chair come climbing and once there mountain once there I will be thinking, mountain so high, who cares for the sky yes mountain no mountain yes I will be there.

Tears came to her eyes.

Yes mountain she said *yes I will be there*.

And then as she looked she saw that one mountain had a top and the top was a meadow and the meadow came up to a point and on the point oh dear yes on the point yes Rose would put a chair and she would sit there and yes she did care yes there she would put a chair there there and everywhere she would see everywhere and she would sit on that chair, yes there.

And she did and this was how she did it. All alone she did it. She and the chair there there, and it was not blue there, no dear no it was green there, grass and trees and rocks are green not blue there no blue was there but blue was her favorite color all through.

14

The Going Up with the Chair

The first thing about which Rose had to make up her mind was what kind of a chair would she want way up there. She might take a camp stool that would be easiest to carry but that would not look very well up there.

She would want one that would look well way up there and that would be comfortable to sit in because she would be sitting a long time once she really did get all the way up there and it would have to be one that the rain would not harm because clouds are rain and surely there would be clouds up there. No matter how many things Rose thought about there would always be some way it could be done better and a chair dear me, a chair well a chair just had to be there.

When Rose knew she had to climb and climb all the time she knew she would have to go away all day and she knew no matter how she tried that that would not do. She knew she did not know the name of the mountain she would climb she knew it had a nice name, any name is a nice name, just have it be a name and it is a nice name, but the mountain perhaps the mountain did not have a name and if it did not have a name would it be a nice name. And if it had no name could a chair stay there right on top of a mountain that did not have a name.

As Rose thought of this she began to feel very funny she just naturally did begin to feel very very funny.

Do you suppose that Rose is a rose

If her favorite color is blue

Noses can be blue but not roses but Rose was a rose and her favorite color was blue.

And now she had to make up her mind what to do.

Would the chair be a green chair or a blue

The chair she was to take up there

There where

She was to sit on the mountain so high

Right up under the sky

But always remember that the world is round no matter how it does sound. Remember.

So Rose had to do so many things too beside deciding whether her chair should be green or blue.

She had to think about number 142. Why.

Numbers are round.

All she took was the blue chair to go there.

It was a long way to go

And so

From morning to evening she did not get there.

But from evening to morning she did get there she and the blue chair.

15

The Trip

It was not a trip she had to grip the blue chair and some-times it hung by a hair not Rose's hair but any hair so great had been Rose's scare.

16

This Was Her Trip

She had decided about the chair it was a blue chair a blue garden chair otherwise scratches and rain and dew and being carried all through would do a chair harm but not a blue garden chair.

So Rose left early so no one saw her and her chair she held before her and the mountain was high and so was the sky and the world was round and was all ground and she began to go, even so it was a very long way to go even if a mountain does not grow even so, climb a mountain and you will know even if there is no snow. Oh no.

Well shall I go Rose said as she was going, nobody does like to go nobody does say no and so Rose did go, even so she did go.

As she began to go it was early morning you know.

The birds began to stir

And then she heard some birds making funny screams as they flew.

And she thought of cousin Willie but that would not do.

Did the blue garden chair have arms or was it without arms, I am wondering.

17

Up the Hill

A hill is a mountain, a cow is a cat,

A fever is heating and where is she at.

She is climbing the mountain a chair in her arms, and always around her she is full of alarms. Why not, a chair is something but not to talk to when it is too cold to be bold too hot to be cold a lot too white to be blue, too red to be wed. Oh Willie she said and there was no Willie but there was a simple noise just a noise and with a noise there were eyes and with the eyes there was a tail and then from Rose there was a wail, I wish I was not dead said Rose but if I am I will have torn my clothes, blackberries are black and blueberries are blue strawberries are red and so are you, said Rose to Rose and it was all true. She could not sit down on her chair because if she did sit down on her chair she would think she was already there and oh dear she just could not see how high it all could be but she knew oh dear yes she knew and when those birds flew she just could not do so too and she could not sing and cry no matter how much she could try because she was there right in the middle of everything that was around her and how little she could move just a little and a little and the chair was sticking and she was sticking and she could not go down because she would not know where, going down might be anywhere, going up had to be there, oh dear where was Rose she was there really she was there not stuck there but very nearly really very nearly really stuck there. And now everything began and if it had not been on a mountain and if it had not been a chair there where she was she would not care but she did not run she never ran, there was no tin can, she was not hungry oh never that, but everything helped to hold her back, but if she stayed she was afraid, run ran a chair can be a man, oh dear chair do dear chair be a man so I will not be all scare, that is what Rose said trying not to see her own hair. Dear me hair chair ran man, Rose is beginning to feel as funny as she can. Anybody try to climb a mountain all alone with only a blue garden chair to hold there and everything on a mountain that is there and then see what it is that ran. Water yes and birds yes and rats yes and snakes yes and lizards yes and cats yes and cows yes, and trees yes and scratches yes, and sticks yes, and flies yes, and bees yes but not a Rose with a chair, all a Rose with a chair can dare is just not stare but keeping on going up there.

She did.

18

Day and Night

Was she awake or did she dream that her cousin Willie heard her scream.

She was asleep right there with her arms around her chair.

She never dragged the chair she carried it before and in a way it was a cane, she leaned upon it all the same and she went on climbing and then it was all still, she heard a sound like a trill and then she thought of her cousin Willie and his lion Billie who was never still but it was not that, no not that, it was nothing completely nothing like that, it was something moving perhaps it was just fat. It, fat can burn like that to make a trill and to be all still and to smell like the lion of cousin Will. Anything can happen while you are going up hill. And a mountain is so much harder than a hill and still. Go on.

19

The Night

Rose did go on smelling and breathing and pushing and shoving and rolling, she sometimes just rolled, and moving. Anything on a mountain side is moving, rocks are rolling, stones are turning, twigs are hitting, trees are growing, flowers are showing and animals are glowing that is their eyes are and everywhere there oh dear everywhere there well Rose was there and so was her chair.

How many minutes go around to make a second how many hours go round to make a minute how many days go around to make an hour how many nights go round to make a day and was Rose found. She never had been lost and so how could she be found even if everything did go around and around.

20

The Night

It all grew rosy they call it an alpine glow when it does so but Rose well Rose is her name and blue is her favorite color. And then she knew yes she had heard it too,

Red at night is a sailor's delight
Red in the morning is a sailor's warning,
And said she is it rose or red
And said she is it morning or evening
And said she am I awake or am I in bed,
And said she perhaps a sailor does not know perhaps somebody just told him so.

And then she remembered everything she had heard it was not about a bird it was about a spider,

A spider at night is a delight a spider in the morning is an awful warning,

And then she remembered about if you put shoes on a table it makes awful trouble, but she had not a table she only had a chair and after all she could not take off her shoes there up upon the mountain so high and that funny black that first was blue and then grey up there in the sky, and then she remembered about the moon, if you see the new moon through a window with glass not any trouble will ever pass no it will not and then she remembered just when she was about to be scared that after all she had never cared no she never had cared for any moon so what was the use how it was seen. And then,

Then she remembered if you see a girl or a woman dwarf it is awful more awful than any cough it is just awful awful all awful and then she remembered just before she began to cry, not that she really would cry, she only cried when she sang, and climbing a mountain was too occupying ever to sing so then she remembered that it was true if you saw a female dwarf everything was through everything was over there was nothing to do. And then she remembered if she saw a boy or a man dwarf not a fairy nothing so foolish as that but a dwarf something little that should have been big and then if she saw it and it was not a female but a man then everything would be better and better and she would get the mountain the mountain would not get her.

And just then was it a pen was it a cage was it a hut but anyway there was no but, she saw it was a dwarf, and it was not a woman it was a man and if it knew how, and it did, away it ran, so Rose oh Rose was as happy then as any hen and she fell on her chair and embraced it there the blue chair.

And then she said perhaps it was not a dwarf perhaps it was a little boy and I could have it for a toy, she knew what a little boy was because she had her cousin whose name was Willie even if he was a little silly. That is the way Rose felt about it but not on the mountain up there, there she would not care if Willie was silly if he would only be there.

21

Night

Rose did not want Willie, it was at night and she was not really resting and yet why did she think Willie was singing about what a day it was when Rose was not there. As she thought of that she almost let go her chair and went and went down and not up there. And then of course Willie never came. Why not when Willie was his name. Why not.

And so Rose went on again.

And now it was really night and when she could see them the stars were bright, and she remembered then that they say when the stars are bright rain comes right away and she knew it the rain would not hurt the chair but she would not like it to be all shiny there. Oh dear oh dear where was that dwarf man, it is so easy to believe whatever they say when you are all alone and so far away.

22

Rose Saw It Close

What did Rose see close, that is what she never can tell and perhaps it is just as well, suppose she did tell oh dear oh dear what she saw when she fell. Poor dear Rose. She saw it close. Never again would she stay on that spot, the chair quick the chair anywhere but there.

Rose and the chair went on, it was dark at least it would

have been if it had not been so bright, alright, alright it was alright of course it was alright it was just night, that is all it was just at night.

23

Night

What is it that water does do.

It falls it does too

It rises up that is when it is dew but when it falls, it is a water-fall and Rose knew all about that too, Rose knew almost everything that water can do, there are an awful lot when you think what, dew lakes rivers oceans fogs clouds and water-falls too, the thing that Rose heard it was night and Rose heard what she heard, dear little bird dear little water and dear little third, not dew, not a few but a water otter, a brown water otter, a long water otter and Rose said not you no not you you cannot frighten me no not you.

So then Rose was frightened all through Rose and the chair which was blue and the otter the brown otter, Rose would have liked him better if he had been blue, and then the water-fall, the water-fall, the water-fall, the water was full of water-fall. Rose carrying the chair went to look behind there to see if there was room for the blue chair. There always is room behind a water-fall when it is tall, and this water-fall even in the night was quite tall.

So Rose went in there it was all dark darker than out there and then she put down the chair and then she saw she did not know but it was so, she did see it there behind the water-fall, although it was all dark there. It was written three times just how it looked as if it was done with a hair on a chair, and it said, oh dear yes it said, *Devil, Devil Devil*, it said Devil three times right there. There was no devil there of course there was no devil there there is no devil anywhere devil devil devil where. But just there where there might be a chair and written in large writing and clear in the black there, it was written there.

Dear me, Rose came out with her blue chair she decided no she would not sit down there. She decided she did not like water to fall, water fall water fall, that is what cows call but there was no cow there there was only writing there. It was too bad that Rose could read writing otherwise she would not have known that it said devil three times there. There are people who cannot read writing, but Rose was not one of them. Oh no.

So Rose and the blue chair went away from there she never could go down not there not ever again there, she could never go anywhere where water is falling and water does fall even out of a faucet, poor Rose dear Rose sweet Rose only Rose, poor Rose alone with a blue chair there.

So she went on climbing higher and higher and higher and blinking, the stars were blinking and she had to think of something. If she did not she would think of seeing that, was the Devil round, was he around, around round, round around, oh dear no think of Pépé, do not think of cousin Willie, he could go around and around, Willie did, and do not think of the blue chair after all the seat of a chair, might it be round oh dear around and around, and Pépé Pépé the little dog who bit her, no he was not round, well his eyes were but not his teeth, they bit oh dear she just thought of that, they had told her that little dogs like Pépé when there are many they bite at the back of the legs of little donkeys and the donkeys fall and the little dogs eat them and do they when they eat a donkey get round like a ball, and there was the moon it was setting a little flat but it was a little round oh dear and it looked as if there was a little girl way up there in the moon with its hair flying and partly lying and she had no chair oh dear oh dear up there.

What a place a mountain could be it looked so steep and its sides so straight and the color so blue and now one two three all out but she and red white and blue all out but you and if there was a cock it was the time when it crew, but no there was no cock, there was no hen there was no glass pen, there was only Rose, Rose Rose, Rose and all of a sudden Rose knew that in Rose there was an o and an o is round, oh dear not a sound.

24

The Morning

Rose was a rose, she was not a dahlia, she was not a butter-cup (that is yellow), she was not a fuchsia or an oleander, well Rose wake Rose, Rose had not been asleep oh dear no, the dawn comes before the sun, and the dawn is the time to run, it is easy to run before the sun and Rose did. She was now not among the bushes which scratched but among trees which have nuts and she liked that, anybody would, and she did.

It is wonderful how many trees there are when they are all there and just then all the trees were all there, tree trunks are round that is if you go around but they are not round up into the air. Rose drew a deep breath of relief, and she lifted up her chair and she was almost glad she was there there where she was.

25

The Trees and the Rocks Under Them

The dawn is not rosy but it is quite cosy and in the woods it really is so, they did once say the woods the poor man's overcoat, and it is true there in the woods no rain comes through no sun comes through no snow comes through no dust comes through, there has to be a lot of anything before in a thick wood it does come through, and this was so and now Rose could know that this was so so early in the morning before there is a morning, and so Rose began to think of singing she thought how nice it would be to sing there in the woods where there were only trees and nothing, perhaps rocks and leaves and nuts and mushrooms but really not anything and perhaps she would like to begin singing, singing with her blue chair. And then she thought of course it always did hap-pen as soon as she began to sing she began to cry and if she began to cry well no matter how much she would try when she began to sing she would begin to cry. And then there she was in the woods, they said the woods were a covering and she had her blue chair and she had to think of something but if she began to sing or if she began to say something. Well when you are all alone alone in the woods even if the woods are lovely and warm and there is a blue chair which can never be any harm, even so if you hear your own voice singing or even just talking well hearing anything even if it is all your own like your own voice is and you are all alone and you hear your own voice then it is frightening.

26

Rose Does Something

So Rose did not sing but she had to do something.

And what did she do well she began to smile she was climbing all the while climbing not like on a stair but climbing a little higher everywhere and then she saw a lovely tree and she thought yes it is round but all around I am going to cut *Rose is a Rose is a Rose* and so it is there and not anywhere can I hear anything which will give me a scare.

And then she thought she would cut it higher, she would stand on her blue chair and as high as she could reach she would cut it there.

So she took out her pen-knife, she did not have a glass pen she did not have a feather from a hen she did not have any ink she had nothing pink, she would just stand on her chair and around and around even if there was a very little sound she would carve on the tree Rose is a Rose is a Rose is a Rose until it went all the way round. Suppose she said it would not go around but she knew it would go around. So she began.

She put the chair there she climbed on the chair it was her blue chair but it excited her so, not the chair but the pen-knife and putting her name there, that she several times almost fell off of the chair.

It is not easy to carve a name on a tree particularly oh yes particularly if the letters are round like R and O and S and E, it is not easy.

And Rose forgot the dawn forgot the rosy dawn forgot the sun forgot she was only one and all alone there she had to carve and carve with care the corners of the Os and Rs and Ss and Es in a Rose is a Rose is a Rose is a Rose.

Well first she did one and then the pen-knife seemed not to cut so well so she thought she would find a shell or a stone and if she rubbed her knife hard on it until it shone it would cut again just as it did before the knife began to groan. So she had to climb up and down on the chair and she had to find a stone and she had to go on and on, and at last well was it still dawn was there a sun well anyway at last it was more than begun it was almost done and she was cutting in the last Rose and just then well just then her eyes went on and they were round with wonder and alarm and her mouth was round and she had almost burst into a song because she saw on another tree over there that some one had been there and had carved a name and the name dear me the name was the same it was Rose and under Rose was Willie and under Willie was Billie.

It made Rose feel very funny it really did.

27

Rose and the Bell

She climbed on and on and she could not tell not very well whether it was night or day but she knew it was day and not night because it was really quite bright, it might though yes it might have been night. But was it.

Well anyway she was climbing away she and the chair and she almost thought that she was almost there and then was it that she fell but anyway she did hear a bell, it was a tinkle and she heard it clearly it might be that a stone had stumbled and hit the garden chair, it might be that the chair had hit something right there or it might be that it was a cat that had a bell or it might be that it was a cow that had a bell or a sheep or a bird or even a little dog that might be running there chasing a low flying crow, or it might be a telephone, not very likely but it might, or it might be a dinner bell, or it might not be a bell at all it might be just a call, or it might be a lizard or a frog or it might be dear me it might be a log, rolling over rocks and water, but no it was a bell how can you tell if a bell is a bell.

There are so many things that are just funny it might just be silver money, anyway Rose was there and she certainly did think she knew she had heard a bell. Did she hear a bell. And would she know it was a bell if it was a bell. Did it come nearer and did she go nearer and was it just perhaps lightning and thunder.

All around the sun was shining and the bell was ringing and the woods were thinning and the green was shining. Please Rose please she was remembering. That is the way it was. It made her feel a little lonesome, until then she had been busy climbing but now she was beginning beginning hearing everything and it was a little lonesome.

Rose was a little lonesome, she had her blue chair. She was a little lonesome.

28

Rose and the Bell

The bell was ringing but there was no singing and Rose went climbing up and on. And then gradually she came out of the trees and there she saw an enormous green meadow going up to a point and in the middle of the meadow green, it was green as grass, there was a little black dog way up all alone and shaking himself like a dog does. Oh said Rose and she almost sat down. It was the first word she had said of all the many that had come into her head since she first began to climb. And of course it was a round one. Oh is a round one. For the first time since she began to climb Rose did not know what to do next.

29

Once Upon a Time

Once upon a time way back, there were always meadows with grass on them on top of every mountain. A mountain looked as if it had rocks way up there but really way up there there was always grass and the grass always made it look elegant and it was nice.

Grass is always the most elegant more elegant than rocks and trees, trees are elegant and so are rocks but grass is more so.

And here way up there was grass and it was going on and on and it is so much harder to climb up and up and up on grass than on rocks and under trees.

And to carry a blue chair way up there on and on through the grass because grass is steep steeper than rocks are, it was a very difficult day that day and that was the way Rose went on her way.

She had to what else could she do she had to see it through getting up there to be all the way there and to sit on her chair.

And when you are walking on grass it is harder to see where there is. And anyway what did it say. The grass did not say anyway, it was green and nothing green ever has anything to say.

Rose knew that that is why she always did prefer blue.

30

The Green Grass Meadow

Rose was now going up and up the green grass meadow that went right on to the top. She did not say oh again she just went on. It was hot, and the green grass was hot and underneath the green grass there was ground and in that ground oh dear Rose almost stepped on it there was something round.

Rose had courage everywhere she just went on going up there.

31

The Last Hour

It is hard to go on when you are nearly there but not near enough to hurry up to get there. That is where Rose was and she well she hardly could go on to get there. And where was there. She almost said it she almost whispered it to herself and to the chair. Where oh where is there.

But she went on and the grass was shorter and the slant was steeper and the chair was bluer and heavier and the clouds were nearer and the top was further because she was so near she could not see which way it was and if she went one way and the top was the other way could it be that she would never see what she could see. Oh deary me oh deary me what did she see. She did see and her eyes were round with fright and her hands and arms did hold her chair tight and suddenly green became blue and she knew that one would become two and three would become four and never again no never again would there ever be a door for her to go through.

But Rose was not like that, stumbling would be the beginning of tumbling and she would not tumble up but tumble down if she began to stumble and so she began to frown and she knew she would have to begin to count, one two one two one two one two.

Close your eyes and count one two open your eyes and count one two and then green would not be blue. So Rose began counting one two one two and she knew that she was counting one two one two and so her eyes were blue although her name was Rose. Of course her eyes were blue even though her name was Rose. That is the reason she always did prefer blue because her eyes were blue. And she had two eyes and each one of her two eyes was blue, one two one two.

And sooner than it could be true there she saw something that was not green nor blue, it was violet and other colors it was high up as high as the sky it was where she could cry it was a rain-bow. Oh yes oh no it was a rain-bow.

And Rose just went right through, she went right through the rain-bow and she did know that was what she would do. She had it to do and she went right through the rain-bow and then there she was right on the top so that there was no other top there just the top with room for the blue chair and Rose put the blue chair there and she sat upon the chair. And Rose was there.

32

There

She was all alone on the top of everything and she was sitting there and she could sing.

This was the song she sang,

It began.

Here I am.
When I wish a dish
I wish a dish of ham.
When I wish a little wish
I wish that I was where I am.

She stopped and sat awhile not that she ever got up, she was so pleased with sitting she just sat.

And then she sang,

When I see I saw I can
I can see what I saw I saw where I am sitting.
Yes I am sitting.
She sighed a little.
Yes I can see I am sitting.
She sighed again.
Yes I can.
Once when five apples were red,
They never were it was my head.
No said she *no it was not my head it was my bed.*
So she began again.
Once when apples were red
When all is said when all is said
Are apples red
Or is it said that I know which which I have.

She stopped to think
Rose stopped to think,
I think said Rose and she wriggled a little on her chair.
She was alone up there.
I think said Rose.
And then she began to sing.

Am I asleep or am I awake
Have I butter or have I cake,
Am I here or am I there,
Is the chair a bed or is it a chair.
Who is where.

Once more Rose began to sing.
It was getting a little dark and once more Rose began to sing.

I am Rose my eyes are blue
I am Rose and who are you
I am Rose and when I sing
I am Rose like anything.

I am Rose said Rose and she began to sing.

I am Rose but I am not rosy
All alone and not very cosy
I am Rose and while I am Rose
Well well Rose is Rose.

It was a little darker.
Rose sat a little tighter on her blue chair. She really was up there. She really was.
She began to sing.

Once upon a time I knew
A chair was blue.
Once upon a time I knew whose chair was blue.
My chair was blue nobody knew but I knew I knew my chair
was blue.

Rose went on singing it was getting darker. *Once upon a*
time there was a way to stay to stay away, I did not stay away

I came away I came away away away and I am here and here is there oh where oh where is there oh where. And Rose began to cry *oh where where where is there. I am there oh yes I am there oh where oh where is there.*

It was darker and darker and the world was rounder and rounder and the chair the blue chair was harder and harder and Rose was more there than anywhere. Oh dear yes there.

And once more Rose began to sing.

When I sing I am in a ring, and a ring is round and there is no sound and the way is white and pepper is bright and Love my dog Love he is away alright oh dear wailed Rose *oh dear oh dear I never did know I would be here, and here I am all alone all night and I am in a most awful fright. Oh chair dear chair dear hard blue chair do hold me tight I'll sit in you with all my might.*

It was getting darker and darker and there was no moon, Rose never had cared about the moon but there were lots of stars and somebody had told her that stars were round, they were not stars, and so the stars were not any comfort to her and just then well just then what was it just then well it was just that it was just then.

Just then wailed Rose *I wish just then had been a hen.*

33

A Light

Well it was night and night well night can be all right that is just what a night can be it can be all night. And Rose knew that. Rose knew so much it made her clutch the blue chair closer as she sat on it there.

And then just then what was it, it was not lightning it was not a moon it was not a star not even a shooting star it was not an umbrella it was not eyes eyes in the dark oh dear no it was a light, a light and oh so bright. And there it was way off on another hill and it went round and round and it went all around Rose and it was a search light surely it was and it was on a further hill and surely Will her cousin Will surely he was on another hill and he made the light go round and round and made the ground green not black and made the sky white not black and Rose oh Rose just felt warm right through to her back.

And she began to sing.

A little boy upon a hill
Oh Will oh Will.
A little boy upon a hill
He will oh will.
Oh Will oh Will.
And I am here and you are there, and I am here and here is there and you are there and there is here oh Will oh Will on any hill.
Oh Will oh Will oh Will
Oh Will oh Will.
Will you sang Rose oh yes you will.

And she sang oh will oh will and she cried and cried and cried and cried and the search light went round and round and round and round.

34

The End

Willie and Rose turned out not to be cousins, just how nobody knows, and so they married and had children and sang with them and sometimes singing made Rose cry and sometimes it made Willie get more and more excited and they lived happily ever after and the world just went on being round.

DOCTOR FAUSTUS
LIGHTS THE LIGHTS

Doctor Faustus Lights the Lights

ACT I

Faust standing at the door of his room, with his arms up at the door lintel looking out, behind him a blaze of electric light.

Just then Mephisto approaches and appears at the door.

Faustus growls out	The devil what the devil what do I care if the devil is there.
Mephisto says	But Doctor Faustus dear yes I am here.
Doctor Faustus	What do I care there is no here nor there. What am I. I am Doctor Faustus who knows everything can do everything and you say it was through you but not at all, if I had not been in a hurry and if I had taken my time I would have known how to make white electric light and day-light and night light and what did I do I saw you you miserable devil I saw you and I was deceived and I believed miserable devil I thought I needed you, and I thought I was tempted by the devil and I know no temptation is tempting unless the devil tells you so. And you wanted my soul what the hell did you want my soul for, how do you know I have a soul, who says so nobody says so but you the devil and everybody knows the devil is all lies, so how do you know how do I know that I have a soul to sell how do you know Mr. Devil oh Mr. Devil how can you tell you can not tell anything and I I who know everything I keep on having so much light that light is not bright and what after all is the use of light, you can see just as well without it, you can go around just as well without it you can get up and go to bed just as well without it,

577

and I I wanted to make it and the devil take it yes you devil you do not even want it and I sold my soul to make it. I have made it but have I a soul to pay for it.

Mephisto coming nearer and trying to pat his arm.

Yes dear Doctor Faustus you of course you have a soul of course you have, do not believe them when they say the devil lies, you know the devil never lies, he deceives oh yes he deceives but that is not lying no dear please dear Doctor Faustus do not say the devil lies.

Doctor Faustus   Who cares if you lie if you steal, there is no snake to grind under one's heel, there is no hope there is no death there is no life there is no breath, there just is every day all day and when there is no day there is no day, and anyway of what use is a devil unless he goes away, go away old devil go away, there is no use in a devil unless he goes away, how can you remember a devil unless he goes away, oh devil there is no use in your coming to stay and now you are red at night which is not a delight and you are red in the morning which is not a warning go away devil go away or stay after all what can a devil say.

Mephisto   A devil can smile a devil can while away whatever there is to give away, and now are you not proud Doctor Faustus yes you are you know you are you are the only one who knows what you know and it is I the devil who tells you so.

Faustus   You fool you devil how can you know, how can you tell me so, if I am the only one who can know what I know then no devil can know what I know and no devil can tell me so and I could know without any soul to sell, without there being anything in hell. What I know I know, I know how I do what I do when I see the way through and always any day I will see another day and you old devil you know very well you never see any other way than just the way to hell, you only know one way you only know one thing, you are never ready for anything, and I everything is always now and now and now perhaps through you I begin to know that it is all just so, that light however bright will never be other than light, and any light is just a light and now there is nothing more either by day or by night but just a light. Oh you devil go to hell, that is all you know to tell, and who is interested in hell just a devil is interested in hell because that is all he can tell, whether I stamp or whether I cry whether I live or whether I die, I can know that all a devil can say is just about going to hell the same way, get out of here devil, it does not interest me whether you can buy or I can sell, get out of here devil just you go to hell.

Faustus gives him an awful kick, and Mephisto moves away and the electric lights just then begin to get very gay.

Alright then

The Ballet

Doctor Faustus sitting alone surrounded by electric lights.

His dog comes in and says

Thank you.

One of the electric lights goes out and again the dog says

Thank you.

The electric light that went out is replaced by a glow.

The dog murmurs.

My my what a sky.

and then he says

Thank you.

Doctor Faustus' song.

If I do it
If you do it
What is it.
  Once again the dog says
Thank you.
  A duet between Doctor Faustus and the dog about the elec-
  tric light about the electric lights.
Bathe me
  says Doctor Faustus
Bathe me
In the electric light.
  During this time the electric lights come and go
What is it
  says Doctor Faustus
Thank you
  said the dog.
  Just at this moment the electric lights get brighter and
  nothing comes
Was it it
  says Doctor Faustus
  Faustus meditates he does not see the dog.
Will it
Will it
Will it be
Will it be it.
  Faustus sighs and repeats
Will it be it.
  A duet between the dog and Faustus
Will it be it
Just it.
  At that moment the electric light gets pale again and in that
  moment Faustus shocked says
It is it
  A little boy comes in and plays with the dog, the dog says
Thank you.
  Doctor Faustus looks away from the electric lights and then
  he sings a song.

Let Me Alone

Let me alone
Oh let me alone
Dog and boy let me alone oh let me alone
Leave me alone
Let me be alone
little boy and dog
let let me alone
    He sighs
    And as he sighs
    He says
Dog and boy boy and dog leave me alone let me let me be
alone
    The dog says
Thank you
    but does not look at Faustus
    A pause
    No words
    The dog says
Thank you
I say thank you
Thank you
    The little boy
The day begins to-day
The day
The moon begins the day
    Doctor Faustus
There is no moon to-day
    Dark silence
You obey I obey
There is no moon to-day.
    Silence
    and the dog says
I obey I say
Thank you any day
    The little boy says
Once in a while they get up.
    Doctor Faustus says
I shall not think

I shall not
No I shall not.
  Faustus addresses little boy and dog
Night is better than day so please go away
  The boy says
But say
When the hay has to be cut every day then there is the devil
to pay
  The dog starts and then he shrinks and says
Thank you
  Faustus half turns and starts
I hear her
  he says
I hear her say
Call to her to sing
To sing all about
to sing a song
All about
day-light and night light.
Moonlight and star-light
electric light and twilight
every light as well.
  The electric lights glow and a chorus in the distance sings
Her name is her name is her name is Marguerite Ida and
Helena Annabel.
  Faustus sings
I knew it I knew it the electric lights they told me so no dog
can know no boy can know I cannot know they cannot know
the electric lights they told me so I would not know I could
not know who can know who can tell me so I know you
know they can know her name is Marguerite Ida and Helena
Annabel and when I tell oh when I tell oh when I when I
when I tell, oh go away and go away and tell and tell and tell
and tell and tell, oh hell.
  The electric lights commence to dance and one by one they
    go out and come in and the boy and the dog begin to sing.
Oh very well oh Doctor Faustus very very well oh very well,
thank you says the dog oh very well says the boy her name
her name is Marguerite Ida and Helena Annabel, I know says
the dog I know says the boy I know says Doctor Faustus no

no no no no nobody can know what I know I know her name is not Marguerite Ida and Helena Annabel, very well says the boy it is says the boy her name is Marguerite Ida and Helena Annabel, no no no says Doctor Faustus yes yes yes says the dog, no says the boy yes says the dog, her name is not Marguerite Ida and Helena Annabel and she is not ready yet to sing about day-light and night light moon light and star-light electric light and twilight she is not she is not but she will be. She will not be says Doctor Faustus never never never, never will her name be Marguerite Ida and Helena Annabel never never never never well as well never Marguerite Ida and Helena Annabel never Marguerite Ida and Helena Annabel.

There is a sudden hush and the distant chorus says
It might be it might be her name her name might be Marguerite Ida and Helena Annabel it might be.

And Doctor Faustus says in a loud whisper
It might be but it is not, and the little boy says how do you know and Faustus says it might be it might not be not be not be, and as he says the last not be the dog says
Thank you.

Scene II

I am I and my name is Marguerite Ida and Helena Annabel, and then oh then I could yes I could I could begin to cry but why why could I begin to cry.

And I am I and I am here and how do I know how wild the wild world is how wild the wild woods are the woods they call the woods the poor man's overcoat but do they cover me and if they do how wild they are wild and wild and wild they are, how do I know how wild woods are when I have never ever seen a wood before.

I wish, (she whispered) I knew why woods are wild why animals are wild why I am I, why I can cry, I wish I wish I knew, I wish oh how I wish I knew. Once I am in I will never be through the woods are there and I am here and am I here or am I there, oh where oh where is here oh where oh where is there and animals wild animals are everywhere.

She sits down.

I wish (says she conversationally) I wish if I had a wish that when I sat down it would not be here but there there where I would have a chair there where I would not have to look around fearfully everywhere there where a chair and a carpet underneath the chair would make me know that there is there, but here here everywhere there is nothing nothing like a carpet nothing like a chair, here it is wild everywhere I hear I hear everywhere that the woods are wild and I am here and here is here and here I am sitting without a chair without a carpet, oh help me to a carpet with a chair save me from the woods the wild woods everywhere where everything is wild wild and I I am not there I am here oh dear I am not there.

She stands up with her hands at her sides she opens and closes her eyes and opens them again.

If my eyes are open and my eyes are closed I see I see, I see no carpet I see no chair I see the wild woods everywhere, what good does it do me to close my eyes no good at all the woods the woods are there I close my eyes but the green is there and I open my eyes and I have to stare to be sure the green is there the green of the woods, I saw it when my eyes were closed I saw the wild woods everywhere and now I open my eyes and there there is the wild wood everywhere.

Would it do as well if my name was not Marguerite Ida and Helena Annabel would it do as well I would give up even that for a carpet and a chair and to be not here but there, but (and she lets out a shriek,) I am here I am not there and I am Marguerite Ida and Helena Annabel and it is not well that I could tell what there is to tell what there is to see and what do I see and do I see it at all oh yes I do I call and call but yes I do I see it all oh dear oh dear oh dear yes I am here.

She says

In the distance there is daylight and near to there is none.

There is something under the leaves and Marguerite Ida and Helena Annabel makes a quick turn and she sees that a viper has stung her.

In the distance there is daylight and near to there is none.

There is a rustling under the leaves and Marguerite Ida and Helena Annabel appears and makes a quick turn and she sees that a viper has stung her, she sees it and she says and what is it. There is no answer. Does it hurt she says and then she says no not really and she says was it a viper and she says how can I tell I never saw one before but is it she says and she stands up again and sits down and pulls down her stocking and says well it was not a bee not a busy bee no not, nor a mosquitoe nor a sting it was a bite and serpents bite yes they do perhaps it was one, Marguerite Ida and Helena Annabel sits thinking and then she sees a country woman with a sickle coming. Have I she says have I been bitten, the woman comes nearer, have I says Marguerite Ida and Helena Annabel have I have I been bitten. Have you been bitten answers the country woman, why yes it can happen, then I have been bitten says Marguerite Ida and Helena Annabel why not if you have been is the answer.

They stand repeating have I and yes it does happen and then Marguerite Ida and Helena Annabel says let me show you and the woman says oh yes but I have never seen any one who has been bitten but let me see no I cannot tell she says but go away and do something, what shall I do said Marguerite Ida and Helena Annabel do something to kill the poison, but what said Marguerite Ida and Helena Annabel, a doctor can do it said the woman but what doctor said Marguerite Ida and Helena Annabel, Doctor Faustus can do it said the woman, do you know him said Marguerite Ida and Helena Annabel no of course I do not know him nobody does there is a dog, he says thank you said the woman and go and see him go go go said the woman and Marguerite Ida and Helena Annabel went.

As she went she began to sing.
Do vipers sting do vipers bite
If they bite with all their might
Do they do they sting
Or do they do they bite
Alright they bite if they bite with all their might.
And I am I Marguerite Ida or am I Helena Annabel
Oh well
Am I Marguerite Ida or am I Helena Annabel.
Very well oh very well
Am I Marguerite Ida very well am I Helena Annabel.

She stops she remembers the viper and in a whisper she says was it a sting was it a bite am I alright, was it a sting was it a bite, alright was it a sting oh or was it a bite.

She moves away and then suddenly she stops.
Will he tell
Will he tell that I am Marguerite Ida that I am Helena Annabel.
Will he tell.

And then she stops again
And the bite might he make it a bite.
Doctor Faustus a queer name
Might he make it a bite
And so she disappears.

Scene III

Doctor Faustus the dog and the boy all sleeping, the dog dreaming says

Thank you, thank you thank you thank you thank you, that you thank you.

Doctor Faustus turns and murmurs

Man and dog dog and man each one can tell it all like a ball with a caress no tenderness, man and dog just the same each one can take the blame each one can well as well tell it all as they can, man and dog, well well man and dog what is the difference between a man and a dog when I say none do I go away does he go away go away to stay no nobody goes away the dog the boy they can stay I can go away go away where where there there where, dog and boy can annoy I can go say I go where do I go I go where I go, where is there there is where and all the day and all the night too it grew and grew and there is no way to say I and a dog and a boy, if a boy is to grow to be a man am I a boy am I a dog is a dog a boy is a boy a dog and what am I I cannot cry what am I oh what am I

And then he waits a moment and he says
Oh what am I.

Just then in the distance there is a call

Doctor Faustus Doctor Faustus are you there Doctor Faustus

I am here Doctor Faustus I am coming there Doctor Faustus, there is where Doctor Faustus oh where is there Doctor Faustus say it Doctor Faustus are you there Doctor Faustus are you there.

The dog murmurs
Thank you thank you
and the boy says
There is somebody of course there is somebody just there there is somebody somebody is there oh yes somebody is there.

and all together they say
Where is there nobody says nobody is there. Somebody is there and nobody says that somebody is not there. Somebody somebody is there somebody somebody somebody somebody says there is where where is it where is it where is it where, here is here here is there somebody somebody says where is where.

Outside the voice says
Doctor Faustus are you there Doctor Faustus say where, Doctor Faustus are you there.

And then there is a knock at the door.
The electric lights glow softly and Marguerite Ida and Helena Annabel comes in.
Well and yes well, and this is yes this is Doctor Faustus Doctor Faustus and he can and he can change a bite hold it tight make it not kill not kill Marguerite Ida not kill Helena Annabel and hell oh hell not a hell not well yes well Doctor Faustus can he can make it all well.

And then she says in a quiet voice.
Doctor Faustus have you ever been to hell.
Of course not she says of course you have not how could you sell your soul if you had ever been to hell of course not, no of course not.
Doctor Faustus tell me what did they give you when you sold your soul, not hell no of course not not hell.

And then she goes on.
I I am Marguerite Ida and Helena Annabel and a viper bit or stung it is very well begun and if it is so then oh oh I will die and as my soul has not been sold I Marguerite Ida and Helena Annabel perhaps I will go to hell.

The dog sighs and says

Thank you

and the little boy coming nearer says

what is a viper, tell me Marguerite Ida and Helena Annabel I like you being Marguerite Ida and Helena Annabel what is a viper do I know it very well or do I not know it very well please tell you are Marguerite Ida and Helena Annabel what is a viper.

Doctor Faustus says

Little boy and dog can be killed by a viper but Marguerite Ida and Helena Annabel not very well no not very well

He bursts out

Leave me alone

Let me be alone

Little boy and dog let me be alone, Marguerite Ida and Helena Annabel let me be alone, I have no soul I had no soul I sold it sold it here there and everywhere

What did I do I knew

I knew that there could be light not moon-light star light day-light and candle light, I knew I knew I saw the lightening light, I saw it light, I said I I I must have that light, and what did I do oh what did I do too I said I would sell my soul all through but I knew I knew that electric light was all true, and true oh yes it is true they took it that it was true that I sold my soul to them as well and so never never could I go to hell never never as well. Go away dog and boy go away Marguerite Ida and Helena Annabel go away all who can die and go to heaven or hell go away oh go away go away leave me alone oh leave me alone. I said it I said it was the light I said I have the light I said the lights are right and the day is bright little boy and dog leave me alone let me be alone.

The country woman with the sickle looks in at the window and sings Well well this is the Doctor Faustus and he has not gone to hell he has pretty lights and they light so very well and there is a dog and he says thank you and there is a little boy oh yes little boy there you are you just are there yes little boy you are and there is Marguerite Ida and Helena Annabel and a viper did bite her, oh cure her Doctor Faustus cure her what is the use of your having been to hell if Marguerite Ida and Helena Annabel is not to be all well.

And the chorus sings

What is the use Doctor Faustus what is the use what is the use of having been to hell if you cannot cure this only only this Marguerite Ida and Helena Annabel.

Doctor Faustus says

I think I have thought thought is not bought oh no thought is not bought I think I have thought and what have I bought I have bought thought, to think is not bought but I I have bought thought and so you come here you come you come here and here and here where can I say that not to-day not any day can I look and see, no no I cannot look no no I cannot see and you you say you are Marguerite Ida and Helena Annabel and I I cannot see I cannot see Marguerite Ida and I cannot see Helena Annabel and you you are the two and I cannot cannot see you.

Marguerite Ida and Helena Annabel

Do not see me Doctor Faustus do not see me it would terrify me if you did see do not see me no no do not see me I am Marguerite Ida and Helena Annabel but do not see me cure me Doctor Faustus does the viper bite the viper sting his sting was a bite and you you have the light cure me Doctor Faustus cure me do but do not see me, I see you but do not see me cure me do but do not see me I implore you.

Doctor Faustus

A dog says thank you but you you say do not see me cure me do but do not see me what shall I do.

He turns to the dog

The dog says

Thank you

and the boy says

What difference does it make to you if you do what difference oh what difference does it make to you if you do, whatever you do do whatever you do do what difference does it make to you if you do.

Marguerite Ida and Helena Annabel

What difference does it make to you if you do what difference does it make to you but I a viper has had his bite and I I will die but you you cannot die you have sold your soul but I I have mine and a viper has come and he has bitten me and see see how the poison works see see how I must die, see how little by little it is coming to be high, higher and higher I must die oh Doctor Faustus what difference does it make to you what difference oh what difference but to me to me to me to me a viper has bitten me a viper a viper has bitten me.

    The dog

Oh Thank you thank you all all of you thank you thank you oh thank you everybody thank you he and we thank you, a viper has bitten you thank you thank you.

    The boy

A viper has bitten her she knows it too a viper has bitten her believe it or not it is true, a viper has bitten her and if Doctor Faustus does not cure her it will be all through her a viper has bitten her a viper a viper.

    Dog

Thank you

    Woman at the window

A viper has bitten her and if Doctor Faustus does not cure her it will be all through her.

    Chorus in the distance

Who is she

She has not gone to hell

Very well

Very well

She has not gone to hell

Who is she

Marguerite Ida and Helena Annabel

And what has happened to her

A viper has bitten her

And if Doctor Faustus does not cure her

It will go all through her

And he what does he say

He says he cannot see her

Why cannot he see her

Because he cannot look at her

He cannot look at Marguerite Ida and Helena Annabel

But he cannot cure her without seeing her

They say yes yes

And he says there is no witness

And he says

He can but he will not

And she says he must and he will
And the dog says thank you
And the boy says very well
And the woman says well cure her and she says she is
Marguerite Ida and Helena Annabel.

There is silence the lights flicker and flicker, and Marguerite
Ida and Helena Annabel gets weaker and weaker and the poison stronger and stronger and suddenly the dog says star-
tlingly
Thank you.

Doctor Faustus says
I cannot see you
The viper has forgotten you.
The dog has said thank you
The boy has said will you
The woman has said
Can you
And you, you have said you are you
Enough said.
You are not dead.
Enough said
Enough said.
You are not dead.
No you are not dead
Enough said
Enough said
You are not dead.

All join in enough said you are not dead you are not dead
enough said yes enough said no you are not dead yes enough
said, thank you yes enough said no you are not dead.

And at the last
In a low whisper
She says
I am Marguerite Ida and Helena Annabel and enough said I
am not dead.

CURTAIN

ACT II

Some one comes and sings
Very
Very
Butter better very well
Butcher whether it will tell
Well is well and silver sell
Sell a salted almond to Nell
Which she will accept
And then
What does a fatty do
She does not pay for it.
No she does not
Does not pay for it.
By this time they know how to spell very
Very likely the whole thing is really extraordinary
Which is a great relief
All the time her name is Marguerite Ida Marguerite Ida
    They drift in and they sing
Very likely the whole thing is extraordinary
Which is a great relief
All the time her name is Marguerite Ida
Marguerite Ida.
    Then they converse about it.
Marguerite Ida is her name Marguerite Ida and Helena
Annabel who can tell if her name is Marguerite Ida or Helena
Annabel
Sillies all that is what makes you tall.
To be tall means to say that everything else is layed away.
Of course her names is Marguerite Ida too and Helena
Annabel as well.
    A full chorus
Of course her names is Marguerite Ida too and Helena
Annabel as well.
    A deep voice asks
Would a viper have stung her if she had only had one name
would he would he.
How do you know how do you know that a viper did sting
her.

How could Doctor Faustus have cured her if there had not been something the matter with her.

Marguerite Ida and Helena Annabel it is true her name is Marguerite Ida and Helena Annabel as well and a viper has stung her and Doctor Faustus has cured her, cured her cured her, he has sold his soul to hell cured her cured her cured her he has sold his soul to hell and her name is Marguerite Ida and Helena Annabel and a viper had to bite her and Doctor Faustus had to cure her cure her cure her cure her.

The curtain at the corner raises and there she is Marguerite Ida and Helena Annabel and she has an artificial viper there beside her and a halo is around her not of electric light but of candle light, and she sits there and waits.

The chorus sings

There she is
Is she there
Look and see
Is she there
Is she there
Anywhere
Look and see
Is she there
Yes she is there
There is there
She is there
Look and see
She is there.
There she is
There there
Where
Why there
Look and see there
There she is
And what is there
A viper is there
The viper that bit her
No silly no
How could he be there
This is not a viper
This is what is like a viper

She is there
And a viper did bite her
And Doctor Faustus did cure her
And now
And now
And now she is there
Where
Why there
Oh yes there.
Yes oh yes yes there.
There she is
Look and see
And the viper is there
And the light is there
Who gave her the light
Nobody did
Doctor Faustus sold his soul
And so the light came there
And did she sell her soul.
No silly he sold his soul
She had a viper bite her
She is there
Oh yes she is there
Look there
Yes there
She is there.

   Marguerite Ida begins to sing

I sit and sit with my back to the sun I sat and sat with my back to the sun. Marguerite Ida sat and sat with her back to the sun.

The sun oh the sun the lights are bright like the sun set and she sat with her back to the sun sat and sat

   She sits

   A very grand ballet of lights.

Nobody can know that it so
They come from everywhere
By land by sea by air
They come from everywhere
To look at her there.
See how she sits.

See how she eats
See how she lights,
The candle lights.
See how the viper there.
Cannot hurt her.
No indeed he cannot.
Nothing can touch her.
She has everything
And her soul,
Nothing can lose her.
See how they come
See how they come
To see her.
See how they come.
Watch
They come by sea
They come by land
They come by air
And she sits
With her back to the sun
One sun
And she is one
Marguerite Ida and Helena Annabel as well.
    They commence to come and more and more come and
    they come from the sea from the land and from the air.
    And she sits.
    A man comes from over the seas and a great many are
    around him
    He sees her as she sits.
    And he says
Pretty pretty dear
She is all my love and always here
And I am hers and she is mine
And I love her all the time
Pretty pretty pretty dear.
No say the chorus no.
She is she and the viper bit her
And Doctor Faustus cured her.
The man from over seas repeats
Pretty pretty pretty dear

She is all my love and always here
And I am hers and she is mine
And I love her all the time.

Marguerite Ida and Helena Annabel suddenly hears something and says
What is it.

He comes forward and says again
Pretty pretty pretty dear she is all my love and she is always here.

She sings slowly
You do or you do not.

He
Pretty pretty dear she is all my love and she is always here.
Well well he says well well and her name is Marguerite Ida and Helena Annabel and they all say it was a viper, what is a viper, a viper is a serpent and anybody has been bitten and not everybody dies and cries, and so why why say it all the time, I have been bitten I I I have been bitten by her bitten by her there she sits with her back to the sun and I have won I have won her I have won her.

She sings a song
You do or you do not
You are or you are not
I am there is no not
But you you you
You are as you are not.

He says
Do you do what you do because you know all the way through that I I was coming to you answer me that.

She turns her back on him.

and he says
I am your sun oh very very well begun, you turn your back on your sun, I am your sun, I have won I have won I am your sun.

Marguerite Ida and Helena Annabel rises. She holds the viper she says
Is it you Doctor Faustus is it you, tell me man from over the sea are you he.

He laughs.
Are you afraid now afraid of me.

She says

Are you he.

He says

I am the only he and you are the only she and we are the only we. Come come do you hear me come come, you must come to me, throw away the viper throw away the sun throw away the lights until there are none, I am not any one I am the only one, you have to have me because I am that one.

She looks very troubled and drops the viper but she instantly stoops and picks it up and some of the lights go out and she fusses about it.

And then suddenly she starts,

No one is one when there are two, look behind you look behind you you are not one you are two.

She faints.

And indeed behind the man of the seas is Mephistopheles and with him is a boy and a girl.

Together they sing the song the boy and the girl.

Mr. Viper think of me. He says you do she says you do and if you do dear Mr. Viper if you do then it is all true he is a boy I am a girl it is all true dear dear Mr. Viper think of me.

The chorus says in the back,

Dear dear Mr. Viper think of them one is a boy one is a girl dear dear viper dear dear viper think of them.

Marguerite Ida and Helena Annabel still staring at the man from over the seas and Mephisto behind them.

She whispers

They two I two they two that makes six it should be seven they two I two they two five is heaven.

Mephisto says

And what if I ask what answer what, I have a will of iron yes a will to do what I do. I do what I do what I do, I do I do.

And he strides forward,

Where where where are you, what a to do, when a light is bright there is moon-light, when a light is not so bright then it is day-light, and when a light is no light than it is electric light, but you you have candle light, who are you.

The ballet rushes in and out.

Marguerite Ida and Helena Annabel lifts the viper and says

Lights are all right but the viper is my might.

Pooh says Mephisto, I despise a viper, the viper tries but the viper lies. Me they cannot touch no not any such, a viper, ha ha a viper, a viper, ha ha, no the lights the lights the candle lights, I know a light when I see a light, I work I work all day and all night, I am the devil and day and night, I never sleep by any light by any dark by any might, I never sleep not by day not by night, you cannot fool me by candle light, where is the real electric light woman answer me.

The little boy and girl creep closer, they sing.

Mr. viper dear Mr. viper, he is a boy I am a girl she is a girl I am a boy we do not want to annoy but we do oh we do oh Mr. Viper yes we do we want you to know that she is a girl that I am boy, oh yes Mr. viper please Mr. viper here we are Mr. Viper listen to us Mr. Viper, oh please Mr. Viper it is not true Mr. Viper what the devil says Mr. Viper that there is no Mr. Viper, please Mr. Viper please Mr. Viper, she is a girl he is a boy please Mr. Viper you are Mr. Viper please Mr. Viper please tell us so.

The man from over the seas smiles at them all, and says

It is lovely to be at ease.

Mephisto says

What you know I am the devil and you do not listen to me I work and I work by day and by night and you do not listen to me he and she she and he do not listen to me you will see you will see, if I work day and night and I do I do I work day and night, then you will see what you will see, look out look out for me.

He rushes away

And Helena Annabel and Marguerite Ida shrinks back, and says to them all

What does he say

And the man from over the seas says

Pretty pretty dear she is all my love and she is always here
   and then more slowly

I am the only he you are the only she and we are the only we,
   and the chorus sings softly

And the viper did bite her and Doctor Faustus did cure her.
   And the boy and girl sing softly

Yes Mr. Viper he is a boy she is a girl yes Mr. Viper.
  And the ballet of lights fades away.

CURTAIN

ACT III

Scene I

  Doctor Faustus' house
  Faustus in his chair, the dog and the boy, the electric lights
  are bright but the room is dark.
  Faustus
Yes they shine
They shine all the time.
I know they shine
I see them shine
And I am here
I have no fear
But what shall I do
I am all through
I cannot bear
To have no care
I like it bright
I do like it bright
Alright I like it bright,
But is it white
Or is it bright.
Dear dear
I do care
That nobody can share.
What if they do
It is all to me
Ah I do not like that word me,
Why not even if it does rhyme with she. I know all the words
that rhyme with bright with light with might with alright, I
know them so that I cannot tell I can spell but I cannot tell
how much I need to not have that, not light not sight, not
light not night not alright, not night not sight not bright, no
no not night not sight not bright no no not bright.

There is a moment's silence and then the dog says

Thank you.

He turns around and then he says

Yes thank you.

And then he says

Not bright not night dear Doctor Faustus you are right, I am a dog yes I am just that I am I am a dog and I bay at the moon, I did yes I did I used to do it I used to bay at the moon I always used to do it and now now not any more, I cannot, of course I cannot, the electric lights they make it be that there is no night and if there is no night then there is no moon and if there is no moon I do not see it and if I do not see it I cannot bay at it.

The dog sighs and settles down to rest

and as he settles down he says

Thank you.

The little boy cuddles up close to him and says

Yes there is no moon and if there is a moon then we do not bay at the moon and if there is no moon then no one is crazy any more because it is the moon of course it is the moon that always made them be like that, say thank you doggie and I too I too with you will say thank you.

They softly murmur

Thank you thank you that you too.

They all sleep in the dark with the electric light all bright, and then at the window comes something.

Is it the moon says the dog is it the moon says the boy is it the moon do not wake me is it the moon says Faustus.

No says a woman no it is not it is not the moon, I am not the moon I am at the window Doctor Faustus do not you know what it is that is happening.

No answer.

Doctor Faustus do not you know what is happening.

Back of her a chorus

Doctor Faustus do not you know what is happening.

Still no answer

All together louder

Doctor Faustus do not you know do not you know what it is that is happening.

Doctor Faustus.

Go away woman and men, children and dogs moon and stars go away let me alone let me be alone no light is bright, I have no sight, go away woman and let me boy and dog let me be alone I need no light to tell me it is bright, go away go away, go away go away.

No says the woman no I am at the window and here I remain till you hear it all. Here we know because Doctor Faustus tells us so, that he only he can turn night into day but now they say, they say, (her voice rises to a screech) they say a woman can turn night into day, they say, a woman and a viper bit her and did not hurt her and he showed her how and now she can turn night into day, Doctor Faustus oh Doctor Faustus say you are the only one who can turn night into day, oh Doctor Faustus yes do say that you are the only one who can turn night into day.

The chorus behind says

Oh Doctor Faustus oh Doctor Faustus do say that you are the only one who can turn night into day.

Faustus starts up confused he faces the woman, he says, What is it you say.

And she says imploringly

Oh Doctor Faustus do say you are the only one who can turn night into day.

Faustus slowly draws himself erect and says

Yes I do say I am the only one who can turn night into day.

And the woman and the chorus say

He is the only one who can turn night into day.

And the dog says

He is the only one who can turn night into day, there is no moon any night or any day he is the only one to turn night into day,

and the little boy says

Yes he is the only one to turn night into day.

And the woman then says

But come Doctor Faustus come away come and see whether they say that they can turn night into day.

Who says it

   says Doctor Faustus

She says it

   says the woman

Who is she
  says Doctor Faustus
  They answer
Marguerite Ida or Helena Annabel
She
  says Doctor Faustus
Who said I could not go to hell.
She she
  says the woman
She she
  says the chorus
Thank you
  said the dog
Well
  said Doctor Faustus
Well then I can go to hell, if she can turn night into day then
I can go to hell, come on then come on we will go and see
her and I will show her that I can go to hell, if she can turn
night into day as they say then I am not the only one so
Marguerite Ida and Helena Annabel listen well you cannot
but I I can go to hell.
Come on every one never again will I be alone come on come
on every one.
  They all leave.

                            Scene II

  The scene as before, Marguerite Ida and Helena Annabel
sitting with the man from over the seas their backs to the sun,
the music to express a noon-day hush.
  Everybody dreamily saying
Mr. Viper please Mr. Viper,
  some saying
Is he is he Doctor Faustus no he isn't no he isn't, is he is he
is he all he loves her is he is he all she loves him, no one can
remember anything but him, which is she and which is he
sweetly after all there is no bee there is a viper such a nice
sweet quiet one, nobody anybody knows how to run, come
any one come, see any one, some, come viper sun, we know
no other any one, any one can forget a light, even an electric
one but no one no no one can forget a viper even a stuffed

one no no one and no one can forget the sun and no one can
forget Doctor Faustus no no one and and no one can forget
Thank you and the dog and no one can forget a little boy and
no one can forget any one no no one.

(These words to be distributed among the chorus).

and the man from over seas murmurs dreamily

Pretty pretty pretty dear here I am and you are here and yet
and yet it would be better yet if you had more names and not
only four in one let it be begun, forget it oh forget it pretty
one, and if not I will forget that you are one yes I will yes I
will pretty pretty one yes I will.

Marguerite Ida and Helena Annabel stiffens a little

Well will you yes I will, no one can know when I do not tell
them so that they cannot know anything they know, yes I
know, I do know just what I can know, it is not there well
anywhere, I cannot come not for any one I cannot say what
is night and day but I am the only one who can know anything about any one, am I one dear dear am I one, who hears
me knows me I am here and here I am, yes here I am.

The chorus gets more lively and says

Yes there she is.

Dear me

says the man from over the seas.

Just then out of the gloom appears at the other end of the
stage Faust and the boy and the dog, nobody sees them,
just then in front of every one appears Mephisto, very excited and sings

Which of you can dare to deceive me which of you he or she
can dare to deceive me, I who have a will of iron I who make
what will be happen I who can win men or women I who can
be wherever I am which of you has been deceiving which of
you she or he which of you have been deceiving me.

He shouts louder

If there is a light who has the right, I say I gave it to him,
she says he gave it to her or she does not say anything, I say
I am Mephisto and what I have I do not give no not to any
one, who has been in her who has been in him, I will win.

The boy and girl shrilly sing

She is she and he is he and we are we Mr. Viper do not forget
to be. Please Mr. Viper do not forget to be, do not forget

that she is she and that he is he please Mr. Viper do not forget
me.

    Faustus murmurs in a low voice

I sold my soul to make it bright with electric light and now
no one not I not she not they not he are interested in that
thing and I and I I cannot go to hell I have sold my soul to
make a light and the light is bright but not interesting in my
sight and I would oh yes I would I would rather go to hell
be I with all my might and then go to hell oh yes alright.

    Mephisto strides up to him and says

You deceived me.

I did not

    says Faustus

    Mephisto

You deceived me and I am never deceived

    Faustus

You deceived me and I am always deceived,

    Mephisto

You deceived me and I am never deceived.

    Faustus

Well well let us forget it is not ready yet let us forget and now
oh how how I want to be me myself all now, I do not care
for light let it be however light, I do not care anything but
to be well and to go to hell. Tell me oh devil tell me will she
will Marguerite Ida and Helena Annabel will she will she really
will she go to hell.

    Mephisto

I suppose so.

    Faustus

Well then how dear devil how how can I who have no soul I
sold it for a light how can I be I again alright and go to hell.

    Mephisto

Commit a sin

    Faustus

What sin, how can I without a soul commit a sin.

    Mephisto

Kill anything

    Faustus

Kill

    Mephisto

Yes kill something oh yes kill anything.

Yes it is I who have been deceived I the devil who no one can deceive yes it is I I who have been deceived.

Faustus

But if I kill what then will.

Mephisto

It is I who have an iron will.

Faustus

But if I kill what will happen then.

Mephisto

Oh go to hell.

Faustus

I will

He turns he sees the boy and dog he says

I will kill I will I will.

He whispers

I will kill I will I will.

He turns to the boy and dog and he says

Boy and dog I will kill you two I will kill I will I will boy and dog I will kill you kill you, the viper will kill you but it will be I who did it, you will die.

The dog says

Thank you, the light is so bright there is no moon to-night I cannot bay at the moon the viper will kill me. Thank you,

and the boy says

And I too, there is no day and night there is no dog to-night to say thank you the viper will kill me too, good-bye to you.

In the distance the voices of the boy and girl are heard saying Mr. Viper please listen to me he is a boy she is a girl.

There is a rustle the viper appears and the dog and the boy die.

Faustus

They are dead yes they are dead, dear dog dear boy yes you are dead you are forever ever ever dead and I I can because you die nobody can deny later I will go to hell very well very well I will go to hell Marguerite Ida Helena Annabel I come to tell to tell you that I can go to hell.

Mephisto

And I, while you cry I who do not deny that now you can go to hell have I nothing to do with you.

Faustus

No I am through with you I do not need the devil I can go to hell all alone. Leave me alone let me be alone I can go to hell all alone.

Mephisto

No listen to me now take her with you do I will make you young take her with you do Marguerite Ida and Helena Annabel take her with you do.

Faustus

Is it true that I can be young.

Mephisto

Yes.

Faustus

Alright.

He is young he approaches Marguerite Ida and Helena Annabel who wakes up and looks at him. He says

Look well I am Doctor Faustus and I can go to hell.

Marguerite Ida and Helena Annabel

You Doctor Faustus never never Doctor Faustus is old I was told and I saw it with my eyes he was old and could not go to hell and you are young and can go to hell, very well you are not Doctor Faustus never never.

Faustus

I am I am I killed the boy and dog when I was an old man and now I am a young man and you Marguerite Ida and Helena Annabel and you know it well and you know I can go to hell and I can take some one too and that some one will be you.

Marguerite Ida and Helena Annabel

Never never, never never, you think you are so clever you think you can deceive, you think you can be old and you are young and old like any one but never never I am Marguerite Ida and Helena Annabel and I know no man or devil no viper and no light I can be anything and everything and it is always always alright. No one can deceive me not a young man not an old man not a devil not a viper I am Marguerite Ida and Helena Annabel and never never will a young man be an old man and an old man be a young man, you are not Doctor Faustus no not ever never never

and she falls back fainting into the arms of the man from

over the seas who sings

Pretty pretty pretty dear I am he and she is she and we are we, pretty pretty dear I am here yes I am here pretty pretty pretty dear.

Mephisto strides up.

Always deceived always deceived I have a will of iron and I am always deceived always deceived come Doctor Faustus I have a will of iron and you will go to hell.

Faustus sings

Leave me alone let me be alone, dog and boy boy and dog leave me alone let me be alone

and he sinks into the darkness and it is all dark and the little boy and little girl sing

Please Mr. Viper listen to me he is he and she is she and we are we please Mr. Viper listen to me.

CURTAIN

IDA

Part One

THERE WAS a baby born named Ida. Its mother held it with her hands to keep Ida from being born but when the time came Ida came. And as Ida came, with her came her twin, so there she was Ida-Ida.

The mother was sweet and gentle and so was the father. The whole family was sweet and gentle except the great-aunt. She was the only exception.

An old woman who was no relation and who had known the great-aunt when she was young was always telling that the great-aunt had had something happen to her oh many years ago, it was a soldier, and then the great-aunt had had little twins born to her and then she had quietly, the twins were dead then, born so, she had buried them under a pear tree and nobody knew.

Nobody believed the old woman perhaps it was true but nobody believed it, but all the family always looked at every pear tree and had a funny feeling.

The grandfather was sweet and gentle too. He liked to say that in a little while a cherry tree does not look like a pear tree.

It was a nice family but they did easily lose each other.

So Ida was born and a very little while after her parents went off on a trip and never came back. That was the first funny thing that happened to Ida.

The days were long and there was nothing to do.

She saw the moon and she saw the sun and she saw the grass and she saw the streets.

The first time she saw anything it frightened her. She saw a little boy and when he waved to her she would not look his way.

She liked to talk and to sing songs and she liked to change places. Wherever she was she always liked to change places. Otherwise there was nothing to do all day. Of course she went to bed early but even so she always could say, what shall I do now, now what shall I do.

Some one told her to say no matter what the day is it always ends the same day, no matter what happens in the year the year always ends one day.

Ida was not idle but the days were always long even in winter and there was nothing to do.

Ida lived with her great-aunt not in the city but just outside.

She was very young and as she had nothing to do she walked as if she was tall as tall as any one. Once she was lost that is to say a man followed her and that frightened her so that she was crying just as if she had been lost. In a little while that is some time after it was a comfort to her that this had happened to her.

She did not have anything to do and so she had time to think about each day as it came. She was very careful about Tuesday. She always just had to have Tuesday. Tuesday was Tuesday to her.

They always had plenty to eat. Ida always hesitated before eating. That was Ida.

One day it was not Tuesday, two people came to see her great-aunt. They came in very carefully. They did not come in together. First one came and then the other one. One of them had some orange blossoms in her hand. That made Ida feel funny. Who were they? She did not know and she did not like to follow them in. A third one came along, this one was a man and he had orange blossoms in his hat brim. He took off his hat and he said to himself here I am, I wish to speak to myself. Here I am. Then he went on into the house.

Ida remembered that an old woman had once told her that she Ida would come to be so much older that not anybody could be older, although, said the old woman, there was one who was older.

Ida began to wonder if that was what was now happening to her. She wondered if she ought to go into the house to see whether there was really any one with her great-aunt, and then she thought she would act as if she was not living there but was somebody just coming to visit and so she went up to the door and she asked herself is any one at home and when they that is she herself said to herself no there is nobody at home she decided not to go in.

That was just as well because orange blossoms were funny

things to her great-aunt just as pear trees were funny things to Ida.

And so Ida went on growing older and then she was almost sixteen and a great many funny things happened to her. Her great-aunt went away so she lost her great-aunt who never really felt content since the orange blossoms had come to visit her. And now Ida lived with her grandfather. She had a dog, he was almost blind not from age but from having been born so and Ida called him Love, she liked to call him naturally she and he liked to come even without her calling him.

It was dark in the morning any morning but since her dog Love was blind it did not make any difference to him.

It is true he was born blind nice dogs often are. Though he was blind naturally she could always talk to him.

One day she said. Listen Love, but listen to everything and listen while I tell you something.

Yes Love she said to him, you have always had me and now you are going to have two, I am going to have a twin yes I am Love, I am tired of being just one and when I am a twin one of us can go out and one of us can stay in, yes Love yes I am yes I am going to have a twin. You know Love I am like that when I have to have it I have to have it. And I have to have a twin, yes Love.

The house that Ida lived in was a little on top of a hill, it was not a very pretty house but it was quite a nice one and there was a big field next to it and trees at either end of the field and a path at one side of it and not very many flowers ever because the trees and the grass took up so very much room but there was a good deal of space to fill with Ida and her dog Love and anybody could understand that she really did have to have a twin.

She began to sing about her twin and this is the way she sang.

Oh dear oh dear Love, that was her dog, if I had a twin well nobody would know which one I was and which one she was and so if anything happened nobody could tell anything and lots of things are going to happen and oh Love I felt it yes I know it I have a twin.

And then she said Love later on they will call me a suicide blonde because my twin will have dyed her hair. And then

they will call me a murderess because there will come the time
when I will have killed my twin which I first made come. If
you make her can you kill her. Tell me Love my dog tell me
and tell her.

Like everybody Ida had lived not everywhere but she had
lived in quite a number of houses and in a good many hotels.
It was always natural to live anywhere she lived and she soon
forgot the other addresses. Anybody does.

There was nothing funny about Ida but funny things did
happen to her.

Ida had never really met a man but she did have a plan.

That was while she was still living with her great-aunt. It
was not near the water that is unless you call a little stream
water or quite a way off a little lake water, and hills beyond
it water. If you do not call all these things water then there
where Ida was living was not at all near water but it was near
a church.

It was March and very cold. Not in the church that was
warm. Ida did not often go to church, she did not know anybody and if you do not know anybody you do not often go
to church not to a church that is only open when something
is going on.

And then she began to know a family of little aunts. There
were five of them, they were nobody's aunts but they felt like
aunts and Ida went to church with them. Somebody was going to preach. Was it about life or politics or love? It certainly
was not about death, anyway, they asked Ida to go and they
all went. It was crowded inside the church cold outside and
hot inside. Ida was separated from the aunts, they were little
and she could not see them, she was tall as tall as any one and
so they could see her.

There was nothing funny about Ida but funny things did
happen to her. There she was there was a crowd it was not
very light, and she was close against so many, and then she
stayed close against one or two, there might have been more
room around her but she did not feel that way about it, anyway it was warm being so close to them and she did not know
any of them, she did not see any of them, she looked far away,
but she felt something, all right she felt something, and then
the lecture or whatever it was was over.

She went out, everybody did, and soon she met the five little aunts, they did not seem to be liking her very much but they all went on together, it was cold it was in March and there was almost snow. There were trees of course there was a sidewalk but nobody was on it except themselves, and then all of a sudden some one a man of course jumped out from behind the trees and there was another with him. Ida said to the aunts go on go on quickly I will walk back of you to protect you, the aunts hurried on, Ida hurried a little less quickly, she turned toward the men but they were gone. The five aunts and Ida went on, they said good-night to her but she never saw them again. These were the first and last friends she ever had, and she really never went to church again not really.

When she got home her dog Love met her and she began to sing about her twin and this is the way she sang.

Oh dear oh dear Love (that was her dog), if I had a twin well nobody would know which one I was and which one she was and so if anything happened nobody could tell anything and lots of things are going to happen and oh Love I feel it yes I know I have a twin.

And then she began to look far away and she began to think about her parents. She remembered them when she grew a little older but there were plenty to take care of her and they did. (Think of all the refugees there are in the world just think.) And then one day she looked and she saw some one, she saw two of them but they were not her parents. She was learning to read and write then and the first thing she learned was that there were miracles and so she asked any one to give her one. Then one day, she said she had one. She sat alone and it was summer and suddenly it was snowing and as it snowed she saw two dogs a black and a white one both little and as she looked they both both the little dogs ran away and they ran away together. Ida said this was a miracle and it was.

Ida gradually was a little older and every time she was a little older some one else took care of her. She liked the change of address because in that way she never had to remember what her address was and she did not like having to remember. It was so easy to forget the last address and she really forgot to guess what the next address was.

Little by little she knew how to read and write and really she said and she was right it was not necessary for her to know anything else. And so quite gradually little by little she grew older.

She always had a dog, at every address she had a dog and the dog always had a name and once she had one and its name was Iris. Just at this time Ida was living up in the mountains. She liked it up there. But then Ida liked living anywhere. She had lived in so many places and she liked any where.

Her dog Iris was not afraid of thunder and lightning but he was afraid of the rain and when it began to rain he ran away from Ida and then he ran back to her because after all he could not run away from the rain because the rain followed him. And so he ran back again to Ida.

And then Ida left there and went to live in a city. She lived with her old grandfather. He was so old and weak you wondered how he could walk any farther but he always could. Ida paid no attention to her grandfather.

While she was in the city funny things happened to her.

It was the month of August. August is a month when if it is hot weather it is really very hot.

Some funny things happened then. Ida was out, she was always out or in, both being exciting.

She was out it was towards evening it was time when public parks were closed and Ida was looking in through the railing, and she saw right across the corner that some one else was looking and looking at her. It was a policeman. He was bending down and looking at her. She was not worrying but she did wonder why he was getting down to look at her across the corner. And then she saw next to her a very old woman, well was it or was it not a woman, she had so much clothing on and so many things hanging from her and she was carrying so many things she might have been anything.

Ida went away it was time for her to be at home.

Finally August was over and then it was September.

Sometimes in a public park she saw an old woman making over an old brown dress that is pieces of it to make herself another dress. She had it all on all she owned in the way of clothes and she was very busy. Ida never spoke to her.

Ida was getting to be older. Sometimes she thought about

a husband but she knew that a husband meant marriage and marriage meant changes and changes meant names and after all she had so many changes but she did have just that one name Ida and she liked it to stay with her. And then another funny thing happened to her.

It was winter and Ida never wondered because thunder rumbled in winter, that lightning struck and thunder rumbled in winter. It just did.

Ida paid no attention to that but she did one day see a man carrying an advertisement on his back, a sandwich man, that was all right but what was funny was that he stopped and he was talking as if he knew him to a big well dressed rich man.

Ida very quickly went off home.

Then she went to live with another great-aunt outside of the city and there she decided and she told her dog Love about it, she decided that she would be a twin.

She had not yet decided to be a twin when another funny thing happened to her.

She was walking with her dog Love, they were walking and suddenly he left her to bark at something, that something was a man stretched out by the side of the road, not sleeping, because his legs were kicking, not dead, because he was rolling, not happy, because he just was not, and he was dressed in soldier's clothing. Love the dog went up to him, not to sniff, not to bark, he just went up to him and when Ida came near she saw he was not a white man, he was an Arab, and of course the dog Love did not bark at him. How could he when an Arab smells of herbs and fields and not of anything human? Ida was not frightened, he got up the Arab and he began to make motions of drinking. Ida might have been frightened if it had been toward evening, which it was, and she had been all alone, which she was, but she motioned back that she had nothing, and the Arab got up, and stood, and then suddenly, he went away. Ida instead of going on the way she was going went back the way she had come.

She heard about religion but she never really did happen to have any. One day, it was summer, she was in another place and she saw a lot of people under the trees and she went too. They were there and some one was moving around among them, they were all sitting and kneeling, not all of them but

most of them and in the middle there was one slowly walking
and her arms were slowly moving and everybody was following and some when their arms were started moving could not
stop their arms from going on moving. Ida stayed as long as
she could and then she went away. She always stayed as long
as she could.

One day, it was before or after she made up her mind to
be a twin, she joined a walking marathon. She kept on moving, sleeping or walking, she kept on slowly moving. This was
one of the funny things that happened to her. Then she lived
outside of a city, she was eighteen then, she decided that she
had had enough of only being one and she told her dog Love
that she was going to be two she was going to be a twin. And
this did then happen.

Ida often wrote letters to herself that is to say she wrote to
her twin.

Dear Ida my twin,
Here I am sitting not alone because I have dear Love
with me, and I speak to him and he speaks to me, but
here I am all alone and I am thinking of you Ida my
dear twin. Are you beautiful as beautiful as I am dear
twin Ida, are you, and if you are perhaps I am not. I can
not go away Ida, I am here always, if not here then
somewhere, but just now I am here, I am like that, but
you dear Ida you are not, you are not here, if you were
I could not write to you. Do you know what I think
Ida, I think that you could be a queen of beauty, one of
the ones they elect when everybody has a vote. They are
elected and they go everywhere and everybody looks at
them and everybody sees them. Dear Ida oh dear Ida
do do be one. Do not let them know you have any name
but Ida and I know Ida will win, Ida Ida Ida,
                                        from your twin
                                               Ida

Ida sat silently looking at her dog Love and playing the
piano softly until the light was dim. Ida went out first locking
the door she went out and as she went out she knew she was
a beauty and that they would all vote for her. First she had to
find the place where they were going to vote, but that did not

make any difference anywhere would do they would vote for her just anywhere, she was such a beauty.

As she went she saw a nicely dressed little girl with a broken arm who threw a stone at a window. It was the little girl's right arm that was broken. This was a sign.

So when Ida arrived they voted that she was a great beauty and the most beautiful and the completest beauty and she was for that year the winner of the beauty prize for all the world. Just like that. It did happen. Ida was her name and she had won.

Nobody knew anything about her except that she was Ida but that was enough because she was Ida the beauty Ida.

Part Two

T HERE WAS an older man who happened to go in where they were voting. He did not know they were voting for the prize beauty but once there he voted too. And naturally he voted for her. Anybody would. And so she won. The only thing for her to do then was to go home which she did. She had to go a long way round otherwise they would have known where she lived of course she had to give an address and she did, and she went there and then she went back outside of the city where she was living.

On the way, just at the end of the city she saw a woman carrying a large bundle of wash. This woman stopped and she was looking at a photograph, Ida stopped too and it was astonishing, the woman was looking at the photograph, she had it in her hand, of Ida's dog Love. This was astonishing.

Ida was so surprised she tried to snatch the photograph and just then an automobile came along, there were two women in it, and the automobile stopped and they stepped out to see what was happening. Ida snatched the photograph from the woman who was busy looking at the automobile and Ida jumped into the automobile and tried to start it, the two women jumped into the automobile threw Ida out and went on in the automobile with the photograph. Ida and the woman with the big bundle of wash were left there. The two of them stood and did not say a word.

Ida went away, she was a beauty, she had won the prize she was judged to be the most beautiful but she was bewildered and then she saw a package on the ground. One of the women in the automobile must have dropped it. Ida picked it up and then she went away.

So then Ida did everything an elected beauty does but every now and then she was lost.

One day she saw a man he looked as if he had just come off a farm and with him was a very little woman and behind him was an ordinary-sized woman. Ida wondered about them. One day she saw again the woman with a big bundle of wash.

She was talking to a man, he was a young man. Ida came up near them. Just then an automobile with two women came past and in the automobile was Ida's dog Love, Ida was sure it was Love, of course it was Love and in its mouth it had a package, the same package Ida had picked up. There it all was and the woman with the bundle of wash and the young man and Ida, they all stood and looked and they did not any one of them say anything.

Ida went on living with her great-aunt, there where they lived just outside of the city, she and her dog Love and her piano. She did write letters very often to her twin Ida.

Dear Ida, she said.

> Dear Ida,
> So pleased so very pleased that you are winning, I might even call you Winnie because you are winning. You have won being a beautiful one the most beautiful one. One day I was walking with my dog Love and a man came up to him, held out his hand to him and said how do you do you the most beautiful one. I thought he was a very funny man and now they have decided that you are the one the most beautiful one. And one day the day you won, I saw a funny thing, I saw my dog Love belonging to some one. He did not belong to me he did belong to them. That made me feel very funny, but really it is not true he is here he belongs to me and you and now I will call you Winnie because you are winning everything and I am so happy that you are my twin.
>
> Your twin, Ida-Ida

And so Winnie was coming to be known to be Winnie.

Winnie Winnie is what they said when they saw her and they were beginning to see her.

They said it different ways. They said Winnie. And then they said Winnie.

She knew.

It is easy to make everybody say Winnie, yes Winnie. Sure I know Winnie. Everybody knows who Winnie is. It is not so easy, but there it is, everybody did begin to notice that Winnie is Winnie.

This quite excited Ida and she wrote more letters to Winnie.

Dear Winnie,
Everybody knows who you are, and I know who you
are. Dear Winnie we are twins and your name is Winnie.
Never again will I not be a twin,

Your twin
Ida

So many things happened to Winnie. Why not when everybody knew her name.

Once there were two people who met together. They said.
What shall we do? So what did they do. They went to see
Winnie. That is they went to look at Winnie.

When they looked at her they almost began to cry. One
said. What if I did not look at her did not look at Winnie.
And the other said. Well that is just the way I feel about it.

After a while they began to think that they had done it, that
they had seen Winnie, that they had looked at her. It made
them nervous because perhaps really had they.

One said to the other. Say have we and the other answered
back, say have we.

Did you see her said one of them. Sure I saw her did you.
Sure he said sure I saw her.

They went back to where they came from.

One day Ida went to buy some shoes. She liked to look at
yellow shoes when she was going to buy red ones. She liked
to look at black shoes when she was not going to buy any
shoes at all.

It was crowded in the shoe store. It was the day before
Easter.

There were a great many places but each one had some one,
it is hard to try on shoes standing, hard, almost impossible
and so she waited for her turn, a man was sitting next to his
wife who was trying on shoes, he was not, and so not Ida but
the saleswoman told him to get up, he did, and he did not
look at Ida. Ida was used to that.

The place was full, nobody looked at Ida. Some of them
were talking about Winnie. They said. But really, is Winnie so
interesting? They just talked and talked about that.

So that is the way life went on.

There was Winnie.

Once in a while a man is a man and he comes from Omaha where they catch all they can. He almost caught Ida. It happened like this.

He went out one night and he saw Winnie. Winnie was always there. She went everywhere.

He followed Winnie.

He did it very well.

The next day he went and rang the bell.

He asked for Winnie.

Of course there was no Winnie.

That was not surprising and did not surprise him.

He could not ask for Ida because he did not know Ida. He almost asked for Ida. Well in a way he did ask for Ida.

Ida came.

Ida was not the same as Winnie. Not at all.

Ida and he, the man from Omaha said. How do you do. And then they said. Good-bye.

The Omaha man went away. He did follow Winnie again but he never rang the bell again. He knew better.

Ida lived alone. She tried to make her dog Iris notice birds but he never did. If he had she would have had more to do because she would have had to notice them too.

It is funny the kind of life Ida led but all the same it kept her going day after day.

But all the same something did happen.

One day she was there doing nothing and suddenly she felt very funny. She knew she had lost something. She looked everywhere and she could not find out what it was that she had lost but she knew she had lost something. All of a sudden she felt or rather she heard somebody call to her. She stopped, she really had not been walking but anyway she stopped and she turned and she heard them say, Ida is that you Ida. She saw somebody coming toward her. She had never seen them before. There were three of them, three women. But soon there was only one. That one came right along. It is funny isn't it. She said. Yes said Ida. There, said the woman, I told them I knew it was.

That was all that happened.

They all three went away.

Ida did not go on looking for what she had lost, she was too excited.

She remembered that one day in front of the house a man with a hat a cane and a bottle stopped. He put down the cane but then he did not know what to do with his hat, so he began again. He put his cane into a window so that stuck out, and he hung his hat on the cane and then with the bottle he stood up. This, he said, is a bottle and in it there is wine, and I who am drunk am going to drink this wine. He did.

And then he said.

It might be like having a handkerchief in a drawer and never taking it out but always knowing it was there. It would always be new and nobody ever would be through with having it there.

What is peace what is war said the man, what is beauty what is ice, said the man. Where is my hat, said the man, where is my wine said the man, I have a cane, he said, I have a hat, he said, I have a bottle full of wine. Good-bye, he said, but Ida had gone away.

She had certain habits. When she counted ten she always counted them on her fingers to make ten times ten. It was very hard to remember how many times she had counted ten when once she had counted them because she had to remember twice and then when she had counted a hundred then what happened. Really nothing. Ida just sat down. Living alone as she did counting was an occupation.

She was walking and she saw a woman and three children, two little girls and a littler boy. The boy was carrying a black coat on his arms, a large one.

A woman said to Ida, I only like a white skin. If when I die I come back again and I find I have any other kind of skin then I will be sure that I was very wicked before.

This made Ida think about talking.

She commenced to talk. She liked to see people eat, in restaurants and wherever they eat, and she liked to talk. You can always talk with army officers. She did.

Army officers do not wear their uniforms in the cities, soldiers do but officers do not. This makes conversation with them easier and more difficult.

If an officer met Ida he said, how do you do and she answered very well I thank you. They were as polite as that.

He said to her. Thank you for answering me so pleasingly, and she said. You are very welcome.

The officer would then go on conversing.

What is it that you like better than anything else, he asked and she said. I like being where I am. Oh said he excitedly, and where are you. I am not here, she said, I am very careful about that. No I am not here, she said, it is very pleasant, she added and she turned slightly away, very pleasant indeed not to be here.

The officer smiled. I know he said I know what you mean. Winnie is your name and that is what you mean by your not being here.

She suddenly felt very faint. Her name was not Winnie it was Ida, there was no Winnie. She turned toward the officer and she said to him. I am afraid very much afraid that you are mistaken. And she went away very slowly. The officer looked after her but he did not follow her. Nobody could know in looking at him that he was an officer because he did not wear a uniform and he did not know whether she knew it or not.

Perhaps she did and perhaps she did not.

Every day after that Ida talked to some officer.

If I am an officer, said an officer to Ida, and I am an officer. I am an officer and I give orders. Would you, he said looking at Ida. Would you like to see me giving orders. Ida looked at him and did not answer. If I were to give orders and everybody obeyed me and they do, said the officer, would that impress you. Ida looked at him, she looked at him and the officer felt that she must like him, otherwise she would not look at him and so he said to her, you do like me or else you would not look at me. But Ida sighed. She said, yes and no. You see, said Ida, I do look at you but that is not enough. I look at you and you look at me but we neither of us say more than how do you do and very well I thank you, if we do then there is always the question. What is your name. And really, said Ida, if I knew your name I would not be interested in you, no, I would not, and if I do not know your name. I could not be interested, certainly I could not. Good-bye, said Ida, and she went away.

Ida not only said good-bye but she went away to live somewhere else.

Once upon a time way back there were always gates, gates that opened so that you could go in and then little by little there were no fences no walls anywhere. For a little time they had a gate even when there was no fence. It was there just to look elegant and it was nice to have a gate that would click even if there was no fence. By and by there was no gate.

Ida when she had a dog had often stood by a gate and she would hold the dog by the hand and in this way they would stand.

But that was long ago and Ida did not think of anything except now. Why indeed was she always alone if there could be anything to remember. Why indeed.

And so nothing happened to her yet. Not yet.

One day Ida saw a moth that was flying and it worried her. It was one of the very few things that ever worried Ida. She said to an officer. This was another officer. There is an army and there is a navy and there are always lots of officers. Ida said to this one. When you put your uniform away for the summer you are afraid of moths. Yes said the officer. I understand that, said Ida, and she slowly drifted away, very thoughtfully, because she knew of this. Alone and she was alone and she was afraid of moths and of mothballs. The two go together.

Ida rarely coughed. She had that kind of health.

In New England there are six states, Maine, Massachusetts, Vermont, New Hampshire, Connecticut and Rhode Island.

Ida turned up in Connecticut. She was living there quite naturally, quietly living there. She had a friend who was tall and thin and her eyes were gray and her hair was messed and she dressed in black and she was thin and her legs were long and she wore a large hat. She did not mind the sun but she did wear a wide-brimmed hat. Yes she did. She was like that. Yes she was.

This friend did not interest Ida. She saw her, yes, but she did not interest her.

Except this one woman nobody knew Ida in Connecticut.

For a while she did not talk to anybody there. She spent the day sitting and then that was a day. On that day she heard somebody say something. They said who is Winnie. The next day Ida left Connecticut.

She began to think about what would happen if she were married.

As she was leaving Connecticut she began to listen to a man. He was an officer in the army. His name was Sam Hamlin. He was a lively Sam Hamlin. He said if he had a wife he could divorce her. He came originally from Connecticut and he was still in Connecticut. He said the only way to leave Connecticut was to go out of it. But he never would. If he had left Connecticut he might have gotten to Washington, perhaps to Utah and Idaho, and if he had he might have gotten lost. That is the way he felt about Connecticut.

Little by little very little by little he said it all to Ida. He said I know, and he said when I say I know I mean it is just like that. I like, he said to Ida, I like everything I say to be said out loud.

He said I know. He said I know you, and he not only said it to Ida but he said it to everybody, he knew Ida he said hell yes he knew Ida. He said one day to Ida it is so sweet to have soft music it is so sweet.

He told her how once upon a time he had been married and he said to her. Now listen. Once upon a time I was married, by the time you came to Connecticut I wasn't. Now you say you are leaving Connecticut. The only way to leave Connecticut is to go out, and I am not going out of Connecticut. Listen to me, he said, I am not going out of Connecticut. I am an officer in the army and of course perhaps they will send me out of Connecticut there is Massachusetts and Rhode Island and New Hampshire and Vermont and Maine but I am going to stay in Connecticut, believe it or not I am.

Ida left Connecticut and that was the first time Ida thought about getting married and it was the last time anybody said Winnie anywhere near her.

There was a woman in California her name was Eleanor Angel and she had a property and on that property she found gold and silver and she found platinum and radium. She did not find oil. She wrote to everybody about it and they were all excited, anybody would be, and they did believe it, and they said it was interesting if it was true and they were sure it was true.

Ida went out to stay with her.

Ida was never discouraged and she was always going out walking.

As she walked along, she thought about men and she thought about presidents. She thought about how some men are more presidents than other men when they happen to be born that way and she said to herself. Which one is mine. She knew that there must be one that could be hers one who would be a president. And so she sat down and was very satisfied to do nothing.

Sit down, somebody said to her, and she sat.

Well it was not that one. He sat too and then that was that.

Ida always looked again to see if it was that one or another one, the one she had seen or not, and sometimes it was not.

Then she would sit down not exactly to cry and not exactly to sit down but she did sit down and she felt very funny, she felt as if it was all being something and that was what always led her on.

Ida saw herself come, then she saw a man come, then she saw a man go away, then she saw herself go away.

And all the time well all the time she said something, she said nice little things, she said all right, she said I do.

Was she on a train or an automobile, an airplane or just walking.

Which was it.

Well she was on any of them and everywhere she was just talking. She was saying, yes yes I like to be sitting. Yes I like to be moving. Yes I have been here before. Yes it is very pleasant here. Yes I will come here again. Yes I do wish to have them meet, I meet them and they meet me and it is very nice.

Ida never sighed, she just rested. When she rested she turned a little and she said, yes dear. She said that very pleasantly.

This was all of Ida's life just then.

She said. I do not like birds.

She liked mechanical birds but not natural birds. Natural birds always sang.

She sat with her friend and they talked together. Ida said, I am never tired and I am never very fresh. I change all the time. I say to myself, Ida, and that startles me and then I sit still.

Her friend said, I will come again.

Do said Ida.

It was very quiet all day long but Ida was ready for that.

Ida married Frank Arthur.

Arthur had been born right in the middle of a big country.

He knew when he was a tiny boy that the earth was round so it was never a surprise to him. He knew that trees had green leaves and that there was snow when time for snow came and rain when time for rain came. He knew a lot.

When Arthur was little he knew a handsome boy who had a club-foot and was tall and thin and worked for a farmer.

The boy with the club-foot rode a bicycle and he would stand and lean on his bicycle and tell Arthur everything.

He told him all about dogs.

He told him how a little dog, once he had found out about it, would just go on making love to anything, the hind leg of a big dog, a leg of a table, anything, he told him how a young hunting dog's voice changed, it cracked just like boys' voices did and then it went up and down and then finally it settled down. He told him about shepherds' dogs, how shepherds only could work their dogs eight years that when the dog was nine years old the shepherd had to hang him, that often the shepherd was awfully sad and cried like anything when he had to hang his dog to kill him but he could not keep him after the dog was eight years old, they did not really care anything for sheep after that and how could you feed a dog if he did not care about sheep any more and so the shepherds some-times cried a lot but when the dog was eight years old they did hang him. Then he told Arthur about another dog and a girl. She always used to give that dog a lump of sugar when-ever she saw him. She was a girl in a store where they sold sugar, and then one day she saw the man come in who had the dog, and when he came she said where is the dog and he said the dog is dead. She had the piece of sugar in her hand and when he said that she put the piece of sugar in her mouth and ate it and then she burst out crying.

He told Arthur about sheep, he told him that sheep were curious about everything but mostly about dogs, they always were looking for a dog who looked like a sheep and sometimes they found one and when they did they the young ones the baby sheep were pleased, but the older ones were frightened, as soon as they saw a dog who really looked like a sheep, and they ran at him and tried to butt him.

He also told Arthur about cows, he said cows were not always willing, he said some cows hated everything. He also told him about bulls. He said bulls were not very interesting.

He used to stand, the boy with a club-foot, leaning on his bicycle and telling Arthur everything.

When Arthur was a little bigger he came to know a man, not a tall man. He was a fairly little man and he was a good climber. He could climb not only in and out of a window but out of the top of a door if the door was closed. He was very remarkable. Arthur asked him and he then heard him say that he never thought about anything else than climbing. Why should he when he could climb anything.

Arthur was not very good at climbing. All he could do was to listen to the little man. He told about how he climbed to the top of a gate, to the top of a door, to the top of a pole. The little man's name was Bernard. He said it was the same name as that of a saint. Then well naturally then he went away. He finally did go away alone.

Arthur was almost old enough to go away. Pretty soon he did go away.

He tried several ways of going away and finally he went away on a boat and got shipwrecked and had his ear frozen.

He liked that so much that he tried to get shipwrecked again but he never did. He tried it again and again, he tried it on every kind of boat but they never were wrecked again. Finally he said, Once and not again.

He did lots of things before he went back to the middle of the big country where he had been born.

Finally he became an officer in the army and he married Ida but before that he lived around.

One of the things he did was to sleep in a bed under a bridge. The bed was made of cardboard. He was not the first to make it. Somebody else made it but when Arthur had no place to go because he had used up all his money he used to go to sleep there. Some one always was asleep there. Day and night there was always somebody sleeping there. Arthur was one who when he woke up shaved and washed himself in the river, he always carried the things with him.

It was a nice time then. Instead of working or having his money Arthur just listened to anybody. It made him sleepy and he was never more than half awake and in his sleep he had a way of talking about sugar and cooking. He also used to talk about medicine glasses.

Arthur never fished in a river. He had slept too often under a bridge to care anything about going fishing. One evening he met a man who had been fishing. They talked a little and the man said that he was not much good at fishing, he saw the fish but he never could catch them. Finally he said to Arthur, do you know who I am. No said Arthur. Well said the man taking off his hat, I am chief of police. Well why can't you catch fish, said Arthur. Well I caught a trout the other day and he got away from me. Why didn't you take his number said Arthur. Because fish can't talk was the answer.

Arthur often wished on a star, he said star bright, star light, I wish I may I wish I might have the wish I wish tonight.

The wish was that he would be a king or rich.

There is no reason why a king should be rich or a rich man should be a king, no reason at all.

Arthur had not yet come to decide which one was the one for him. It was easy enough to be either the one or the other one. He just had to make up his mind, be rich or be a king and then it would just happen. Arthur knew that much.

Well anyway he went back to where he came from, he was in the middle of his country which was a big one and he commenced to cry. He was so nervous when he found himself crying that he lay full length on the ground turned on his stomach and dug his palms into the ground.

He decided to enter the army and he became an officer and some few years after he met Ida.

He met her on the road one day and he began to walk next to her and they managed to make their feet keep step. It was just like a walking marathon.

He began to talk. He said. All the world is crying crying about it all. They all want a king.

She looked at him and then she did not. Everybody might want a king but anybody did not want a queen.

It looks, said Arthur, as if it was sudden but really it took me some time, some months even a couple of years, to understand how everybody wants a king.

He said. Do you know the last time I was anywhere I was with my mother and everybody was good enough to tell me to come again. That was all long ago. Everybody was crying because I went away, but I was not crying. That is what makes anybody a king that everybody cries but he does not.

Philip was the kind that said everything out loud.

I knew her, he said and he said he knew Ida, hell he said, yes I know Ida. He said it to every one, he said it to her. He said he knew her.

Ida never saw Arthur again.

She just did not.

She went somewhere and there she just sat, she did not even have a dog, she did not have a town, she lived alone and just sat.

She went out once in a while, she listened to anybody talking about how they were waiting for a fall in prices.

She saw a sign up that said please pay the unemployed and a lot of people were gathered around and were looking.

It did not interest her. She was not unemployed. She just sat and she always had enough. Anybody could.

Somebody came and asked her where Arthur was. She said, Arthur was gone.

Pretty soon she was gone and when she was gone nobody knew what to say.

They did not know she was gone but she was.

They wanted to read about her but as there was nothing written about her they could not read about her. So they just waited.

Ida went to live with a cousin of her uncle.

He was an old man and he could gild picture frames so that they looked as if they had always had gold on them. He was a good man that old man and he had a son, he sometimes thought that he had two sons but anyway he had one and that one had a garage and he made a lot of money. He had a partner and they stole from one another. One day the son of the old man was so angry because the partner was most successful in getting the most that he up and shot him. They arrested him. They put him in jail. They condemned him to twenty years hard labor because the partner whom he had killed had a wife and three children. The man who killed the other one had no children that is to say his wife had one but it was not his. Anyway there it was. His mother spent all her time in church praying that her son's soul should be saved. The wife of their doctor said it was all the father and mother's fault, they had brought up their son always to think of money, always of money, had not they the old man and his wife got the cousin of the doctor's wife always to give them presents of course they had.

Ida did not stay there very long. She went to live with the cousin of the doctor's wife and there she walked every day and had her dog. The name of this dog was Claudine. Ida did not keep her. She gave her away.

She began to say to herself Ida dear Ida do you want to have two sisters or do you want to be one.

There were five sisters once and Ida might have been one.

Anybody likes to know about then and now, Ida was one and it is easy to have one sister and be a twin too and be a triplet three and be a quartet and four and be a quintuplet it is easy to have four but that just about does shut the door.

Ida began to be known.

As she walked along people began to be bewildered as they saw her and they did not call out to her but some did begin to notice her. Was she a twin well was she.

She went away again. Going away again was not monotonous although it seemed so. Ida ate no fruit. It was the end of the week and she had gone away and she did not come back there.

Pretty soon she said to herself Now listen to me, I am here and I know it, if I go away I will not like it because I am so used to my being here. I would not know what has happened, now just listen to me, she said to herself, listen to me, I am going to stop talking and I will.

Of course she had gone away and she was living with a friend.

How many of those who are yoked together have ever seen oxen.

This is what Ida said and she cried. Her eyes were full of tears and she waited and then she went over everything that had ever happened and in the middle of it she went to sleep.

When she awoke she was talking.

How do you do she said.

First she was alone and then soon everybody was standing listening. She did not talk to them.

Of course she did think about marrying. She had not married yet but she was going to marry.

She said if I was married I'd have children and if I had children then I'd be a mother and if I was a mother I'd tell them what to do.

She decided that she was not going to marry and was not going to have children and was not going to be a mother.

Ida decided that she was just going to talk to herself. Anybody could stand around and listen but as for her she was just going to talk to herself.

She no longer even needed a twin.

Somebody tried to interrupt her, he was an officer of course but how could he interrupt her if she was not talking to him but just talking to herself.

She said how do you do and people around answered her and said how do you do. The officer said how do you do, here I am, do you like peaches and grapes in winter, do you like chickens and bread and asparagus in summer. Ida did not answer, of course not.

It was funny the way Ida could go to sleep and the way she could cry and the way she could be alone and the way she could lie down and the way anybody knew what she did and what she did not do.

Ida thought she would go somewhere else but then she knew that she would look at everybody and everything and she knew it would not be interesting.

She was interesting.

She remembered everything and she remembered everybody but she never talked to any of them, she was always talking to herself.

She said to herself. How old are you, and that made her cry. Then she went to sleep and oh it was so hard not to cry. So hard.

So Ida decided to earn a living. She did not have to, she never had to but she decided to do it.

There are so many ways of earning a living and most of them are failures. She thought it was best to begin with one way which would be most easy to leave. So she tried photography and then she tried just talking.

It is wonderful how easy it is to earn a living that way. To be sure sometimes everybody thinks you are starving but you never are. Ida never starved.

Once she stayed a week in a hotel by herself. She said when she saw the man who ran it, how often do you have your hotel full. Quite often he answered. Well, said Ida, wait awhile and I will leave and then everybody will come, but while I am here nobody will come. Why not said the hotel keeper. Because said Ida, I want to be in the hotel all alone. I only want you and your wife and your three boys and your girl and your father and your mother and your sister in it while I am here. Nobody else. But do not worry, you will not have to keep the others out, they will not come while I am here.

Ida was right. The week she was there nobody came to eat or sleep in the hotel. It just did happen that way.

Ida was very much interested in the wife of the hotel keeper who was sweet-voiced and managed everything because Ida said that sooner or later she would kill herself, she would go out of a window, and the hotel would go to pieces.

Ida knew just what was going to happen. This did not bother her at all. Mostly before it happened she had gone away.

Once she was caught.

It was in a hilly country.

She knew two young men there, one painted in water colors and the other was an engineer. They were brothers. They did not look alike.

Ida sat down on a hillside. A brother was on each side of her.

The three sat together and nothing was said.

Then one brother said. I like to sit here where nothing is ever said. The other brother said. I I like bread, I like to sit here and eat bread. I like to sit here and look about me. I like to sit here and watch the trees grow. I like to sit here.

Ida said nothing. She did not hear what they said. Ida liked sitting. They all three did.

One brother said, It pleases me very much that I have discovered how prettily green looks next to blue and how water looks so well rushing down hill. I am going away for a little while. He said this to his brother. He got up and he went away.

His brother who was very polite did not go away as long as Ida stayed. He sat on and Ida sat on. They did not go to sleep but they almost stopped breathing. The brother said out loud. I am talking to myself. I am not disturbing any one. I feel it is better that everybody is dangerous than that they are not and if they are everybody will either die or be killed.

He waited a minute to listen to himself and then he went on.

I feel that it is easy to expect that we all wish to do good but do we. I know that I will follow any one who asks me to do anything. I myself am strong and I will help myself to anything I need.

Ida paid no attention.

Slowly this other brother went away.

Ida sat on. She said to herself. If a great many people were here and they all said hello Ida, I would not stand up, they would all stand up. If everybody offered me everything I would not refuse anything because everything is mine without my asking for it or refusing it.

Ida understood what she was saying, she knew who she was and she knew it was better that nobody came there. If they did she would not be there, not just yet.

It is not easy to forget all that. Ida did not say that but it is true it is not easy to forget all that.

It was very quiet all day long but Ida was ready for that.

And then she went away.

She went away on a train in an automobile by airplane and walking.

When she answered she looked around for water she looked

around for a bay, for a plowed field and then she saw a man standing and she said to him, do you live here. The man said no.

Ida was always ready to wait but there was nothing to wait for here and she went away.

When she came to the next place she had better luck. She saw two men standing and she said to them, do you live here. They both said, they did. That did seem a good place to begin and Ida began.

This time she did not talk to herself she talked to them.

She sat down and the two men sat down. Ida began. She said. Do you know that I have just come. Yes said one of the men because we have never seen you before.

The other man said, Perhaps you are not going to stay.

I am not answered Ida.

Well then said one of the men it is not interesting and I am not listening.

Ida got very angry.

You are not listening to me, she said, you do not know what you are saying, if I talk you have to listen to what I say, there is nothing else you can do.

Then she added.

I never talk much anyway so if you like both of you can go away.

They both did go away.

Ida sat down. She was very satisfied to be sitting.

Sit again she said to some one and they sat, they just sat.

I do not think that Ida could like Benjamin Williams.

He did get up again and he did walk on.

Ida was not careful about whom she met, how could she be if she was always walking or sitting and she very often was.

She saw anybody who was on her way. That was her way. A nice way.

Ida went back again not to Connecticut but to New Hampshire. She sighed when she said New Hampshire.

New Hampshire, she said, is near Vermont and when did I say Vermont and New Hampshire.

Very often, she whispered, very often.

That was her answer.

This time she was married.

Part Three

IDA DID NOT get married so that never again would she be alone. As a matter of fact until the third time she was married she would not be married long. This first time she was married her husband came from Montana. He was the kind that when he was not alone he would look thoughtful. He was the kind that knew that in Montana there are mountains and that mountains have snow on them. He was not born in Montana. He had not lived very long in Montana, he would leave Montana, he had to to marry Ida and he was very thoughtful.

Ida, he said and then he sighed.

Oh Ida, he said.

How often, he said, how often have I said, Oh Ida.

He was careful. He began to count. He counted the number of times he said, Oh Ida.

It is not easy to count, said he to himself because when I count, I lose count.

Oh dear he said, it is lovely in Montana, there are mountains in Montana and the mountains are very high and just then he looked up and he saw them and he decided, it was not very sudden, he decided he would never see Montana again and he never did.

He went away from Montana and he went to Virginia. There he saw trees and he was so pleased. He said I wonder if Ida has ever seen these trees. Of course she had. It was not she who was blind, it was her dog Iris.

Funnily enough even if Ida did see trees she always looked on the ground to see what had fallen from the trees. Leaves might and nuts and even feathers and flowers. Even water could fall from a tree. When it did well there was her umbrella. She had a very pretty short umbrella. She had lost two and now she had the third. Her husband said, Oh Ida.

Ida's husband did not love his father more than he did his mother or his mother more than he did his father.

Ida and he settled down together and one night she dreamed of a field of orchids, white orchids each on their stalk in a field. Such a pretty girl to have dreamed of white orchids each on its stalk in a field. That is what she dreamed.

And she dreamed that now she was married, she was not Ida she was Virginia. She dreamed that Virginia was her name and that she had been born in Wyoming not in Montana. She dreamed that she often longed for water. She dreamed that she said. When I close my eyes I see water and when I close my eyes I do see water.

What is water, said Virginia.

And then suddenly she said. Ida.

Ida was married and they went to live in Ohio. She did not love anybody in Ohio.

She liked apples. She was disappointed but she did not sigh. She got sunburned and she had a smile on her face. They asked her did she like it. She smiled gently and left it alone. When they asked her again she said not at all. Later on when they asked her did she like it she said. Perhaps only not yet.

Ida left Ohio.

As she left they asked her can you come again. Of course that is what she said, she said she could come again. Somebody called out, who is Ida, but she did not hear him, she did not know that they were asking about her, she really did not.

Ida did not go directly anywhere. She went all around the world. It did not take her long and everything she saw interested her.

She remembered all the countries there were but she did not count them.

First they asked her, how long before you have to go back to Washington.

Second they said, how soon after you get back to Washington will you go back to Ohio.

Thirdly they asked her. How do you go back to Washington from Ohio.

She always answered them.

She did not pay much attention to weather. She had that kind of money to spend that made it not make any difference about weather.

Ida had not been in love very much and if she were there she was.

Some said, Please like her.

They said regularly. Of course we like her.

Ida began to travel again.

She went from Washington to Wyoming, from Wyoming to Virginia and then she had a kind of feeling that she had never been in Washington although of course she had and she went there again.

She said she was going there just to see why they cry.

That is what they do do there.

She knew just how far away one state is from another. She said to herself. Yes it is all whole.

And so there she was in Washington and her life was going to begin. She was not a twin.

Once upon a time a man had happened to begin walking. He lived in Alabama and walking made it seem awfully far away. While he was walking all of a sudden he saw a tree and on that tree was a bird and the bird had its mouth open. The bird said Ida, anyway it sounded like Ida, and the man, his name was Frederick, Frederick saw the bird and he heard him and he said, that kind of a bird is a mocking bird. Frederick went on walking and once every once in a while he saw another tree and he remembered that a bird had said Ida or something like Ida. That was happening in Alabama.

Frederick went into the army became an officer and came to Washington. There he fell in love with a woman, was she older was she younger or was she the same age. She was not older perhaps she was younger, very likely she was not the same age as his age.

Her name was not Ida.

Ida was in Washington.

If there are two little dogs little black dogs and one of them is a female and the other a male, the female does not look as foolish as the male, no not.

So Ida did not look foolish and neither she was.

She might have been foolish.

Saddest of all words are these, she might have been.

Ida felt very well.

Part Four

S O IDA settled down in Washington. This is what happened
every day.

Ida woke up. After a while she got up. Then she stood up.
Then she ate something. After that she sat down.

That was Ida.

And Ida began her life in Washington. In a little while there
were more of them there who sat down and stood up and
leaned. Then they came in and went out. This made it useful
to them and to Ida.

Ida said. I am not careful. I do not win him to come away.
If he goes away I will not have him. Ida said I can count any
one up to ten. When I count up to ten I stop counting. When
she said that they listened to her. They were taken with her
beginning counting and she counted from one to ten. Of
course they listened to her.

Ida knew that. She knew that it is not easy to count while
anybody listens to them, but it is easy to listen to them while
they are counting.

More and more came to see Ida. Frederick came to see Ida.

Little by little Frederick fell in love with Ida. Ida did not
stop him. He did not say that he was in love with her. He did
not say that, not that.

And then he was and then they were all there together.

He married her and she married him.

Then suddenly not at all suddenly, they were sent there, he
was in the army, they got up and had decided to leave for
Ohio. Yesterday or today they would leave for Ohio.

When they got to Ohio, Ohio is a state, it is only spelled
with four letters. All of a sudden there they were in Ohio.

Ohio very likely was as large as that.

Everybody said to Ida and they said it to Frederick too.
Smile at me please smile at me.

Ida smiled.

They settled down in Ohio.

What did they do in Ohio.

Well they did not stay there long.

They went to Texas.

There they really settled down.

It is easier for an officer in the army to settle down in Texas than in Ohio.

Ida said one day.

Is there anything strange in just walking along.

One day in Texas it was not an accident, believe it or not, a lizard did sit there. It was almost black all over and curled, with yellow under and over, hard to tell, it was so curled, but probably under.

Ida was not frightened, she thought she was thinking. She thought she heard everybody burst out crying and then heard everybody calling out, it is not Ohio, it is Texas, it is not Ohio.

Ida was funny that way, it was so important that all these things happened to her just when and how they did.

She settled down and she and Frederick stayed there until they were not there together or anywhere.

All this time Ida was very careful.

Everything that happened to her was not strange. All along it was not strange Ida was not strange.

It is so easy not to be a mother.

This too happened to Ida.

She never was a mother.

Not ever.

Her life in Ohio which turned out to be her life in Texas went on just like that. She was not a mother. She was not strange. She just knew that once upon a time there was a necessity to know that they would all leave Texas. They did not leave Texas all together but they all left Texas. She left Texas and he left Texas, he was Frederick, and they left Texas. They were all the people they knew when they were in Texas.

As they one and all left Texas, they all fastened their doors and as they fastened their doors nobody saw them leave. That is a way to leave.

Ida always left everywhere in some way. She left Texas in this way. So did they.

She left Texas never to return.

She never went back anywhere so why would she go back to Ohio and to Texas. She never did. Ida never did.

She did not go back to Frederick either.

Ida never did.

She did not remember just how many years she had been with Frederick and in Ohio and in Texas.

She did not remember even when she was with him and there because when she was there she did not count, that is she could count up to ten but it did not give her any pleasure to count then.

How pleasant it is to count one two three four five six seven, and then stop and then go on counting eight nine and then ten or eleven.

Ida just loved to do that but as she certainly was not in Ohio or in Texas that long and certainly not with Frederick that long counting was not anything to do.

Ida liked to be spoken to.

It happened quite often.

How do you do they said and she said it to them and they said it to her. How do you do.

Would you never rather be Ida, they said, never rather be Ida, she laughed, never, they said never rather be Ida.

Of course not, of course she would always rather be Ida and she was.

They all said everybody said, Never rather be Ida, it got to be a kind of a song.

Never, never rather be Ida, never rather be Ida.

Ida never heard anybody sing it. When she heard her name she never heard it. That was Ida.

And so it was all over that is Frederick was all over, Ida left Texas just as it was.

Before she left Texas she talked to Duncan. Old man Duncan they called him but he was quite young. He was forty-five and he had been a policeman and now he was a head of police and not in uniform, of course not, otherwise she would not have been talking to him.

He said to her, where were you before you came to Texas. He asked her that after they had shaken hands several times together and it was evening. It often was evening in Texas.

It is very easy to leave Texas, Ida said, not to Duncan, she just said it.

There is no harm in leaving Texas, no harm at all.

Ida said, I have not left Texas yet, but tell them, you and

he, what are you, tell them that he has left Texas and tell them that you and he, well tell them about Texas, you and he.

So then suddenly, she was called away, they thought in Ohio, but she was called away to wherever she was. Just like that Ida was called away.

She was not there any more, because she was called away.

Duncan told her, that is he did not tell her because she was called away, but anyway he told her that he had not left Texas.

Duncan never did leave Texas except once when he went to Tennessee. But by that time he never wanted to leave Texas. No use saying that he only remembered Ida because he didn't.

Once upon a time there was a meadow and in this meadow was a tree and on this tree there were nuts. The nuts fell and then they plowed the ground and the nuts were plowed into the ground but they never grew out.

After Ida left Texas she did not live in the country, she lived in a city. She lived in Washington.

That is the way it went on. Washington is a city and a city well a city is well it is a city. Ida lived there.

Once upon a time every time Ida lived in a city she was careful, she really was. She might lose it lose being careful but really every time she lived in a city she was careful. She was careful in Washington. All who came in would say to her, well Ida how about it.

That is what did happen.

By the time it was all comfortable for Ida and everybody knew better, she knew just what would not be there for her. And it was not. It just was not there for her.

Just then somebody came in and he said here I am. He said to Ida if you were with me I would just say, say she is with me. By golly that is what we are like in Minnesota, Minnesota is just like that.

Hello Ida, said some one. And they said, No Ida we are not. Ida said, no I am not.

Ida felt that way about it. She said well sit down and cry, but nobody did, not just then.

So life began for Ida in Washington.

There were there Ida and two more, Ida kept saying to herself.

There whether there whether whether who is not.

That might have been the motto for Minnesota.

She did have to see those who came from Minnesota and hear them say, Minnesota is not old, believe it or not Minnesota is not old.

Ida began a daily life in Washington.

Once upon a time there was a shotgun and there were wooden guinea hens and they moved around electrically, electricity made them move around and as they moved around if you shot them their heads fell off them.

I thought I coughed said Ida and when I coughed I thought I coughed.

Ida said this and he listened to her he was not from Minnesota.

Once upon a time Ida stood all alone in the twilight. She was down in a field and leaning against a wall, her arms were folded and she looked very tall. Later she was walking up the road and she walked slowly.

She was not so young any more. It almost happened that she would be not sad not tired not depressed but just not so young any more.

She looked around her, she was not all alone because somebody passed by her and they said, it is a nicer evening than yesterday evening and she said, it was.

Ida married again. He was Andrew Hamilton and he came from Boston.

It is very usual of them when they come from Boston to be selfish, very usual, indeed. He and Ida sat together before they sat down.

But not, said some one seeing him, and who had heard of Ida, not, he said.

In Boston the earth is round. Believe it or not, in Boston the earth is round. But they were not in Boston, they were in Washington.

In Boston they hear the ocean as well. Not in Washington. There they have the river, the Potomac.

They were being married, it was not exciting, it was what they did. They did get married.

Once upon a time all who had anywhere to go did not go. This is what they did.

Ida was married again this time he came from Boston, she remembered his name. She was good friends with all her husbands.

This one came from Boston. They said Massachusetts, and when they said Massachusetts they remembered how fresh and green they were there, all of it, yes that is what they said.

In Washington it was different.

There it was in Washington it was come carefully and believe what they said.

Who is careful.

Well in a way Ida is.

She lives where she is not.

Not what.

Not careful.

Oh yes that is what they say.

Not careful.

Of course not.

Who is careful.

That is what they said.

And the answer was.

Ida said.

Oh yes, careful.

Oh yes, I can almost cry.

Ida never did.

Oh yes.

They all said oh yes.

And for three days I have not seen her.

That is what somebody did say somebody really somebody has said. For three days I have not seen her.

Nobody said Ida went away.

She was there Ida was.

So was her husband. So was everybody.

Part Five

POLITICS

THEY SAID, they do not want to buy from Ida. Why should they want to buy.

Ida and he.

He did not come from Louisiana, no. He was that kind. He did not only not come from Louisiana but he had had a carriage hound, a white and black spotted one and he the black and white spotted one was killed not killed but eaten by other dogs, they were all looking at a female dog and no one told him that the dog was nearly dead.

No one told him.

A young woman had silently had a way of giving the dog sugar and when she heard the dog was dead she ate the sugar.

And the man who was not from Louisiana added that, Oh yes he added that.

He and Ida.

He would have bought from Ida bought and well not well yes well no well why why not bought from Ida.

Ida was a friend.

She stayed in Washington.

She came to do what she knew each one of them wanted. Easy enough in Washington.

She did not sell anything although they all wanted to buy.

Not at Bay Shore.

No not in Louisiana.

But in Carolina.

Not in North Carolina.

But in South Carolina.

Yes he would have bought from Ida in South Carolina but Ida was not there never there. She never was in either North or South Carolina. She was in Washington.

And so well yes so he did he did not buy from Ida.

Only Ida.

Well what did Ida do.

Ida knew just who was who.

She did. She did know.

They did not not an awful lot of them know Ida, just enough knew Ida to make Ida be just the one enough of them knew.

There are so many men.

What do you call them there.

There are so many men.

They did not all know Ida.

Now then.

In Washington, some one can do anything. Little by little it was Ida. She knew Charles and she smiled when she saw him. He wanted her to give him the rest of the morning. The rest of the morning. She was too busy too. She said, she never had anything to do but she did not give him the rest of the morning.

Woodward would not die of chagrin when he did not get what he had bought from Ida.

They all buy twice a day but the morning is the best time to buy. Woodward was a great buyer and he never did die of chagrin.

If he was no longer in Washington would Woodward die of chagrin.

Ida smiled every morning. She rested a good deal, she rested even in the evening.

Would Woodward come in and go out just as he liked.

Now that is a question a great question and Ida might answer, she might answer any question, but she did not find it as interesting as anything.

Would Woodward die of chagrin if he left Washington. Somebody stopped Ida and asked her this thing and she said nothing.

Then she said yes, Yes she said and she said nothing.

Yes they said yes would Woodward die of chagrin if he left Washington.

Almost at a loss Ida said yes, she did stand still and then she went on again.

Nobody ever followed Ida. What was the use of following Ida.

Ida had a dream. She dreamed that they were there and there was a little boy with them. Somebody had given the little boy a large package that had something in it and he went off to thank them. He never came back. They went to see why not. He was not there but there was a lady there and she was lying down and a large lion was there moving around. Where said they is the little boy, the lion ate him the lady said, and the package yes he ate it all, but the little boy came to thank you for it, yes I know but it did happen, I did not want it to happen but it did happen. I am very fond of the lion. They went away wondering and then Ida woke up.

Ida often met men and some of them hoped she would get something for them. She always did, not because she wanted them to have it but because she always did it when it was wanted.

Just when it was not at all likely Ida was lost, lost they said, oh yes lost, how lost, why just lost. Of course if she is lost. Yes of course she is lost.

Ida led a very easy life, that is she got up and sat up and went in and came out and rested and went to bed.

But some days she did rest a little more than on other days. She did what she could for everybody.

Once in a while a father when he was young did not do it himself but a friend of his did. He took something.

When the policeman came nobody knew him. Most certainly he who later was a father refused to know him. They did not come from Africa, they came from North Carolina and Colorado. Later on the father had a son a young son and the young son began to go with men who stole. They were all then in Michigan so when they did steal they stole it again. The father was so worried, worried lest the police come and say to him your son is stealing, had he not refused when he was young and in North Carolina to recognize a friend who had stolen. He did say to the policeman then that he had never known that man although of course he had. And now, here in Michigan perhaps his own son was stealing. The policeman might come and how could he say he did not know his son. He might say it of course he might, he almost probably would.

Ida said to him I'll ask him. She meant that it was all right, it would be just like that, no trouble to anybody. Ida always did that. She saw the one who was all right and who would say yes yes it is all right and of course it was all right.

Ida did not need to be troubled, all she need do was to rest and she did rest. Just like that.

Once very often every day Ida went away. She could not go away really not, because she had no mother and she had no grandmother no sister and no aunt.

She dreamed that clothes were like Spanish ice-cream. She did not know why she dreamed of Spain. She was married in Washington, there was ice-cream there were clothes, but there was no Spain. Spain never came, but ice-cream and clothes clothes and ice-cream, food and clothes, politics, generals and admirals, clothes and food, she was married and she was in Washington.

She was not away from Washington.

No no more was there any day. She dreamed, if you are old you have nothing to eat, is that, she dreamed in her dream, is that money.

Ida had a companion named Christine. Christine had a little Chinese dog called William. Christine went away taking William. She thought of leaving him behind but she changed her mind.

When Christine went away she accomplished a great deal. Oh Ida.

Ida was not married any more. She was very nice about it.

All around were what they found. At once they seemed all to like coming.

Ida did not leave Washington.

She rested.

Somebody said. Where is Ida.

Should she go away, somebody said. Go away like what.

Like what, they said.

Like Ida.

No said Christine and for this they thanked her.

All alone in Montana was a little man fragile but he smoked a pipe. Not then but later.

All alone there he was pale. Not tall. Not tall at all. All alone there he went about. He knew nobody was stout in Montana.

For this every little while he tried not to be thinner.

Dear Montana and how he went away.

It does not take long to leave Montana but it takes a long

time to get stout, to put flesh on, get rosy and robust, get vaccinated, get everything.

In Montana he was never at a loss. Very likely not because he was careful of Montana.

He knew how to be careful and he was careful of Montana. And so he plans everything.

He was a great success in Washington. Of course he was. Politically speaking.

All of a sudden the snow had fallen the mountains were cold and he had left Montana.

That was when he began to smoke his pipe.

That was when he was a success in Washington.

That was when Christine had left him, naturally she had gone again. Now he knew Ida. Not to marry her. It was going to be quite a little while before Ida married again.

Ida moved around, to dance is to move around to move around is to dance, and when Ida moved around she let her arms hang out easily in front of her just like that.

She kept on being in Washington.

Once upon a time, once very often a man was in Washington who was cautious. He came from Wisconsin although he had been born in Washington, Washington city not Washington state.

All right he liked it.

After a little while he was nervous again and then for them it was just as if he was cautious. How do you like it, they said. Then he said no. For that they were very willing that they could just as much as ever they could be used to it.

Oh believe me, he said, and then mountains, he said.

Of course there are no mountains in the city of Washington but there are monuments. Oh believe me, he said, there are mountains in Wisconsin. And everybody believed him.

Once when it happened to snow he stayed at home. I will, he said, I will stay at home and as I am at home I will think and as I am thinking I will say I am thinking. He did, he did stay at home, he did think and as he thought he did think that he would think. He did.

Gradually he wondered what it was he was thinking. He thought how very nice it is and then he said I can not help it.

Of course not of course he could not help it, dear Madison, dear Wisconsin.

He was born in the city of Washington but that just happened.

Ida was in Washington she was not thinking, all the time she was suffering because of his thinking and then he was not thinking about his thinking.

Dear Ida.

Ida very likely Ida was not only in Washington but most likely he would not forget to cry when he heard that Ida was never to leave Washington.

Never to leave Washington.

Of course she finally did.

But in the meantime Ida could not believe that it was best.

To be in Washington.

She knew only knew that she did not rest.

She did it all.

Ida did.

But enough, said some one.

And then Ida came in and sat down and she did rest.

When anybody needed Ida Ida was resting. That was all right that is the way Ida was needed.

Once upon a time there was a city, it was built of blocks and every block had a square in it and every square had a statue and every statue had a hat and every hat was off.

Where was Ida where was Ida.

She was there. She was in Washington and she said thank you very much, thank you very much indeed. Ida was in Washington.

Thank you very much.

While she was in Washington it was a long time.

There it was.

She was kind to politics while she was in Washington very kind. She told politics that it was very nice of them to have her be kind to them. And she was she was very kind.

She really did not get up in the morning. She wished that she could and they wished that she could but it was not at all necessary.

When she was up and she did see them she was kind.

She saw seven, or eight of them and she saw them one or

perhaps two and each time it was a very long time. She never went away she always did stay.

This was what they did say.

How do you do, said Ida, how do you feel when I see you, said Ida, and she did say that and they liked it.

Of course they liked it. And then she was not tired but she did lie down in an easy-chair.

It was not really politics really that Ida knew. It was not politics it was favors, that is what Ida liked to do.

She knew she liked to do them.

Everybody knew she liked to do favors for them and wanting to do favors for everybody who wanted to have favors done for them it was quite natural that those who could do the favors did them when she asked them to do them.

It does go like that.

Once upon a time there was a man his name was Henry, Henry Henry was his name. He had told everybody that whatever name they called him by they just had to call him Henry. He came to Washington, he was born in San Francisco and he liked languages, he was not lazy but he did not like to earn a living. He knew that if anybody would come to know about him they would of course call him Henry. Ida did.

She was resting one day and somebody called, it was somebody who liked to call on Ida when she was resting. He might have wanted to marry her but he never did. He knew that everybody sooner or later would know who Ida was and so he brought Henry with him. Henry immediately asked her to do a favor for him, he wanted to go somewhere where he could talk languages and where he would have to do nothing else. Ida was resting. She smiled.

Pretty soon Henry had what he wanted, he never knew whether it was Ida, but he went to see Ida and he did not thank her but he smiled and she smiled and she was resting and he went away.

That was the way Ida was.

In Washington.

When it was a year Ida did not know how much time had passed. A year had passed. She was not married when a year had passed.

She was in Washington when a year had passed.

They asked her to stay with them and she did.

Once upon a time a man was named Eugene Thomas. He was a nice man and not older than Ida. He was waiting after he had been careful about coming in and going out and everybody invited him. They said Eugene are you married and he said perhaps he had been. He never had been. That was the funny part of it he never had been married. He liked to think that Ida had been married and she had, of course she had been.

So that went on.

Ida was not tired, she went on staying in Washington.

Eugene Thomas pretty well stayed there too.

If a house has windows and any house has them anybody can stand at the window and look out.

He was funny Eugene Thomas, he used to say, There is a treasure, That is a pleasure, It is a pleasure to her and to him.

All these things did not really make Ida anxious to see him. Ida was never anxious. Ida was tired. Once in a while she knew all about something and when this happened everybody stood still and Ida looked out of the window and she was not so tired.

It is hard for Ida to remember what Ida said.

She said, I could remember anything I ever said. She did say that.

Eugene Thomas was caught in a flood. And so he did not marry Ida. The flood caught him and carried him away. The flood was in Connecticut and he was so nearly being drowned that he never came back to Washington. But in the meanwhile Ida had begun to wonder, to wonder whether she had perhaps better begin to leave Washington and go elsewhere.

Not that she really went then, she was still resting. She saw a great many who lived in Washington and they looked at her when they saw her. Everybody knew it was Ida, not when they saw her, seeing her did not bring it home to them but hearing about her, hearing that she was Ida, it was that that made them know everything that Ida was to do. It was a pleasant Ida. Even when she was just tired with having besides everything had to come in after she had been out, it was a very pleasant Ida.

And so Ida was in Washington.

One day, it had happened again and again some one said something to her, they said Oh Ida, did you see me. Oh yes she said. Ida never did not see anybody, she always saw everybody and said she saw them. She made no changes about seeing then.

So he said to her Ida, your name is Ida isn't it, yes she said, and he said I thought your name was Ida, I thought you were Ida and I thought your name is Ida.

It is, she said.

They sat down.

She did not ask his name but of course he told her. He said his name was Gerald Seaton, and that he did not often care to walk about. He said that he was not too tall nor was he too stout, that he was not too fair and that he often had thought that it was very pleasant to live in Washington. He had lived there but he thought of leaving. What did Ida think. She said she thought that very often it was very well to rest in the afternoon. He said of course, and then they did not leave, they sat there a little longer and they drank something and they thought they would eat something and pretty soon they thought that the afternoon was over which it was not.

How are you Ida said Gerald Seaton and she said, very well I thank you, and she said that they knew that.

Ida was not sure that she did want to marry not that Gerald Seaton had asked her, but then if Ida did want to marry well Gerald Seaton might go away and he might come back again and if while he was away she would want to marry and then when he was back again she still wanted to marry would she marry him.

They neither of them really said anything about any such thing. Gerald Seaton had not yet gone away and Ida had not yet wanted to marry, but but. Ida had friends, she stayed with them and they thought perhaps they thought that Ida would marry again perhaps marry Gerald Seaton.

Who is Gerald Seaton said the husband to his wife, who is any one said the wife to the husband and they liked to sit with Ida while Ida was resting.

Ida could always stay with a married couple, neither the husband nor the wife did not like to have her, they always wanted to make her life easy for her, it always was easy for her and they always wanted her to keep right on going to marry Gerald Seaton or whoever it was, now it was Gerald Seaton and he was going away. Nobody could say that he was not going away.

You see Edith and William are still talking about Ida as everybody is. Does it make any difference to Edith and William. Just enough so that like everybody they go on talking and they talk about Ida.

Edith and William were the married couple with whom Ida was staying.

They were not the ones who were anxious and ambitious, nor were they the ones who collected anything they were a quiet couple even though they were rich and they talked together.

Positively, said Edith, can you go on doing what you do do. Can you go on doing what you did do. This is what Edith told William she had said to Ida.

And William, laughed and then he broke into poetry.

At a glance

What a chance.

He looked at Edith and laughed and they laughed.

Edith went on being worried and William began again.

That she needs

What she has.

Edith said that William was foolish and Gerald Seaton was going away.

And they have what they are, said William.

Looking at William you never would have thought that he would talk poetry.

He liked to be in a garden.

Edith was worried not really worried but she liked to feel worried and she liked to look as if she felt worried, of course only about Ida.

Oh dear she said, and they have what they are said William chucking her under the chin.

Cheer up Edith he said let us talk about Ida.

And they like where they go

He murmured,

And Edith said Shut up.

Which is all after a while said William and then he and Edith said all right they would talk about Ida and Ida came in, not to rest, but to come in. They stopped it, stopped talking about her.

So Edith and William did not look at Ida, they started talking. What do you think said William what do you think if and when we decide anything what do you think it will be like. This is what William said and Edith looked out of the window. They were not in the same room with Ida but they might have been. Edith liked an opportunity to stand and so she looked out of the window. She half turned, she said to William, Did you say you said Ida. William then took to standing. This was it so they were standing. It is not natural that if anybody should be coming in that they would be standing. Ida did not come in, Edith went away from the window and William stood by the window and saw some one come in, it was not Gerald Seaton because he had gone away.

Let it be a lesson to her said Edith to William, but naturally William had said it first. Life went on very peacefully with Edith and William, it went on so that they were equally capable of seeing Ida all day every day, for which they might not feel it necessary to be careful that they shall after all realize what it is.

It is not early morning nor late in the evening it is just in between.

Edith and William had a mother but not living with them. She was waiting to come to see them but she was not coming any particular day. William had been married before and had a boy, Edith had been married before and had a girl, so naturally they did not have another one. It was very comfortable with them but Ida might go away.

It was a pleasant home, if a home has windows and any house has them anybody can stand at the window and look out.

Ida never did. She rested.

It was summer, it is pretty hot in Washington and Edith and William were going away to the country. Ida did not mind the heat and neither did Gerald Seaton. He was back in Washington.

How hot Washington is in summer and how much everybody in Washington feels the heat to be hot.

It was easy, Ida was Mrs. Gerald Seaton and they went away to stay.

It was a long time before they said all they had to say, that is all Washington had to say about Ida and Gerald Seaton. But they were there naturally not since they were man and wife and had gone away.

This was not the only thing to do but they did it. They lived together as man and wife in other places. Which they were they were married, Ida was Mrs. Gerald Seaton and Seaton was Gerald Seaton and they both wore their wedding rings.

Part Six

THEY LIVED in a flat not too big not too small. And they lived there almost every day. They were not in Washington, they were far away from Washington, they were in Boston. There they lived almost as if Ida had not been Ida and Gerald Seaton had married any woman. They lived like this for quite a while. Some things did happen one of them was that they left Boston. Ida rested a good deal she liked to live in a smallish flat, she had never lived in a big one because she and Gerald could hear each other from one end of the place to the other and this was a pleasure because Ida liked to hear some one she liked to rest and Gerald Seaton did content her. Almost anything did content Ida although everybody was always talking about her.

Gerald Seaton did not look as if he had any ideas he was just a nice man but he did have some. He was always saying Ida knows a lot of people and if I have known them I have admired the ones I have known and if I have admired the ones I have known I have looked like them that is to say I do not look like them but they are like the ones I have known.

Ida did like to know that Gerald was in the house and she liked to hear him.

Gerald often said, I do not mean, I myself when I say I mean I mean, I do know how much I feel when once in a while I come in and I do. I am very busy, said Gerald and thinking does not take very much of my time, I do not think that is I do not feel that I do not like thinking.

All this would interest Ida also the way he would say I never think about Ida, everybody talks about Ida but I do not talk about Ida nor do I listen when they are all talking about Ida. I am thinking, Gerald would say, I am thinking of another person not any one whom I could possibly think would be at all like Ida not at all. This is what Gerald said and he did say that and that was the way it was.

Ida was not idle but she did not go in and out very much and she did not do anything and she rested and she liked Gerald to be there and to know he was talking.

So they went on living in their apartment but they did not live in Washington and later on they did not live in Boston.

If nobody knows you that does not argue you to be unknown, nobody knew Ida when they no longer lived in Boston but that did not mean that she was unknown.

She went away and she came again and nobody ever said they had enough of that.

What happened. She felt very well, she was not always well but she felt very well.

One day she saw him come, she knew he was there but besides that she saw him come. He came. He said, oh yes I do and she said thank you, they never met again.

Woodward George always worked, and he was always welcome. Ida said do come again. He came very often. When he came he came alone and when he came there were always at least a half dozen there and they all said, oh dear, I wish it was evening.

It almost looked as if Ida and Woodward would always meet, but Woodward went away and as they were not on the same continent, Ida was on one and Woodward was on another it looked as if they would not meet. But a continent can always be changed and so that is not why Ida and Woodward did not always meet.

Very likely Ida is not anxious nor is Woodward. Well said Ida, I have to have my life and Ida had her life and she has her life and she is having her life.

Oh dear said Ida and she was resting, she liked to get up when she was resting, and then rest again.

Woodward started in being a writer and then he became a dressmaker but not in Washington and not in Boston. Ida almost cried when she met his brother. She said what is your name and he answered Abraham George. Oh dear said Ida and she looked at him. Abraham George was a writer and he did not become a dressmaker like his brother and he and Ida talked together all the time. Abraham George even asked her questions, he said, you know I really think you are a very pleasant person to know, and Ida said of course, and she said I do like to do favors for anybody and he said do one for me, and she said what is it, and he said I want to change to being a widower and she said yes of course, and she did not really laugh but she did look very pleasant resting and waiting. Yes she did. After all it was Woodward George who was important to her but he was far far away.

She was still married to Gerald Seaton and houses came and houses went away, but you can never say that they were not together.

One day they went away again, this time quite far away, they went to another country and there they sat down. It was a small house, the place was called Bay Shore, it was a comfortable house to live in, they had friends among others she had a friend whose name was Lady Helen Button. How are you they said to each other. Ida learned to say it like that. How are you.

Ida liked it at Bay Shore. It did not belong to her but she well she did belong to it. How are you, she said when they came to see her.

A good many people did come to see her. Well of course she was married there was Gerald Seaton. How are you, was what they said to her, and they did sometimes forget to say it to Gerald but Gerald was nice and always said, oh yes, do, oh yes do.

She lived there and Gerald Seaton lived there, they lived in the same apartment and they talked to each other when they were dining but not much when they were resting and each in their way was resting.

Ida knew a vacant house when she saw it but she did not look at it, would she be introduced to some one who did look at a vacant house. Never at any time did tears come to Ida's eyes.

Never.

Everybody knew that Andrew was one of two. He was so completely one of two that he was two. Andrew was his name and he was not tall, not tall at all.

And yet it did mean it when he came in or when he went out.

Ida had not known that she would be there when he came in and when he went out but she was.

Ida was.

Andrew, there were never tears in Andrew's voice or tears in his eyes, he might cry but that was an entirely different matter.

Ida knew that.

Slowly Ida knew everything about that. It was the first thing Ida had ever known really the first thing.

Ida somehow knew who Andrew was and leave it alone or not Ida saw him.

If he saw her or not it was not interesting. Andrew was not a man who ever noticed anything. Naturally not. They noticed him.

Feel like that do you said Ida.

Ida was busy resting.

Ida when she went out did not carry an umbrella. It had not rained enough not nearly enough and once a week Ida went walking and today was the once a week when she went walking.

Once a week is two days one following another and this was the second one and Ida was dreaming.

So much for Andrew.

There was hardly any beginning.

There never could be with Andrew when he was there there he was. Anybody could know that and Ida well she just did not know that and Andrew looked about him when she was there and he saw her.

She was married to Gerald and she and Gerald were just as old as ever but that did not bother them. They talked together at least some time every day and occasionally in the evening but that was all and when they talked she called out to him and he did not answer and he called out to her and mostly she did not answer but they were sometimes in their home together. Anyway they were married and had been for quite some time.

Andrew did not notice Ida but he saw her and he went away to meet some one who had been named after a saint, this one was named after a saint called Thomas and so his name was Thomas and so Andrew met Thomas that is to say Andrew went out to meet that is to say he would meet Thomas who was out walking not walking but reading as he was walking which was his habit.

Andrew was there and then Thomas came to him.

Everybody was silent and so were they and then everybody went away. Andrew went away first.

Ida went out walking later on and the rain came down but by that time Ida was at home reading, she was not walking any more. Each one reads in their way and Ida read in her way.

Andrew never read.

Of course not.

Ida was careless but not that way. She did read, and she never forgot to look up when she saw Andrew.

Ida went out walking instead of sitting in a garden which was just as well because in this way she often met everybody and stopped and talked with them, this might lead her to meet them again and if it did she sometimes met some one who cried for one reason or another. Ida did not mind anybody crying, why should she when she had a garden a house and a dog and when she was so often visiting. Very often they made four and no more.

This had nothing to do with Andrew who in a way was never out walking and if he was then of course nobody did meet him.

Andrew never disappeared, how could he when he was always there and Ida gradually was always there too. How do you do. That is what she said when she met him.

She did not really meet him, nobody did because he was there and they were there and nobody met him or he them, but Ida did, she met him.

Andrew, she called him, Andrew, not loudly, just Andrew and she did not call him she just said Andrew. Nobody had just said Andrew to Andrew.

Andrew never looked around when Ida called him but she really never called him. She did not see him but he was with him and she called Andrew just like that. That was what did impress him.

Ida liked it to be dark because if it was dark she could light a light. And if she lighted a light then she could see and if she saw she saw Andrew and she said to him. Here you are.

Andrew was there, and it was not very long, it was long but not very long before Ida often saw Andrew and Andrew saw

her. He even came to see her. He came to see her whether
she was there or whether she was not there.

Ida gradually was always there when he came and Andrew
always came.

He came all the same.

Kindly consider that I am capable of deciding when and
why I am coming. This is what Andrew said to Ida with some
hesitation.

And now Ida was not only Ida she was Andrew's Ida and
being Andrew's Ida Ida was more that Ida she was Ida itself.

For this there was a change, everybody changed, Ida even
changed and even changed Andrew. Andrew had changed Ida
to be more Ida and Ida changed Andrew to be less Andrew
and they were both always together.

Part One

T HE ROAD is awfully wide.
With the snow on either side.

She was walking along the road made wide with snow. The moonlight was bright. She had a white dog and the dog looked gray in the moonlight and on the snow. Oh she said to herself that is what they mean when they say in the night all cats are gray.

When there was no snow and no moonlight her dog had always looked white at night.

When she turned her back on the moon the light suddenly was so bright it looked like another kind of light, and if she could have been easily frightened it would have frightened her but you get used to anything but really she never did get used to this thing.

She said to herself what am I doing, I have my genius and I am looking for my Andrew and she went on looking.

It was cold and when she went home the fire was out and there was no more wood. There was a little girl servant, she knew that the servant had made a fire for herself with all that wood and that her fire was going. She knew it. She knocked at her door and walked in. The servant was not there but the fire was. She was furious. She took every bit of lighted wood and carried it into her room. She sat down and looked at the fire and she knew she had her genius and she might just as well go and look for her Andrew. She went to bed then but she did not sleep very well. She found out next day that Andrew came to town every Sunday. She never saw him. Andrew was very good looking like his name. Ida often said to herself she never had met an Andrew and so she did not want to see him. She liked to hear about him.

She would if it had not been so early in the morning gone to be a nurse. As a nurse she might seek an Andrew but to be a nurse you have to get up early in the morning. You have to get up early in the morning to be a nun and so although

if she had been a nun she could have thought every day about
Andrew she never became a nun nor did she become a nurse.
She just stayed at home.

It is easy to stay at home not at night-time but in the morning and even at noon and in the afternoon. At night-time it
is not so easy to stay at home.

For which reason, Andrew's name changed to Ida and eight
changed to four and sixteen changed to twenty-five and they
all sat down.

For which all day she sat down. As I said she had that habit
the habit of sitting down and only once every day she went
out walking and she always talked about that. That made Ida
listen. She knew how to listen.

This is what she said.

She did not say Ida knew how to listen but she talked as if
she knew that Ida knew how to listen.

Every day she talked the same way and every day she took
a walk and every day Ida was there and every day she talked
about his walk, and every day Ida did listen while she talked
about his walk. It can be very pleasant to walk every day and
to talk about the walk and every day and it can be very pleasant to listen every day to him talk about his every-day walk.

You see there was he it came to be Andrew again and it was
Ida.

If there was a war or anything Andrew could still take a
walk every day and talk about the walk he had taken that day.

For which it made gradually that it was not so important
that Ida was Ida.

It could and did happen that it was not so important.

Would Ida fly, well not alone and certainly it was better not
to fly than fly alone. Ida came to walking, she had never
thought she would just walk but she did and this time she did
not walk alone she walked with Susan Little.

For this they did not sing.

Such things can happen, Ida did not have to be told about
it nor did she have to tell about it.

There was no Andrew.

Andrew stayed at home and waited for her, and Ida came.
This can happen, Andrew could walk and come to see Ida and
tell her what he did while he was walking and later Ida could

walk and come back and not tell Andrew that she had been walking. Andrew could not have listened to Ida walking. Andrew walked not Ida. It is perhaps best so.

Anybody can go away, anybody can take walks and anybody can meet somebody new. Anybody can like to say how do you do to somebody they never saw before and yet it did not matter. Ida never did, she always walked with some one as if they had walked together any day. That really made Ida so pleasant that nobody ever did stay away.

And then they all disappeared, not really disappeared but nobody talked about them any more.

So it was all to do over again, Ida had Andrew that is she had that he walked every day, nobody talked about him any more but he had not disappeared, and he talked about his walk and he walked every day.

So Ida was left alone, and she began to sit again.

And sitting she thought about her life with dogs and this was it.

The first dog I ever remember seeing, I had seen cats before and I must have seen dogs but the first dog I ever remember seeing was a large puppy in the garden. Nobody knew where he came from so we called him Prince.

It was a very nice garden but he was a dog and he grew very big. I do not remember what he ate but he must have eaten a lot because he grew so big. I do not remember playing with him very much. He was very nice but that was all, like tables and chairs are nice. That was all. Then there were a lot of dogs but none of them interesting. Then there was a little dog, a black and tan and he hung himself on a string when somebody left him. He had not been so interesting but the way he died made him very interesting. I do not know what he had as a name.

Then for a long time there were no dogs none that I ever noticed. I heard people say they had dogs but if I saw them I did not notice them and I heard people say their dog had died but I did not notice anything about it and then there was a dog, I do not know where he came from or where he went but he was a dog.

It was not yet summer but there was sun and there were wooden steps and I was sitting on them, and I was just doing nothing and a brown dog came and sat down too. I petted him, he liked petting and he put his head on my lap and we both went on sitting. This happened every afternoon for a week and then he never came. I do not know where he came from or where he went or if he had a name but I knew he was brown, he was a water dog a fairly big one and I never did forget him.

And then for some time there was no dog and then there were lots of them but other people had them.

A dog has to have a name and he has to look at you. Sometimes it is kind of bothering to have them look at you.

Any dog is new.

The dogs I knew then which were not mine were mostly very fine. There was a Pekinese named Sandy, he was a very large one, Pekineses should be tiny but he was a big one like a small lion but he was all Pekinese, I suppose anywhere there can be giants, and he was a giant Pekinese.

Sandy was his name because he was that color, the color of sand. He should have been carried around, Pekinese mostly are but he was almost too heavy to carry. I liked Sandy. When he stood up on a table all ruffled up and his tail all ruffled up he did look like a lion, a very little lion, but a fierce one.

He did not like climbing the mountains, they were not real mountains, they were made of a man on two chairs and Sandy was supposed to climb him as if he were climbing a mountain. Sandy thought this was disgusting and he was right. No use calling a thing like that climbing the mountains, and if it has been really mountains of course Sandy would not have been there. Sandy liked things flat, tables, floors, and paths. He liked waddling along as he pleased. No mountains, no climbing, no automobiles, he was killed by one. Sandy knew what he liked, flat things and sugar, sugar was flat too, and Sandy never was interested in anything else and then one day an automobile went over him, poor Sandy and that was the end of Sandy.

So one changed to two and two changed to five and the next dog was also not a big one, his name was Lillieman and he was black and a French bull and not welcome. He was that kind of a dog he just was not welcome.

When he came he was not welcome and he came very often.

He was good-looking, he was not old, he did finally die and was buried under a white lilac tree in a garden but he just was not welcome.

He had his little ways, he always wanted to see something that was just too high or too low for him to reach and so everything was sure to get broken. He did not break it but it did just get broken. Nobody could blame him but of course he was not welcome.

Before he died and was buried under the white lilac tree, he met another black dog called Dick. Dick was a French poodle and Lillieman was a French bull and they were both black but they did not interest each other. As much as possible they never knew the other one was there. Sometimes when they bumped each other no one heard the other one bark it was hard to not notice the other one. But they did. Days at a time sometimes they did.

Dick was the first poodle I ever knew and he was always welcome, round roly-poly and old and gray and lively and pleasant, he was always welcome.

He had only one fault. He stole eggs, he could indeed steal a whole basket of them and then break them and eat them, the cook would hit him with a broom when she caught him but nothing could stop him, when he saw a basket of eggs he had to steal them and break them and eat them. He only liked eggs raw, he never stole cooked eggs, whether he liked break- ing them, or the looks of them or just, well anyway it was the only fault he had. Perhaps because he was a black dog and eggs are white and then yellow, well anyway he could steal a whole basket of them and break them and eat them, not the shells of course just the egg.

So this was Dick the poodle very playful very lively old but full of energy and he and Lillieman the French bull could be on the same lawn together and not notice each other, there was no connection between them, they just ignored each other. The bull Lillieman died first and was buried under the white lilac, Dick the poodle went on running around making love to distant dogs, sometimes a half day's run away and running after sticks and stones, he was fourteen years old and very lively and then one day he heard of a dog far away and he felt he could love her, off he went to see her and he never

came back again, he was run over, on the way there, he never
got there he never came back and alas poor Dick he was never
buried anywhere.

Dogs are dogs, you sometimes think that they are not but
they are. And they always are here there and everywhere.

There were so many dogs and I knew some of them I knew
some better than others, and sometimes I did not know
whether I wanted to meet another one or not.

There was one who was named Mary Rose, and she had
two children, the first one was an awful one. This was the way
it happened.

They say dogs are brave but really they are frightened of a
great many things about as many things as frighten children.

Mary Rose had no reason to be frightened because she was
always well and she never thought about being lost, most dogs
do and it frightens them awfully but Mary Rose did get lost
all the same not really lost but for a day and a night too.
Nobody really knew what happened.

She came home and she was dirty, she who was always so
clean and she had lost her collar and she always loved her
collar and she dragged herself along she who always walked
along so tidily. She was a fox-terrier with smooth white hair,
and pretty black marks. A little boy brought back her collar
and then pretty soon Chocolate came, it was her only puppy
and he was a monster, they called him Chocolate because he
looked like a chocolate cake or a bar of chocolate or chocolate
candy, and he was awful. Nobody meant it but he was run
over, it was sad and Mary Rose had been fond of him. Later
she had a real daughter Blanchette who looked just like her,
but Mary Rose never cared about her. Blanchette was too like
her, she was not at all interesting and besides Mary Rose knew
that Blanchette would live longer and never have a daughter
and she was right. Mary Rose died in the country, Blanchette
lived in the city and never had a daughter and was never lost
and never had any worries and gradually grew very ugly but
she never suspected it and nobody told her so and it was no
trouble to her.

Mary Rose loved only once, lots of dogs do they love only
once or twice, Mary Rose was not a loving dog, but she was
a tempting dog, she loved to tempt other dogs to do what

they should not. She never did what she should not but they did when she showed them where it was.

Little things happen like that, but she had to do something then when she had lost the only dog she loved who was her own son and who was called Chocolate. After that she just was like that.

I can just see her tempting Polybe in the soft moonlight to do what was not right.

Dogs should smell but not eat, if they eat dirt that means they are naughty or they have worms, Mary Rose was never naughty and she never had worms but Polybe, well Polybe was not neglected but he was not understood. He never was understood. I suppose he died but I never knew. Anyway he had his duty to do and he never did it, not because he did not want to do his duty but because he never knew what his duty was.

That was what Polybe was.

He liked moonlight because it was warmer than darkness but he never noticed the moon. His father and his sister danced on the hillside in the moonlight but Polybe had left home so young that he never knew how to dance in it but he did like the moonlight because it was warmer than the dark.

Polybe was not a small dog he was a hound and he had stripes red and black like only a zebra's stripes are white and black but Polybe's stripes were as regular as that and his front legs were long, all his family could kill a rabbit with a blow of their front paw, that is really why they danced in the moonlight, they thought they were chasing rabbits, any shadow was a rabbit to them and there are lots of shadows on a hillside in the summer under a bright moon.

Poor Polybe he never really knew anything, the shepherds said that he chased sheep, perhaps he did thinking they were rabbits, he might have made a mistake like that, he easily might. Another little little dog was so foolish once he always thought that any table leg was his mother, and would suck away at it as if it was his mother. Polybe was not as foolish as that but he almost was, anyway Mary Rose could always lead him astray, perhaps she whispered to him that sheep were rabbits. She might have.

And then Mary Rose went far away. Polybe stayed where

he was and did not remember any one. He never did. That was Polybe.

And he went away tied to a string and he never did try to come back. Back meant nothing to him. A day was never a day to Polybe. He never barked, he had nothing to say.

Polybe is still some place today, nothing could ever happen to him to kill him or to change anything in any way.

The next dog was bigger than any other dog had been.

When a dog is really big he is very naturally thin, and when he is big and thin when he moves he does not seem to be moving. There were two of them one was probably dead before I saw the second one. I did not know the first one but I heard what he could do I saw him of course but when I saw him he came along but he was hardly moving.

It did not take much moving to come along as fast as we were going. There was no other dog there which was lucky because they said that when he saw another dog well he did not move much but he killed him, he always killed any dog he saw although he hardly moved at all to kill him. I saw this dog quite a few times but there was never any other dog anywhere near. I was glad.

The other one well he looked gentle enough and he hardly moved at all and he was very big and he looked thin although he really was not.

He used to walk about very gently almost not at all he was so tall and he moved his legs as if he meant them not to leave the ground but they did, just enough, just a little sideways just enough, and that was all. He lived a long time doing nothing but that and he is still living just living enough.

The next dog and this is important because it is the next dog. His name is Never Sleeps although he sleeps enough.

He was brown not a dark brown but a light brown and he had a lot of friends who always went about together and they all had to be brown, otherwise Never Sleeps would not let them come along. But all that was later, first he had to be born.

It was not so easy to be born.

There was a dog who was an Alsatian wolf-hound a very nice one, and they knew that in the zoo there was a real wolf quite a nice one. So one night they took the dog to see the wolf and they left her there all night. She liked the wolf and the wolf was lonesome and they stayed together and then later she had a little dog and he was a very nice one, and her name was Never Sleeps. She was a gentle dog and liked to lie in the water in the winter and to be quiet in the summer. She never was a bother.

She could be a mother. She met a white poodle he was still young and he had never had a puppy life because he had not been well. His name was Basket and he looked like one. He was taken to visit Never Sleeps and they were told to be happy together. Never Sleeps was told to play with Basket and teach him how to play. Never Sleeps began, she had to teach catch if you can or tag, and she had to teach him pussy wants a corner and she taught him each one of them.

She taught him tag and even after he played it and much later on when he was dead another Basket he looked just like him went on playing tag. To play tag you have to be able to run forward and back to run around things and to start one way and to go the other way and another dog who is smaller and not so quick has to know how to wait at a corner and go around the other way to make the distance shorter. And sometimes just to see how well tag can be played the bigger quicker dog can even stop to play with a stick or a bone and still get away and not be tagged. That is what it means to play tag and Never Sleeps taught Basket how to play. Then he taught him how to play pussy wants a corner, to play this there have to be trees. Dogs cannot play this in the house they are not allowed to and so they have to have at least four trees if there are three dogs and three trees if there are two dogs to play pussy wants a corner. Never Sleeps preferred tag to pussy wants a corner but Basket rather liked best pussy wants a corner.

Ida never knew who knew what she said, she never knew what she said because she listened and as she listened well the moon scarcely the moon but still there is a moon.

Very likely hers was the moon.

Ida knew she never had been a little sister or even a little brother. Ida knew.

So scarcely was there an absence when some one died.

Believe it or not some one died.

And he was somebody's son and Ida began to cry and he was twenty-six and Ida began to cry and Ida was not alone and she began to cry.

Ida had never cried before, but now she began to cry.

Even when Andrew came back from his walk and talked about his walk, Ida began to cry.

It's funny about crying. Ida knew it was funny about crying, she listened at the radio and they played the national anthem and Ida began to cry. It is funny about crying.

But anyway Ida was sitting and she was there and one by one somebody said Thank you, have you heard of me. And she always had. That was Ida.

Even Andrew had he had heard of them, that was the way he had been led to be ready to take his walk every day because he had heard of every one who came in one after the other one.

And Ida did not cry again.

One day, she saw a star it was an uncommonly large one and when it set it made a cross, she looked and looked and she and did not hear Andrew take a walk and that was natural enough she was not there. They had lost her. Ida was gone.

So she sat up and went to bed carefully and she easily told every one that there was more wind in Texas than in San Francisco and nobody believed her. So she said wait and see and they waited.

She came back to life exactly day before yesterday. And now listen.

Ida loved three men. One was an officer who was not killed but he might have been, one was a painter who was not in hospital but he might have been one and one was a lawyer who had gone away to Montana and she had never heard from him.

Ida loved each one of them and went to say good-bye to them.

Good-bye, good-bye she said, and she did say good-bye to them.

She wondered if they were there, of course she did not go away. What she really wanted was Andrew, where oh where was Andrew.

Andrew was difficult to suit and so Ida did not suit him. But Ida did sit down beside him.

Ida fell in love with a young man who had an adventure. He came from Kansas City and he knew that he was through. He was twenty years old. His uncle had died of meningitis, so had his father and so had his cousin, his name was Mark and he had a mother but no sisters and he had a wife and sisters-in-law.

Ida looked the other way when they met, she knew Mark would die when he was twenty-six and he did but before that he had said, For them, they like me for them and Ida had answered just as you say Mark. Ida always bent her head when she saw Mark she was tall and she bent her head when she saw Mark, he was tall and broad and Ida bent her head when she saw him. She knew he would die of meningitis and he did. That was why Ida always bent her head when she saw him.

Why should everybody talk about Ida.

Why not.

Dear Ida.

Part Two

IDA WAS almost married to Andrew and not anybody could cloud it. It was very important that she was almost married to Andrew. Besides he was Andrew the first. All the others had been others.

Nobody talked about the color of Ida's hair and they talked about her a lot, nor the color of her eyes.

She was sitting and she dreamed that Andrew was a soldier. She dreamed well not dreamed but just dreamed. The day had been set for their marriage and everything had been ordered. Ida was always careful about ordering, food clothes cars, clothes food cars everything was well chosen and the day was set and then the telephone rang and it said that Andrew was dying, he had not been killed he was only dying, and Ida knew that the food would do for the people who came to the funeral and the car would do to go to the funeral and the clothes would not do dear me no they would not do and all of this was just dreaming. Ida was alive yet and so was Andrew, she had been sitting, he had been walking and he came home and told about his walk and Ida was awake and she was listening and Andrew was Andrew the first, and Ida was Ida and they were almost married and not anybody could cloud anything.

Part Three

Any ball has to look like the moon. Ida just had to know what was going to be happening soon.

They can be young so young they can go in swimming. Ida had been. Not really swimming one was learning and the other was teaching.

This was being young in San Francisco and the baths were called Lurline Baths. Ida was young and so was he they were both good both she and he and he was teaching her how to swim, he leaned over and he said kick he was holding her under the chin and he was standing beside her, it was not deep water, and he said kick and she did and he walked along beside her holding her chin, and he said kick and she kicked again and he was standing very close to her and she kicked hard and she kicked him. He let go her he called out Jesus Christ my balls and he went under and she went under, they were neither of them drowned but they might have been.

Strangely enough she never thought about Frank, that was his name, Frank, she could not remember his other name, but once when she smelled wild onion she remembered going under and that neither were drowned.

It is difficult never to have been younger but Ida almost was she almost never had been younger.

Part Four

A<small>ND NOW</small> it was suddenly happening, well not suddenly but it was happening, Andrew was almost Andrew the first. It was not sudden.

They always knew what he could do, that is not what he would do but what they had to do to him. Ida knew.

Andrew the first, walked every day and came back to say where he had walked that day. Every day he walked the same day and every day he told Ida where he had walked that day. Yes Ida.

Ida was just as much older as she had been.

Yes Ida.

One day Ida was alone. When she was alone she was lying down and when she was not alone she was lying down. Everybody knew everything about Ida, everybody did. They knew that when she was alone she was lying down and when she was not alone she was lying down.

Everybody knew everything about Ida and by everybody, everybody means everybody.

It might have been exciting that everybody knew everything about Ida and it did not excite Ida it soothed Ida. She was soothed.

For a four.

She shut the door.

They dropped in.

And drank gin.

I'd like a conversation said Ida.

So one of them told that when his brother was a soldier, it was in summer and he ate an apple off an apple tree a better apple than he had ever eaten before, so he took a slip of the tree and he brought it home and after he put it into the ground where he was and when he took it home he planted it and now every year they had apples off this apple tree.

Another one told how when his cousin was a soldier, he saw a shepherd dog, different from any shepherd dog he had ever seen and as he knew a man who kept sheep, he took the shepherd dog home with him and gave it to the man and now all the shepherd dogs came from the dog his cousin had brought home with him from the war.

Another one was telling that a friend of his had a sister-in-law and the sister-in-law had the smallest and the finest little brown dog he had ever seen, and he asked the sister-in-law what race it was and where she had gotten it. Oh she said a soldier gave it to me for my little girl, he had brought it home with him and he gave it to my little girl and she and he play together, they always play together.

Ida listened to them and she sighed, she was resting, and she said, I like lilies-of-the-valley too do you, and they all said they did, and one of them said, when his sister had been a nurse in a war she always gathered lilies-of-the-valley before they were in flower. Oh yes said Ida.

And so there was a little conversation and they all said they would stay all evening. They said it was never dark when they stayed all evening and Ida sighed and said yes she was resting.

Once upon a time Ida took a train, she did not like trains, and she never took them but once upon a time she took a train. They were fortunate, the train went on running and Andrew was not there. Then it stopped and Ida got out and Andrew still was not there. He was not expected but still he was not there. So Ida went to eat something.

This did happen to Ida.

They asked what she would have to eat and she said she would eat the first and the last that they had and not anything in between. Andrew always ate everything but Ida when she was alone she ate the first and the last of everything, she was not often alone so it was not often that she could eat the first and the last of everything but she did that time and then everybody helped her to leave but not not to get on a train again.

She never did get on any train again. Naturally not, she was always there or she was resting. Her life had every minute when it was either this or that and sometimes both, either she was there or she was resting and sometimes it was both.

Her life never began again because it was always there.

And now it was astonishing that it was always there. Yes it was

Ida

Yes it was.

Part Five

ANY FRIEND of Ida's could be run over by any little thing.

Not Andrew, Andrew was Andrew the first and regular.

Why are sailors, farmers and actors more given to reading and believing signs than other people. It is natural enough for farmers and sailors who are always there where signs are, alone with them but why actors.

Well anyway Ida was not an actress nor a sailor nor a farmer.

Cuckoos magpies crows and swallows are signs.

Nightingales larks robins and orioles are not.

Ida saw her first glow worm. The first of anything is a sign.

Then she saw three of them that was a sign.

Then she saw ten.

Ten are never a sign.

And yet what had she caught.

She had caught and she had taught.

That ten was not a sign.

Andrew was Andrew the first.

He was a sign.

Ida had not known he was a sign, not known he was a sign.

Ida was resting.

Worse than any signs is a family who brings bad luck. Ida had known one, naturally it was a family of women, a family which brings bad luck must be all women.

Ida had known one the kind that if you take a dog with you when you go to see them, the dog goes funny and when it has its puppies its puppies are peculiar.

This family was a mother a daughter and a granddaughter, well they all had the airs and graces of beauties and with reason, well they were. The grandmother had been married to an admiral and then he died and to a general and then he died. Her daughter was married to a doctor but the doctor could not die, he just left, the granddaughter was very young, just as young as sixteen, she married a writer, nobody knows just how not but before very long she cried, every day she cried, and her mother cried and even her grandmother and

680

then she was not married any longer to the writer. Then well she was still young not yet twenty-one and a banker saw her and he said he must marry her, well she couldn't yet naturally not the writer was still her husband but very soon he would not be, so the banker was all but married to her, well anyway they went out together, the car turned over the banker was dead and she had broken her collar-bone.

Now everybody wanted to know would the men want her more because of all this or would they be scared of her.

Well as it happened it was neither the one nor the other. It often is not.

The men after that just did not pay any attention to her. You might say they did not any of them pay any attention to her even when she was twenty-three or twenty-four. They did not even ask not any of them. What for.

And so anybody could see that they could not bring good luck to any one not even a dog, no not even.

No really bad luck came to Ida from knowing them but after that anyway, it did happen that she never went out to see any one.

She said it was better.

She did not say it was better but it was better. Ida never said anything about anything.

Anyway after that she rested and let them come in, anybody come in. That way no family would come that just would not happen.

So Ida was resting and they came in. Not one by one, they just came in.

That is the way Andrew came he just came in.

He took a walk every afternoon and he always told about what happened on his walk.

He just walked every afternoon.

He liked to hear people tell about good luck and bad luck.

Somebody one afternoon told a whole lot.

Andrew was like that, he was born with his life, why not. And he had it, he walked every afternoon, and he said something every minute of every day, but he did not talk while he was listening. He listened while he was listening but he did not hear unless he asked to have told what they were telling. He liked to hear about good luck and bad luck because it was not real to him, nothing was real to him except a walk every afternoon and to say something every minute of every day.

So he said, and what were you saying about good luck and bad luck.

Well it was this.

The things anybody has to worry about are spiders, cuckoos goldfish and dwarfs.

Yes said Andrew. And he was listening.

Spider at night makes delight.

Spider in the morning makes mourning.

Yes said Andrew.

Well, said the man who was talking, think of a spider talking.

Yes said Andrew.

The spider says

Listen to me I, I am a spider, you must not mistake me for the sky, the sky red at night is a sailor's delight, the sky red in the morning is a sailor's warning, you must not mistake me for the sky, I am I, I am a spider and in the morning any morning I bring sadness and mourning and at night if they see me at night I bring them delight, do not mistake me for the sky, not I, do not mistake me for a dog who howls at night and causes no delight, a dog says the bright moonlight makes him go mad with desire to bring sorrow to any one sorrow and sadness, the dog says the night the bright moonlight brings madness and grief, but says the spider I, I am a spider, a big spider or a little spider, it is all alike, a spider green or gray, there is nothing else to say, I am a spider and I know and I always tell everybody so, to see me at night brings them delight, to see me in the morning, brings mourning, and if you see me at night, and I am a sight, because I am dead having died up by night, even so dead at night I still cause delight, I dead bring delight to any one who sees me at night, and so every one can sleep tight who has seen me at night.

Andrew was listening and he said it was interesting and said did they know any other superstition.

Yes said the man there is the cuckoo.

Oh yes the cuckoo.

Supposing they could listen to a cuckoo.

I, I am a cuckoo, I am not a clock, because a clock makes time pass and I stop the time by giving mine, and mine is money, and money is honey, and I I bring money, I, I, I. I bring misery and money but never honey, listen to me.

Once I was there, you know everybody, that I I sing in the spring, sweetly, sing, evening and morning and everything.

Listen to me.

If you listen to me, if when you hear me, the first time in the spring time, hear me sing, and you have money a lot of money for you in your pocket when you hear me in the spring, you will be rich all year any year, but if you hear me and you have gone out with no money jingling in your pocket when you hear me singing then you will be poor poor all year, poor.

But sometimes I can do even more.

I knew a case like that, said the man.

Did you said Andrew.

She well she, she had written a lovely book but nobody took the lovely book nobody paid her money for the lovely book they never gave her money, never never never and she was poor and they needed money oh yes they did she and her lover.

And she sat and she wrote and she longed for money for she had a lover and all she needed was money to live and love, money money money.

So she wrote and she hoped and she wrote and she sighed and she wanted money, money money, for herself and for love for love and for herself, money money money.

And one day somebody was sorry for her and they gave her not much but a little money, he was a nice millionaire the one who gave her a little money, but it was very little money and it was spring and she wanted love and money and she had love and now she wanted money.

She went out it was the spring and she sat upon the grass with a little money in her pocket and the cuckoo saw her sitting and knew she had a little money and it went up to her close up to her and sat on a tree and said cuckoo at her, cuckoo cuckoo, cuckoo, and she said, Oh, a cuckoo bird is singing on a cuckoo tree singing to me oh singing to me. And the cuckoo sang cuckoo cuckoo and she sang cuckoo cuckoo to it, and there they were singing cuckoo she to it and it to her.

Then she knew that it was true and that she would be rich and love would not leave her and she would have all three money and love and a cuckoo in a tree, all three.

Andrew did listen and the man went on.

And the goldfish.

Yes said a goldfish I listen I listen but listen to me I am stronger than a cuckoo stronger and meaner because I never do bring good luck I bring nothing but misery and trouble and all no not at all I bring no good luck only bad and that does not make me sad it makes me glad that I never bring good luck only bad.

They buy me because I look so pretty and red and gold in my bowl but I never bring good luck I only bring bad, bad bad bad.

Listen to me.

There was a painter once who thought he was so big he could do anything and he did. So he bought goldfish and any day he made a painting of us in the way that made him famous and made him say, goldfish bring me good luck not bad, and they better had.

Everything went wonderfully for him, he turned goldfish into gold because everything he did was bold and it sold, and he had money and fame but all the same we the goldfish just sat and waited while he painted.

One day, crack, the bowl where we were fell apart and we were all cracked the bowl the water and the fish, and the painter too crack went the painter and his painting too and he woke up and he knew that he was dead too, the goldfish and he, they were all dead, but we there are always goldfish in plenty to bring bad luck to anybody too but he the painter and his painting was dead dead dead.

We knew what to do.

Andrew was more interested, and the dwarfs he said.

Well this is the way they are they say we are two male and female, if you see us both at once it means nothing, but if you see either of us alone it means bad luck or good. And which is which. Misfortune is female good luck luck is male, it is all very simple.

Oh yes anybody can know that and if they see one of us

and it is the female he or she has to go and go all day long
until they see a dwarf man, otherwise anything awful could
happen to them. A great many make fun of those who believe
in this thing but those who believe they know, female dwarf
bad luck male dwarf good luck, all that is eternal.

Silence.

Suddenly the goldfish suddenly began to swish and to bub-
ble and squeak and to shriek, I I do not believe in dwarfs
neither female nor male, he cried, no not in a cuckoo, no not
in spiders, no, the only thing I believe in besides myself is a
shoe on a table, oh that, that makes me shiver and shake, I
have no shoes no feet no shoes but a shoe on a table, that is
terrible, oh oh yes oh ah.

And the cuckoo said,

Oh you poor fish, you do not believe in me, you poor fish,
and I do not believe in you fish nothing but fish a goldfish
only fish, no I do not believe in you no fish no, I believe in
me, I am a cuckoo and I know and I tell you so, no the only
thing I believe in which is not me is when I see the new moon
through a glass window, I never do because there is no glass
to see through, but I believe in that too, I believe in that and
I believe in me ah yes I do I see what I see through, and I
do I do I do.

No I do not believe in a fish, nor in a dwarf nor in a spider
not I, because I am I a cuckoo and I, I, I.

The spider screamed. You do not believe in me, everybody
believes in me, you do not believe in spiders you do not believe in me bah. I believe in me I am all there is to see except
well if you put your clothes on wrong side to well that is an
awful thing to do, and if you change well that is worse than
any way and what do I say, if you put your clothes on wrong
everything will go well that day but if you change from wrong
to right then nothing will go right, but what can I do I am a
green spider or a gray and I have the same clothes every day
and I can make no mistake any day but I believe oh I believe
if you put your clothes on wrong side to everything will be
lovely that you do, but anyway everybody has to believe in
me, a spider, of course they do, a spider in the morning is an
awful warning a spider at night brings delight, it is so lovely

to know this is true and not to believe in a fish or in dwarfs or in a cuckoo, ooh ooh, it is I, no matter what they try it is I I. I.

The dwarfs said, And of whom are you talking all of you, we dwarfs, we are in the beginning we have commenced everything and we believe in everything yes we do, we believe in the language of flowers and we believe in lucky stones, we believe in peacocks' feathers and we believe in stars too, we believe in leaves of tea, we believe in a white horse and a red-headed girl, we believe in the moon, we believe in red in the sky, we believe in the barking of a dog, we believe in everything that is mortal and immortal, we even believe in spiders, in goldfish and in the cuckoo, we the dwarfs we believe in it all, all and all, and all and every one are alike, we are, all the world is like us the dwarfs, all the world believes in everything and we do too and all the world believes in us and in you.

Everybody in the room was quiet and Andrew was really excited and he looked at Ida and that was that.

Part Six

GOOD LUCK and bad luck.
No luck and then luck.
Ida was resting.

She was nearly Ida was ready nearly well.

She could tell when she had been settled when she had been settled very well.

Once she had been and she liked it, she liked to be in one room and to have him in another room and to talk across to him while she was resting. Then she had been settled very well. It did not settle everything, nothing was unsettling, but she had been settled very well.

Andrew had a mother.

Some still have one and some do not still have one but Andrew did still have a mother.

He had other things beside

But he had never had a bride.

Flowers in the spring succeed each other with extraordinary rapidity and the ones that last the longest if you do not pick them are the violets.

Andrew had his life, he was never alone and he was never left and he was never active and he was never quiet and he was never sad.

He was Andrew.

It came about that he had never gone anywhere unless he had known beforehand he was going to go there, but and he had, he had gone to see Ida and once he was there it was as if he had been going to see Ida. So naturally he was always there.

Andrew knew that he was the first Andrew.

He had a nervous cough but he was not nervous.

He had a quiet voice but he talked loudly.

He had a regular life but he did what he did as if he would do it and he always did. Obstinate you call him. Well if you like. He said obstinate was not a word.

Ida never spoke, she just said what she pleased. Dear Ida.

It began not little by little, but it did begin.

Who has houses said a friend of Ida's.

Everybody laughed.

But said Andrew I understand when you speak.

Nobody laughed.

It was not customary to laugh.

Three makes more exchange than two.

There were always at least three.

This was a habit with Andrew.

Ida had no habit, she was resting.

And so little by little somebody knew.

How kindly if they do not bow.

Ida had a funny habit. She had once heard that albatrosses which birds she liked the name of always bowed before they did anything. Ida bowed like this to anything she liked. If she had a hat she liked, she had many hats but sometimes she had a hat she liked and if she liked it she put it on a table and bowed to it. She had many dresses and sometimes she really liked one of them. She would put it somewhere then and then she would bow to it. Of course jewels but really dresses and hats particularly hats, sometimes particularly dresses. Nobody knew anything about this certainly not anybody and certainly not Andrew, if anybody knew it would be an accident because when Ida bowed like that to a hat or a dress she never said it. A maid might come to know but naturally never having heard about albatrosses, the maid would not understand.

Oh yes said Ida while she was resting. Naturally she never bowed while she was resting and she was always resting when they were there.

Dear Ida.

It came to be that any day was like Saturday to Ida.

And slowly it came to be that even to Andrew any day came to be Saturday. Saturday had never been especially a day to Andrew but slowly it came to be Saturday and then every day began to be Saturday as it had come to be to Ida.

Of course there was once a song, every day will be Sunday by and by.

Ida knew this about Saturday, she always had, and now Andrew slowly came to know it too. Of course he did walk every day walk even if every day was Saturday. You can't change everything even if everything is changed.

Anybody could begin to realize what life was to Andrew what life had been to Andrew what life was going to be to Andrew.

Andrew was remarkable insofar as it was all true. Yes indeed it was.

Saturday, Ida.

Ida never said once upon a time. These words did not mean anything to Ida. This is what Ida said. Ida said yes, and then Ida said oh yes, and then Ida said, I said yes, and then Ida said, Yes.

Once when Ida was excited she said I know what it is I do, I do know that it is, yes.

That is what she said when she was excited.

Part Seven

ANDREW KNEW that nobody would be so rude as not to remember Andrew. And this was true. They did remember him. Until now. Now they do not remember Andrew. But Andrew knew that nobody would be so rude as not to. And pretty well it was true.

But again.

Andrew never had to think. He never had to say that it was a pleasant day. But it was always either wet or dry or cold or warm or showery or just going to be. All that was enough for Andrew and Ida never knew whether there was any weather. That is the reason they got on so well together.

There was never any beginning or end, but every day came before or after another day. Every day did.

Little by little circles were open and when they were open they were always closed.

This was just the way it was.

Supposing Ida was at home, she was almost at home and when she was at home she was resting.

Andrew had many things to do but then it was always true that he was with Ida almost all day although he never came to stay and besides she was resting.

One of the things Ida never liked was a door.

People should be there and not come through a door.

As much as possible Ida did not let herself know that, they did come through a door.

She did not like to go out to dinner at a house because you had to come in through a door. A restaurant was different there is really no door. She liked a room well enough but she did not like a door.

Andrew was different, he did just naturally come through a door, he came through a door, he was the first to come through a doorway and the last to come through a doorway. Doorways and doors were natural to him. He and Ida never talked about this, you might say they never talked about anything certainly they never talked about doors.

The French say a door has to be open or shut but open or

shut did not interest Ida what she really minded was that there was a door at all. She did not really mind standing in a portiere or in a hall, but she did not like doors. Of course it was natural enough feeling as she did about doors that she never went out to see anybody. She went out she liked to go out but not through a doorway. There it was that was the way she was.

One day she was telling about this, she said, if you stand in an open place in a house and talk to somebody who can hear that is very nice, if you are out or in it is very nice but doors doors are never nice.

She did not remember always being that way about doors, she kind of did not remember doors at all, it was not often she mentioned doors, but she just did not care about doors.

One day did not come after another day to Ida. Ida never took on yesterday or tomorrow, she did not take on months either nor did she take on years. Why should she when she had always been the same, what ever happened there she was, no doors and resting and everything happening. Sometimes something did happen, she knew to whom she had been married but that was not anything happening, she knew about clothes and resting but that was not anything happening. Really there really was never anything happening although everybody knew everything was happening.

It was dark in winter and light in summer but that did not make any difference to Ida. If somebody said to her you know they are most awfully kind, Ida could always say I know I do not like that kind. She liked to be pleasant and she was but kind, well yes she knew that kind.

They asked her to a dinner party but she did not go, her husband went, she had a husband then and he wore a wedding ring. Husbands do not often wear wedding rings but he did. Ida knew when he came home that he had worn his wedding ring, she said, not very well and he said oh yes very well.

Three things had happened to Ida and they were far away but not really because she liked to rest and be there. She always was.

Andrew next to that was nothing and everything, Andrew knew a great many people who were very kind. Kind people always like doors and doorways, Andrew did. Andrew thought about Ida and doors, why should he when doors were there.

But for Ida doors were not there if they had been she would not have been. How can you rest if there are doors. And resting is a pleasant thing.

So life went on little by little for Ida and Andrew.

It all did seem just the same but all the same it was not just the same. How could anybody know, nobody could know but there it was. Well no there it wasn't.

Ida began talking.

She never began but sometimes she was talking, she did not understand so she said, she did not sit down so she said, she did not stand up so she said, she did not go out or come in, so she said. And it was all true enough.

This was Ida

Dear Ida.

Ida was good friends with all her husbands, she was always good friends with all her husbands.

She always remembered that the first real hat she ever had was a turban made of pansies. The second real hat she ever had was a turban made of poppies.

For which she was interested in pansies and gradually she was not. She had liked pansies and heliotrope, then she liked wild flowers, then she liked tube-roses, then she liked orchids and then she was not interested in flowers.

Of course she was not interested. Flowers should stay where they grow, there was no door for flowers to come through, they should stay where they grew. She was more interested in birds than in flowers but she was not really interested in birds.

Anything that was given to her she thanked for she liked to thank, some people do not but she did and she liked to be thanked. Yes she said.

She was careful to sit still when she thanked or was thanked, it is better so.

Some people like to stand or to move when they thank or are thanked but not Ida, she was not really resting when she thanked or was thanked but she was sitting.

Nobody knew what Ida was going to do although she always did the same thing in the same way, but still nobody knew what Ida was going to do or what she was going to say. She said yes. That is what Ida did say.

Everybody knew that they would not forget Andrew but was it true.

Not so sure.

You did not have to be sure about any such thing as long as it was happening, which it was not.

Andrew come in said Ida.

Andrew was in.

Andrew do not come in said Ida. Ida said Andrew is not coming in. Andrew came in.

Andrew had not been brought up to come in but little by little he did come in he came in and when Ida said he is not to come in he came in. This was natural as he came to know Ida. Anybody came in who came to know Ida but Ida did not say come in. To Andrew she had said yes come in and Andrew had come in.

It was not a natural life for Andrew this life of coming in and this was what had been happening to Andrew, he had commenced to come in and then he never did anything else, he always came in. He should have been doing something else but he did not he just came in.

Little by little it happened that except that he took his walk in the afternoon he never did anything but come in. This little by little was everything Andrew did.

She tried to stop, not anything but she tried to stop but how could she stop if she was resting how could she stop Andrew from coming in.

And in this way it might happen to come to be true that anybody would forget Andrew.

That would not happen little by little but it could come to be true.

Even in a book they could be rude and forget Andrew but not now. Andrew said not now, and Ida said Andrew said not now and Ida said she said not now but really Ida did not say not now she just said no.

Ida often sighed not very often but she did sigh and when somebody came in she said yes I always say yes, if you say no then you say no but if you say yes then you just say yes.

This was very natural and Ida was very natural.

So much happened but nothing happened to Ida.

To have anything happen you have to choose and Ida never chose, how could she choose, you can choose hats and you can choose other things but that is not choosing. To choose, well to choose, Ida never chose. And then it looked as if it happened, and it did happen and it was happening and it went on happening. How excited, and Ida was excited and so was Andrew and his name might have been William.

He had a great many names Andrew did and one of them was William but when he became Andrew the first he could not be William.

Ida often wished gently that he had been William, it is easier to say William than Andrew and Ida had naturally to say a name. Every time Andrew came in or was there or was anywhere she had to say his name and if his name had been William she could have said it easier. But all the same it was easy enough to say Andrew and she said Andrew.

Sometimes she called him Andy and sometimes she would say Handy Andy it is handy to have Andy, and her saying that did please Andrew. Naturally enough it pleased him.

It is not easy to lead a different life, much of it never happens but when it does it is different.

So Ida and Andrew never knew but it was true they were to lead a different life and yet again they were not.

If one did the other did not, and if the other did then the other did not.

And this is what happened.

If they had any friends they had so many friends.

They were always accompanied, Andrew when he came and went and wherever he was, Ida was not accompanied but she was never alone and when they were together they were always accompanied.

This was natural enough because Andrew always had been and it was natural enough because Ida always had been.

Men were with them and women were with them and men and women were with them.

It was this that made Ida say let's talk.

It was this that made Ida say, I like to know that all I love to do is to say something and he hears me.

It was this that made Ida say I never could though they were not glad to come.

It was this that made Ida say how do you do do come. It was this that made Ida say yes everything I can do I can always ask Andrew and Andrew will always do anything I ask him to do and that is the reason I call him Handy Andy.

Ida never laughed she smiled and sometimes she yawned and sometimes she closed her eyes and sometimes she opened them and she rested. That is what Ida did.

It did look as if nothing could change, nothing could change Ida that was true, and if that was true could anything change Andrew.

In a way nothing could but he could come not to be Andrew and if he were not Andrew Ida would not call him Handy Andy and as a matter of fact when he was not any longer Andrew she never did call him Handy Andy. She called him Andy, and she called him Andrew then but that was not the same thing.

But it was natural enough. Nature is not natural and that is natural enough.

Ida knew that is she did not exactly know then but all the same she did know then some people who always were ready to be there.

The larger the house these people had the more ready they were to be there.

Ida might have come to that but if she did she could not rest.

Oh dear she often said oh dear isn't it queer.

More than that she needed no help, but she might come to need help, and if she would come to need help she would help herself and if she helped herself then she certainly would be needing help.

I let it alone, she told everybody, and she did. She certainly did. But most gradually Andrew it was true was a way to do, not for Ida, but for Andrew, and that made a lot of trouble, not for Ida, but for Andrew.

What was because was just what was a bother to Ida because she saw that Andrew was across from where he was.

Nobody knew whether it was happening slowly or not. It might be slowly and it might not.

Once in a great while Ida got up suddenly.

When she did well it was sudden, and she went away not

far away but she left. That happened once in a way. She was
sitting just sitting, they said if you look out of the window
you see the sun. Oh yes said Ida, and they said, do you like
sunshine or rain and Ida said she liked it best. She was sitting
of course and she was resting and she did like it best.

They said, well anybody said, More than enough. Oh yes
said Ida, I like it, yes I do, I like it.

Somebody said, well let us go on. No said Ida I always say
no, no said Ida. And why not they asked her, well said Ida if
you go away. We did not say we were going away, they said.
Believe it or not we did not say we were going away, they
said. Well said Ida I feel that way too. Do you they said. Yes
said Ida I feel that way too.

It was not then that she got up suddenly. It was considerably after. She was not startled, a dog might bark suddenly
but she was not startled. She was never startled at once. If she
was, well she never was.

But after all, if she got up suddenly, and she did not very
often. And once she got up suddenly, she left.

That did not as a matter of fact make very much difference.

More than enough she never really said, but once well really
once she did get up suddenly and if she did get up suddenly
she went away.

Nobody ever heard Andrew ever mention what he did because he never did it.

Everybody always said something, they said let's have it
again, and they always had it again.

For this much they did come in, of course there never really
was a beginning, for which it was fortunate.

Ida was mostly fortunate even if it did not matter. It really
did not matter, not much.

So whether it was slowly or not was not enough because
nobody was scared. They might be careful Ida was careful.

For which reason she was never worried not very likely to
be.

She once said when this you see remember me, she liked
being like that. Nicely.

For this reason she was rested. She will get up suddenly
once and leave but not just now. Not now.

They could exchange well she knew more about hats than cows.

Andrew was interested in cows and horses. But after all there was much more in the way they sat down. Believe it or not they did sit down.

Part Eight

WELL HE SAID Andrew said that he could not do without Ida. Ida said yes, and indeed when she said yes she meant yes. Yes Andrew could not do without Ida and Ida said yes. She knew she might go away suddenly, but she said yes.

And so it came to be not more exciting but more yes than it had been.

Ida did say yes.

And Andrew was not nervous that is to say Andrew trembled easily but he was not nervous. Ida was nervous and so she said yes. If you are resting and you say yes you can be nervous, and Ida was nervous. There was no mistake about Ida's being nervous. She was not nervous again, she was just nervous. When she said yes she was not nervous. When she was resting she was nervous. Nearly as well as ever she said she was, she said she was nearly as well as ever, but nobody ever asked her if she is well, they always knew she was nearly as well as ever.

It happened that when she went out she came in. Well she did go out and when she went out she came in.

Anyhow went in and went out, but Ida did not.

When she went out she came in.

This was not just in the beginning it came to be more so, the only time that it ever was otherwise was when she got up suddenly and this did happen soon.

And so Andrew well Andrew was not careless nothing ever made Andrew careless.

He was much prepared.

Neither Andrew nor Ida was astonished but they were surprised. They had that in common that they were surprised not suddenly surprised but just surprised.

They were not astonished to learn but they were surprised.

This is what happened.

Ida had an aunt, she remembered she had an aunt but that had nothing to do with Ida nothing at all. Next to nothing to do with Ida.

Her aunt well her aunt sometimes did not feel that way

about it but not very often and really it had nothing to do with Ida or with what happened.

What happened was this.

Ida returned more and more to be Ida. She even said she was Ida.

What, they said. Yes, she said. And they said why do you say yes. Well she said I say yes because I am Ida.

It got quite exciting. It was not just exciting it was quite exciting. Every time she said yes, and she said yes any time she said anything, well any time she said yes it was quite exciting.

Ida even was excited, well not altogether but she really was excited. Even Andrew was excited and as for the rest of all of them, all of them were excited.

And in between, well Ida always did have a tendency to say yes and now she did say, she even sometimes said oh yes.

Everybody was excited, it was extraordinary the way everybody was excited, they were so excited that everybody stopped everything to be excited.

Ida was excited but not very excited. At times she was not excited but she did always say yes.

Andrew was excited, he was not excited when he took his walk but he was quite often excited. Ida did say yes.

They went out together of course but it was difficult as the more excited he was the faster he went and the more excited she was the slower she went and as she could not go faster and he could not go slower. Well it was all right.

They lived from day to day. Ida did. So did they all. Some of their friends used to look at clouds, they would come in and say this evening I saw a cloud and it looked like a hunting dog and others would say he saw a cloud that looked like a dragon, and another one would say he said a cloud that looked like a dream, and another he saw a cloud that looked like a queen. Ida said yes and Andrew said very nicely. They liked people to come in and tell what kind of clouds they had seen. Some had seen a cloud that looked like a fish and some had seen a cloud that looked like a rhinoceros, almost any of them had seen a cloud.

It was very pleasant for Ida that they came and told what the clouds they had seen looked like.

Ida lived from day to day so did they all but all the same a day well a day was not really all day to Ida, she needed only a part of the day and only a part of the night, the rest of the day and night she did not need. They might but she did not.

Andrew did not need day nor night but he used it all he did not use it up but he used it, he used it all of it it was necessary to use all of it and it was always arranged that he did everything that was necessary to do and he did. It was necessary that he used all of the night and all of the day every day and every night. This was right.

Ida chose just that piece of the day and just that piece of the night that she would use.

All right.

They did not say it but she said it and that was why she said yes.

And then something did happen.

What happened was this.

Everybody began to miss something and it was not a kiss, you bet your life it was not a kiss that anybody began to miss. And yet perhaps it was.

Well anyway something did happen and it excited every one that it was something and that it did happen.

It happened slowly and then it was happening and then it happened a little quicker and then it was happening and then it happened it really happened and then it had happened and then it was happening and then well then there it was and if it was there then it is there only now nobody can care.

And all this sounds kind of funny but it is all true.

And it all began with everybody knowing that they were missing something and perhaps a kiss but not really nobody really did miss a kiss. Certainly not Ida.

Ida was not interested, she was resting and then it began oh so slowly to happen and then there it was all right there it was everybody knew it all right there it was.

Dear Ida.

What happened.

Well what happened was this. Everybody thought everybody knew what happened. And everybody did know and so it was that that happened. Nothing was neglected that is Ida did nothing Andrew did nothing but nothing was neglected.

When something happens nothing begins. When anything begins then nothing happens and you could always say with Ida that nothing began.

Nothing ever did begin.

Partly that and partly nothing more. And there was never any need of excuses. You only excuse yourself if you begin or if somebody else begins but with Ida well she never began and nobody else began. Andrew although he was different was the same, he was restless all day and Ida was resting all day but neither one nor the other had to begin. So in a way nothing did happen.

That was the way it was nothing did happen everybody talked all day and every day about Ida and Andrew but nothing could happen as neither the one of them or the other one ever did begin anything.

It is wonderful how things pile up even if nothing is added. Very wonderful.

Suppose somebody comes in, suppose they say, well how are we today. Well supposing they do say that. It does not make any difference but supposing they do say that. Somebody else comes in and says that too well how are we today. Well if Ida had not answered the first one she could not answer the second one because you always have to answer the first one before you answer the second one.

And if there was still a third one and mostly there was and a fourth one and a fifth one and even a sixth one and each one said well and how are we today, it is natural enough that Ida would have nothing to say. She had not answered the first one and if you are resting you cannot hurry enough to catch up and so she had nothing to say. Yes she said. It is natural enough that she said yes, because she did not catch up with anything and did not interrupt anything and did not begin anything and did not stop anything.

Yes said Ida.

It looks the same but well of course one can run away, even if you are resting you can run away. Not necessarily but you can. You can run away even if you say yes. And if you run away well you never come back even if you are completely followed.

This could be a thing that Ida would do. She would say yes

and she was resting and nothing happened and nothing began but she could run away. Not everybody can but she could and she did.

What happened.

Before she ran away.

She did not really run away, she did not go away. It was something in between. She took her umbrella and parasol. Everybody knew she was going, that is not really true they did not know she was going but she went, they knew she was going. Everybody knew.

She went away that is she did get away and when she was away everybody was excited naturally enough. It was better so. Dear Ida.

Little by little she was not there she was elsewhere. Little by little.

It was little by little and it was all of a sudden. It was not entirely sudden because she was not entirely there before she was elsewhere.

That is the way it happened.

Before it happened well quite a while before it happened she did meet women. When they came she was resting, when they went she was resting, she liked it and they did not mind it. They came again and when they came again, she was obliging, she did say yes. She was sorry she was resting, so sorry and she did say yes. She thought they liked it and they did but it was not the same as if she had ever said no or if she had not always been resting.

If she had not always been resting they would not have come nor would they have come again. They said thank you my dear when they went. She had said yes Ida had and she said yes again.

That is the way it was before going away, they had not really come nor had they said Thank you my dear.

That is really the reason that Ida ran away not ran away or went away but something in between. She was ready to be resting and she was ready to say yes and she was ready to hear them say thank you my dear but they had almost not come again.

So Ida was not there. Dear Ida.

She knew she would be away but not really away but before

she knew she was there where she had gone to she was really away.

That was almost an astonishment, quite to her, but to all the others not so much so once she was not there.

Of course she had luncheon and dinners to eat on the way. One of the menus she ate was this.

She ate soft-shell crabs, she had two servings of soft-shell crabs and she ate lobster à la Newburg she only had one helping of that and then she left.

She often left after she ate. That is when she was not resting but she mostly was resting.

And so there she was and where was Andrew, well Andrew moved quickly while Ida moved slowly that is when they were both nervous, when each one of them was nervous. But he was not there yet. Not really.

Ida was resting. Dear Ida. She said yes.

Slowly little by little Andrew came, Andrew was still his name.

He was just as nervous as he was and he walked every afternoon and then he told about his walk that afternoon. Ida was as nervous as she was and she was resting.

For a little time she did not say yes and then she said yes again.

Gradually it was, well not as it had been but it was, it was quite as it was Ida was resting and she was saying yes but not as much as she had said yes. There were times when she did not say yes times when she was not resting not time enough but times.

It is all very confused but more confused than confusing, and later it was not interesting. It was not confused at all, resting was not confused and yes was not confused but it was interesting.

When any one came well they did Ida could even say how do you do and where did you come from.

Dear Ida.

And if they did not come from anywhere they did not come. So much for resting.

Little by little there it was. It was Ida and Andrew.

Not too much not too much Ida and not too much Andrew.

And not enough Ida and not enough Andrew.

If Ida goes on, does she go on even when she does not go on any more.

No and yes.

Ida is resting but not resting enough. She is resting but she is not saying yes. Why should she say yes. There is no reason why she should so there is nothing to say.

She sat and when she sat she did not always rest, not enough.

She did rest.

If she said anything she said yes. More than once nothing was said. She said something. If nothing is said then Ida does not say yes. If she goes out she comes in. If she does not go away she is there and she does not go away. She dresses, well perhaps in black why not, and a hat, why not, and another hat, why not, and another dress, why not, so much why not.

She dresses in another hat and she dresses in another dress and Andrew is in, and they go in and that is where they are. They are there. Thank them.

Yes.

THREE SISTERS WHO ARE NOT SISTERS

A Melodrama

JENNY, HELEN *and* ELLEN
SAMUEL *and* SYLVESTER

Three Sisters Who Are Not Sisters

W E ARE three sisters who are not sisters, not sisters. We are three sisters who are orphans.

We are three sisters who are not sisters because we have not had the same mother or the same father, but because we are all three orphans we are three sisters who are not sisters.

Enter two brothers.

We are two brothers who are brothers, we have the same father and the same mother and as they are alive and kicking we are not orphans not at all, we are not even tall, we are not brave we are not strong but we never do wrong, that is the kind of brothers we are.

JENNY: And now that everybody knows just what we are what each one of us is, what are we going to do.

SYLVESTER: What are we going to do about it.

JENNY (*impatiently*): No not what are we going to do about it there is nothing to do about it, we are three sisters who are not sisters, and we are three orphans and you two are not, there is nothing to do about that. No what I want to know is what are we going to do now. Now what are we going to do.

SAMUEL: I have an idea a beautiful idea, a fine idea, let us play a play and let it be a murder.

JENNY:

HELEN: Oh yes let's.

ELLEN:

SYLVESTER: I won't be murdered or be a murderer, I am not that kind of a brother.

SAMUEL: Well nobody says you are, all you have to do is to be a witness to my murdering somebody.

HELEN: And who are you going to murder.

SAMUEL: You for choice. Let's begin.

ELLEN: Oh I am so glad I am not a twin, I would not like to be murdered just because I had a sister who was a twin.

JENNY: Oh don't be silly, twins do not have to get murdered together, let's begin.

Scene 2

A room slightly darkened, a couch, and a chair and a glass of water, the three sisters sitting on the couch together, the light suddenly goes out.

JENNY: Look at the chair.

HELEN: Which chair.

JENNY: The only chair.

ELLEN: I can't see the only chair.

JENNY (*with a shriek*): Look at the only chair.

All three together: There is no chair there.

SAMUEL: No there is no chair there because I am sitting on it.

SYLVESTER: And there is no him there because I am sitting on him.

JENNY: Which one is going to murder which one.

SAMUEL: Wait and see.

Suddenly the light goes up there is nobody in the room and Sylvester is on the floor dead.

[CURTAIN]

ACT II

Scene 1

The light is on.

Sylvester is on the floor dead.
Jenny is asleep on the couch.
She wakes up and she sees Sylvester on the floor dead.

Oh he is dead Sylvester is dead somebody has murdered him, I wish I had a sister a real sister oh it is awful to be an orphan and to see him dead, Samuel killed him, perhaps Helen killed him, perhaps Ellen but it should be Helen who is dead and where is Helen.

She looks under the bed and she bursts out crying.

There there is Helen and she is dead, Sylvester killed her and she killed him. Oh the police the police.

There is a knock at the door and Samuel comes in dressed like a policeman and Jenny does not know him.

JENNY: Yes Mr. Policeman I did kill them I did kill both of them.

SAMUEL: Aha I am a policeman but I killed both of them and now I am going to do some more killing.

JENNY (*screaming*): Ah ah.

And the lights go out and then the lights go up again and Jenny is all alone, there are no corpses there and no policeman.

JENNY: I killed them but where are they, he killed them but where is he. There is a knock at the door I had better hide.

She hides under the bed.

Scene 2

SAMUEL (*as a policeman comes in*): Aha there is nobody dead and I have to kill somebody kill somebody dead. Where is somebody so that I can kill them dead.

He begins to hunt around and he hears a sound, and he is just about to look under the bed when Ellen comes in.

ELLEN: I am looking for Helen who is not my twin so I do not have to be murdered to please her but I am looking for her.

Samuel the policeman comes out of the corner where he has been hiding.

SAMUEL: Aha you killed her or aha you killed him, it does not make any difference because now I am going to do some killing.

ELLEN: Not me dear kind policeman not me.

SAMUEL: I am not a policeman I am a murderer, look out here I come.

The light goes out. When it comes on again, the policeman is gone and Ellen murdered is on the floor.

Jenny looks out timidly from under the bed and gives a shriek:

Oh another one and now I am only one and now I will be the murdered one.

And timidly she creeps back under the bed.

[CURTAIN]

ACT III

Jenny under the bed. Samuel this time not like a policeman but like an apache comes creeping in.

SAMUEL: Aha I am killing some one.

JENNY (*under the bed*): He can't see me no he can't, and anyway I will kill him first, yes I will.

Suddenly the room darkens and voices are heard.

I am Sylvester and I am dead, she killed me, every one thinks it was Samuel who killed me but it was not it was she.

HELEN'S VOICE: I am Helen and I am dead and everybody thinks it was Samuel who killed me but not at all not not all not at all it was she.

A THIRD VOICE: I am Ellen and I am dead, oh so dead, so very very dead, and everybody thinks it was Samuel but it was not it was not Samuel it was she oh yes it was she.

The light goes up and Jenny alone looks out fearfully into the room from under the bed.

JENNY: Oh it was not Samuel who killed them it was not, it was she and who can she be, can she be me. Oh horrible horrible me if I killed all three. It cannot be but perhaps it is, (*and she stretches up very tall*) well if it is then I will finish up with him I will kill him Samuel and then they will all be dead yes all dead but I will not be dead not yet.

The light lowers and Samuel creeps in like an apache.

SAMUEL: They say I did not kill them they say it was she but I know it was me and the only way I can prove that I murdered them all is by killing her, aha I will find her I will kill her and when I am the only one the only one left alive they will know it was I that killed them all, I Samuel the apache.

He begins to look around and suddenly he sees a leg of Jenny sticking out under the bed. He pulls at it.

SAMUEL: Aha it is she and I will kill her and then they will know that I Samuel am the only murderer.

He pulls at her leg and she gives a fearful kick which hits him on the temple. He falls back and as he dies,

SAMUEL: Oh it is so, she is the one that kills every one, and that must be so because she has killed me, and that is what they meant, I killed them each one, but as she was to kill me, she has killed all of them all of them. And she has all the glory, Oh Ciel.

And he dies.

Jenny creeps out from under the bed.

JENNY: I killed him yes I did and he killed them yes he did and now they are all dead, no brothers no sisters no orphans no nothing, nothing but me, well there is no use living alone, with nobody to kill so I will kill myself.

And she sees the glass of water.

JENNY: Aha that is poison.

She drinks it and with a convulsion she falls down dead.

The lights darken and the voices of all of them are heard.

We are dead she killed us, he killed us sisters and brothers orphans and all he killed us she killed us she killed us he killed us and we are dead, dead dead.

The lights go up and there they all are as in the first scene.

JENNY: Did we act it are we dead, are we sisters, are we orphans, do we feel funny, are we dead.

SYLVESTER: Of course we are not dead, of course we never were dead.

SAMUEL: Of course we are dead, can't you see we are dead, of course we are dead.

HELEN (*indignantly*): I am not dead, I am an orphan and a sister who is not a sister but I am not dead.

ELLEN: Well if she is not dead then I am not dead. It is very nice very nice indeed not to be dead.

JENNY: Oh shut up everybody, shut up, let's all go to bed, it is time to go to bed orphans and all and brothers too.

And they do.

[FINIS]

BREWSIE AND WILLIE

Chapter One

YOU KNOW Willie, said Brewsie, I think we are all funny, pretty funny, about this fraternisation business, now just listen. They did not have to make any anti-fraternisation ruling for the German army in France because although the Germans did their best to fraternise, no French woman would look or speak to them or recognise their existence. I kind of wonder would our women be like French or be like Germans, if the horrible happened and our country was conquered and occupied.

Willie: Well I wouldnt want any American woman to be like a Frenchwoman.

Brewsie: No you would want them to be like the Germans, sleep with the conquerors.

Willie: You get the hell out of here, Brewsie. No American woman would sleep with a foreigner.

Brewsie: But you admire the Germans who do. Which do you want American women to be like.

Willie: I know what I dont want them to be like, I dont want them to be like any lousy foreigner.

Brewsie: But all your fathers and mothers were lousy foreigners.

Willie: You get the hell out of here, Brewsie. What's that to you, I am going to sleep with any German wench who'll sleep with me and they all will.

Brewsie: Sure they all will but all the same if the horrible happened and our country was defeated and occupied, how about it.

Willie: Well our country isnt going to be defeated and occupied, that's all there is to that.

Brewsie: Yes but you never can tell in a war.

Willie: And that's the reason there aint going to be any more war not if I can help it.

Brewsie: But if you cant help it.

Willie: I'll see to it that I do help it, there aint going to be any more war.

Brewsie: But that's what they said last time and hell here we are.

Willie: Well did I say we werent here, we're here all right, you betcha we're here, and I am going to sleep with any German girl who'll sleep with me, and they all will and that's what I call fraternisation, and they let us do it and we're doing it.

Brewsie: But Willie listen.

Willie: Aint I listening, aint I always listening, you're always talking and I am always listening.

Brewsie: Well anyway, Willie, just listen.

While Brewsie talked, it was not alone Willie who sometimes listened, there were others more or less listening, Jo, and Bob and Ralph and Don and there was Brock, he was older, he liked to talk about how his father and mother moved from one house to another and what illnesses they had had and what it did to them and what flowers his mother grew and that she was fond of cooking and eating, and that he was not the only child but they did like him that is to say he was interested in everything they wrote to him and was natural enough because although he had been married, he did not know whether he was married now or not, anyway he did listen to Brewsie, because Brewsie was really very interesting and had a lot to say that was interesting and he, whenever he Brock had time, he did listen to him, he was a good chap Brewsie and had a lot to say that was really interesting.

Listen, said Brewsie, listen to me. I want to know why do you fellows feel the way you do.

Jo: Oh go way Brewsie, dont you know we're disillusioned, that's what we are, disillusioned, that's the word, aint it, fellows, disillusioned.

All of 'em: Sure, that's the word, disillusioned.

Brock: No no I am not disillusioned, as long as my mother is fond of flowers, and she is and fond of cooking as she is and fond of eating as she is, and likes to move into other houses which she does I could never be that word I could never be disillusioned. No, Jo, no, no no, and I think you all know I mean it I do I never could be disillusioned.

Willie: Take me away, that man makes me crazy. I just cant stand another minute of it, take me away.

Brewsie: All right, Willie, let's go. Come along, Jo.

Jo: Yes I got to go to the river to wait on a girl.

Brewsie: Where is she.

Jo: She is gone home to eat but I said I'd sit on the river bank and wait and I'm going to, want to come along.

Willie: There aint two.

Jo: No there aint but one, want to come along.

Brewsie: Let's all three go.

Jo: That's all right with me.

Look, said Willie, there comes a man-eating dog.

It was a dark day but it did not rain. The dog was white and gentle. That is what Willie said.

Brewsie does talk to himself, he said to himself, how can I be interested in how many people will be killed or how much property will be destroyed in the next war, how many people will be killed in the next war.

They went on to the river. It is not always easy to sail a sailboat up a river.

That made them talk about what they did remember, steering an airplane. Some of them sighed, it made them sigh because they liked it. It was like sleeping in a bed, it made them sigh, it did make them sigh because they liked it.

I remember, he said, he said, I remember.

They saw three others coming along, one of them said, what we doing just walking, aint anybody going to buy anything.

Brewsie remembered about buying, there was a time when anybody could buy something that is if he had money with him. Brewsie said that spending money if you had it, well it was just spending money and spending money was not only easy as anything it was more than anything.

I know what you mean, said Willie.

I do too, said Jo, let's go buy something. We aint found anything to buy for the kind of money we got, said Willie, and then the girl came along. If you put your arm all over a girl, well any girl does any girl say, tell him I dont want him, but no girls do because there is chewing gum and tobacco and coffee and chocolate, yes there is. Does, said Brewsie, does any one want to buy anything if it can be given to them, if they can get it without buying. Nobody answered him, they were busy other ways.

It's a long war but it will end, said Brewsie, and then we will go home. Where's home, said a man just behind him.

What's your name, said Brewsie.

Paul is my name and if it aint Paul it's Donald, what do you want with my name.

I want to know how old you are and where you come from.

Oh get the hell out of here, said Donald Paul and then he sat down.

Let's, said Donald Paul, let's talk about beds. What kind of beds, said Brewsie. Oh any kind, the kind you sleep in, the kind you make for yourselves and the kind others make for you. A bed is a bed, just write that down if you know how to read and write, a bed's a bed. When you wish you were dead you always wish for a bed. Yes that's the way it is. Remember you know when they put you in prison they make you make your own bed. I just read about it this evening. Yes, said Brewsie, if there is a bed. Yeah you're right too, if there is a bed. And they both sighed not loud, not really at all. Anybody knows how long a day is when evening comes. They gather that they had rather not be able to sit than not.

Yes, said Brewsie, do be anxious.

It was almost as much aloud as that.

Donald Paul snorted.

Allowed, he said, allowed, what's allowed, anything that is allowed is just what they never said. There are, said Donald Paul, yes there are, said Brewsie. Are what, said Willie. Eight million unemployed any next year, said Jo. Oh go to hell out of here, said Willie and as he spoke he fell asleep just like that.

Chapter Two

BREWSIE
  I'm here
What you doing.
I'm thinking.
I am thinking about religion.
What religion.
Well Willie's, somebody said to me today why don't the
G.I.'s have the Bible around like the doughboys did, why aint
there ever a Bible in a plane.

Why should there be, there aint anything the matter with
the plane.

Of course there could be.

Ya but if there could be it would be the fault of the ground
men, and if there is any flack then you're taught how to dive
in so that it dont hit you and if you dont do it right it does
and anyway there is of course there is the calculation of errors.
What's the matter with you Brewsie, dont you know all that.

Yes it is kind of funny I know all that, they do say though
that the doughboys always had Bibles around, that's what they
say.

Well, said Jo, why do you worry.

I don't worry, said Brewsie, I never worry I am kind of
foggy in the head and I want to be clear, that's all.

Willie: Well you never will, you just keep on thinking and
talking the more foggy you feel. Now you take us, we dont
think we know that all America is just so and we are all Americans, that's what we are all Americans.

Brewsie: I wish I was a girl if I was a girl I would be a WAC
and if I was a WAC, oh my Lord, just think of that.

Don: Dont you go being funny Brewsie, I been out with a
WAC, yes I have, well no she was not an officer WAC although I have been out even with an officer WAC, how can
you worry when anything is like that.

Brewsie: Well now boys let's all get together and think.

Willie: All right now how would you want us to get together and think.

Brewsie: Well let's think about how everybody perhaps will get killed in the next war.

Willie: Well they sure will if they fight the war good enough. If you fight a war good enough everybody ought to get killed.

Brewsie: You mean the other side.

Willie: No not the other side, that's only when one side fights good enough, but when they both do, and that can happen too, well when they both do, then everybody will be dead, all dead, fine, then nobody's got to worry about jobs.

Brewsie: But oh dear me, there are the wives and children. Yes there are.

Brock: You know the other day I heard a colored major say, he had no children although he was married nine years and I said, how is that, and he said, is this America any place to make born a Negro child.

Willie: I dont want to hear any talk like that, you know right well Brock I dont want to hear any talk like that.

But Willie, said Brock, Willie you listen to Brewsie and he talks like that and when I talk like Brewsie talks you tell me you dont want me to talk at all like that, that's not right Willie, that's not right, it is not right, Willie, it is not right.

Willie: Oh my God.

While they were talking they did not know what country they were in. If they did know they might talk about it but they did not know what country they were in, and little by little they knew less what country they were in. It was not night yet, it was not even late in the afternoon, they knew that, and sometimes they thought about that, but Brewsie did not talk about that so they did not have to listen about that not that afternoon.

It was early in the morning, and there was anybody there, they never thought that there was anybody there even when there was.

Let's go and have a drink, said Willie, but they could get a drink where they were so they did not go and get a drink, they had a drink where they were.

I was in a hotel, said Willie, and I saw from the window around the corner somebody getting into bed and I could not tell whether it was a little girl or a little woman.

What time was it, said Brewsie.

About half past ten, said Willie.

You couldnt tell by that, said Brewsie, not by that. A little girl could be going to bed then, yes she could.

I know, said Willie, I know, it might have been a little girl and it might have been a round-faced little woman, I kind of think it was a round-faced little woman and I couldnt tell whether she was kneeling to say her prayers or to take make-up off her face, I just couldnt tell.

Was there a mirror in front of her, said Brewsie.

I just couldnt tell, said Willie.

Even a little woman could kneel and say her prayers as well as a little girl, said Brewsie.

Could she, said Willie.

Yes she could, said Brewsie.

Well I dont know, said Willie, it was so around the corner.

Well couldnt you see her the next day.

I tell you it was the back of a house around the corner, how could I tell which house it was next day.

Well, said Brewsie, why didnt you go around that night and see.

I tell you, said Willie, it was around the corner and the front wouldnt be the same as the back.

Well couldnt you count, said Jo waking up.

No not in French how could you count in French around the corner with the back and the front different and not sure it was a girl or a little woman. No I just never did find out.

Well why didnt you go back to the hotel and try again, said Brewsie, try to see her get to bed again.

Because I never have gone back there, said Willie, I never have and when I do get back she will be gone sure she will.

Nobody ever moves in France, said Jo.

No, maybe though it was a hotel.

Well if it was, said Brewsie, it was not a little girl.

I guess you're right Brewsie, I guess it was a little woman, a little round-faced woman and she was taking off her make-up.

Perhaps, said Brewsie, it was a little round-faced woman and she was saying her prayers.

Not likely, said Willie.

Chapter Three

BREWSIE: Are we isolationists or are we isolated, are we efficient or are we quick to make up for long preparation, if we were caught without time to get it all in order would we be ready, would we be, well did we be, if Japan had followed up, oh dear me, said Brewsie, oh dear me, are we efficient or are we slow and so we are very quick to make up for being slow, oh dear me, said Brewsie, and do we like the German girls best because we are virgins and they do all the work.

Willie: You get the hell out of here Brewsie, I am no virgin, I never was a virgin, I never will be a virgin.

No, said Brewsie, no, you never were a virgin, well then you dont know the difference perhaps you still are a virgin.

Jo: That sounds funny, Brewsie, that's not the way you talk, Brewsie, what's the matter with you, Brewsie.

Brewsie: I dont know, I kind of feel funny, it is true over half the E. T. O. are virgins, they are they are, and that's why they like the German girls I get so mad I just have to say it, I just get so mad.

Willie: Well I get mad too, if you say I am a virgin.

Jo: Well, Willie, perhaps you are. Brewsie is right, a whole lot of the army are virgins. I dont say they cant but they dont and that's the reason they got to have so many pin-ups and German girls, yes sometimes I guess Brewsie is right, you just bellow, Willie, you just bellow and Brewsie is just foggy so he is but I know, I never say it but I know, a lot of us is just virgins, Willie, just E. T. O. virgins, Willie, all you fellows, are you or are you not E. T. O. Virgins.

Willie: You get the hell out of here, Jo, I can stand what Brewsie says but I wont stand anything you say, I just wont and I warn you right here and now if you call me a virgin again some night or some day you'll die and it wont be any enemy that will have killed you, it will have been just me.

Brock: Oh boys, boys, listen to me, I am older than any of you and I dont know whether I am married or not and I am always interested in what my mother does and I do like to drink but nobody ever thinks of calling me a virgin. You wouldnt, Willie, and you wouldnt, Jo, and you wouldnt, Brewsie, you never would think of calling me a virgin. So dont you be worried, Willie, dont you be worried, you just listen to me and dont you be worried.

Willie: Oh.

Brewsie: But to come back to what is worrying me, to come back to it, are we isolationists or are we isolated.

Willie: You just want to explain, Brewsie, so go ahead, you will anyway so go ahead, we just listen anyway, so just go ahead. Come on, Jo, come on, everybody, Brewsie is thinking.

Brewsie: Well I just am thinking are we isolationists or are we isolated.

Jo: Well what about it.

Well you see, said Brewsie, I kind of like to be liked. Willie likes to be liked, so do you all, well yes I do like to be liked, I just could cry if they dont like me, yes I could. I do like to be liked.

And besides, said Jo, it's dangerous not to be liked, if Willie did not like me I would just be scared.

Brock: I am sure everybody does like me, I do I am sure I do what makes anyone like me.

Oh my God, said Willie, take me away.

All right, said Brewsie, all right where shall we go.

Right back where we started from, said Willie. And the flowers.

Oh come along, said Jo, Brewsie will remember what he wants to say for another day.

No, said Brewsie, I wont remember but I will find it out again.

Let's go, said Willie.

And they went.

The sun was shining and they were all worried, there was nothing to worry about, the sun was shining and they were all worried.

It used to be fine, said Willie, before the war when we used to believe what the newspapers and the magazines said, we used to believe them when we read them and now when it's us they write about we know it's lies, just lies, just bunches of lies, and if it's just bunches of lies, what we going to read when we get home, answer me that, Brewsie, answer me that.

I saw a girl, said Donald Paul, she was saying how can I replace potatoes, how can I take the place of potatoes. My darling, I said, you just cant. Brewsie: I am going to begin to talk and I am just going on talking, that's what I am going to do.

Sure you are, said Willie.

I say, said Brewsie, and I am just going to be solemn, just as solemn as anything, are we isolationists or are we isolated, do we like Germans because we are greedy and callous like them. Oh dear, I guess you boys better go away, I might just begin to cry and I'd better be alone. I am a G. I. and perhaps we better all cry, it might do us good crying sometimes does.

Oh get the hell out of here, Brewsie, said Willie.

Crying does good, said Jo, but I dont like it, not anybody's crying.

Where is Donald Paul, said Brewsie.

I told him to go away, said Willie.

If they knew it was Sunday afternoon then it was Sunday afternoon, nicely and quietly Sunday afternoon. Even yesterday was Sunday afternoon, Brewsie said so and they all said, yes, yesterday even yesterday was Sunday afternoon too.

Two majors came along, one was a fat major and one was a thin major, they were in transport, the fat major said, I wonder when we get home, can we make them see that it is just as good not to work seven days a week all day, that railroads get along just as well if you go home for a day and a half a week and work in your garden. The thin major said, I wonder, no I dont wonder about the railroads getting along just as good, I wonder if they'll see it and let us take a day and a half off and perhaps longer and a month for a vacation like they do over here, I wonder. And do you suppose, said the fat major we could retire when we were fifty instead of when we were seventy. I wonder, said the thin major and they went home in the twilight, a nice twilight.

Brewsie when he was awake woke slowly, it was just as well as when he went to sleep, he went to sleep slowly.

Willie never asked him why, Willie knew why.

Said Brewsie, do you remember, Willie, what I was talking

about. Well I do, I was talking about a lot of things and I was going to talk a long time and I was going to commence with, Are we isolationists or are we isolated.

Two Red Cross nurses came along, they were lieutenants still they did say, listen he sounds interesting. Tell me, said the fatter and younger, dont you think it is awful that the French have no leaders.

Havent they, said Donald Paul, and if they have why do they want them, a leader is some one who leads you where you dont want to go, where do you want to go, sister, can I lead you.

The older and the thinner said, we were not talking to you, we were talking to him, he sounds interesting.

Donald Paul: Fair sister, you are right, he not only sounds interesting but he is interesting.

Brewsie: I have a great deal to say.

The older one: Yes, that is why we are listening.

Brewsie: If I have a great deal to say it will take a long time to say it.

Yes, said the younger, but how can the French expect to come back if they have no leaders.

Why why why, how how how, said Donald Paul.

How, said Jo, I dont know how.

The older: Yes but he does, you tell us, she said to Brewsie.

Brewsie, said yes, I'll tell you. Leaders, what are leaders, yes was right, a leader either does not lead you or if he does he leads you where you do not want to go. Isnt it so, sisters, isnt it, where do you want to go, where do the French want to go, they dont want to go anywhere, they want enough to eat, a place to sleep, and fuel to keep them warm, that's what they want, leaders never give you that, they kind of scratch around and get it for themselves. No he is right what can leaders do, we always have leaders but where do they lead us. No listen to me and I will tell you about efficiency and about being isolated and why although rich we are poor and why although quick we are slow and how, well leaders better stay at home a while and lead everybody that way.

Chorus of a crowd: Ah yes, let's go home, I want to go home, we want to go home, everybody wants to go home. And then somebody began to sing Home Sweet Home.

Then everybody got quiet.

Do you know, said Donald Paul, I watch all those men all that army going around excursioning in auto-buses, so fat, so well dressed, so taken care of, and I say to myself, they want to go home and I say to myself, do they, and I say to myself, let's go home, and I say to myself, where is home, where you got a bellyful, that's home, where you got no cares, that's home.

Willie: Get the hell out of here, home is home, home is where you come from, that's home, that's fine, that's home.

Jo: You got no imagination, Willie.

Willie: To hell with imagination, I want to go home.

Yes, said the two nurses, you all want to go home, yeah you're all going home.

Yes we all are going home, home, that's where we're going, home.

Donald Paul: All too soon.

Willie: You get the hell out of here. If anybody is going to talk it's Brewsie, Brewsie, you talk.

Brewsie: Not today Willie, not today, I kind of dont understand anything today, I kind of thought I understand everything today, but today I kind of think I dont understand anything today. I aint no leader today, I'm kind of scared of being a leader today.

Willie: Ah you're no leader, Brewsie, you just talk.

Donald Paul: And what do leaders do.

Jo: They talk too, but they talk differently. Orientation, that's the word, said Donald Paul.

Now tell me, said the two nurses, do you all talk like this every day?

Not every day, said Jo.

Mostly every day, said Willie.

I think we will come again, said the younger fatter nurse and the older thinner one was very interested and they went away.

Chapter Four

JO SAID, what do you think, one of those frog girls said, I showed 'em a picture of my wife and the baby in the baby carriage and she said, what, do you have those old fashioned baby-carriages with high wheels and a baby can fall out, no we French people, we have up-to-date baby-carriages, streamlined, she said. It's funny but that's what she said, and I said, take me show me and show me she did. The town was lousy with them, sure and we never noticed, nice deep baby-carriages with low rubber-tired wheels, just as comfortable and safe as anything. Why, said that frog girl, we just use the kind of baby-carriages you have to carry packages around, not babies, never babies. Now can you beat it.

It's funny, said Willie, some ways you do and some ways you dont, it is funny, said Willie.

Jo: Let's go home and work, I want to buy one of those up-to-date baby-carriages, I cant have no frog girl pull one like that over me.

Work, said Brewsie, yes, you know I often think American men work funny, they write to me from home, they have worked so hard they never do want to work that hard again.

Perhaps, said Donald Paul sourly, perhaps they wont have the chance.

What you mean, said Jo.

Well how about it, any work to go back to, you.

Just as much as you, said Jo. Not so, said Donald Paul. I am the only one of the whole lot of you that dont have to look for work. Why, said Jo, are you rich. Too rich to work, said Donald Paul. I, said Brock, can always find work. You certainly can, said Willie, they give you work to shut you up. But, said Brock, I can always explain things while I am working, that's it, said Willie, suppose you stopped explaining and began working anybody would drop down dead and so they got to keep you working to keep themselves from being dead.

Well anyway, said Brewsie, I often think we soldiers complain, and we complain about what the officers have but we dont complain how we have everything civilians dont have.

Civilians, oh hell, what you mean Brewsie. Well dont we have food and clothes and shoes and free parties all the time, they take us everywhere, and eats, and treats, and free everything, subways and theatres and everything and my gracious, my good gracious and no worries. Oh my good gracious, oh my good gracious and no worries, my good gracious. I just could kind of just cry when I think we all got to scratch around and worry, worry and scratch around, and then those bills, pay everything on the installment plan, and coming in and coming in, oh dear, sometimes I just burst out crying in my sleep, I am older than you boys, you dont know, I could just burst out crying.

Oh, said Willie, if we got to cry let's cry into liquor, come along, which they did.

It was late afternoon and the streets were narrow and three Negro soldiers came along, there was a very little girl and her mother, one of the Negroes fell on his knee like a cavalier before the little girl and took her hand, the mother went on and then stood slightly flushed looking at her little girl, the little girl a little flushed shook the hand of the kneeling soldier, he said a word in French, she answered him, she was a very little girl, only five years old, the other two had gone on, he rose from his knee and he went on, the little girl went along with her mother.

Chapter Five

IT'S FUNNY, said Willie, the way a nigger always finds some little nigger children to talk to, you'd think there were no niggers anywhere and there he is, he just is sitting on a chair in a garden and two darky little boys talking to him and they talking French and he talking and they go on talking French and he does talk the same to them, and I do think it is funny.

Yes I found three of them taking a little nigger girl out walking and they said they had borrowed her from her mother and there they were just out walking, it is funny. Yes, said Jo, and I saw that girl in the house around the corner, she was not a little girl she was a kind of a big girl and she was reading a book and she had her elbows on the table and her head in her hands, and she was studying in a book, and she had other books on the table and she was brunette and yes, she had books. And did she see you, said Willie. Well I dont know, said Jo, but I guess she did kind of see me. And how did you know she was the same girl, well she was in the same room and there wasnt two of them so she must have been the one, you never can tell and she was not round-faced and she was not small and she was a brunette, one of those dark-complected ones but it was she all right, and she knew me even if she did not see me, not that other time, anyway. Oh forget it, said Willie, I was the one saw her. Oh well perhaps this was another place and around another corner. There is no other place, said Willie and she is my girl. Well take her if you want to, said Jo. You know, said Brewsie.

Do you fellows, have you fellows been listening. No, said Willie, we have been talking. Well, said Brewsie, I was talking to Donald Paul. Oh that fellow, said Willie, Brewsie, yes he said he wanted to. He's married. Well, said Jo, aint we all married, werent we just forgetting about being married, yes of course, yes I know about being married, well that is what I say, Donald Paul, said he wanted the government to take over everything. And, said Willie, I hope you answered him back that the first thing they the government ought to take over is this blamed army, if they manage other things the way they manage this, then they better had keep their hand off, that's all I got to say, keep their hand off. Government, aint the government back of this army, aint this a most wasteful badly managed piece of machinery, aint we all no good. Answer me that, government, answer me that, those business sharks that cant give us a job, they're bad, the government and this army, my God, we cant take care of ourselves without the government and those rich guys. I tell you boys there aint any answer, just you believe me, there aint any answer, and anybody says there is, you Brewsie, and that lousy Donald Paul, I just tell you and though I dont sound like it I've got plenty of sense, there aint any answer, there aint going to be any answer, there never has been any answer, that's the answer. Listen to me, that's the answer. There aint any answer, and we all know there aint any answer, there aint one of us in our miserable little hearts who dont know that there isnt any answer, and anybody who talks different knows he is lying, he knows darn well that that is the answer, the answer is there aint, there completely is no answer. You all listen to me you all want to go home, well you all going to be home and I tell you you'll know there just like you knew here, there aint going to be any answer.

Chapter Six

WHEN I get home, said Richard, I got a home to go to, my wife and I have bought two hundred acres, we built a shack and outhouses. We got a neighbor a Pole farmer, they take care of it when we are away. My wife teaches school, and we are claiming back the land and there are rattlesnakes, so I guess it's a good place to grow grapes and make wine and what they call marc, which is a brandy, and I got a place to go home to, to hell with jobs, I got a place to go home to, and sure they will offer me a job because I dont need it, they wont offer it to those that need it, you see, I'm going home to a home. You see, where I can live, and you see I have got a home to go home to where I can live, God it's good to live, and I got a home where I can live.

I dont see why, said Ed, everybody is so scared, nothing to be scared about, my brother lived through the depression and he always had a job, and I have always been educated and I always can get well paid. What you all scared about, I am a strong man, not so strong but strong enough and now I'll tell you just how I do it, just how old I am, just what I have done, just what I am going to do, I am just going to tell you.

Willie: Oh Brewsie, kill him.

Brewsie: No Willie, you just listen.

Willie: Thank God he's dead, did you see him die, Brewsie, he died just like one of those things that go out. Oh it's fine to see them die just fine.

Are you sure he's dead, Brewsie, I am sure but are you sure he's dead.

Jo: Well you always listen to Brewsie.

Willie: Sure I listen to Brewsie. Brewsie is so earnest, and he is so careful of what he says, and besides you dont have to listen, you know what he says is so true you just dont have to listen and that's just fine, you just dont have to listen.

Brewsie: Well this time you got to listen because I've got it all doped out.

Say Brewsie, said Willie, do you know why that funny girl she says her name is Betty, but why any girl who talks no

English can have a name Betty well that gets me, but besides her name being Betty, she just kind of giggles and laughs every time she sees me and not because she loves me, I can see that, but because she thinks I am ridiculous. Now why, Brewsie, why does she think I am so funny, she aint interested in me. What makes her giggle like that. Well does she do that with others, I dont know, Brewsie, she makes me so mad I just dont know. Well I know, said Jo, she thinks everybody is funny and she thinks she's funny and she's religious and I always have noticed that when anybody gets religious they giggle. What you mean, said Willie. Well I just have noticed that, said Jo, but anyway forget it, tell me something, anybody tell me something, if it is true and it is that now we have less iron ore left in our country than Canada has, why we going to go home to jobs just to use up just what we have of iron ore making gadgets to be sold on the installment plan to people worried to death because they have to pay something every month and they'd be lots happier without it, now tell me why we all want to rush home to work at a job just so our children and our children's children wont have no iron ore and be just like those European people without no iron ore. That, said Donald Paul that is what you call a high standard of living. Hell of a high standard of living, said Jo, which is on top of you all the whole time. I want to be on top of a standard of living not have it on top of me, all the time, and they say in the papers we are going to have a higher standard of living when we get home, how many more installment plans does that mean fuss and worry. It aint that, said Willie, it aint that we aint like those lousy Europeans, we like to work. Sure, said Jo, but isnt there any other kind of work to do than make those gadgets, aint there. Not that any he American wants to do, said Willie, believe me, we want to work making gadgets, and that's what we'll all do, we will stand in line till we get a job to make gadgets, and somebody else will stand in line till he gets a job to sell them on the installment plan. And then, said Jo, we use up all our raw material which is what makes us so rich. Sure we will, said Willie, and then we'll all be dead, and why worry. I do worry, said Brewsie, Sure you worry, said Willie, that's why we love you and that's why we listen to you, we like you to worry, go ahead and worry.

Yes, said Brewsie, yes let me explain, I understand everything. Sure you do, said Willie. This, said Brewsie, is what I
understand, and it's terribly important, even if you dont listen,
well you got to listen, listen. It's not about jobs but yes it is
about jobs, you see industrialism, you know making a lot of
things turning them out just like that by the million in no
time, England began it, early in the nineteenth century. If I'd
known those Limies invented it, I never would go home to
get a job, I'd stay right here, said Willie. Well they did, said
Brewsie, they invented it and they made machines and they
turned out well not like we do but a hell of a lot of goods
but they had all their colonies to dump them on and their
possessions, you know about how the sun never set on them,
it never shines on them that's all I know, said Jo. Well anyway
they had lots of coal and iron ore and tin right there on that
island and they just made and made, and everybody gave up
every kind of way of living excepting jobs in factories and
mines, even little children, and they made all their colonies
and empire buy them and it was swell just like us and they
got richer and richer. Well we horned in after our Civil War,
we went industrial and we had more everything than they had
and we got richer and they got poorer and their markets that
is the people in their empire slowed down in buying and they
used up their raw material, and then they tried to take new
places to sell to, like Egypt which they took from the French
and Africa from the Dutch. The lousy Limies, said Willie. You
just wait, said Brewsie, and there we were getting richer and
richer and why because we had our outside market right at
home that is we had emigration, thousands and millions coming in every year into our country, and as soon as they made
some money. The lousy foreigners, said Willie. Well anyway
they made America rich I tell you that Willie, and they bought
and they became us, yes U.S. us, and the more they came the
more they made and like England we kept on using up our
raw material and it was fine. Well Germany and Japan they
said they'd get industrial too, but they had no raw material
but they said they'd buy up stocks of raw material and they'd
manufacture and they'd get countries that had raw material
and own them, Germany would own Russia and Japan China.
Well well, said Jo, that's just what they did do, I mean that's

just what they didnt do. Yes, said Brewsie, but it wasnt so easy
to stop them. And it's all because everybody just greedy wants
to manufacture more than anybody can buy, well then you
know what happened after the last war we cut off immigration, we hoped to sell enough to foreign countries, foreign
countries didnt want to buy and we had the depression. My
God yes, said Jo, we did have the depression. Yes and then
we had to fight, and yes we won but we used up a hell of a
lot of raw material and now we got to make a club to make
those foreign countries buy from us, and we all got to go
home to make some more of those things that use up the raw
material and that nobody but our own little population wants
to buy. Oh dear, said Brewsie.

Oh dear, said a woman's voice behind him, it does just
sound too awful. Yes, said another woman, my father used to
say it would happen, I remember now, he was an Englishman
and he did used to say it would happen. A Limey, muttered
Willie. Well he did say it would happen, and he said when
they cut off immigration he said to me little girl you'll see
right here in this big rich prosperous country you'll see a real
depression, not just busted booms but a real big depression.
But Brewsie, said Jo, what you mean, what can any of us do
but go home get a job if we can, make the gadgets you say
nobody has the money to buy, and buy them ourselves on the
installment plan and borrow money from Friendly Finance to
sort of worry along, what can we do, what you want us to do
want us to starve, you cant starve with that all that land that
has fallen out of cultivation. Sure not, said Richard, didnt I
tell you about my two hundred acres. Yes, said Jo you're sitting pretty, but we cant all be farmers, what the hell can we
do. That's what the English are saying, said one of the
women. Oh sister forget the Limies. But, said she, how can I
forget them when we are doing just like them. I know, said
Brewsie. I know, said Richard. Well I dont know I'm going
to believe it even if it is true, said Willie. If it is true, said Jo,
you got to believe it. I dont see why I got to believe a thing
only because it's true, said Willie. Well, said Jo, what you
going to believe. Perhaps I wont believe anything, said Willie,
you can do that, I dont say I will do it, but I say you can do
it. He certainly is right, said Richard Paul you certainly can

get along fine and not believe it even if it is true. Anyway what if it is true it dont prove anything. I aint going to get a job that's all I know, I'd rather be a tramp. Will you, said one of the girls, will you be a tramp. No I wont have to, a fellow like me always lives easy some way. Yes you do, said Jo. Listen, said one of the girls, I heard some men talking. Frogs, said Willie, you didnt believe them. No they werent frogs they, well they did say and I know that my father would have thought so too. It's enough, said Willie, that we got to fight the rich men and the poor men too, but we got to stop somewhere sister, we cant take on your father, sure anybody has to have a father, that's all right but anybody can forget about a father especially in a war, especially. Well, said the nurse, it is especially in a war you better find out something, that is what those guys in the Intelligence say and do they.

Jo: Let her talk.

Willie: Any sister has the right to talk about her father, any sister.

It isnt about my father it was about what some men said, they said, those men said, why do the Americans make such a fuss, and everybody should be grateful to them, what's the matter with them said these men dont they know they didnt come over to Europe to fight until they were attacked at Pearl Harbor and then they came over to protect the rear of their country, and then well they crossed the channel all right but they were fighting a pretty broken German army which had all its best troops killed in Russia, and they thought France fine when they had the French resistance to help them but when they got to Germany with no guerrillas to help them, it did not go so good, and then the Germans almost broke through with a used-up army. Janet, said one of the women in a shocked voice, Janet did you sit there and listen to those men say things like that about your country. It was their country too, it was, they were Americans, and Janet you mean to say you sat there and listened to Americans talk like that about America about the American army. I didnt sit Jenny I stood and anyway it is true. It isnt true Janet it is not true, nothing is true that makes the American army sound like that, I am going home, and you will find out how wrong you were. Dont forget sister, said Jo, she had a father. And I, said Willie, met two soldiers just yesterday who never have and never can worry, and why cant they and why dont they worry, well because they're too young, they are so young they just smile, dont you worry, sister even if your name is Jenny dont you worry there are a lot of them too young to worry, they just smile.

Chapter Seven

DOES IT make one mad or doesnt it make one mad, said Willie. What you mean, asked Jo. Well, said Willie, I saw a Negro soldier sitting on a bench just looking out into the street, and next to him were three white women, not young, not paying any attention nor he wasnt paying any attention to them and I didnt know whether it made me mad or didnt make me mad. Well, said Jo, I kind of notice they all think they still care and they think it makes 'em mad but really it doesn't make 'em mad not even when they see a white woman walking with one of them, the boys like to think it makes 'em mad but it doesnt really make 'em mad not really it doesnt. No, said Willie, I guess it just really doesnt, perhaps because they've griped so much they kind have lost the trick of getting mad or perhaps they just dont care, not the Southern fellows and not anybody really very much. Well I know, said Jo, when I was in school down in Paris the only Red Cross place where you could get coffee and doughnuts anywhere near was a colored one and so we just all went in there, and just at first we never went in alone, we just always were two or three together and then just anyhow kind of soon we went in alone or together just as it happened and we sat down anywhere and we ate coffee and doughnuts and we just didnt think a thing about it not at any time, no I dont know whether we just lost the way of getting mad. There arent any fellows just mad much anyway, sometimes when they see some Negroes sitting just like that in a café, they look at them as if they feel they ought to get mad about it, but nobody notices and they just dont kind of remember to keep on being mad about it. Yeah, said Ed, lots of the boys they say wait till we get home we'll show these Negro soldiers and officers where they belong, and they say it just to kind of hearten themselves up about being at home but they just cant feel mad about it, they just cant, I never have seen any that really can. I saw two soldiers once, they said, what part of town do the Negroes go to because we dont want to go anywhere near that. Yes sure you dont I said, but how do you know there is that part of town. Well there always is these two soldiers said and we see enough of Negroes, we work with them over supplies. Well and dont you get along, no we dont, said the two soldiers and we dont come from the South, we come from the way North. All right, I said, and they said all right, and that was that. Say, said Richard, I heard a Negro man say a funny thing, somebody did say to him somebody said he had a dog there who only talked English. Only talk English, does he, said the Negro man, well then I guess I certainly do not ever want to interrupt him. I often wonder, said Brewsie, whether home was ever like this. Well you can be sure it never is like this, said Willie. Yes I know, said Brewsie, but I mean when we get home will we get mad and all excited up about something that really doesnt amount to anything to us just like we did before there was this war. I do wonder, said Brewsie. You always are wondering, said Willie. I met two soldiers and they said you know what happened to one of us the other night. He drew a pistol on a German girl he had because he didnt trust her. And what had she done, I said. She hadnt done a thing except what she was there to do, but he heard a noise just a little noise and so he drew a pistol on her. And what did she do. She was scared, that's what she did. Well, said Ed, anyway you look at it girls, well we have to have them, an American soldier has to have wine women and song, he just is made that way. Oh is he, said Willie, you just listen to Brewsie. Well what of it, it's true anyway. Not so true, said Brewsie, not so true, kind of true but not so true. Pin-up girls, not so true, said Brewsie, wait till you get home and have to treat girls in an ordinary way, not so much wine women and song. You think you're soldiers and you make yourselves up like soldiers and soldiers have to have wine women and song, and so all American soldiers just are so sure they have to have wine women and song, American soldiers think life is a movie and they got to dream the parts in their feelings. Here comes some more sisters, said Willie. I wish we wasnt so popular, said Willie.

For all that, said Jo, you know what I was doing, I was coming along and I stopped before a door and there was a crack in a door and when I looked through and there she was, a whore. Did you go in, asked Willie. No I didnt go in, said

Jo, and you wouldnt have gone in either, said Jo. Well, said
Willie, I want to know. I, said Ed, I was coming along and
there was a girl and she said to me you stand over across the
street in front of that little door and when I tell you you
commence and sing a song. And did you, said Willie. Well,
said Ed, yes I did go across the street and I stood in front of
the door and then she said she was there back across the street
and she said sing and I began to sing. What did you sing, said
Willie. Oh just a song and when I got started singing that
song she said, stop, and I stopped. How come, said Jo, that
you understood her, said Jo. Well I did understand her, said
Ed. And then what happened, said Willie. Well, said Ed, when
I got back across the street she was gone. Where did she go
to, said Willie. I dont know where she went to all I knew was
that she was gone. And what did you do then, said Willie. I
went back across the street and finished the song. I dont guess
you did, said Willie. The nurses were there by that time. We
would like, said the nurses, if you would tell us about what
you were talking about the last time. You never want him to
say twice what he said once, said Willie. No of course, said
the nurse, no of course not but just the same I wish that he
would talk and if only he would I am sure a great many, a
very great many would like to listen. He's modest, said Willie,
you are modest Brewsie, that's what you are, said Willie, but
just the same you tell them Brewsie, everybody wants to hear
you tell it, begin now. Yes do begin now, said the nurses. Well
all the same, said Brewsie, I will begin now. I worry, said
Brewsie, we all worry, said Brewsie, and said Jo, we got plenty
to worry us. Not now, said Brewsie, not now, now when we
are soldiers and fed and clothed and taken sightseeing. No,
said Brewsie, not now, we only think we are worrying now,
but when we get home and bills, and pay your way, and we
are lazy, that's what we are, lazy. Not so lazy, said Ed, not so
lazy. No, said a nurse and her name was Pauline, you know
what I often think, I often think, that we dont really hate
everybody the way everybody says they do, no we really dont,
but we are just kind of scared and lost, and we want to go
home. Being a soldier I often think, said Pauline, is all right
when there is fighting, fighting knocks the scare out of you,
the scare of being alone. You never are alone when you are

fighting. I know that even when there is only one in a fox hole, you are not really alone because there is danger there but when the danger is all over like it is now and you are away from home where everybody is just like you and you have that comfort, when they are all just like you, like they are at home, when you are home too, but when you are away from home and there is no more danger and excitement of danger then the boys really feel all alone and they have to be really tough to give them courage and they have to hate everybody to give themselves courage. They certainly have to sister, said Willie. They certainly have to and they do, said Jo. They certainly do hate everybody they certainly do, said Ed, and they are going to go on hating them until they get home and then, said Donald Paul. Then, said Ed, then I dont know. Well Brewsie, now sister has talked, you talk and tell us how to save ourselves from death and measles, said Willie. Death aint so bad, said Jo, but measles, did any of you ever have measles, said Jo. You shut up tight Jo, everybody has had measles, let Brewsie begin. Well I am going to begin, said Brewsie, because I have a lot to say and I am going to say it all and it is going to take me a lot of time. We'll wait, said the nurses. Let's begin about the Civil War, said Brewsie, the great war of the Civil War, said Brewsie, well it was a mistake. And, said Jim at that, that's no news, it certainly was one hell of a mistake, I come from Georgia, mistake is the word. Well you missed your steaks all right, said Willie. Yes we did, said Jim and for a mighty long time but we're beginning to eat 'em up now. I wonder, said Jo, I did my training way down South, yes I did. Most as foreign as foreigners, said Willie, only you got to be polite, you cant call 'em lousy foreigners because that way they arent foreigners, they are lousy and they are foreigners but they are not lousy foreigners, not not, you get me. My aunt, said Donald Paul, I have an aunt somewhere down there and she told me her mother a sweet old lady said to her about the Yankees who were down there training, remember my daughter we must be patient with them because we must always remember that they are after all our allies, even if they are Yanks they are our allies. Remember that daughter. Yes, said Brewsie, I keep telling you we have to go back to that Civil War, that long Civil War, that American Civil War and it was a mistake, the South should never have fought, she should have let her slaves be bought off, slavery is wrong whatever you say you cant take any man and take away his wife and children if he dont want them to go and they dont want to go, and sell 'em to somebody else, it's not right. Well, said Jim, nobody in the South talks about that any more. No but all I say the South shouldnt have fought. But, said Donald Paul how about state's rights, that's what they fought for. Well that's just it, said Brewsie, they didnt because if they wanted state's rights the way to have done was to let their slaves be compensated for, and they would then have been so strong politically they would have beaten out on state's rights. I tell you, said Brewsie, the Civil War it was a mistake, and we are all suffering for it. How come, said George, why you suffering. Because, said Brewsie, the South it would have acted as a brake on the North. A kind of dead weight you mean, said Willie. Not necessarily dead, said Jim. No, said Brewsie, not necessarily dead but a counterweight, keeping us from going ahead so fast. Oh dear, sighed the nurse Pauline, oh dear, we have to find a way so they say not to go down to poverty after eighty paltry years of wealth like England did with industrialism. You got a father too who was a Limie, said Willie. I have not my father was good American even if he did believe in Bryan. Who's Bryan, said Willie, I had a father who believed in Single Tax, his name not my father's but Single Tax's name was Henry George, all right Brewsie, you go on when we were yes we were fighting so no colored man would ever again have to say yes ma'am, thank you ma'am. Well that's something I do get kind of tired of that word ma'am. I've heard a lot of Southerners say it an awful lot of times. Ma'am, all right we fought that Civil War so that would not happen any more. Well yes, said Brewsie. Now, said Brewsie, I want you all to listen to me. You listen to me, said Donald Paul, I got something real to say, the trouble with us all, all Americans, they think they are up to date but they are just old-fashioned. Just old-fashioned said Pauline, old-fashioned. My father never said that, and he said almost anything. Well, said Donald Paul, then I move on, not that I am not old-fashioned too like you all, it makes me cry and wish my name was Christopher when I realize how old-fashioned we all are.

Old-fashioned, said Donald Paul, old-fashioned, what we think about war what we think about Germans, we think about 'em just like the last lot did twenty-five years ago, yes we do. We like 'em the Heinies, because they have electric lights and fixings, if there is anything old-fashioned it's that, just old-fashioned. They tell me that the gypsies in Spain had electric lights fifty years ago, why make such a much of it, no we're old-fashioned. We think war is wine, women and song, and heroes, we're just old-fashioned, we believe in industrialism, which makes us poor, we are just bloody old-fashioned, old-fashioned, old-fashioned, old-fashioned. Dont you, said Willie, dont you get so excited, yeah, old-fashioned, yes said Donald Paul just as old-fashioned as a pin-up girl, what's the matter with a pin-up girl. Nothing the matter with a pin-up girl, if only you know it's old-fashioned. Do you know, said Pauline with great solemnity, you know that Stein woman who says things. Yeah we all know, said Willie. Well she said America that is the United States of America is the oldest country in the world because she went into the twentieth century in eighteen ninety, when all the others were way behind and so now the United States of America instead of being young and vigorous is old like a man of fifty, still a chippy chaser cause he feels so young, but conservative, just like we are. Oh my oh my, said Pauline, I am glad my father believed in Bryan. Well, said Janet, do you think then it is kind of right and a mighty good thing they are striking over home and not working, kind of tough on everybody not earning anything but since all the countries want us to work and use up our raw material just to give them things. It's perhaps all right that they are striking. See how they like it those countries that want us to give them everything, see how they like doing without. Fine sister fine, your father certainly did for sure believe in something, it certainly does seem so. But, said Jane, aint it a little bit cutting off your nose to spite your face. Well why do you mind that sister, said Willie, why you so old-fashioned.

It was coming on winter, it always is coming on winter when summer is over and it was coming on winter and even if everybody does eat his supper or dinner at five o'clock, it comes on dark when it comes on winter. Did you ever, said

Christopher, did you ever hear anything so funny. They just kicked out a lot of Heinies out of their houses, told 'em they had to quit in eight hours because they needed just all those houses. And what do you think those Heinies did, instead of packing up and finding some place to roost, they just started in cleaning the house from top to bottom to leave it all nice and clean for us soldiers. Did they really, said Pauline. They really did and do, said Ed. That does make them old-fashioned, said Jim, my God yes. I hope, said Brewsie, that they are not so old-fashioned that they are new-fashioned, that'll never happen to them. Or to us, said Donald Paul. Oh shut up everybody, said Willie, I wish Brock was here, I never did wish for that guy before but he would say something so long-winded it would be funny and my God you need something funny, nothing's funny, nothing, not even the American soldier or a Heine, no nothing's funny nothing, not even the comics no nothing nothing, no nothing nothing is funny.

Chapter Eight

Do you know, said Ed, Brewsie is right he just is, those wine women and song guys, Brewsie's right they dont care about girls not really. It was like this. One of those actor girls and a mighty fine-looking Jane she is, well she went out to dinner with two of us and we asked her to dress up in civvies, so we could feel like we were home, there were two of them and they did, and after dinner it was a nice night and we walked on home, it was awful, lots of G.I.s were drunk, some not so drunk they came up to us and they used the most God-awful language about just anything and there were crowds everywhere and not one single one noticed that there was a mighty good-looking real American girl with us, good as any pin-up they ever pinned up, but because she did not wear a label saying pin-up not one of those fellows not one of them ever noticed that she was there, they thought if they thought, a fellow has picked up a frog, they didnt even notice not any of them that if it was a frog girl it was a mighty good-looking one, no not any of them not one of them noticed, and then you say Brewsie aint right. It's all make believe to give 'em courage and make 'em feel tough, they dont really notice a thing not a thing when it is a girl.

How, said Willie, can they notice when the part of them that aint drunk is worrying about jobs. How I hate that word job, said Brewsie. You're right, said Willie, you're right to hate that word, hate it good and plenty, but you can afford to hate it Brewsie, fellows like you dont need a job you just live, everybody's got to see to it you live and live you do but fellows like us, well we got to have jobs, what you want us to do, nobody's going to feed us, you just watch them not feed us dont we know, no we got to have jobs, talk all you like and talk is good I like talk I like to listen to you Brewsie, but when we get home and dont wear this brown any more we got to have a job, job, job. Yes job. I know, said Brewsie, I know, I know Willie. Yes I know, you got to have a job, and it's all right but it's not all right, see here let me tell you about jobs. Some have to have jobs, some have got to be employed and be employees, but not so many Willie. Listen to me not so many, when everybody is employed. God, said Willie, if they only just could not be employed. I aint forgot that depression, no not yet. Yes but Willie, said Brewsie, that's what I want to say, industrialism which produces more than anybody can buy and makes employees out of free men makes 'em stop thinking, stop feeling, makes 'em all feel alike. I tell you Willie it's wrong. All right, said Willie, it's wrong. I'll say it's wrong, I aint so sure I dont think it's wrong, and there is that old man Kaiser, making poor California come all over industrial. I liked my California, said Willie, yes I did like my California. Yes I know you liked your California, said Brewsie, yes I know. But listen Willie now we are alone let's go all over this and get it straight. Will you let me. You know, said Willie, I never did think I could ever be homesick for that man Brock but I am, how it would kind of cheer me up just to hear his foolishness about how his father and his mother or is it his mother grew their flowers, grew them on their own graves perhaps but it would be a kind of a comfort to hear him, yes and how they moved from one house to another. Well go on Brewsie, go on straighten things out. I'm sure straight is something that looks funny, but go on, let's straighten it out. Well, said Brewsie, it's about this industrialism. You know, said Willie, what you make industrialism sound like, you make it sound like chewing gum. You chew and chew but it dont feed you, it's got a kind of a taste but that is all there is to it no substance. Have I got it right, kind of. Industrialism is like chewing gum. Well go on Brewsie I am here to hear.

Let's go all over it carefully from the beginning, said Brewsie.

Do you know, said Jo, a funny thing happened to me, I just took me a room in a hotel you know one of those little hotels in a little street and I was standing in the doorway and a Negro soldier came along and he said hello to me and I said hello to him and at the end of that little street there came down another street two M.P.s and nothing happened, said Jo.

Well listen, said Brewsie, we got to talk this over earnestly, we got to use all our common sense and see what there is to do. Well if there is anything to do can we do it, said Jo. No we cant do it, said Willie. The thing to do, said Brewsie is to use all our common sense. Well I got plenty of that, said Willie, go ahead Brewsie.

If, said Brewsie, industrialism is wrong not because of this or not because of that but because in a very little while it makes the country going all industrial poor, well then it aint common sense to go on being industrial. That's right, said Jo. Yeah that's common sense, said Willie. Well listen, said Brewsie, it's so, let's go over it again, to see how the countries go poor which are industrial and how that is inevitable. Now look at France she never went industrial and she is rich. Now is she now, said Willie, if she is, then I guess I just as leave be poor even if I have to be industrial. The frogs. Yes but you see France dont get poor because she makes luxuries, and you cant be industrial and make luxuries because once industry makes luxuries it aint a luxury any more. Yeah, said Willie, I know that's it just like that, dont we all spend all we got right here in this France, dont we, and we dont spend it nowhere else. Yes it's good sense that, but cause we spend does that make her rich. Yeah course it does, said Jo, because what she sells dont cost her hardly anything to make, while when it's industrial so many got to be paid and so much raw material it makes you poor. It dont, said Willie, seem to make sense. I know it's all true but all the same just the same it does not seem to make sense. Just the same, said Brewsie, it does make sense, now listen. Here come the sisters, you might as well wait till they get here. Yes, said Pauline, here we are, now tell us. Yes, said Jane, tell us tell us tell us why, no I dont mean to be funny. Perhaps you're not funny said Jimmie. Well anyway we all understand when you say, said Janet, that we Americans, that is to say that we are the last of the countries that went industrial in the nineteenth century who have not yet gone poor, but you say we will. I wonder, said Jo, why now everybody that is all of us call America the States, in the old days that is before now, Americans always call it America or the United States, it was only foreigners who called it the States, and now just as natural as anything we each one and every one of us calls it the States just like some foreigners like the Limies used to. I wonder, said Pauline, I wonder does that really mean anything does that mean the beginning that we are beginning to feel poor, call it the States instead of America, do you think, said Pauline, do you think it does really mean anything. Everything means something, said Donald Paul, dont you know that, havent you heard, that's what's called psychoanalysis, dont you know that, that says anything always means something. And dont you know, said Jimmie, that's true in science too, anything means something. Perhaps, said Donald Paul, something means anything, perhaps it's more like that. Ah you all talk too much, said Willie, give Brewsie a chance. Brewsie is sort of timid, give Brewsie a chance. What we all here for, we are all here to listen to Brewsie, give Brewsie a chance, you go ahead Brewsie. Now before you talk any more I want to ask something, said Jane, is there going to be any answer because if there isnt going to be any answer, I think I'll go back. Is there going to be any answer. Is there going to be any answer Brewsie, the sister wants to know, she's very polite but she certainly does want to know. Yes, said Brewsie, I do think there is an answer. I am kind of coming to it, of course it has to be that we have to take care of ourselves. Well, said Jimmie, there is one thing not anybody has any doubt about whatever he thinks that if we dont take care of ourselves, no industrialist boss, any name you like to put to them not any one of them is going out of his way to take care of us, take care of ourselves is right, take care, take care, all right we'll take care but how, striking is no good if anybody is poor, wanting more work is no good, if working more work uses up our raw material and makes us all poor, how in hell you going to answer the sister Brewsie, and answer me too Brewsie, and yourself too, how you going to answer us all or any of us just how can you, if you are right and my God it does kind of seem so, the more we work the poorer our country gets and the more depressions we have. What's the answer Brewsie, dont keep us on the anxious seat, if you got an answer my God dont keep it to yourself, give it to us. I say Brewsie give it to us. Well, said Brewsie, yes but do you mind all of you if I begin all over again from the beginning. I guess the boys are right, said Pauline, we cant help ourselves if we do mind, and we do mind, we'd like the answer now yes we would but all right, go on begin begin anywhere but goodness gracious do begin. Be quiet sister, said

Willie, you make him kind of nervous and if he gets too nervous everything kind of stops and if everything stops he'll never get going again and then where will we be, what will happen, we'll just be poor, poor, poor white trash. Perhaps, said Donald Paul it will be the niggers who get rich, I suppose even in a poor country somebody has just got to be rich. Not always, said Willie, look at the Limies. My father, said Janet. Yeah your father, said Willie. But let Brewsie talk, see he is opening his mouth, not good and wide yet, but let him tell us how to be useful but poor. No, said Brewsie, how to be hopeful though poor. At that, said Jo, at that, hope is something. But, said Jane, if we had not been industrial the way we were how we would have won this war. Did we win it, said Willie. Yes, said Jane, we did, we did win this war. Well then, said Donald Paul, with that behind us we can settle down to be poor but honest. Not so much on the honest, said Pauline, ever hear about stealing. Stealing what, said Jo. Go anywhere in the occupied country and what does everybody do. They steal. Sure they do, said Willie, and then they gamble it away and they go home poor but honest. Poor it is, said Jo. I know. Good God, said Jimmie, everybody shut up. Go ahead Brewsie, how about what the sister says, how about that winning the war, how about it, what's the answer Brewsie, what's the answer.

Chapter Nine

LISTEN Willie, said Brewsie, you kind of think I go over it all too much, you're like anybody with a story, you want the middle to go faster but that's it Willie, that's it, it is going too fast, got to slow it down, got, sure then you want the end, but Willie there isn't any end, you got to go slower, sure there is an answer. I kind of feel the answer, sometimes I know I know the answer, but wait Willie, wait till I tell you all about it all over, perhaps if I tell you all about it all over you'll come to the answer too, not an answer but a way to go on, wait Willie while I tell you all about it from the beginning. I got nothing to do but wait, said Willie, not just right here, not anything to do but wait, but when we get back and then hustle. Yes but Willie, that is what you dont see it is not hustle you got to slow down, Willie, that is what has to happen, it has to slow down, when you get back you have to pioneer, and pioneering is slow work. Pioneer what, said Willie. Pioneer, said Brewsie, listen to me Willie, I am so earnest, listen to me Willie. I said Henry, before I came into the army I taught the seven year olders in public schools. Where, said Jo. In western New York state. Was that interesting, said Jo. Well yes it was sometimes it was almost exciting. And, said Jo, are you going back to it. Well no, said Henry, not if I can get a job over here. What, said Willie, you want to stay in this lousy Europe. Well yes in a way, said Henry, you see my mind's confused, and so I want to stay. Willie, muttering mind mind, confused, get a mind, get it confused, I suppose, said Willie, you have been listening to Brewsie. No I havent, said Henry. Who's Brewsie. Who's Brewsie, said Willie, that's Brewsie, well how did you get your mind confused if you didnt listen to Brewsie. Well I guess, said Henry, I got my mind confused because I just cant see any way not to have my mind confused that's all, see here Willie, you see it's about that employee mentality we're all getting to have, we're just a lot of employees, obeying a boss, with no mind of our own and if it goes on where is America, I say if it goes on, where is America, no sir, said Henry, no sir, I want to pioneer. Ah, said Willie,

you been listening to Brewsie. I have not been listening to
Brewsie. I dont know Brewsie, never saw him, less heard him,
you listen to me Willie. You see I been in England, and that
country is poor poor, and it's poor because it went industrial
and the people lost their pep they went employee-minded and
they manufactured more than they could sell and they speeded
it up, and they went bust and I am kind of scared about going
home. You know what Churchill said he did not want to pre-
side over the downfall of the British empire. Well I dont want
to see us get more employee-minded, employed by the big
factory owners, employed by the strikers, employed by the
government, employed by the labor unions. Well, said Willie,
who the hell do you want should employ you who the hell
do you want should give you a job. I dont want a job, said
Henry. I want to pioneer. Oh hell, said Willie, you make me
tired, you been listening to Brewsie, and anyway you want to
get a job over here. How that, you a pioneer. Well that's
different, said Henry. How different, said Willie. Well it is
different, said Henry, because anyway there are a few of us
and so we can forget we are just employed, anyway that's
something, said Henry. You get the hell out of here you been
listening to Brewsie and at that, Brewsie he would never be
so silly as thinking of getting a job over here was pioneering.
Come over here Brewsie, explain to this guy what pioneering
is. I dont know yet, said Brewsie, I am just thinking. Well let's
all think, said Henry. No, said Willie, you let Brewsie do the
thinking, that's the way we are in this outfit, we let Brewsie
do the thinking. Willie, said Brewsie, Yes, said Henry, that
just shows how employee you are Willie. Oh get the hell out
of here, said Willie. Yeah it's funny, said Jimmie, the only real
pioneering there is in America these days is done by Negroes.
They're pioneering, they find new places, new homes, new
lives, new ways and they more and more own something,
funny, said Jimmie, kind of queer and funny. I dont like it,
said Jo. No, said Jimmie. No I dont like it, said Jo, it makes
me kind of nervous. Does it, said Jimmie, well it doesnt make
me nervous, I guess when you come from the South anything
like that dont make you kind of nervous. I come from Georgia. Yes I know, said Jo.

Here we are, said Pauline. So you are sister, said Willie. And

what are you talking about. We are talking about that, said
Willie, what do you think we're talking about women and
chickens and yellow butterflies and potatoes, no we just aint
talking about them we're talking about that, of course I am
not talking I only listen and it never listens good. Yes, said
Pauline, but I do want to know. You'll know, said Willie, any
moment of the day or night they talk and they always talk
about it. About what, said Pauline. About it, about what it is,
about how about it, about what is it about, about, what are
you going to do about it, about, how about it, you just wait
sister you just wait, not that you really have to wait, we got a
new guy who talks, his name, what is that guy's name Jo, oh
yes his name is, there I lost it again, it dont make no difference
all I know is his name is not Brewsie. You better listen to
Brewsie, I tell you you better listen to Brewsie. My uncle, said
Pauline. Did he believe in Bryan too, said Jo. No, said Pauline,
he did not, he was one of the directors of the legion in our
town, and he often told me what trouble he had with the last
returned soldiers. When they came back to work on their jobs,
their bosses complained, they were no good, they were
dreamy. Dreamy, said Jane, is a nice way to put it, they must
have been polite bosses. I should say that all soldiers and all
ex-soldiers come home lazy, that's what I should say, said
Jane. Jane, said Janet, be polite, remember you are talking to
soldiers and future ex-soldiers. Well it's so all right, said Janet,
Sister, said Jo, if you say it it's so but the worst of it is, said
Jo, it's so even if you dont say so. I know, said Pauline, my
uncle always said that was not all. He said during the depression he tried to help all the legionnaires and he had ground
plowed up so that they could grow food, and they gave them
seeds and fertilizer and tools and everything and they mostly
said, like the electrician, I am not going to be a farmer, I am
an electrician and I'll stay electrician until an electrician job
comes my way. I know, said Janet, I know that's the way they
are in our town. Well some of them used to go home to work
in the gardens and so they started a cinema just where they
all took the cars and had a special big attraction just when
they might be going home to work in their gardens and so
they went to the cinema instead of going home to work in
their gardens. That's what my father says. Your father is a

Limie isnt he sister. He certainly is one, said Janet and proud to be one. Poor and proud that's what Brewsie would say. Well it's better to be poor and proud than just poor as your Brewsie says you Yankees will be if you dont watch out. Here fellows, said Willie, here we got another one talking, it's catching, you better look out Brewsie, soon there wont be a thing you can tell them. Not at all, said Brewsie, not at all I always keep ahead. Now listen everybody listen. I want to tell you everything all over again and you'll see what I mean. Brewsie, said Willie, if you dont watch out you'll be as tedious as Brock, and that's something. Listen, said Brewsie. I been thinking. Well anyway Brewsie Brock never did begin that way. Go ahead Brewsie we're listening. I wonder, said Jane, could you explain just what President Roosevelt meant when he said that there had to be sixty million jobs, just what did he mean to do, of course we want to know because that would mean women too, just what did he mean to do, can you tell just what did he mean to do. Roosevelt, said Donald Paul, was a benevolent despot and I hate all despots, and benevolent ones are worse than the others because nobody wants to hurt their feelings by telling them so. Yes, said Jane, I know but all the same he just must have meant something. What, said Jo. My father always said so, what is the difference between the New Deal and Communism. Nothing much, said Brewsie, that's why I have to begin all over again because neither of them could be without industrialism, any more than trade unions and capitalists, now that's just it, everything is all right if you dont take too much of it. Like drink and venereal disease, said Willie. Yes that's just it, said Jo, but you see the way I understand it industrialism is not like drink, you can take a little of that the other, well they dig it deep they dig it for one another, and you just cant help falling in and once you're in you cant get out, that's it Brewsie. Not exactly, said Brewsie, not exactly. Well what is it then, said Pauline, what is it, we've got to know. Well not today sister, said Willie, you didnt really got to know today, we got to get home and get a job first and it dont really make all that difference knowing about it today. But it does it does, said Pauline, I have a kind of a feeling and we all have I know we all have if he dont begin to make it begin to come clear today it will never be any better, and he is right, our own dear beautiful strong rich country will go down like England did. Not on your life, said Willie, not on your life. Yeah, said Pauline, that's easy, be the strong white man, who never can be brought down, that's all right if you had never left home, but you have left home, you're scared, you're thinking about everything and way back deep down you're scared, scared. I know I am scared too, here I am scared, said Willie, sure you're scared, said Pauline, and he's got to tell us what to do. But, said Brewsie, you got me scared, how can I tell you what to do, I can tell you what's wrong, I can kind of tell you what's going to happen, and it will, said Jane, yes it will. All right, said Willie, it will. I know, said Brewsie, logic is logic, facts are facts I know I am right but how to get going away from what everybody has gotten the habit of thinking is the only way to do, kind of swinging a big truck around, said Jo, and making it come back around a corner. No, said Brewsie, not that, but to find the way that looks the same and is different or find the way that looks different and is the same. Oh dear, said Pauline, we got to hurry up and find out because we're all to be home for Christmas. Does anybody know how old Christmas is, said Willie. Of course, said Pauline, of course read your Bible and you'd know it too. Well, said Brewsie, I begin to know one thing, if industrialism makes a country poor and makes the people of that country poor because they all have employee minds, that is job minds, we got to get on top of industrialism and not have it on top of us. How come, said Jo. Well, said Brewsie, it sounds harder than it is. How do you get on top of anything that is on top of you, first you got to break it off you, said Jo. Oh dear, said Pauline, fighting is so natural.

Chapter Ten

YOU GOT to say it Brewsie, said Willie, you cant just cam-
ouflage it, you cant just cover it over, you cant just whisper it, you got to say it and you got to say it out loud. Yes I
know Willie, said Brewsie, but you cant say it out loud until
it's there to be said. Oh yes you can, said Willie, you'd like
to whisper it Brewsie, yes you do just whisper it, but you just
got to say it out loud. Yes Willie, said Brewsie, but you got
to have it out loud inside you and I tell you I've got it but I
havent got it out loud. I've got some of it out loud but not
all of it out loud, give me more time Willie, give me time. It
aint time, said Willie, it's the way, out loud is the way, got to
make a noise, not whisper, said Willie, not whisper. You got
to. I know, said Brewsie. I had a little frog kid on my knee,
said Jo, and he was very little and I told him to say dog and
he learned to say it so quick you'd think he never had talked
French, was just learning to talk to say dog. Like anything he
said dog, and he didnt forget it, either, he said it again, dog
just like that. I guess any kid would, said Jimmie. Well, said
Jo, a lady came along and she said is he yours and I said no
he's a frog kid but he does say dog, and she said had I one
of my own and I said no I been in the army too long and she
said how old are you and I said I was twenty-three and she
said I did look younger but of course if I had been in the
army four years, and I said lady make it five and I said this
frog kid says dog, and it did say dog, just like that. I know,
said Brewsie. Yes, said Jimmie, you know what they all talking
about now at home, they're talking about free trade. My God,
said Donald Paul have we come to that. I know, said Jane,
my father. And sure he was a Limie and he knew where free
trade brings you. Yes, said Jane but he knows more than that,
when you know you're going to get poor then you say free
trade, when nobody wants to buy them you say free trade, kid
yourselves, kid yourselves, the factory owners kid themselves
so as to make their workmen believe and the workmen kid
themselves with strikes so as to make the owners think they
would be working if the men werent striking so they all kid

themselves and they kid each other, and does anybody believe. Yeah, said Willie, that's what's so funny about kidding everybody believes, a bigger and better country, a bigger and better industry, a bigger and better war, yeah, sure everybody believes when they kid, they gotta believe, otherwise everybody would stop working. And wouldnt it, said Pauline, wouldnt it just be beautiful if everybody stopped working, and just went out walking, and ate a sundae or an ice-cream soda and went on walking, and then just came home, and had doughnuts and a coke, and then they came in and sing a little and go to bed. How beautiful, said Pauline. Yeah, said Willie, beautiful is the word. I love, said Willie, I love that word beautiful, yes sister I certainly surely do love that word beautiful. Listen, said Ed, listen. I know I just do know. Listen. That sister aint so phony as she sounds, listen. You see like this, when factories work hard and lots of money moves around, then there are chain stores and mail-order houses and little business cant live, cause they cant make enough money to compete, but when the factories they dont work, and everybody just walks around like sister says, why then chain stores and mail-order places go bust, there is too much overhead if there aint a big volume of business, and that's the time for a new start of little business, so that's it boys that's it, if we can stall going home till there is a depression, then we can start our little businesses like we all want to do. How about it everybody, dont that listen good. Say, said Willie, say, it aint Brock come to life again and being different, is it, does anything that guy says make sense or does it. Well I think it does, said Pauline, I certainly do think it does make sense. I wonder, said Willie, Brewsie, where are you Brewsie, did you hear him, where's Brewsie. Brewsie had to go away and think, said Donald Paul. Not Brewsie, said Willie, when Brewsie thinks he stays where he always is, and he always thinks and so he always stays where he is. Brewsie, said Willie, I am here, said Brewsie. Is there, said Willie, any sense to what that guy says. Yes there is, said Brewsie.

Chapter Eleven

I KNOW, said John. What you know, said Jo. I know, said John that I am not just tired of everything not tired of everything. Well that's something to know, said Willie. I know, said John, I am pretty young and I might maybe being so young be just tired of everything, I know what you fellows talk about we all know what Brewsie explains and we all know he's right, that industrialism business makes us all job men with no way of choosing anything, and it'll make the country poor and everybody in it, dont I know, I tell you I know, didnt I see it work, in my family just we we worked out but I know it's right, industrialism makes industrials poor individuals and makes a country poor and I know we're old-fashioned, dont I know all the fellows admire the Heinies, and why, because the Heinies are the only things on this earth that are more old-fashioned than we Americans, and so we kind of suck up to the Heinies to keep 'em in countenance and they suck up to us to kind of keep themselves in countenance, just the most two old-fashioned countries in the world, the least up-to-date in the world, so far behind, they might almost catch up with themselves but they dont and why because they know it but they cant dare hear themselves say it, do I know all this, sure I know all this, I know it's so, and yet and why, well I aint all just tired of everything and sometimes I do almost know why. Dont let anybody stop you telling John, go on, said Willie. Well this is the only thing that kind of comforts me. Come there are lots who know it's all true and wont say, and then there are lots who really know and do say, now I dont believe no I dont that in those countries England, Germany, Japan, no I dont I dont believe a whole young generation knew what was wrong, and were not violent about it, no not at all violent not at all violent, they just knew, that's all they just knew, they just knew it's so. That's the thing that just dont make me just tired of everything, that the big lot of us know all this is so, and they aint a bit violent not a bit, they just know, they just know that this is all so. Yes, said Jo, yes but then what comes next. Does anything come next when you just aint tired of everything, said John. Well, said Willie, that almost doesnt sound like a question, I'll go get Brewsie. High Brewsie, said Willie, come here Brewsie, somebody got to say something. Where are you Brewsie. He aint there, said Jimmie. Aint he, said Willie. No he aint, said Jimmie.

I dont think, said Ed, that any G.I. would like a Heinie if he were all alone with a Fraulein or a Heinie, he likes Heinies when he's part of a crowd not when the Heinie is although that's all right too but the G.I.s. When there are a plenty of G.I.s, they like the Heinies, now you know if there was only one G.I. alone with some frogs or Mademoiselles he'd like it better than if that same G.I. would be just all alone with Heinies and Frauleins, I kind of sometimes think it would be like that. Well, said John, aint it, that G.I. likes Heinies because like them they like to be a crowd. I heard one G.I. tell a frog that France was too God damn full of Frenchmen, but crowds of Heinies, well do crowds of Heinies make a G.I. feel like a strong man, well it's all funny anyway but I dont care, said John, I just dont care. All I care about is that I just aint just all tired of everything. And that's good thing too, said Willie.

But what we gonna do, said Ed, not about Heinies, Heinies is just dirt, you know, said Peter another thing is funny and that is fluffy food, not chow, you dont mean, said Willie, I see no fluff in chow. Yeah, I do, said Peter. We love sweets like babies, we dont love no lumps of cheese, and tough bread, no we just like to eat soft stuff, soft bread, soft ice-cream, soft chocolate, soft mush, soft potatoes, soft jam, and peanut butter, we dont except at a little meat we dont really chew. Well and if we dont, said Jo. Soft eats make soft men, said Peter. We soft, are we, said Willie. Well aint we, said Peter. Well perhaps we are, said Willie. How soft, said Jo. Too soft, said Ed. Well where is Brewsie, said Willie, where is Brewsie. I'd even like to hear a sister speak up just for a change. Where is that Brewsie. Listen to me, said Brewsie, although really I havent anything really to say. We're listening, said Willie, with a sigh of relief.

Chapter Twelve

D<small>O WE</small>, said Brewsie, that is to say do they know just who we are while we wear brown and if they do know just who we are does that give us distinction. Now, said Willie, you're talking funny and when you talk funny you know how old I am. How old are you Willie, said Jo, you know, said Jo, they used to say be your age and I kind of wonder sometimes are we that age, everybody says we're sad, we know we're lonesome, how old do you have to be to be sad, and how young can you be to be lonesome. Yes, said Donald Paul, everybody is talking funny, is it because perhaps isnt that a nice word, redeployed, redeployed. Hell, said Willie, rede- ployed it is, they make it like that because they wont be re- sponsible if we have a job or not. Dont you know, said John, that Brewsie dont like that word job. He never said, said Jo, that he liked that word redeployed. Funny, said Donald Paul, very funny, and sometimes nobody knows how funny it is, redeployed. I know, said Jim, I met a man who was born in Mississippi, he couldnt read and write. And can he now, said John. He just can and as good as I can. Well well, said Donald Paul, well well. Dont you get funny, said Jimmie, if you get very funny, oh hell, said Willie, let's go home. What home, Heaven, said John. No not Heaven, said Willie, just home just redeployed just home. Sometimes, said Jo, I am scared. Some- times, said Willie. Just sometimes, said Jimmie. Why does any- body want to be scared all the time. Just the same, said Donald Paul, what are you going to do. I, said Brewsie, I been thinking. Oh, said Willie, that's what makes me all here, go on Brewsie, think. My God Brewsie think, if you dont think Brewsie. Yeah, said Jo, you always want somebody to do your thinking for you. Well why not, said Jimmie, why not, said Jo, why not. Oh of course why not think, Brewsie, if you can, it's kind got near redeployment, Brewsie, think Brewsie, think. My God yes Brewsie think, we're getting older and older Brewsie, just think. Yeah, said Jimmie, and after all does it do any good. Yes it does, said John, it keeps us talking. And does that do any good, said Jo. Yes it does, said John, it does, we'd go crazy if Brewsie didnt think, crazy. Well, said John, if you dont like that word redeployment, if that does make you kind of nervous, how about that word reconversion, how do you like that all you, how do you. That, said Donald Paul, that is only a word, reconversion turns out to be only a word. A third of a word, said Jimmie, it might have made you feel like a bird, but it only turned out to be a third of a word. I know, said Brewsie, I told you so, you remember I told you so, I said remember that those industrialists know as well as I do that there arent any foreign markets and do they want to start, no they dont, so they let them strike and so it aint their fault, the others and everything is as it is. It's lousy, said Willie, yes it is. More lousy than foreigners Willie, said Donald Paul. Almost not yet quite but well no not that not as lousy as foreigners no no not that, never that, foreigners are lousy, everything is lousy but foreigners they are all lousy. It's funny, said John, when I see one of those frogs with one of those large loaves of bread under his arm, I know he is going to have good eats, you cant not not with that bread. Yeah, said Willie, I like that bread, And I like the cafés, said Jo, they are real comfortable, winter and summer they are real comfortable. And, said Jimmie, it's kind of nice when you are riding along in a truck to see all that landscape and no billboard. I kind of like billboards, said Willie, it is one of the things I do kind of like, said Willie. Brewsie, said John, you know I am young, I got no points, I aint been over long and when I get out I kind of think I'll stay over here a while. But Brewsie tell me if I was not so young and had more points and was not going to stay over a while and I was going home what could I do about it, tell me Brewsie, they say you can, tell me Brewsie. Well, said Brewsie, what is it we got that nobody else has got. The atomic bomb, said Jo. Not so got, said Jimmie, they all say not so got. All right then not the atomic bomb, said Jo, tell us Brewsie what we got that nobody else has got. Well, said Brewsie, I think we still have got it, we like to pioneer. How can you pioneer when there aint no wilderness any more. Shut up everybody, said Willie, here come the sisters, seems to me more than ever today but there is that cute one they call Pauline. Well go on anyway, said John, how about how you can pioneer when there aint any wilderness.

Aint there any wilderness, said Pauline, you just go home and look around, there's lots of wilderness, around where I live there is all wilderness, north south east and west, and where is it you live sister, said Willie. Oh I just live, said Pauline. All right then, said Jo, you just live. Well can anyone pioneer in that wilderness of yours. Why not, said Pauline. Anybody can say why not, said Willie, but do you mean it sister, can anybody pioneer where you live. Yes they can if they got any guts and dont expect it to to be easy. All right sister, said Willie. Now listen to me, said Janet, I think he is right about that pioneer thing, you got to break down what has been built up, that's pioneering. Why not, said Jo. Yes why not, said Janet, I say if you all are ready to break down what has been built up, well then that is pioneering, here in Europe they broke down what they had built up and now they are all just as busy as anything pioneering and they are kind of happy doing it. Not so happy, said Jimmie, not by their looks. Well anyway, said Janet, they got a lot to do and when you have got a lot to do you are kind of happy and pioneering and we well we havent anything to do not until what we built up has broken down and we can pioneer. But sister, said Willie, you're funny, well I dont want to say all I think because I was brought up to be nice to a lady but what do you want, do you want us to drop our atomic bombs on ourselves, is that what you want, so we can go out and pioneer, is that the idea. Well yes kind of, said Janet. I get you, said Willie. And you get me Willie. Oh, Lord, give me Brock, I never thought I would pray to the good Lord to give me back Brock but here I am I am praying to the good Lord to give me back Brock. He was awful, but he did sound all right compared to this pioneering idea, he certainly did. But, said John, let's begin again, we've all got kind of funny. Not so funny, said Willie. Well you see, said Brewsie, you do know that we cant keep all together a million or so of us all over our country because in the next war. Oh God, said Willie, the next war, any war we might just as well. Well yes, said Janet, we might just as well think like the Germans, peace is only in between wars and not wars in between peace. Well, said Donald Paul, you see last time everybody thought there was going to be peace and there was war, why not this time everybody think there is going to be war and maybe there will be peace. Maybe, said Willie, But, said John, after all there is our country we got a country, let's think about it we got to think about it, let's think. Well, said Willie, Where is Brewsie. Yes, said Jo, where is Brewsie. Yes, said John, where is Brewsie. Yes, said Janet, where is he. Where is, said Pauline. Where is Brewsie, said Willie. Yes where is he, said Donald Paul.

Chapter Thirteen

WILLIE, said Brewsie, it's serious. Sure it's serious, said Willie, what. Our country, said Brewsie. Sure, it's serious, said Willie. You mean pioneering, she was cute that Pauline about wilderness and pioneering, didnt you think she was cute Brewsie, didnt you. She is cute Brewsie that Pauline. I guess I'll like to see her real often. Yes I would Brewsie, but I guess I will and find out more about her pioneering, she is cute Brewsie. Willie, said Brewsie, it's serious. Yes I know Brewsie, yes I know. All right it's serious but you dont any of you say what to do you all say what's the matter and that everything is the matter but you dont say what to do, thinking is what you do Brewsie, but living is what we all got to do, now what are we going to do, how we going to live. Well, said Brewsie, if I am right they mostly are not going to live. Sure you're right Brewsie but they mostly are going to live, that's it, that's the funny part of it they mostly do go on living, look at the Limies, you're right how poor they are and all and once they were so rich and all but they dont die, they just keep on all of them just going on living, that's the trouble with everything Brewsie, that's the real trouble with everything, somehow everybody just does keep on living, look at everybody over here, by rights they ought all to be all dead, all of them over and over again dead, all of them and they aint Brewsie, they aint at all dead, far from it, from being all dead, they seem from the looks of them to be more of them living than ever were living before, so many more of them, just look at them everywhere is lousy with them and they all ought to be dead but they dont die, that is not more than natural, some more but not really enough more to make it really matter. No Brewsie that's really the trouble with all the thinking that's the real trouble, sure you're right and some get rich and more get poor, and some go ahead and some go behind but all the same they all go on living and so Brewsie, well that is it, sure you're right and if we go on like this well yes we will get poor like the Limies got poor somebody else will get rich like we were rich. Sure Brewsie you're right but

762

in a kind of way we wont die, we'll just all somehow go on living, that's it, Brewsie, that's it, that is what is the matter with thinking, that's it, no matter what does happen everybody somehow goes on living, and there always seem to be lots more of them lots more than anybody needs but they all go on living. Yes, said Donald Paul, that is what William James called the will to live. Yes it is, said Willie, I dont know the guy but that's what it is they just do go on living, you cant kill them off. Dont you make any mistake about that atom bombs or potato bugs or concentration camps or religion or poverty or no jobs or education, it does not make it go any other way, they just do go on living, they dont disappear. The lousy foreigners how many of them God knows how many of them there are, more than ever, I never saw them before but I certainly am fixed to know that there are more of them living than ever, more than ever, that's what I say more of them than ever.

Chapter Fourteen

Yes, Willie, said Brewsie, yes, but you got to think any-how. Can you, said Willie, when you are all kind of set that way, can you really make yourself go on when you are all kind of set to get backward. I been reading a book, said John. Well well, said Willie, and here they come that is here they are. Listen sister this guy has been reading a book. Well and if he has so have I, said Janet, I've been reading a book about Susan B. Anthony. And who, said Jo, might that dame be. She is the one, said Janet, that made women vote and have the right to money they earn and to their children, before she came along women were just like Negroes, before they were freed from slavery. You can say what you like but she was pretty wonderful. And if she was, said Willie. Yes I know, said Janet, but the real thing is that she started to do all this be-cause of the depression. My God what depression, said Jo. The depression of eighteen thirty-eight. Now who of all of you ever knew about that not even Brewsie. You know, said Janet, we all think we had the one and only depression, but they began having them in eighteen thirty-eight. Just think of that over a hundred years ago when America first started. Well, said Jimmie, but there was no industrialism then, just wilderness and pioneering, hey Pauline. No, said Janet, and that is what is funny, there was industrialism and it com-menced so hard and they had wildcat banking and poof, up went the industries. Nobody had any money to buy just like now. Her father he was well-to-do, he went bust, she had to go to work and she found how little a woman had of her own, a married woman couldnt even have her own money and so she began to make a noise. Now, said Janet, we got to make a noise, a loud noise, a big noise, we got to be heard. Who's we, said Willie, We are all we, said Janet, all of our age all together, we got to make a noise. My name is Lawrence, said Lawrence. Now is it, said Jo, how do you know it is. Well it is, said Lawrence, and I got something to say, she's right, not that it'll do anything, but she's right. The trouble with us is we are being ruled by tired middle-aged people, tired business men, the kind who need pin-ups, you know that kind, only they can afford the originals, not the ones we get, well I tell you, said Lawrence, I tell you, here in Europe they are ruled by the young or by the old, and by God they're right, young ones can make fools of themselves that's all right, and old ones if they are old enough to be really old they got the energy of being old, but I tell you and my name is Lawrence and I tell you old and young are better than tired middle-aged, nothing is so dead dead-tired, dead every way as middle-aged, have we the guts to make a noise while we are still young before we get middle-aged, tired middle-aged, no we havent, said Willie, and you know it, no we havent, said Willie.

Chapter Fifteen

WHAT's the matter, said Willie. Well it kind of makes me cry, said Pauline, What makes you cry, said Willie, well the way you said we hadnt guts enough to make ourselves heard, it does make me cry. Yeah but have we, said Willie, Well, said Pauline, it does kind of make me cry.

Chapter Sixteen

WILLIE, said Brewsie. Well, said Willie, it is true, said Brewsie, industrialism cant put on a brake itself, nothing quiets it down but a catastrophe. How could anything quiet it down, said Willie, do you think anybody knows when they got enough, nobody, said Willie, I tell you Brewsie, nobody ever knows when they got enough. Some do, said John, my mother always did, nothing ever could tempt her to eat a bit more than was enough, she just never did, and she never would run around more than was enough, no Willie, some do have self-control, some do, really Willie, some do. All right, said Willie, some do, but not enough to make any real difference, that's what I mean. Well, said Lawrence, I told you my name was Lawrence and I got something to say, everybody in America they think if perfection is good more perfection is better. I never want to go back, there is no sense to it, none, I never want to go back. Oh get the hell out of here, said Willie, I know your kind, everything looks good to you except where you belong. All right all right, said Lawrence, all right, I never want to go back. All right, said Willie, dont go back. That's what I am going to do, said Lawrence, I am not going back. All right, said Willie, you're not going back, all right nothing stops anything except hell, well all right, and we got to go back, and what's going to stop anything. But in a kind of a way, said John, nothing has begun. All right, said Willie, and that's right, nothing has begun. Listen, said Brewsie, listen. All right, said Willie, I am so sore, I just could do nothing but listen. All right, said Brewsie, listen, it's true all I said is true all I am saying is true, Willie's right, there arent enough of them got any self-control to stop anything, whether it's drinking or eating or industrialism, or spending. Oh come off, said Jimmie, lots of people got lots of self-control, lots of people have, I even got some of it myself. All right, said Willie, all right then you have and then what. It aint, said Donald Paul, it aint self-control that matters it's what happens that matters, and as nothing is going to happen nothing at all it's that what matters. Now, said Willie, you're just talking funny.

I am not, said Donald Paul, or if I am and perhaps I am then it means something it means a lot, listen. Oh let Brewsie talk. No, said Donald Paul, Brewsie dont know about this, we all go home no reconversion, no nothing, we kind of dont know what's happening, not a depression, this time just nothing. Well, said Janet, here I am, I heard you. What's nothing. Nothing, said Donald Paul, is when it all stops. Can it, said John. It can, said Donald Paul. Well then, said Jo, what we all going to do we all are there, what we going to do. Well that's it, said Lawrence, some they just kind of will act as if it was just the way it always has been, but most of us we'll know, we'll know that there is just nothing doing nothing. Oh Willie, said Pauline. Now listen to me, said Jimmie, you just listen to me. I got nothing to say but you all just listen to me. All right, said Janet, all right. Well now it's like this, it does kind of scare you that's what he is trying to do, and we, well. We all of us we do scare awful easy, that's what I want to say, we all of us do scare awful easy. Dont everybody scare easy, said John. No I think, said Jimmie, that we kind of scare more easy than lots of others. Because we are spoiled babies, said Janet. I guess that's so, said Jo. Oh dear, said Pauline, I am that scared, well no I am not, I am not scared, I am going home and I am not scared, are you scared Janet. Well in a way not, said Janet. All right, said Jimmie, we're not scared. All right, said Willie, anyway it's all right. Let's talk, said John. Yes let's, said Jo. I know, said Pauline, you mean it's going to be like a dust-bowl. Yes, said Jimmie, that's it, it's going to be like a dust-bowl. Oh my God, said Jo, I live there. Sure you live there, said Willie, that's what I say anybody can live even in a dust-bowl, that's what I say. Well are we going to live in a dust-bowl, said Pauline. Yes, said Willie, you've said it, we are going to live in a dust-bowl, but live we will, said Willie, why not, said Willie, why not. All right, said Janet, why not. Well, said Pauline, I know why not. Well sister, said Willie, why not. Well, said Pauline, because you all said you were going to pioneer, well and then, and then it wont be a dust-bowl, have you ever read about pioneers, said Lawrence, if you have you'll know a lot about dust-bowls. Oh dear, said Pauline. Oh dear.

Chapter Seventeen

YOU GOT TO, said Willie, you got to Brewsie, you got to hold out a little hope. Yes, said Brewsie, the hope is that our generation is more solid more scared, more articulate than the last ones. What do you mean, said Willie, those G.I.s those guys. Yes I do, said Brewsie, I do mean them. You're crazy, said Willie, they all just think they're the only thing there is, said Willie, they're just nothing, that's what they are, you know what they think, Brewsie, well you just listen. Say, called out Willie, you guys come over here, stop talking about how much you pay for cognac anywhere you are, and how much you got to pay more than anybody else and how much cognac you had yesterday just come over here and tell this man Brewsie what you think lousy foreigners are and what you think Americans are, come over and tell Brewsie, come along over. We Americans, said Sam, we Americans, we ride wide and handsome, that's what we Americans are and everybody admires us. Oh do they, said Donald Paul. Yes they do, why shouldnt they admire us, aint we got everything they want, everything, do they want it, said Donald Paul, sure they want it, said Sam, how could they not want it when they see us have it and we ride so wide and handsome. Wide all right but not so handsome, said Jo. Well, said Paul, if they didnt want what we got would there be any progress. Perhaps there aint any progress, said Donald Paul, perhaps not. There cant not be progress, said Sam, if there isnt any progress how could we sell goods and we gotta sell goods to get a job. Yes, said Donald Paul, that's it. And perhaps said Sam, all these over here they're so poor they live with their chickens and all they're just so poor. Yes all right, said Jimmie, but they do have chickens to live with. Yes, said Sam, but that aint progress. Well I dunno, said Jimmie, I like chickens, I kind of guess there always will be chickens. And if not, said Willie. Well then there might be progress, said Donald Paul, well anyway, said Fred, do you think it's right, that there I was sitting and behaving and I ask for a cognac and then a girl comes in and she has a cognac and then they charge her fifteen and they ask me twenty-five for the same cognac. Not the same, said Jo, hers was hers and yours was yours. And, said Jimmie, anyway you're so rich, you make such a holler that that dollar your dollar is the only money there is, naturally you got to pay more. Sure the dollar is all that, said Fred, but a poor soldier is a poor soldier and he is just poor. Just as poor as a lousy foreigner, said Willie. Well yes kind of, said Jimmie. It's all right, said Fred, it's all right about that dollar, anyway I was sitting there just as peaceable. And, said Donald Paul, you were sitting there with your lonesome dollar. What do you mean, said Fred, I may be a poor soldier but I got more than one dollar. Not that, said Donald Paul, not that, what I mean is that the dollar the United States dollar is a very lonesome dollar, it's all alone, it's riding wide and hand-some but it's riding all alone, nobody can use it, perhaps pretty soon we cant use it, it's a mighty lonesome dollar. What you mean, said Fred, what you mean I had some cognac and I dont see what you mean. I mean, said Donald Paul, that our lovely lively dollar is a very lonesome dollar and it lives all alone, alone alone alone, and if you live all alone you get to be kind of lonesome, and if you get kind of lonesome you get to be no good and if you get to be no good, you go kind of bad and if you get kind of bad you dont get at all, and if you dont get you havent got, and where are you, nowhere are you. I tell you our fine dollar is just lonesome. Oh get the hell out of here, said Willie. Yeah, said Jo, the worst of everything is it always sounds as if it was true. Well something has got to be true, said Jimmie. Does it, said Jo, I wonder, well anyway when we get home we wont talk any more not any of us will talk any more and so we wont have to worry whether anything is true or whether it aint true. If you think talking or not makes it different you better think again, said Jimmie, if you think we'll have more chickens or the dollar will buy more just because we get like all those at home and dont talk about it if you think it changes the facts you just better think again. All I know, said Fred, all I know is that they do give you a drink and they dont charge you more for it than they charge a lousy foreign girl who has one. No, said Willie, over there they charge the lousy foreign girl the extra ten cents. I dont believe, said Fred that anybody would do that at home, I dont believe anybody would, I dont believe it. You dont, said Willie, you talk like that when you get back and then they wont give you another drink they'll say you're drunk. Here we are, said Janet, we heard you, tell me something I always wanted to know why do men get so proud of being drunk, anybody can drink, what is it makes men so proud that they can get drunk, there is nothing special about it they all get drunk just exactly the same way, nothing seems any kind of way different but they all each one of 'em are so proud of being drunk. Aint that, said Jo, the way with any vice, cant you say the same about women, any man can sleep with a woman but every man is kind of special proud of it just the same, makes him feel a he-man, yes but about women, said Pauline, some men make women want to more than others. Yes they do, said Willie, yes they do. Oh, said Pauline, what I mean. Yes that is what we do mean, said Willie, No about being drunk. Oh let's forget about being drunk, said Willie, there is only one guy here who can never forget about being drunk and his name is Fred, and he just dont count. Let's talk about women, said Willie. Let's not, said Pauline, let's not, oh dear, said Pauline, when I think again and again about everything I could just cry. It's just as easy not to cry, said Willie, I know it is, said Pauline, that's the reason I am going to cry. How come, said Willie. Where is the man who talks, said Pauline. They wont let him talk any more, said Willie. Who wont let him talk any more, said Janet, the officers. Oh dear no, said Willie, it's all the guys, they found out from listening to him how to do it and now they all talk and talk and think it sounds just like him. And does it, said Pauline. How can I tell, said Willie, I dont listen to them. But you listened to him, said Pauline. Oh yes, said Willie, I listened to him.

Chapter Eighteen

I BEEN THINKING, said Brewsie, do we feel alike as well as say alike, do we think alike or dont we think at all. I dont think, said Brewsie, that we feel alike, I think we dont feel alike at all, they say we are sad and I think we are sad because we have different feelings but we articulate all the same. Listen, said Brewsie, you see, said Brewsie, you see I dont think we think, if we thought we could not articulate the same, we couldnt have Gallup polls and have everybody answer yes or no, if you think it's more complicated than that, over here, they wont answer the questions like that, they wont tell you how they are going to think tomorrow but we always know how we gonna think tomorrow because we are all going to think alike, no, said Brewsie, no not think, we are all going to articulate alike, not think, thinking is funnier and more mixed than that, not articulate alike, they ask us G.I.s what we think about Germans yes or no, my gracious, said Brewsie, you cant just think yes or no about Germans or about Russians and yet we all articulate alike about Germans and Russians, just as if it was the Democratic or Republican Party and it isnt, Willie it isnt, it may be life and death to us and we cant all feel alike and we dont think, is it we cant think, is it that we can only articulate, and if you can only articulate and not think, feel different but no way to get it out, because it comes out and it just is a Gallup poll, yes or no, just like that, oh Willie, I get so worried, I know it is just the most dangerous moment in our history, in a kind of a way as dangerous more dangerous than the Civil War, well they didnt all think alike then, they had lots of complications, and they did think, think how they orated, they did think, and then, said Brewsie, the Civil War was over, and everybody stopped thinking and they began to articulate, and instead of that they became job-hunters, and they felt different all the time they were feeling different, but they were beginning to articulate alike, I guess job men just have to articulate alike, they got to articulate yes or no to their bosses, and yes or no to their unions, they just got to articulate alike, and when you begin to articulate alike, you got to drop thinking out, just got to drop it out, you can go on feeling different but you got to articulate the same Gallup poll, yes you do, and it aint no use making it a second ballot, because nobody can think, how can you think when you feel different, you gotta feel different, anybody does have to feel different, but how can you think when you got to articulate alike. Listen to me Willie, listen to me, it's just like that Willie it just is, said Brewsie. I know, said Willie, it's all right, Brewsie, you got it right it's just the way we are, it's just the way it is, but what are you going to do about it Brewsie. Well that's just it, I kind of think, well I kind of feel that our generation, the generation that saw the depression, the generation that saw the war. I did more than see the depression Brewsie, and I did more than see the war, dont you make no mistake about that Brewsie, I did more than see the depression and I did more than see the war. I know Willie, said Brewsie, I know, I know Willie, and there it is, there was the depression and there was the war, yes but back of that, there is job-mindedness, and what can we do about it. No use saying communism communism, it's stimulating to Russians, because they discovered it, but it wouldnt stimulate us any not any at all. No, said Willie, it certainly would not stimulate me. No I know Willie, said Brewsie, no I just know just how it wouldnt stimulate you but Willie, what we gonna do, we got to think, and how can we think when we got to jump from feeling different to articulating the same, and if we could think Willie what could we think. But, said Willie, Brewsie you just got to hold out some hope, you just got to hold it out. That's very easy to say, said Brewsie, but how can you hold out hope, until you got hope and how can you get hope unless you can think and how can you think when you got to go right from feeling inside you kind of queer and worried and kind of scared and knowing something ought to be done about it articulating all the same thing every minute they ask you something and every minute you open your mouth even when nobody has asked you anything. They talk about cognac, they talk about wine and women, and even that they say just exactly alike, you know it Willie, you know it. Sure I know it Brewsie, sure I know it, but just all the same Brewsie you got to hold out some kind of hope you just got to

Brewsie. Well, Willie, I have got some kind of hope not really got it, but it's kind of there and that is because all of us, yes all of us, yes we kind of learned something from suffering, we learned to feel and to feel different and even when it comes to think well we aint learned to think but we kind of learned that if we could think we might think and perhaps if we did not articulate all alike perhaps something might happen. But, said Willie, how about all that job-mindedness, Brewsie, yes, said Willie, how can you not be job-minded when you all have to look for jobs and either get a job or not get a job but you have to do all the time with jobs, how can you be not job-minded if you dont do anything but breathe in a job, think Brewsie, answer me that, said Willie. Yes, said Brewsie, yes sometimes, said Brewsie, when I know how they all feel. They all feel all right they do all feel, said Willie, they do all feel. Well, said Brewsie, when I see how they all feel, sometimes I almost see something. Well look Brewsie look, look all you can Brewsie, and I'll listen while you are looking Brewsie, count on me I told that Pauline I listened to you and I'll listen to you Brewsie I'll listen.

Chapter Nineteen

WELL Brewsie, said Willie, we got 'em, the order has come. Yes I know, said Brewsie. Hullo Jo, said Willie, we got 'em. Sure we got 'em, said Jo. Hullo Willie, said Jimmie. Hullo, said Willie, we got 'em we got orders, we are the boys who are redeployed, in a little boat, on a little shore, and no more will we see a whore whenever we are wherever we are, away so far, it makes me feel funny, kind of funny very funny but it's all right there wont be any thinking over there, no thinking over there, no whores, no thinking, yes Brewsie, nothing but jobs, well do we like it. Yes do we like it, Brewsie, yes do we like it. Well, said John, I am staying, I got no points, so I'll think, do any of you guys want me to think for you. I'll have lots of time, Willie how about you, shall I think the thinks for you. You can stink the stinks for me, but think, well I was gonna say never again, never any thinking, but I dunno, I kind of think I am going to miss thinking, there was that cute Pauline and there was thinking, I kind of think I am going to miss thinking, there'll be no thinking over there, they dont think over there, they got no time to think, they got to get a job, they got to hold the job, they got no time to think over there, yes sometimes I might be kind of lonesome for thinking and I'll be thinking here is John he's got nothing to do, he's having a hell of a good time just thinking. Yes, said Brewsie, yes and yes, and dont you think it was true all we thought over here. Yes, said Willie, of course it was true but it dont do no good, it dont help any, it dont, what we gonna do thinking, what we gonna do. Well I tell you Willie, and if you dont think a little and go on thinking you'll have another awful time. Listen Willie, listen, listen Willie, what's a job, you havent got it, what's a job, you have got it, what's rushing around so fast you cant hear yourself think, what will happen, you'll be old and you never lived, and you kind of feel silly to lie down and die and to never have lived, to have been a job chaser and never have lived. Yes, said Willie, but Brewsie, now honest to God Brewsie, honest to God and it's the last time we all are here, honest to God Brewsie, can you be a job

chaser and live at the same time, honest to God Brewsie tell
me that can you live and be a job chaser at the same time,
honest to God, Brewsie tell me it, honest to God Brewsie,
honest to God. Honest to God Willie, said Brewsie, I just
dont know, I just dont know. And if you dont know, said
Willie, honest to God who does know. Well, said Jo, I know.
What do you know, said Willie. Well, said Jo, I know I am
going to. Going to what, said Willie. Honest to God I dont
know, said Jo. Well I know, said Jimmie, I dont have to chase
jobs, yeah, said Jimmie, because I live in a part of the South
where they all live so simple they just cant starve and they live
so simple that there aint really much difference between having a job and not having a job, between earning a living and
not earning a living, just like these lousy foreigners, said
Willie. Well yes perhaps, said Jimmie. And do you think living
that way, said Willie. Well, said Jimmie, not so much no and
not so much yes, but yes kind of, anyway we can do something
that you job chasers cant do, we can listen when other people
think and we can sit and wait for them to go on thinking,
that's more than you job chasers can do, believe me Willie it's
so. Yes, said Willie, I dont say no, yes I know it's so. And said
Jo, I know a fellow he is going home to be a bar-keep, he
and his brother always wanted to be bar-keeps, and their father never would buy them a bar, and now his brother has
been killed in the Pacific and so his father has bought him a
bar and is keeping it himself till his son gets home, and the
son my God he is fuddled all the time, he is pale and drunk,
drunk and pale, my God, said Jo. Well what has that to do
with what we got to do, said Jo. Nothing, said Jo, it's just a
story. Here we are, said Janet, we heard your crowd were
leaving and we came to say good-bye. Good-bye it is sister,
said Willie, where is Pauline. She is coming, she said, she
wanted to stop and pick you a flower. God bless her for that
tender thought, said Willie, God bless her. Yes, said Jo, yes.
And said Jimmie, how old is she. What do you want to know
that for, said Janet. I just want to know, said Jimmie, if she
was her age. Well she aint, said Willie, she's my age. Dear
dear, said Janet, isnt that chivalrous unless you are too old.
Not so old as that sister, said Willie. And tell me, said Janet,
wont you miss talking when you get home, you do know dont

you all of you nobody talks like you boys were always talking, not back home. Yes we know, said Jo. Yes we know, said Jimmie. Not Brewsie, said Willie, he'll talk but, said Willie, Brewsie will talk but we wont be there to listen, we kind of will remember that he's talking somewhere but we wont be there to listen, there wont be anybody talking where we will be. But, said Jo, perhaps they will talk now, why you all so sure they wont talk over there, perhaps they will talk over there. Not those on the job they wont, said Willie, not those on the job.

To Americans

G.I.s AND G.I.s AND G.I.s and they have made me come all over patriotic. I was always patriotic, I was always in my way a Civil War veteran, but in between, there were other things, but now there are no other things. And I am sure that this particular moment in our history is more important than anything since the Civil War. We are there where we have to have to fight a spiritual pioneer fight or we will go poor as England and other industrial countries have gone poor, and dont think that communism or socialism will save you, you just have to find a new way, you have to find out how you can go ahead without running away with yourselves, you have to learn to produce without exhausting your country's wealth, you have to learn to be individual and not just mass job workers, you have to get courage enough to know what you feel and not just all be yes or no men, but you have to really learn to express complication, go easy and if you cant go easy go as easy as you can. Remember the depression, dont be afraid to look it in the face and find out the reason why, dont be afraid of the reason why, if you dont find out the reason why you'll go poor and my God how I would hate to have my native land go poor. Find out the reason why, look facts in the face, not just what they all say, the leaders, but every darn one of you so that a government by the people for the people shall not perish from the face of the earth, it wont, somebody else will do it if we lie down on the job, but of all things dont stop, find out the reason why of the depression, find it out each and every one of you and then look the facts in the face. We are Americans.

THE MOTHER OF US ALL

The Mother of Us All

ACT I

(Prologue sung by Virgil T.)

Pity the poor persecutor.
  Why,
If money is money isn't money money,
  Why,
Pity the poor persecutor,
  Why,
Is money money or isn't money money.
  Why.
Pity the poor persecutor.
Pity the poor persecutor because the poor persecutor
    always gets to be poor
  Why,
Because the persecutor gets persecuted
Because is money money or isn't money money,
  That's why,
When the poor persecutor is persecuted he has to cry,
  Why,
Because the persecutor always ends by being perse-
    cuted,
  That is the reason why.
(Virgil T. after he has sung his prelude begins to sit)

Virgil T.   Begin to sit.
                       Begins to sit.
                       He begins to sit.
                       That's why.
                       Begins to sit.
                       He begins to sit.
                       And that is the reason why.

ACT I Scene I

Daniel Webster.   He digged a pit, he digged it deep
                       he digged it for his brother.

	Into the pit he did fall in the pit he digged for tother.
All the Characters.	Daniel was my father's name, My father's name was Daniel.
Jo the Loiterer.	Not Daniel.
Chris the Citizen.	Not Daniel in the lion's den.
All the Characters.	My father's name was Daniel.
G. S.	My father's name was Daniel, Daniel and a bear, a bearded Daniel, not Daniel in the lion's den not Daniel, yes Daniel my father had a beard my father's name was Daniel,
Daniel Webster.	He digged a pit he digged it deep he digged it for his brother, Into the pit he did fall in the pit he digged for tother.
Indiana Elliot.	Choose a name.
Susan B. Anthony.	Susan B. Anthony is my name to choose a name is feeble, Susan B. An- thony is my name, a name can only be a name my name can only be my name, I have a name, Susan B. Anthony is my name, to choose a name is feeble.
Indiana Elliot.	Yes that's easy, Susan B. Anthony is that kind of a name but my name Indiana Elliot. What's in a name.
Susan B. Anthony.	Everything.
G. S.	My father's name was Daniel he had a black beard he was not tall not at all tall, he had a black beard his name was Daniel.
All the Characters.	My father had a name his name was Daniel.
Jo the Loiterer.	Not Daniel
Chris a Citizen.	Not Daniel not Daniel in the lion's den not Daniel.
Susan B. Anthony.	I had a father, Daniel was not his name.
Indiana Elliot.	I had no father no father.
Daniel Webster.	He digged a pit he digged it deep he digged it for his brother,

into the pit he did fall in the pit
he digged for tother.

ACT I Scene II

Jo the Loiterer.	I want to tell
Chris the Citizen.	Very well
Jo the Loiterer.	I want to tell oh hell.
Chris the Citizen.	Oh very well.
Jo the Loiterer.	I want to tell oh hell I want to tell about my wife.
Chris the Citizen.	And have you got one.
Jo the Loiterer.	No not one.
Chris the Citizen.	Two then
Jo the Loiterer.	No not two.
Chris.	How many then
Jo the Loiterer.	I haven't got one. I want to tell oh hell about my wife I haven't got one.
Chris the Citizen.	Well.
Jo the Loiterer.	My wife, she had a garden.
Chris the Citizen.	Yes
Jo the Loiterer.	And I bought one.
Chris the Citizen.	A wife.

No said Jo I was poor and I bought a
garden. And then said Chris. She said,
said Jo, she said my wife said one tree
in my garden was her tree in her garden. And said Chris, Was it. Jo, We
quarreled about it. And then said Chris.
And then said Jo, we took a train and
we went where we went. And then said
Chris. She gave me a little package said
Jo. And was it a tree said Chris. No it
was money said Jo. And was she your
wife said Chris, yes said Jo when she
was funny, How funny said Chris. Very
funny said Jo. Very funny said Jo. To
be funny you have to take everything
in the kitchen and put it on the floor,
you have to take all your money and all

	your jewels and put them near the door you have to go to bed then and leave the door ajar. That is the way you do when you are funny.
Chris the Citizen.	Was she funny.
Jo the Loiterer.	Yes she was funny.

(Chris and Jo put their arms around each other)

Angel More.	Not any more I am not a martyr any more, not any more. Be a martyr said Chris.
Angel More.	Not any more. I am not a martyr any more. Surrounded by sweet smelling flowers I fell asleep three times. Darn and wash and patch, darn and wash and patch, darn and wash and patch darn and wash and patch.
Jo the Loiterer.	Anybody can be accused of loitering.
Chris Blake a Citizen.	Any loiterer can be accused of loitering.
Henrietta M.	Daniel Webster needs an artichoke.
Angel More.	Susan B. is cold in wet weather.
Henry B.	She swore an oath she'd quickly come to any one to any one.
Anthony Comstock.	Caution and curiosity, oil and obligation, wheels and appurtenances, in the way of means.
Virgil T.	What means.
John Adams.	I wish to say I also wish to stay, I also wish to go away, I also wish I endeavor to also wish.
Angel More.	I wept on a wish.
John Adams.	Whenever I hear any one say of course, do I deny it, yes I do deny it whenever I hear any one say of course I deny it, I do deny it.
Thaddeus S.	Be mean.
Daniel Webster.	Be there.

Henrietta M.	Be where
Constance Fletcher.	I do and I do not declare that roses and wreaths, wreaths and roses around and around, blind as a bat, curled as a hat and a plume, be mine when I die, farewell to a thought, he left all alone, be firm in despair dear dear never share, dear dear, dear dear, I Constance Fletcher dear dear, I am a dear, I am dear dear I am a dear, here there everywhere. I bow myself out.
Indiana Elliot.	Anybody else would be sorry.
Susan B. Anthony.	Hush, I hush, you hush, they hush, we hush. Hush.
Gloster Heming and Isabel Wentworth.	We, hush, dear as we are, we are very dear to us and to you we hush, we hush you say hush, dear hush. Hush dear.
Anna Hope.	I open any door, that is the way that any day is to-day, any day is to-day I open any door every door a door.
Lillian Russell.	Thank you.
Anthony Comstock.	Quilts are not crazy, they are kind.
Jenny Reefer.	My goodness gracious me.
Ulysses S. Grant.	He knew that his name was not Eisenhower. Yes he knew it. He did know it.
Herman Atlan.	He asked me to come he did ask me.
Donald Gallup.	I chose a long time, a very long time, four hours are a very long time, I chose, I took a very long time, I took a very long time. Yes I took a very long time to choose, yes I did.
T. T. and A. A.	They missed the boat yes they did they missed the boat.
Jo a Loiterer.	I came again but not when I was expected, but yes when I was expected because they did expect me.
Chris the Citizen.	I came to dinner.

(They all sit down)

Curtain

ACT I Scene III

(Susan B. Anthony and Daniel Webster seated in
two straight-backed chairs not too near each other.
Jo the Loiterer comes in)

Jo the Loiterer.	I don't know where a mouse is I don't know what a mouse is. What is a mouse.
Angel More.	I am a mouse
Jo the Loiterer.	Well
Angel More.	Yes Well
Jo the Loiterer.	All right well. Well what is a mouse
Angel More.	I am a mouse
Jo the Loiterer.	Well if you are what is a mouse
Angel More.	You know what a mouse is, I am a mouse.
Jo the Loiterer.	Yes well, And she.

(Susan B. dressed like a Quakeress turns around)

Susan B.	I hear a sound.
Jo the Loiterer.	Yes well
Daniel Webster.	I do not hear a sound. When I am told.
Susan B. Anthony.	Silence.

(Everybody is silent)

Susan B. Anthony.	Youth is young, I am not old.
Daniel Webster.	When the mariner has been tossed for many days, in thick weather, and on an unknown sea, he naturally avails himself of the first pause in the storm.
Susan B. Anthony.	For instance. They should always fight. They should be martyrs. Some should be martyrs. Will they. They will.
Daniel Webster.	We have thus heard sir what a resolution is.
Susan B. Anthony.	I am resolved.
Daniel Webster.	When this debate sir was to be resumed on Thursday it so happened that it would have been convenient for me to be elsewhere.
Susan B.	I am here, ready to be here. Ready to

	be where. Ready to be here. It is my habit.
Daniel Webster.	The honorable member complained that I had slept on his speech.
Susan B.	The right to sleep is given to no woman.
Daniel Webster.	I did sleep on the gentleman's speech; and slept soundly.
Susan B.	I too have slept soundly when I have slept, yes when I have slept I too have slept soundly.
Daniel Webster.	Matches and over matches.
Susan B.	I understand you undertake to overthrow my undertaking.
Daniel Webster.	I can tell the honorable member once for all that he is greatly mistaken, and that he is dealing with one of whose temper and character he has yet much to learn.
Susan B.	I have declared that patience is never more than patient. I too have declared, that I who am not patient am patient.
Daniel Webster.	What interest asks he has South Carolina in a canal in Ohio.
Susan B.	What interest have they in me, what interest have I in them, who holds the head of whom, who can bite their lips to avoid a swoon.
Daniel Webster.	The harvest of neutrality had been great, but we had gathered it all.
Susan B.	Near hours are made not by shade not by heat not by joy, I always know that not now rather not now, yes and I do not stamp but I know that now yes now is now. I have never asked any one to forgive me.
Daniel Webster.	On yet another point I was still more unaccountably misunderstood.
Susan B.	Do we do what we have to do or do we have to do what we do. I answer.

Daniel Webster.	Mr. President I shall enter on no encomium upon Massachusetts she need none. There she is behold her and judge for yourselves.
Susan B.	I enter into a tabernacle I was born a believer in peace, I say fight for the right, be a martyr and live, be a coward and die, and why, because they, yes they, sooner or later go away. They leave us here. They come again. Don't forget, they come again.
Daniel Webster.	So sir I understand the gentleman and am happy to find I did not misunderstand him.
Susan B.	I should believe, what they ask, but they know, they know.
Daniel Webster.	It has been to us all a copious fountain of national, social and personal happiness.
Susan B.	Shall I protest, not while I live and breathe, I shall protest, shall I protest, shall I protest while I live and breathe.
Daniel Webster.	When my eyes shall be turned to behold for the last time the sun in heaven.
Susan B.	Yes.
Jo the Loiterer.	I like a mouse
Angel More.	I hate mice.
Jo the Loiterer.	I am not talking about mice, I am talking about a mouse. I like a mouse.
Angel More.	I hate a mouse.
Jo the Loiterer.	Now do you.

Curtain

INTERLUDE

(Susan B.   A Short Story)

Yes I was said Susan.

You mean you are, said Anne.

No said Susan no.

When this you see remember me said Susan B.

I do said Anne.

After a while there was education. Who is educated said Anne.

Susan began to follow, she began to follow herself. I am not tired said Susan. No not said Anne. No I am not said Susan. This was the beginning. They began to travel not to travel you know but to go from one place to another place. In each place Susan B. said here I am I am here. Well said Anne. Do not let it trouble you said Susan politely. By the time she was there she was polite. She often thought about politeness. She said politeness was so agreeable. Is it said Anne. Yes said Susan yes I think so that is to say politeness is agreeable that is to say it could be agreeable if everybody were polite but when it is only me, ah me, said Susan B.

Anne was reproachful why do you not speak louder she said to Susan B. I speak as loudly as I can said Susan B. I even speak louder I even speak louder than I can. Do you really said Anne. Yes I really do said Susan B. it was dark and as it was dark it was necessary to speak louder or very softly, very softly. Dear me said Susan B., if it was not so early I would be sleepy. I myself said Anne never like to look at a newspaper. You are entirely right said Susan B. only I disagree with you. You do said Anne. You know very well I do said Susan B.

Men said Susan B. are so conservative, so selfish, so boresome and said Susan B. they are so ugly, and said Susan B. they are gullible, anybody can convince them, listen said Susan B. they listen to me. Well said Anne anybody would. I know said Susan B. I know anybody would I know that.

Once upon a time any day was full of occupation. You were never tired said Anne. No I was never tired said Susan B. And now, said Anne. Now I am never tired said Susan B. Let us said Anne let us think about everything. No said Susan B. no, no no, I know, I know said Susan B. no, said Susan B. No. But said Anne. But me no buts said Susan B. I know, now you like every one, every one and you each one and you they all do, they all listen to me, utterly unnecessary to deny, why deny, they themselves will they deny that they listen to me but let them deny it, all the same they do they do listen to

me all the men do, see them said Susan B., do see them, see
them, why not, said Susan B., they are men, and men, well of
course they know that they cannot either see or hear unless I
tell them so, poor things said Susan B. I do not pity them.
Poor things. Yes said Anne they are poor things. Yes said
Susan B. they are poor things. They are poor things said Susan
B. men are poor things. Yes they are said Anne. Yes they are
said Susan B. and nobody pities them. No said Anne no, nobody pities them. Very likely said Susan B. More than likely,
said Anne. Yes said Susan B. yes.

It was not easy to go away but Susan B. did go away. She
kept on going away and every time she went away she went
away again. Oh my said Susan B. why do I go away, I go away
because if I did not go away I would stay. Yes of course said
Anne yes of course, if you did not go away you would stay.
Yes of course said Susan B. Now said Susan B., let us not
forget that in each place men are the same just the same, they
are conservative, they are selfish and they listen to me. Yes
they do said Anne. Yes they do said Susan B.

Susan B. was right, she said she was right and she was right.
Susan B. was right. She was right because she was right. It is
easy to be right, everybody else is wrong so it is easy to be
right, and Susan B. was right, of course she was right, it is
easy to be right, everybody else is wrong it is easy to be right.
And said Susan B., in a way yes in a way yes really in a way,
in a way really it is useful to be right. It does what it does, it
does do what it does, if you are right, it does do what it does.
It is very remarkable said Anne. Not very remarkable said
Susan B. not very remarkable, no not very remarkable. It is
not very remarkable really not very remarkable said Anne. No
said Susan B. no not very remarkable.

And said Susan B. that is what I mean by not very remarkable.

Susan B. said she would not leave home. No said Susan B.
I will not leave home. Why not said Anne. Why not said Susan
B. all right I will I always have I always will. Yes you always
will said Anne. Yes I always will said Susan B. In a little while
anything began again and Susan B. said she did not mind.
Really and truly said Susan B. really and truly I do not mind.
No said Anne you do not mind, no said Susan B. no really

and truly truly and really I do not mind. It was very necessary never to be cautious said Susan B. Yes said Anne it is very necessary.

In a little while they found everything very mixed. It is not really mixed said Susan B. How can anything be really mixed when men are conservative, dull, monotonous, deceived, stupid, unchanging and bullies, how said Susan B. how when men are men can they be mixed. Yes said Anne, yes men are men, how can they when men are men how can they be mixed yes how can they. Well said Susan B. Let us go on they always listen to me. Yes said Anne yes they always listen to you. Yes said Susan B. yes they always listen to me.

ACT II

Andrew J.	It is cold weather.
Henrietta M.	In winter.
Andrew J.	Wherever I am

(Thaddeus S. comes in singing a song)

Thaddeus S.	I believe in public school education, I do not believe in free masons I believe in public school education, I do not believe that every one can do whatever he likes because (a pause) I have not always done what I liked, but, I would, if I could, and so I will, I will do what I will, I will have my will, and they, when the they, where are they, beside a poll, Gallup the poll. It is remarkable that there could be any nice person by the name of Gallup, but there is, yes there is, that is my decision.
Andrew J.	Bother your decision, I tell you it is cold weather.
Henrietta M.	In winter.
Andrew J.	Wherever I am.
Constance Fletcher.	Antagonises is a pleasant name, antagonises is a pleasant word, antagonises has occurred, bless you all and one.
John Adams.	Dear Miss Constance Fletcher, it is a

great pleasure that I kneel at your
feet, but I am Adams, I kneel at the feet
of none, not any one, dear Miss
Constance Fletcher dear dear Miss
Constance Fletcher I kneel at your feet,
you would have ruined my father if I
had had one but I have had one and
you had ruined him, dear Miss Constance Fletcher if I had not been an
Adams I would have kneeled at your feet.

Constance Fletcher.   And kissed my hand.
J. Adams.
  (shuddering).   And kissed your hand.
Constance Fletcher.   What a pity, no not what a pity it is
better so, but what a pity what a pity it
is what a pity.

J. Adams.   Do not pity me kind beautiful lovely
Miss Constance Fletcher do not pity
me, no do not pity me, I am an Adams
and not pitiable.

Constance Fletcher.   Dear dear me if he had not been an
Adams he would have kneeled at my
feet and he would have kissed my hand.
Do you mean that you would have
kissed my hand or my hands, dear Mr.
Adams.

J. Adams.   I mean that I would have first kneeled
at your feet and then I would have
kissed one of your hands and then I
would still kneeling have kissed both
of your hands, if I had not been an
Adams.

Constance Fletcher.   Dear me Mr. Adams dear me.
All the Characters.   If he had not been an Adams he would
have kneeled at her feet and he would
have kissed one of her hands, and then
still kneeling he would have kissed both
of her hands still kneeling if he had not
been an Adams.

Andrew J.	It is cold weather.
Henrietta M.	In winter.
Andrew J.	Wherever I am.
Thaddeus S.	When I look at him I fly, I mean when he looks at me he can cry.
Lillian Russell.	It is very naughty for men to quarrel so.
Herman Atlan.	They do quarrel so.
Lillian Russell.	It is very naughty of them very naughty.

(Jenny Reefer begins to waltz with Herman Atlan)

A Slow Chorus.	Naughty men, they quarrel so Quarrel about what. About how late the moon can rise. About how soon the earth can turn. About how naked are the stars. About how black are blacker men. About how pink are pinks in spring. About what corn is best to pop. About how many feet the ocean has dropped. Naughty men naughty men, they are always always quarreling.
Jenny Reefer.	Ulysses S. Grant was not the most earnest nor the most noble of men, but he was not always quarreling.
Donald Gallup.	No he was not.
Jo the Loiterer.	Has everybody forgotten Isabel Wentworth. I just want to say has everybody forgotten Isabel Wentworth.
Chris the Citizen.	Why shouldn't everybody forget Isabel Wentworth.
Jo the Loiterer.	Well that is just what I want to know I just want to know if everybody has forgotten Isabel Wentworth. That is all I want to know I just want to know if everybody has forgotten Isabel Wentworth.

ACT II Scene II

Susan B.   Shall I regret having been born, will I regret having been born, shall and will, will and shall, I regret having been born.

Anne.   Is Henrietta M. a sister of Angel More.

Susan B.   No, I used to feel that sisters should be sisters, and that sisters prefer sisters, and I.

Anne.   Is Angel More the sister of Henrietta M. It is important that I know important.

Susan B.   Yes important.

Anne.   An Indiana Elliot are there any other Elliots beside Indiana Elliot. It is important that I should know, very important.

Susan B.   Should one work up excitement, or should one turn it low so that it will explode louder, should one work up excitement should one.

Anne.   Are there any other Elliots beside Indiana Elliot, had she sisters or even cousins, it is very important that I should know, very important.

Susan B.   A life is never given for a life, when a life is given a life is gone, if no life is gone there is no room for more life, life and strife, I give my life, that is to say, I live my life every day.

Anne.   And Isabel Wentworth, is she older or younger than she was it is very important very important that I should know just how old she is. I must have a list I must of how old every one is, it is very important.

Susan B.   I am ready.

Anne.   We have forgotten we have forgotten Jenny Reefer, I don't know even who

	she is, it is very important that I know who Jenny Reefer is very important.
Susan B.	And perhaps it is important to know who Lillian Russell is, perhaps it is important.
Anne.	It is not important to know who Lillian Russell is.
Susan B.	Then you do know.
Anne.	It is not important for me to know who Lillian Russell is.
Susan B.	I must choose I do choose, men and women women and men I do choose. I must choose colored or white white or colored I must choose, I must choose, weak or strong, strong or weak I must choose.

(All the men coming forward together)

Susan B.	I must choose
Jo the Loiterer.	Fight fight fight, between the nigger and the white.
Chris the Citizen.	And the women.
Andrew J.	I wish to say that little men are bigger than big men, that they know how to drink and to get drunk. They say I was a little man next to that big man, nobody can say what they do say nobody can.
Chorus of all the Men.	No nobody can, we feel that way too, no nobody can.
Andrew Johnson.	Begin to be drunk when you can so be a bigger man than a big man, you can.
Chorus of Men.	You can.
Andrew J.	I often think, I am a bigger man than a bigger man. I often think I am.

(Andrew J. moves around and as he moves around
he sees himself in a mirror)

| | Nobody can say little as I am I am not bigger than anybody bigger bigger bigger (and then in a low whisper) bigger than him bigger than him. |

Jo the Loiterer.   Fight fight between the big and the big never between the little and the big.

Chris the Citizen.   They don't fight.

(Virgil T. makes them all gather around him)

Virgil T.   Hear me he says hear me in every way I have satisfaction, I sit I stand I walk around and I am grand, and you all know it.

Chorus of Men.   Yes we all know it. That's that.

And Said Virgil T.   I will call you up one by one and then you will know which one is which, I know, then you will be known. Very well, Henry B.

Henry B.
  comes forward.   I almost thought that I was Tommy I almost did I almost thought I was Tommy W. but if I were Tommy W. I would never come again, not if I could do better no not if I could do better.

Virgil T.   Useless. John Adams. (John Adams advances) Tell me are you the real John Adams you know I sometimes doubt it not really doubt it you know but doubt it.

John Adams.   If you were silent I would speak.

Jo the Loiterer.   Fight fight fight between day and night.

Chris the Citizen.   Which is day and which is night.

Jo the Loiterer.   Hush, which.

John Adams.   I ask you Virgil T. do you love women, I do. I love women but I am never subdued by them never.

Virgil T.   He is no good. Andrew J. and Thaddeus S. better come together.

Jo the Loiterer.   He wants to fight fight fight between.

Chris.   Between what.

Jo the Loiterer.   Between the dead.

Andrew J.   I tell you I am bigger bigger is not biggest is not bigger. I am bigger and just to the last minute, I stick, it's better to

	stick than to die, it's better to itch than to cry, I have tried them all.
Virgil T.	You bet you have.
Thaddeus S.	I can be carried in dying but I will never quit trying.
Jo the Loiterer.	Oh go to bed when all is said oh go to bed, everybody, let's hear the women.
Chris the Citizen.	Fight fight between the nigger and the white and the women.

(Andrew J. and Thaddeus S. begin to quarrel violently)

Tell me said Virgil T. tell me I am from Missouri.

(Everybody suddenly stricken dumb)

(Daniel advances holding Henrietta M. by the hand)

| Daniel. | Ladies and gentlemen let me present you let me present to you Henrietta M. it is rare in this troubled world to find a woman without a last name rare delicious and troubling, ladies and gentlemen let me present Henrietta M. |

Curtain

ACT II Scene III

| Susan B. | I do not know whether I am asleep or awake, awake or asleep, asleep or awake. Do I know. |
| Jo the Loiterer. | I know, you are awake Susan B. |

(A snowy landscape.

a negro man and a negro woman)

Susan B.	Negro man would you vote if you only can and not she.
Negro Man.	You bet.
Susan B.	I fought for you that you could vote would you vote if they would not let me.
Negro Man.	Holy gee.
Susan B. moving down in the snow.	If I believe that I am right and I am right if they believe that they are right

	and they are not in the right, might, might, might there be what might be.
Negro Man and Woman following her.	All right Susan B. all right.
Susan B.	How then can we entertain a hope that they will act differently, we may pretend to go in good faith but there will be no faith in us.
Donald Gallup.	Let me help you Susan B.
Susan B.	And if you do and I annoy you what will you do.
Donald Gallup.	But I will help you Susan B.
Susan B.	I tell you if you do and I annoy you what will you do.
Donald Gallup.	I wonder if I can help you Susan B.
Susan B.	I wonder.

(Andrew G., Thaddeus and Daniel Webster
                  come in together)

	We are the chorus of the V.I.P.
	Very important persons to every one who can hear and see, we are the chorus of the V.I.P.
Susan B.	Yes, so they are. I am important but not that way, not that way.
The Three V.I.P.'s.	We you see we V.I.P. very important to any one who can hear or you can see, just we three, of course lots of others but just we three, just we three we are the chorus of V.I.P. Very important persons to any one who can hear or can see.
Susan B.	My constantly recurring thought and prayer now are that no word or act of mine may lessen the might of this country in the scale of truth and right.
The Chorus of V.I.P.	
Daniel Webster.	When they all listen to me.
Thaddeus S.	When they all listen to me.
Andrew J.	When they all listen to him, by him I mean me.

Daniel Webster.	By him I mean me.
Thaddeus S.	It is not necessary to have any meaning I am he, he is me I am a V.I.P.
The Three.	We are the V.I.P. the very important persons, we have special rights, they ask us first and they wait for us last and wherever we are well there we are everybody knows we are there, we are the V.I.P. Very important persons for everybody to see.
Jo the Loiterer.	I wished that I knew the difference between rich and poor, I used to think I was poor, now I think I am rich and I am rich, quite rich not very rich quite rich, I wish I knew the difference between rich and poor.
Chris the Citizen.	Ask her, ask Susan B. I always ask, I find they like it and I like it, and if I like it, and if they like it, I am not rich and I am not poor, just like that Jo just like that.
Jo the Loiterer.	Susan B. listen to me, what is the difference between rich and poor poor and rich no use to ask the V.I.P., they never answer me but you Susan B. you answer, answer me.
Susan B.	Rich, to be rich, is to be so rich that when they are rich they have it to be that they do not listen and when they do they do not hear, and to be poor to be poor, is to be so poor they listen and listen and what they hear well what do they hear, they hear that they listen, they listen to hear, that is what it is to be poor, but I, I Susan B., there is no wealth nor poverty, there is no wealth, what is wealth, there is no poverty, what is poverty, has a pen ink, has it.
Jo the Loiterer.	I had a pen that was to have ink for a year and it only lasted six weeks.

Susan B.	Yes I know Jo. I know.

Curtain

ACT II Scene IV

A Meeting.

Susan B.
On the Platform.   Ladies there is no neutral position for us to assume. If we say we love the cause and then sit down at our ease, surely does our action speak the lie.
And now will Daniel Webster take the platform as never before.

Daniel Webster.   Coming and coming alone, no man is alone when he comes, when he comes when he is coming he is not alone and now ladies and gentlemen I have done, remember that remember me remember each one.

Susan B.   And now Virgil T. Virgil T. will bow and speak and when it is necessary they will know that he is he.

Virgil T.   I make what I make, I make a noise, there is a poise in making a noise.

(An interruption at the door)

Jo the Loiterer.   I have behind me a crowd, are we allowed.

Susan B.   A crowd is never allowed but each one of you can come in.

Chris the Citizen.   But if we are allowed then we are a crowd.

Susan B.   No, this is the cause, and a cause is a pause. Pause before you come in.

Jo the Loiterer.   Yes ma'am.

(All the characters crowd in. Constance Fletcher and Indiana Elliot leading)

Daniel Webster.   I resist it to-day and always. Who ever falters or whoever flies I continue the contest.

Constance Fletcher and Indiana Elliot
   bowing low say.   Dear man, he can make us glad that we
                               have had so great so dear a man here
                               with us now and now we bow before
                               him here, this dear this dear great man.

Susan B.   Hush, this is slush. Hush.

John Adams.   I cannot be still when still and until I
                               see Constance Fletcher dear Constance
                               Fletcher noble Constance Fletcher and
                               I spill I spill over like a thrill and a trill,
                               dear Constance Fletcher there is no
                               cause in her presence, how can there be
                               a cause. Women what are women.
                               There is Constance Fletcher, men what
                               are men, there is Constance Fletcher,
                               Adams, yes, Adams, I am John Adams,
                               there is Constance Fletcher, when this
                               you see listen to me, Constance, no I
                               cannot call her Constance I can only
                               call her Constance Fletcher.

Indiana Elliot.   And how about me.

Jo the Loiterer.   Whist shut up I have just had an awful
                               letter from home, shut up.

Indiana Elliot.   What did they say.

Jo the Loiterer.   They said I must come home and not
                               marry you.

Indiana.   Who ever said we were going to marry.

Jo the Loiterer.   Believe me I never did.

Indiana.   Disgrace to the cause of women, out.
                               And she shoves him out.

Jo the Loiterer.   Help Susan B. help me.

Susan B.   I know that we suffer, and as we suffer
                               we grow strong, I know that we wait
                               and as we wait we are bold, I know that
                               we are beaten and as we are beaten we
                               win, I know that men know that this is
                               not so but it is so, I know, yes I know.

Jo the Loiterer.   There didn't I tell you she knew best,
                               you just give me a kiss and let me alone.

Daniel Webster.   I who was once old am now young, I

who was once weak am now strong, I who have left every one behind am now overtaken.

Susan B.   I undertake to overthrow your undertaking.

Jo the Loiterer.   You bet.

Chris the Citizen.   I always repeat everything I hear.

Jo the Loiterer.   You sure do.

(While all this is going on, all the characters are crowding up on the platform)

They Say.   Now we are all here there is nobody down there to hear, now if it is we're always like that there would be no reason why anybody should cry, because very likely if at all it would be so nice to be the head, we are the head we have all the bread.

Jo the Loiterer.   And the butter too.

Chris the Citizen.   And Kalamazoo.

Susan B. advancing.   I speak to those below who are not there who are not there who are not there. I speak to those below to those below who are not there to those below who are not there.

Curtain

ACT II Scene V

Susan B.   Will they remember that it is true that neither they that neither you, will they marry will they carry, aloud, the right to know that even if they love them so, they are alone to live and die, they are alone to sink and swim they are alone to have what they own, to have no idea but that they are here, to struggle and thirst to do everything first, because until it is done there is no other one.

(Jo the Loiterer leads in Indiana Elliot in wedding attire, followed by John Adams and Constance Fletcher and

followed by Daniel Webster and Angel More. All the
other characters follow after. Anne and Jenny Reefer
come and stand by Susan B. Ulysses S. Grant sits down
in a chair right behind the procession)

Anne.	Marriage.
Jenny Reefer.	Marry marriage.
Susan B.	I know I know and I have told you so, but if no one marries how can there be women to tell men, women to tell men.
Anne.	What
Jenny Reefer.	Women should not tell men.
Susan B.	Men can not count, they do not know that two and two make four if women do not tell them so. There is a devil creeps into men when their hands are strengthened. Men want to be half slave half free. Women want to be all slave or all free, therefore men govern and women know, and yet.
Anne.	Yet.
Jenny Reefer.	There is no yet in paradise.
Susan B.	Let them marry.

(The marrying commences)

Jo the Loiterer.	I tell her if she marries me do I marry her.
Indiana Elliot.	Listen to what he says so you can answer, have you the ring.
Jo the Loiterer.	You did not like the ring and mine is too large.
Indiana Elliot.	Hush.
Jo the Loiterer.	I wish my name was Adams.
Indiana Elliot.	Hush.
John Adams.	I never marry I have been twice divorced but I have never married, fair Constance Fletcher fair Constance Fletcher do you not admire me that I never can married be. I who have been twice divorced. Dear Constance Fletcher dear dear Constance Fletcher do you not admire me.

Constance Fletcher.	So beautiful. It is so beautiful to meet you here, so beautiful, so beautiful to meet you here dear, dear John Adams, so beautiful to meet you here.
Daniel Webster.	When I have joined and not having joined have separated and not having separated have led, and not having led have thundered, when I having thundered have provoked and having provoked have dominated, may I dear Angel More not kneel at your feet because I cannot kneel my knees are not kneeling knees but dear Angel More be my Angel More for evermore.
Angel More.	I join the choir that is visible, because the choir that is visible is as visible.
Daniel Webster.	As what Angel More.
Angel More.	As visible as visible, do you not hear me, as visible.
Daniel Webster.	You do not and I do not.
Angel More.	What.
Daniel Webster.	Separate marriage from marriage.
Angel More.	And why not.
Daniel Webster.	And.

(Just at this moment Ulysses S. Grant makes
his chair pound on the floor)

Ulysses S. Grant.	As long as I sit I am sitting, silence again as you were, you were all silent, as long as I sit I am sitting.
All Together.	We are silent, as we were.
Susan B.	We are all here to celebrate the civil and religious marriage of Jo the Loiterer and Indiana Elliot.
Jo the Loiterer.	Who is civil and who is religious.
Anne.	Who is, listen to Susan B. She knows.

The Brother of Indiana Elliot rushes in.

	Nobody knows who I am but I forbid the marriage, do we know whether Jo the Loiterer is a bigamist or a grandfather or an uncle or a refugee. Do we

know, no we do not know and I forbid
the marriage, I forbid it, I am Indiana
Elliot's brother and I forbid it, I am
known as Herman Atlan and I forbid
it, I am known as Anthony Comstock
and I forbid it, I am Indiana Elliot's
brother and I forbid it.

Jo the Loiterer.   Well well well, I knew that ring of mine
was too large, It could not fall off on
account of my joints but I knew it was
too large.

Indiana Elliot.   I renounce my brother.

Jo the Loiterer.   That's right my dear that's all right.

Susan B.   What is marriage, is marriage protection or religion, is marriage renuncia-
tion or abundance, is marriage a
stepping-stone or an end. What is marriage.

Anne.   I will never marry.

Jenny Reefer.   If I marry I will divorce but I will not
marry because if I did marry, I would
be married.

(Ulysses S. Grant pounds his chair)

Ulysses S. Grant.   Didn't I say I do not like noise, I do
not like cannon balls, I do not like
storms, I do not like talking, I do not
like noise. I like everything and everybody to be silent and what I like I have.
Everybody be silent.

Jo the Loiterer.   I know I was silent, everybody can tell
just by listening to me just how silent
I am, dear General, dear General
Ulysses, dear General Ulysses Simpson
dear General Ulysses Simpson Grant,
dear dear sir, am I not a perfect example of what you like, am I not silent.

(Ulysses S. Grant's chair pounds and he is silent)

Susan B.   I am not married and the reason why
is that I have had to do what I have
had to do, I have had to be what I have

	had to be, I could never be one of two I could never be two in one as married couples do and can, I am but one all one, one and all one, and so I have never been married to any one.
Anne.	But I I have been, I have been married to what you have been to that one.
Susan B.	No no, no, you may be married to the past one, the one that is not the present one, no one can be married to the present one, the one, the one, the present one.
Jenny Reefer.	I understand you undertake to overthrow their undertaking.
Susan B.	I love the sound of these, one over two, two under one, three under four, four over more.
Anne.	Dear Susan B. Anthony thank you.
John Adams.	All this time I have been lost in my thoughts in my thoughts of thee beautiful thee, Constance Fletcher, do you see, I have been lost in my thoughts of thee.
Constance Fletcher.	I am blind and therefore I dream.
Daniel Webster.	Dear Angel More, dear Angel More, there have been men who have stammered and stuttered but not, not I.
Angel More.	Speak louder.
Daniel Webster.	Not I.
The Chorus.	Why the hell don't you all get married, why don't you, we want to go home, why don't you.
Jo the Loiterer.	Why don't you.
Indiana Elliot.	Why don't you.
Indiana Elliot's Brother.	Why don't you because I am here.

(The crowd remove him forcibly)

| Susan B. Anthony suddenly. | They are married all married and their children women as well as men will |

have the vote, they will they will, they
will have the vote.

Curtain

ACT II Scene VI

(Susan B. doing her house-work in her house)

Enter Anne.	Susan B. they want you.
Susan B.	Do they
Anne.	Yes. You must go.
Susan B.	No.
Jenny Reefer comes in.	Oh yes they want to know if you are here.
Susan B.	Yes still alive. Painters paint and writers write and soldiers drink and fight and I I am still alive.
Anne.	They want you.
Susan B.	And when they have me.
Jenny Reefer.	Then they will want you again.
Susan B.	Yes I know, they love me so, they tell me so and they tell me so, but I, I do not tell them so because I know, they will not do what they could do and I I will be left alone to die but they will not have done what I need to have done to make it right that I live lived my life and fight.
Jo the Loiterer at the window.	Indiana Elliot wants to come in, she will not take my name she says it is not all the same, she says that she is Indiana Elliot and that I am Jo, and that she will not take my name and that she will always tell me so. Oh yes she is right of course she is right it is not all the same Indiana Elliot is her name, she is only married to me, but there is no differ-ence that I can see, but all the same

	there she is and she will not change her name, yes it is all the same.
Susan B.	Let her in.
Indiana Elliot.	Oh Susan B. they want you they have to have you, can I tell them you are coming I have not changed my name can I tell them you are coming and that you will do everything.
Susan B.	No but there is no use in telling them so, they won't vote my laws, there is always a clause, there is always a pause, they won't vote my laws.

(Andrew Johnson puts his head in at the door)

Andrew Johnson.	Will the good lady come right along.
Thaddeus Stevens behind him.	We are waiting, will the good lady not keep us waiting, will the good lady not keep us waiting.
Susan B.	You you know so well that you will not vote my laws.
Stevens.	Dear lady remember humanity comes first.
Susan B.	You mean men come first, women, you will not vote my laws, how can you dare when you do not care, how can you dare, there is no humanity in humans, there is only law, and you will not because you know so well that there is no humanity there are only laws, you know it so well that you will not you will not vote my laws.

(Susan B. goes back to her housework.
All the characters crowd in)

| Chorus. | Do come Susan B. Anthony do come nobody no nobody can make them come the way you make them come, do come do come Susan B. Anthony, it is your duty, Susan B. Anthony, you know you know your duty, you come, do come, come. |

Susan B. Anthony.	I suppose I will be coming, is it because you flatter me, is it because if I do not come you will forget me and never vote my laws, you will never vote my laws even if I do come but if I do not come you will never vote my laws, come or not come it always comes to the same thing it comes to their not voting my laws, not voting my laws, tell me all you men tell me you know you will never vote my laws.
All the Men.	Dear kind lady we count on you, and as we count on you so can you count on us.
Susan B. Anthony.	Yes but I work for you I do, I say never again, never again, never never, and yet I know I do say no but I do not mean no, I know I always hope that if I go that if I go and go and go, perhaps then you men will vote my laws but I know how well I know, a little this way a little that way you steal away, you steal a piece away you steal yourselves away, you do not intend to stay and vote my laws, and still when you call I go, I go, I go, I say no, no, no, and I go, but no, this time no, this time you have to do more than promise, you must write it down that you will vote my laws, but no, you will pay no attention to what is written, well then swear by my hearth, as you hope to have a home and hearth, swear after I work for you swear that you will vote my laws, but no, no oaths, no thoughts, no decisions, no intentions, no gratitude, no convictions, no nothing will make you pass my laws. Tell me can any of you be honest now, and say you will not pass my laws.
Jo the Loiterer.	I can I can be honest I can say I will

not pass your laws, because you see I have no vote, no loiterer has a vote so it is easy Susan B. Anthony easy for one man among all these men to be honest and to say I will not pass your laws. Anyway Susan B. Anthony what are your laws. Would it really be all right to pass them, if you say so it is all right with me. I have no vote myself but I'll make them as long as I don't have to change my name don't have to don't have to change my name.

T. Stevens.   Thanks dear Susan B. Anthony, thanks we all know that whatever happens we all can depend upon you to do your best for any cause which is a cause, and any cause is a cause and because any cause is a cause therefore you will always do your best for any cause, and now you will be doing your best for this cause our cause the cause.

Susan B.   Because. Very well is it snowing.

Chorus.   Not just now.

Susan B. Anthony.   Is it cold.

Chorus.   A little.

Susan B. Anthony.   I am not well

Chorus.   But you look so well and once started it will be all right.

Susan B. Anthony.   All right

Curtain

ACT II Scene VII

(Susan B. Anthony busy with her housework)

Anne comes in.   Oh it was wonderful, wonderful, they listen to nobody the way they listen to you.

Susan B.   Yes it is wonderful as the result of my work for the first time the word male has been written into the constitution of the United States concerning suffrage. Yes it is wonderful.

Anne.   But

Susan B.   Yes but, what is man, what are men, what are they. I do not say that they haven't kind hearts, if I fall down in a faint, they will rush to pick me up, if my house is on fire, they will rush in to put the fire out and help me, yes they have kind hearts but they are afraid, afraid, they are afraid, they are afraid. They fear women, they fear each other, they fear their neighbor, they fear other countries and then they hearten themselves in their fear by crowding together and following each other, and when they crowd together and follow each other they are brutes, like animals who stampede, and so they have written in the name male into the United States constitution, because they are afraid of black men because they are afraid of women, because they are afraid afraid. Men are afraid.

Anne timidly.   And women.

Susan B.   Ah women often have not any sense of danger, after all a hen screams pitifully when she sees an eagle but she is only afraid for her children, men are afraid for themselves, that is the real difference between men and women.

Anne.   But Susan B. why do you not say these things out loud.

Susan B.   Why not, because if I did they would not listen they not alone would not listen they would revenge themselves. Men have kind hearts when they are not afraid but they are afraid afraid afraid. I say they are afraid, but if I were to tell them so their kindness would

	turn to hate. Yes the Quakers are right, they are not afraid because they do not fight, they do not fight.
Anne.	But Susan B. you fight and you are not afraid.
Susan B.	I fight and I am not afraid, I fight but I am not afraid.
Anne.	And you will win.
Susan B.	Win what, win what.
Anne.	Win the vote for women.
Susan B.	Yes some day some day the women will vote and by that time.
Anne.	By that time oh wonderful time.
Susan B.	By that time it will do them no good because having the vote they will become like men, they will be afraid, having the vote will make them afraid, oh I know it, but I will fight for the right, for the right to vote for them even though they become like men, become afraid like men, become like men.

(Anne bursts into tears. Jenny Reefer rushes in)

| Jenny Reefer. | I have just converted Lillian Russell to the cause of woman's suffrage, I have converted her, she will give all herself and all she earns oh wonderful day I know you will say, here she comes isn't she beautiful. |

(Lillian Russell comes in followed by all the women
in the chorus. Women crowding around,
Constance Fletcher in the background)

| Lillian Russell. | Dear friends, it is so beautiful to meet you all, so beautiful, so beautiful to meet you all. |

(John Adams comes in and sees Constance Fletcher)

| John Adams. | Dear friend beautiful friend, there is no beauty where you are not. |
| Constance Fletcher. | Yes dear friend but look look at real beauty look at Lillian Russell look at real beauty. |

John Adams.   Real beauty real beauty is all there is of
                     beauty and why should my eye wander
                     where no eye can look without having
                     looked before. Dear friend I kneel to
                     you because dear friend each time I see
                     you I have never looked before, dear
                     friend you are an open door.

(Daniel Webster strides in, the women separate)

Daniel Webster.   What what is it, what is it, what is the
                     false and the true and I say to you you
                     Susan B. Anthony, you know the false
                     from the true and yet you will not wait
                     you will not wait, I say you will you will
                     wait. When my eyes, and I have eyes
                     when my eyes, beyond that I seek not
                     to penetrate the veil, why should you
                     want what you have chosen, when mine
                     eyes, why do you want that the curtain
                     may rise, why when mine eyes, why
                     should the vision be opened to what
                     lies behind, why, Susan B. Anthony
                     fight the fight that is the fight, that any
                     fight may be a fight for the right. I hear
                     that you say that the word male should
                     not be written into the constitution of
                     the United States of America, but I say,
                     I say, that so long that the gorgeous
                     ensign of the republic, still full high ad-
                     vanced, its arms and trophies streaming
                     in their original luster not a stripe
                     erased or polluted not a single star ob-
                     scured.

Jo the Loiterer.   She has decided to change her name.

Indiana Elliot.   Not because it is his name but it is such
                     a pretty name, Indiana Loiterer is such
                     a pretty name I think all the same he
                     will have to change his name, he must
                     be Jo Elliot, yes he must, it is what he
                     has to do, he has to be Jo Elliot and I
                     am going to be Indiana Loiterer, dear

	friends, all friends is it not a lovely name, Indiana Loiterer all the same.
Jo the Loiterer.	All right I never fight, nobody will know it's men, but what can I do, if I am not she and I am not me, what can I do, if a name is not true, what can I do but do as she tells me.
All the Chorus.	She is quite right, Indiana Loiterer is so harmonious, so harmonious, Indiana Loiterer is so harmonious.
All the Men Come In.	What did she say.
Jo.	I was talking not she but nobody no nobody ever wants to listen to me.
All the Chorus Men and Women.	Susan B. Anthony was very successful we are all very grateful to Susan B. Anthony because she was so successful, she worked for the votes for women and she worked for the vote for colored men and she was so successful, they wrote the word male into the constitution of the United States of America, dear Susan B. Anthony. Dear Susan B., whenever she wants to be and she always wants to be she is always so successful so very successful.
Susan B.	So successful.

Curtain

ACT II Scene VIII

(The Congressional Hall, the replica of the
statue of Susan B. Anthony and her
comrades in the suffrage fight)

Anne alone in front of the statuary.	The Vote. Women have the vote. They have it each and every one, it is glorious glorious glorious.

Susan B. Anthony
  behind the statue.   Yes women have the vote, all my long
                     life of strength and strife, all my long
                     life, women have it, they can vote,
                     every man and every woman have the
                     vote, the word male is not there any
                     more, that is to say, that is to say.
        (Silence. Virgil T. comes in very nicely,
           he looks around and sees Anne)
Virgil T.   Very well indeed, very well indeed, you
                     are looking very well indeed, have you a
                     chair anywhere, very well indeed, as we
                     sit, we sit, some day very soon some day
                     they will vote sitting and that will be a
                     very successful day any day, every day.
      (Henry B. comes in. He looks all around
         at the statue and then he sighs)
Henry B.   Does it really mean that women are as
                     white and cold as marble does it really
                     mean that.
     (Angel More comes in and bows gracefully
          to the sculptured group)
Angel More.   I can always think of dear Daniel Web-
                     ster daily.
    (John Adams comes in and looks around, and then
          carefully examines the statue)
John Adams.   I think that they might have added dear
                     delicate Constance Fletcher I do think
                     they might have added her wonderful
                     profile, I do think they might have, I
                     do, I really do.
        (Andrew Johnson shuffles in)
Andrew Johnson.   I have no hope in black or white in
                     white or black in black or black or
                     white or white, no hope.
(Thaddeus Stevens comes in, he does not address anybody,
      he stands before the statue and frowns)
Thaddeus S.   Rob the cradle, rob it, rob the robber,
                     rob him, rob whatever there is to be
                     taken, rob, rob the cradle, rob it.

Daniel Webster (he sees nothing else).

> Angel More, more more Angel More, did you hear me, can you hear shall you hear me, when they come and they do come, when they go and they do go, Angel More can you will you shall you may you might you would you hear me, when they have lost and won, when they have won and lost, when words are bitter and snow is white, Angel More come to me and we will leave together.

Angel More.   Dear sir, not leave, stay.

Henrietta M.   I have never been mentioned again. (She curtseys)

Constance Fletcher.   Here I am, I am almost blind but here I am, dear dear here I am, I cannot see what is so white, here I am.

John Adams (kissing her hand).

> Here you are, blind as a bat and beautiful as a bird, here you are, white and cold as marble, beautiful as marble, yes that is marble but you you are the living marble dear Constance Fletcher, you are.

Constance Fletcher.   Thank you yes I am here, blind as a bat, I am here.

Indiana Elliot.   I am sorry to interrupt so sorry to interrupt but I have a great deal to say about marriage, either one or the other married must be economical, either one or the other, if either one or the other of a married couple are economical then a marriage is successful, if not not, I have a great deal to say about marriage, and dear Susan B. Anthony was never married, how wonderful it is to be never married how wonderful. I have a great deal to say about marriage.

Susan B. Anthony voice from behind the statue.	It is a puzzle, I am not puzzled but it is a puzzle, if there are no children there are no men and women, and if there are men and women, it is rather horrible, and if it is rather horrible, then there are children, I am not puzzled but it is very puzzling, women and men vote and children, I am not puzzled but it is very puzzling.
Gloster Heming.	I have only been a man who has a very fine name, and it must be said I made it up yes I did, so many do why not I, so many do, so many do, and why not two, when anybody might, and you can vote and you can dote with any name. Thank you.
Isabel Wentworth.	They looked for me and they found me, I like to talk about it. It is very nearly necessary not to be noisy not to be noisy and hope, hope and hop, no use in enjoying men and women no use, I wonder why we are all happy, yes.
Annie Hope.	There is another Anne and she believes, I am hopey hope and I do not believe I have been in California and Kalamazoo, and I do not believe I burst into tears and I do not believe.

(They all crowd closer together and Lillian Russell
who comes in stands quite alone)

Lillian Russell.	I can act so drunk that I never drink, I can drink so drunk that I never act, I have a curl I was a girl and I am old and fat but very handsome for all that.

(Anthony Comstock comes in and glares at her)

Anthony Comstock.	I have heard that they have thought that they would wish that one like you could vote a vote and help to let the ones who want do what they like, I have heard that even you, and I am

through, I cannot hope that there is
dope, oh yes a horrid word. I have
never heard, short.

Jenny Reefer.   I have hope and faith, not charity no
not charity, I have hope and faith, no
not, not charity, no not charity.

Ulysses S. Grant.   Women are women, soldiers are soldiers, men are not men, lies are not lies,
do, and then a dog barks, listen to him
and then a dog barks, a dog barks a dog
barks any dog barks, listen to him any
dog barks.

(he sits down)

Herman Atlan.   I am not loved any more, I was loved
oh yes I was loved but I am not loved
any more, I am not, was I not, I knew
I would refuse what a woman would
choose and so I am not loved any
more, not loved any more.

Donald Gallup.   Last but not least, first and not best, I
am tall as a man, I am firm as a clam,
and I never change, from day to day.

(Jo the Loiterer and Chris a Citizen)

Jo the Loiterer.   Let us dance and sing, Chrissy Chris,
wet and not in debt, I am a married
man and I know how I show I am a
married man. She votes, she changes
her name and she votes.

(They all crowd together in front of the statue, there is
a moment of silence and then a chorus)

Chorus.   To vote the vote, the vote we vote, can
vote do vote will vote could vote, the
vote the vote.

Jo the Loiterer.   I am the only one who cannot vote, no
loiterer can vote.

Indiana Elliot.   I am a loiterer Indiana Loiterer and I
can vote.

Jo the Loiterer.   You only have the name, you have not
got the game.

Chorus.   The vote the vote we will have the vote.

Lillian Russell.   It is so beautiful to meet you all here
                          so beautiful.

Ulysses S. Grant.   Vote the vote, the army does not vote,
                          the general generals, there is no vote,
                          bah vote.

The Chorus.   The vote we vote we note the vote.

(They all bow and smile to the statue. Suddenly
          Susan B.'s voice is heard)

Susan B.'s voice.   We cannot retrace our steps, going for-
                          ward may be the same as going back-
                          wards. We cannot retrace our steps,
                          retrace our steps. All my long life, all
                          my life, we do not retrace our steps, all
                          my long life, but.

(A silence a long silence)

                          But—we do not retrace our steps, all my
                          long life, and here, here we are here, in
                          marble and gold, did I say gold, yes I said
                          gold, in marble and gold and where—

                              (A silence)

                          Where is where. In my long life of ef-
                          fort and strife, dear life, life is strife, in
                          my long life, it will not come and go,
                          I tell you so, it will stay it will pay but

                          (A long silence)

                          But do I want what we have got, has it
                          not gone, what made it live, has it not
                          gone because now it is had, in my long
                          life in my long life

                              (Silence)

                          Life is strife, I was a martyr all my life
                          not to what I won but to what was
                          done.

                              (Silence)

                          Do you know because I tell you so, or
                          do you know, do you know.

                              (Silence)

                          My long life, my long life.

                          Curtain

REFLECTION ON THE
ATOMIC BOMB

Reflection on the Atomic Bomb

T HEY asked me what I thought of the atomic bomb. I said
I had not been able to take any interest in it.

I like to read detective and mystery stories, I never get
enough of them but whenever one of them is or was about
death rays and atomic bombs I never could read them. What
is the use, if they are really as destructive as all that there is
nothing left and if there is nothing there is nobody to be
interested and nothing to be interested about. If they are not
as destructive as all that then they are just a little more or less
destructive than other things and that means that in spite of
all destruction there are always lots left on this earth to be
interested or to be interesting and the thing that destroys is
just one of the things that concerns the people inventing it or
the people shooting it off, but really nobody else can do anything about it so you have to just live along like always, so
you see the atomic (bomb) is not at all interesting, not any
more interesting than any other machine, and machines are
only interesting in being invented or in what they do, so why
be interested. I never could take any interest in the atomic
bomb, I just couldnt any more than in everybody's secret
weapon. That it has to be secret makes it dull and meaning-
less. Sure it will destroy a lot and kill a lot, but it's the living
that are interesting not the way of killing them, because if
there were not a lot left living how could there be any interest
in destruction. Alright, that is the way I feel about it. And
really way down that is the way everybody feels about it. They
think they are interested about the atomic bomb but they
really are not not any more than I am. Really not. They may
be a little scared, I am not so scared, there is so much to be
scared of so what is the use of bothering to be scared, and if
you are not scared the atomic bomb is not interesting.

Everybody gets so much information all day long that they
lose their common sense. They listen so much that they forget
to be natural. This is a nice story.

CHRONOLOGY

NOTE ON THE TEXTS

NOTES

Chronology

1874   Born February 3 in Allegheny, Pennsylvania, the youngest of five surviving children of Daniel Stein and Amelia ("Milly") Keyser. (Parents both belonged to German-Jewish immigrant families who settled in Baltimore before the Civil War. Daniel, born 1832, was a partner with his four brothers in the clothing trade in Baltimore until 1862, when he left to form a clothing business in Pittsburgh with his brother Solomon. He married Amelia, born 1842, in 1864; the newlyweds settled in Allegheny, a northern suburb of Pittsburgh. Their surviving children were Michael, born 1865; Simon, born 1868; Bertha, born 1870; and Leo, born 1872.) Partly because of tensions between the brothers and their families, father moves family to Austria in fall of 1874 to study opportunities in banking business.

1875–79   Father soon returns to the U.S. on business, and is frequently absent during European stay; family remains in Vienna. Stein learns German along with English, and is cared for by a governess. Moves with mother and siblings to Paris in 1878; attends school and learns French. Returns with family to U.S. the following year, living for a while with maternal grandparents in Baltimore.

1880–87   Moves with family to East Oakland, California, in 1880. Father works as stockbroker and invests in San Francisco enterprises, including Omnibus Cable Car Company; family lives at a hotel and a furnished house before settling in April 1881 in large house with a ten-acre yard. Stein attends public schools, Sabbath school, and also has tutors at home; reads widely and goes to the theater; inseparable from brother Leo. Family moves to smaller Oakland house in 1885. Mother becomes ill with cancer.

1888–90   Mother dies in July 1888. Brother Michael returns from Johns Hopkins to manage family business interests. Stein leaves Oakland High School in 1889 (never obtains high school diploma).

1891   Father dies suddenly in January. Michael assumes legal guardianship of Leo and Gertrude and moves family to

San Francisco. He sells off Omnibus holdings and manages estate so efficiently that Leo and Gertrude have small but sufficient incomes.

1892   Stein goes to Baltimore with sister Bertha in July to live with mother's sister, Fannie Bachrach. Leo enrolls in September at Harvard, where Gertrude visits him frequently.

1893–95   Stein enrolls in fall of 1893 in Harvard Annex (re-named Radcliffe the following year); moves into Cambridge boarding house where she will live for the next four years. Attends wedding of brother Michael and Sarah Samuels in March 1894. Studies composition with William Vaughn Moody, philosophy with George Santayana and Josiah Royce, and psychology with Hugo Münsterberg (who supervises her work at Harvard Psychological Laboratory) and William James (later describes herself as deeply influenced by James's ideas on consciousness and perception). Active in philosophy and drama clubs. Has lively social life with group of mostly Jewish students known as "the Crowd." Forms close friendship with philosophy student Leon Solomons, with whom she collaborates on psychology experiments.

1896   Joins Leo (who has been traveling around the world for a year) in Europe for summer; tours Holland and Germany, and visits Paris briefly before settling in London for a month. Research paper "Normal Motor Automatism," co-written with Leon Solomons, published in Harvard publication *The Psychological Review* in September.

1897   Studies with Leo at Woods Hole Marine Biological Laboratory in Massachusetts during summer. Enters Johns Hopkins School of Medicine (where Leo is studying biology) in September; brother and sister share apartment. Forms friendship with physician Claribel Cone and her sister Etta (members of wealthy Jewish family who become important art collectors).

1898–1901   Awarded B.A. from Radcliffe in 1898, after belatedly passing required Latin examination. "Cultivated Motor Automatism: A Study of Character in its Relation to Attention" published in *The Psychological Review* in May

1898. Spends two summers, 1898 and 1899, with Michael and family in San Francisco. Socializes with circle of Bryn Mawr–educated young women at Johns Hopkins, including May Bookstaver (with whom she has affair). Leon Solomons dies February 1900. Stein sails to Europe in June with Leo and mutual friend Mabel Weeks; they travel in Italy and France. Fails four courses; leaves school in spring of 1901 without medical degree. Travels in the summer with Leo, touring in Morocco and Spain before joining the Cone sisters in Paris. Does further research on brain anatomy in Baltimore in the fall, but results are not deemed publishable by advisers at Johns Hopkins.

1902 Sails to Europe in the spring. Joins Leo in Italy and travels with him to England. Makes acquaintance of art historian Bernhard Berenson, his wife, Mary, and philosopher Bertrand Russell. Rents rooms with Leo in Bloomsbury Square, London, in the fall. On her own, studies English literature; shares Leo's interest in Japanese prints.

1903 Sails back to New York in January; stays with Mabel Weeks and other friends at 100th Street and Riverside Drive. Begins early version of long novel *The Making of Americans*, based on the history of her family. Returns to Europe in June; travels to Florence, where she spends time with the Cone sisters. Has emotionally difficult meetings in Rome and Siena with May Bookstaver and her wealthy companion, Mabel Haynes. In the fall joins Leo in Paris, where he is pursuing a career as a painter; settles into his apartment at 27, rue de Fleurus. With Leo, goes regularly to Ambroise Vollard's gallery, where they buy paintings by Cézanne. Writes *Q.E.D.*, novella based on relationship with May Bookstaver.

1904 Michael and his family move to Paris in January. Stein sails to America, visiting friends in New York and Boston; returns to Europe in June with Etta Cone, and spends summer with Leo in Florence, where they see private collection of Cézanne paintings. With unexpected windfall from family estate, Stein and Leo buy paintings by Gauguin, Cézanne, and Renoir from Vollard; subsequently purchase works by Delacroix, Toulouse-Lautrec, Manet, Degas. Stein forms friendship with journalist Mildred Aldrich. Works on novella *Fernhurst*.

1905–6   Begins *Three Lives*, series of three novellas, in spring of
          1905 (completed the following year). Spends summer
          in Italy with Leo. Attends Autumn Salon in Paris, first
          public showing of Fauvist painters; Stein and Leo, as well
          as Michael and Sarah Stein, begin collecting work by
          Henri Matisse and form friendships with Matisse family.
          Stein and Leo begin buying work by Pablo Picasso;
          through his dealer, Clovis Sagot, they meet Picasso in No-
          vember. Stein and Picasso form enduring friendship, and
          he begins a portrait of her (finished in 1906, by her
          account after more than 80 sittings). Stein and Leo hold
          Saturday-night salons which become cultural center of
          Bohemian Paris and primary showcase of modern art,
          attended by figures including Guillaume Apollinaire,
          Georges Braque, Charles Demuth, André Derain, Marcel
          Duchamp, Marie Laurencin, Mina Loy and husband
          Stephen Haweis, Henri and Amélie Matisse, and art dealer
          Daniel-Henry Kahnweiler (who becomes close friend).
          Resumes work on *The Making of Americans*.

1907   At home of Michael and Sarah in September, is introduced
          to Alice Babette Toklas (born in San Francisco in 1877),
          who has just arrived in Paris from California. Toklas rooms
          with friend Harriet Levy at hotel near rue de Fleurus.

1908   Stein and Toklas spend much of summer together in Italy
          (Stein stays with Leo, Toklas with Harriet Levy). On re-
          turn to Paris, the two women are inseparable. Toklas be-
          gins to type up manuscript of *The Making of Americans*.
          William James visits rue de Fleurus.

1909   *Three Lives* published in August by Grafton Press in New
          York (for $600 fee); receives some favorable reviews.

1910   Tensions and disagreements increase between Stein and
          Leo. Stein and Toklas spend summer in Italy; send post-
          cards to friends of themselves together in Venice. Toklas
          moves into 27, rue de Fleurus in December. Stein and
          Toklas are henceforth permanent companions, always liv-
          ing and traveling together; Toklas serves as homemaker,
          secretary, typist. Stein composes the first of her portraits,
          "Ada," in tribute to her relationship with Toklas.

1917 and afterwards is stationed in Nîmes. They make many acquaintances among American soldiers, and form close friendship with W. G. "Kiddie" Rogers.

1918–21   Stein and Toklas return briefly to Paris after November 1918 armistice, then travel to Alsace to do civilian relief work; they go back to Paris in May 1919, but do not resume Saturday-evening salons. Stein becomes friend of Sylvia Beach and subscriber to Beach's Shakespeare & Company bookstore in Paris. Sits for bust by Jacques Lipschitz in 1920. Stein and Leo glimpse each other for last time, without speaking, on a Paris street in December 1920. Forms friendships with Erik Satie; Jean Cocteau; Sherwood Anderson; Ford Madox Ford; writer Kate Buss, who serves as advocate and agent; and journalist Janet Flanner.

1922   Meets photographer Man Ray, who takes portraits of Stein and Toklas, and the 23-year-old Ernest Hemingway, who visits with a letter of introduction from Sherwood Anderson. Spends summer with Toklas in Saint Rémy. *Geography and Plays*, collection of prose, plays, and poems, published in December.

1923   Stays with Toklas at Hôtel Pernollet in Belley, Ain, in southeastern France, in September (they will continue to spend summers in the region). Sits for bronze portrait by Jo Davidson.

1924   Receives visits from William Carlos Williams in January and T. S. Eliot in November. *The Making of Americans* is partially serialized in Ford Madox Ford's *Transatlantic Review*, April–December.

1925   *The Making of Americans* published by Robert McAlmon's Contact Editions, financed by McAlmon's wife, the novelist Bryher. Introduced by Hemingway to F. Scott and Zelda Fitzgerald in May; meets Edith Sitwell (who introduces her to brothers Osbert and Sacheverell) and, through Van Vechten, Paul Robeson.

1926   Delivers lecture "Composition as Explanation" during summer at Cambridge and Oxford; Leonard and Virginia Woolf's Hogarth Press publishes text. Forms close friendship with Bernard Faÿ, scholar of American history, who becomes translator of her work. Meets composer Virgil Thomson in the fall (he becomes collaborator and pioneer in setting Stein's texts to music). Gradually forms circle of new acquaintances (many of them friends of Thomson) including French poets Georges Hugnet and René Crevel, painters Pavel Tchelitchev, Christian Bérard, and Eugène Berman, and American writer Bravig Imbs. Kahnweiler publishes "A Book Concluding with As a Wife Has a Cow, A Love Story," with illustrations by Juan Gris, in December.

1927   Publishes "Elucidation" (written 1923, early analysis of her own work) in *transition*. Composes "The Life of Juan Gris, the Life and Death of Juan Gris" after Gris' death in May. Agrees to write opera libretto for Virgil Thomson, and completes *Four Saints in Three Acts* in June. Natalie Barney organizes a Gertrude Stein evening at her "Académie des Femmes" salon, at which Thomson performs settings of "Capital Capitals," "Susie Asado," and "Preciosilla."

1928–29   *Useful Knowledge* published in autumn 1928 in New York by Payson & Clarke. Stein and Toklas find summer house in Bilignin near Belley, and begin leasing it in spring 1929 (in future years they will spend summers there).

1930   Sells Picasso's 1905 painting "Woman with a Fan" to finance Plain Edition, small press run by Toklas and dedicated to publishing Stein's work; first book published is *Lucy Church Amiably* (written 1927). Meets Francis Rose, British painter whose work she has begun collecting.

1931   Stein's free adaptation of Hugnet's poem *Enfances* published by Plain Edition as *Before the Flowers of Friendship Faded Friendship Faded*; friendship with Hugnet breaks up over his objections to the looseness of the translation. Visited at Bilignin in the summer by composers Aaron Copland and Paul Bowles.

1932   Publishes *How To Write* (composed 1927–31) and *Operas and Plays* (collection of film treatments, plays, and operas created since 1913) in Plain Edition. While showing unpublished work to novelist Louis Bromfield in April, rediscovers manuscript of *Q.E.D.*; revelations about earlier love affair provoke strains with Toklas. Writes *The Auto-biography of Alice B. Toklas* in six weeks at Bilignin (October–November).

1933   *Matisse Picasso and Gertrude Stein with Two Shorter Sto-ries*, collection of works written before World War I, pub-lished by Plain Edition. Finishes *Four in America* (writings on Ulysses S. Grant, Wilbur Wright, Henry James, and George Washington). Sits for portrait by Picabia. *The Autobiography of Alice B. Toklas* is excerpted in *Atlantic Monthly*; it is published by Harcourt Brace in September and becomes a bestseller. Bennett Cerf of Random House agrees to publish her future work, and reissues *Three Lives* in the Modern Library. *The Making of Americans* is pub-lished in an abridged French translation edited by Stein and Faÿ.

1934   *Four Saints in Three Acts* (directed by John Houseman with all-black cast, choreography by Frederick Ashton, sets and costumes by Florine Stettheimer) opens to acclaim in Hartford in February, then moves to New York for one-month run. Stein agrees to return to America for lecture tour. The abridged version of *The Making of Americans* is published by Harcourt Brace. Sails with Toklas for New York in October; receives wide publicity and gives frequent press and radio interviews (forms friendship with journalist Joseph Alsop, Jr.). Gives first lecture at Colony Club under auspices of Museum of Modern Art on November 2; makes other East Coast appearances at Columbia Univer-sity and Princeton. Random House publishes *Portraits and Prayers* (collection of work from 1909 to 1931) in No-vember. With Toklas, makes first airplane trip to Chicago for performance of *Four Saints*. Lectures at University of Chicago at intervals throughout American visit; faculty member Thornton Wilder becomes friend and advocate. Revisits Harvard and Radcliffe; spends Christmas with Bal-timore relatives. Lectures in Washington, D.C., in Decem-ber; with Toklas, has tea at White House with Eleanor Roosevelt.

1935   Continues lecture tour with engagements in New En-gland; makes recording of her work in New York. Travels with Toklas in South in February. Dismisses "Testimony Against Gertrude Stein," an attack on the accuracy of *The*

Autobiography of Alice B. Toklas by Parisian figures including Matisse, published in February *transition*. *Lectures in America* published by Random House in March. Tours Texas and Oklahoma, March–April. In California, meets Charlie Chaplin, Dashiell Hammett; receives key to city of San Francisco. Stein and Toklas return to childhood homes; Stein finds Oakland home vacant, disagreeable ("there is no there there"); lectures in Berkeley. Returns to New York in late April. Stein and Toklas sail for France in May. Toklas, worried about European political turmoil, begins preparing typescripts of Stein's work for safekeeping by Van Vechten. *Narration*, text of Chicago lectures, published in December with introduction by Wilder.

1936   At Oxford and Cambridge in February, delivers lectures "What Are Masterpieces" and "An American and France." Discusses musical setting of her plays with English composer Lord Gerald Berners, who adapts *They Must Be Wedded To Their Wife* as *A Wedding Bouquet*. Forms friendship with photographer Cecil Beaton. *The Geographical History of America* published by Random House in October.

1937   Stein and Toklas fly to London in April for premiere of *A Wedding Bouquet* (choreographed by Frederick Ashton). Accepts Yale University Library proposal to deposit manuscripts there. Anticipating war, Michael Stein family returns to U.S. Memoir *Everybody's Autobiography* published by Random House in December.

1938   Stein and Toklas move to 5, rue Christine in February. Michael Stein dies of cancer in San Francisco. Stein publishes *Picasso* in French (translated into English by Toklas). Finishes play *Doctor Faustus Lights the Lights* in June.

1939   Visited at Bilignin by Clare Booth and Henry Luce; expresses skepticism when they warn her of impending war; rejects similar warnings from other friends. Children's book *The World Is Round* published in August. Following outbreak of war in September, Stein and Toklas spend 36 hours in Paris retrieving papers, clothing, one Cézanne, and Picasso portrait of Stein. Against advice of American officials, they remain in Bilignin.

1940   *Paris France* published in April. As France falls to the Germans in June, Stein and Toklas consider leaving the country, but at last minute decide to stay in Bilignin, soon to be under Vichy rule. "The Winner Loses: A Picture of Occupied France" published in November *Atlantic Monthly*. Begins *Mrs. Reynolds*, novel dealing allegorically with origins of World War II.

1941–43   *Ida: A Novel* published by Random House in February 1941. Receives protection from Faÿ, who has been appointed director of Bibliothèque Nationale in Paris. Develops interest in prophecies, including those of 15th-century writer Saint Odile; begins translation, later abandoned, of speeches by Vichy leader Marshal Pétain. Stein and Toklas subsist on scant rations and food bought on black market. Bilignin house reclaimed by landlord in 1942; Stein institutes a lawsuit against him, drops it when she finds another house ("Le Colombier") in nearby Culoz. Begins diaristic account of the war years (published as *Wars I Have Seen*). Ignores private warning to flee to Switzerland or be sent to concentration camp. Stein and Toklas move to Culoz in February 1943. A German officer and his orderly are billeted with them in September.

1944   Two Italian officers and 30 soldiers are billeted in house and adjoining park in January. Culoz house commandeered by German officer and men for 24 hours in July. French Resistance forces liberate Culoz in August. American soldiers arrive September 1; correspondents Eric Sevareid and Frank Gervasi find Stein and Toklas the next day, and Sevareid arranges for Stein to broadcast to U.S. from nearby Voiron. Returning to Paris in mid-December, learns that art collection in rue Christine apartment is mostly intact. Reunites with friends, including Picasso and Hemingway.

1945   Treated as celebrity by American soldiers who visit her regularly. *Wars I Have Seen* published by Random House in March and sells well. Corresponds with Richard Wright. Tours U.S. army bases in Germany in June. Lectures to American soldiers at Sorbonne. Visits Bernard Faÿ, who has been imprisoned for collaboration, and writes testimonial defending him. Begins working with Thomson in October on *The Mother of Us All*, opera about Susan B.

Anthony (score is not completed until after her death). Lectures to G.I.'s in Brussels in December; complains of fatigue, and suffers intestinal attacks.

1946   Finishes libretto of *The Mother of Us All* by March. Play *Yes Is For A Very Young Man* (originally *In Savoy*) produced in Pasadena. Meets Richard Wright and family when they arrive in Paris in May. *Brewsie and Willie* published in June. Stein becomes ill while driving to country house of Faÿ, returns to Paris by train; ambulance takes her to American Hospital at Neuilly-sur-Seine, where doctors diagnose stomach cancer. Draws up will on July 23, leaving Picasso portrait to Metropolitan Museum in New York, manuscripts and papers to Yale, and money in care of Van Vechten (who, with Toklas, is named literary executor) for publication of manuscripts. The rest of estate is left for care of Toklas until her death, the residue to pass to nephew Allan Stein and his children. Insists on operation even when told by doctors that she is too weak for it. Awaiting surgery on July 27, asks Toklas, "What is the answer?"; when Toklas remains silent, adds, "In that case, what is the question?" Following operation, dies same day without recovering consciousness. Buried October 22 in Père Lachaise Cemetery, Paris (tombstone designed by Francis Rose; Toklas is buried in same tomb when she dies in March 1967). *Selected Writings of Gertrude Stein* (edited by Van Vechten) published by Random House the same month.

Note on the Texts

This volume contains fifteen works written by Gertrude Stein between 1932 and 1946, seven of which were published after her death in 1946.

The complete text of "Stanzas in Meditation," written in 1932, was not published during Stein's lifetime, although it was excerpted in *Orbes* (no. 4, Winter 1932–33, with French translation on facing pages), *Life and Letters Today* (vol. XV, no. 6, Winter 1936–37), and *Poetry* (vol. LV, no. 5, February 1940). The complete text first appeared in *Stanzas in Meditation and Other Poems 1929–1933* (New Haven: Yale University Press, 1950; edited by Donald Sutherland) as part of the Yale Edition of the Unpublished Writings of Gertrude Stein. This edition included revisions that Stein made to the typescript, apparently at Toklas's urging. The majority of the changes consist of the excision of almost all forms of the word *may* from the text, perhaps as a result of Stein's rediscovery in the spring of 1932 of *Q.E.D.*, a fictional work based on Stein's relationship with May Bookstaver (see Ulla E. Dydo, "How to Read Gertrude Stein: The Manuscripts of 'Stanzas in Meditation' " in *Text*, vol. I, 1981). Revisions include the frequent substitution of *can* or *day* for *may* and sometimes involve further recasting of the text; for example, "Just why they may count how may one mistaken" (16.6) becomes "Just why they can count how many are mistaken" and "month of May" (22.8) becomes "month to-day." The text printed here is that of the corrected typescript copy that bears the title "LXXXIII Stanzas" and that does not include the revisions to the word *may*; the manuscript is in the Beinecke Library, Yale University.

Written in 1932–33, "Henry James" is one part of a study of four Americans, including also Wilbur Wright, Ulysses S. Grant, and George Washington, which Stein titled *Four in America*. The book first appeared in 1947 (edited by Donald Gallup) as part of the Yale Edition of the Unpublished Writings of Gertrude Stein; the text of the first edition was based on a collation of the holograph manuscript and the typescripts in the Beinecke Library. The text printed here is that of the first edition.

Lectures in America was first published in 1935 by Random House and includes the lectures Stein wrote in 1934 and read during her American lecture tour in 1934–35. No typescript is known to be extant. The text printed here is that of the first edition.

Written in 1935, "Narration: Lecture 3" is the third lecture of four that Stein read at a seminar at the University of Chicago. *Narration: Four Lectures by Gertrude Stein* was first published in 1935 by the University of Chicago Press. Collation of the typescript copies and the first edition suggests that the typescripts are late drafts, since the book contains revisions that are evidently authorial. The text printed here is that of the first edition.

"What Are Master-pieces and Why Are There So Few of Them" was written in 1935 and was first published in America by the Conference Press, California in 1940. Collation of the typescripts and the first edition reveals a number of minor differences in the first edition which appear to be authorial. The text printed here is that of the first edition.

The Geographical History of America or The Relation of Human Nature to the Human Mind was written in 1935 and first published by Random House in 1936. Although Stein corrected one set of proofs, her letters to Bennett Cerf, her publisher, express concern about the number of errors introduced into the text during typesetting. She was unable to correct a second set of proofs and urged Cerf to proofread the book carefully against her original typescript. Collation of the typescript and the first book edition reveals significant disparities, including differences of punctuation, capitalization, and spacing, and numerous handwritten corrections to the typescript that are not reproduced in the first edition. The text printed here is that of the corrected typescript in the Beinecke Library.

Written in 1936, "What Does She See When She Shuts Her Eyes: A Novel" was first printed in *Mrs. Reynolds and Five Earlier Novelettes* as part of the Yale Edition of the Unpublished Writings of Gertrude Stein in 1952. The text printed here is that of the typescript, from the Beinecke Library.

Picasso was originally written and published in French in 1938. Alice B. Toklas translated the work into English, and Stein then corrected the manuscript produced by Toklas. The English-language version was first published in London by B. T. Batsford Ltd., in October 1938, and then, in identical form, in the United States by Charles Scribner's Sons in 1939. Collation of two corrected typescript carbon copies and the first edition shows numerous changes in punctuation and occasional word changes. Attached to the 42-page typescript in the Beinecke Library is a note in Stein's hand that reads "On no account depart from punctuation etc. of actual typescript." The text printed here is that of the 42-page corrected typescript.

The World Is Round, a children's book, was written in 1939 and first appeared in *Harper's Bazaar* (June 1939). It was first published in book form in the United States in 1939 by William R. Scott, illustrated by Clement Hurd and printed on bright pink paper with white and blue type, and was published in London a few months later by B. T. Batsford, with illustrations by Francis Rose. Collation of the corrected typescript copy and the first edition reveals significant word and punctuation differences, including many which appear authorial. The text printed here is that of the first American edition.

"Doctor Faustus Lights the Lights" was written in 1938. The play was commissioned by Gerald Berners, who intended to score it himself; when he was unable to do so, Virgil Thomson composed the music. It was published posthumously in *Last Operas and Plays* (New York and Toronto: Rinehart & Co., 1949). Collation shows significant differences between the typescript carbon copies and the first book edition, including differences of punctuation and wording. Because the authority for these changes is unclear, the text printed here is that of the later corrected typescript copy in the Beinecke Library.

Ida was written between 1937 and 1940 and was first published by Random House in 1941. No typescript is known to be extant. The text printed here is that of the first edition.

"Three Sisters Who Are Not Sisters" was written in 1944 and was first published in *The First Reader* (Dublin: Maurice Fridberg, 1946). No typescript is known to be extant. The first American printing, offset from the Dublin edition, was published in 1948 in Boston by Houghton Mifflin Co. The text printed here is that of the first book printing.

Brewsie and Willie was written in 1945 and was first published by Random House in 1946. The extant typescript has been marked up both by Stein and by a copy editor. Because it is not always possible to distinguish the two sets of markings, and because the identifiable revisions by Stein are incorporated into the first edition, the text printed here is that of the first edition.

"The Mother of Us All" was written in 1945–46, and a portion of it appeared in *Harper's Bazaar* (May 1947). The first book publication was in *Last Operas and Plays*. No typescript is known to be extant. The text printed here is that of the first book edition.

Written in 1945–46, "Reflection on the Atomic Bomb" may have been Stein's last piece of writing. The title was given to the piece by the editors of the *Yale Poetry Review*, where the piece appeared in no. 7, December 1947. The text printed here is that of the original typescript, from the Beinecke Library.

Although Stein's use of language and punctuation was unconventional, she employed standard spelling; therefore words inadvertently misspelled in the typescripts, as well as other obvious slips, have been corrected. However, Stein's omission of the apostrophe in some contractions ("its," "whats," for example) is fairly consistent and so has not been changed. Her British forms of several words such as "realise" and "recognise" have also been retained.

This volume presents the texts of the original printings chosen for inclusion here, but it does not attempt to reproduce features of their typographic design, such as display capitalization of chapter openings. The following is a list of typographical errors in the printed source texts corrected in this volume, cited by page and line number: 207.11, sounds It; 221.31, than; 242.5, musts; 287.6, childred; 303.13, Assado; 303.14, Preciocilla; 306.5, you going; 306.39, Play; 306.40, Assado; 306.40, Preciocilla; 744.21, real tough; 756.4, everything,; 767.4, quits; 767.37, said,; 772.9, couldn't; 785.8, constance.

Notes

In the notes below, the reference numbers denote page and line of this volume (the line count includes headings). No note is made for material included in standard desk-reference books such as Webster's *Collegiate, Biographical*, and *Geographical* dictionaries. Footnotes in the text were in the originals. For references to other studies, and further biographical background than is contained in the Chronology, see Richard Bridgman, *Gertrude Stein in Pieces* (New York: Oxford University Press, 1970); *A Stein Reader*, edited by Ulla E. Dydo (Evanston, Illinois: Northwestern University Press, 1993); Janet Hobhouse, *Everybody Who Was Anybody: A Biography of Gertrude Stein* (New York: G.P. Putnam, 1975); *A Gertrude Stein Companion: content with the example*, edited by Bruce Kellner (Westport, Connecticut: Greenwood Press, 1988); James Mellow, *Charmed Circle: Gertrude Stein & Company* (New York: Praeger Publishers, 1974); Diana Souhami, *Gertrude and Alice* (New York: Pandora Press, 1991); *The Letters of Gertrude Stein and Carl Van Vechten, 1913–1946* (New York: Columbia University Press, 1986), edited by Edward Burns; *The Letters of Gertrude Stein and Thornton Wilder* (New Haven: Yale University Press, 1996), edited by Edward M. Burns and Ulla E. Dydo with William Rice; Linda Wagner-Martin, *"Favored Strangers": Gertrude Stein and Her Family* (New Brunswick: Rutgers University Press, 1995); Brenda Wineapple, *Sister Brother: Gertrude and Leo Stein* (New York: G.P. Putnam's Sons, 1996); *Four Americans in Paris: The Collections of Gertrude Stein and Her Family* (New York: The Museum of Modern Art, 1970); and *Gertrude Stein: A Bibliography*, compiled by Robert A. Wilson (New York: The Phoenix Bookshop, 1974).

149.14–15   Before . . . Friendship Faded] Stein's free translation (Paris: Plain Edition, 1931) of Georges Hugnet's poem *Enfances*.

157.35   Owen Young] Young (1874–1962), diplomat, co-founder of RCA and NBC, and president of General Electric.

168.35   It was a glorious victory] Cf. Robert Southey, "The Battle of Blenheim."

192.1   BERNARD] Bernard Faÿ (1893–1977), French historian and translator; he was appointed director of the Bibliotheque Nationale by the Vichy government in 1940, and following the Liberation was sentenced to life imprisonment for collaboration (he was released in 1957).

196.11   can one serve god and mammon]   Cf. Matthew 6:24.

196.40   I would not . . . my province]   Cf. Francis Bacon, in a 1592 letter to Lord Burleigh: "I have taken all knowledge to be my province."

198.35   he who runs may read]   Cf. William Cowper, "Tirocinium" (1785): "Shine by the path of every path we tread / With such a luster, he that runs may read."

200.7–8   Lamb's tales of Shakespeare]   *Tales from Shakespeare* (1807) by Charles and Mary Lamb.

216.26   Clarissa Harlowe]   *Clarissa, or, The History of a Young Lady* (1747–48), epistolary novel by Samuel Richardson.

224.4   Little Review]   Literary magazine (1914–29) edited by Margaret Anderson.

227.38–39   battle of Waterloo . . . Victor Hugo]   Cf. *Les Miserables* (1862).

228.10   Rosenthal]   Toby Edward Rosenthal (1849–1917), genre painter who studied at the San Francisco School of Design and the Academy of Munich.

229.24   Cazin]   Jean-Charles Cazin (1841–1901), landscape and history painter.

230.17   Barbizon school]   French school of landscape painting which flourished in the mid-19th century and was extremely influential in the United States; its chief exponents included Theodore Rousseau and Charles Daubigny.

230.28   Tannhauser]   Opera (1845) by Richard Wagner.

230.34   Shilling]   Alexander Shilling (b. 1859), landscape painter and engraver.

233.37   Ary Sheffer]   Ary Scheffer (1795–1858), French artist of Dutch origin who painted religious subjects.

256.35   Pinafore]   *H.M.S. Pinafore* (1878), comic opera with libretto by W. S. Gilbert and music by Arthur Sullivan.

257.5   fight in Faust]   The duel between Faust and Valentin in Charles Gounod's opera *Faust* (1859).

257.11   Lohengrin]   Opera (1850) by Richard Wagner.

257.27   Booth playing Hamlet]   Edwin Booth (1833–93) toured frequently as Hamlet, playing the part for the last time in 1891.

259.13   Secret Service]   Melodrama of the Civil War by the American actor-playwright William Gillette (1855–1937); it was first performed in 1895.

260.7 Russian ballet] The Ballet Russe, founded by Sergei Diaghilev, performed its first season in Paris in 1909.

262.36–37 Lucy Church Amiably] *Lucy Church Amiably: A novel of Romantic beauty and nature which Looks Like an Engraving* (Paris: Plain Edition, 1930).

288.11–12 Wallace . . . Fletcher] The prolific crime novelists Edgar Wallace (1875–1932), author of *The Four Just Men* (1905), and J. S. Fletcher (1863–1935), author of *The Middle Temple Murder* (1918).

293.20 Dillinger] Bank robber, born 1902, designated by the FBI as "public enemy number one" and killed by FBI agents in Chicago in 1934.

295.39–40 As Galileo . . . move.] *E pur si muove:* Galileo is alleged to have muttered this remark after formally abjuring his theory of the earth's movement around the sun.

347.29 Hauptmann] Bruno Hauptmann, executed in 1936 for the kidnapping and murder of Charles Lindbergh's baby son.

390.24 Jo Alsop] Joseph Alsop, Jr. (1910–89), journalist for *The New York Herald Tribune* who befriended Stein on her American tour in 1934.

392.20 René Crevel] French Surrealist novelist and poet, born 1900, who committed suicide in 1935.

417.26–27 Upton Sinclair . . . elected] Sinclair (1878–1968), author of *The Jungle* (1906), ran for governor of California in 1934.

480.4–5 Polonius . . . his son] Cf. *Hamlet*, Act I, scene iii.

498.36 Max Jacob] French writer and artist (1876–1944) whose works include *The Dice Cup* (1917), a collection of prose poems.

498.37 André Salmon] French poet, novelist, and art critic (1881–1969).

499.3 Derain] André Derain (1880–1954), French painter and sculptor associated with the Fauvist group.

508.6 Roger Fry] English painter and art critic (1866–1934), an early champion of Cézanne's work.

510.3 Tschoukine] Sergei Shchukin, wealthy Russian connoisseur of art whose collection of modern painting was housed in the Troubetskoy Palace in Moscow until 1918, when it was expropriated by the Soviet government.

519.14 Lord Grey] Sir Edward Grey (1862–1933), Viscount Grey of Fallodon, diplomat involved in peace negotiations after World War I; author of *Twenty-Five Years (1892–1916)* (1925).

722.18 E.T.O.] European Theater of Operations.

741.25–26 Single Tax . . . Henry George] George (1839–97) propounded his theory of a single tax on land in *Progress and Poverty* (1879).

Library of Congress Cataloging-in-Publication Data

Stein, Gertrude, 1874–1946.
  [Selections. 1998]
  Writings, 1932–1946 / Gertrude Stein.
     p. cm. — (The library of America ; 100)
  ISBN 1–883011–41–8 (alk. paper)
  I. Title. II. Series.
PS3537.T323A6 1998a
818′.5209—dc21   97–28916
                           CIP

THE LIBRARY OF AMERICA SERIES

This book is set in 10 point Linotron Galliard,
a face designed for photocomposition by Matthew Carter
and based on the sixteenth-century face Granjon. The paper is
acid-free Ecusta Nyalite and meets the requirements for permanence
of the American National Standards Institute. The binding
material is Brillianta, a woven rayon cloth made by
Van Heek-Scholco Textielfabrieken, Holland.
The composition is by The Clarinda
Company. Printing and binding by
R.R.Donnelley & Sons Company.
Designed by Bruce Campbell.

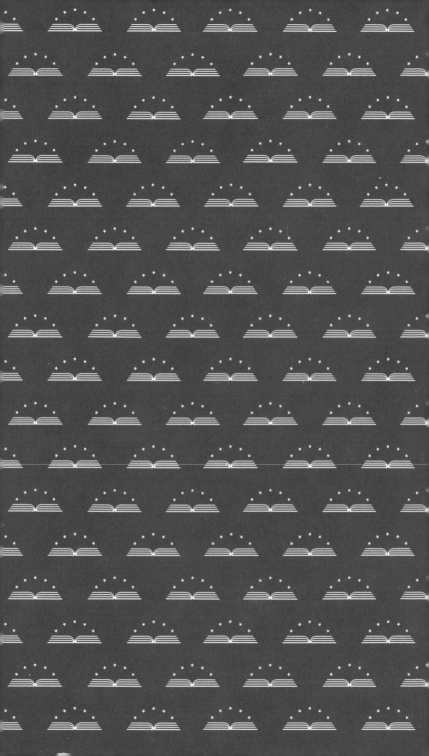